[

2

EDEN
TE

1

2 8 M

M.

D.

2   IAI

A

WITH THE GURKHAS IN THE FALKLANDS

A WAR JOURNAL

A proportion of the royalties from the sale of *With the Gurkhas in the Falklands* will be donated to the Gurkha Welfare Trust.

WITH THE GURKHAS IN THE FALKLANDS

A WAR JOURNAL

by

Mike Seear

LEO COOPER

To Victoria, Emily and Kristina.

First published in Great Britain in 2003 by
LEO COOPER
an imprint of Pen & Sword Books
47 Church Street
Barnsley
South Yorkshire
S70 2AS

ISBN 0 85052 916 6

A catalogue record for this book
is available from the British Library

Typeset in 10/12pt Baskerville by
Phoenix Typesetting, Burley-in-Wharfedale, West Yorkshire

Printed by CPI UK

CONTENTS

The deployment of the 7th Duke of Edinburgh's Own Gurkha Rifles to the Falkland Islands as part of 5 Infantry Brigade had a special significance for two reasons. It was the first time since the Second World War that Gurkha troops had been involved in active operations other than in the Far East. It was also because the 'Falkland Islands' Battle Honour proved to be the last to be earned by the Regiment before it became part of the newly formed Royal Gurkha Rifles in 1994.

Although the Battalion was not directly involved in any of the major battles of the campaign, it probably took it further from home than any other Gurkha unit of the British Army. This is a valuable account of the participation of these tough warriors in the extraordinary events in the South Atlantic in 1982.

FOREWORD BY HRH THE PRINCE PHILIP,
DUKE OF EDINBURGH, KG, KT

GLOSSARY

2IC – Second-in-Command of a unit or sub-unit.

44-pattern webbing – British Army infantry canvas webbing and pouches designed for jungle warfare first introduced in 1944.

58-pattern webbing – British Army general issue infantry webbing and pouches first introduced in 1958.

66 – American 66-mm calibre infantry section hand-held light anti-tank weapon (LAW) with a range of 200 metres. It is thrown away after use.

84 – Infantry platoon 84-mm Swedish-built Carl Gustav medium anti-tank weapon (MAW).

ADAT – Army Dependants' Assurance Trust.

Adjutant – Commanding Officer's staff officer for personnel and discipline.

Alternative Battalion HQ – Back-up HQ for 1st/7th Gurkha Rifles' Tactical HQ.

AOA – Amphibious Operating Area.

ARA – Armada de la Republica Argentina (the equivalent of HMS)

ARO – Area Recruiting Officer in Nepal.

Assembly Area – Area where an infantry battalion first assembles to carry out battle preparation before going into battle.

ATO ('a-toe') – Ammunition Technical Officer.

BAOR – British Army of the Rhine (Germany).

Battalion – infantry brigade sub-unit comprising three rifle companies (four in a Gurkha battalion), support company, HQ company and Battalion HQ, totalling about 650 men (1,000 in a Gurkha battalion) commanded by a lieutenant colonel.

BC – Artillery Battery Commander.

Beasting – British Army expression for extending oneself physically.

Bergen – British Army generic term for a military-type rucksack.

BFT – Battle Fitness Test.

BIT – Battle Individual Training.

BLESMA – British Limbless Ex-Servicemen's Association.

Blowpipe – Shoulder-held ground-to-air missile.

Blue-on-blue – Accidental clash between forces of the same side.

BM – Brigade Major – the chief of staff of a Brigade HQ.

BO – British Officer.

BOR – British Other Ranks.

Brigade – a formation comprising three infantry battalions, supporting artillery, cavalry, engineer and logistic units, and Brigade HQ and signals squadron totalling about 3,200 men, commanded by a brigadier.

Brigade Rear HQ – Reserve HQ for Brigade HQ.

CAP – Combat Aircraft Patrol.

CBF – Commander British Forces.

CEI – Communication Electronic Instruction for all Battalion Signallers.

Chaff – Plastic coated aluminium and fibreglass pins discharged by Royal Navy warships to deceive and deflect away incoming missiles from their course.

Chinook – American-built large CH-47 double-rotored transport helicopter.

C.-in-C. ('Sink') – Commander-in-Chief.

Clansman – A reliable battalion radio communications system used in the Falklands' War.

CLFFI ('Cliffy') – Commander Land Forces Falkland Islands.

CO – Commanding Officer with rank of lieutenant colonel.

Commandant – 7th Gurkha Rifles title for its CO.

Company – infantry battalion sub-unit comprising three platoons and HQ, totalling about 100 men commanded by a major. Similar-sized units of other arms are squadrons, batteries etc.

Compo – British Army generic term for composite rations which are eaten in the field.

CPO – Control Post Operator for the mortars. ACPO is his assistant.

CPX – Command Post Exercise.

CrabAir – British Army slang for Royal Air Force, so called because of a belief that the RAF tends to move sideways rather than forwards.

CT – Communist Terrorist.

Cymbeline – Artillery radar target locating system.

Dagger – Israeli-built Argentine fighter-bomber aircraft.

DF – Defensive Fire: pre-recorded and adjusted artillery, mortar or machine-gun fire by troops in defensive positions against attacking troops.

DMS boots – Direct moulded sole British Army boots which leaked to cause trench foot during the Falklands' campaign.

DQ – Deputy Assistant Quartermaster and Adjutant General.

Endex – British Army expression for 'end of exercise'.

EPC – Education Promotion Certificate for British Army other ranks.

EPS – Exercise Planning Staff.

Exocet – French-built anti-ship missile capable of being fired from the air, sea, and in the case of the Falklands' War, land.

FAC – Forward Air Controller for Harrier GR3 ground attack jump jet aircraft.

FIBUA – Fighting in built-up areas.

Field dressing – Sterile pad with attached bandages for emergency first aid in the field. A shell dressing is a larger type of field dressing.

FIMEZ – Falkland Islands Maritime Exclusion Zone.

FOD – Foreign Object Damage.

FOO – Forward Observation Officer (artillery), usually a captain who accompanies front-line infantry and brings down artillery fire onto enemy targets.

FOP – Frequent Overwater Flier.

Force Maintenance Area – Logistics storage area.

Fuerza Aerea Argentina – Argentine Air Force.

FUP – Forming Up Place – Area where an infantry battalion assembles before moving to its start line for an attack.

Forward Tac – Commanding Officer's small forward recce group.

G3 Ops – Staff Officer Grade 3 Operations.

GPMG – Belt-fed 7.62-mm General Purpose Machine Gun.

GPMG(SF) – General Purpose Machine Gun in the sustained-fire role.

Gurkha Welfare Trust – the official Brigade of Gurkhas' charity to assist pensioned British Army Gurkha soldiers.

Hawkeye – radio appointment title for a pilot or aviation representative.

Helarm request – Armed helicopter request.

Helquest – Helicopter transport request.

Herkey bird – Fleet Air Arm colloquialism for Hercules C-130 Transport Aircraft.

H-hour – the time by which a unit crosses its start line to begin an attack.

Holdfast – radio appointment title for an engineer representative.

II – Illegal Immigrant.

IO – Intelligence Officer of a battalion HQ responsible for compiling and providing intelligence information on the enemy.

Kelper – Nickname for the Falkland Islanders.

LCU – Landing Craft Utility.

LFFI ('Liffy') – HQ Land Forces Falkland Islands.

LGB – laser-guided bomb.

Locstat – Location State.

LOLA – Logistics and Loitering Area.

LS – Landing site.

LSL – Landing Ship Logistics.

MBE – Member of the British Empire.

Mesco – message code.

MFC – Mortar Fire Controller is a forward observer for the Mortar Platoon who can observe and correct the fall of shot on a chosen target.

MFO – Movement Freight Organization.

MID – Mention in Dispatches.

Milan – Wire-guided infantry anti-tank missile.

Mirage – French-built Argentine fighter-bomber aircraft.

MTO – Mechanical Transport Officer.

MT Platoon – Mechanical Transport Platoon.

NAAFI – Navy, Army and Air Force Institute.

NBC – Nuclear, Biological, Chemical.

NCO – Non-Commissioned Officer.

ND – Negligent discharge of a weapon.

Nitesun – Powerful searchlight mounted on a helicopter.

Northern Ireland 'Yellow Card' – Rules of engagement printed on a yellow card for soldiers on Northern Ireland operations.

NOSH – Naval Ocean-going Surgical Hospital.

Nuco – numbers code.

OC – Officer commanding a battalion sub-unit.

O Group – The Commanding Officer's formal Orders Group where he gives out operational orders to subordinates which are then, in turn, passed on down the chain of command.

OP – Observation Post.

Opdem – Operational demand.

Operations and Training Officer (Ops Officer) – The Battalion Ops Officer is responsible for the coordination of the unit's operational tasks and assisting the CO in planning. He is also responsible for coordinating training.

Part I Orders – Battalion written daily orders, routines and notices issued by Battalion HQ.

P and D – Battalion Pipes and Drums band.

PIRA – Provisional Irish Republican Army.

PLA – Peoples' Liberation Army.

Platoon – infantry company sub-unit comprising three sections and HQ, totalling thirty to thirty-five men commanded by a lieutenant.

Playtime – radio appointment title for a transport representative.

PNG – Passive infra-red night goggles for helicopter pilots.

PQS – Progressive Qualification Scheme for British Army Staff College candidates.

Psyops – psychological operations.

Pucará – Argentine twin turbo-prop fighter for close air support operations.

QGO – Queen's Gurkha Officer.

QRF – Quick Reaction Force

RAP – Battalion Regimental Aid Post where wounded are assessed, stabilized and prepared for evacuation.

Rapier – Royal Artillery surface-to-air missile system.

RAS – Replenishment At Sea.

RCT – Royal Corps of Transport.

Re-bro station – Rebroadcast station for relaying radio messages.

REME – Royal Electrical and Mechanical Engineers.

RFA – Royal Fleet Auxiliary.

RSO – Battalion Regimental Signals Officer.

RUC – Royal Ulster Constabulary.

SAM-7 – Soviet manufactured surface-to-air missile.

SARBE ('sabre') – Search and Rescue Beacon.

Sangar – A defensive position built above the ground which, during the Falklands' campaign, consisted of stone, earth and peat.

Scimitar – light tank equipped with a Rarden rapid-firing 30-mm cannon.

Scorpion – light tank equipped with 76-mm cannon.

Section – platoon sub-unit of eight to ten men commanded by a corporal.

Sheldrake – radio appointment title for an artillery representative.

Sitrep – Situation Report.

SLR – British Army 7.62-mm self-loading rifle.

Snotrac – Tracked supply vehicle used in Arctic climates.

SOP – Standard Operating Procedures.

Spearhead Battalion – The infantry element of the UK short-notice rapid-reaction force.

SS-11 missile – Helicopter mounted air-to-ground missile.

Stag – Sentry or radio-watch duty.

Starlight – Radio appointment title for a doctor or medical orderly.

Starlite scope – The bulky first generation Individual Weapon Sight (IWS) mounted on a SLR and used for night operations.

Start Line – A natural feature on the ground which marks the start line for a battalion attack which is crossed at H-hour.

Stick – A group of soldiers comprising eight men to ten men flown in a helicopter.

STUFT – Ship taken up from trade.

Sunray – radio appointment title for a commander of a unit or sub-unit.

Sunray Minor – radio appointment title for second-in-command of a unit or sub-unit.

Supdem – Supply demand.

TA – Transport Area.

Tab – Tactical advance to battle.

Tac HQ – Tactical Headquarters of the Battalion HQ.

TACP – Tactical Air Control Party.

TAOR – Tactical Area of Responsibility.

TEWL – Tactical Exercise Without Land (Gurkha *QE2* variant of a TEWT).

TEWT – Tactical Exercise Without Troops.

TEZ – Falkland Islands' Total Exclusion Zone.

TRALA – Tug, Replenishment and Loitering Area.

Triage – Casualty Sorting Area.

War Cabinet – A sub-committee of the Oversea and Defence Committee of the Cabinet. Its abbreviated title was OD(SA) (SA – South Atlantic).

Woodentops – The remainder of the British Army's nickname for the Guards' Division.

GURKHALI VOCABULARY

bahaduri – bravery

bayalis sataunna – forty-two, fifty-seven

bhat – standard rice meal

bis bis – twenty, twenty

bujhnu – to understand

burho – old boy

chitto – hurry

chiya – tea

dhanyabad – thank you

dumba – sheep

dushman/dush – enemy

galla wallah – intake recruiter

gora sahibharu – white officers

gurujiharu – instructors

hajur – (honorific) You

hags – duck

jadu – magic

jai – long live

jat – clan, tribe

jhaure – folk-song

josh – enthusiasm

kaida – method, rule

kasam khane – oath-eating

kepat – land

keta – boy

khaini – tobacco mixed with lime

khorsani – chilli

madal – Nepalese drum

maharindi – queen

mandir – temple

maruni – male dancer playing a female's part

memsahib – madam, mistress

namaste – greetings

naramro – bad

nautch – party

panchayat – council

pandit – priest

phursunge – male dancer

puja – worship

raja-hags – goose

ram ram – hello

ramro – good

roti – orderly

sahib – sir, master

shyabash – well done

sipai – soldier

tato pani – hot water, whisky

umedwar – candidate (also hopeful)

ACKNOWLEDGEMENTS

I would like to thank:

Herbert Seear, my late father, for the Gurkha introduction, and motivation from his island war description: 'Locked up in Malta by Rommel 1941–43. Let out by Montgomery. Lost two and a half stones in weight, but gained a Mention in Dispatches.'; Kay Seear, my mother, for her art; the British officers, Queen's Gurkha Officers, Gurkha soldiers and British other ranks of the 1st/7th Gurkha Rifles for their anecdotes; Keith Baillie, for the Goose Green wartime stories and hospitality from him and Ginnie, his wife; David Grey, for a kelper's opinion of the Gurkhas; Warrant Officer Ramsing Limbu and Sergeant Dipak Subba for typing draft one aboard SS *Uganda*; Nancy Seear, the late Baroness Seear of Paddington, for exhorting under-statement and rationing 'very' to twice throughout (allocated to the Gurkha chilli's heat); Yasmin Sibley for typing draft two; the 1st/7th Gurkha Rifles orderly room clerks Sergeant Nawin Rai and Corporal Rakamsingh Limbu for typing drafts three and four in Hong Kong while exercising Gurkha patience with an impatient OC sahib; Regimental Quartermaster Sergeant Jasbahadur Gurung and Rifleman Baliprasad Rai for the latter's story; Corporal Anandkumar Rai for his cartography; Norma Higson, Maria Emilia Bosio, Charles Seear and Natalia Alemanno for Spanish translations; Lieutenant David Wright, Major Mark Willis, Major Corin Pearce, and my ex-wife Tove Grindhaug for draft reading and comments; Professor Lars Weisæth and Dr. Pål Herlofsen of the Office for Disaster Psychiatry in Oslo for teaching me the theory after my 'practical'; Mike Nicholson for a copy of his book *A Measure Of Danger*; Robin Neillands, military history author, for encouragement and advice; Alberto Peralta Ramos and Marisabel Clausen de Bruno for support, information, and being wonderful hosts in Argentina; Lieutenant General Diego Soria, Rear Admiral Carlos Robacio, Commander Diego Quiroga (the war's first casualty), Lieutenant Colonel Tomás Fox, Lieutenant Commander Eduardo Gerding, Lieutenant Jorge Perez Grandi, and First Sergeant Nicolás Urbieta for superb contributions; Brigadier David Morgan for support, lobbying and casting a Gurkha eye over my tale; the 7th Gurkha Rifles' Regimental Trust for 'Regimental support'; Brigadier Henry Wilson, Publishing Manager of Pen & Sword, for lessons on brevity; Major Nigel Price for poems, infor-mation and outstanding guidance; all those authors permitting me to quote from their books; and finally Else, my second Norwegian wife, for countless cups of tea and enduring the final two years.

Because without these people, this book would not exist.

Mike Seear
Oslo, September 2002

You have never lived until you have almost died. For those who fight for it,
life has a flavour the protected will never know. – Anon.

INTRODUCTION

War is by far the most traumatic 'life event' that any human can experience, a damaging combination of danger, uncertainty and horror. Civilian experiences, no matter how terrible, are simply not in the same league.[1] – Hugh McManners, who served in the Falklands' War as a Captain in 148 Commando Forward Observation Battery.

We needed luck to survive amongst humming Argentine shrapnel behind the Tumbledown on the final morning of Britain's last colonial war. Some of the world's toughest, strongest and fiercest fighters from Nepal, our most faithful ally, made a significant contribution to the British victory. But the Gurkhas' professionalism camouflaged a chaotic and frightening experience. As a seconded officer to the 1st Battalion, 7th Duke of Edinburgh's Own Gurkha Rifles, my appointment as the Operations and Training Officer not only gave me a unique opportunity to observe matters from the Battalion's hub during all phases of that 1982 Falklands' War, but also a qualification to write about it.

This resulting book attempts to be honest, so I can admit to never being a budding lieutenant colonel, rather only an average officer who could not boast of having a particularly good Falklands' War. The years have passed and, with a modicum of regret, I am a civilian now. But locked into my mind remains a plethora of pictures from that English spring and South Atlantic winter of 1982. So, as 2 April annually rears its head to start that four-month period again, I find myself once more charting the daily occurrances to 14 June – that day of ceasefire, surrender, liberation and peace after an unpredicted military operation. Indeed being prepared for the unexpected should be the bread and butter for peacetime soldiers, yet during my two years of training at the Royal Military Academy, Sandhurst the syllabus lacked an explanation of how a unit, or officer, prepares for such a short-notice war as this, or information of possible long-term psychological reactions from the fighting.

One week there were no problems, then suddenly plenty that affected one's life to an unimaginable degree. Unlike the 1991 Gulf War, there was no slow methodical build-up of forces. Everything happened so fast without the luxury of referring to a staff officer's sophisticated list of 'transition from peace to war measures'. This was non-existent and improvised solutions had to be found immediately. Operation CORPORATE was about rapid deployment and planning on the move which made this a unique crisis management operation par excellence. The media's hype also resulted in affected servicemen and their families reading, watching and listening almost hourly to external events and consequent decision-making by persons who were in total control of *our* immediate future. Of those mentally unprepared for going to war in April 1982, which must have been many in the Task Force, a significant proportion would consequently have had psychological difficulties to 'hang in' and tackle their allotted job responsibilities.

Twenty months accumulated service in Northern Ireland during the first decade of 'the Troubles' never prepared me psychologically for going to war in the purest sense. Once in-theatre, dealing with operational demands was easier than the build-up phase, but afterwards I had stress reactions in the short- and long-term which psychiatrists specializing in trauma counselling would put in the 'no pain, no gain' category. There must be many others affected because, five years after the war, two highly limited studies carried out on some serving Falklands' War British Army veterans revealed post-traumatic stress disorder symptoms associated with their experiences.[2] Furthermore, two decades since the war at least ten Falklands' veterans annually on average have committed suicide. As this is a conservative figure, the total of 200 suicides could be soon approaching the number of 255 British fatalities in the war.[3] Other veterans have taken a less drastic but, nevertheless, eye-catching action by suing the Ministry of Defence in London with alleged failure in its 'duty of care' for them and others from Northern Ireland, the Gulf War and Bosnia.

But did I also gain from this unique experience where a lack of immediate post-war *preventive* information to us, the war's front-line participants, about such reactions becomes more obvious as the years roll by? The answer is a qualified 'yes' because the Falklands' War not only contributed to changing my life both in a negative but also, ultimately, positive way with a psycho-traumatology phenomena known as post-traumatic growth. Many might then ask a Falklands' veteran like myself, 'What was it like as a soldier fighting in that war?'

My answer starts by maintaining that war belongs to the extreme end of the emergency response and crisis management spectrum where the pervading sword of Damocles threat from enemy action exists for all in-theatre troops regardless of whether they are at the front line or not. The professional soldier's introduction to his tools of trade is to prepare him for combat, and not the profound before and after phases. In particular those long drawn-out weeks prior to combat, which victims of civilian disasters never experience, are particularly onerous. That, and the fighting, is like being put into a cake mixer where there are additional ingredients – the professional, the personal, the emotional and, not least, the comical – and then switching on to maximum speed. It is when hostilties end and the cake mixer is switched off that the soldier emerges to a supposedly 'normal' life. But many discover this is never quite the same as before because, during the blending process, a major complication has occurred. The ingredients did not bind together because of the severe turbulence, and many find new attitudes have been created. The soldier might then experience a soft- or hard-landing or combination of both with his revised priority values, and there might be increased vulnerability in how his subsequent behaviour and actions are perceived by the 'peacetime' society who sent him to war.

His next of kin and friends are also beaten around in their own cake mixer. War commentators and many others forget them, to focus instead on the fighting. But any married soldier who has experienced war will know his family brings a mental image of comfort on the battlefield and gives a grain of structure. Extracts from my Norwegian wife's letters depict the burden of living in a vacuum of specific information about a war fought 13,000 kilometres away, exemplified by the immediate aftermath of the attack on two landing ship logistics RFA *Sir Galahad* and RFA *Sir Tristram* where many 5 Infantry Brigade troops were casualties. However, stress from Government-imposed restrictions to public information had been greater for the Gurkhas' wives in Nepal as their access to news was highly limited.

From a plethora of Falklands' War books, only a handful have been written by servicemen describing their experiences at the sharp end and, unlike me, most distinguished themselves in one way or another. But married or single, we often have a mutual aim of providing a worm's-eye view of the fighting. Maybe, too, cartharsis has been a mutual motive for our writings. Nonetheless I have another of more importance. Falklands' War books are still published which mention the Gurkhas, but omissions and errors about the latter continue. For example, a 1999 Gurkha publication on 'the inside story of the world's most feared soldiers' also contained a chapter on the 1st/7th Gurkha Rifles' role in the Falklands. No less than the book reviewer in the 7th Gurkha Rifles *Regimental Association Journal* claimed that this chapter had been '. . . particularly well done'.[4] But the thirty-seven errors I spotted on those fourteen pages merely supported the view that, 'A civilian who attempts to write a military history is of necessity guilty of an act of presumption'.[5]

My account attempts to put the record straight on a Gurkha performance of which their forefathers would have approved. The bald facts are compelling. Descendants of Gurkha recruitment into the former Honourable East India Company's Army that began at the time of the Battle of Waterloo, the 7th Gurkha Rifles had participated in both World Wars with distinction. One of ten Gurkha regiments in the British Indian Army, they were among the four transferred to the British Army under the UN-ratified 1948 Tripartite Agreement between Great Britain, Nepal and India. In the van of the Malayan and Borneo campaigns, the Regiment was marooned afterwards in the backwaters of Hong Kong and tasked with internal security and border duties. But a formidable battlefield reputation remained intact and, with an order of battle of 637 Gurkha officers and men plus forty-three attached British officers and other ranks, the Battalion went to the Falklands' War as the largest and most dangerous Task Force unit for its Argentine opposition.

Yet little was written about them. One major reason is that the media must always prioritize stories that most concern their readers. This meant, despite their popularity, that the Nepalese soldiers did not command as much 'readability' as their British counterparts. Apart from one press call at the Gurkhas' camp in Church Crookham, Hampshire, prior to embarkation, an improvised press briefing I gave in the shop-cum-post office at Goose Green, and limited coverage given by BBC's Brian Hanrahan and ITN's Mike Nicholson, none of the twenty-seven accredited Task Force journalists was attached to the Battalion. Small wonder then that soldiers of the 6th Gurkha Rifles on jungle exercise in Brunei after stopping daily to set up a radio aerial in any tall tree so they could receive BBC World Service News broadcasts, were always disappointed at the lack of 1st/7th information. Another explanation came from Patrick Bishop of *The Observer* in a November 1982 letter written to the Gurkhas' Commandant, Lieutenant Colonel David Morgan:

> . . . the Gurkhas got rather a raw deal in terms of Press and TV coverage and deserved more media attention and credit than they received. This was due, I feel, to the haphazard way the MOD (Ministry of Defence) allocated journalists to units and I for one regret that contact with your men was minimal.

This domestic vacuum of information also affected the international description of our operations, such as in the *New York Herald Tribune*:

> (The Gurkhas) arrived two weeks before the war ended, fired few shots, took three prisoners, suffered only a handful of casualties and never reached the Falklands capital . . .[6]

So being also the Battalion's Public Information Officer during the war, I have always felt that telling this unknown story has been, in a way, my responsibility. Argentines and British still have not understood what the Gurkhas did or did not do in the war: the tendency amongst Argentines is to believe that the Gurkhas were everywhere, whilst the British tendency is to think the Gurkhas did nothing. My fighting these two misconceptions was begun on the reverse side of a signals message form in post-war Goose Green. I never kept a war diary but made rough notes on my raw impressions in those first ten days or so after returning from the battlefield. Afterwards the skeleton account was tucked away into a combat jacket pocket and lay dormant for a couple of weeks before being expanded into a first draft during the three-week return sea voyage to Southampton.

Its structure has evolved as the years have passed. Phase I – On Standby provides accounts of a Nepalese teenager's selection and first experiences with the 7th Gurkha Rifles, my first Gurkha encounters, secondment and initial training for war at the Gurkha camp in Church Crookham. Participation in a 5 Infantry Brigade exercise at Sennybridge where the Battalion honed its battle skills to perfection leads on to Phase II – Going To War which chronicles the final preparations, departure, *QE2* cruise south to South Georgia and unpleasantness of mass Gurkha seasickness during the second leg to San Carlos. Once on Falklands' terra firma, Gurkha operations in Lafonia and elsewhere are described in Phase III – In-Theatre as well as the frustrations of a phoney war period at the settlement of Goose Green. This leads to the campaign's final days and Phase IV – At The Front where the Battalion's move by sea and air into the hills surrounding the capital of Stanley, and coming under artillery fire, is described. The climax comes with frenzied battle preparations prior to advancing behind the Scots Guards onto the enemy 5th Marine Infantry Battalion at the Tumbledown and Mount William and, underway, being 'ambushed' by enemy artillery. Reference is also made to the psychological effect that the Gurkhas had on the Argentine Army, summed up in that same Patrick Bishop letter:

. . . I was very interested in your various observations . . . particularly where you say 'the Argies were scared stupid of the Gurkhas'. You and your men may be interested to learn of an article which appeared recently in the Spanish newspaper 'Pueblo'. A correspondent who has recently visited Argentina reported that one returned soldier was still in a state of shock as a result of his experiences.

He was in a military hospital where he lay in silence except for occasional moments of panic when he scrambled under the bed shouting: 'Los Gurkhas! Los Gurkhas!'

Lastly Phase V – Aftermath not only describes the first forty-eight hours post-hostilities on a blizzard-lashed battlefield and our eventual voyage home but, more important, how the Gurkhas won the peace in the context of the Duke of Wellington's phrase on that matter, 'We are English and we pride ourselves on our deportment'. The effect of their impact can be gauged two decades later during Brigadier David Morgan's official visit to the Falklands when he was told by two independent persons that, given the choice, ninety-eight per cent of the Islanders would select the Gurkhas as their Garrison troops.

Once back at Church Crookham, I agonized over a title to my writing. An idea came from the redeployment of many Battalion sub-units around the Islands. One, C Company, was located at Port Stephens on West Falkland. The Company Commander there, Major 'Taj' Alan Lewis, one day received a visit from the Commandant who was duly shown the settlement. His walkabout included the tiny school on whose walls a number of pro-British slogans had been written by the teacher. These were coloured in vividly by her twelve pupils, and both officers read with pride 'God Bless the Task Force', 'Gurkhas are Great', and delightful 'Nepals are our Pals'; but their favourite was definitely 'Penguins Prefer Peace'.

In a regiment renowned for its gentleness in peace and ferocity in battle, those words symbolized the futility of war. They were adopted as a slogan incorporated in the design of a new battalion T-shirt. It sold like hot cakes at Church Crookham and I chose initially *Penguins Prefer Peace* as the embryo manuscript's title. A minor shock came therefore twenty years later when my publishers advised that trading heavily in Gurkha mystique and a fiercesome reputation required another title which should highlight the nouns 'Gurkha', 'Falklands' and 'War'. I capitulated to their professional judgement, but maintain that the original title more accurately sums up the feeling of many who returned from the war.

Meanwhile other writers would continue to comment on the Gurkhas' performance in the Falklands. One more notable than most was the fifty-five year-old Columbian journalist and novelist Gabriel García Márquez who won the 1982 Nobel Prize for Literature. His article, *The Malvinas, One Year Afterwards*, published in the Bogotá newspaper *El Espectador de Columbia* on 3 April 1983 merely provided me with just one more reason to tell the true story since his description of how the Gurkhas fought both during *and* after (!) the Battle of Puerto Argentino was as wildly distorted as the alleged nightmares of the wounded Argentine soldier in the military hospital. Like any Márquez novel containing 'magic realism', such an account makes colourful reading and is in keeping with his philosophy, 'Life is not that which happened, but what you remember and the way you remember it.' However, if telling the truth is also a criteria for a Nobel literature prizewinner, then perhaps the *Svenska Akademien* should check their candidates a fraction more carefully – even though, paradoxically, his article does sustain and reinforce that battle-winning Gurkha reputation:

> The memory most terrible which remains with the Argentine survivors is the savagery of the battalion of 'Gurkhas', the legendary and ferocious decapitators from Nepal who preceded the English in the battle of Puerto Argentino (Stanley). 'They advanced shouting and cutting throats,' one witness of that pitiless butchery has written. 'The speed at which they decapitated our poor lads with their assassins' scimitars was one every seven seconds. On one rare occasion the head which had been cut remained attached by its skin, and they cut off its ears as well.' The Gurkhas confronted the enemy with such a blind determination that, of the 700 that disembarked, only 70 survived. 'These beasts were so worked up that, once the battle of Puerto Argentino was finished, they continued killing even the Englishmen until these had to resort to the ultimate to overcome them.'

Contrary to such revelations, *With the Gurkhas in the Falklands – A War Journal* describes accurately what happened then, before and afterwards. But no manuscript about war's effects which deliberately avoids mentioning and analysing *casus belli*, becomes readable literature overnight. Any combat veteran who strives to become a novice author can encounter difficulties in later-life as my final chapter reveals, even though this and the Epilogue also describe the positive spin-offs. That is why it has taken two decades to complete this book. I finished writing it in 2002 – the centenary year of the raising of the 7th Gurkha Rifles and the twentieth anniversary of the Falklands' War.

So I hope you enjoy reading my war journal as much as I enjoyed writing it.

PROLOGUE

by Professor of Disaster Psychiatry Lars Weisæth, MD PhD. Director, Division of Disaster Psychiatry, Department Group of Psychiatry, University of Oslo and Medical Staff, HQ Defence Command Norway.

I first met Mike Seear seven years after the Falklands' War had ended. By then he was Scandinavian Airline's Security Manager in Norway with an additional responsibility for emergency response. Although I am Norwegian and psychiatrist by profession, we quickly discovered a Gurkha common denominator. In Mike's case it was as a seconded officer to the 1st/7th Duke of Edinburgh's Own Gurkha Rifles; and, in mine, as an attached Medical Officer to a Nepalese Army Gurkha infantry battalion for two weeks during a three-month period of service with UNIFIL, the United Nations Force in Southern Lebanon, whose task was to act as a buffer between the warring factions. My main appointment was as the UNIFIL Hospital's clinical psychiatrist where I examined all cases referred from the various national units. I also later served with UNIFIL's two Norwegian battalions.

During this period and afterwards I carried out a study on the general stress and psychiatric problems in the UNIFIL infantry battalions of Fiji, France, Ghana, Ireland, Nepal, Netherlands, Nigeria, Norway and Senegal. Of particular interest were the Gurkha soldiers of the Nepalese battalion because they had the lowest incidence of mental disorders within UNIFIL compared with the Norwegians who scored the highest. The neighbouring Norwegian and Gurkha battalions had fundamental differences in material, psychological, socio-cultural and religious matters. These account for much of the difference in psychiatric morbidity which was almost non-existent amongst the Gurkhas. The latter could be rated highly on almost all criteria known to increase the ability of a soldier to withstand military stress, such as positive selection, upbringing, physical fitness, motivation, training, competence, group spirit, leadership, etc. The Gurkhas' remarkable coolness in danger was partly a consequence of their belief in reincarnation and an absolute deterministic view of life. To die in combat was progress. Their only fear was somatic illness, illustrated during one particular medical consultation I had with a Gurkha who defined shame as, 'If I died in my bed because of illness, I might return in another life as a dog!'

The Norwegians did better in technical competence and individual autonomy and, during times of crisis, were allowed to express their emotions more freely. By comparison, Gurkhas who had legs blown off by Israeli booby traps concealed under sandbags only laughed and smiled when I visited them in hospital. When conflicting demands of peacekeeping and military action was felt as stress to the Gurkha, it seemed due to the challenge to his identity as a soldier, and not to a feeling of psychological helplessness manifesting itself in stress symptoms. The strong and proud soldier identity could pose problems however, as when a Gurkha, taken hostage by the Palestine Liberation Organization, was consequential to his Battalion's motto, 'It is better to die than be a coward', and asked to be shot by his captors. An honourable military sacrifice is not necessarily relevant in UN service.

More than a decade later my second, and more lasting, Gurkha encounter was with Mike who can be safely described as an 'officer gentleman' of best British tradition. During the intervening thirteen years we have built up a solid professional relationship. Reliable, conscientious, thorough and possessing great personal integrity, he has an ability to motivate personnel in the emergency response arena and carried out pioneer work for SAS in planning, organization building, implementing educational and training programmes and setting new airline standards for the provision of support to emergency affected passengers, crew and next of kin both during and after emergency situations. His broad international perspective gave such responsible work new dimensions. The necessary qualifications came from British Army and NATO staff exercise and contingency planning appointments, Light Infantry and Belfast Brigade HQ emergency tours of duty in Northern Ireland and, of most significance, his Falklands' War active service with the 7th Gurkha Rifles.

Mike's book is not just a detailed, fascinating and often amusing glimpse behind the scenes of a British Army Gurkha infantry battalion's participation in the Falklands' War. It also contains an excellent in-depth description and self-analysis of an officer's psychological reactions before, during, and in the short- and long-term aftermath of front-line warfare – the worst case 'disaster' scenario any human being can experience. I am convinced that *With the Gurkhas in the Falklands* is the alternative textbook for civilian professionals and others who have a vested interest in modern emergency response and crisis management concepts, methods and procedures. These underlying themes include the necessary attitude, plans and planning, training, mental preparedness, leadership, strategic management, C3-I – command, control, communications and internal information – as well as operational coordination, media-handling, psycho-traumatology and psychosocial support. They reoccur constantly throughout a narrative rich in dialogue between men involved in demanding operations, but who simultaneously must confront the stresses of extreme crisis management.

Original in treatment, this book's overall aim is to tell a 'living' military history in a personal way. When I read it my attention was captured. As a Professor of Disaster Psychiatry with decades of operational psychiatry experience with Norwegian and international civilian disasters, combat veterans and war victims, and of leading UN World Health Organization international missions to post-Gulf War Kuwait and afterwards all the Balkan wars, I therefore have no hesitation in recommending Mike Seear's war journal.

Lars Weisæth

The Falkland Islands

PHASE 1 – ON STANDBY

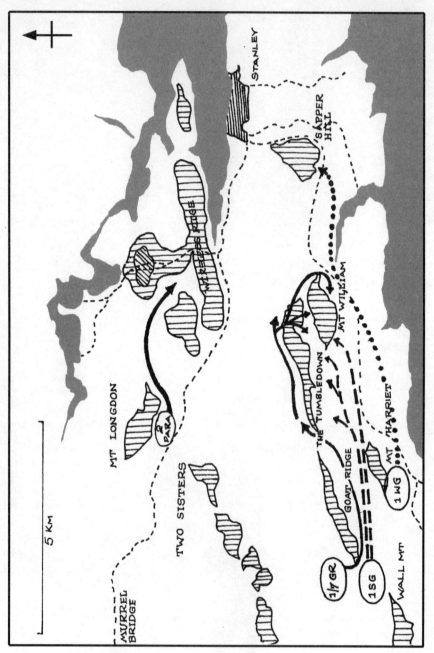

The Final Phase 13–14 June 1982

Chapter One

THE LAD FROM CHOKUM

When God first chose a Gurkha
As a vessel of his own,
He took a chunk of cheerfulness
And laid on flesh and bone,
A face, well some deny it
But a soul that no one could,
For anyone who's seen it
Wishes his was half as good.

William Ross Stewart

The Falkland Islands and South Atlantic are thousands of miles from Mount Everest; but Edmund Hillary's and Tenzing Norgay's conquest is only four days walk for the 200 villagers of Chokum in the Diktel district of Eastern Nepal. They are amongst the six per cent of Nepal's population from which Gurkha soldiers are chosen, with their village once having been in the recruiting district for the 7th Duke of Edinburgh's Own Gurkha Rifles. There, amongst the Limbu *jat* and Rai *jat* (clans) who make up the inhabitants, lived an ex-Regimental Sergeant Major of the 1st Battalion who had advised the *galla wallah* (intake recruiter) by letter in the first half of 1979 of some potential candidates for the Regiment.

In the middle of the *Asoj* month (end of September), the *galla wallah* paid a visit. He was an ex-Gurkha sergeant of unimpeachable record who supplemented his Army pension as a member of the Corps of Recruiters. His duties involved scouring the villages for suitable recruiting material and this entailed long hours tramping up and down the hills and along the many tracks that criss-cross the countryside. Remuneration would come from a commission he would earn if the hopefuls he selected were, in turn, chosen for the Brigade of Gurkhas. On this first visit to Chokum he had been accommodated overnight at the house of the ex-RSM *burho* (old boy) whom he did not know too well. However the offer of lodgings to a comparative stranger and president of the local village *panchayat* (council) was perfectly normal as these hill people are naturally hospitable. 'And besides,' the ex-RSM had said to the *panchayat*, 'the *galla wallah* is important because he would bring honour to the village if any of our local *keta* (boys) succeeded.'

3

The following day, five *keta* were selected. 'You'll have to wait another six weeks until after the end of the dewy season for the ARO sahib to visit Chokum in *Mangsir* (December) and cast his eye over you,' they were told by the *galla wallah*. 'You'll be checked on your basic physical abilities, any external medical problems, proof of age, birthplace and village residence. And remember that the ARO sahib is a retired Queen's Gurkha Officer who knows better than most as to who will probably make the grade in the final selection tests at the Brigade of Gurkhas' cantonment in Dharan!'

The five hopefuls re-assembled at the ex-RSM's house on the appointed day for the visit of the Area Recruiting Officer. All were nervous. 'This is the first obstacle to overcome if you are to stand a chance of fulfilling your dream of becoming a Gurkha soldier in the British Army, who has possibilities of promotion, decorations, travel, adventure, status and, not least, money which could be used primarily to buy *kipat* (land),' the *galla wallah* informed them. 'But don't worry, *keta*. In recent years I've recruited successfully from Chokum!'

The omens seemed good, but the ARO sahib was ruthless in his selection. 'There's only one likely lad for the next Brigade of Gurkhas *galla* in Hong Kong,' he told the *galla wallah* and pointed to a slight youth by the name of Baliprasad Rai. The latter had given his age as seventeen and a half but, in reality, he was sixteen and a half because Nepalese babies at birth are automatically one year old. The others were dismissed, crestfallen at not having been chosen. Still, this result was better than the average rate of only one in seven applicants achieving hill selection for Dharan.

Baliprasad Rai was then given instructions from the *galla wallah* for his big adventure, the first time he would live away from his home, 'We'll leave for Dharan next month. You must pack food, and you'll also need a blanket to sleep in. The journey will take some days, but if you pass the tests at Dharan you'll get to know this route well in the years to come. We'll depart at dawn, together with others from nearby villages that also have been selected.'

The teenager nodded. He was given the date to be ready and then, too tongue-tied to reply, ran quickly back to his home at the top end of the village. His father had just returned from working in the fields and was delighted with his son's news. 'At last,' he thought, 'there would be a possibility of honour for the family as well as the village in having a Hong Kong Gurkha son. And if Baliprasad should have a successful Army career, he would more than likely become headman in the village – just like the ex-RSM!' 'This is a chance to aim for something far better than simply scratching a living out of the soil here at Chokum,' said Baliprasad's father to his excited son, 'because, as a Gurkha, you will earn a hundred times more than your friends!'

Baliprasad's mother, however, sighed. Although any military career had positive points, she knew if her son was accepted into the Army there would be years of separation from his family. However she did not voice any objections to her husband's enthusiasm because of one important advantage. With her son gone from the nest there would be one less family mouth to feed if he succeeded. The couple's children had been brought up in a hard and hungry land where natural disasters were commonplace. Earthquakes occurred sometimes, but the weather was the main difficulty with a rainy season whose monsoons could produce floods and hailstones as large as golf balls which had been known to hammer down so powerfully that they ripped roofs off

4

houses. The only method to combat the cold at nights was by burning wood, but this had started to become a scarce natural resource because it had been cut down so much. Deforestization increased the rate of soil erosion which, in turn, made farming even more difficult. It was a vicious circle, resulting in the family surviving barely above subsistence level.

Wealth in this harsh yet paradoxically beautiful environment, apart from ownership of *kepat*, is measured in unlikely forms to people from the western world. For example, possession of a corrugated tin roof for one's house thus affording a more permanent protection against the natural elements than dried mud or straw, or of goats which would ensure an easily accessible daily supply of milk, let alone shoes and western clothes or, to provide the ultimate status symbols unobtainable for most, a transistor radio, watch or camera. Despite the deprivations, everyone in Chokum was cheerful, close-knit and accustomed to hard work. Roads, vehicles, or pack-animals did not exist here, so everyone had to carry everything everywhere. This included the vegetable produce grown by the villagers. It was taken down the hills to be sold on Wednesdays and Thursdays in the local markets, just outside the nearby town of Bagsila, the main shopping centre of the district and home for 9,000 inhabitants.

Unlike many of the other villagers whose body frames and huge leg muscles had been developed in struggling daily with loads up to seventy kilos, young Baliprasad Rai was slight in appearance. Such work at altitude was a significant factor that contributed to his high standard of fitness. He did his fair share of work in the fields and humping the back-breaking loads, interspersed with attendance at school. There he had attained the minimum Brigade of Gurkhas' recruiting standard of eighth grade, but his progress had been slow because more than eighty pupils were in his class and his number of daily lessons limited accordingly. The school, in excess of two hours walk from his home, split its classes so that the lower were taught in the single school building in the morning, and the upper attended in the afternoon. His remaining school day was spent walking. For relaxation, he was fond of music and enjoyed beating out rhythms on his *madal*. This tom-tom drum was always used at a Chokum campfire *nautch* (party) to accompany the singing of *jhaures* (folk songs).

Small wonder Baliprasad Rai was so excited at the prospect of service in the 7th Gurkha Rifles. This was, indeed, the big chance for adventure; but failure at the recruiting depot in Dharan was the one nagging doubt which kept him from sleeping well that night. He had heard that some, so ashamed of being refused entry into the British Gurkha regiments and rather than face their family and friends with the bad news, ran away from home to try their luck in the Gurkha regiments of the Indian Army. Maybe he would be faced with a similar decision, so he began to prepare thoroughly with daily training sessions of running up and down the hill next to his home.

The following month the lad from Chokum set out with the *galla wallah* and six other *keta* who had also passed 'preliminary selection' from the Sagarmatha hills area. 'Remember the paths we take southwards,' the *galla wallah* reminded them, 'because successful or not, you'll have to walk back home on your own.'

This did not dampen their excitement as the group made their way down the hour-long track to Bagsila. Baliprasad Rai knew the town's bazaars well, but this time the Chokum villager did not stop at these and, carrying his blanket and food, he and the others began their march along a stoney track which soon began to snake up and down the steep hills. The few roads in Nepal lay much further to the south and west, so their journey to Dharan would be undertaken on foot and last for days. Theirs was a seven day track. The beautiful scenery compensated for the sweat of their exertions. Several times daily they would be cooled by fording the same fast-flowing river which curved around the valleys. At night they stopped to eat and sleep in the small huts specially built for travellers. There the *galla wallah* lectured as how they ought to reply to questions if the interview stage of the tests was reached. They set out again early each morning and made good progress. At least the trek was not being made during the rainy season which would begin in the next few months, but Baliprasad Rai's heart jumped at every thought of his approaching ordeal – the most important of his life.

After a week's walking they finally reached the *terai* (plain) of eastern Nepal and sprawling town of Dharan with its 100,000 inhabitants. The Dharan Cantonment lay half a mile away and housed the recruiting depot for the Gurkhas, headquarters for the British Gurkhas, Nepal, a large hospital where Gurkha pensioners from Chokum had been treated in the past, and other units. Baliprasad Rai's group were just a few of more than 400 other candidates who had also drifted down from the hills. His *galla wallah* now became only a spectator during the day who could only give encouragement to his protégés at night.

The first full day was devoted to initial documentation, and it amused Baliprasad Rai to have his candidate's number 'branded' on his chest with indelible ink. A quarter of all the hopefuls failed next day's first hurdle, tuberculosis being the common failure reason at this medical examination. The following day's programme consisted of a timed one-mile run to familiarize the survivors with the battle fitness test route, then came educational tests in mathematics, *Nagri* script writing, and an IQ test. The next day, their physique was subjected to stringent fitness tests, such as heaves to the bar and sit ups. These had a grading system of far higher values than those used to measure the average British recruit as the latter possesses an overall body strength far weaker than his Gurkha counterpart. Selection was again deliberately ruthless and only fifty per cent remained. Included in this batch was Baliprasad Rai.

'OK, you are through to the interview stage,' said his *galla wallah* that evening, 'so remember what I told you! It's going to be the worst part of the ten days.' With this he confirmed again what Baliprasad Rai had been dreading. It turned out to be just such an ordeal, too, and consisted of a preliminary filter board to establish Baliprasad Rai's claim of birth and residence in Chokum, and then a searching interview with many questions to judge his character. He tried to answer as the *galla wallah* had told him on the way down to Dharan, but the questions proved to be many and were difficult. He gave up and just tried to answer as best he could. The final selection rounds were based on more physical tests. These included a three-mile timed run, ascending and descending a hill the size of Hong Kong's *Nameless* with a heavy load on the back, participation in pairs wrestling, an ultra-aggressive game of team scrabble otherwise known as 'murder ball', as well as racing round an obstacle course. All this provided Baliprasad

Rai with the chance of demonstrating his determination and fitness: the names of those finally selected were called out.

'Baliprasad Rai!'

Unbelievably, he was one of them. A quarter of those who had arrived at Dharan passed, or in other words, only one in thirty who had originally applied for the *galla* had succeeded. It did not take into account the thousands of *galla wallah* rejections before the ARO sahib selection round. This was irrelevant now. Not even a minor problem could dampen Baliprasad Rai's euphoric grin, so enormous it nearly split his face in two.

'The next recruiting *galla* will not start at the Gurkhas' Hong Kong training depot until April,' he was then told, 'so, Rifleman Baliprasad Rai, here is 135 rupees for you to go back home and tide you over for the spring!'

He had never been so rich, having now the equivalent of £7 sterling in his pocket. The new Gurkha rifleman tramped back to Chokum along with the others who had also come down from the Diktel area. One of these had also been selected, and both felt as though they were riding on the crest of a wave after their recent traumas. They had that simple ability of unsophisticated people to live in the present and make the best use of it. During the day they laughed with delight at their success, whilst in the evenings sang themselves hoarse accompanied by the throb of Rifleman Baliprasad Rai's *madal* as they rested in the wayside huts. The return did not feel nearly so long or arduous as their outward trek.

Once Rifleman Baliprasad Rai arrived back at Chokum, his family and friends were beside themselves at his success, although his mother had a few private reservations. She knew her son would be gone for three years initially but, even when returning for a six-month leave period, he would have become something of a hybrid. Although still a villager of Chokum, his calling would be to the Regiment. Once in the final phase of his leave, he would have to begin his seven-day trek to Dharan in order to reach Kathmandu in time for the onward flight to Hong Kong. She had seen it all before with the few other youths of the village who had also been accepted into the 7th Gurkha Rifles. One thought did, however, console her. 'At least my son will now have meat to eat twice a day on most days of his Army service,' she told her husband, 'compared to only five times a year here at home!'

For the time being, Rifleman Baliprasad Rai continued his schooling and helped his family in the nearby fields. The concept of time now began to have some meaning beyond previous indistinct approximations as he waited impatiently. He experienced a new calmness. It stemmed from his achievement and embryonic sense of commitment which allowed him to accept whatever was to come his way. His future could not be worse than the past.

When the time arrived for his departure, the ex-RSM called him to his house. The old soldier's farewell was of a serious nature. 'Rifleman Baliprasad Rai, you are going on the biggest adventure of your life, one for which many boys in this village would give their right arm,' he reminded the new British Army recruit. 'Remember that although you will eventually take part in the Regimental *kasam khane* (oath eating) parade on joining your Battalion, that binds you to the 7th Gurkha Rifles and its officers, this Regiment is also part of the Brigade of Gurkhas. You must not therefore

7

just content yourself with resting on past deeds and honours of your predecessors because, from these, has grown a dangerous myth that the Gurkha is invincible. A myth, I might add, which seems to feed on itself.'

The *burho* leaned forward, and looked the future recruit to the 7th Gurkha Rifles squarely in the eyes before ending his pep talk, 'In short, what I am saying is that it is not enough to let the name honour us, we must honour the name too.'

Rifleman Baliprasad Rai listened carefully to these pearls of wisdom and took mental note. He bade farewell to his mentor because he would leave early next day for Dharan on the first stage of his journey. At home he packed his few belongings, including his trusty *madal*, for the seven-day journey. In three years, when it would be time for his first leave, he might need a porter to assist in bringing back luxuries from the outside world. The porter might also be needed for personal protection from the attentions of thieves after his newly acquired wealth.

'. . . And prostitutes and gamblers are other traps to avoid as well,' the ex-RSM had advised him adding though his usual 'suggestion' to any new Gurkha from the village, 'and on your safe return a donation to the *panchayat* would be most welcome!'

Rifleman Baliprasad Rai would also start looking for a wife on that leave, even though another three years of separation would have to be endured if they got married. Eventually he might also save money and buy *kepat* without being saddled with an enormous debt and punitive interest rates of more than thirty per cent that many struggled to repay. So the next morning after a tearful farewell, he set out alone to Dharan. The rainy season still had not begun, otherwise some of the route he was about to take would have been impassable with river flood water. The way was familiar, so he arrived without incident at Dharan to prepare for his departure to the Brigade of Gurkhas' Training Depot in Hong Kong.

Life was busy in the ten days at Dharan. Issued with military kit that included a Gurkha service kukri, he received a short back-and-sides haircut, learnt how to eat with a knife, fork and spoon and was introduced to the rudiments of drill. The climax came in his recruit *kasam khane* parade where allegiance was sworn to the English *maharindi*, Queen Elizabeth. It was time to begin the long journey to Hong Kong. This particular party of Gurkhas was just one of many such groups which made up that never-ending two-way aerial street known as 'the Gurkha Airlift' to the Pearl of the Orient. None in Rifleman Baliprasad Rai's party had ever flown before so, quite understandably, their excitement was barely containable, and even more so as they were told, 'Rather than flying from the local Biratnagar Airport here, you will board an aircraft of the Royal Nepalese Airlines at the capital for your flight to Hong Kong!'

Shortly afterwards, the recruits set out on the dusty bus drive westwards to Kathmandu and its airport. On board their aircraft were not only the recruits, but also other Gurkhas. Some had their dependants – wives and children – who were also flying for the first time. Such was the anticipation in the cabin that many applauded at take-off. Nevertheless, as is normal for Gurkhas, most slept nearly all of the six hours flying time. Only in the final twenty minutes did anticipation rise again as the descent began on the western approach path to Hong Kong.

This was the so-called scenic route, arguably the most dangerous of its type in the world. Sparsely-populated islands of Lantau, Tsing-Yi and Stonecutters appeared in rapid succession before the main undercarriage gear was lowered, groaning in protest. 'Look!' said Rifleman Baliprasad Rai to the Gurkha next to him, and pointed to the first glimpse of Kowloon Peninsula's concrete jungle as they crossed the coast. With a near ninety-degree starboard turn, they were virtually inside the old walled city of Kowloon. Only 100 metres above fourteen-storey flats, the wing tips seemed in danger of scraping the rooftops of buildings which, at every window-level, were bedecked with washing hung on bamboo poles known locally as 'the flags of a thousand nations'. Kai Tak Airport's runway lay 800 metres ahead extending south-east into the harbour on reclaimed land. The aircraft straightened onto its final approach with little daylight between undercarriage and city market rooftops, then there was wild Gurkha applause as smoking tyres bit into runway asphalt.

It was the start of the uncomfortable summer season in the Colony with temperatures of thirty degrees plus centigrade and ninety per cent humidity, but all part of Rifleman Baliprasad Rai's adventure. Driving in the hurly-burly of Kowloon was also more than just an eye-opener to a lad from Chokum's somnolence. So many people, suicidal taxi-drivers and crowded buses in the streets where the awful thump of piledrivers amongst the high-rise buildings seemed to increase the stress of life. Like all Gurkhas, he enjoyed shopping and quickly noticed the large number of Chinese shops which sold gold jewellery that could come in useful for a marriage exchange during his first Nepal leave.

The recruits were destined for the quieter recesses of the New Territories and training depot at the village of Sek Kong, a stone's throw from 48 Gurkha Infantry Brigade Headquarters. There he settled in for the start of an intensive nine-month course to turn him from raw recruit into trained soldier. The time needed was double that which Rifleman Baliprasad Rai's British contemporaries needed but, nonetheless, necessary to counter the Gurkha's bewilderment over a meteoric projection from a Nepalese environment, comparable to the start of Britain's eighteenth-century industrial revolution.

'You have many new lessons to learn, *sipai* (soldier)!' he was told by his *gurujiharu* (instructors). 'To cross a busy road, answer the telephone, switch on an electric light or fan, turn on the water tap, and flush the toilet are some of the twentieth-century skills that you will be taught – and which most Westerners take for granted!' Furthermore he lost his name and was informed, 'So now, number 21164257 Rifleman Baliprasad Rai, you are to be known as Bayalis Sataunna (4257)!'

To the uninitiated this could be construed as merely a quaint and dehumanizing custom of Regimental discipline. But there was a logical necessity for the *gurujiharu* to address the recruits by their 'last four', a method also adopted by the recruits with each other. It was caused by the fact that three-quarters of those in his *galla* who would join the 7th Gurkha Rifles had *jat* surnames of Rai, Limbu, or Gurung. All this was the tip of a mountain of changes for the newly-arrived recruits. However the *gurujiharu* teaching Rifleman Bayalis Sataunna at the Malaya Lines depot in Sek Kong were experienced Gurkha NCOs who exercised considerable patience. Years ago they had also been exposed to this bewildering transformation to their lives. Some had completed their basic training in the Depot at Sungei Patani, Malaya where herculean toil was necessary with their kit and, in a moment of frustration, one made a mysterious

9

comment about Rifleman Bayalis Sataunna and his fellow *sipai* (soldiers) which sounded distinctly derogatory.

'Excuse me, *hajur*, but what do you mean?' asked Rifleman Bayalis Sataunna using the honorific form of 'you' to his elder and, without question, his better.

The Sergeant replied to the ramrod stiff recruit who had summoned up courage to speak, 'I'll repeat that, compared to us Gurkhas, your generation are nylon *sipai*. You are like instant noodles, with all the cheap qualities of the latter. At Sungei Patani we were taught things the hard way and used our spare time on bulling boots and other parts of our uniform, as well as scrubbing or polishing barrack-room paraphernalia for endless inspections. Everything on issue now, is made of either plastic, nylon, chrome, or other equally cheap material. There is little time and effort needed these days to keep it clean!'

The recruit looked at the Sergeant without replying, and then completed a smart right turn to dismiss himself. He could not stop wondering if the Sergeant was correct. Perhaps his superior had wasted much time with cleaning because, as a recruit, he was certainly busy and effective. Rifleman Bayalis Sataunna found himself back in the classroom again tackling the uphill battle of basic English. His school reports in Nepal described him as 'hard-working and laborious' although he had finished in the bottom half-dozen of his class. This applied to his Malaya Lines classroom progress braked by his agrarian upbringing. The emphasis had shifted from that harsh barrack-room discipline decades ago, to an environment for Rifleman Bayalis Sataunna and his *galla* more conducive to creating a modern, thinking soldier. This applied to other parts of the training syllabus such as weapon training, fieldcraft, physical fitness, minor tactics and shooting which made up the bulk of their day. The former lad from Chokum thrived, describing his new world with typical Gurkha innocence:

> It was the first time I had ever been outside the area of Bagsila, apart from my first trip to Dharan, and I was immensely thrilled and a bit bewildered. Within a short space of time we were turned from raw recruits into trained soldiers by our *gurujis* at Sek Kong. I was seeing a new world altogether and each day brought new revelations.[1]

His life-quality was far better than in Nepal, despite the Depot's rigid rules. He discovered that personal advancement in his new career lay entirely in his own hands, as opposed to partiality or nepotism so common in parochial Chokum. His judges, the British officers in particular, were all part of the same highly-motivated and trained team. Their sole cause for determining who would be the best, was service to the Crown. These *gora sahibharu* (white officers) all spoke Gurkhali, were smart, liked saluting and had a religion that worshipped time. Tradition dictated that Rifleman Bayalis Sataunna should trust these *sahibharu* who were so surprisingly impartial towards all recruits.

'They can be relied upon whether marking examination papers,' said the *guruji* sergeants, 'or making a plan for battle.' Thus the Rifleman accepted everything without question, having been positively influenced by this new system and way of life. He had come under the influence of 'the British Connection' – a Brigade of Gurkhas' invisible and unique Anglo-Nepalese bond that has made the synergy effect between Gurkha soldier and British officer so effective since Gurkha military service with the British began in the early nineteenth century. The months ticked by rapidly and, at the end of that year, the Depot passing-out parade marked a new phase in Rifleman Bayalis Sataunna's military career:

> In January 1981, I, along with forty of my comrades, were told that we were being posted to 7GR, and I was happy at the news. We joined the regiment in Gallipoli Lines where I was sub-posted again to the pipes and drums platoon, possibly due to my preference for music.[2]

The camp of Gallipoli Lines was tucked into the north-east corner of the New Territories just behind the expanding town of Fanling, and only a couple of miles from the Sino-Hong Kong border. Rifleman Bayalis Sataunna's immediate impression as he entered the whitewashed barracks was of a seemingly endless sea of basketball courts. This suited him well because, like others in his draft, he was not only fond of this sport but football and volleyball as well. Many of the Battalion's British officers despaired at this 'three-ball syndrome' believing it dominated the Gurkhas' sporting life too much, with traditional Khud Racing a victim.

Sport, though, was not on this new 7GR soldier's mind in those early days of 1981. There was a two-week introductory Regimental cadre and, most important of all, selection for his initial job. He had nurtured a secret desire for some months of becoming a piper in the Pipes and Drums band ever since he heard them play at one of the many Depot parades. Liking music was important, but the decisive factor was that the Regiment's 2nd Battalion would be re-raised in Hong Kong later that year with half of the current band being transfered across to the new unit. Volunteers were therefore asked for the 1st Battalion's P and D, as it was known. Rifleman Bayalis Sataunna leapt at the chance. However at his initial interview with the Pipe Major he learnt that, unlike British battalions, the P and D had a more offensive role in battle than operating as stretcher bearers.

The Pipe Major spelt this out in his introductory interview, 'Welcome to the P and D, Bayalis Sataunna. We enjoy playing the bagpipes, but one important fact you must never forget. We are first and foremost machine-gunners. Playing musical instruments always comes second. This means that we shall concentrate on training you as a gunner on the GPMG (General Purpose Machine Gun) in the sustained-fire role. You will learn to be both the number one and number two on the gun, as well as learning to play the pipes – and I promise you're going to be busy.' But the Pipe Major was an expert at understatement as the P and D's new piper noted:

> It was not all blowing bagpipes though, as our platoon doubled as the GPMG(SF) platoon, and I was again moving up and down all the familiar Hong Kong hills on exercises as the No. 1 gunner.[3]

He became immersed in the technicalities of the 'SF' gun. 'Laying-on' to pre-selected targets by day and night, unravelling mysteries of the dial-sight system, and man-handling the heavy and awkward tripod legs all required mastering before moving out to the firing range. Once there, long hours were spent firing a gun that, much to the surprise of Rifleman Bayalis Sataunna, had a capability of hitting targets nearly two kilometres distant. It was also great fun. Combined with piping lessons, formation marching, and a band uniform to maintain, this training would have been enough for most. But this was the Hong Kong exercise season with temperatures at their coolest, so he participated in his first ten-day Battalion exercise, followed by a four-week Sino-Hong Kong border tour at Sha Tau Kok and Tolo Peninsula.

The P and D were tasked to reinforce one of the rifle companies operating there. Split into a northern and southern village by the border, Sha Tau Kok had been the scene of tension at the height of the Cultural Revolution in 1967. Then the 1st/7th Gurkha Rifles were subjected in their sector to provocation from loudspeakers and the Red Guards. It had also been a reminder to the Gurkhas that Chairman Mao Tse-tung's Red China overshadowed its small neighbour of Nepal. The Communist media labelled them, '. . . the mercenary Gurkhas helping the Reactionary British'[4] and the Chinese waved Mao's famous *Little Red Book* tauntingly at them. It contained not only his political thoughts, but also a war doctrine based on *The Art of War* written in 490 BC by the Chinese General, Sun Tzu, 'That is why Sun Wu Tzu's axiom, "Know the enemy and know yourself, and you can fight a hundred battles with no danger of defeat", remains a scientific truth.'

The Gurkhas knew their enemy and themselves in the current illegal immigrant threat. Rifleman Bayalis Sataunna's first taste of operations was at the tail end of a two-year period when there had been a great upsurge in 'IIs' (illegal immigrants) attempting to escape from the Peoples' Republic, with the Battalion capturing 27,000 of them. '*Sipai!* This can be dangerous work,' he and his fellow riflemen had been briefed earnestly by the Pipe Major. 'After spending weeks on the run, they are desperate to avoid capture when crossing the border. If caught, they will be handed over to the Royal Hong Kong Police for repatriation via the Peoples' Liberation Army soldiers at the police post of Man Kam To. Their punishment will be incarceration in *lao-gai* or "Thought Reform Through Labour" camps. To avoid all this, they will use their fists, makeshift clubs, and knives when confronted by you Gurkha soldiers armed only with a baton and kukri. These are the rules of the game. No firearms can be carried, and only minimum force permitted!'

But on Tolo two years before, a Lance Corporal from the Battalion, Aimansing Limbu, had nearly drowned in a desperate struggle with three of these IIs. He finally apprehended not only them, but another five on their raft single-handed: a near comparable feat to the famous Gurkha story of Rifleman Gane Gurung who also bagged eight German prisoners during an individual assault in the 1915 Battle of Neuve Chapelle. A few days before Aimansing's achievement, Sergeant Dalbahadur Rai, had also grappled with another vicious II intent on avoiding capture. A dagger was drawn, and the Sergeant countered with his kukri to make the arrest. Arguably the Battalion's smallest Gurkhas, they were awarded the Queen's Gallantry Medal and Queen's Commendation for Brave Conduct respectively.

'So there are real chances of action, *sipai,* and maybe also a chance of receiving a medal from the *Maharindi* in London!' Rifleman Bayalis Sataunna and the others had been told.

To counter this huge influx of humanity into overcrowded Hong Kong's restricted land area, more money had been spent by the Government in reinforcing the border fence. This was now ten-feet high with barbed-wire rolls on top and a built-in intruder alarm system. Rifleman Bayalis Sataunna's operational tasks were restricted to the landside west of Sha Tau Kok where various methods had been implemented to capture the IIs. So patrolling on foot or bicycles, sitting in ambushes or in-depth 'stop' positions mainly by night, and manning observation posts on a twenty-four hour basis became the routine for him and his fellow riflemen. They caught single IIs and others who were in pairs or more. If the IIs escaped then other resources were set in to track them down – like the 'Nitesun' helicopters mounted with powerful searchlights, or tracker dogs from the Hong Kong Dog Unit.

Most Gurkhas, including Rifleman Bayalis Sataunna, found these occasional incidents exciting and rewarding after hours of patient waiting. But in his first year yet another adventure awaited that did not often come to Gurkhas as the busy piper explained:

> In March 1981 came more good news. The Battalion was going to England for a two-year tour. I was thrilled, and could not wait to see the 'gora saheb's' land about which I had heard so much. Yes, I was lucky I told myself.[5]

After weeks of preparation the Battalion moved in mid-1981. Flying from Nepal to Hong Kong did not compare to the twenty-two hour RAF trooping flight to Brize Norton and journey to the Gurkhas' UK camp which Rifleman Bayalis Sataunna came to regard quickly as a surrogate village to Chokum and provider of most needs. Experiences were many during the first few months in a country where, though so far from his native Nepal, the local English people appeared to hold the Gurkha name in high esteem:

> Our barracks at Church Crookham were cold, but comfortable inside, and I found the people friendly. We were kept busy since our arrival with various commitments – the Bisley (Army Championships) shooting competition, training, exercises and numerous band shows to perform all over the country, but it was a good and fairly cheap way of seeing Britain! We did a lot of training in the Stanford area especially during that bitterly cold English winter when I had my first real taste of snow. I thought that whatever Bagsila's shortcomings, it was never as cold as this. Little did I know that this was nothing to what I was about to endure . . . The high point of our training season was when our team won the GPMG(SF) United Kingdom Land Forces competition at Warminster, Wiltshire in late January 1982. We had become a good, professional team.[6]

. . . which is what would be required because, like the remainder of those Gurkhas serving in the Battalion then, Rifleman Bayalis Satunna was about to be sucked into the Falklands' War that began later in the spring of that year. Becoming a battlefield casualty, he returned from the Falklands in the early summer. A member of the Battalion's Rear Party, Regimental Quartermaster Sergeant Jasbahadur Gurung of the Quartermaster's Department, then wrote an account of the Rifleman's war experiences which was circulated to the wives of the Battalion's British officers in early July as the first, though partly exaggerated, account of the Gurkhas' role in the campaign.

'Send it to the *Reader's Digest* as a possible article for publication,' also suggested Major Bill Dawson, the Battalion's 2IC, to the Training Officer sahib who had just returned from the Falklands' War. But the seconded Light Infantry officer had another plan. Having completed already draft one of a possible book about the Gurkhas in the Falklands, he decided that the RQMS' story might become original Gurkha input to his next draft. With the Training Office's Sergeant Sarankumar Limbu interpreting, the Training Officer sahib then interviewed Rifleman Bayalis Sataunna who seemed surprised at the interest shown. The extra information gleaned plus original story, then resulted in this background perspective of a Nepalese teenager from the hills east of Kathmandu recruited into the 7th Gurkha Rifles and who became a representative Gurkha soldier of the Battalion which went to war in the Falkland Islands – and is where he, Rifleman Bayalis Sataunna, will also be encountered in this Training Officer sahib's war journal.

Chapter Two

FIRST ENCOUNTERS

The Gurkha in the mountains is as much superior to the British soldier as the Urial is to the Southdown sheep.[1] – Colonel Sir T.H. Holdich c. 1900[2]

Enduring the longest siege in British history alongside the other starving garrison personnel during the Axis Powers' Second World War blitz on the Mediterranean island of Malta whetted my father's appetite for more action. Herbert Seear was a Royal Air Force Squadron Leader in the Secretarial Branch but, post-war, qualified as an Intelligence Officer. Promotion to Wing Commander followed and, in January 1954, he was seconded to the Malayan Police Special Branch which was battling against the 'Emergency's' Communist Terrorist threat. His family accompanied him to the capital, Kuala Lumpur, and we eventually moved into a vast wooden bungalow in Damansara Road. Once home of a rubber plantation manager, by its entrance grew some beautiful bougainvillea bushes named after the Frenchman who first colonized the Falklands in the eighteenth century with settlers from St Malo, thus providing the Islands' Argentine name of Malvinas.

The bushes contrasted to the bungalow's ugly concrete stilts. 'These,' I was told, 'act as protection against possible floods from the monsoon rains and any inquisitive snake!' Although the convectional rain crashed down as regular as clockwork every afternoon, there were no floods and, despite our Chinese amah Lo Ying decapitating a cobra in the outside bath house, no snake managed to slither into the bungalow. Gold-toothed Lo Ying was kind to my twin brother and me. We developed a habit of eating an occasional bowl of her rice and small dried fishes whilst sitting Chinese hunker-style on the servants' verandah. It was excellent training for my later life appreciation of Gurkha food. But after our normal supper and to a background of the insects' hum from the garden, swish of the living room ceiling fan's blades and buzz of a mosquito, my ears would always twitch at the mention of 'CTs', and also that other name – 'Gurkha'.

Coincidentally both battalions of the 7th Gurkha Rifles in the adjacent states of Pahang and Negri Sembilan were engaged in operations against the CT full-time and, whilst we sat out on our veranda during the evenings, bombs from RAF Lincoln aircraft detonated on CT prey in the jungle nearby. More impressive to a seven-year-old was father's service pistol and its clip of ammunition. Frequently he would put the pistol into its holster strapped on his belt and disappear early in the morning to work – in the jungle. Often killed or captured in Gurkha ambushes, the CTs' plight was once

15

explained to me by father, 'You see, Mickey m'boy, those Gurkhas have an ability to wait days and nights like mice in an ambush. They're armed with a long knife called a kukri, so woe betide any CT who walks into their killing area. And when a Gurkha opens fire with his rifle he doesn't have a habit of missing.'

Waiting daily for the 6 o'clock radio news to report ambush results, father's fist once thumped on the table after hearing the 'kills' tally, his blow making the radio jump as he exclaimed, 'Gotcha! That's a really big fish landed!' Never one to divulge his 'hush-hush' work to my mother, on this particular occasion he added, 'God, those little men are good.' Or on other evenings, if CTs had been captured, it would be a terse, 'That'll mean business again tomorrow m'dear.'

It implied interrogation work on captured CTs assisted by a Chinese police inspector at the Special Branch Headquarters secret Holding Centre hidden behind a Kuala Lumpur rubber plantation. This would produce more operational intelligence for the Gurkhas and other British Army units. As a little boy who enjoyed his *Eagle* comic and spaceman Dan Dare's eternal struggle against the green Treens, in addition to fighting mock battles with his toy fort and soldiers against the doomed enemy forces of his twin, Philip, I became positively influenced by such comings and goings. 'Surely then,' was my simple conclusion, 'a soldier's life had to be anything but dull?'

But our idyllic existence was ended all too soon by father's unreasonable logic, 'You've fallen a year behind your education here, so now you must catch up in England!'

Always wanting to be a soldier, father put me on the traditional path towards a Queen's Commission in the next decade – first prep school in South Croydon, then Whitgift Public School at nearby Haling Park and, finally, the Royal Military Academy Sandhurst. Lacking academic motivation, my priorities always went to rugby and the modern pentathlon's diverse disciplines of horse-riding, fencing, pistol shooting, swimming, and cross-country running. I also met my future wife on a winter warfare course sponsored by the Norwegian Military Academy. The end-of-course party was held in Oslo where fifty schoolgirls had been mustered for fifty tanned and opposite-sex deprived Sandhurst cadets. The girls were deposited into one room of *Den Gamle Krigskolen*, and the cadets in another. Raffle tickets were distributed, partition doors flung open, and the order shouted, 'Call out your numbers gentlemen!' So I mumbled nervously to the waiting line of Viking females,' Anyone got sixteen?'

'Yes! That's me!' replied the blonde, green-eyed Tove, daughter of Oslo's Police CID Chief. It was also how number sixteen changed my life.

Commissioned in August 1968, my choice of Regiment was heavily influenced by promises of more pentathlon glory. But the Royal Corps of Transport was a grind. An eight-month detachment to the 2nd Battalion, Light Infantry with an exercise in Malaysia and London Public Duties, provided the motivation that my troop commander's life with twenty-two ten-ton lorries had to end. Belonging to a 'corporate' group like the LI with its express marching speed of 140 paces to the minute and skirmishing history in the American War of Independence and Battle of Waterloo, would have better status. So I transferred to 2LI in September 1971.

As a platoon commander my next four years were busy with Northern Ireland – two emergency tours in South Armagh 'bandit country' and Londonderry, and two

Spearhead Battalion 'crash-out' operations. Wedged in between was marriage to twenty-two year-old Tove (pronounced Tor-vah) and a peaceful posting to Shropshire. Then a pause from the whims of the Provisional IRA, other Irish extremist groups and politicians, which in blacker moments led me to believe the only solution to 'the Troubles' was to tow the Province out into the North Atlantic and sink it, arrived with a January 1976, 1st Battalion move to Kowloon, Hong Kong. By now I was a Captain and 2IC of B Company.

Our pre-departure briefing in Colchester was interesting. 'You'll be involved in Hong Kong internal security duties, the Sino-Hong Kong border guard, and ceremonial duties,' we were informed. 'This part of colonial Britain has been branded by the Communist Chinese as the "City of Imperial Decadence Run by the White Skinned Pigs". You, the hairy Europeans, are known as *kwai-lo* or "pale ghosts", stink of dairy fats, particularly cheese, and your barbarian women are a most loose form of species!'

Kowloon was indeed fascinating, but by early February the daily military routine had been established in our colonial-style barracks. The inmates of Battalion HQ then allocated different tasks to each rifle company as an initial Hong Kong orientation. 'B Company is to enter a team for the Khud Race,' the Battalion 2IC informed me. Perhaps his decision represented a surrogate form of chastisement, but I was curious and decided there and then to become the runner-manager.

Our Sergeant Major was the key to recruiting my team. 'Mighty mouse' Dudard-Aberdeen ruled with a rod of ron, did not take to fools gladly, and was a self-declared enemy of all B Company subalterns and its Captain. Standing to the rear of the serried ranks of soldiery, I listened to his Muster Parade oration on company routine and pitfalls of the Wanchai red-light district before the all-important item. '. . . we've been allocated the Khud Race. This is not an eating race against cows, but a run between other Hong Kong Service units. It'll take place in a couple of weeks up and down a steep bare-arsed hill, somewhere in the New Territories near the Sino-Hong Kong border!' He paused as eighty-odd soldiers guffawed, then threw down the gauntlet with a pinch of Clint Eastwood and basinful of sergeant major pseudo-democracy. 'I want volunteers. If I don't get them, I'll start press-ganging. Anyone feeling lucky? All you've to do is put up your arm!'

This time-honoured British Army form of selection did not deter ten fit LI privates. A briefing was needed, so the map and previous year's race programme proved useful. The 1,887 foot hill's official name was *Kai Keung Leng*. Located in the Colony's north-west corner near the border, it had another name of *Nameless*. I understood why a degree of anonymity was desirable. 'So how could anyone remember its real name in the exhaustion of climbing one mile and 614 yards with total elevation of 1,300 feet, followed by a corresponding descent fifty feet longer, and where the average gradient was 1 in 2.54?' I asked myself. 'Some vital statistics!'

One race for the major units with more than 300 men on establishment was for the Gurkha battalions. The other would be ours for minor units with less than 300. To finish in the top three individual places required a time of about sixteen minutes thirty seconds. A programme footnote explained that the modern British Forces' Hong Kong Khud Race origins came from the late nineteenth-century Indian North-West Frontier campaigns. It continued:

All movement in the mountainous terrain called at this time for deployment of pickets to secure high ground overlooking the route of the main column. Speed of deployment for the pickets both up and down the hills or khuds, was essential in securing the column's route of advance. Not unnaturally rivalry began to develop therefore between the pickets from different companies and detachments, and this led directly to hill racing as a sport.

'Some of you are cross-country runners, but we've got to start training tomorrow,' I urged my men, 'since there's only a fortnight before the race.' Despite two months of physical inactivity with UK posting preparations, embarkation leave, Christmas, and tiring flight to Hong Kong, their motivation was high. Exercises to strengthen calf muscles were interspersed with repetition running on the Gun Club barracks' football pitch and relay races up and down flights of stairs. This removed cobwebs from lungs so, after week one, I held another briefing. 'You've done well, but we've only got Monday and Tuesday to sample the course. To make maximum use of each trip, we'll have to start at 06.00 hours from Kowloon in order to arrive early at the New Territories and conquer *Nameless* twice daily!'

Some wrinkled their noses. 'Why *so* early? And why *twice*, sir?' they demanded. 'It's a limited gesture,' I conceded, 'but our climbing and descending techniques need practice to improve chances of not breaking our necks!'

We drove north in a cramped Army Land-Rover and, forty minutes later, reached the Tam Mei camp for Gurkha families behind Cassino Lines. Driving through the camp and along a narrow winding road, we finally reached our objective at the base of a green and brown mottled *Nameless*. Confronted by this beast silhouetted against the blue sky, its contour lines on the map were unrecognisable. 'A minor unit we might be,' I thought, 'but this is no minor assignment.' Then we noticed small stocky figures hurtling down a path on the hill's frontal spur. This was my first encounter with the Gurkhas. Their low centre of gravity produced a spectacular method of hill-running as, with arms flung outwards to preserve balance, they leapt over rocks with ease. Feet impacting into the hillside created mini-dust clouds as bulging thigh and calf muscles assisted these human projectiles' balance and speed. My Light Infanteers gasped.

'Blimey! Look up there! Wot's that bouncin' down like the clappers out of 'ell?'

'Dunno. Never realized Superman had been breeding!'

'Look. There's more of them nifty little bleeders. Must be them Gurkhas, but it's more like an avalanche of slimmed-down Michelin men bouncing down if yer ask me.'

Another team of Brit soldiers pointed out to us a large rock marking the course's halfway point and start of its descent, so we began the first session. More than thirty minutes later at the finish, my prostrate body told me the Khud Race would be no picnic. One team member voiced our collective thoughts by panting, 'It's not a hill, sir . . . it's a bloody mountain!'

He was bloody right, too.

We spoke again to the other Brits. One had competed in the previous year's race. His story confirmed our fears about the speed and agility of Gurkhas accustomed since birth to hills, and who had completed three months of hard Khud Race training.

'So what was it like then?'

'Well, it wasn't much fun. One Gurkha ran so fast he jumped on top of me coming down, and I was well and truly flattened.'

'But surely that must have helped your downward momentum a bit?'

'Nah, 'fraid not mate. I was still climbing up the bleedin' thing at the time!'

We tried again in the afternoon. It was difficult to judge what was worst, going up or coming down. Reaching the top, one considered other methods of descent like hang-gliding or para-gliding. Somehow we managed the descent again, but most feet were in a sorry state.

'Cor, look at my heel, sir. It's just become one gigantic blister!' complained one of my sockless team members as every other man discovered the same. To alleviate this, a raid was launched on the Battalion's Medical Inspection room from where we removed vast quantities of elastic bandages, gauze pads, plasters and antiseptic creams for treating our tortured flesh. Methylated spirits were also rubbed into our feet twice a day – supposedly to harden the soles. We also searched the local Kowloon Stinkies' market for that elusive *Nameless* capability of 'better foot-grip on descent' and eventually found a Chinese Peoples' Republic ten-dollar gym shoe with serrated soles. Another was not encouraged by this, exclaiming, 'Yeah, great stuff! That footwear's not going to help much against them Gurkhas, is it? But I suppose it might, at a pinch, prevent the owner from 'aving to slide down *Nameless* on the seat of his pants!'

There was another problem. Late February was still in the subtropical Hong Kong winter, but on *Nameless* our thirst had been unquenchable and gulping down iced orange from large Norwegian containers and cans of orange and lemonade became the vital catalysts that injected life into dehydrated bodies limping off the hillside. After the second day's training a couple of days remained to rest and lick self-inflicted wounds. We arrived early on race day. Tove had driven up with me from Kowloon as a mildly interested spectator of the event but, although she came from mountainous Norway, even her eyes began watering at the sight of our objective. Dressed in their Regimental mufti of dark green blazers and grey flannels and accompanied by their sari-clad wives, many Gurkhas were already walking up the road on their annual pilgrimage from Tam Mei Camp. Opposite *Nameless* was a small rise and there, chatting and laughing amongst themselves, they sat down to wait patiently. Luckily the temperature was only twenty degrees centigrade and relative humidity of seventy-five per cent. Ideal for uninitiated Europeans about to discover the Khud Race proper.

Soon other teams materialized as did our smooth-talking Commanding Officer. In his dark-green double-breasted Regimental blazer, Lieutenant Colonel Tony Wilson trod gingerly over the rough ground in his thin black leather moccasin shoes. He gazed at the finishing stretch of the course, then his eyes wandered upwards along its main part marked by six-foot flag poles which disappeared along the brutal *Nameless* gradients. Turning around to his 1LI racers, the CO then muttered, half to himself and half to us, 'Goodness! All I can say is that you're braver men than me . . .'

Having grown wise as to what *Nameless* could inflict on the lesser man, methylated spirits had been rubbed into our feet the last few days. This was more for a psycho-logical boost than scientific contribution towards hardening our soles. With another 100 hopefuls, we made our way along a narrow path at the hill's base to the start line, 200 metres from the finishing area. Turning right to face the summit, tufts of dry grass protruded between footholds pock-marking the course that angled away at seventy degrees. An Army PT Corps instructor swung his flag down and optimistically the charge began but, after only fifty metres, the gradient forced most into a hands-on-knees walk. The exceptions were a few better-trained Brits – and Gurkha competitors.

Lungs ballooned already. Body temperature increased. Sweat blurred vision. Thigh and calf muscles transformed into lead as ears popped with the gain in height. The terrain channelled runners into single file and those tufts of grass were grabbed for upward leverage in this nightmare. Occasionally a plateau of semi-level ground appeared, but any attempt to overtake others became fruitless since muscles refused to respond. Higher up a LI green running vest flashed past on my right. I had reached the large rock and turn round point. No time to admire stunning views of the sea dotted with small islands, the start of the steep descent knocked my legs from first gear direct into overdrive. My feet now had an impetus of their own. The Gurkha ability of braking to avoid yet another rock and selecting a new line of descent as well as maintaining speed was absent in us Westerners used to moving in straight lines. An inherent personal lack of coordination was another negative factor as my legs grew heavier and grunts of other runners behind neared. Several passed by and one had the temerity to suggest, 'Keep it up mate! Don't worry, it's all in the mind!'

Lacking breath to reply, I made a mental note of disbelief. Halfway down, the crowd came into view. Those colourful saris caught the eye again as cheers and whistles from the sea of black-haired Gurkha spectators floated upwards. Then two LI runners leapt past me. They emphasized once more my lack of balance and speed needed for Khud Race success, and in the last hundred metres of a near-vertical drop I tumbled head over heels. Crossing the finishing line, a legs-to-dough and knees-to-jelly metamorphosis already had occurred as my two 'catcher' officials carried out their task to perfection. Soon I was master of my senses again, although still wading through a proverbial sea of treacle.

The hors d'oeuvre over, a hush settled over the spectators. Amused by our antics, they began taking life seriously as the four Gurkha battalion[3] teams started their perfect demonstration of how to assault *Nameless*. They cruised up it as if running a flat 800 metres, then bored back down with such finesse that we in the first event resembled tortoises attempting the north face of the Eiger. Like most Brits my instinct had been to lean back, thereby braking downward momentum. Not so with the Gurkhas confident and strong enough to hold their bodies upright and maintain a rocket speed.

There was little surprise when a Lance Corporal of the 7th Gurkha Rifles set a new record time of fifteen minutes and thirty-four seconds. TV recorded the distribution of prizes by the smiling Commander of British Forces in Hong Kong, Lieutenant General Sir Edwin 'Dwin' Bramall. A former Royal Greenjacket infantry officer asked by the 2nd Gurkha Rifles to be their Colonel when appointed CBF, he understood the significance to the Gurkha soldier of winning in their unofficial national sport. However medals were presented not only to the drill-stamping Gurkhas, but also to us who captured the title of best non-Gurkha team. In addition, one Light Infanteer finished behind the first six Gurkhas of our race to become the best non-Gurkha 'minor' individual. This made up for our discomforts but, walking away from this razzmatazz, I was aware that this *Nameless* flirtation had awoken my latent curiousity about the Gurkhas.

Later, before a forthcoming 'Captain to Major' practical promotion examination, I met more of them. My first attempt in Colchester had caused much gnashing of teeth in the higher echelons of 1LI's Battalion HQ which made my ears wag red. 'Infantry officers don't fail an exam with an infantry scenario and ditto questions!' was one reprimand during the 'hot wash-up' debriefing. Seear's achievement of the impossible meant an encore and participation on a tactics study day at the Gurkha Officers' Mess under the shadow of *Nameless*. It was also an opportunity to sample the colonial atmosphere. Diminutive Gurkha waiters dressed in white uniform and small black hats, wielded enormous silver platters brimful with *bhat*. This was their version of Indian curry, not the violently hot Vindaloo or Tendaloo categories, but spicy meat and lentils accompanied by steaming silver tureens of silky-soft white rice. An undeniable delicious love at first taste and, perhaps, inspiration that ensured eventual exam success.

There then followed a one-month operational tour guarding the Sino-Hong Kong border against intrusion from Chinese IIs. 'B Company will be deployed, in depth, to the north-eastern sector of the Tolo Peninsula to face the seaward II threat,' our Company Commander directed us at his Orders Group. 'Mission – to seek out and capture any II who has swum or rafted across Mirs Bay. And I want you, Mike, to command an advance party of the three platoon commanders and two senior NCOs to prepare the handover/takeover from the 2nd Gurkha Rifles' Company who are currently on operations there.'

The only approach to our TAOR (Tactical Area of Responsibility) was by assault boat from the border village of Sha Tau Kok. Skippered by a Gurkha, the flat-bottomed craft with capacity for a dozen waited for us at the southern side of the jetty because its northern side was inside the Peoples' Republic. We skimmed across Starling Inlet to stop at the jetty of a semi-abandoned village. There we met the 2GR British officers for several hours.

After our oppos' departure, we were entertained by two of their Gurkha Sergeants with a 'tactical' meal of *bhat*. It had an excess of bones, but the conversation was more palatable. One of them had been chopping wood with his short wide-bladed kukri. So I asked him, 'Why does it have such a shape?'

In excellent English he explained, 'It represents, sahib, the three Hindu gods of *Brahma*, *Vishnu* and *Shiva*. That is – the Creator, the Caretaker of Heaven and the Destroyer of Evil. Over 200 years ago the King of Gorkha won the Kathmandu Valley because of the kukri. Most fighting was hand-to-hand, but his enemies were unsuccessful in defending themselves against the kukri. See. Here's mine,' he said, letting me feel its weight. He then showed us the heavier and blunt outer edge which gave a balance to the slightly elliptical blade of this slashing weapon. 'And pretty good for decapitation puposes,' I surmised as the Gurkha demonstrated a curious upward motion of his arm if an alternative stabbing action was required. The sharp inner edge performed the cutting. With assistance from the other Sergeant's kukri, he demonstrated that the notch near the base of the blade was responsible for the weapon's efficiency in battle.

A blow of a sword or, indeed, thrust of a bayonet, could be caught in the kukri blade and slipped down into the notch. A quick twist, normal to the kukri holder – but back-handed to his opponent, frequently disarmed the latter. 'The notch also stops blood from dripping onto the handle sahib,' grinned the Sergeant, 'but it is *not* used, as some would believe, as a rifle sight for aiming at any enemy target before throwing! Since that fighting for the Kathmandu Valley, our kukri has become Nepal's national weapon. And every Gurkha soldier, as you might know, is issued with a kukri as part of his uniform. But it's not just a battle weapon. Even the hill people in Nepal carry a kukri and it's used in everyday jobs such as butchering, tree cutting, and vegetable peeling.'

He showed us the two miniature knives fixed into the back of the scabboard. One was blunt. Known as the *chutna*, it was used for making sparks to light a fire or sharpen the main blade. The other, a *karda*, was sharp so that meat could be cut from bone. 'There's a good story about the kukri's sharpness,' continued the NCO. 'Have you heard of the Gurkha who met a German Afrika Korps soldier in the Western Desert during a Second World War battle there?' Although an old hat Gurkha yarn, we were ignorant of their folklore and shook our heads. Chuckling, our storyteller was having a field day with these *gora sahibharu*.

'Both had run out of ammunition, and the Gurkha rose up from behind a small sand dune,' began our host. 'Then the Gurkha attacked the German by slashing at his head so quickly with his kukri that it was impossible to see if the target had been hit. Nothing happened. Then the German grunted loudly, 'Ach, you have missed, Gurkha!' Raising his rifle, ready to thrust with his fixed bayonet, he then shouted, 'Und now it is my turn!' But the Gurkha had full confidence in his kukri. 'Oh no, German soldier,' he replied with a smile, 'try shaking your head first!''

This could be classified as a form of 'cutting humour', and the evening continued in the same enjoyable vein. I recounted our struggle with *Nameless* and that next year we might compete in the Major Units' race. Both Gurkhas laughed, shook their heads, and the talkative one exclaimed, 'Sahib, Gurkhas describe *Nameless* and the other hills around Tam Mei camp as, "*Hamro pahar jasto chha*". This means "it is just like our hills" and, of course, is why Gurkhas are so good at Khud Racing!' However they seemed impressed that a British officer actually wanted to try his luck again.

Later, when most had wandered off to their sleeping bags, the informative Sergeant asked me, 'Have you considered serving in a Gurkha battalion, sahib? You'll then see how the Battalion Khud Race team is trained and might even see Nepal in your leave! You know, we usually get officers from other British regiments joining us for two years to get some different experiences.' His sales technique had given me extra food for thought to which he added, 'If you do want to join the Gurkhas, sahib, remember we work hard and so, too, will you. Also liking *bhat* is a most important qualification!'

He assured me that II captures had been prolific during their Tolo company tour. This sounded promising as we were equipped with the first generation individual weapon sight known as the 'Starlite' image-intensifying night telescope. But we caught few IIs during that long April, and became convinced that the Gurkhas had much better natural night vision. Neither could our tactics have been as polished for, as we learnt later, the next Gurkha company on Tolo brought the II capture rate quickly back up to normal.

Meanwhile my wife had become even more enchanted with life in 'Fragrant Harbour' – the euphemistic Chinese name for Hong Kong. Her enthusiasm was neither undimmed by contracting dysentry, or her husband returning to Warminster for a six-week course at the School of Infantry. She took a break in Oslo, then I caught up with Tove at *Damansara*, my parent's West Sussex Rustington home, prior to returning to Hong Kong and Typhoon Ellen. Sixteen inches of rain in twenty-four hours, flooding, landslides, twenty-six Chinese killed, and many more injured was nothing compared to the bad news afterwards. Colonel Tony's interview preamble, 'I like you, Mike . . .' was the softing-up before my relegation to training Army cadets in Shropshire. To rub salt into the wound, I also had to sign an unflattering annual confidential report. Nonetheless as we took off from Kai Tak Airport in September, I was determined to experience Hong Kong and the Gurkhas again.

But first came those two years in the Shrewsbury wilderness, another fourteen months in Northern Ireland as a 2LI Company 2IC and watchkeeper at Belfast's HQ 39 Infantry Brigade, followed by a posting to Germany. 'OK, that's it. I've done my bit for Queen and country,' I sighed, en route to Belfast's Aldergrove Airport for the last time in January 1980. Perhaps that relaxing of professional attitudes led to later difficulties. A two-year junior Grade 3 appointment on the 1st British Corps HQ staff at Bielefeld, West Germany made a welcome change. Promoted Major that summer I was, to quote the Army vernacular, on the first leg of the 'sq ladder'. There were three legs for the slower bretheren like myself who failed to obtain a place at Staff College, with the staff-qualified ladder being a back door route to further promotion. The second leg had to be a Regimental company commander appointment, whilst the final one would be a Grade 2 staff job. The six-year process had no guarantee of success. Ticks in the correct profile boxes and a flattering pen picture on six successive confidential reports were vital, and anything less than a 'key' appointment brought the kiss of death to promotion prospects.

Although the 'Exercise Planning Staff' sign outside our office door possessed a grandiose aura, there were only two occupants inside. My fellow EPS office mate was a Queen's Own Highlander. Work consisted of assisting Major Philip Forster on command post exercises, and processing myriad BAOR unit applications to exercise over the German countryside. I enjoyed life which included sport such as orienteering and running in the inaugural Bielefeld marathon, but during the summer of 1981 received grapevine news that my next job would be at the Light Infantry depot in Shrewsbury. A third round of Shropshire did not appeal, so I dug out the necessary paperwork from our department's Chief Clerk and applied for a secondment to the Gurkhas. A couple of months later, an upper-crust officer's voice on the telephone from the LI Regimental HQ in Winchester provided the result: 'Well, Mike, I'm afraid that there's only one vacancy the Brigade of Gurkhas have come up with, and that's with 7GR at Church Crookham in Hampshire . . .'

'Oh, no. Not England again!' I thought.

'. . . but they're going to Hong Kong in '83 . . .'

My depression switched to an instant inner, 'Better!'

'. . . however they're scheduled for a six-month unaccompanied tour to Belize before leaving England!'

'Damn!' I cursed silently as my heart sank. Stories about 1LI's tour in 1974–75 to Belize in Central America indicated this was the arsehole of the world, enjoying a continued threat from neighbouring Guatemala. '*And* be without my family?' I thought. 'What was the answer then? OK! Buy some time from an HQ of which one staff officer had once described me during a interview as, 'an officer lacking panache". He was probably right, too.

'OK, understood,' was my worried response, 'but can I have twenty-four hours to think it through?'

I was relieved to hear: 'Yes, but only twenty-four hours!'

Putting down the receiver, contemplation began. 'Were the Gurkhas of the British Army really an anachronism in the twentieth century? Perhaps I could organize the Khud Race? Teach the Gurkhas orienteering? Train Gurkhas for a marathon? Gorge myself stupid on *bhat*? And, not least, sample Hong Kong again . . . ?'

CPX Philip looked up. This kilted officer's forte was throwing four armoured divisions, pitted against Orange Forces, around his enormous West Germany map for months, in designing six-day long paper command post exercises. Although a workaholic in moulding together precise detail and correct chronological sequence to achieve realistic play, he now spared a few seconds from such labours by saying, 'You'd be a fool not to accept the secondment, Mike!'

He seemed to have a positive opinion about the Nepalese. After all, his Regiment was affiliated to the 7th Gurkha Rifles, having operated with them during both World Wars in Mesopotamia, North Africa and Italy – *and* in the Malayan Emergency.

'Oh? Why's that?' I queried.

Philip's repartee contained a concealed challenge, 'For it'll be your only chance of experiencing nineteenth-century soldiering!'

Agreement was still required from my wife. It was never in doubt. 'Even though you'll get a Belize unaccompanied tour, I didn't get enough of Hong Kong last time round,' Tove reminded me. 'There's also our long-term plan to live in Norway, and we Norwegians don't send our children to boarding school!' Four year-old Victoria and one year-old Emily had become other major reasons why compulsive 'career-planning' did not affect our decision-making. For once we would steer our own future, so I accepted next day. A reminder of our decision came several weeks later after switching on TV to the British Forces' channel. It was broadcasting the London Royal Tournament with no less than 1st/7th Gurkha Rifles' B Company executing a demonstration company attack in the arena. A flashing kukri's decapitation of a dummy enemy soldier caused a big-eyed Tove to comment, 'Mm!'

When my posting order eventually arrived, I excitedly informed her, 'Looks like my new job'll begin in March 1982 as a Gurkha Company Commander for two and a half years!'

'Surely you'll need more information,' she replied, thoughts firmly on Hong Kong.

'OK, I'll ring the 7GR Adjutant tomorrow,' I assured her.

However the CO's personal staff officer was out. Instead I spoke to the Operations and Training Officer, Captain David Llewelyn-Davies. 'Oh, yes! Hello! I'm another seconded officer,' he informed me. 'You'll be in England for Christmas and want to visit us at the end of December? Couldn't agree more! It'll be well worth while.'

'Could you also inform the Commanding Officer that I'd like to . . . ?'

'Sorry, we don't refer here to the Colonel of 7GR as "Commanding Officer", or "CO". He's the "Commandant", y'know!'

Ignoring this clue that the posting might be like no other I had experienced, my main concern during the intervening period was of learning a little Gurkhali. Alas, foreign languages were, and still are, my blind spot. So I rang a 6GR British Captain serving on the 3rd Armoured Division's HQ staff at Paderborn. 'Gurkhali is the military version of Nepali which, in turn, is an off-shoot of Sanskrit,' he informed me, 'and Nepali is also the lingua franca of the many caste languages and dialects existing in Nepal.'

'Great,' I replied, 'but that doesn't help me a lot. Have you any Gurkhali grammar books so I can start swotting up for next year?' My Gurkha friend turned up trumps immediately: 'Don't worry. If Napoleon Bonaparte said every soldier has a field marshal's baton in his knapsack, then he forgot to mention an item vital for any Gurkha British officer – the standard issue "Basic Gurkhali Dictionary". Its author has the wonderful name of M. Meerendonk and so the book's simply known in the Brigade as "Meerendonk"! I'll post you mine tomorrow – then you can get cracking!'

A few days later this unique 'tactical' dictionary arrived. Fitting snugly into the palm of my hand, the outer covers were dark green – good camouflage when out in the field. But flicking through it that evening did not sooth my anxiety. 'Crumbs, this looks diffi-cult,' I complained to Tove who had such a natural linguist talent that any new acquaintance would be unaware she was Norwegian until told. 'For example, in Appendix B there's no less than seventy-three different expressions for family relation-ships and relatives!'

Gurkhali continued to cause headaches, but my recce went ahead. The wooden-hutted camp of Queen Elizabeth Barracks was a familiar stamping ground from my 1968 RCT Junior Officers Course. I drove up to the main gate where a Gurkha sentry stood. Wearing a large bush hat, he was clad in a khaki greatcoat. A menacing kukri dangled from his belt. He came smartly to attention as my car stopped, and then asked politely, 'Could I see your ID-card please, sahib?' I had not exchanged it for the latest type, and the sentry squinted repeatedly at my face and mugshot like a Wimbledon tennis spectator. Five minutes elapsed before his guard commander and he agreed I had no PIRA connections. A salute then rocked his stocky body as he barked, 'Sahib!' so fiercely it still rang in my ears as I parked outside Battalion HQ. Perhaps the sun had not yet set over the British Raj in this corner of England.

The redundancy of 'sir' as a form of address was even more evident inside the verandah-fronted HQ. In his office an irritated Adjutant was issuing a whirl of instruc-tions to the Gurkha RSM. It was a fluent demonstration of the diminutive warrant officer's language and my first encounter with Gurkhali. The Gurkha's, 'Sahib . . . sahib . . . *hunchha* (very well) . . . sahib . . .' replies indicated that the Battalion's impossible problems always landed here. The Adjutant finished his tirade and the RSM promptly whipped up the smartest of salutes to march out. Smiling benignly, the British officer then focused on me. Captain David Willis was a batchelor, workmanlike, and thorough

– as befitted a future Battalion Commandant. A little later he ushered me into the boss's office. In his third month of command, Lieutenant Colonel David Morgan was an approachable person bubbling over with enthusiasm and an inexhaustable supply of ideas. Awarded an MBE after a previous three-year job as Brigade Major of Hong Kong's Gurkha Field Force coordinating measures to stem the invasion of IIs, he was small in stature like his Gurkhas and explained their big future role within 5 Infantry Brigade.

'This'll be re-formed next month as the only regular British Army formation not tied to NATO's apron strings. It'll be committed not only to defending UK, but also have a world-wide "fire brigade" role. This "out of area" priority will focus on the Paratroopers of 2 and 3 Para seizing an airhead with us flown in afterwards as the airhead guard force,' enthused Colonel David. 'The possible scenarios for such an operation could be similar to those encountered by the Israelis on their raid at Entebbe in 1976,' he continued with a glint in his eye, 'or the dropping of French Foreign Legion paratroopers on Kolwezi four years ago to rescue foreign nationals caught up in the insurrection there. So we've got to be well prepared!'

He also talked about his men. 'The Gurkha's a dependable soldier who needs, nonetheless, good leadership from up front. Give him that, and he'll go through a brick wall for you. You'll find out before the end of your time here if you've succeeded. And, no doubt, you'll receive a silver kukri from your company as a parting present. The Queen's Gurkha Officers, that is the rank structure under the British officers, all speak English like most of the NCOs. As a BO you must rely on your QGOs. It'll also be handy to learn Gurkhali so you can get your message across. The language is top-heavy, with 100 words for different types of rice and a few English ones for such modern expressions as "beer", "radio", "GPMG" and . . .' he gesticulated towards a piece of furniture in the corner of his office, '. . . "table".'

Then came the news I dreaded. 'It'll be to your advantage to do a language course soon. We've applied for you to go on the four-week Hong Kong course in May next year. There's an exam at the end of it. Don't worry. You'll pass. Everyone does!' Although the Colonel was unaware of my blind spot for foreign languages, unforeseen events in the South Atlantic would postpone these Gurkhali academics. The interview ended, he made a phone call. 'Hello, David. Yes, we're finished. Can you take Mike up to the Mess for tea now?'

Whilst waiting I asked, 'Um, could you give me an idea of the current availability and location of married quarters, sir?' It was a case of once bitten, twice shy after having three homes in Germany during the past two years. Also fear of being cooped up daily in human cattle wagons to and from the City had been an important factor in joining the Army. Colonel David confirmed the Gurkha posting perk, 'No problem. There's plenty, and they're only a stone's throw from our camp.'

My relief at this ease of getting to work was short-lived when my future boss added, 'And that's a big advantage. Married quarters close by are a necessity in a Gurkha battalion since we start the day with BIT at seven sharp!' This sounded painful, and he strengthened my suspicions by explaining, ' BIT, in case you're confused, means "battle individual training" of running and physical jerks. You'll train with HQ Company, then afterwards can shower and breakfast with the other BOs in the Mess!'

26

Although I enjoyed being fit, this information represented the coin's downside. Every morning was an individual battle to terminate my Egyptian PT in bed. Now there would be an additional fight with the Gurkha variety. There was a knock on the door. In came Captain David Llewelyn-Davis. His crevassed face revealed an age of mid-forty, far removed from my impression on the telephone of a youthful seconded Ops/Training Officer. 'OK, David'll look after you now,' smiled the Colonel. 'Oh, and pencil into your diary next October's Belize tour. We'll be taking over from 2 Para.'

My host drove me by car to the Officers' Mess explaining en route, 'Normally there're separate Messes for both sets of officers but, for this tour, a shortage of space exists. All the QGOs live-in here, since their wives aren't permitted on UK tours. Hence our joint British and Queen's Gurkha Officers' Mess is a compromise!'

We walked into the ante-room where there were a few seated QGOs. 'Hello sahibs!' said David breezily. Although a Gurkhali speaker, he conversed with them in English.

Their reply was a unison, 'Good afternoon sahib!' whilst my eyes flicked around. Silver ornaments of all shapes and sizes were placed on various small tables, including a large attractive elephant. Bookshelves overflowed with Regimental histories. Several fearsome kukris hanging in Nepalese silver scabbards engraved with a multitude of intricate designs also hit my eye. On the walls were cases of campaign medals and pictures that included a magnificent Terence Cuneo painting of the 7th Gurkha Rifles mounting guard at Buckingham Palace. I felt a little like royalty, too, as the QGOs stood up. With years of Battalion service behind them, they had been promoted from the ranks.

'They're mostly the company 2ICs, platoon commanders, and deputies of other departments,' David whispered as we strode over to them.

'Meet Seear sahib from The Light Infantry. He'll be taking over A Company,' fussed David. The QGOs stepped forward to shake hands and the personal introductions began. 'Here's Tekbahadur sahib, Mike. He's one of your future platoon commanders!'

'How do you do, sahib,' said Lieutenant Tekbahadur Limbu sahib gravely, 'you're most welcome to the 7th Gurkha Rifles!'

I picked up the ritual – add 'sahib' to either a name or the second person singular. My reply was textbook correct, 'Thank you, sahib. I'm looking forward to working here.'

'Mike, this is Captain Khile Rai sahib, Support Company's OC sahib,' continued my guide using a further modification of address.

'So, one could add sahib to a title as well,' I thought whilst shaking hands with the even graver-looking Khile sahib. All this was most useful, but also dangerous. 'Sahib', it seemed, could be used in any context but could also promote laziness if the name of the officer being addressed had been forgotten.

'Do you like being in England, sahib?' I asked the OC Support Company sahib.

'Oh, it's nice, thank you sahib – except for the freezing weather, ' replied Khile sahib. His discontent was justified because the winter was exceptionally cold. Snow and floods were good acclimatization, though, for the austral winter to come. All were dressed in thick sports jackets, and some had even replaced their green Regimental tie with polo-necked pullovers. Introductions over, we sat down.

'They use the title "sahib" a lot,' I whispered over my cup of tea.

'Standard custom,' David muttered back as those deep wrinkles puckered into twenty different expressions per minute, 'and even 10GR's Major Rambahadur Limbu who, during the Borneo Confrontation, became the thirteenth Gurkha ever to win the Victoria Cross, is known as "VC sahib"! But, tell me, why did you decide to second?'

I mentioned the Khud Race and conversation with the 2GR sergeants on Tolo after they had been deserted by their BOs. David laughed, lit up a third cigarette in as many minutes, and exhaled the pithy comment of one seasoned in matters Gurkha, 'Typical 2GR officers. Within Brigade folklore they've always been known to be so idle and snobbish that they only converse with the Lord Almighty, whilst we 7th Gurkhas are labelled as being uneducated, unwashed, and undisciplined. Must be something to do with being flexible and always winning the Khud Race. You've definitely joined the right Regiment!'

He then chatted about his maverick background. 'I was commissioned as a Gunner, also served with the Royal Marine Commandos, and then transferred to the Army Air Corps. I spent five years as a Hong Kong helicopter squadron pilot where many of my customers were Gurkhas. This gave me the idea to second, but it'll be my swansong,' he sighed. 'You see, my wife's not keen in following the drum for the rest of her life.' Known as L-squared, David Llewelyn-Davis was a Battalion institution. Violently pro-Gurkha, amusing and sometimes charming, he mentioned two vital Gurkhali words before I left that evening, 'Look Mike, you'll do well to remember that *kaida* dominates this Regiment. *Kaida* is stronger than tradition, roughly translating to method or rule. Also if you've any communication problems with the *keta* and all else fails, then don't forget to say "*shyabash*". They'll love that because it means "well done"! OK?'

This is where my Gurkha and Falklands' War journal, unhindered by the blind devotion often apparent in those with a more intimate knowledge of these small warriors from the Kingdom of Nepal, really begins.

Chapter Three

SECONDMENT

Square-built, sturdy men with fine, muscular and large chest and lung development, ... a merry-hearted race, intensely fond of soldiering ... hardy and extremely single-minded, kind-hearted and generous and absolutely truthful, ... very proud and sensitive, very independent ... intensely loyal to each other and their officers, delighting in all sports. – Major E. Vansittart c. 1900[1]

The next couple of months went by slowly. In that first March week came the packing and formal 'marching-out' of my Gumbinner Strasse married quarter at Bielefeld. My girls flew from RAF Gütersloh, while I travelled on the Townsend-Thoresen Ostend-Dover ferry. Unaware that such vessels would soon be part of a more significant collective cruise south, and apart from an obstinate customs officer insisting my heavily-laden car be emptied in his hunt for a registration number on a TV-set, the trip was uneventful – unlike that soon to come. After 'marching-in' to 80, Wakefords Park, I met up with my family and, at the weekend, began the attempt to create order from chaos. I should have been more superstitious: not only were Tove and I about to live in our thirteenth home in ten years of married life, this would also be my thirteenth job in the Army. But then serendipity had never featured too much in my life.

Monday, 8 March would be my first day with the Gurkhas. The first officer I met in Battalion HQ was the new Adjutant. This slighly-built Captain had just finished a rapid exchange of Gurkhali with his Chief Clerk, Lieutenant Rupman Thapa. 'Obviously an expert in the QGO's language,' I noted before introducing myself with a breezy, 'Hello, I'm Mike Seear, the new OC A Company. And if I could speak Gurkhali like you then I'd be more than happy!'

Mark Willis smiled in reply, 'Then I recommend a five-month Nepal trek, like I did, paying out Gurkha pensions!'

And later that morning Rupman sahib would reinforce to me his master's opinion, 'It is, sahib, the best method of learning Gurkhali because there are few who speak English in the hills. Also,' he beamed proudly, 'the Adjutant sahib is probably the best Battalion BO Gurkhali speaker!'

Ushered into Colonel David's office, its incumbent had news of a reshuffle, 'I've decided, Mike, you'll take over L-squared's job as the Ops/Training Officer since he's now going to the 2nd Battalion in Hong Kong. David Willis will become OC A Company after returning from the course he's on. Then, in October, you'll be cross-posted to A Company and take over from David as OC. Perhaps it's no bad change of plan. Working in Battalion HQ will be an ideal "running-in" period before becoming Company Commander.'

Week One continued with our handover/takeover. Meeting my QGO Assistant Training Officers had priority. 'Hello sahibs!' beamed the chain-smoking L-squared as he marched into their office. 'Here's your new Training Officer sahib!'

This was to be my title even when under enemy fire three months later. Captain Dilbahadur Newar and Lieutenant Harkabahadur Rai stood up. Typically dark, short, efficient, and good English speakers, their deadpan expressions broke into instant smiles at the hint of a joke. They were so ultra respectful to their new Light Infantry sahib that my ego risked becoming dangerously inflated. Their office was a hum of activity and covered in maps, charts, calendars and training programmes. 'They've a tight grip on the Battalion's training,' I was assured by L-squared afterwards, 'so there'll be little to do except tweak the rudder.'

There were twenty BOs. They held all the key appointments and one was also next door. Fond of a dram or two, Major Bill Dawson was the larger than life 2IC sahib. He was another excellent Gurkhali speaker and enthused about his men. 'I couldn't even begin to think of serving with other soldiers,' he declared. Collecting handguns was his hobby, and he praised the Gurkhas' marksmanship in the Borneo jungle during the 'Confrontation' with Indonesia. His aim was also good. L-squared's in-tray had been constantly shelled with Bill's 'yellow peril' memo slips on which were scrawled many a directive.

'You'll be guaranteed no relaxation when I've gone, Mike, because Buffalo Bill's bombardments are bound to continue,' warned L-squared after we left the 2IC's office and on to another nearby HQ hut where the enthusiastic Second Lieutenant Redding stalked.

'Hi! I'm Paddy!' said the newly appointed Intelligence Officer with a radio signals appointment title of 'Acorn', as opposed to my fiercer one of 'Kestrel'. But we had something in common as the young IO's father, Colonel Desmond Redding, had been on the staff at my previous posting in Bielefeld. By virtue of impending circumstances I would become acquainted with the Colonel's son quickly enough.

Next day was spent reviewing company training programmes, and briefings on a rifle company night exercise and Battalion airportability exercise. 'The companies are also into nuclear, biological and chemical warfare training at Porton Down's NBC battle simulator, and you'll also have to start planning a Battalion exercise in May at Stanford. So don't forget to skim through this copy of the Battalion's Standard Operating Procedures before you begin!' the outgoing Training Officer sahib reminded me.

We visited Aldershot Range Office on the Wednesday. On Thursday, my thirty-fifth birthday, I was 'walked' around the camp to visit the BO company commanders located in the maze of wooden huts. L-squared continued to ply me with information en route, 'A British battalion, as y'know, has three rifle companies. But 1,000 Gurkhas on our establishment means that 1st/7th Gurkha Rifles has an extra rifle company. About a quarter of the soldiers at any one time are rotated through their six-month Nepal leave which occurs for each man every third year . . .'

At each corner my right arm pumped piston-like in returning salutes. B Company commanded by Major Guy Pearson was in the Belize jungle for seven months and not due back until May. First stop was D Company. The broad-shouldered, craggy-faced Company Commander, Major Mike Kefford, was an adventure training and Himalayan rock-climbing fanatic. 'D'you canoe or climb?' he demanded. I beat a sensible retreat to C Company and the more relaxed Major T.A.J. Lewis. Alan, otherwise known as Taj, had been in my Sandhurst intake, was married to Australian Meg, and had an eye already on retirement to kangeroo land.

'What's on your current training programme, then?' I enquired.

To Taj a spade was a spade. 'Well, we're escaping shortly from the powers that be in Battalion HQ and also this bloody winter to an overseas training exercise and a lot of sun-bathing in Cyprus!'

HQ Company's boss was Major Rory Stewart, seconded on tour number two from the King's Regiment. Responsible for camp administration and logistics on exercises or operations, he was also stone-deaf in one ear. Only after the introduction did he realize belatedly I was talking. 'Oh sorry!' he suddenly said, 'you're addressing the wrong ear!' Lesson learnt. Always face Rory if you wanted to speak to him.

Finally, A Company. My future Company 2IC, Captain Narainprasad Rai, seemed *kaida* personified – dependable, polite and all smiles. He was talking to another visitor, Captain Pratapsing Limbu who was a foot taller than the average Gurkha five feet two. He was being groomed for the top Battalion QGO job of Gurkha Major, and currently detached to Buckingham Palace as a Queen's Gurkha Orderly Officer. 'Unusually, Pratapsing sahib has been the previous A Company Commander,' said L-squared to me later, 'which reflects the general shortage of Gurkha BOs. But Pratapsing's also an excellent QGO!'

It had been a busy morning. But any BO newcomer has to be entertained in the Gurkha Sergeants' Mess. Our host, RSM Karnabahadur Rai, stood ready in the doorway. 'He's got bulldozer-like skills on the football pitch, and a fearful parade square voice,' whispered L-squared in my ear. It was not apparent now. His hands clasped together as if offering a prayer, Karnabahadur bowed slightly to utter the traditional Nepalese greeting of, '*Namaste*, sahib!' Arguably the British Army's smallest RSM, his stocky body frame matched his nickname of One-Ton earned years before. Driving a one-ton Land-Rover that simulated an aircraft during an airportability exercise, he was late on parade. 'Where's the one-ton?' everyone asked. Inevitably the name stuck, but his *bhat* was superior to the exercise and cookhouse 'beaks 'n' bones' norm served to me six years before on Tolo Peninsula.

'Don't worry. If you get fed up with *bhat*, there's a further menu sophistication in our Mess,' L-squared assured me afterwards, 'and we'll try it tomorrow.' I wondered what awaited me there as my guide pointed to the multitude of football matches that seemed to occur daily on the camp's football fields. 'And you should take serious note that besides *bhat*, there's another Gurkha passion!' he warned. 'So take an interest, Mike, because you're also the Battalion Sports Officer. Remember representing the Battalion in the annual Gurkha inter-unit football Nepal Cup championship, is every Gurkha's ambition!'

Eighteen months later during one of my A Company orders parades, I discovered

31

footballing ability could also be used as a Gurkha bargaining chip. The BOs' Battalion promotion board had decided that one of my Sergeants did not qualify for promotion, but no civilian firm could even begin to match the agony of our deliberations or fairness. My planned five-minute interview with the NCO stretched to an hour as our dialogue ping-ponged backwards and forwards:

'Sahib, I cannot understand this decision! It is not right!'

'Why? You know the system. You've not been selected for promotion, and this means a retirement course before returning to Nepal on pension in six months.'

'But sahib! I am a good soldier who should be promoted after seventeen years of service!'

'Why?'

'Because I have been a good sportsman – *and* Battalion team footballer!'

Currently I was little the wiser, however, as to the strength of the spell that football held on Gurkhas. The handover/takeover was nearly complete. On Friday we visited Aldershot and Ash Ranges to observe Gurkha shooting, before moving on to 5 Brigade HQ's training and ops staff. Returning to the Gurkha Officers' Mess and its dining room, my guide showed me the sideboard on which stood steaming rice, and meat and lentils swimming in a thick sauce, to remark, 'That's *bhat* GT – Gurkha Type. The other dish on offer is *bhat* BT!'

I was confused. 'But isn't there only one type?' I queried.

'No,' he replied, 'in a British Gurkha Battalion there's British Type too – meat and two veg. That's the menu sophistication!'

Most BOs opted for *bhat* BT. The exception was a languid subaltern by the name of Lieutenant David Wright. A short-service university entrant to the Regiment, he exuded a distinct laid-back impression that his military career was a hobby. This young Deputy P and D President's philosophy of, 'It's simply not British to say how good you are!' was reflected in his professionalism towards the consumption of *bhat* GT. I joined him where he sat amongst a number of the QGOs. David had such an enormous plate of *bhat* before him that it could have competed quite happily with the heights of *Nameless.* 'Just can't get enough of the stuff!' he gasped between the heavenly-tasting mouthfuls as our agreement on this matter quickly became a mutual gastronomic reality.

Afterwards L-squared and I returned to the Training Office. Proud to have become a member of the Battalion, my closer encounters with the Gurkhas had been positive. But one item remained. 'Oh, damn!' exclaimed the ex-Training Officer sahib, on his way out to the Mess to pack for Hong Kong, 'I nearly forgot! You're also the Unit Public Information Officer, so you'll be the media's Battalion contact man!'

'You're joking, aren't you?' I exclaimed. 'My CV's got a zero public relations entry in it!'

'Don't worry, old boy,' soothed L-squared, 'there's a PR Officer at South-East District HQ in Aldershot to give advice, and the Army's easiest PR job is right here. Nothing ever happens in sleepy hollow. But if you're so inclined, there's no problem in acquiring plenty of media coverage. The local civilians, y'know, always want a Gurkha home for Christmas!'

My predecessor had timed his disappearance perfectly, because I would find out soon enough that the 1st/7th Gurkha Rifles' Public Information Officer was anything *but* a Rip van Winkle sinecure. But, for now, that weekend was kept busy with continued unpacking of the many boxes of family bric-a-brac – and then, on 15 March and the second Monday with the Gurkhas, I ascended my new throne in the Training Office still dripping sweat from a BIT workout. After a while I stuck my head around the neighbouring door to ask my two Assistant Training Officers, 'How's the planning getting on for the Battalion airportability exercise taking place later this week, sahibs?'

'It's all OK, sahib. Nothing to worry about!' came their firm reply, signalling that current tasks of the new Training Officer sahib should be restricted to reading himself into his new job, answering the occasional telephone call, and dealing with the constant flood of Dawson yellow perils.

Opportunities also soon arose to observe the other QGOs and Gurkha other ranks. The twenty-six QGOs put the BOs' ideas into practice, dealt with all the mundane problems, and were the conduit between British and Gurkhas. Three *burho* officers had special charisma. Captain Khile Rai commanded Support Company comprising the Anti-Tank, Mortar and Reconnaissance Platoons. In dark-green Regimental blazer and tie, grey flannels and black shoes, Khile sahib with his almost permanent expressionless face, seemed a cross between an elegant James Bond and robot Arnold Schwarzenegger. 'Definitely unwise,' I thought on my second meeting with him, 'to have a nocturnal encounter with this Gurkha Terminator leading a Gurkha fighting patrol!'

Another was the 'Number 1 Quartermaster' – Captain Rambahadur Gurung. Awarded the British Empire Medal for coordinating the Church Crookham barracks' refurbishment a decade before, he was promoted three years later from a QGO captain to Gurkha commissioned officer. Only seven others in the Brigade held such a commission which equated to that of the Battalion's 'Number 2 Quartermaster' – Captain Les Peacock, an ex-3 Para RSM. 'Ram's' service in 7GR had been for as long as I had lived. It included the Malayan Emergency and Borneo Confrontation. He had seen Commandants come and go. Sometimes cantakerous, always willing to debate issues, he was nonetheless loyal and a respected Battalion institution. I knocked on his door and entered. He looked up from his desk to say, 'Welcome to the 7th Gurkha Rifles! Please sit down, Mike. You'd like some tea? So, how long will you be staying with us?' He appeared willing to tolerate the fumblings of a freshman *gora* sahib.

'The normal two and a half year tour for seconded officers,' I replied, relaxing in my chair whilst a Gurkha scurried in and put a cup of tea on the table in front of me.

'Hospitality's clearly a Gurkha hallmark,' I thought as his boss provided a friendly warning of, 'Well, you'll find things a little different to what you've been used to in the Light Infantry!'

Ram's understated prophesy was already fact, and we chatted about matters military, the Battalion, and my becoming its Ops/Training Officer. We seemed to find a mutual wavelength. 'You're also a bit different from the others,' he remarked. Although L-squared and Rory were of a similar vintage, seconded BO officers were normally a lot younger. Viewed retrospectively, perhaps this was a disadvantage for one a bit too set in his ways. 'OK, nice to meet you,' finished off Ram – to add in a kindly manner, 'and, if I can give you some advice, you'd do well to rely on your QGOs when you get your rifle company in the autumn.'

The last *burho* was the senior QGO, Major Lalbahadur Rai. He was the Battalion Gurkha Major, but his informality and urbane sophistication took me unawares. Lalbahadur sahib's grin stretched from ear to ear as he shook my hand and exclaimed, 'Hello sahib! It's good to have you with the Regiment!' Within the hierarchy he equated to a British RSM. Colonel David deferred to GM sahib's judgement on all Gurkha matters of custom and religion and, in contrast to the British RSM-CO partnership, this duo walked in tandem on inspections and parades. It was rumoured Lalbahadur sahib had a secondary career as 'in-house' consultant on a matter dear to the Gurkhas' agricultural heart – the purchase of Nepal *kepat*, and also took pride in 'his' Church Crookham camp *kepat*, as I would witness at the end of the week.

On Wednesday I had the privilege of being invited into the Gurkhas' *mandir* by DB sahib. This was their local Hindu temple, and turned out to be a low wooden barrack hut on the far side of the parade square converted into an operational centre for the *Pandit*, a non-English speaking Hindu priest, and his teaching of this non-pacifist religion with its multi-god choice. He was of the upper-class *bahun* caste and served on contract to the Battalion where no religious ceremony is complete without his presence. He stood by proudly as DB sahib said, 'You know, of course sahib, that cows are regarded as sacred by Hindus and eating of beef is forbidden.'

The QGO raised his eyebrows to indicate this was why my leather Highland brogue shoes had to be removed on entry. The interior was empty except for the altar on which rested a large gold idol of the Gurkhas' main deity, *Durga* the Goddess of War, who fights against evil. 'It's a paradox, *Durga* in such a male-orientated environment is female!' I thought while gazing at the idol draped in red ribbon – a colour also painted by Hindus on their dead.

'The October festival of *Dashera*, the Hindu equivalent of Christmas, is when *Durga* is honoured on *Mar*, the third day,' DB sahib informed me. 'We gather the Battalion's weapons of war in the temple to be blessed and, in Nepal, a male buffalo is sacrificed by cutting his head off with a kukri. This must be done by one blow because more than one means bad luck.' After admiring the *mandir* and *Durga*, we began putting on our footwear to leave, DB sahib found it necessary to continue his explanation of how the pragmatic Gurkhas tailor made their gory customs when serving abroad, 'Our battalions in Hong Kong don't kill a buffalo because of the expense so, instead, a goat is sacrificed. But here at Church Crookham,' he added a trifle embarrassed, 'we cannot risk offending the British animal protection society, the RSPCA. So therefore, sahib, we always use a large cucumber as a substitute goat which is then cut in half!'

However that autumn, despite DB's assurances, I bumped into a Gurkha walking along a hut corridor with a goat on a leash. He pulled it around the next corridor corner to rush out of sight, thereby strengthening my suspicion that the vast majority of Gurkhas knew nothing about the existence of the RSPCA or its honourable philosophy and aims. This was reinforced by a later story I heard of a Gurkha soldier out and about in the nearby town of Fleet. In front of one shop he encountered an old lady attired in a smart tweed two-piece suit rattling an RSPCA collection box and requesting donations. The Gurkha was impressed and generously inserted a 10p coin into the box, only to remark back in camp, 'English beggars are far more respectable and better dressed than those in Nepal!'

Thursday's airportable exercise demonstrated Gurkha pride in their equipment. Most of the Battalion were transported to the South Cerney Movement Control Centre for RAF Brize Norton. As Unit Emplaning Officer, I took an interest in the details. Each Gurkha had full equipment scales which would be spot-checked. Three men per platoon were singled out. The first batch shuffled forward. An infringement of *kaida* would be a Regimental disaster, and their apprehensive look asked silently, 'Have we done anything wrong?'

'Right! You men take out the contents of your kit bags, and these'll be matched against checklists held by us,' instructed one of the two RCT Movements NCOs hovering nearby. The Gurkhas complied. But their bulled-up field training (note: *not* parade) boots, precision-ironed creases in towels and clothing such as PT shorts, PT vests, combat jackets and trousers, sparkling eating utensils, mess tins so gleaming that they could be used as mirrors, delicately rolled up individual spare bootlaces, and other immaculate equipment only brought forth British expressions of stunned disbelief. There were equally worried Gurkha ones as they registered the British NCOs' reaction. The latter looked at each other and exchanged a few words. One of them then approached me. 'Cor blimey, sir,' he exclaimed, 'We don't have to continue with this any more. You'd never get British squaddies producing such fantastic kit as this!'

He looked again at the Gurkhas' possessions as if to make sure he was not hallucinating, then shook his head muttering to himself, 'Are these guys real?' The Gurkhas had misunderstood. They froze, stunned. Their eyes narrowed. This was *naramro* (bad). Personal kit to a Gurkha soldier is sacrosanct and always well maintained, far better than any British soldier's. So to receive derogatory comments from these British NCOs on this matter was quite beyond the pale. Someone had to allay their fears, but my Gurkhali vocabulary was hopeless.

'Prevent an international incident, Seear – for God's sake, try to convert *naramro* into something much better than the tepid *ramro* (good)!' I urged myself, only to remember L-squared's advice. And my immediate, '*Ramro! Shyabash! Ramro!*' worked like a charm too, judging by all the Gurkha grins and chuckles as they repacked their kit bags.

The following morning was my turn to be grilled in an interview with the Brigadier at Aldershot. That six-mile journey in a Land-Rover stretched to double that distance by my Gurkha chauffeur's non-existent sense of direction. This first encounter with the Gurkha achilles heel of motorized vehicles and driving was underlined by his employment of steering and gear-changing techniques that would have caused even the most daring of World Championship Formula 1 Grand Prix racing drivers to refuse the offer of becoming his passenger. Only exceedingly good luck ensured my arrival at the 5 Brigade HQ just before the appointed hour, albeit scarcely fit enough to be ushered into the office of my ex-CO.

Brigadier Tony Wilson was a stylish officer. He been awarded the Military Cross as the 2LI A Company Commander of Newry in 1971 when I was a platoon commander at Dungannon on the same Battalion emergency tour. His decoration was the result of outstanding leadership during a period when the PIRA carried out some of their worst excesses and the local township had burnt and rioted for several days after the introduction of internment. Two reinforcing artillery batteries converted to the infantry role, plus an armoured car squadron, had been placed under his command to assist his Company quell the violence. He had also been my CO in 1LI when I had competed in the Khud Race.

His appearance remained unchanged. Of slim build, dark, with a heavily-jowled face, the Brigadier's inquisitive eyes summed up a person with ease. He also had a ladies' man reputation. His elegant wife was, to mimic that special Light Infantry officer phraseology and intonation, a 'su-pah' lady. In three months Janet would become ultra-super when, with the going getting rougher, she demonstrated her innate Brigade mother-hen ability to provide effective psychosocial support for the other officers' wives – including Tove – by hosting supper parties, visiting married quarters, and giving optimistic encouragement. But though my interview with her husband that day might have begun with a similar, 'Welcome to 5 Brigade and I hope that you'll have a good time here,' type of approach, his actual opening line, 'Well, Mike, I see that you've fallen on your feet now that you're with 7GR . . .' was articulated with the precision of a diamond cutter. It indicated my past indiscretions had been remembered, although the ensuing conversation was pleasant enough.

I returned to Church Crookham in time to observe the weekly Friday afternoon ritual of the GM's Fatigues Party which launched a merciless offensive against dirt, rubbish and anything else that blemished the local environment. At the appointed hour, cohorts of green track-suited Gurkhas paraded behind my office to be given their proxy battle orders by the RSM. I understood nothing of what was being said, but Captain Mark Willis saw me watching and remarked, 'You should be aware of a neat Gurkha digital system of address.'

'How's that done then?' I asked as, post battle briefing, the Gurkhas commenced hostilities with their brooms, shovels, pickaxes, and ubiquitous kukris.

'The RSM and *keta* utilize the last four digits of their Regimental number to prevent the confusion that'd be caused by using the few *jat* surnames in existence. Believe it or not,' Mark added, 'this also applies to wives, with their husband's last two digits used. That's why, for example, the wives of Sergeants Gurung 27 and Gurung 39, Mrs Gurung and Mrs Gurung, are known respectively as Mrs *Sattais-ni* (27-sy) and Mrs *Unanchalis-ni* (39-sy)!'

The *kaida* of brushing, digging, hacking and slashing all grass and weeds on roads and pathways produced a sparkling camp. Conversely, it was the week's black spot for the company commanders. 'All their military training has to stop, sahib,' explained DB sahib to me once again, 'because the GM's Fatigues Party takes priority – over everything!' My QGO Assistant Training Officers also supplied more information on Gurkhas' first names and their aspirations, 'Harkabahadur, Tekbahadur, Mohanbahadur and Lalitbahadur are also common. Their parents expect great things of them – for *bahadur* means brave!' said HB sahib – to which DB added, 'But wars only happen once every so often, therefore promotion is important. Many want to be GM, but only those exceptional have a chance.'

Promotion was important for other reasons. It not only affected the time a soldier could serve with the Regiment, thereby increasing his income that was worth a hundred times more than his contemporaries in Nepal, but also the size of his pension. This meant the difference between scratching a living in Nepal on retirement or being in relative comfort. Promotion to senior NCO also implemented the right of being accompanied on Battalion tours by one's family. But all this took time. Unlike a British battalion, no soldier left the unit before his official 'run out' date due to the financial carrot. 'Competition within each *galla* is hard, sahib, because it takes five years before a rifleman can be promoted to lance corporal. The *Umedwar* Cadre for NCO candidates is therefore important for all Gurkhas as they only get one chance,' was HB sahib's sober explanation.

'Goodness me, sahib!' exclaimed the seconded Light Infanteer, 'that's an unheard of rate in a British battalion!' I understood this a little more after consulting my Meerendonk which gave an alternative meaning to *umedwar* (candidate) as 'hopeful'.

Much emphasis was therefore placed on education. Typical was Sergeant Sarankumar Limbu of my Training Team. An industrious NCO tipped by DB and HB *sahibharu* for promotion, he had asked me earlier that week, 'Sahib, have I spelt this word correctly?' Putting a piece of paper in front of me, he pointed to his mistake – parlament. Puzzled, I glanced at the page. It was a correspondence course on English Constitutional History. Sergeant Saran had shown that Gurkhas were not born unintelligent. Traditional stories of a mule going lame after kicking a Gurkha's head, or of a BO being hit by a bullet ricocheting off another Gurkha bean, had no substance. The Gurkha lacked education opportunities. British Army enlistment was not only for status and money, but also to improve their education.

Colonel David also wanted to optimize their versatility. 'Will you investigate the possibility of parachute training for our Recce Platoon?' he asked me. 'We missed out participating on a Brigade parachute drop during the recent Exercise GREEN LANYARD where our out of area role was also discussed in depth on this initial 5 Brigade battle camp. If trained, the platoon could drop with the Paras on operations and prepare for the Battalion Main Body's later arrival.' It seemed, at the time, an off-beat idea which had to be postponed because of a shortly looming maritime event.[2]

Domestic activity that third weekend also reached record levels. Our tenth year of living in Army married quarters proved this one was no different from the others. 'I want *all* curtains in the quarter and furniture cushions exchanged,' Tove had demanded. 'Their colours simply don't match the decor schemes provided by our Ministry of Defence landlord!' These now had to be collected and put up. Our washing machine needed plumbing in, an extra but necessary expense. Worst were paper-thin walls and electric heating unable to cope with the cold. There was also a fat file of complaints from the previous occupants. 'Oh, for an insulated wooden Norwegian house. And roll on sunny Hong Kong,' Tove urged the Viking gods above. These irritating domestic problems overshadowed everything. They gave minimal time for newspaper reading, although I did scan a footnote on *The Daily Telegraph*'s front page of something about Argentine scrap metal merchants illegally landing on an island near the Antarctic. It was this, however, that soon became *the* domestic problem.

The Battalion's officers were scheduled to participate in another training exercise at the start of my third week. A two-year UK tour for a Gurkha battalion was considered the highlight of a ten-year Brigade of Gurkha battalion roulement cycle, and every effort was made to participate in the many training facilities not available in Hong

37

Kong. The UK-based battalion was also the Brigade's shop window, hence the fast pace of life. It was tempting to think later that this particular event had been ordered by a clairvoyant. Exercising in a command post on the Battle Group Trainer simulator at Bovington, Dorset would also be a novelty and the QGOs looked forward to it. There would be outdoor training the first day. Abbreviations and jargon are rife in the Army and the name of this first phase was no exception. Without any troops on the ground, we would partake in a TEWT, an acronym which meant a 'tactical exercise without troops' where the Battalion was in a mobile defence battle scenario. This involved all officers put into syndicates to assess the ground, match it to available resources, discuss the problems and produce solutions. In addition, the Brigadier would visit us.

'We'll have to make the Brigadier sahib comfortable,' said a QGO displaying typical Gurkha hospitality. So, in a nearby barn, some of them built an intricate seat of hay bales. On arrival the Brigadier was ushered to this improvised throne, while we gathered around and then, one by one, the syndicates presented their solutions.

'I've enjoyed sitting up there,' he remarked afterwards, 'and look forward to returning to the 7th Gurkha Rifles whenever possible!'

'And who,' I thought to myself, 'would not, after being treated like a king by the Gurkhas?'

The warm-up completed, our Battalion HQ next day entered the building where the command post was housed in an armoured personnel carrier mock-up. Here we had to prepare for, and eventually fight, the scripted battle. 'This BAOR mobile defence battle against a Warsaw Pact Orange Forces scenario is like a dream that's come true for us, Training Officer sahib,' commented one happy QGO to me. In an adjacent room they and other BOs were explained the rules and introduced to an enormous battle board on which stood miniature pieces of military hardware. Everyone began poring over it when the exercise started. They represented commanders manoeuvering their combat teams and other sub-units around this field of play and reporting by radio their progress, or lack of it, to us in the HQ. For several hours the 'battle' continued against unconvincing canned sound-effects. As is traditional in British Army defence planning and exercises, focus was on the worst case scenario which, even politically, did not seem to have been considered for the South Atlantic.

After a while whistles were sounded for a notional chemical attack and, with the prescribed shouts of, 'Gas! Gas! Gas!' HQ personnel donned respirators and protective NBC 'noddy' suits as rapidly as possible to continue fighting the war. To most this was a realistic way to exercise Battalion HQ, but the effect of adverse weather conditions, lack of information, fog of war and ensuing confusion and, most important of all, requirement to withstand combat exhaustion and the corrosive effect of fear on the battlefield were all absent. In truth, the latter cannot be simulated on any exercise – but none expected we would soon be experiencing this live as the mid-week return to Church Crookham was made.

Despite South Atlantic diplomatic sabre-rattling, Thursday's *kasam khane* parade had been foremost on the agenda there. GM sahib had already been rehearsing with the latest draft of recruits for some time. Unlike British regiments, this oath to the Gurkha Regiment and its officers would be in addition to that taken to the *maharindi*, Queen Elizabeth, at their recruit *khasam khane* parade in Dharan, Nepal. It contributes significantly to the Gurkhas' special respect for their officers. The oath was considered sacred, so the 'oath-eating' ceremony would be administered by the *Pandit* just as he would oversee the blood-letting on *Mar.* 'One who claims to be an authority' is the English derivitive from his title, but on the *kasam khane* parade that morning his dress of a worn out tweed sports jacket, beige trousers that resembled riding jodphurs, brown leather shoes and small cloth hat created the opposite impression. The 7th Gurkha Rifles were the only British Gurkha Regiment to have a *kaida* of flying the Nepalese flag for such occasions and the *Pandit*, standing under the flag, read out the oath and offered a prayer. The Battalion did not possess Regimental colours. Their thirty-two battle honours were emblazoned instead on the three P and D side drums and, as a parade climax, these were trooped down the ranks of the new draft with each man touching a drum as it passed. Soon they would contribute to the thirty-third and final Regimental battle honour of 'Falkland Islands 1982' being eventually added to the drums two years later.

In the evening, my Regimental 'dining-in night' would take place in the Officers' Mess. It also was for Tim Morris, a newly arrived cherub-faced subaltern who had taken command of the Assault Pioneer Platoon. Previously the owner of longer than normal locks of hair, he had entered the dining room for breakfast earlier that month after completing a Battalion Battle Fitness Test. These locks combined with, understandably, an even ruddier cherubic complexion than normal, had prompted Colonel David to ask, 'Where have you come from?' L-squared beat Tim to the draw with a lightening-fast, 'Crufts, by the look of him!' Formal mess kit was now our dress. Tim's dark green 7GR super-tight trousers, short jacket, and Mess wellingtons was, with the exception of my red waistcoat and jingling spurs denoting an officer of field rank, similar to mine. *Bhat* BT was on the menu, and P and D on standby. Another enormous Cuneo painting, this time of a four-man Gurkha squad escorting two Yeomen of the Guard being challenged by an SLR and kukri-armed Gurkha sentry in the Tower of London Ceremony of the Keys, presided over the drinking and eating officers.

After the port and madeira had been passed around anticlockwise and 'Mr. President' of the Mess Committee had requested the evening's chosen 'Mr. Vice' (Vice President) to propose toasts first to the Queen and then to the Regiment, a haze of cigarette and cigar smoke then began drifting up as the after dinner chat began. The P and D soon broke into the peace. With droning bagpipes, rapping drumsticks on side drums, and thumping on the big drum, pipers and drummers entered the dining room and marched clockwise around the tables. Numerous tunes were played before Pipe Major Meherman Tamang went solo. Colonel David cocked an ear, looking down at the gleaming mahogany table top in his concentration to detect any off-key note. To my untrained ear the Pipe Major's recital was without blemish. As a finale, the P and D returned marching not to the Regimental March of *All the Blue Bonnets are over the Border* which, with its LI speed would have been impossible in the dining room's confines, but *Black Bear* – a popular Battalion tune I was to hear often during my secondment. It produced goose pimples and sent a shiver of pride down a green-about-the-ears seconded Light Infantry officer whilst other officers' hands all around me pounded the tables in appreciation so hard after the performance that coffee cups and spoons engaged in an impromptu jig of some violence.

Then came a special Anglo-Gurkha touch neatly symbolizing 'the British Connection' between Gurkha and British officer and requirement for *mel-milap* or cooperation between the ranks. The Pipe Major received his traditional tot of whisky in a silver quaich. Before drinking, he raised it and stated solemnly, '*Sabai sahibharu, lagra rahauna hawas.*' The reciprocal response from the BOs around me was, '*Tagru rahau.*' I was mystified, but later received an explanation that this custom amounted to a mutual wish of continued good health. This formal *kaida* was replaced afterwards by the informal. It included Mess rugby, tug of war, and a race involving lateral hand-stands on upturned glass beer tankards, but the highlight was provided by an attached 2GR officer, Lieutenant Jeremy McTeague.

'Come on, folks! It's time to gather around because I'm about to start taking bets for tonight's first big race,' declared the gung-ho Jeremy. Determined to challenge the skills of TV's horse racing commentator, Richard O'Sullivan, he proudly showed us his large wooden box race course placed in one corner of the Mess anteroom in which had been constructed six parallel lanes for the six mice runners. All had been painted in different racing colours. The betting and races continued into the small hours but, much later that day, arrived official displeasure of my *kaida* violation on the *kasam khane* parade. Although obtaining a 7GR side-hat, I had omitted to exchange my LI No. 2 Service Dress jacket brass buttons for black Gurkha ones. My failure to acquire an orderly had contributed to this cock-up. A visiting Gurkha senior officer noticed the shortfall and mentioned it to Colonel David. My two Assistant Training Officers must have been informed because a mound of Gurkha buttons were now conspicuous on my office desk as I clocked in for the day's work still tired from the night's activities. Nothing more was done, unlike an LI battalion which would have meted out extra orderly officer duties, drinks all round the Officers' Mess, and replaced my RCT nickname of 'Wheels' with 'Buttons'.

All this socializing and lack of sleep should have led to a relaxing weekend at home. It was not to be. My attention was drawn towards the intensifying TV and newspaper reports of the scrap metal merchants' activities on South Georgia and alarming increase of Argentine naval movement in that part of the South Atlantic. 'My God,' I thought after a cursory squint, then thorough examination of *The Sunday Telegraph*, 'we're in this out of area Brigade, and just *might* get involved in what's happening down south!'

I showed Tove the newspaper. But her mind had been targeted elsewhere for such a long time, that she just laughed at my far-fetched worry of something which could not happen in a month of Sundays.

'Don't be so idiotic. We're going to Hong Kong!'

Chapter Four

GETTING TO GRIPS
WITH REALITY

I am very anxious, if possible, to get a brigade of Gurkhas, so as to complete the New Zealand Divisional Organisation with a type of man who will, I am most certain, be most valuable on the Gallipoli peninsula. The scrubby hillsides on the south-west faces of the plateau are just the sort of terrain where these little fellows are their brilliant best . . . each little 'Gurk' might be worth his full weight in gold at Gallipoli. – Extract from a letter written on 25 March 1915 by General Sir Ian Hamilton, the Gallipoli Expeditionary Force Commander, to Lord Kitchener.

On Monday, 29 March, my first telephone customer was an ex-fellow Sandhurst cadet, Major Peter Dennison of 3 Para. Now based at Tidworth, his Gurkha size had prompted his cadet peers to nickname him Little Peter.

'I'm keen to continue the Para-Gurkha cooperation, Mike, which began three months ago on Exercise GREEN LANYARD,' he began. 'I'm planning a company escape and evasion exercise which'll take place soon in Scotland, and I'd like some of your Gurkhas to act as the hunter force. Could you assist?'

'Of course, shouldn't think it'll be a problem,' I replied benevolently.

He followed up my optimism with, 'Great! So can I visit you on Wednesday?'

My response, 'OK, just come to my office and I'll be pleased to see you,' did not take into account the next forty-eight hours when matters worsened in the South Atlantic. Nonetheless Peter descended on my office. Not having seen each other for years, we had a lengthy chat and decided to get together with our families for tea in the near future before discussing his exercise and manpower requirement. I assumed the Gurkhas would be happy to play the enemy – after all, another Gurkha unit at Sandhurst was employed full-time in that role. Eleven years before, 7GR had formed the Demonstration Company which provided all exercise 'enemy' against the cadets. This unit now recruited from all Gurkha units and its soldiers took pride in their work, illustrated by one at the end of his year's service when answering, '145, sahib!' after a senior officer asked, 'And how many times have you been "killed" on exercise?'[1]

As he left my office, the Para and SAS officer with startlingly bright blue eyes joked half seriously, '3 Para becomes the UK Spearhead Battalion next month on seventy-two hours notice to move worldwide and, as things are shaping up down south, we

41

might have to change the exercise venue and you won't have to produce the enemy!' Two days later Lieutenant General Leopoldi Fortunato Galtieri, leader of the Argentine junta and that country's President, gave new meaning to the expression 'The lights are on, but there's nobody at home' by pressing the button to invade the Falklands. This cancelled our tea party and Little Peter's exercise, thereby permitting us to participate in one that would be the most realistic of our lives.

When I got out of bed on Saturday, 3 April elements of the Carrier Battle Group of Rear Admiral Sandy Woodward already had turned left and not right on leaving the Straits of Gibraltar. The next invasion, of South Georgia, was only hours away. Munching my cornflakes, I listened to the Prime Minister's radio speech during that House of Commons debate in the first Saturday re-call of Parliament since 1956. Mrs. Thatcher's announcement: '. . . a large Task Force would sail as soon as preparations are complete' was crisis management 'overkill', once described by Napoleon Bonaparte as, 'Great operations . . . require speed in movements and as much quick-ness in conception as in execution . . . We require therefore unity of thought – military, diplomatic, and financial.' All this, including European Economic Community sanc-tions, would be implemented – but current developments were not of significance to Tove.

'Sounds quite big, doesn't it?' she commented, putting a slice of brown Norwegian goat cheese on her toast. 'Still, 'spect your Navy'll sort out the problem, so we won't have to worry.'

'I'm not so sure,' I replied. 'We're in a Brigade with this out of area role thing. It looks as though Peter and 3 Para are going. So why not us as well in order to fight? After all, we're at five days notice to move.'

Maybe I was the born pessimist – but my prediction, as Tove called it, would gather pace as the weeks passed. Being an officer in the British Army meant there was nothing new to my vanishing out of her life on Northern Ireland operations. But this current operation and its potential would be different. Failing abjectly to cease worrying, I accompanied my family for a spring afternoon walk on Tweseldown Racecourse. Competing for Britain there in the 1967 Junior World Modern Pentathlon Championships' riding event had been an exciting experience, but would soon pale into insignificance with this rapidly escalating South Atlantic crisis in which Mrs Thatcher described the Argentine action as 'military hooliganism'.

Next morning's news that the UN Security Council had passed Resolution 502 demanding an immediate withdrawl of all Argentine forces from the Falkland Islands, implied there would not be long to wait in 80, Wakefords Park during this 'golden hour' response period. Nor was there. After breakfast the telephone rang and, polite as ever, a Gurkha voice asked: 'Training Officer sahib? Battalion 2IC sahib wants all officers in the Mess for a briefing at 14.00 hours. Can you be there, please sahib? And will you have tea afterwards?'

'Who was it then?' asked a worried Tove.

'That, my dear,' I replied, sickly sweet, while my stomach began filling with a swarm of lead-heavy butterflies, 'is the start of the Gurkha irresistable force towards Galtieri's immovable objects on the Falklands.'

It was to be the first of many such conferences. In the Mess ante-room excitement laced the atmosphere. Burdened with silver trays laden with ritual tea cups and saucers, Gurkha waiters bustled among arriving BOs and QGOs many of whom were dressed in Regimental blazers and ties. It was not difficult to imagine a corresponding nineteenth-century scene in a Gurkha Officers' Mess of the British Raj after marching orders to the North-West Frontier had been received. One QGO, Lieutenant Chandrakumar Pradhan who commanded the Mechanical Transport Platoon, had propped himself up by a table and was reading a newspaper. He was regarded as a Battalion up-and-coming star and, after grabbing a cup of tea, I asked him, 'Hello, sahib! So what do you think of the situation in the South Atlantic? Think we'll go in against the Argies?'

A beaming Chandra sahib looked up. 'Oh, I do hope so, sahib,' he replied with gusto, 'because then we'll all become famous!'

Unconcerned at the prospect of travelling by ship rather than air if deployed, he wanted to emulate his Gurkha predecessors – even though they and others could easily succumb to sea-sickness like those, post-Second World War, on board the British India Steam Navigation Company's ships sailing between Calcutta, Rangoon, Penang and Singapore. Another Gurkha officer, however, was not so excited. Ram relaxed in a leather armchair nearby. His expressionless face with the heavy-hooded eyes, spoke the body language of one who had seen it all before. But the *burho* was not asleep. He exuded boredom, despite overhearing my conversation with Chandra sahib.

I was concerned however, needed to converse, and began questioning him in a similar vein to his younger colleague, 'So what d'you think'll happen, Ram? How will the Battalion get on if we are sent down to the Falklands?'

There was an artificial pause. If the Battalion was to be deployed then Ram had no doubt of the outcome. With eyes remaining half closed, rather like those of a tiger lazing under a tree in the shadow of the midday sun, the *burho* murmured somnolently, 'No problem. We'll chop them into little pieces.'

'Gentlemen!' called out Bill Dawson. 'It's time for the conference!' Everyone moved into the adjoining TV room and sat down. Colonel David arrived. He was dressed in his No. 2 Service Dress and exuded the air of being *the* Regimental Gurkha British Officer in the right place at the right time. His career apogee had arrived. Bill Dawson called us to attention. Gurkha *kaida* prevailed – sitting to attention, backs straightened, arms straight out and ram-rod stiff and clenched fist on knees with knuckles uppermost. A pin could have been heard to drop. We were about to receive a rare briefing to start preparations for war.

The Colonel had a captive audience and began by saying, 'I've just come from a Brigade conference. As you're aware, there's been no long-term warning scenario prior to the invasion. Hence we don't know much about the Falklands, operation, or opposition. Neither do we know if we're going. 3 Para are now under command to 3 Commando Brigade, and they'll be leaving next week. Meanwhile, this Battalion's still part of 5 Brigade. We've an out of area role, so it'll be wise to start preparing with a view to being ordered south. This'll be done by sea, not air, so we'll have a different logistics problem to tackle than in the current Brigade concept of operations. And if there's going to be any action then it'll be quite a scrap, for we must assume the Argentine Army'll be a tough nut to crack.'

The possibility of Gurkha involvement was being taken seriously and Colonel David had his strategy clear for our training. Rather than wait for the situation to dictate to him, he would proactively launch the Gurkha version of 'overkill' as this would optimize time and effort if orders eventually came for our deployment. So my stomach started twitching as he issued concrete instructions at machine-gun rate, 'Our notice to move remains unchanged. However we might become involved soon in events that are going on down south. Adjutant, you must therefore start re-calling men on external training courses back to Church Crookham. Training Officer? Where are you? We've got to make use of all available training time. Seek authority to override other units' range bookings as this'll enable us to start zeroing in all Battalion small arms. I also want helicopters booked for basic helicopter training here at camp. There'll also be a requirement for intelligence briefings, and combat and cold-weather survival lectures. Furthermore all rifle companies must intensify their weapon-handling training, and our soldiers must become so slick that they can do this blindfolded. We must also prioritize first aid training – and this has to begin immediately!'

His underlying message had a similar tone to Mao Tse-tung's, a legendary strategic enemy of the Gurkhas from Malaya and Hong Kong, 'Fight no battle unprepared . . . make every effort to ensure victory in the given set of conditions between the enemy and ourselves . . .' As 5 Brigade's third infantry battalion, we remained at five days notice to move but, unofficially, the Colonel told me that he reckoned on being at twenty-four hours notice because the QGOs and other ranks were without families and could therefore react faster than other units.

Such a rapid response was not needed at the moment but, faced with the possibility we might participate in the liberation of the Falklands, his aim was to crank start the Battalion's training immediately. Coordinating the programme was my responsibility. It began early next morning on 5 April when 'Battle Individual Training' stopped being a euphemism for a long-distance Gurkha run and suddenly became an important part of preparing for war. The BIT pace that Monday around the narrow minor roads behind the camp was severe for a seconded British officer. Most 7GR soldiers came from the *pahar*, Nepal's middle hills, 1,000 to 3,000 metres above sea level. This altitude advantage and no roads, so everything has to be carried everywhere, was reflected in the Gurkhas' fleetness of foot. One QGO told me of their bi-annual Battalion Battle Fitness Test standard.

'It's the normal run of one and a half miles, sahib, except that our "pass" time for the BFT is ten minutes or under!' he said. I blinked. At a mere eleven minutes thirty seconds my British pass time was more than ninety seconds slower.

After breakfast, first aid lectures were held for the QGOs and younger BOs in the Officers' Mess. I attended the first led by the Battalion's Royal Army Medical Corps doctor, Captain Martin Entwhistle. 'OK sahibs, this series of hands-on lessons is based on the "train the trainer" concept,' he explained. 'In other words, the knowledge I'm going to give you now must be passed on to your companies by yourselves, and the aim of these lessons will be to show how your men can stabilize casualties with battle-field gunshot wounds.'

Martin's expertise came from his Belfast and PIRA sniper experiences. The basic mechanics were explained, 'First, it's vital to stop the bleeding by applying pressure to the wound. You then must plug up the entry and exit holes with your field dressings. Remember in the case of high-velocity rounds that the exit holes are much larger, so it will be necessary for you to use many dressings. OK, let's begin!'

Laughter punctuated the class as they received an expert demonstration before trussing each other up with the field dressings of a thick gauze pad and attached long bandages. Splints were also used in simulating treatment of shattered bones, and explanation made of how to use a shock-reducing saline drip. I paused to ask for a cup of tea from the Mess kitchen, but foghorn laughter made me return to the dining room class where a QGO was asking, 'Is this alright, sahib?' Martin's foghorn hooted again. 'Goodness! Are you trying to kill your poor patient? Even the job on King Tutankhamun couldn't have been done better!' was the young doc's diagnosis of the blue-faced victim mummified by a straitjacket of bandages. Nonetheless, the Gurkhas would improve with practice and, two years later, realism reached such a standard during my A Company overseas exercise in Malaysia, that smiling Gurkha battle 'casualtics' were having saline drips inserted into their arms by others after a victorious company attack on the Royal Malaysian Army 'enemy'.

When I returned home early evening and turned on the TV news this, too, had intensified its blitz on the Falklands' crisis. The Royal Navy aircraft carriers HMS *Invincible* and HMS *Hermes* departing Portsmouth Harbour stuffed with twenty Fleet Air Arm Sea Harrier jump-jet all-weather fighters and twenty-one anti-submarine and assault Sea King helicopters was superb Rule Britannia jingoism. But I never gave any thought that my other function as the Battalion Public Information Officer might imply becoming an eventual microscopic part of this circus, with its artists like General Galtieri, Mrs Thatcher, General Alexander Haig, John Nott, Lord Carrington, Francis Pym and Nicanor Costa Mendez.

Next day the *keta* continued zeroing their small arms on the shooting range and began basic helicopter training of emplaning and deplaning drills, and familiarization flying. They were also quick to focus on the two main protagonists, issuing each with a Gurkha *nom de guerre*. When I visited the Orderly Room on a minor errand that morning, Mark Willis divulged General Galtieri's. 'So what does *Galti garyo* mean, Mark?' I asked, quite baffled.

'The *keta* have a point,' replied the smiling Adjutant, 'because it means "Mistake made"!'

But the Gurkhas had no monopoly in twisting the meaning because, oddly enough, the Norwegian words *gal* and *galt* also mean 'mad' and 'wrong' respectively. That afternoon I was using the same Gurkhali terminology as Mark's in referring to 'the boys' when asking HB sahib, 'And how are the *keta* keeping themselves updated on the situation, sahib?'

My Assistant Training Officer replied, 'Come and have a look at A Company's restroom, sahib. They're really interested in the Fokland Creesis!' In the room many were watching TV. A recording of the scenes from Buenos Aires' central Plaza de Mayo where thousands of Argentine flag waving demonstrators had gathered at *Galti garyo*'s pink Casada Rosada Presidential Palace to listen to his emotional speech delivered from a lofty balcony whilst, in between the pauses, they chanted, '*Las Malvinas es Argentina!*' seemed to raise the phlegmatic riflemens' eyebrows a little.

'It is good for their geography education, sahib,' explained HB sahib. 'Initially the *keta* had problems locating Argentina and the Foklands. But, as you can see, the Company has put up a large map of the world on the wall there, and stuck pins into Buenos Aires, Foklands, Church Crookham and Nepal. So now they understand a little more the distances involved!' This did nothing to persuade the Gurkhas that they would eventually sail with the Task Force, even though all wanted to participate in what could be the first Gurkha active service since Borneo. But apprehensive of offending other Third World countries by committing Gurkhas to a colonial war, the Foreign Office mandarins were no crisis managers. A hopeless interpretation of the situation leading up to the invasion which had caused Lord Carrington's resignation as the Foreign Secretary was one major error. Now the mandarins promoted further heartache at Church Crookham in applying their bureaucratic brakes by writing to the King of Nepal seeking permission to commit his countrymen to the South Atlantic. The Gurkhas, paradoxically, were a unit of gilt-edged quality which could deliver the Foreign Office from its mistakes.

The men's eagerness for deployment was reinforced by their fatalistic philosophy towards war's realities as HB sahib explained, 'I'll teach you a jingle about this, Training Officer sahib. There are two different types of death to the Gurkha, even though the result is the same. "*Ki marnu rana ma – ki marnu banama*" means "it's good to die in the jungle" – in other words, in peaceful solitude – "or in a war".'

Hinduism contributed to this attitude. A belief in reincarnation is as valid a spiritual support for Gurkhas as Christian hope for British soldiers when push comes to shove. It might be needed, too, by that 7 April announcement that a Maritime Exclusion Zone, centred just north of Swan Island in the Falkland Sound with a radius of 200 nautical miles around the Falklands, would be imposed in five days. The Nepalese opponents of *Galti garyo* could have been forgiven for thinking that Mrs Margaret Thatcher was a Mark II version of *Durga*, their Goddess of War. For the latter, after a fierce battle, had beheaded *Mahishura*, an evil demon that had terrorized heaven and earth. Some of the thirty-two ancient rules of Hindu womanly virtue, or *lakchhin*, could also never have applied to Maggie in her dealings with *Galti garyo*, such as rule number seven – Be soft and sweet spoken; or rule number eight – Be kind and sympathetic to all people; or rule number twenty – Understand the status and position of other men and women and give due respect. This must have made her *nom de guerre* even more amusing. It also demonstrated Gurkha black humour at its best.

'If Galtieri's is *Galti garyo*, then what's Mrs. Thatcher's?' I asked HB sahib.

'The *keta* call her *Thatcher le Thecharyo*,' replied the deadpan faced QGO, 'which means "wrestle and knock down", sahib!'

In the afternoon a second conference was held in the Officers' Mess. This had an agenda to discuss the Battalion's current training status and any other preliminary planning and preparation matters for a possible South Atlantic deployment. It soon became apparent that one QGO did not rate our unit's chances of making the trip. His priorities were dictated by Battalion shooting *kaida* and he complained to Colonel David, 'Sahib, I am worried that all these preparations for operations in the South Atlantic might hinder the training schedule of our team who are preparing for the shooting championships at Bisley!'

The Colonel's face went from a state of shock, to amusement, and then, finally, anger in a matter of microseconds. This querying QGO, to put it mildly, had still not comprehended the situation which the Battalion could soon be facing. Getting to grips with reality was not his strong point. 'Goodness me, sahib!' exclaimed the senior sahib with twitching eyebrows and ditto movement of feet under the table which indicated a certain amount of steam on the boil. 'Don't you understand that it's precisely these Bisley shooting experts of ours who are exactly the men that our Battalion'll require if we are to fight in such an operation?'

The following day, 8 April, the situation's seriousness grew again with not only news of the 1st Battalion, Welsh Guards' inclusion in 5 Brigade, thereby replacing 3 Para, but also of Argentina announcing its own Exclusion Zone incorporating *Islas las Malvinas*. At home, pressure intensified. 'Note my prediction's a little closer!' I warned Tove after this reciprocal sabre-rattling which, a month later, would include the kukri and its Argentine equivalent. My pessimism was infectious as Tove's face had become more strained in the past forty-eight hours. A personal lock on to the media coverage of the crisis made it even more so. Getting up in the morning to listen to breakfast time radio, studying my newspaper and those in the Officers' Mess, catching the early evening television news, followed by an update on the BBC's *Nine O'clock News* and check for changes on ITN's *News at Ten* all that week had a negative effect on domestic bliss. Information and assessments were lopsided and pessimistic, overestimating Argentine capabilities and under-estimating British. Mentally I was caught with trousers down. My sixteen years of military training had been for a war that would never begin and was beyond reality. 'So why take work too seriously?' had been my naive attitude. 'Life was, after all, supposed to be fun!'

'I don't know,' I despaired to Tove, 'our grand plan had been to return to Hong Kong and enjoy a last British Empire titbit, rather than be faced with going to war on a wind-blasted and desolate leftover. So what the hell did we do wrong?'

My denial had become a psychological burden. The challenge lay in getting to grips with reality that had arrived with a capital R – and its consequences. I was also in a vulnerable soldier category. Having a young family, my possibility of fighting in offensive operations far from home created a semi-subconscious dilemma between the roles of soldier and father. Reconciling the two was more than difficult, particularly when my job's sudden extra workload required more concentration and effort. It would become far worse. But like Lord Carrington, we had also experienced enough for now. 'Thank goodness for the long weekend!' exclaimed Tove, 'I'm looking forward to Easter at your parents' home.'

It was envigorating to stroll along the seashore at Rustington on Good Friday, 9 April. As Tove and I inhaled the sea breeze watching Victoria and Katie, her three-year old cousin, playing 'chicken' with the waves, we offered no thoughts to Peter Dennison and other troops on P&O's cruiseship SS *Canberra* further down the coast at Southampton, who were preparing to sail that evening as part of Maggie's continuing game of 'chicken' with the Argentine junta. Over lunch and supper my father listened to our news. Retiring from the RAF, he had become immersed in local politics as an Arun district councillor. His knowledge of Gurkha jungle operations during the Malayan Emergency guaranteed interest with my possible participation in the South

Atlantic crisis. That his appearance resembled Sir Winston Churchill made the situation eerie. The Gurkha 'we might go' or 'might not go' theme of our conversation that evening was interrupted by the television news reporting *Canberra*'s departure, and further intensive media coverage of the crisis ruined a potentially pleasant weekend. It only strengthened my conviction that the Gurkhas would be deployed.

'Oh, Daddy! We do like our Easter eggs!' enthused Victoria as Emily tucked into hers during Sunday's breakfast. But our stay at *Damansara* had to be cut short. I was rostered as the Battalion Duty Field Officer starting on Easter Monday, so we had to return to Church Crookham. In the South Atlantic, events possessed a momentum of their own. Whilst we were tucked up in our beds at 80, Wakefords Park, the Falkland Islands Maritime Exclusion Zone came into effect at midnight Falkland Islands local time or 04.00 hours GMT. The Falklands/*Malvinas* War time zone currency of *Victor, Whisky, Zulu,* and *Alpha* had begun. Royal Navy submarines enforcing the FIMEZ were now on *Victor*: however the above-surface Task Force which would operate around, over, and subsequently on the Falklands did not move forward four hours in time to GMT or *Zulu* until eleven days later. This time change included all forces on or at Ascension Island, the forward mounting base in mid-Atlantic 3,500 nautical miles from the Falklands. 5 Brigade was still on local British Summer Time or *Alpha* – and five hours ahead of *Victor*. To compound this muddle, the Argentines at Stanley operated on *Whisky* (Buenos Aires time) three hours behind *Zulu*, but elsewhere on the Islands they were on *Victor*. It ensured a chaotic foundation for Falklands' War historians.

To any soldier with 'stag' or sentry duty experience, 04.00 hours was easy to remember, being ironically known as 'dead-man's hour'. FIMEZ implementation meant a naval blockade – an act of war. This and *Canberra*'s sailing triggered a reinforcement by air of the Argentine 2,000-man garrison on the Islands, the news of which made my kitchen radio buzz as I left our married quarter on 12 April to take over my duties in camp. Unlike the twenty-four hour Orderly Officer duty, performed by a QGO or junior BO, the not too onerous Duty Field Officer's job lasted all week and was known as 'stooge of the week'. Easter Monday was also a good day to complete a number of that week's irritatingly small routine tasks. Checking a meal in the cookhouse where, as always, *bhat* was the only menu item, making the weekly spot check of the spices and rice treasure trove in the Battalion food store of which oriental gourmets and paddy field farmers would have been in awe, and viewing a smart guard-mounting in the evening all provided temporary distractions from South Atlantic happenings. Nevertheless the TV news that early evening continued to confirm the rapidity of the Argentine reinforcement.

'When are you coming to bed?' demanded my disenchanted wife. Her irritation was turning to anger because I spent most of my spare time following events on the 'box'. 'Damn the Argies, and for goodness sake turn it off!' she commanded.

'Sorry, but the *News at Ten* on ITN is beginning now and maybe it'll have a new update on the situation!' I replied stubbornly whilst thinking, 'And at 11 p.m. there's also BBC2's late news round-up.' It had become an unhealthy and compulsive habit. Neither did tranquillity endure from a final cup of tea before turning out the light. My main role as the Duty Field Officer was to provide a backstop for the Orderly Officer in fielding anything awkward that came the latter's way. This arrived now. Just before midnight the telephone rang.

'You'd better answer it,' said Tove sleepily. I got up.

'Could I speak to the Training Officer sahib, please?' a Gurkha voice requested.

'Yes, speaking,' I answered, afraid that the Gurkha call to arms from Memsahib *Thatcher le Thecharyo* had finally arrived to counter *Galti garyo*'s cheek.

'Sahib,' said the polite voice, 'this is the Duty Clerk in Battalion Headquarters. There's a secret signal that's just arrived from Brigade Headquarters. Could you come and read it?'

'In order to do that I'll have to get dressed. Can't you get the Duty Driver to bring it round to my quarter?' I asked irritably.

A pause of doubt was followed by: 'Alright, sahib. But where's your quarter?'

My explanation followed – even though 80, Wakefords Park was only 600 metres from camp.

'OK, sahib,' said the worried Gurkha clerk, 'but I hope there won't be any difficulty.'

After he rang off I recalled the Gurkha driver who had chauffeured me to the Brigadier. As a precaution I waited some minutes and then, clad in only pyjamas and dressing gown, stepped outside our quarter to wave down the courier. Twenty minutes later his vehicle's high pitched whine orbiting aimlessly around its unidentified target only reinforced my total distrust with Gurkha orientation abilities. I threw in the towel and stormed upstairs to fling on my uniform.

'Where on earth are you now going, then?' asked a fed up Tove.

'I'm about to play Postman Pat if you must know and, as an educated guess, will soon collect the latest news from the wretched South Atlantic!' was my equally annoyed response.

On arrival at the Orderly Room I read the signal. It contained the latest Operation CORPORATE intelligence, but the red 'secret' stamp on the top and bottom of the signal only demonstrated an ability to overclassify its information. This minor episode, amusing in parts had also contributed to generating even more family stress. 'Uh! What a waste of rations! I could've stayed in bloody bed!' I cursed at Tove on returning home. 'That epistle's military intelligence author didn't put a lot of research into his work. He must have been glued to a TV set earlier this evening because the content is nearly identical to that shown on the *News at Ten.* So good night – and sweet dreams!'

There was no let up in the Battalion's preparations that week for a possible deployment. Briefings continued. An officer who had been on the Falklands visited the Battalion, and a topography description of the Islands was included in his briefing to the officers. His message was bleak, but important, '. . . as for the coastlines, gentlemen, they have an abundance of penguins and kelp seaweed. That's why the 1800 inhabitants are known as "kelpers". A multitude of sheep thrive on the open and rolling countryside. But, beware! The valleys are full of bogs, peat, and stone runs. The going underfoot is atrocious. And, as for cover, the only trees are a few sorry-looking specimens at the capital Port Stanley!'

Unlike the Ministry of Defence, Colonel David had already decided that the Battalion's planning should be proactive i.e. based on a worst case scenario of fighting in any war rather than assuming we would only become part of a post-war garrison force. Attack, not defence, would be the prime phase of war employed. So he decided to take advantage of the briefer's information on open ground and later requested our establishment of GPMGs be doubled. This was approved, and two GPMGs per eight-man rifle section with a grand total of ninety-four such guns therefore became the Battalion's most prized part of its weapon inventory.

Training did not cease despite this extra operational planning. It included Milan anti-tank missile firing at Netheravon, and artillery target indication practice for all officers on the Gunners' Aldershot puff range where chalk dust blown up from a model land-scape simulated shell explosions and aided practising radio procedures to bring down accurate fire on a given target. But still no decision had been taken to include the Gurkhas in the Task Force. Colonel David had been wrestling with a scenario over Easter for the imminent Battalion exercise and walked into my office the following day. 'Mike, I think we must continue to plan for the Stanford training area exercise next month despite events down south,' he said. 'So you must recce the area this week for a defensive exercise followed by a Battalion advance to contact. Take DB sahib and HB sahib with you. Here, I'll show you what I've got in mind!'

His South Atlantic motives were obvious as he then strode over to my map on the wall and began his invasion of the training area. He swept his hands over it, pointing up terrain corridors, blocking defiles, moving around obstacles and explaining options. I had some ideas also, but the recce would reveal more about the possibilities. Next day seemed as good as any for the trip and preparations were made with the two QGOs. Prior to the journey there was yet another interruption to Tove's and my sleep. The telephone was ringing again.

'There's a secret signal that's just arrived here, sahib!'

It was the Duty Clerk again.

'Oh dear, signal number two,' I sighed to myself. However I had learnt from the night before about such Cinderella-hour trips to Battalion Headquarters. The situation 13,000 kilometres distant was as per the TV news reports two hours before. Of more interest was the address list that included the 1st Battalion, Queen's Own Highlanders at Tidworth. They had pedigree. Twenty years before the QOH had been deployed with 1st/2nd Gurkha Rifles and 42 Commando to snuff out a revolt in Brunei. Now equipped and trained for cold-weather climates, as a 1 Infantry Brigade unit they were earmarked for NATO Allied Command Europe Mobile Force operations. They had just returned from a NATO exercise in Norway with the Royal Marine Commandos and, if chosen, would be a better bet operationally than the Welsh Guards who had been a London Public Duties battalion. This did not happen but, in 1991, the QOH got their chance in the Gulf War.

Our Land-Rover left camp early the following day for the Norfolk training area located north of Thetford. I had forgotten to take a packed lunch, but there was no need to worry. 'Here you are, sahib,' said HB sahib, passing to me a large white carton.

'Oh! Yes. Well . . . er . . . thanks sahib!' I stuttered, feeling an idiot. Typical. I was becoming too spoilt.

We started to talk about the recce's aim, but our conversation always drifted back to the South Atlantic. The inexorable progress of the Task Force southwards, with conno-tations of nineteenth-century Palmestonian gun boat diplomacy, must have concentrated junta minds on the wisdom of their actions. The Task Force's existence as a diplomatic bargaining counter reminded me of Sandhurst military history lessons. These had included a study of the early nineteenth century Prussian General and philosopher of war, Karl Maria von Clausewitz. His book *On War* written 150 years before, contained the famous maxim, 'War is an extension of the diplomatic process by other means'. Such a process had begun, but diplomatic failure might mean the Gurkhas fighting for the *Maharindi.* I asked DB sahib therefore about the consequences of his role as a pawn in this chess game, 'So what do you think of combat thousands of miles away in a war where Nepal has no argument, sahib?'

DB sahib was a Newar, a *jat* that traditionally produced traders rather than Gurkha soldiers. The Newars were grouped together with two others, the Brahmans and Chetris, the three being collectively known as the 'NBCs'. Nineteenth century BOs had regarded the 'NBCs' as a non-martial constellation. They had got it wrong, judging by DB's reaction. He looked at me a little puzzled but, shrugging his shoulders, his answer to my loaded question was rather good and certainly to the point, 'I am a soldier, sahib.'

He was also an infantry foot soldier, a type about to be in demand in the Falklands, a fact even more apparent when, back at home, I watched the latest TV news. The main garrisons appeared to be at Stanley and Goose Green in East Falkland, and Port Howard and Fox Bay in the west, but were too spread out for a coherent defence. 'Nonetheless, to remove them means our ground forces will have to go in on foot,' I told a worried Tove, 'and that concept's a bit out of fashion in a British Army with heady plans for an armoured mobile defence on the north-west German plain!'

The principle for any attack was that a defended position could only be attacked by a force with numerical superiority of three to one. So my wife continued to be plagued by, 'Surely then there's a requirement for more infantry as the directors of the operation only have the equivalent of four infantry battalions pitted against a Brigade plus?'

Again the midnight signal at Battalion HQ confirmed the TV news content. Two birds would be killed with one stone that night as my Field Officer duty book indicated the requirement of carrying out 'Grand Rounds'. This was a weekly post-midnight tour around camp with spot checks on security and sentry alertness. It proved unnerving as the lost Land-Rover driver had been annoying. In India 'Gurkha' is synonymous with watchkeepers who guard office blocks, private housing and building sites. Now I discovered why. In one palpitating moment, the Training Officer sahib experienced how past Gurkha enemies must have felt on the battlefield. At one darkly lit camp corner a prowler sentry suddenly leapt out from behind a hut. He brandished a pickaxe helve and screamed an intimidating Gurkhali challenge. 'Useful to learn the language,' I had been told but, alas, no Meerendonk was at hand. This Gurkha was not going to give way. However I was saved by sudden inspiration as my strangled shout of 'Grand Rounds!' placated the small dervish.

He stood to attention immediately.

'*Shyabash!*' I said, convinced no Argentine officer would have been let off so easily.

The morning after my Norfolk excursion Colonel David rang and invited me into his office. As is the custom I went in via the Adjutant's office, and Mark Willis escorted me into the Colonel. The three of us had a common denominator as family men with young children. Hannah, the youngest of the Colonel's three, would become my

51

Victoria's playmate in a month's time. If the Battalion was deployed, then we all had a vested interest in coming back – alive. I thought that the Colonel wanted a back briefing on the results of my previous day's recce. Not so. Now Thursday, 15 April and nearly a week since *Canberra* had sailed, his keenness mirrored that of the Gurkha sentry ten hours before as he briefed me on the latest developments.

'Mike, things are hotting up a bit. 5 Brigade are holding a conference tomorrow and I want you to come along with me. With luck, the Battalion'll be involved in any eventual scrap down south. Should be interesting. Oh, yes, ' he added as an afterthought, 'and could you also do something for me?' He motioned through the office windows to his wife, Belinda, standing on the verandah outside. Bin Morgan came in. She was an attractive lady, usually full of smiles. Today there were none. Signing a document on his table, Colonel David gesticulated for me to come nearer as he offered his pen. His request gave food for thought, 'So can you do me a favour please, and witness my signatures on my new will?'

Matters were taking a new turn. This informal signal in the dynamic crisis management situation, marked my arrival at the border of uncharted territory to which peacetime Army units give too little thought – the administrative and, not least, psychological processes to be traversed in order to go to war. The latter was the most difficult. American Civil War combatants of the nineteenth century talked about their first experience of the enemy's advance towards them, coming under fire, and fear on the battlefield as 'seeing the elephant'. Better known by the modern term 'battlefield stress', this animal had crashed around me in the Northern Ireland undergrowth. 'But now,' I thought while looking for the place to witness the Colonel's signature on his Last Will and Testament, 'the current opposition and rules of the game will be different, for a herd of Argentine "elephants" were waiting on the plain, not in the undergrowth, and visible to all and sundry!'

After I had countersigned, the grim-faced Bin followed suit. It was not an everyday occurrence that an infantry battalion CO's wife had to prepare at such short notice for the ultimate consequences of her husband's profession. There was no mention of my recce and Colonel David had given the strongest possible hint that the Stanford exercise was no longer a priority. The Falklands' crisis was a fortnight old and, with the situation suddenly being ratcheted up several notches, personal pressures had increased significantly. People react differently to such situations and afterwards, alone with the Colonel, I gave vent to personal doubts about the operation into which we were being sucked, nearly shooting myself in the foot by taking such a line. Even today I have a guilty conscience about such an unprofessional reaction. Maybe it was part of my process in trying to get to grips with reality, just like that QGO moaning about the Bisley team's irrelevant problems a week before.

Colonel David was professional enough to listen and respond positively by including me in next day's conference.

Chapter Five

SENNYBRIDGE TROPICS

As for the training courses the main objective should still be to raise the level of technique in marksmanship, bayoneting, grenade throwing and the like, and the secondary objective should be to raise the level of tactics, while special emphasis should be laid on night operations. – Mao Tse-tung

That tense tête-à-tête and, after the children had been put to bed, all the evening TV news programmes on every channel which contained nothing but news of the Argentines reinforcing the Falklands, the progress southwards of the Task Force, and doomed shuttle diplomacy of US Secretary of State, Alexander Haig, between London, Buenos Aires, and Washington, concentrated my grey matter wonderfully. 'Looks like that original prediction I made to you is bang on course,' I told an increasingly worried Tove, 'because it seems 5 Brigade is about to gear itself up for going to war, and we're going to find out about this tomorrow.'

She needed to offload fears in Norwegian and had been ringing her family in Oslo frequently. Another half-hour on the telephone temporarily eased the strain. 'They're concerned, send their love and are following closely what's happening on Norwegian TV and in the newspapers,' she told me. 'Nobody believes Britain will go to war against Argentina.'

I was not too interested in what the Norwegians thought. They were out of touch with reality. 'Bombing the Argentine mainland's a non-starter,' I continued to reason selfishly to Tove, 'but where would be the landings? And, indeed, would there be any? Would they be in West Falkland with a slow build-up for an assault on East Falkland? Or a direct frontal assault on Stanley that risked large casualties? Or unopposed landings in Lafonia with the threat of air attack in country devoid of cover?'

I gave up my personal think tank – not that Tove was interested in any of its meaningless outcomes. Everything had become overwhelming and the alternatives endless. We went to bed in a fog of anxiety, but soon the telephone rang at the Cinderella hour. Secret signal number four had been received at the Orderly Room. The usual request: 'Would you come and read it, sahib?' meant my familiar outing to camp and unsurprising discovery that the situation remained the same down south as I read the summary of the TV news. Returning to my married quarter afterwards, I wondered if the Gurkhas' future might become more clear-cut at the Brigade conference a few hours later.

Colonel David and I arrived twenty minutes before its start. Situated next to 2 Para's barracks on Aldershot's outskirts, the HQ's building was a modern but characterless concrete and glass structure typical in this area. Security was tight. The PIRA had bombed this part of Aldershot after Londonderry's Bloody Sunday, and they could never choose a better time than now to strike again. In the conference room covered with Falkland maps on its walls, unit commanders were gathering. One was absent. 2 Para's CO, 'H' Jones, had been issued with a warning order the previous day to deploy his unit to the South Atlantic under command of 3 Commando Brigade.

With two out of three Parachute Regiment battalions now committed, the CO of 1 Para had already tried to replace the Gurkhas. He travelled from his Battalion's operational tour in Belfast to London and the Ministry of Defence to present the argument that his unit should be next for a cruise south.[1] This met stout resistance from Gurkha proponents. After all, John Nott, the Secretary of State for Defence was an ex-2GR officer who, by strange coincidence, had served for three years with this Regiment in Malaya precisely during the period I had also lived there as a little boy. General Sir Edwin Bramall, Chief of the General Staff, was also the Colonel of his Regiment and the officer who had presented me with my Khud Race medal six years before. Perhaps this was the first time therefore that the British Armed Forces' political boss had to bow to the wishes of his military 'boss'. Both mens' support for the Battalion had proved effective in the verbal boxing ring against the Foreign Office. They were backed up by Lieutenant Colonel Keith Robinson, the British Defence Attaché in Kathmandu, also a 7GR officer, who had worked overtime to win the King of Nepal's approval of Gurkha deployment. The end result was the attendance of Colonel David and myself at this Aldershot conference.

2 Para's replacement unit was not the QOH, but 2nd Battalion, Scots Guards based at London's Chelsea Barracks. To infantry of the line this selection was yet another illogical decision, only demonstrating the Woodentops' political power in the British Army. 5 Brigade now owned two Guards battalions which, a few days before, had not only been geared to guarding Buckingham Palace, the Queen Mother's residence at St James's Palace, known to them as Jimmy's, the Tower and its royal trinkets, and Windsor Castle, but were about to begin the annual Woodentop ritual of pulverizing their Pirbright drill square into dust prior to that June's Trooping the Colour ceremony. Their new mission in a Brigade gearing up to fight was light years away from a current combat capability that could not be compared to the Gurkhas'. These two major units were not the only eleventh-hour Brigade additions. Also present were other commanders of extra gunner, helicopter, medical, and logistic support Minor Units and attachments[2] vital for the Brigade's operational viability, but a severe challenge to incorporate into the Brigade in the limited time available.

The Brigadier, determined to overcome his formation's standing start, began his briefing with a concise, 'OK gentlemen. We're going to present you with our current plans regarding a possible deployment south.' His Brigade IO, Captain David Baldwin of the Worcestershire and Sherwood Foresters' Regiment, then launched into the usual Falkland topography brief, followed by another on local climate. It was foreboding.

'The austral autumn is well advanced,' intoned the pleasant IO, soon to be known as Diddy David by his Intelligence Section because of his Gurkha-like height. 'Winter temperatures in June can fall well below zero centigrade. The UK's average wind speed is four knots. In the Falklands there's a constant wind averaging sixteen knots. It can increase to sixty and result in a dangerous chill-factor . . .'

By using the wall maps to highlight the Argentine current build-up and assisted by the Brigade RAF liaison officer's input, Captain Baldwin provided yet more perspective, 'Probably two infantry brigades are now in place. These are being reinforced by so many logistic support units and supplies, that we believe the Stanley Airport runway might start cracking up with daily landings of so many heavily-loaded aircraft!'

Apart from this later disproved aviation problem, there was still no change to the midnight 'secret' intelligence reports I had been receiving or to the content of the BBC's seven o'clock radio news that morning. Nevertheless, 5 Brigade's task remained unclear. As a strategic reserve there were various possibilities. 'Would we be a back-up to 3 Commando Brigade? Or actually fight in the recapture of the Islands? Or be part of a post-war garrison?' I wondered.

The Brigadier pointed out the facts, his strategy, and challenges ahead, 'Gentlemen, if we're going to fight then our modus operandi will be as foot soldiers supported by helicopters. Logistics will be a challenge, and the sea a decisive factor. The Cunard liner *QE2* is a possible vessel for the Brigade's transportation requirements southwards, however she's at the eastern seaboard of the States at the current moment. This'll make time an even more crucial factor after any eventual requisition. Modifications will be necessary that must include the construction of two helicopter landing pads and stripping out of her luxury fittings such as furniture, sculptures, paintings and other more general stores. Concurrently Brigade freight, not least ammunition and food, will also have to be loaded aboard her and other shipping. So delay to our departure is a real possibility.'

After lunch the Brigadier presented his short-term plans and, typically, came to the point with short, clipped sentences, 'You'll now realize there's a good chance we might be deployed to the South Atlantic. However it might take time before any political decision is made. Meanwhile we can't sit back like fat cats and do nothing. We've many new faces here. The Brigade's been reorganized and must train together. I've therefore asked for, and got, Sennybridge training area in South Wales from 22 to 29 April. All other unit bookings for that period have been cancelled. And you might ask, why not Salisbury Plain? Well, although both have similar terrain to the Falklands, there's one thing that Sennybridge has that others lack. Vile weather – similar to what we can expect in the Falklands. So for the first time in my career I'm praying it'll pour cats and dogs whilst I'm out on exercise!'

The Brigadier knew Sennybridge. Located on the north-east side of the Brecon Beacons, my memories of exercises there, including one on my platoon commanders course when it rained non-stop for a week, burned bright as repeat experiences to avoid. Also Colonel David was right. Gurkha chances of participating in the operation had improved, and thoughts of Hong Kong were now placed firmly on my back burner. After the six-hour conference I returned to 80, Wakefords Park. The domestic tension continued to rise.

'So you *are* probably going to war!' exclaimed Tove when she heard about the exercise.

'Maybe so,' I replied, 'and our weekend's also ruined because I'm flying to Wales on Sunday for a training conference!'

'This teaches us for being too greedy in wanting to return to Hong Kong,' retorted my wife, whose country's most important event in December, apart from the Christmas and New Year Eves, was the Nobel Peace Prize ceremony. Such a cultural gap between us never did close, but neither had two years administrating unit exercise applications in Germany been the ideal psychological preparation for this situation. Nonetheless my taking the oath of allegiance to the Queen and her heirs at Norbury Army Recruiting Office as a naive nineteen year-old on 23 August 1966, and acceptance of the 'Queen's shilling' on that day's inflated rate of £2 10s. was now bearing fruit for Her Majesty.

Planning a Battalion training programme for war would begin immediately. DB sahib had told me that the first part of the SAS unofficial motto plagiarized from the Soviet Red Army of, 'Train hard, fight easy . . .' also had a Gurkha equivalent, '*Training ma pasina bagae larain ma khun joginchha.*' (If you sweat during training, you can save blood during the real thing.) Lieutenant Robert Lawrence, a Scots Guards subaltern who would be deployed to the Falklands' War, had already experienced this phenomenon two years before during a 'work-up' exercise for a six and a half-month Battalion emergency tour of Belfast:

> We were trained for Northern Ireland in mock villages which the Army built for the purpose. Gurkhas would pretend to be rioters, but were pretty serious about it. One hit me across the side of the head with a baseball bat and burst one of my eardrums despite the fact that I had a steel helmet on.[3]

Psychological pressures and training intensity prior to my previous Northern Ireland Light Infantry battalion tours of duty would not be in the same league as those soon to be encountered on Exercise WELSH FALCON. My overriding thought was one of, 'Lad, you're growing up quickly this week,' as I went to bed. Sleep came fitfully. Then the telephone rang. It was just after midnight. Of course, the Gurkha voice in the receiver politely reeled off the message: 'Sahib, we have just received a secret signal . . .'

That, and twenty-four hours later the next, confirmed the serious Falklands' situation and need for Exercise WELSH FALCON. This would be split into two phases. 22 to 25 April was for live-firing exercises, followed by a four-day Brigade field training exercise to practise battle and logistic resupply procedures. To participate in the coordination of training area and range allocations at Sennybridge, I boarded a Puma helicopter at Aldershot on 18 April with HB sahib and the other unit training officers. The Sennybridge permanent staff supervised the conference where the meticulous HB sahib recorded our allocations.

'Can we carry out night live-firing not just individually, but also section and platoon fire and movement exercises?' pleaded the QGO. I backed up his request. But the Small Arms Service Corps Instructor chairing the conference had an inflexible tone, 'Sorry, sir. We've strict night live-firing restrictions and rule-bending is totally forbidden!'

This was incompatible peacetime bureaucracy for units about to go to war. Unlike us, he had not done the exhausting psychological quantum leap. Night fighting had to be exercised realistically because, once we were engaged on Falkland operations, this basic infantry skill would be needed. But as if to emphasize the official shyness to such nocturnal activity, came another incredible announcement, 'So only *six* one-inch Very flares will be allocated to your Battalion for the week!'

HB sahib and I were flown back home late that afternoon. While waiting in the 5 Brigade Headquarters guardroom for transport back to Church Crookham, we observed 2 Para's advance party loading up their vehicles for a move to the port of Hull and embarkation onto the P&O North Sea ferry MV *Norland* which, in due course, would provide the Gurkhas with some stormy maritime experiences. My report next day to Colonel David on the conference results and night restrictions also hoisted his comments to gale force. 'No way!' he objected. 'Contrary to these hopeless range orders, this Battalion *will* carry out section and platoon night live-firing practices so that the basic tactics of manoeuvring with two machine guns per section can be learnt!' With that, a Nelsonian blind eye was turned to the 'illegality' aspect of such vital training.

The day also marked the completion of my week as Duty Field Officer. 'A peaceful Monday,' I thought, 'in which to prepare for the rigours of Sennybridge.' It was not to be. The idyll was soon disturbed by two excited journalists who, having cheekily enlisted Gurkha Provost staff assistance, knocked on my door, came in, and began firing questions, 'We've heard that the Gurkhas'll be going on exercise in Wales prior to joining the Task Force. Could you confirm this? And when's your likely departure date?' A breather was needed from these aggressive gentlemen – and some advice. 'Could you give me a moment, please?' I asked.

With the dynamic duo sent out, guidelines were acquired from the Public Relations office of South-East District HQ at Aldershot. The boss there, Lieutenant Colonel David Dunn, provided an official guideline which set the future tone in my responses to media enquiries about the Gurkhas and the Task Force. This uneasy and not too truthful answer dictated by my PR master who also happened to be a Light Infanteer, was repeated to numerous other national and local paper journalists' telephoned enquiries later the same day, 'As far as I know the Gurkhas have no connection whatsoever with current military activities in the South Atlantic. 5 Brigade will only be exercising in Wales as part of its routine training programme because two new infantry units have joined the formation!'

During any big crisis situation, newspaper editors will engage all available staff on the 'hot story'. These are the media 'experts' who use a technique that is broad-brush in approach, exemplified by that familiar civilian expression 'there was heavy fighting today', to describe the complicated execution of a professional military operation. No doubt these words would be read and heard many times in the UK media during the latter end of May and first half of June. Nevertheless, irritating as it was now to answer their queries, such people could not be so stupid as to believe my ridiculous statement from the HQ at Aldershot.

Next day I said goodbye to my girls at Wakefords Park to join the 30 mph Brigade convoy chugging along the M4 to Wales. It produced only monotony and, at the stop near Cheltenham, I glanced at what one national tabloid newspaper had concocted that day. **NAVY MOVES IN ON PENGUIN ISLAND** blazed its headline but, although South Georgia's Operation PARAQUET recapture was imminent, the Gurkhas were more focused on consuming coke and cardboard-tasting sandwiches in the restaurant. We seemed far removed from reality. The Sennybridge weather did not help. Sun and blue sky during our stay would wreck the Brigadier's prime reason for selecting the training area where the dry grassland was a severe fire hazard. Taj Lewis' C Company, flown home prematurely from their Cyprus exercise, could not complain about lost sunbathing opportunities.

Sharing a room in the Officers' Mess spartan accommodation on arrival, Taj and I talked. He was not amused at the possibility of a permanent disruption to his antipodean retirement plans or that the Battalion's possible deployment 'down-under' would miss Australia by the width of the South Pacific. The conversation ended and reality returned when he told me, 'My brother's in the SAS and already near the Falklands.'

We began our training area recces and administrative work early next morning on 21 April as only twenty-four hours were available. My first task was to be updated by the 5 Brigade staff on the training facilities. In the sprawl of single-storey buildings and maze of one-way circuits I found their offices where, outside, was a pile of equipment and boxes beside parked-up Land-Rovers and trailers. There was more of this kit in the vehicles, and men had to hump it all into the headquarters. Major Barnie Rolfe-Smith, a red-bereted Para and Brigade's chief logistician, with imposing title of Deputy Assistant Adjutant and Quartermaster General, passed by. The DQ viewed the sweating workers then, prophetically, remarked to me, 'Going to war's a chaotic business. No doubt it'll be just as chaotic down south.'

After the informal meeting, I made my way to our nearby Battalion HQ. Outside stood our first British attachments, six Signallers from 30 Signals Regiment at Blandford. They had never worked with Gurkhas before, but were more preoccupied with the South Atlantic and repeatedly asked me, 'D'ya think we'll go, sir?' Unconvinced this would happen, they had no doubt the Gurkhas meant business by our comprehensive training programme. Captain Kit Spencer, who had only recently begun his job as the Regimental Signals Officer, would need their expertise. He had received a consignment of the new Clansman radio system which would replace the older Larkspur system. The former would be used on Operation CORPORATE and was being issued to Battalion sub-units but, although many other Army units already possessed Clansman, the Gurkhas had never seen or operated the new system and would have to be trained on it during the exercise and beyond. So Kit would need his British Signallers plus Lieutenant Don Macauley, also attached from the Royal Signals, to provide the vital expertise.

'Where's all this stuff coming from, Kit?' I asked the hard-pressed RSO who was emptying wooden crates of radio equipment. His reply indicated how low 5 Brigade's concept of operations had been prioritized, 'I've heard that a lot has been withdrawn from University Officer Training Corps units, but this is only a first consignment. We should get even more after the exercise!'

The policy appeared to be that officer recruitment took priority over military operations and need for thorough training to succeed. This was the key to the Battalion's

Exercise WELSH FALCON programme. Although tough, the Gurkhas responded because the second part of that SAS saying about training, '. . . but – train easy, fight hard – and die', was inapplicable to any Gurkha preparing for the Falklands' War. Gaining confidence in daylight live fire and movement exercises of personal and support weapons on 22 April, and then again 'illegally' that night, they focused on perfecting their basic weapon drills. If all else failed, at least this could be relied upon in combat's moment of truth when a weapon jams and charging enemy are only twenty metres away. But unevenness in unit standards meant that Gurkha instructors had to be provided for the Guards' GPMG weapon training.

St George's Day, 23 April, came and went, but the Gurkhas' appetite for more ammunition remained. A lack of Very flares was not the only shortfall attributable to the penny-pinching attitudes towards live ammunition. The Battalion's officers had been briefed at Church Crookham of the potential Argentine armour threat which had been taken most seriously. However the soft Falkland ground surface meant the only Argentine armour to be deployed there was a handful of French-built Panhard cars with movement restricted to the Port Stanley area. In April the Battalion was unaware of this, and concern mounted at the recently formed Milan Anti-Tank Platoon's desperate shortage of live-firing practice. Its wire-guided missile with a range of 2,000 metres and twelve seconds' flight time would become the main bunker-busting weapon of the Falklands' War. But because each missile cost £8,000 at 1982 prices, none were available for the Gurkhas on Exercise WELSH FALCON – although *Canberra*'s troops after arrival at Ascension Island fired nine training-years' worth of missiles in a day.

The Swedish-made 84-mm Carl Gustav medium anti-tank gun, however, was fired at Sennybridge. An unpopular platoon shoulder-held weapon, the '84's' weight made it unsuitable for protracted offensive operations. Even at Sandhurst no cadet volunteered to be the 'Charlie G gunner' on exercise and hump the damn thing around for eternity. At section level the 'throw-away-after-use' shoulder-held 66-mm light anti-tank weapon would be a far more potent Falklands' weapon, but most Gurkhas had little experience firing its live rocket. I visited the range to observe many missing their targets by a worrying margin.

'The problem, sahib, is not their fault,' one QGO told me. 'They're finding a big difference between the trigger pressure of a 66's live round compared to a practice round, and need more live rounds to improve their marksmanship!'

More would not be forthcoming to an unbelievably miserly allocation of a vital weapon supposed to prepare infanteers for what would become an infantry war. Other ammunition shortages became evident. For their SLRs (Self Loading Rifles) Gurkha riflemen carried five magazines filled with twenty rounds each. Placing two tracer rounds on top and one on the bottom of each seemed a clever ploy for enhancing target indication and reminding the rifleman to change magazines after firing the twentieth round.

'But the real truth,' one BO revealed, 'is that it's the most effective method we've found of rationing the pitiful amount of tracer ammunition made available to us by the powers above!'

During this period the first Brigade casualties occurred when a Battalion Land-Rover overturned, killing Sergeant Ramparsad Limbu and seriously injuring three other

Gurkhas. 'I hope this doesn't have a detrimental effect on morale,' said a worried Colonel David who knew Gurkhas better than most BOs. Command was lonely. To compensate he talked on the telephone frequently with an 'external advisor', 7GR's Colonel of the Regiment, Brigadier 'Birdie' Smith, a Second World War, Malaya and Borneo combat veteran. A wise ploy. There was shock at the news of Ramparsad's death, but focus was retained on training geared to offensive Falkland operations amidst news of the continued Argentine build-up. Driving around to observe the companies' activities, I noted Gurkhas digging trenches as a background activity on one of the shooting ranges. Unlike chalky Salisbury Plain, the earth's softness made the work easy. Nonetheless strength, motivation, and a traditional expertise in defence matters meant that two- and three-man trenches were constructed in double-quick time with a blur of pickaxe, shovel, and kukri. I was also becoming more aware of one side to the Gurkha 'Jekyll and Hyde' character as a determined, but placid individual who was the most polite and smartly dressed soldier in uniform – and civilian clothes – ever to grace the British Army, particularly with my father's claim that, 'Gurkhas in the heat of battle launch themselves at their enemy with a red mist over their eyes after they've witnessed fellow Gurkhas killed,' – and when such paradoxical behaviour might occur in a few weeks.

Meanwhile happy Sergeant Hemkumar Gurung, the Officers' Mess Head Steward, typified the Gurkhas' polite and laughing side. He was like a shadow whenever I entered the Mess dining room, pulling out my chair and pouring water into my glass. This later-in-life owner of a Nepalese restaurant in Colorado, USA, chuckled sonorously as I gorged myself daily at lunch and supper with Himalayan platefuls of *bhat*. The difference between the lentils of *dal-bhat* and plain meat of *bhat* became more apparent but, whatever type was served, it still remained a delicious, spicy heaven without compare. Yet, personifying Gurkha politeness and hospitability, Sergeant 'Hem' never did make any remarks about my gluttony.

At Sennybridge I enjoyed at least twenty consecutive meals of *bhat*, including an introduction to *khorsani*. Like a bloated pea pod, the QGOs consumed these chillis without blinking an eyelid. HB sahib enlightened me on the Gurkhas' favourite vegetable, 'Some say that eating them improves the Gurkhas' marksmanship. We also have a saying, "*Khorsani khane Gurkhali ko rish*" which means "Having a temper like Gurkhas who eat chillis"! Would you like some, sahib?' he asked, pushing the bowl across to me. Perhaps it was an alternative cause for their alleged red mist. But after my first bite there was no time for further thought. The green *khorsani* was hot. 'No, it's *really* hot!' I thought two seconds later. 'Oh God, it's *very, very* hot, Hem!' I gasped after another five seconds, trying to suck in cool air over my over-heating tongue. Thank goodness for his fireman's instinct in providing a tumbler of water to douse that scorching heat. His rescue action was appreciated, but the attempted cool-down of my melt-down had a zero effect. The Training Officer sahib just managed to whimper, 'More!' before refilling his tumbler and swallowing the water so rapidly that even Hem had no time to begin chuckling again.

In a further attempt to simmer down afterwards, I did find time to call Tove from my usual telephone box outside the Mess. Training for war needed its counterbalances with non-military input from elsewhere to maintain some equilibrium, and news about family activities did just this. All the same, the burning taste of that green *khorsani* still existed two hours later on Sunday, 25 April, the eve of the Brigade field-training exercise. So when Bill Dawson rushed into Battalion HQ's cramped offices I wondered if his haste might have been related to a similar eating experience as mine. This was not so. The 2IC looked exceptionally excited and exclaimed, 'Have you lot heard what's happened?'

We looked up blankly as he enlightened those present with a flood of words equating to, 'No? Well, there's bloody good news on the radio! The Argies have lost a submarine[4] at Grytviken, and the Navy's recaptured South Georgia!'

Such an event indicated that the Argentines might need a few green chillis to put fire into their bellies. It would also add spice to our exercise whose scenario was based on the seizure of a bridgehead by 'amphibious' heliborne assaults on the western 'shores' of Sennybridge, now rechristened Caleb Island. This would be followed by an eastern advance across the 'Island' on foot and by helicopter, in addition to practising battle procedures from platoon level upwards. Using this almost identical strategy to that employed five weeks later on the Falklands, our final objective would be the mythical Port Picton. The Brigadier's message was clear. Rather than lame acceptance of becoming the Islands' post-war garrison, his intention was that we would fight if ordered to deploy to the Falklands and this field exercise would now test his concept of operations and exercise all personnel.

Monday, 26 April began at sparrow's fart with the Battalion's move to a football pitch at the camp's far end to the waiting 'burning and turning' CrabAir Puma helicopters. A dozen years before as a Light Infantry platoon commander I had participated in an amphibious heliborne assault from the Royal Marine Commando carrier HMS *Bulwark* during Exercise GRANADA off the north-east Malaysian coast. Minus the carrier, there were operational similarities, including the glorious tropical Sennybridge weather. Taj's Company emplaned since they would be the first Battalion sub-unit to deploy, followed by Tac HQ. Taj's job was to secure the Battalion's landing site on Caleb Island. Ten minutes after his Company took off, Tac HQ took to the air. We circled the landing site before finally landing and I quickly located the C Company Commander. He was walking around rather disconsolately with a sour look on his face which prompted me to ask, 'What's wrong, Taj?'

'Great start! We were ambushed by an enemy force dug in nearby as we were landing, and have been cut to ribbons!' he shouted back above the noise of more arriving helicopters. Not even the efforts of C Company's Forward Air Controller, Major Mike Howes, could compensate for the notional disaster. The Royal Welsh Fusilier FAC tried directing a belated air strike onto the enemy position by a direct radio link with the CrabAir Jaguar pilots. He tramped around the hill-top searching for a better transmission location and calling into his handset with a Welsh baritone that echoed around the hillside from loud to deafening: 'This is Red Dragon! This is Red Dragon! Jaguar pilot come in please! Come in!'

Alas, his Red Dragon call sign failed to ignite any fire. This and C Company's holocaust on touchdown were indicators that the exercise would mercilessly expose 5 Brigade's many operating weaknesses. Most units had their problems and the fighting-fit Gurkhas were no exception. The seeds of our distrust with the Brigade resupply system were sown early when A Company left behind their bergens for the CrabAir Pumas to pick up and deliver later. In reality this meant the Gurkhas had kissed goodbye to their kit and provoked many an irritated Gurkhali comment on the Battalion radio net. Judging also from conversations on the Brigade radio net, both Guards' battalions had embarrassing night navigation difficulties. Too much public duties. Furthermore a firepower demonstration by RAF Strike Command Jaguar and Harrier GR3 ground attack fighters with artillery support was more a public relations event for visiting journalists than an vital work-up exercise for us soon to sample live combat. Troops had been held so well back that binoculars were required to view the explosions of this aerial strike. Not surprisingly the general comment made in Tac HQ about that CrabAir equivalent to the Farnborough Air Show was an irritated, 'What a waste of rations!'

On the final day, a sweating steel-helmeted Colonel David with map and results of a Gurkha recce in his hand called out, 'Right, I need some help!' Unfortunately there was no time to prepare his orders for an assault on Port Picton because a stony-faced Lieutenant General Sir Frank Kitson arrived inconveniently at Tac HQ. The Deputy Commander of UK Land Forces had been the PIRA's *bête noire* in Northern Ireland during the previous decade. He now became ours as time and effort were sucked up taking care of this VVIP. This diverted energy away from preparing our only chance of practising the infanteer's nightmare of fighting in a built-up area. The subsequent lengthy and sweaty 'advance to contact' across open and rising ground ended with the enemy firing on us from their empty two-storey block houses of Sennybridge's 'fibua' complex. We launched a sweeping left-flank attack, gained access to a number of buildings, and Tac HQ set up a temporary command post in one. A panting shirt-sleeved order umpire followed, pointed at Colonel David, and said, 'You're dead, sir!'

A surprised Bill Dawson received the message by radio and ran into our building to assume command as the umpire declared, 'So now it's a Sunray Minor show!' It was exactly the nightmare that 2 Para's 2IC would experience during a similar, but 'live', moment four weeks later. In any event, at the end of that last half-hour of the Battle of Port Picton it was judged that the Gurkhas had avenged their Commandant's 'death' by total victory.

At the Battalion debriefing, though, more helicopter exercise problems were revealed. 'No means exists for a pilot to talk direct to a company commander, and this deficiency is causing great confusion whenever a rapid tactical move is required,' said one BO. The solution lay in SARBE, pronounced sabre, which was a small two-way emergency transmitter-receiver search and rescue beacon. Harrier pilots and the SAS possessed these on Falklands operations, but there were not enough for 5 Brigade.

'The bidding system for helicopters has severe limitations,' another commented, but post-exercise corrections remained untested.

'We should also be training on the Navy's Sea King,' one more observed. Only the Puma and Wessex had been made available for Exercise WELSH FALCON, but the Sea King would be in constant use on the Falklands and no Gurkha had, as yet, even seen one. Impacting negatively on Battalion morale, these and other shortfalls did not bode well for the future. To cap everything, that Sennybridge dry grass generated extra fires for the UK's out of area fire Brigade with its own Headquarters, 4 Field

Regiment Royal Artillery, and 81 Ordnance Company all losing equipment, tents and stores. Probably there were also a few long Brigade HQ staff faces at their debriefing. Apparently the UK Land Forces' umpires were unimpressed even though a bad exercise can, in reality, be good because discovering weaknesses during 'the real thing' must be avoided. Deployment of more troops to the South Atlantic on the field training exercise eve had been a War Cabinet agenda item, so the real problem would be an acute shortage of time to make adjustments if we were deployed.

At Brigade 'endex' their decision was finally made as Argentina sent final reinforcements to the Falklands comprising 3 Infantry Brigade from the northerly province of sub-tropical Corrientes. Nine infantry regiments out of twenty-eight in the Argentine Army and a Marine Infantry Battalion had been committed. To ensure repossession of the Islands would now require a 5 Brigade reinforcement of 3 Commando Brigade; but when 10 Downing Street's tenant received information that a Gurkha battalion would, after all, be included in the Brigade order of battle, her response was rumoured to be, 'What? Only one?'

It would be enough.

This decision had not arrived at Sennybridge and, instead, Colonel David received another directive on 29 April. 'You're not going to enjoy a Bank Holiday weekend because our notice to move has now been reduced to seventy-two hours, and we're to remain here for another four days!' he informed his officers. 'We'll make use of our time by more range work and, to mark the end of our stay, the 2IC will organize a Battalion live-firing exercise.' 'OK,' said Bill, 'I'll begin immediately but we've only got less than seventy-two hours, and a tight liaison is needed with the Range Office to comply with their strict safety rules.'

An initial visit to its staff early on 30 April predictably revealed a night-firing prohibition. The detailed planning continued with, by now, most BOs realizing that 5 Brigade would be committed soon as the Total Exclusion Zone, inside which both ships and aircraft could be attacked, came into force and US President Ronald Reagan's diplomatic and matériel 'tilt' swung towards Britain. Next afternoon Bill held his briefing. 'The exercise will start tomorrow evening,' he confirmed, having thrown heart and soul into the project. 'Phase One will be the Battalion's move to the training area and digging a defensive position on one side of a valley whilst targets are placed out on the other. Phase Two starts at first light when from our trenches we'll engage a notional enemy advance with all available weapons. Finally Phase Three will involve manoeuvring all three rifle companies in a counter-attack around an intricate pattern of supporting SLR, GPMG, and mortar fire!' Issuing the technical detail, he finished with an eyebrow-raising boast of, 'The Range Office have approved all of this, and I've also been told by them that this'll be the biggest exercise of its type at Sennybridge since 1944 just before the D-Day Normandy landings!'

Although training continued, administrative support was reduced and eating facilities of the various unit Officers' Messes centralized in the Brigade Mess. After dinner Gurkha BOs and QGOs were gathered around the TV waiting for transport to the training area. The early evening ITN news was reporting the start of the real 'shooting war' with Operation BLACK BUCK Vulcan bombing of Stanley Airport, Harrier attacks on Goose Green, and Royal Navy bombardment around Port Stanley. An excited newsreader continued: 'We're just receiving reports that three Argentine aircraft, maybe Mirages, have also been shot down . . . !'

The Brigadier entered the crowded ante-room. He had made up his mind how a deployed 5 Brigade would operate in the Falklands and growled, 'A pity . . . three less for us!' These events underscored the need for a Battalion live field-firing exercise climax. So with the Scots and Welsh Guards packed by the following evening and fleeing back to London's bright lights, the Gurkhas moved out of camp to the khuds.

'Looks like we've chosen the correct time for our final Falklands exercise,' I observed to Mark Willis as rain began falling.

PHASE II – GOING TO WAR

Chapter Six

PROJECTING THE IMAGE

'The renowned Gurkha troops with their foot-long kukris will be no match for Argentine fighters who grew up with the eighteen-inch gaucho's knife,' a Buenos Aires military source said yesterday. Advised of British reports that 650 of the Nepalese troops are being sent to the Falkland Islands, the military source, who declined to be identified, said they will be met by 1,000 Argentine soldiers from the northern province of Corrientes. 'Let the Gurkhas come with their foot-long daggers,' he said. 'The boys from Corrientes will have their terrible 'Facones' unsheathed.' – From an article in *The Daily Telegraph* about the deployment of the Argentine Army's 3 Infantry Brigade, and published a few days before 1st/7th Gurkha Rifles' embarkation onto RMS *Queen Elizabeth II.*

The tropical climate cursing most of Exercise WELSH FALCON had vanished. Instead weather that the Brigadier had hoped for at Aldershot now hit the Gurkhas. Conditions deteriorated rapidly and, by nightfall, became a classic Sennybridge nightmare. Thirty-knot gusts of wind, rain, hail, sleet and finally snow resembled more the forecasted evils of a Falklands' winter. Beating arms on his body in an unsuccessful attempt to maintain blood circulation, Bill exclaimed, 'I realize who was responsible for the exercise planning, but I had nothing to do with this weather! For God's sake someone send a radio message to camp for them to despatch two bottles of *tato pani*. Tell 'em we need it pronto to warm ourselves up,' he demanded to an informal BO gathering.

'It's *kaida* to use *tato pani* in these circumstances,' explained Mark to me. 'The literal translation of *tato pani* is "hot water", however to Gurkhas it's also their favourite beverage of "whisky"!'

But Bill's message was misinterpreted by the Gurkhas in camp and, instead, two large field containers brimful with hot water arrived for the Battalion HQ's BO *sahibharu* to thaw freezing limbs. So the night remained long until the second phase at first light when our 81-mm mortars fired ranging shots onto the opposite hillside above us. The regular crump of mortar bomb explosions followed by a full Battalion shoot gave seldom-experienced realism.

Despite the weather, any remaining inhibitions with live rounds 'up the spout' disappeared in the final phase as sections skirmished forward firing their 7.62-mm SLRs and GPMGs. 'Oh, yes! That's pretty, Mike!' commented Bill in observing the warlike gymnastics of Mike Kefford's D Company.

Nonetheless, afterwards we shivered with cold whilst waiting for transport back to camp. 'I'll tune into the frequency for the BBC World Service to get the latest news,' offered Mark to kill time. Despite frozen fingers, flipping the dials on his high-frequency Clansman radio set presented little difficulty to the ex-RSO. The broadcast made us rub our eyes even harder a second time on that grey, icy morning of 3 May with news of the cruiser ARA *General Belgrano*'s sinking by a Royal Navy submarine and attacks on more minor shipping.[1]

'Seems as though the South Atlantic's nicely on the boil,' another BO remarked prior to the arrival of two Brigade staff officers fifteen minutes later. One was the Brigade Major, Brendon Lambe. In our trench Mark and I looked up into their serious faces. The BM bent down to give *his* news to us. It was no surprise.

'OK, your unit's going,' he confirmed. 'We've just been informed that the War Cabinet has ordered *QE2*'s requisition, and that 5 Brigade is to embark on her and sail south.'

So the Gurkhas would cross the element they dreaded most – the *kala pani* or black water. Deploying to the First World War in Flanders and elsewhere, their forefathers were subject to the general ban of carrying out a *kala pani* journey because of their Hindu religion. However special permission could be sought providing a purification ceremony, the *pani patiya*, was performed after arriving back at home. To my knowledge the Gurkhas of 5 Brigade did not have to submit to such religious bureaucracy from the *Pandit* for this *QE2* cruise. But I should have bet a bottle of *tato pani* on the answer to my reflex question, 'OK, but do you have any idea when we'll leave?'

Brendon's reply, 'It looks as though departure has been pencilled in for 12 May,' briefly stunned us. Only nine days. 'If victory is a brightly coloured flower, transport is the stem without which it would never have blossomed' was Churchill's aphorism, but *QE2* represented more than just transport to the South Atlantic. She was *the* flower of the Merchant Navy and, approaching the English Channel from Pennsylvania, USA, received her requisition order the same day. A Mediterranean cruise was cancelled; the liner would need six days for conversion work to be carried out on her at Southampton.

Increased chances of being in a shooting war made our shortfall of sleep irrelevant. With the Mess closed, all officers ate their *bhat* and scanned newspapers in the other ranks' cookhouse before our Church Crookham return. Not only fatigue and warmth after fourteen hours of intense cold stopped conversation, but also a realization that time horizons had contracted. Only short-term thoughts and planning existed in response to non-controllable external strategic decisions as if we were strapped into a big dipper with a momentum of its own. Exercise WELSH FALCON had generated Gurkha team spirit and some adrenalin, but the greatest leveller of the battlefield remained missing. An inoculation of fear might have increased my chances of a more efficient personal performance if 'the boys from Corrientes' dared draw their gaucho knives against the Gurkhas from Church Crookham.

Once back there on Tuesday, 4 May and during the first daily post-exercise conference, Bill Dawson declared, 'Going to the Falklands is the best thing that could have happened to this Battalion.' It was the Gurkhas' biggest chance since Borneo to demonstrate that they could operate on the modern battlefield with their particular skills – the night attack, surprise from the rear, small patrols, and hand-to-hand fighting. At stake was the Gurkha's long-term future in the British Army. Failure was unthinkable. Yet we would go to war with one disadvantage compared to our Falkland Major Unit contemporaries, because political restrictions had prevented the Battalion from experiencing Northern Ireland operations.

Before Exercise WELSH FALCON Bill Dawson had also suggested to me, 'We need a thorough amendment of the Battalion's Standard Operating Procedures, Mike. Look here, I've gone through one page and have already indicated where some changes are needed.' He had put the page in front of me covered with his scribble. The year before I had revised the BAOR Standing Instructions for Exercises, but that self-imposed task had taken months to complete. Amending the Gurkhas' SOPs would require sending a rewritten draft out to the companies for their comments, and maybe chairing a co-ordinating meeting or two before final publication. Because the Scots Guards had been a Public Duties Battalion, their Ops Officer had to compile the Guards' Battalion SOPs from scratch for the Falklands. But he also had the advantage of knowing their system.

'OK,' had come my dutiful promise to the 2IC sahib, 'I'll take a look at it.'

That copy of SOPs had been put into my pending tray – and was still there on return from Wales. Rightly or wrongly, I deemed Bill's proposal unrealistic. My decision did not produce a bad conscience. Like any civilian disaster contingency plan, SOPs had to be rich in detail for, as Napoleon claimed, 'In war nothing is accomplished except through calculation. Anything that is not profoundly meditated in its details will produce no result.' It included information on the Battalion's organization, equipment, battle procedures, logistics and communications – and had to be structured into a simple format for the reader to arrive quickly at his relevant pages. Cutting out detail to make SOPs thinner was the amateur's approach. But I had no detailed knowledge of this bible and meddling with it in the limited time available would court disaster. Besides, my telephone all that Tuesday possessed a life of its own. Newspaper, radio and TV journalists pestered me non-stop about our deployment with their calls of: 'Hello, could we have some information about the Gurkhas? When are you leaving for the Falklands? Is it possible to interview you or anybody else today? Can we film and take pictures of your soldiers?'

I rang Lieutenant Colonel David Dunn at the South-East District HQ and agitatedly sought advice, 'So what should we do in order to cope with this deluge of enquiries, Colonel? The Battalion's pressed for time as it is with all our preparations for deploying south and has precious little left for these Fleet Street buggers.'

His instructions felt like a soothing breeze for an officer who, in addition to dealing with the irritating media, was also preoccupied in psyching himself up for the toughest experience of his life. 'The only way to resolve this mayhem, Mike,' replied my fellow Light Infanteer officer who had become 5 Brigade's Public Relations Officer, 'is by contacting the Press Association and inform them of a Battalion 'press-call' at Church Crookham tomorrow. You'll also need to plan and organize a programme for that morning, and then give a lunch afterwards to all those journalists who turn up.' So the novice Public Information Officer sahib swung into action with this seemingly unnecessary diversion but, surprisingly, the eventual dividend would be immense.

Colonel David also called me into his office that afternoon to give further instructions after returning from a Brigade conference. We've got to refine the reorganization

69

of Battalion HQ and its split into two parts,' he said, 'and this means enlarging Tac HQ to control the rifle companies' operations and coordinate their logistic support.'

So this became another priority of mine. Thirty-eight personnel would eventually make up Tac HQ's establishment. We had already received our Signaller attachments, and would later receive more with Gunners and an FAC and his small team. Redesigning Tac HQ's defensive lay-out in two-, three- and four-man trenches became important as the correct persons had to be domiciled in the correct trench to ensure efficient cooperation and communication. Other suggestions came and my designs had to be remodified several times. Our back-up organization would be an Alternative Battalion HQ commanded by Bill Dawson. Half Tac HQ's size, it also would maintain a constant standby status.

'We'll assume command immediately if Tac HQ and you are blown away on the battlefield, Mike,' Bill informed me later in a matter-of-a-fact tone, 'and if you're alive, your job'll be to coordinate Tac HQ's daily operations, thereby enabling Colonel David to command with his small Forward Tac party.'

The Battalion's emphasis, though, was on administration. 'Be aware that a major in a Gurkha battalion is well looked after by his personal orderly,' I remembered Philip Forster telling me at Bielefeld. The moment was now ripe, so I asked DB sahib, 'Can you find me an orderly sahib to collect my Falklands kit?' Naturally he agreed. Distribution of such equipment now led to Gurkhas wrestling with unfamiliar Arctic clothing outside the Quartermaster's Department.

'The choice of issue is excellent,' Ram said to me as I walked past his office later to take a breather from the media, 'but it's what *not* to take which is the big problem!' He showed me an example. Two windproof suits were on offer: a Northern Ireland model, and a superior CrabAir 'foul-weather' equivalent. But when moving in the latter, a sound was produced reminiscent of two sheets of sandpaper being rubbed together. Not an advisable outcome if crawling up close to the enemy but then, of course, no CrabAir personnel would ever find themselves in such a situation.

Back at home that evening we also started to receive phone calls from relatives and friends. They all had the same wish and advice: 'Good luck, and keep your head down!' Tove's telephone calls to relatives in Oslo had also intensified. An international marriage drains the family budget, but the Falklands' crisis exacted an extra toll. 'Watch it! We're going to have a vicious quarterly bill!' I warned her. She continued to ring and my financial prognosis became fact; the Falklands' War still owes me that £200 extra sum on my telephone bills. However someone was thinking about our financial problems. After my departure on *QE2*, Tove received a letter from my Rustington bank manager. Her husband's cruise and ultimate destination prompted him to provide the offer 'of any assistance if it was required'. Alas, such generosity has never been repeated when peacetime financial crises struck me in the years after the war.

That the Gurkhas *were* now part of Operation CORPORATE also heightened our information craving. We locked ourselves again into the TV news. A Harrier had been shot down over Goose Green and its pilot killed. The activities of the lugubrious Peruvian UN Secretary-General, Javier Perez de Cuellar, seemed proof that, like the military operations, international mediation had become a growth industry, with involvement of his fellow countryman President Fernando Belaunde Terry. Then came that announcement of the fatal Exocet attack on the frigate HMS *Sheffield*. I groaned, 'Oh, shit alive!' as my stomach sagged between my knees and Tove's face whitened.

Mumbling from the temporary safety of my sofa, 'This war's going to be no pushover,' my inner concerns grew for the imminent *QE2* 'cruise' and implications of this first-ever 'ship against missile' encounter. Our married quarter was silent after the robot monotone of Ian McDonald, the Ministry of Defence TV spokesman, had ceased its cant which had started with what would become a well-known refrain of doom that week and next: 'In the course of their duties within the Total Exclusion Zone around the Falkland Islands . . .' We retired to bed in sombre mood. A continued presence at home was now counter productive as my acute awareness of mortality and fear of the unknown had driven, slowly but surely, such a wedge between us that the first fissures in our marriage began appearing.

'I wish you'd stop worrying and get to sleep,' complained my wife, 'because it's bound to be better once all you warriors are together at sea.'

B Company on their way back to the UK from Belize did not, however, have the same reaction. After hearing the distressing news of *Sheffield*'s loss, their Company Commander, Major Guy Pearson, had decided it was his duty to brief the men about this Royal Navy disaster at sea. Nevertheless, on being informed of this frightful news there erupted a loud cheer of joy from them. Such a reaction puzzled even Guy who, it must be said, should have been acquainted with the mechanics of Gurkha logic. So he queried his 2IC.

'Did they really understand what I've just said?' he asked Captain Dalbahadur Sunwar, hardly believing what he had just heard and seen.

'Yes, sahib, they understood extremely well!' acknowledged the B Company QGO. 'Your information means to them that no longer are they simply "on exercise" but, instead, as from now the *keta* will be going to war – and this has raised their morale accordingly!'

Of course explaining such Gurkha thinking had its difficulties, particularly post-war when Colonel David attempted this for a speechless Royal Navy Captain who had lost men on his ship in the South Atlantic. B Company would also soon receive Rifleman Baliprasad Rai of the P and D as a GPMG(SF) gunner attachment. He described his feelings about this deployment:

> It was on a fairly hectic day in the first week of May that I knew I was going to war in the Falklands – a place I had never heard of before. I was not unduly surprised because all of us in the Battalion were expecting to go there sooner or later. We had just arrived in camp after (a two-week) exercise in the wilds of the Brecon Beacons and I remember having mixed feelings of elation and appre-hension – elation at the prospect of adventure in a far off land, and apprehension in not knowing if I would ever come back alive – but the overwhelming feeling was one of excitement.[2]

Next morning's conference was chaired by Colonel David. 'We're going to receive extra weapons,' he informed us. 'The M-79 grenade launcher will be useful, but we've no time for any training on it or carrying out test-firing. The Brigadier has also insisted that each battalion be issued with six .5-inch Browning heavy machine guns which are being dug out of mothballs to bring our total machine-gun arsenal to 100! A new Machine Gun Platoon will therefore be created from the Mechanical Transport Platoon as limited roadway on the Falklands means under employment for its drivers.'

It was unlikely that any Gurkha battalion in history had so many machine guns at its disposal, and compared most favourably to a Gurkha battalion which entered the 1915 Neuve Chapelle trenches possessing two. With its range of 2,600 metres the Browning was considered a potent weapon for the open Falklands' terrain even though it had a weight of fifty-eight kilos, heavy ammunition and proved wildly in-accurate. Only anti-aircraft sights had been fitted, and no night sights existed like those infrared ones later found on some of the enemy Brownings. So any chance of hitting the target at night depended on the Mortar Platoon's illumination bombs. A gun team of three was required but, as yet, no Gurkha had handled the weapon, let alone fire it. One candidate for commanding this new platoon was the hawk-eyed Captain Steve Crowsley, a free-fall parachutist and class marathon runner who had just arrived from Hong Kong. Scheduled to participate in a pre-SAS selection course, I met him later as he was walking out of Colonel David's office. 'Great stuff!' he beamed, 'I've just hitched a lift on *QE2* for some special pre-training for the SAS course instead, and a Sergeant Major Instructor from the Small Arms Service Corps is to be attached to us for the next two weeks to assist in heavy machine gun training!'

A little later DB sahib wheeled Rifleman Prembahadur Limbu of the Signals Platoon into my office to announce, 'This man's been nominated as your orderly, sahib!'

'Oh! Jolly good, sahib!' I replied before looking at Prembahadur to continue, 'I'm too busy to collect my kukri and Falklands kit, so can you fetch it for me?'

The rifleman nodded his head vigorously with a beaming, 'Yes, sahib!' Alas, it would be too easy. For the time being though, I breathed a sigh of relief and turned my mind to the imminent press call. *Sheffield*'s fate did not now prevent the camp from being swamped by the media. It simply created more interest for the Gurkhas. Originally designed as a public relations stunt, the press call initiated an unintended psychologi-cal operation which would profoundly affect our eventual Falkland operations. Gurkhas charged around brandishing small arms, anti-tank weapons and mortars whilst others carried out live-firing on the thirty-metre range. Interviews were held. GM sahib was adept in answering questions about the Gurkhas; and his articulate replies this day and on others contributed to his later MBE award for services rendered during Operation CORPORATE. Questions also came my way:

> Among the Gurkhas were most of the prize-winning shooting team from Bisley who had been training up for this year's event. As Major Mike Seear, their Ops/Training Officer said:
> 'Time and time again, they come away from Bisley with the top prizes. They are extremely good shots and really first class marksmen.'[3]

To the *Soldier* journalist who interviewed me, Gurkhas were synonymous with the steamy jungles of Burma, Malaya and Borneo. He had not read his history books. These were men for all seasons as demonstrated in those Flanders, Gallipoli and Italian winters. So I conveniently forgot the wonderful Sennybridge weather and milked that final Battalion field firing exercise for all it was worth in reply to his tricky question:

> But how would they stand up to an Antarctic winter, coming as they do from the sweltering Indian sub-continent? Major Seear was confident. 'They are mostly from the mountain areas which are cool in the winter, but they do seem to adapt and function in extreme climates. They have just done very, very well on the recent Welsh Falcon exercise on the Brecon Beacons. There they withstood 30 mile-an-hour winds, rain, snow, sleet, and hail while digging into defensive positions. They came out of it smiling.'[4]

Seemingly satisfied, he then fired off another loaded question with a personal angle, 'And how then do you feel, Major, about going to the Falklands?'

His covert challenge was parried by, 'Well, if one has to go, then I wouldn't dream of going with any other soldier than the Gurkha.'

And back came the oily response, 'Nice answer, Major, nice answer!'

A pretty interviewer of an Austrian TV crew also expressed her surprise to me at, '... the way in which two civilized countries were going about settling the dispute'. She must have been horrified then to observe laughing Gurkhas sharpening their kukris on a large millstone outside one company armoury. During the *bhat* lunch, I voiced my concern to DB sahib about this press call climax, 'Maybe we overdid those kukris at the millstone, sahib!'

As I renewed attacking my overladen plate with apparent undiminished vigour, but partly also to camouflage anxiety, DB sahib was quick to reassure me of that day's 'psyops' gain, 'No, sahib, I believe this will put the fear of the Gurkhas into the enemy.'

'Do you really think so, sahib?' queried the Training Officer sahib.

The QGO's rationale contained no doubt, 'Of course, sahib. Anyway the kukri must be sharp so that "*Hamile dushmanlai mula katai katyaun*" can be achieved.'

My Gurkhali still retained its countless imperfections. 'So what does that mean, sahib?'

'Chopped the enemy like radishes cut into little pieces, sahib!' replied the stoic QGO.

His belief in those millstone photos was incorrigible. They were to save many lives as the Gurkha public relations bandwagon began rolling next day. In the Mess prior to our daily conference I picked up *The Sun*. This newspaper's series of banal Falklands front-page headlines continued by its proclaimation of **COLD STEEL FOR JOHNNY GAUCHO**. 'God! Was I responsible for that?' became my paranoid worry, little knowing that the Argentine media would reinforce this image by more lurid articles about our men. The lawyer Eduardo Roca, leader of the Argentine delegation at the UN General Assembly in New York would become involved and, with support from Cuba, he protested to Nepal about the 'mercenary' status of the Battalion as *Flash*, a Buenos Aires weekly periodical, would report:

> Concerning this new aberration of the delirious Margaret Thatcher, a Latin American diplomat in the UN declared: 'Great Britain absurdly pretends to go back in time and re-shape its now dying grasp on colonial power, by resorting to

73

use ferocious mercenaries in a lame attempt of reclaiming the Malvinas Islands, as if it was possible in the middle of 1982 to repeat the episode from the novel Gunga Din.'[5]

On reflection however, to receive mention at this level of international diplomacy was a unique compliment no other Task Force unit received. Propaganda aside, the administrative drive towards our 12 May embarkation deadline had forged ahead, but at the daily conference Ram startled most with his comment, 'We're going to have to paint many of the civilian bergens which have been issued to us!'

'Why's that?' was the collective chorus of amazement.

'Because many have been issued with their original bright blue or yellow colour which is far from suitable camouflage for the Falklands,' he replied dryly.

'OK, a decor conversion is required to standard khaki green,' ordered Colonel David, 'and this'll include a re-paint of all SLR bodywork. Also on Falkland operations all slings will be removed to make riflemen carry their SLRs in the alert position at all times.'

Such an artistic measure for the rifle was unpopular, and some company commanders chose not to implement this. Furthermore, although their men's old-fashioned Second World War 44-pattern webbing did eventually become exchanged with the modern 58-pattern that had larger ammunition pouches in the front and additional kidney pouches at the back, they had another equipment complaint of, 'Why hasn't the delivery promise of the latest combat boot been kept?' But this footwear never did materialize. It would be sorely missed

There were other headaches. Constantly changing numbers and names on the Battalion nominal roll continued to be a nightmare for Mark Willis. The Adjutant also had to deal with a large number of unexpected letters arriving on his desk. 'Look at these,' he said, throwing a couple of examples at me, 'they're all from Regimental officers currently serving in external posts!' They all contained the same message: an affirmation of Regimental loyalty by requesting an immediate return to the Battalion. It would not be possible, for the 1st/7th Gurkha Rifles was already overmanned with officers.

I also received a similar epistle from an irate L-squared in Hong Kong. We had talked before about my taking over a married quarter temporarily there whilst attending my Gurkhali language course. But his request was doomed to fail:

I've tried to get back to the Battalion, but failed . . . So you're my last chance. I can't understand what the hell they think they're doing in leaving me out of this Falklands operation with all my military experience as a Gunner, Royal Marine Commando, helicopter pilot, and infanteer . . . Mike, do you think we could possibly swop jobs when you arrive here for your Gurkhali language course? Then I'll simply get the first flight back to the UK.

Yet there *was* one last officer arrival to replace the B Company Commander. Guy Pearson was a high-calibre officer who would not go to the Falklands since he had been already earmarked for the Canadian Staff College. So, having just completed a School

74

of Infantry platoon commanders course, the new OC met his men for the first time on that day when they arrived from Belize. Only five days remained in the relentless battle against time, but Acting Captain Lester Holley was used to pressure. Two years before as a trooper of B Squadron, 22 SAS Regiment he had been part of the legendary Operation NIMROD that resolved the Iranian Embassy siege at Prince's Gate, London. Arguably the only officer ever to attend his platoon commanders' course eligible for two separate British Army units in the same Theatre of Operations, he had taken a course intermission by attending a South Atlantic briefing at the SAS's Hereford base but chose to go to war with the Gurkhas instead. Sporting dark good looks and Che Guevara moustache, Lester would succeed impressively in the Falklands despite, like myself, a total lack of Gurkhali knowledge. Force of personality, fearlessness, humour and a professional obssession with detail and the value of snipers were attributes that brought him much Gurkha respect.

In addition to Lester's arrival, Operation CORPORATE also provided a speedy re-think and changes to the Regimental Aid Post with a prospect of treating mass battlefield casualties. This resulted in British soldier reinforcements to Martin Entwhistle's original medical organization of five Gurkha orderlies, and consisted of a medical collection section of ten orderlies from 16 Field Ambulance led by another doctor, Captain Paul Edmondsen-Jones, plus five medical orderlies from 19 Field Ambulance at Colchester. Twelve were distributed to the rifle companies who received three each, whilst the other eight plus the two doctors formed the RAP. Some in the Battalion, including myself, were also reminded of such ultimate battlefield conse-quences that afternoon.

The Aldershot Crematorium provided a death *puja* ceremony venue for Sergeant Ramparsad Limbu killed at Sennybridge. Led by GM sahib and *Pandit*, the ceremony had flexibility since the Hindu requirement of it taking place in sunlight was ignored as East met West with the religious bumblings inside the building and firing party's discipline outside. Ramparsad's death also prompted more South Atlantic administra-tive action as he had been insured with an official scheme known as ADAT – the Army Dependants' Assurance Trust – and £95 per month would now be paid out to next of kin until his fifty-fifth birthday. ADAT could not have had a better advertisement. Many Gurkhas applied to join because such potential income was a fortune in Nepal. This was also one part of the outstanding shortfalls in my personal administration. I had found only a kukri on my office desk that day which gave me a horrible feeling that Rifleman Prembahadur Limbu had believed this to be the only piece of Falklands kit which the Training Officer sahib needed. 'Or was this proof that my assumed prin-ciple of Gurkha orderly dotage to BOs did not apply to the Training Officer sahib about to go to war?' I thought.

As a company commander I would have benefited from the tight control exercised by my QGO 2IC on 'matters orderly'. Indeed, the system did work when I became A Company's OC sahib. For example two years later, after a hard day's march through leech-infested Malaysian jungle I retired to my sleeping bag to find that not only had my orderly laid this out on a kukri-constructed bamboo-stilted bedframe enclosed in a mosquito net, but also had supplied slippers and a lighted candle. Such bedside service made me feel like a jungle version of Wee Willie Winkie.

But now, at Church Crookham, going solo to achieve my personal administration goals had become a critical priority. Filling out my Army Will form was a maudlin task at home that evening with the TV news of two Harriers missing at sea off the Falklands after an apparent mid-air collision. It consisted of a sheet of A4 paper, not as exotic as Colonel David's, but sufficient enough and would be valid after active service had been declared with only Tove's signature witnessing mine. An interruption came from a phone call made by my father's sister, the indomitable Aunt Nancy alias the Baroness Seear of Paddington. Promoter of the Sex Discrimination Act of 1975, and soon to become Leader of the Liberal Party peers in the House of Lords and model political television panellist, Lady Seear was unusually supportive in remarks about Mrs. T. as her rhetorical questions turned quite warlike with: 'Well, for goodness sake, she had to do something, didn't she? And when it came to the crunch there wasn't much choice, was there?'

Maybe the Baroness had 'insider' information. Perhaps this peer, who never used notes a few years later in making the House of Lords maiden televised speech, had a tinge of jealousy. If she had been Conservative or Labour and had won a parliamentary seat for one of these parties, my aunt might well have become Britain's first female Prime Minister. She would definitely have sat in the Cabinet as Minister. Four months living with a German family in 1932 had taught Lady Seear all about the effect of totalitarianism on people. Her nephew, surprised at her forthrightness, became even more so when the Baroness added aggressively: 'And I expect you must be dying to get down there!' I did assume her ambiguity *was* unintentional, nonetheless my crystal-clear appreciation of the precision and lethality of modern weapon systems tempted me to respond: 'Not if that becomes my final predicament after arrival!' But I wisely refrained.

Next morning, 7 May, my administration drive continued. Like other BOs, I visited the Orderly Room to collect an ADAT brochure and fill out its application form. Another on the same errand was Captain Nigel Price, the Mortar Platoon Commander. Displaying an inexhaustible enthusiasm for work and Regiment, Nigel had an efficient partner in his 2IC, Lieutenant Bhimbahadur Gurung, whose grin was so enormous that it would have reduced the Cheshire Cat's to a frown. We two BOs began a morbid discussion.

'It's obvious who's going to benefit regarding myself becoming a battlefield casualty,' I confided with Nigel, 'because that'll be my wife who'll receive the jackpot immediately. But you're a bachelor, so who's going to enjoy the windfall that you'll be leaving behind?'

There was no doubting the sincerity of Nigel's reply, 'Oh, that's easy. I'm nominating the Gurkha Welfare Trust!' Such thoughtfulness typified the bond that exists between BO and Gurkha soldier.

Determined next to rectify my critical kit situation with a do-it-yourself procurement initiative, I made my way to the HQ Company stores. A group of heavily-loaded Gurkhas were on their way out, and I surprised the storeman with my entry. Excepting inspections, BOs did not appear in his domain, so this one was out of line with *kaida*. His eyes narrowed. 'Where is your orderly, sahib?' he asked in halting English.

But my explanation, 'I know I'm late, but you'll just have to give me as much

Falklands kit as possible since I've received nothing from my orderly,' seemed to work as the elderly Corporal scuttled off to the dark recesses of his stores.

A pile of equipment grew. It included a bergen, sleeping bag and karrimat foam underlay, underwear, three pairs of arctic socks, parka jacket and hood, the two wind-proof suits, quilted Chairman Mao combat jacket and trouser liners, 58-pattern webbing, arctic cap and outsize eye goggles for wind protection. One missing item had been at the top of my shopping list.

'Have you got any of those rubber overboots left?' I asked hopefully.

'Oh yes, sahib!' grinned my supplier, beckoning me to a corner of his store. 'Cold feet no good, sahib, if you want to sleep in the Foklands. These special boots with zips on the front are popular, but many *keta* will not get them because not enough were given to me. But you will be OK. I have many BO pairs left. See! Here!'

My heart dropped like a brick. The sizes available were a few Gurkha fours to sixes – and numerous BO twelves. However ours would be a Falklands, not moon, destination and my size was a sober nine. At last, after more searching, a pair of oversize eights were located. Back at home and stacking my kit in the spare room, I wondered over the logic which delivered astronaut twelves to the Gurkhas. Extra items would have to be packed i.e. more underwear, spare combat suit, steel helmet, towel, shaving kit, two bulky Brigade and Battalion SOP files, water sterilizing tablets, a silver-foil space blanket in a packet that fitted into the palm of my hand, a half-litre intravenous saline drip solution in a thick plastic cylinder, and two large shell dressings stuffed into the top two pockets of combat jacket – but no personal omnipom (morphine) issue, implying that military chiefs elsewhere than the Aldershot area did not expect 5 Brigade to fight.

This internal load matched the external. A large battle board with map slung over my shoulder guaranteed impeded movement, whilst gas respirator, decontamination kit, 9-mm Browning pistol, two empty ammo magazines, and kukri all slung from my belt represented defensive and offensive intent for several scenarios. An entrenching tool in the form of a pickaxe strapped onto my back webbing provided the ultimate prospect of landscaping the Falklands. Finally, my six year-old Hong Kong Canon camera was shoved into my respirator pouch so that experiences, maybe, might be reviewed in old age. It was a lighter load than the Gurkha rifleman who carried far too much.

The weekend prior to going to war arrived and most in the Battalion had been granted leave. Different people did different things. Bill Dawson would continue to decorate his home, whilst Tove and I escaped from reality. It would be no success. Leaving our daughters in the care of Philip, my twin-brother and Jackie, his wife, we took the train to London and a hotel near Piccadilly Circus. On the Saturday, first stop was at an Oxford Street departmental store.

'I'll need some extra thermal vests, long johns, and woollen socks,' I told Tove, trying to be practically-minded. However it was early summer – and the girl behind the counter cooed disbelievingly, 'You going somewhere near the Antarctic then, love?' Embarrassed to reveal my destination, I replied, 'Hmm – not too far away.' Her prognosis, 'Well, you'd be a bit daft to go anywhere near the Falklands. What with all them Argies on them Islands and more of our blokes sailing there as well, there'd be no point wearing this stuff as it's going to get a lot hotter there soon,' would be correct.

'Let's go to a musical,' suggested Tove, 'but not to *Evita* because there's no way I want to hear *Don't Cry for Me Argentina*.' We had seen this two years before, so our choice was the Palace Theatre's catchy *Song and Dance* with the voice of Marti Webb and agility of Wayne Sleep. I half-pushed the Falklands to the back of my mind, but reality soon intervened. Strolling through Leicester Square, we noticed the Sunday newspapers were already on sale.

'Look at that,' I said to Tove pointing to a headline of **INVASION JUST DAYS AWAY**, 'if that's the case then the Battalion had better put its skates on!' My mono-logue led to a tunnel vision of worry clamping around a short-term future. The Falklands' crisis was everywhere.

'I can't see the point of us having come to London,' protested Tove back at the hotel, 'so please tell me what we're going to do tomorrow?' This was awful. Our last weekend together spent arguing. The psychological stress had never been worse.

'Come on, at least let's get some fresh air and go for a walk along the Embankment,' I suggested next morning after breakfast.

'OK,' agreed a dispirited Tove, 'as long as we leave London at lunchtime so I can get back to Victoria and Emily.'

The stroll, though, did succeed in planting one healthy long-term aim as we became caught up in the crowds watching that year's London Marathon. Travelling back to Church Crookham later, I remarked, 'Well *that* could be something for the Gurkhas next year!' But deliberately did not add, '. . . *if* I return.'

Re-united with our girls at 80, Wakefords Park, we said goodbye to our babysitters. My twin was a solicitor who specialized in conveyancing – and probate. 'You got a will?' he asked with detached professional interest, and then added a piece of well-meaning psychosocial support, 'Don't worry, if there's a tragedy we'll take care of all three of them.'

Badly timed, this capped that dreadful weekend. I failed to cope and had a most un-Gurkha-like reaction as emotions flooded embarrassingly to the surface. Philip and Jackie were shocked at my unexpected reaction, perhaps because it ran counter to their conviction that a professional British Army soldier, and officer to boot, *never* behaves like that. They left, but not before my kind sister-in-law gave me a hug. She had *never* done that before. Afterwards, the telephone continued to interrupt our strained domes-ticity as friends and more relatives rang to say goodbye. My father finished his conversation with an untypically emotional: 'God bless you my son.' The TV news, between the phone calls that Sunday evening, had also become more relevant person-ally. Reports of more Royal Navy bombardments around Port Stanley, two enemy Skyhawk aircraft and a helicopter shot down, and capture of the spy trawler *Narwal* preceded another item that had me shouting to Tove, 'Come and look at this!'

The coverage of *QE2*'s preparations at Southampton gave me a psychological lift in place of brooding over the unknown future. That weekend Gurkhas had loaded equip-ment onto eleven Battalion Land-Rovers and these were now aboard the requisitioned Swedish Stena Line roll-on roll-off ships MV *Baltic Ferry* and *Nordic Ferry* together with Brigade guns and heavy equipment. The non-tactical loading would result in severe logistic shortfalls on the Falklands. *Baltic Ferry* passengers included Gurkha drivers under the command of the gangling David Wright, who had recently been appointed the Mechanical Transport Officer; and on *Nordic Ferry* Lieutenant Budhibahadur Rai from the Anti-Tank Platoon was the Gurkhas' OC. Had she known, Tove would have disapproved of Gurkhas on board such *'söta bror'* (sweet brother) transport, given the traditional abrasiveness between the two Scandinavian countries.

These ships then departed Southampton seventy-two hours before the Battalion's main body.

Chapter Seven

SAILING

The stage of action for a military strategist is built upon objective material conditions, but on that stage he can direct the performance of many a drama, full of sound and colour, power and grandeur. – Mao Tse-tung

Two days remained before embarkation. The final preparations though, including a conference, continued at a frantic pace. Another two 81-mm mortars were received to add to the Mortar Platoon's existing six. But as no Gurkhas had been trained to man them, these had to be taken as battle replacement spares. Neither would the vehicles of this forty-five man strong platoon be taken, so their drivers, together with attachments from the Recce Platoon, formed an eleven-man group whose main job was the defence of a mortar line which would comprise three sections rather than the textbook four.

At Sennybridge the Signals Platoon had exchanged some of the Battalion's old Larkspur radio system for the first load of the modern Clansman type. Exercise WELSH FALCON had demonstrated the vastly improved capabilities that the more user-friendly Clansman offered in terms of transmission range and weight. Such assets would be vital for efficient operations in the harsh Falklands' winter. Now another load had also arrived, but the time available for its distribution was short and further complicated by accounting for incoming Larkspur sets. Outside the Signals Platoon's offices Kit Spencer, the puckish RSO, was working furiously on that 10 May Monday morning. Masterminding this radio changeover had put great demands on him, but his sense of humour did not suffer. Kit was assisted by his Gurkha Signals Officer, the relaxed and urbane Lieutenant Sange Tamang. Both could barely be seen outside the Signals Platoon office directing unpacking operations amongst piles of empty crates and boxes. They were well behind schedule.

'My God!' moaned Kit as two more Gurkha Signallers scuttled away with radios tucked under their arms, 'at the rate we're going the *keta* will be running up and down *QE2*'s gangways on Wednesday still delivering radios to the rifle companies. I tell you Mike, I wouldn't have wished this hell on my grandmother!'

He was to meet his deadline, but would spend the forthcoming twenty days at sea preparing and issuing all the Battalion's radio instructions and codes in five-day packets for the first thirty days of Gurkha operations on the Falklands. The moral was obvious.

Never become a Battalion RSO. Furthermore, after the campaign Kit was instructed to withdraw Clansman – only to reissue it the year afterwards.

Tuesday was reserved for tidying my office, coffee drinking, and perusal of Officers' Mess newspapers full of reports about the frigate HMS *Alacrity* blowing up a ship in the Falkland Sound[1] and continued Navy bombardment around Stanley. Visiting the barber in Fleet was my main objective afterwards. The Gurkhas would cut their own hair on *QE2* because, unlike the Marine Commandos, there was no time to hold a Falklands embarkation parade, and therefore no parade preparations required. Colonel David issued only a valedectory 'Special Order of the Day' in both English and *Nagri*. It contained a simple challenge to the Gurkhas. In summary, this was:

> The Battalion has trained well during the past six weeks for our forthcoming task, and we are now as well prepared as we can ever be . . . However the enemy should not be under-estimated. They have had time to prepare their defences and can be expected to fight hard for what they believe in . . . Furthermore the winter climate is going to be extreme and the going tough, but such conditions are ones that the Battalion revels in. I am confident that you will acquit yourselves well. . . . And all should be aware that this Battalion will be representing the Brigade of Gurkhas, and other Gurkha Battalions will be watching our performance with the utmost of interest. *Jai Seventh!*

I enquired politely about the only incomprehensible item, 'Excuse me DB sahib, could you tell me what "*Jai Seventh*" means?' The QGO replied with a proud whiff of nine-teenth century British Indian Army *kaida*, 'Ah! That, sahib, is our formal Regimental salute of "Long Live the Seventh!"'

I sincerely hoped so, given the order's allusion to blood, sweat and tears in the not too-distant future. Furthermore, although '*Jai Seventh*' was uniquely Gurkha in providing such an effective expression to the 1st/7th Gurkha Rifles' Falklands War *esprit de corps,* I could not even begin to imagine any copy of my own Regiment's Part I Orders ending with 'Long live The Light Infantry!'

'So what on earth will happen,' I asked myself, 'once we've landed on the Falklands?'

At home, embarkation eve was awful. In addition to my bergen, two suitcases had to be packed that puzzled our little daughters. Twenty-three month-old Emily could scarcely string two words together, but four-year-old Victoria, a blonde, blue-eyed kindergarten pupil interested in ballet, had a logical mind in the circumstances. 'Are we going on holiday Daddy?' she asked.

As a qualified kindergarten teacher, Tove believed explanations to children were important. So she insisted, 'We've got to tell them why!' Camouflaging facts was achieved by my combat kit and arctic cap mannequin show, squinting, sticking out my tongue, pulling yet more weird faces, and Tove's assurances, 'All this, girls, is going to frighten all of those other men right off the Islands, and then Daddy will be able to come home!'

This unintentionally accurate forecast was accepted by our wide-eyed daughters. If aware of the stark facts, soldiers are superstitious beings and many believe in a talisman.

'Here's my gold engagement ring mounted with a bismark chain,' said my wife, 'you can hang it around your neck alongside your two dog tags. That'll give you good luck during the *QE2* trip and then on the Falklands!' Hopefully her gesture would prevent the ultimate of one of these metal identity discs engraved with my name, number, blood type and religion being removed for unit records and the other left on my body for identification purposes.

Tove and the girls would not be at Southampton to watch 5 Brigade's embarkation and departure. Upset enough, we did not want Victoria and Emily exposed to more extremes. So early next morning came those dreaded goodbyes. There was Tove's final optimistic, 'We'll be waiting here for you when you get back.' Emily smiled. Victoria looked angrily at me. 'Would they still have a father next month?' I thought. 'Or get the same one back?'

I drove my car to the parade square, parked and unloaded my kit. The Gurkhas were already under fire from RSM One-Ton amidst the weapon-rolls, baggage and assorted stores piled everywhere. Like most BOs, I waited on the sidelines whilst all companies were busy with their roll-calls. Unlike the Scots Guards' officers at Chelsea Barracks, we did not indulge in a farewell glass of champagne, although B Company's Rifleman Baliprasad Rai and other Gurkhas had celebrated the night before:

> *Je hola hola* (whatever will be, will be) was the general consensus of opinion. Our forefathers had earned us our enviable reputation and we were proud of our name. But it is not enough to let the name honour us, we must honour the name. And here was the chance to do it. The last night in camp before embarkation was a fun-filled night in the Junior Ranks Club. Hardly anyone slept – we were all there, sitting, talking, drinking, dancing and making jokes. At six o'clock in the morning we were all on the parade square in full battle order for a final check-up before boarding the buses to take us to the *QE2*.[2]

The Commandant was the last to arrive gripping a stout silver-topped cane walking stick. Belonging previously to his medical missionary grandfather in China during the 1900 Boxer Rebellion, this inheritance possessed a hint of 'Rod, Moses, Mark II' which would lead the Gurkhas to their promised (is)land(s). Their Hindu persuasion led them to think of only two things: victory on the battlefield and a sackful of gallantry medals. Although not awarded the latter, they would be destined to achieve the former – if not quite in the manner now envisaged. Their Commandant did not carry a firearm because his safety had been delegated to a bodyguard, Sergeant Bernie Durkin, the Battalion's Army Physical Training Corps instructor. But chunky Durkin was unhappy. 'This is ridiculous,' sighed the Gurkhas' cockney BIT *guruji* to me. 'I know the boss is unarmed, but there's little point in givin' me this bodyguard job,' he continued while waving a despairing arm towards the gathered Gurkha host, ' because 'ell, just look at all of them lot over there! Once them Argies clap eyes on 'em,' he bubbled on, 'they'll soon realize the sense in not gettin' involved with Johnnie Gurkha or their Colonel sahib. After all 'e's already got well over 600 personal minders in 'is Battalion. Wot's the bleedin' point in usin' yet another poor sod like me? It's all a waste of time!'

Poor Durkin, despite his protests, was not given another job.

The arrival of four-ton lorries and civilian coaches to transport us to the Cunard cruise costing Her Majesty's Government more than £2,000,000, signalled our embussing onto them. Driving out through the camp's main entrance, we passed a small group of waving children, a limp Union Jack hanging in a private garden, and a thirty-strong cheering Gurkha UK Rear Party left behind to provide the camp security guard. Their consolation prize was enlistment as extras in a John Cleese film as the barracks would be one of the main film locations. A signal that work was about to commence on *Privates on Parade* had been the overnight growth of a full-size palm tree outside the Gurkha Sergeants' Mess. The film portrayed a group of British Army entertainers during the Malayan Emergency and its script included a kukri-charge by these 7GR riflemen against their CT arch-enemy.

A pity this celluloid clash would not be available in time for distribution to Argentine cinemas, but the media's coverage of the Gurkhas at Southampton Docks after our two-hour drive was a good substitute. In the empty warehouse ground floor of the Queen Elizabeth II terminal, TV cameras rolled and flashlights popped as hundreds of bewildered Gurkhas shuffled into line prior to embarkation. Rifleman Baliprasad Rai was among them:

> I had heard what a big ship the *QE2* was, but I was totally unprepared for the sight that greeted my eyes as I got down from the bus. Such a ship had to be seen to be believed. Why, it was even larger than any building I had seen back home.[3]

One-Ton was in his element. His stentorian Gurkhali cracked out order after order as he strutted up and down like a Falklands' King Penguin. The *Pandit* then began an impromptu *Puran* scripture reading to some waiting Gurkhas on the ethics of war from the *Gita*, one of the three holy Hindu books. 'Come on, let's get away from this lot and take a closer look at her,' muttered Mark Willis to me nodding towards the liner parked up outside the building. We sneaked outside to the *QE2* now converted to a troop ship or, in military logisticians' language, a LPL(L), i.e. Landing Platform Luxury (Large). The Marine Commandos had irreverently nicknamed Cunard's flagship 'The Black Pig' and, from ground-level looking upwards towards the stern, a multitude of rust-patches on the dark charcoal-grey hull did not make her so awe-inspiring as we had been led to believe. A large helicopter landing pad, built by Vosper Thornycroft Ship Repairers the previous weekend, covered the upper superstructure over the aft quarter deck area where passengers normally sunned themselves, and another had been constructed on One Deck in front of the Bridge. It had taken:

> . . . two days to destore the caviare etc. and restore to 60 x 4000 man days endurance of troops' food and drink including 12 tons of chips, 100 tons of meat, 80 tons of flour, 150 tons of groceries, 75 tons of dairy products and 18,500 cases of beer.[4]

Weighed down with their bergens almost as big as them, the Gurkhas' turn to embark arrived and the Guards, already on board, cheered our march up the main gangway accompanied by a tune on the Pipe Major's bagpipes. Next to him was a TV cameraman. Opposite, the *Pandit* muttered a blessing and threw dried *dublo* (thin) grass over each passing soldier. However he, unlike the Guards' padres, could not travel to the South Atlantic. There were salient reasons. No facilities were available on board for him to cook *bhat* with his religious status decreeing that no one else could make his food. Furthermore no alternative cuisine could be provided because his high caste prevented him from consuming *bhat* BT. So the GM sahib became his deputy, and thereby responsible for the Gurkhas' spiritual needs. In the circumstances perhaps this senior QGO could have called upon *Shiva*, the Destroyer of Evil, to partner *Durga*, the Goddess of War as the former had an ability to display different forms when the world is threatened by demoniac powers – like *Galti garyo.*

I marched up the gangway to receive the *Pandit's* blessing and handful of holy grass in my face. This was a dried broad-bladed type whose triangular-shaped top represented the Hindu deities of *Brahma, Vishnu* and *Shiva.* Later I concluded that, in this situation, (a) it was comforting the Gurkhas offered to share their religion with a BO non-churchgoing Church of England Protestant, but (b) that the mix of Hindu fatalism with Christian expectation could have a volatile potential. However the wholehearted support of the Hindu gods on the gangway did not enter my thoughts as an index finger became even more tightly clamped over my damaged briefcase's unshuttable lid. I had visions of being enveloped in a flood of cascading A4 pages and TV cameraman recording such a disaster for posterity.

My worry was replaced by another once on board. I was lost. Maybe the 2IC sahib behind me would know where to go. 'Bill, where on earth is our cabin?' I asked a red-faced and panting Bill Dawson who was equally as heavily-laden and disorientated as myself.

'Haven't a clue, Mike,' was his frustrated reply, 'and don't forget the word "cabin" is taboo on *QE2*. There's going to be four of us living in a "room" for the next fortnight!'

We looked around for our other 'room-mates'. There was no sign of Captain Graham Stewart-Smith, the Battalion's Paymaster, and Rory Stewart. So we remained lost, as were many of the Gurkhas from their confused looks. Bergens banged against the walls in a crush of bodies as the hunt for rooms intensified with a continuous tramp of boots up and down the maze of corridors. None wore anything that resembled the standard *QE2* male passengers' Armani suit and equivalent fancy shoe uniform. So it had been a wise decision to cover the wooden-panelled walls and carpeted floors with hardboard sheeting fixed together with black masking tape.

Locating our £600 per day outside starboard boat deck room was achieved by pure chance. Inside was a different pedigree to the formica and linoleum-clad, double-tiered bunk, single porthole, smelly toilet, and prison cell-dimensions of a standard cabin in a North Sea ferry. 'Oh boy! Look at this!' we gasped.

Our residence boasted a terrace with panoramic sea view partially obscured by a lifeboat bow, full-length floral curtains framing the large windows, fitted carpet, large table lamps, two expansive single beds, comfortable sofa and armchairs, chests of drawers and cupboards. The room was large enough to accommodate two extra camp beds; a measure duplicated in every other room of the liner which normally carried 1800 civilian passengers compared with the current 3,200 embarked troops.

'It's even got a bidet!' noted Bill, peeping into a spacious bathroom that was also equipped with bath, shower and toilet. So, notwithstanding the overcrowding, this sixteen-day cruise with full board was a bargain at £700 per head.

Bill and I then dumped our kit to make a premature return to land via the other gangway at the stern. Our goal was the retrieval of our suitcases from the baggage vehicles before attempting re-embarkation up the main gangway. It was not possible. Blocking our path was the Commandant and media. They were bombarding him with questions verging on the farcical.

'Are you happy with the preparations that your Battalion has made?'

'Are your men looking forward to being part of the Task Force?'

'Is it the case that a kukri's never drawn unless there's blood about to flow?'

'We've heard that your men don't like travelling on ships. Is it true that they're bad sailors?'

'How's your Battalion going to cope with any seasickness?'

And so on. We turned back to the stern gangway and marched away from the Commandant's rapid-fire explanations.

'These are mountain men, not sailors . . .'

'They're armed with thousands of seasickness pills . . .'

'They'll get at least one *bhat* meal a day . . .'

'The men are appalling sailors so, as a preventive measure, their quarters are in that part of the ship which is at sea-level!'

Once again navigation back to our room took an embarrassingly and irritatingly long time, but finally we safely deposited our suitcases there as Bill's stomach rumbled. He was not going to wait anymore and declared, 'Come on, I'm starving. The time's come to sample the haute cusine of the Queen's Grill. Good job it's so close by.'

Before our embarkation this had been a restaurant for the penthouse suite passengers and, prior to that, a nightclub and casino. Now it was the Brigade Officers' Mess dining room with two sittings required for each meal. This first, eaten under a multitude of candelabras, indicated the quality of food augured well for the cruise. Afterwards in a renewed search for our room, I suddenly found myself outside in the commotion on a crowded boat deck. Departure was an hour away, but the Scots Guards' red-tuniced band on the quayside below were already into their programme of *Men of Harlech, Scotland the Brave, Rule Britannia, Super Trouper, Sailing* and other appropriate renditions.

Spurred on by Ken Baily, the English soccer team cheerleader, 3,000 placard and banner-waving well-wishers were making their presence felt. The civilian workers of Queen Elizabeth Barracks held aloft the only Gurkha banner with an inevitable *Jai Seventh!* scrawled over it. The only vantage points left for latecomers on board to watch these proceedings were in the ten starboard-side lifeboats. So despite some half-hearted opposition from the Military Police, I joined other soldiers in one. This was 5 Brigade's improvised version of the Royal Navy's *Procedure Alpha* when crew line the decks on port departures and arrivals, but I also hoped it would be the only cruise occasion we had to take to these boats.

The top brass visiting on board included the cheerful Secretary of State for Defence John Nott, accompanied by a smiling Ian McDonald and exiled Governor of the Falklands, Rex Hunt. That day the War Cabinet had rubber-stamped Operation

SUTTON, the plan for the British landings and its choice of San Carlos on East Falkland as the amphibious landing area, so these *QE2* visitors had every reason to be in a jolly mood. Overcome by the moment, one spectator went topless in the Ocean Terminal opposite. The hook of a dockside crane passed her bra across to her husband on board. Another female appeared on the quayside clad in black lingerie, suspenders, and nylons. She was the bearer of a 'singing telegram', but her message had as much chance of being heard above the hullabaloo as that of *QE2* sailing up the River Plate to launch a Gurkha assault on *Galti garyo*'s Presidential Palace.

Nepalese eyes grew wider as necks were strained to sunflower length for a better view of these ladies. 'Randy little sods!' muttered one BO good-naturedly behind me. There was more than a grain of truth to the observation. At Church Crookham my office was sited opposite the main gate and I had been witness to local girls approaching the Guardroom to ask whether so-and-so Rai and so-and-so Limbu could be found. This open secret that some Gurkhas had English girlfriends was frowned upon by those in the higher parts of the Regiment's hierarchy.

16.00 hours and departure time had arrived. Moorings and emotions were slipped free. There was a lump in my throat. From the band rose *Sailing* and *Auld Lang Syne*. Swallowing was impossible. Tears trickled down my cheeks. I bit my lip and sat glumly in my lifeboat. Sun Tzu, the Chinese General for the King of Wu in 512 BC, had written about this phenomenon in *The Art of War*, 'On the day they are ordered out to battle, your soldiers may weep, those sitting up bedewing their garments, and those lying down letting the tears run down their cheeks.'

Would I see my family again? And my home? And my country? were grim reflections that traversed around in my head. Fifty-eight of us on board would not, with more than treble that number returning as casualties. Such pangs of homesickness possibly affected many Gurkhas. In Nepal it was *Jeth*, the annual peak period for planting rice and other crops, so Gurkha thoughts must have wandered to their families tending the fields and goats.

I clutched the side of the lifeboat so hard that my knuckles turned white. To cheer was also impossible. And irrelevant. That narrow strip of water between ship and quay widened. I waved farewell. Not to those below, but to my family at Church Crookham and old life. There would be a new one as from now. We turned through 180 degrees as three tugs at the bow and the two aft pointed us towards the Solent. Gurkha pipers echoed the sentiment being played quayside. Climbing out of my lifeboat for a better portside view, I passed the Brigade Commander enthusing with Nelsonian pride over the 5 Brigade flag that the fifty-nine year-old Senior Master of the Cunard Fleet, Captain Peter Jackson, had hoisted high over the Bridge as a gesture to his gun-toting passengers. However *QE2* could not market herself as a 'one-up-the-spout' vessel, so her formal non-combatant status was marked by flying the Merchant Services' Red Ensign.

Media helicopters clattered overhead. They took pictures and waved, just like the sightseers in a private boat flotilla with flapping Union Flags that accompanied our wallow down Southampton Water. Against a near Force Five wind, the tugs slowly battled up-river with their 67,107-ton load. *QE2* had a problem. Only one engine boiler was available. Of the other two, one leaked twenty tons of distilled water per hour, while maintenance work continued on the other. Power was therefore provided by the only operative boiler and unusually large number of tugs to ensure clearance out of Southampton Harbour. Seriously under-powered at seven knots and contravening Board of Trade Regulations, the liner's propaganda value of sailing 5 Infantry Brigade punctually to war overrode everything.

Eventually two of the tugs were slipped free at the Brambles buoy. Another pair departed a short while afterwards, leaving one attached for extra manoeuvrability if required. Thousands lined the Hamble beaches. The private boats continued to bob alongside whilst *QE2*'s over-worked siren tested limits near to meltdown. Perspective was also needed as it had been busier further south. The Navy's bombardment around the Port Stanley area had preceded its shooting down of three enemy aircraft whose bombs had badly damaged the destroyer HMS *Glasgow*. By then, shadows had lengthened as we passed the village of Beaulieu to starboard, before heading out into the Solent. Two Fleet Air Arm Sea King helicopters of 825 Naval Air Squadron which were to accompany us south, then landed on the aft flight deck. 'So, it looks as though the Gurkhas will receive their first training on Sea King helicopters while at sea,' I noted to myself.

A few of the small boats still attempted to intercept the *QE2*, but only when she finally slipped away en route to the Isle of Wight did I return to our boat deck room. The other three BOs were already unpacking there as the local Radio Solent continued to report on our departure. No one paid much attention, for sobriety had replaced the afternoon's excitement as we silently contemplated an uncertain future. Our departure had also been a trial at 80, Wakefords Park as Tove described in her first letter to me:

> Well done! You got yourself on telly as you almost ran up the gangway. We made an occasion of South Today on TV, which was specially devoted to *QE2* leaving . . . but at the end it proved too much for Victoria and she cried her little heart out when the boat (sorry – ship!) left. There was no stopping her . . . She was terribly upset about not spotting you on the telly as well – I'm afraid I got a bit excited. Anyway, we both cried, while Emily munched crisps and drank Fanta. . . . I am glad we didn't go down to Southampton though – we would have just dissolved completely. There is another special programme on BBC1 at 11.20 p.m. about *QE2* leaving, but I don't think I'll watch it again. Once is enough . . .
>
> There is still cautious optimism about UN progress – but if you lot are going to keep on shooting Argentine 'planes like the three this afternoon, they'll probably stop talking again! I shall not waste time, breath, and paper on the ifs and buts of the political situation. I will write to you every day so that you can hear about all the exciting things we do at home! Good news about the Post Office giving us free letters to send to the Task Force. I shall go down tomorrow and get my fair share.

The anti-climax came after the last tug was released. At about 20.00 hours off Spithead and three miles south of the Nab light tower, a broadcast on the liner's Tannoy system, otherwise known as a 'pipe' to Navy buffs, interrupted our thoughts. The message was an unexpected: 'D'ya hear there? Due to urgent repair work on our engines, we'll drop anchor shortly. It's anticipated that we'll get under way again tomorrow morning.'

I could not care less. It was not my problem. Bidding one's farewell to family and country had been an emotionally wearying matter. Mental recovery was needed so, after dinner, I retired unsocially early into the sheets of my campbed to be fresh for next day's planning activities. But lack of vibrations indicated *QE2*'s anchored state off the Isle of Wight. She was still there at breakfast next morning. Only at 09.35 hours did her real UK departure take place after the discovery that the boiler leak had been caused by a carelessly left open valve.

Although another eleven days were to pass before being registered as STUFT, an acronym for a 'ship taken up from trade', the liner would become a worthy successor to the *Queen Elizabeth*. The latter transported five times as many servicemen in a single Atlantic sailing during the Second World War but, unlike *QE2*, she did not have to provide training facilities as there were only three activities on board – sleeping, reading, or playing cards standing up. Conversely, *QE2*'s embarked troops required all of her 40,500 square feet of open deck space. Although this might be perceived by the layman as ample for military training, the opposite was true, so tight coordination of unit training area space and time allocations would be needed at the daily 14.00 hours Brigade training conference. There Bill and I would declare the Battalion's requirements and negotiate compromises, thereby creating the basis for my early-evening publication of the Gurkha training programme.

First though, on the morning of 13 May, a general muster stations drill was held prior to evacuating to the lifeboats. A rethink of this and the boat stations drill's mechanics was required because, as one BO commented afterwards, 'God! *That* was *the* organizational disaster of the century!' Even more appropriate was the Royal Naval 'snafu' acronym of 'situation normal, all fucked up' and precursor to many more experienced by the Gurkhas during the campaign. Such major readjustments were necessary because, despite the last serviceable enemy submarine's decision to withdraw to its mainland base two days before, there remained a significant air and surface threat nearer the Falklands. The Gurkhas were particularly vulnerable. Their accommodation was on five deck, ten decks down from the uppermost signal deck and near the waterline. The standard model was four Gurkhas to a double room – a third the size of ours on the boat deck – additionally furnished with two campbeds. According to Rifleman Baliprasad Rai, they thrived in these cramped conditions:

> And what luxurious quarters! Never had I slept in such beautiful surroundings or in such a big, soft bed, nor perhaps I ever will! If I was to go to war, then there was no better way to go.[5]

Nevertheless, the Gurkhas' horror of sea travel is such that their forefathers had been known to complain of seasickness when aboard their vessel still tied up at the quayside. Once at sea their desire to set foot on land is similarly overwhelming with, on this occasion, not much trust put in the deployment of *QE2*'s twin stabilizers. The Church Crookham soldiers' 'rooms' were therefore allocated on this particular deck to avoid the greater roll higher up when seas became rough.

An enemy Aerospatiale air-launched AM-39 Exocet strike would have presented a few more problems. *Sheffield*'s demise as the first Royal Navy warship to be lost by enemy action since the Second World War caused us great concern. The worst scenario was a 655-kilo Exocet missile with its 165 kilos of explosives bursting in at Mach 0.9 amidships and a programmed nine feet above the waterline explosion, and fire that generated dense, suffocating smoke. This, in turn, would produce zero visibility in an environment several decks down in the liner without electrics and, therefore, no light. So the Commandant decided priority be given to finding the most effective training method which would ensure, faced with such an emergency, that as many Gurkhas as possible could have the best possible chance of reaching their boat stations. Indeed there were two minor emergencies on board before noon that first day, signalled by a Tannoy pipe of:

D'ya hear there? Hands to flying stations! Hands to flying stations! No more gash to be ditched overboard! No smoking or naked lights!

This indicated Fleet Air Arm Sea King activity and apotheosis of 'foreign object damage'. Those FOD countermeasures in the announcement were to prevent any inadvertent ingestion of rubbish into a helicopter engine, but the words of this first aviators' call to flying stations would, all too soon, become our *QE2* cruise motto. On this occasion the Sea Kings were required to evacuate ashore one serviceman with suspected appendicitis and another with a ruptured achilles tendon.

After lunch, preparations were made for a 'replenishment at sea' exercise with the Royal Fleet Auxiliary *Grey Rover* hooking up and 'rassing' *QE2* with a test RAS of one ton of oil into her bunkers. Meanwhile Bill and I made our way down the circular steel and glass staircase that connected the boat deck's Double Up Room to the upper deck's Double Down Room. Our destination was the Brigade training conference to be held in the Double Down Bar. To get there we walked past the Double Down Room's rows of six-foot wooden tables and folding chairs that served as a combined training area and Other Ranks' Mess in the 20,000 square feet of this two-tiered Double Room.

With so many troops on board it was essential that training area allocation principles be discussed and agreed. This first conference would also enable us to become acquainted with our opposite numbers in the other units. We sat around a long rectangular table in the Bar's plush red decor. The Brigade Major, Major Brendon Lambe, and his G3 Ops sidekick, Captain Arthur Petrie, presided. Both 5 Infantry Brigade and 3 Commando Brigade HQs were not using the new NATO staff officer titles, even though BAOR had officially adopted these the year before. If this had been implemented then Brendon's title would have been Chief of Staff, but going to war with a brand new system of staff titles and its resulting confusion had to be avoided at all costs.

We started the conference with a tour de table of the three Major Units' and eleven Minor Units' representatives. The BM's opening remarks indicated not even he and his staff had any knowledge of the itinerary prior to any Falklands landfall or that San Carlos would become our final destination, even though troops on board *Canberra* had been informed the day before, 'Gentlemen, welcome aboard this magical mystery tour. *QE2* has now come under command of the Commander South Atlantic Task Force. This is Commander-in-Chief of the Fleet, Admiral Sir John Fieldhouse, based at

Northwood in north-east London.' He paused melodramatically, to continue, 'And I hope, however, that the title of C.-in-C. Fleet doesn't mean that it'll be a bad omen for us.' This Jack Tar abbreviation of 'sink fleet' for the Admiral's title brought forth a muffled groan from the audience. The BM had been on board longer than us and was demonstrating the fruits of his nautical lessons from the Senior Naval Officer of Naval Party 1980. Unabashed, he issued out various plans of the liner's interior, 'The only certainty is that we'll be heading south. Meanwhile we must sing for our supper by continuing to train. But there are two major problems – time and space. Of *QE2*'s thir-teen decks, the top five, bar the signals deck, are available for training. We walked around the liner whilst she was docked at Southampton and earmarked the most important areas. These are marked on the deck plans in front of you. However there's still a severe shortage of space, and if anyone in the next few days can identify any more areas that could be utilized, then please let us know.'

He looked round the table hopefully. But the Gurkhas, for one, would definitely *not* volunteer information on any such valuable discovery. He continued, 'The training priority goes to the three infantry battalions. We've only available fifteen hours in the day for training, from 06.30 to 21.30 hours. After this we can't train because of the noise. Not everyone can train at the same time, so we're going to have to stagger timings. Of course there'll be opportunities for the men to relax, but we've got to plan things carefully.'

The implications of his opening briefing dawned on Majors Ian Mackay-Dick and Jo Griffiths-Eyton who, respectively, were the Scots' and Welsh Guards' 2ICs. They looked concerned. A continuation of the Chelsea and Pirbright comfortable nine to four routine might prove not so easy to engineer on this cruise. Fortunately Bill inter-rupted proceedings to ease Woodentop worries. He had absolute confidence in his Gurkhas and, if this had been the same conference held a decade later, the impression was that he would have continued in the same vein despite Mackay-Dick's promotion to Major General and appointment as Commander British Forces Falkland Islands.

'The Gurkha's a flexible soldier and can provide the solution to this problem,' declared a grinning Bill, with benevolent gesture of understanding to his two Guards colleagues, 'so we'll start at sparrow's fart, take the afternoons off, and then continue until late evening!'

No objections from the relieved Guards officers was the signal for Bill to continue selling his offer, 'I've noticed the main cinema can't possibly house all three Battalions simultaneously as there's seating capacity there for only 532. And I'm quite sure,' he chuckled, 'that the Guards don't want to watch Hindi films. I suggest therefore that the Gurkhas use the cinema in the afternoons, whilst the Brits watch English films in the evenings. Doing it this way, we all can make optimal use of available training time.'

His concept was accepted without complaint, and the detailed allocation of training areas for next day agreed. A smart idea for the Gurkhas to begin so early. Most training would be conducted in warmer latitudes, but the Battalion's hourly BIT exertions on the sports deck and around the promenade part of the boat deck would be finished well before temperatures rose. The Guards might regret their acceptance of Bill's suggestion. Administrative points closed this first conference which set the tone for subsequent ones where any haggling would always be conducted in good humour. But, as we rose to leave, Arthur Petrie warned crisply, 'OK gentlemen, please stick rigidly to these daily deck allocations that we've agreed. Don't freelance around the ship, otherwise things will become chaotic.'

Yet, at times, turning a Nelsonian blind eye is necessary. Space shortages had to be overcome not only by planning, but improvisation and ingenuity. So to achieve Gurkha aims, there had to be some freelancing during the next fifteen days. Indeed perhaps a lecture or two on 'The Art of Freelancing' should have been included in the training programme since it would be used extensively on the Falklands.

And, ironically, Brigade HQ would become its best exponents – with fatal consequences.

Chapter Eight

ACTIVE SERVICE

The fact that a ship can carry only a limited supply of drinking water could not be under-stood by the men. They argued: 'Any amount of water all round, so why should there be any shortage of water on the ship?' Subedar Gambirsing Pun, who had attended King George's Coronation, soon enlightened these philosophers. Selecting a dozen men, he seated them in a row on the deck. He then lowered a bucket into the sea, and administered a pint of salt water all round. There was no further waste of fresh water. – An anecdote from the 1st/6th Gurkha Rifles on board SS *Teesta* in November 1914 when three days out of Karachi bound for Gallipoli via Suez.[1]

After the Brigade training conference, I had a cup of tea before the first 17.00 hours Battalion Orders Group in the boat deck's Reading Room. It was noisy. All Battalion orderly rooms had been squeezed in there and three conferences were being held simultaneously. In our cramped section Bill Dawson, Mark Willis, Khile sahib, Kit Spencer, Ram, Paddy Redding and I were relative bystanders, although we had our moments. The key officers were the Commandant and four rifle company comman-ders. Their leadership, an unspoken theme throughout Operation CORPORATE, always invisibly underpinned any training or operation. Failure, not that there was any, would be infectious as Sun Tzu had registered two and a half millennia before:

> When the general is weak and without authority; when his orders are not clear and distinct; when there are no fixed duties assigned to officers and men, and the ranks are formed in a slovenly and haphazard manner, the result is utter disorganization.

We became well acquainted at these daily gatherings. David Willis was unperturbed by most matters; Lester Holley, full of humour, imagination and still obsessed with sniping skills; Taj Lewis, pithy in his comments and Mike Kefford, the senior and most experienced, always querying any decision with which he did not agree. Observing them throughout this cruise was fascinating as pressure mounted. Men's lives were their responsibility and they did a professional job to prepare their companies for the challenges ahead – even if Mike irritated me with his constant demands. 'The result of stress and pursuit of excellence,' I reprimanded myself.

The Commandant began with such invective that his bushy eyebrows protruded more than ever. 'We'll continue to prepare for war as thoroughly as we've started at Church Crookham and Sennybridge!' was his unequivocal opening. The end of his training directive left no doubt, 'To prepare for any onboard emergency caused by enemy action, company training progammes will include evacuation drill exercises from your mens' accommodation out to their muster stations and boats. They'll put on blindfolds and wear respirators. Then in half-platoon teams, they'll grope their way upwards from their accommodation on five deck through another eight decks to the boat deck. The winners of this orienteering race will be the first to their muster boat station.'

Then came my sub-allocation of the Battalion's quota of training areas. 'We need some give and take', I pointed out, 'because the only decent internal training areas are the Double Down Room and, below that, the Queen's Room where the dance floor's been covered in hardboard sheeting.'

Despite these limitations, bartering began and solutions provided for most needs, but the Commandant's final item on administration had non-negotiable demands. 'Drinking water is already a problem. Our consumption is too high, and if it continues there'll be an acute shortage soon. So the message is: conserve water! Next – dress. To limit damage to floors only plimsols will be worn. Officers can wear crepe sole desert boots. *Tato pani* for the rank and file is also forbidden and beer restricted to three cans daily. There will also be a ban on gambling.'

The Gurkhas' affluence, already a headache, would grow to migraine proportions. Paid a total of £250,000 in cash two days before embarkation, they had only deposited £60,000 of this in the special Gurkha saving fund at Church Crookham leaving, on average, each Gurkha with £350 to spend. The one shop open in the *QE2* shopping arcade could not soak up this amount of money, since it only sold items such as post-cards, stationary, paperback books, shoe-polish, T-shirts, soap, razor blades and camera film. With such limited shopping possibilities the Gurkhas' desire to indulge in their favourite pastime of gambling might increase. 'You see, gambling is only allowed during Diwali, the annual November five-day festival during which sisters also pray for their brothers. This is shortened to three days at Church Crookham when the cook-house becomes a casino inundated with a mass of card-playing Gurkhas intent on winning a fortune,' Mark told me afterwards.

However, I was more concerned with publishing the Battalion's first *QE2* training daily programme for 14 May and relieved after the Duty Gurkha Clerk finally declared, 'OK sahib, here it is,' to produce the first of thirteen such Training Officer sahib epistles. Tove had also written that afternoon:

I didn't get to bed until past midnight, had to watch the special prog about *QE2* going to war late on BBC1 after all. It isn't every day my hubby is on telly! . . . I'm surprisingly cheerful – I honestly cannot believe that you'll be away for six months. Maybe I'm simply hiding my head in the sand – but the world can't be that crazy. Eternal optimist!

Obviously the whole world has heard about the free aerogrammes. I tried three Post Offices this morning and gave up because of the queue. Never mind, you're worth fifteen and a half-pence for a normal letter so far, I'll go and get some aerogrammes next week . . . Emily saw the picture of the *QE2* plastered over the newspaper and immediately observed, 'Pappa boat!' – so the message has got through.

With work done for the day, and after listening to the BBC World Service reporting more air strikes on Stanley Airport, dinner in the Queen's Grill, also earmarked as our lifeboat muster station, was relaxing with the animated Battalion RSO. 'How about a half-bottle of wine?' asked Kit, a Nepal trekking and mountaineering fanatic. So Doc, the little Irish, white-haired wine waiter made an unchallengeable recommendation, 'A-ah! If it's wine yer want then yer won't go far wrong with a wee bottle of the 1978 Chablis, gents!'

Soon one half-bottle became two. Despite an aversion to alcohol and inebriation after only two glasses, this Chablis kick at dinner became my norm throughout the cruise. I was only copying the drinking habits of my British Army predecessors at places like Agincourt, Waterloo and the Somme as it assisted the daily combat against that awful psychological stress of going to war. Amongst the other khaki-clad officers, one person added colour. At the Brigade Commander's table sat Linda Kitson, a Royal College of Art tutor turned Fleet Air Arm and Imperial War Museum commissioned war artist. She wore a blue military jacket reminiscent of the Beatles' Sergeant Pepper's Lonely Hearts Club Band uniform. Throughout the next fortnight this would be alternated with another of pillar-box red so, with a punk hair-do and vital personality, one could not miss her in this male environment. The Commandant, aware of the historical perspective and need to utilize her talents, had told me at the end of that first O Group, 'Finally, Mike, make sure from now on that Linda Kitson gets our Battalion training programme.'

I informed her, and she was 'more than flattered'[2] to find in the Gurkha orderly room a special envelope in which her daily programmes would be put. Soon she was drawing the Gurkhas, but BIT would be too early for her. To participate in the first session at 06.00 hours on 14 May required waking up at 05.30 hours. As we steamed down the Bay of Biscay on two boilers at twenty-four knots, two companies shared the first half-hour of the Battalion's sixty-minute allocation. One ran anti-clockwise on the outer promenade deck where four circuits equated to the mile, whilst the other carried out static exercises led by Sergeant Bernie Durkin on the after sports deck. He had a holiday cruise spirit. 'OK gents, let's get cracking with some gentle Jane Fonda exercises that I've worked out for yer. We'll split up into different groups and rotate around each exercise. Keep working hard, and you'll appreciate your shower afterwards before sitting down to the cruise breakfast!'

This programme was repeated in the second half-hour for the other two companies. With six companies in the Battalion, the other two would get their chance the following day, thereby allowing one rest day in a complete cycle of three. I would latch myself onto HQ Company's single file of 100 Gurkhas who ran – in step and without a pause – for their thirty minutes. No elegant jog as practised by *QE2*'s standard clientele, this bobbing line of black-haired heads was to become one of the sights of the voyage and, even at this early hour, attracted spectators like the moustached waiter with grey streaks in his hair. This dapper veteran of many a *QE2* cruise sidled up to me afterwards, 'Are you with the Gurkhas? I think your boys are smashing! They're always so nicely turned out!' I took a step back, but the obsequious character continued, 'They look beautifully fit and so well organized. I can tell you now, there's absolutely no doubt as to which Battalion I'd want to be with if I had to take part in things on the Falklands!'

'No chance!' I thought while mumbling, 'Yeah, the Gurkhas are pretty tough all right,' and tempted to add, 'but much too tough for the likes of you!' before beating a retreat back to my room for a reviving hot shower and life-giving cup of tea. Support Company's BO platoon commanders also had an admirer. Nigel Price, Steve Crowsley, Quentin Oates and John Palmer, the latter two being the Recce and Anti-Tank Platoon Commanders, all shared a room served by a steward who invited John to stay at his UK home – much to the amused titterings of the other three.

After breakfast it was the other units' turn to beast themselves as training shoes and boots throbbed along the boat deck's outer promenade deck. Vibrations were so intense that caulking between the deck planks fell out towards the end of the cruise. Below on upper deck in the Double Down Room, nobody escaped these acoustics during the twelve hours of daylight. It became so oppressive that the Military Police had to cordon off the boat deck above the Brigade conference room when the latter was in use: a disadvantage the Gurkha early-morning sessions never suffered. Under this on the quarter deck, it was quieter in the Queen's Room where Gurkha and other groups clustered everywhere – listening, learning and practising skills essential to not only taking life, but saving it as well. The training followed Mao Tse-tung's blueprint:

> As for the method of training, we should unfold the mass training movement in which officers teach soldiers, soldiers teach officers and the soldiers teach each other.

Weapon training figured prominently in this early part of the voyage. SLR and GPMG loading, unloading and stoppage clearance drills were repeated ad nauseam. The mechanics of shooting whilst wearing the service-issue Arctic glove also had to be explained carefully to the Gurkhas. 'The glove is in two parts, Training Officer sahib,' explained one QGO to me, 'a thick white woollen inner and a khaki nylon outer. But, look! Many are putting their nylon outer on first and then wollen inner over that, because the nylon outer has a separate index finger section and they can feel the trigger through this!'

This QGO and others used much time and effort to show their men how to wear the Arctic clothing even after reaching the hot equatorial regions. Others, like the Mortar Platoon, were having to undergo a drastic rethink as to how their specialized equipment should be manpacked. Being the Battalion's indirect-fire artillery sub-unit, its mortarmen would play a vital role in the Falklands' open terrain. Fortunately they had trained in the manpack role during an exercise in Cyprus three months before, but the extra articles of clothing and special equipment issued for the Falklands' climate, on top of the usual burden of ammunition, spare radio batteries and rations meant that their mortar kit had to be trimmed to the bare essentials. The total load to be carried per man would be in excess of sixty kilos as Nigel Price later wrote in a report that also alluded to the technical finesses his Gurkhas had to master:

The first articles to be abandoned were the manpack frames – with the mortar barrels, bipods or baseplates being strapped to the bergen. Next to go were the C2 Trilux sight cases, the sights themselves being padded with clothing and put in the bergen pouches of the No. 1s. Apart from the sight and the baseplate strapped to his bergen, the No. 1 also carried a Trilux marker and spare firing pin. The mortar No. 2s had the hardest task with the barrels. Inside the barrel itself was carried one Aiming Post and in a bergen pouch a set of staff sections, a periscope and a firing pin wrench, used to remove the firing pin for cleaning or in the event of a misfire.

The mortar No. 3s carried the bipod, an oilcan, cloth and wire mesh for cleaning the barrel and two spanners for removing the breech plugs; one No. 3 in each section carried an Alignment Sight and a tool for removing jammed or misfired rounds from the barrel. The remainder of the ancillaries from the holdalls, and the holdalls themselves were not carried. The CPO and ACPO each carried a plotter, and a (Clansman) PRC 351 radio with three batteries. Binos, compasses, maps, torches and laser range finders were also carried by the six MFCs. No mortar ammunition was carried . . . this was (to be) carried from place to place in underslung nets by support helicopters wherever these could be obtained.[3]

Always keen to learn, they and the others would pull out notebooks to scribble down copious notes. Many times I would walk through the Double Up Room, only to stop, lean on the red plastic-topped balcony, and look below. Rows of Gurkhas in the Double Down Room seated at the six-foot tables were bent dutifully over their work in contrast to the more relaxed manner of the British soldiers. Despite Brigade HQ displeasure, freelancing also became a necessity. There was room for no more than thirty Gurkhas to train in any area but weapon-training instructors who held the butts of SLRs and GPMGs into their right shoulder, soon became adept at locating suitable passageways and stairways to teach at the apex of right-hand bends. SLR live-firing also took place on that first training day despite the discovery of forced-open lids to ammunition boxes and rumour that PIRA sympathizers were responsible. Targets were full black plastic garbage bags and empty ammunition boxes flung over the stern from an improvised shooting range on the after-quarterdeck Lido area – now a jungle of vertical red-leaded steel girders cemented into the swimming pool and deck to support the overhead heli-copter landing pad.

The Commandant's insistence on 'hands-on' training to counter potential hazards from Exocet, bomb or torpedo explosions was also implemented. Former US Chief of Naval Operations Admiral Elmo Zumwalt had no doubt of *QE2*'s vulnerability. 'It is one big fat target,' he said in a TV interview.[4] But no other unit copied us. Once a line of fifteen blindfolded Gurkhas inadvertently gatecrashed the Scots Guards' cocktail party in the Queen's Grill Lounge. One or two of the Guards officers thought they were practising night movement in a conga, but these Gurkhas had lost their way and, holding each other by the shoulder, were guided twice round the lounge by a smiling Guardsman before their departure, without removing their blindfolds. The following month nobody would be amused at 5 Brigade's sea disaster off Fitzroy, East Falkland.

Hindsight proved the importance of Gurkha dedication to such emergency drill exercises which could only be achieved by freelancing.

At our evening O Group the Commandant, fresh from his Brigade conference, rattled through a long training shopping list, 'I want to focus on signals, first-aid, winter combat survival, mines and aircraft recognition lectures. Intelligence briefings on the enemy and Falkland topography, and life-saving drills in the six deck swimming pool must also be prioritized. Note active service conditions will be declared at midnight. We will then come under the aegis of the Geneva Convention, so we must hold lectures about this. Finally, *QE2* will call in at Freetown, Sierra Leone on the 18th for some eighteen hours or so . . .'

Implementing active service conditions was the nearest Her Majesty's Government came to declaring war. Nonetheless nobody informed me of the possible pecuniary benefits to my meagre estate as it would be freed from death duties in the event of my demise while serving the Crown. Tax avoidance was never my strong point. Neither was my salary which would hardly be boosted by the announcement that the annual pay review had awarded us £2 extra per day, plus £1.70p Falklands and 50p hard-lying allowances for the privilege of Operation CORPORATE participation. In comparison, the 650 crew of merchant seamen on board enjoyed a 150 per cent increase in their salaries for Task Force duties, even though they would never get nearer than 800 nautical miles to the sharp end. Their colleagues in many other merchant ships would do even better as this war supplement would not cease until 28 July – six weeks after cessation of hostilities.

After the dawn's BIT exertions, our expanded training programme cranked into gear on that 15 May. Stern live firing continued and more spectacular shoots off the liner's bows with, at last, the Anti-Tank Platoon firing some Milan missiles. Assisted by Lieutenant Don Macaulay and the other attached Royal Signals personnel, Kit Spencer's signals training for all Battalion sub-units on the recently issued Clansman radio system continued, whilst Paddy Redding gave detailed briefings on our enemy and Falklands' topography. He had an overwhelming quantity of information but irritatingly lacked slides, photographs or even a video about the Islands. Such elementary visual aids had not been made available for 5 Brigade, even though our counterparts on *Canberra* had these in proliferation. As the ship's third boiler became operative, speed increased to twenty-seven knots, and Cape St Vincent slipped over the horizon on the port beam, Linda Kitson observed the Gurkha training:

> The glamourous architecture of the Queen's Room formed an incongruous setting for the units taking part in the different activities there; but the Gurkhas impressed everybody with the intensity of their training . . . They could have found their boat stations in any circumstances. Each day wearing life jackets and in full battledress, they jumped into the frozen water of one of the pools (on six deck). (Neither the sea, nor the degree of cold, is part of their background.)[5]

Training programme misunderstandings were few as coordination functioned well. Interruptions occurred, however, by the Royal Navy's demands to rehearse more muster station drills. The helicopter-flying from the improvised Royal Navy flight deck also meant an incessant Royal Navy verbal interruption to life by harsh Royal Navy 'big brother' pipes on the Royal Navy Tannoy of: 'D'ya hear there? Hands to flying stations! Hands to flying stations! No more gash to be ditched overboard! No smoking or naked lights!' indicating, of course, that such vital Royal Navy Fleet Air Arm aviation activity was perilously imminent and all soldiery should not, on the pain of the cat o' nine tails, forget this.

By lunchtime on Day One of active service the only topic of conversation was of the previous night's Pebble Island raid. Exclamations rang around the Queen's Grill, 'Bloody good show! The BBC say the SAS have taken out quite a few Argie aircraft on the airstrip there without any losses to themselves!'

En route afterwards to the Brigade training conference, my attention was drawn to the huge Falklands map pinned on the blue staircase wall outside the quarterdeck main cinema. Pebble Island lay to the north-west of the Falklands, its threat on the Falkland Sound and San Carlos was now eliminated. A state board also listed inaccurate figures of air and naval enemy assets lined up against us that made me swallow hard. It included nine Canberra bombers, five Dassault-Breuguet Super Etendard AM-39 Exocet-armed bombers, seven Hercules transports, forty-seven Mirage fighters (this should have included figures for the Dagger, an Israeli produced version of the Mirage), forty-five Pucará ground-attack fighters, sixty-eight Skyhawk fighters and sixty-eight helicopters of seven different types. The night's activity had swelled the original total of ten enemy 'splashed' aircraft by another ten.[6]

A warmer climate had also brought a daytime uniform change for the Naval sea dogs from blues to whites on this cruise where training was supplemented by a growing list of off-duty entertainments. The main cinema showed three different films in any twenty-four hour period. Unlike their Hindi counterparts, the English films were mainly of war. Official policy must have been made that audiences required brainwashing before their onshore task with films ranging from the adventures of *Von Ryan's Express* to extremes of *Gallipoli* where a Gurkha Battalion had once disposed of 2,000 Turks in one day's fighting. Those responsible for such blood and guts could not have been ex-Sandhurst cadets because the light relief of *Tom and Jerry*'s eternal cat and mouse war was sorely missing. At the Academy cinema, applause and whistles had been vociferous whenever the credits showed 'Fred Quimby', the name of the cartoon's producer.

The Gurkhas' diet of Hindi films in their post-lunch cinema slot was insatiable. Hindi to the Nepalese is rather similar to a Norwegian's relationship to the Swedish language, or a Glaswegian trying to make himself comprehensible to an Englishman residing south of the Thames. Three-hour long bizarre plots mesmerized their Gurkha audiences by intertwining comedy, violence, dancing, music, tragedy, songs, pretty girls, romance with kissing strictly forbidden, and the invariable triumph of the hero over hardened criminals. *Desh Premee*, an Indian patriotic film about one who loves his country and highly topical, was particularly popular. Life on board made a favourable impression on Rifleman Baliprasad Rai:

Travelling on a ship was a new thrill for me. I never dreamt that I would one day be on a ship, much less the world's greatest liner. Yes, I was lucky I thought.

Where before only millionaires and men of means had wined and dined, strolled and played, there I was, a boy from Bagsila, Nepal, savouring the same air of opulence. My shoes may not have been made by Gucci, but at least they were tramping the same corridors! Life on the *Queen Elizabeth 2* was much the same as in Queen Elizabeth barracks however. BIT in the mornings to keep us physically fit followed by lessons in skill-at-arms . . . Lectures on the history and geography of the Falklands were given and we listened in earnest. Everything possible was done to prepare us for the difficult task ahead. Hundreds of Hindi and English video films provided recreation in the evenings and on the whole voyage; I must have seen 'Desh Premee' at least ten times! We could not complain about the food served since it was excellent and we could have our fill of either 'dal-bhat' or a vast selection of British fare.[7]

Correct attire, for some, became important. A few officers in the Queen's Grill Lounge that evening appeared in Red Sea Rig: a nautical version of mess kit consisting of a white short-sleeved shirt, scarlet cummerbund and Blues No.1 Dress trousers. But in the circumstances, it seemed ostentatious. 'I'm happy to remain in my khaki shirt-sleeve order,' I told Mark.

The Guards subalterns appeared to have similar thoughts with most of them permanently chained to their Walkman boogie packs. Pre-dinner gin and tonic became another enforced, and reinforcing, supplement to the *QE2* diet which, without the early-morning deck pounding, would have wreaked havoc on my waistline. Food had become an obsession. With so many to feed, the other three restaurants – Britannia on the upper deck, and Columbia and Grill Room on the quarterdeck – also had to stagger their meal timings with two sittings. The Gurkhas could choose between *bhat* GT or *bhat* BT. Some would also supplement their diet with *khorsani*. Before going to dinner I had noticed that Sergeant Deoman Limbu of A Company possessed a lot of these Gurkha shiny-green bullets of fire, and asked him, 'Why are these necessary when there's such a fantastic menu on board?' His reply possessed Gurkha versatility of thought:

> You see, sahib, I've got a one pound supply of this *sabji* (vegetable) with me. It's not only to add taste to the food on board, but also to our arctic rations when we are on the Foklands. I'm also afraid of seasickness so, maybe by biting on a *khorsani*, my mind will be taken off such a problem. Also I prefer a burning mouth than falling to sleep whilst on sentry duty in the Foklands!

The entertainments continued after dinner with video films also shown on a large screen in the Queen's Room. One type became available at night in clandestine locations that included the synagogue which, during daytime, housed the Battalion's Intelligence Section. The venue became universally known and, later, one unlucky audience of these celluloid anatomical adventures was raided by the Military Police. After dinner *'Saturday night at the races'*, a traditional ocean-going game, was also to be held in the Cunard Officers' boat deck wardroom from 22.00 hours. I invested £1 in a programme, but publishing my own training programme and inevitable

99

early morning BIT exertions soon ended fancy thoughts of late-night gambling and complimentary drinks up to midnight that from then, according to the programme, '. . . will cost a bloody fortune.' Such *QE2* 'racing' with wooden horse models could never replace the Gurkha BO rodent variety at my Church Crookham dining-in night, although the programme displayed a Jack Tar inventiveness:

The Sierra Leone Selling Place	Flat race . . . one length of the track.
The Freetown Frolic	Hurdle race.
The Galtieri Gallop	Donkey race . . . last horse home is the winner.
The Mid-Atlantic Marathon	Double length race.
The Twelve Mile Limit	Water jump race.
The Costa Mendez Costa Bundle	Auction race . . . triple length race.

Son-Of-A-Gun by *One-Up-The-Spout* out of *Tommy*.
Bunkers Built by *Galtieri* out of *Sheer Terror*.
Ascension Missed by *QE2* out of *Radar*.
Sea King Snafu(ed) by *Fod* out of *Funnel*.
Queens Serviced by *Ras* out of *Rover*.
Belgrano Distinguished by *Slipping* out of *Sight*.

Instead, I strolled through the liner's public areas. Enjoying their own informal gatherings, groups of Gurkhas sat crossed-legged on the floor whilst others sat at tables dressed in grey flannels, white shirts and ties. Sipping beer, some mixed in the palms of their hands powdered *khaini*. This white powder consisted of *surti* (strong tobacco) and *chuna* (lime) which was then placed inside their mouth between the top lip and gum. 'It has no telltale smell sahib,' explained a QGO, 'so I recommend this substitute as a good 'tactical smoke' whilst waiting in an ambush position.' Many savoured its aromatic flavour, but there could be pitfalls. Three Gurkhas earlier that year on a London weekend visit to a Soho theatre of lesser repute had been arrested by a police plain-clothes detective. They had been indulging in their *khaini* during the show, but the detective had mistaken this for something more sinister. The misunderstanding was, happily, soon sorted out at the local police station.

Up again early on 16 May for inevitable BIT; afterwards Bill Dawson and I wandered around observing the Battalion prior to that afternoon's Brigade training conference. All Gurkhas were again hard at work with SLR and GPMG weapon training. Directed by their Small Arms Service Corps instructor, Steve Crowsley's Machine Gun Platoon were being taught to strip down and re-assemble their much-vaunted 800 rounds per minute Browning heavy machine gun which would soon be fired for the first time from the liner's stern. There would also be play that Sunday evening as the Gurkhas had been planning to celebrate their eightieth Regimental birthday with a spectacular *nautch*. Putting on jacket and tie, I listened to the BBC reporting another bombing attack on Stanley Airport. It failed to put me in a party mood. The Brigade Commander and two Guards COs had been invited and, as an official host, I had to meet Lieutenant Colonel Johnny Rickett of the Welsh Guards. Known to play the guitar, he had no such instrument available for the Gurkhas' party. Indeed, the senior officer looked down-right worried.

'How do you think things will be when we arrive down south, sir?' I asked in a clumsy attempt to start a conversation whilst propping up the after sports deck hand-rail.

His prophesy, 'It's going to be tough once we're there,' would be more than accurate for his Battalion.

'And good enough reason to enjoy this evening whilst we can,' I thought as everyone waited for the Brigade Commander. But his non-arrival was unpopular. The start was delayed forty-five minutes until he materialized. Forthright Taj spoke to him and the Brigade Commander's face froze. Later I asked the C Company Commander, 'So what did you say?'

'Ah, nothing much,' he said laconically, 'just complained he was late and the *keta* had waited far too long for him!'

BOs of the 1st/7th Gurkha Rifles cared about their soldiers, just as they enjoyed a Regimental *nautch*. This ranged from the music of the P and D, dressed in dark-green Regimental blazer, grey flannels, and black shoes – to the throb of *madals* accompanying a flamboyant kukri dance of two Gurkhas clad in Regimental T-shirts adorned with kukri prints who leapt around slashing at the warm air with gleaming kukris. There was also a Falklands 'briefing' showing that Gurkhas, like their British counterparts, are not adverse to raw humour. A Gurkha NCO held up his large poster displaying a female model's naked posterior dotted with light bulbs. 'Gentlemen! Here's a map of "Miss Backlands"!' he proclaimed to his audience. 'As a preliminary to our mission in recapturing this objective, I'm going to take you on a recce around her defensive positions. It will be most useful for our land operations planning!' The sightseeing began and, at every stop, a light bulb flashed. Accompanied by lurid navigational instructions, the Gurkha's ten-minute description of her topography had most in stitches.

It was followed by more Nepalese dances, Regimental birthday cake cutting and presentation to the Commandant of a *QE2* framed photograph from her Master, Captain Jackson. A kukri was given in return, and the evening's climax came with the Battalion attempting to dance through the deck to the P and D's repeated piping and drumming of *Black Bear*. Gurkha riflemen approached BOs to insist on participation. 'Seconded officers are *surely* exempt!' I thought, only to be shocked as a grinning Gurkha grabbed my arm.

'Go on, Mike, get cracking!' yelled out Mark, 'It's *kaida!*' There was no alternative but to obey in a near-Red Indian totem pole war dance, which would have been bad news for the enemy if they had met the Gurkhas that night.

The following day, 17 May, would provide dual-hemisphere celebrations. It was both Argentine Naval Day and Norwegian Independence Day. I thought of Tove. However my priority continued to be coordinating, negotiating, writing and publishing Battalion training programmes. The rare opportunity for privacy was devoted to the BBC World Service and its reports on a situation we had been caught up in – and which demanded so much personally. In our room the listening experience was eerie. On surges of static came the announcement: 'This is London', the signature tune *Lillibulero*, followed by the time signal. And from several thousands of miles away, an English voice: 'BBC World Service. The news – read by . . .' The heart fluttered before the lead Falklands item which, today, was about British attacks on two enemy ships and Royal Navy bombarding the Port Stanley area and elsewhere. This caused us four officers to fantasize about participating in this ever-nearing war.

'It'll make Northern Ireland seem like a piece of cake,' I reflected.

Rory Stewart had another opinion. 'Of course there won't be any rules of engagement available like the Northern Ireland yellow card. Despite this absence of a rifleman's guide to kill, I expect it'll be like Ireland – except for a few more bangs,' he said laconically after finishing his Sterling sub-machine gun cleaning. Snapping forward the weapon's working parts, he squinted through its sights to an imaginary target on *Islas las Malvinas* before adding tartly, 'But if the bastards come near me, I'll be ready for 'em.'

As Rory changed into his running gear and disappeared for a quick training spin on deck, I continued staring at the white-flecked blue of the South Atlantic. My mind turned to my 2LI Northern Ireland 'hairy' experiences of a decade before. I thought of the PIRA ambush of our D Company convoy outside Dungannon where, although one soldier was killed by a gunshot wound to his head, the 'players'' oil drum stuffed with fifty kilos of explosives failed to detonate; 'lifting' PIRA suspects with dawn raids on their homes; a Coalisland riot and my maiden coming under fire; nightly attacks on Coalisland's police station and the need for my ordering a petrol bomber to be shot. I remembered patrolling post-Bloody Sunday Londonderry streets; two months' Alamo-like incarceration in that city's Bligh's Lane police station when D Company claimed hits on seventeen gunmen, of which the RUC Special Branch confirmed five, an Armalite rifle sniper wounding a soldier in the leg, and my platoon's participation in Operation CARCAN to gain British Army entry into the PIRA 'nogolands' of 'Free Derry'.

'Yet despite all this,' I reasoned to myself, 'Rory's wrong. The Falklands' War will be something else where a soldier's death can be more easily accepted politically than in a domestic internal security situation.'

It was four o'clock and everything seemed a trifle unreal as *QE2* steamed relentlessly southwards. I wandered off to a nearby steward's pantry which had become my private little kitchen to make another nice cup of tea before yet another O Group. The daily venue for this had now been moved away from the stress of the Reading Room to the green opulence of the Midships Bar – and was where the Commandant outlined the next twenty-four hours' activities. His instructions increased my need to coordinate the Battalion's training programme even more tightly as he said, 'Tomorrow we'll be calling at Freetown to take on more fuel and water. Nobody'll be allowed off the ship, however we'll be busy. Both Guards Battalions have already carried out dry emplaning and deplaning helicopter training drills on the aft flight deck. But at Freetown it'll be our turn with full equipment – including bergens!'

While notices were written and pinned up on the walls around five deck that evening, indicating the location of the Battalion's numerous assault boat stations for next day's training, a band concert was held in which our P and D played and cocktail and dinner parties continued apace. At Church Crookham Tove composed her first letter on the small, blue Task Force aerogramme which could be sent free of charge:

As you could see I made it to the post office. These airletters are a brilliant idea, but it's the least the Government can do for you and us! Now that the *QE2* has left there seems to be a lull – everywhere the newspapers are only reporting about a deepening rift within the Tories etc. about a possible 'sell-out'. I don't care if they sell the Islands, sheep and people to the lowest bidder as long as the fighting ships and you all come back! . . .

It must be getting warmer where you are at the moment – I wish we could see pictures of *QE2* where she sails – at least as far as Ascension Island. After that I suppose it's secret! Only the Russians and Argentinians will know.

The following day, 18 May, with *QE2* moored at Freetown, the Gurkhas practised the drill for assembling in the Double Down room from their five deck assault boat stations. A Fleet Air Arm aviator instructed them how to put on a helicopter life jacket, '. . . and *don't* press this! If you do, then you'll inflate the thing!' Too late. All eyes swung towards the unfortunate Gurkha who had triggered the hiss of escaping air. Silence, followed by a gale of Gurkha laughter. Their sense of humour in the ridiculous is highly developed, but none found it funny that we had never flown in or been inside a Sea King before.

'Coo, it's big inside, isn't it?' we commented on its twenty-two man carrying capacity after emplaning in the heat and sweat. But there was to be no flying, even though the helicopter would become one of the major Gurkha transport workhorses in the Falklands' War. Neither was there any 'hands-on' training of evacuation drill through the escape hatch. It would be another nineteen years before the British Army adopted such an official training policy for 'frequent overwater passengers', thereby creating a FOP competitor to the Navy's FOD.

That evening the BBC reported another Harrier air strike on Stanley Airport and, on the morning of 19 May, more Navy night bombardments of the Port Stanley area. *QE2* was again slicing through the seas. We were in the Doldrums and closer to the equator, the Falklands and war. During these days I had been redesigning Tac HQ's defensive layout, but tropical humidity fermented apprehension as the early morning runs around the boat deck continued, as well as daily writing on blue aerogrammes to Tove describing life on board and subdued private thoughts. This substitute war diary was also a method of emotionally offloading in those down periods. I had been snapping away with my camera at the Gurkha sights. Others had also taken pictures of a 'happy' Training Officer sahib, so I mailed home two rolls of completed film to my young family, slipping even further away.

Sudden squalls of rain often disturbed the calm sea. Many attended the equatorial 'crossing the line' ceremony visited by a 5 Brigade King Neptune and his mermaids. I did not. Psychological pressures had increased so much that a need to talk became of overriding importance and Bill Dawson made the appointment with Padre Peter Brooke, the Chaplain of the Welsh Guards. 'Time to bite on the bullet,' had been father's advice if life's difficulties appeared. On the contrary, for the first time in my military career I now let the bullet drop . . . and learned not only more about myself that day than the sum of all the previous days post-enlistment, but also understood at last why the white-haired Regimental Colonel of The Light Infantry, General Sir

Geoffrey Musson, had leant towards me during his interview eleven years before and asked quietly, 'And do you believe in God?' Too naive and immature to think otherwise, I considered it had just been one of those strange questions from an exceptionally senior officer who, no doubt, had seen a bit of life in his time. . . . Now, on *QE2*, the sympathetic and concerned Padre became an invaluable safety valve as he listened to my emotional off-loading. He was older than many of the other officers aboard, but pointed to the bedside photograph of his wife and four teenage boys. 'I get my strength from that,' was his simple message.

A superb conversation partner, he encouraged me afterwards to say a prayer with him. When I left Padre Brooke's room he also kept his promise by writing to Tove. Never again would I deride the military clergy. He provided for that short period the chance to talk about normal things in life and, for me, this had been a valuable diversion from the bizarre cruise programme mix of training for war and onboard entertainments. Later I felt guilty in having impinged on his time, for Peter Brooke would become even busier with others during the next week as the Falklands loomed nearer and, within three weeks, the poor man would be at the centre of the worst disaster of the war when all his ecclesiastical and psychosocial support skills would be tested to the limit and beyond.

We were also approaching the limit of our first cruise leg. It did not seem we would soon stop, turn around and start paddling back to Southampton as some in the other units unrealistically believed a week before. The stark fact was another 3,500 nautical miles remained – southwards. So our evening O Group convened again, but focus was on the Commandant's crystal gazing. It had an operational ring, 'We'll be arriving near Ascension Island tomorrow and more troops will be embarked. In addition we'll receive a Royal Navy destroyer escort. Afterwards we'll steam south five days, then cross deck onto the amphibious assault ship HMS *Fearless* by helicopter, and move nearer the Falklands before finally flying off in helicopters or, maybe, embarking into landing craft.'

Things were becoming more serious.

The *Pandit* reciting the ethics of war from a Hindu holy book immediately prior to *QE2* embarkation. RSM One Ton Karnabahadur Rai (right) listens. *(Author's collection)*

QE2 muster station drill - Lieutenant Jeremy McTeague (left) and Captain (QGO) Bhuwansing Limbu. *(Author's collection)*

3. The author on board *QE2*. *(Author's collection)*

4. En route to the Falklands - left to right, Second Lieutenant Quentin Oates, Lieutenant John Palmer, Captain Nigel Price, Captain Kit Spencer, Lieutenant Don Macauley, Second Lieutenant Paddy Redding, Major (QGO) Lalbahadur Rai and Second Lieutenant Tim Morris.

(Author's collection)

5. Second Lieutenant Paddy Redding (left) and Major Taj Lewis on board the tug *Typhoon* at South Georgia.

(Author's collection)

6. Gurkha air defence on MV *Norland*'s top deck en route to San Carlos. *(Author's collection)*

7. The Chinook, Bravo November, flying the Battalion from San Carlos to Goose Green on 1 June. *(Author's collection)*

8. An alert Gurkha ready to confront *dush* aircraft with his louch pole-mounted GPMG. *(Author's collection)*

9. A Gurkha rifleman in light assault order for the Battalion's attack on the Tumbledown and Mount William. *(Author's collection)*

10. The Battalion's last operational 81-mm mortar at Goat Ridge surveyed by Rifleman Ganeshbahadur Gurung after the Tumbledown Battle on 14 June.

(Photograph courtesy of Soldier Magazine of the British Army)

12. Major Mike Kefford at post-war Fox Bay. *(Author's collection)*

13. *Cabo* Nicolás Urbieta of the Argentine 4th Infantry Regiment. *(Author's collection)*

1. Inspecting an inhabitant of New Island, which is located off the west coast of West Falkland. *(Author's collection)*

14. Lieutenant Colonel David Morgan, Commissioner Rex Hunt and Major General Jeremy Moore before the Goose Green *nautch* on 10 July. *(HQ UKLF)*

15. A *nautch* kukri dance. *(HQ UKLF)*

16. A *Tamang* dance performed by a *maruni* and *phursunge* on board SS *Uganda*. (*Author's collection*)

17. Singing Gurkhas at the *nautch*. (*HQ UKLF*)

18. Making the point to ex-2GR officer John Nott, Secretary of State for Defence, on board SS *Uganda* prior to disembarkation at Southampton on 9 August. On the extreme left is Major (QGO) Lalbahadur Rai. The first Gurkha on Mr Nott's right is Sergeant Hemkumar Gurung, the Officers' Mess Head Steward. *(Press Association)*

19. The author, Mike Seear. *(Author's collection)*

Chapter Nine

ASCENSION AND BEYOND

'Look how I tremble': The pirates (British) *say they are now bringing cruel mercenaries with knives . . . The presence of the Gurkha knives in the Malvinas Theatre of Operations once again shows the incredible blunders of Thatcher and those following orders from her bloody delirium. – Flash* periodical[1]

By Thursday morning, 20 May, rumours climaxed that British Falklands landings were imminent. This gave our officers an extra training edge as they gathered in the Double Down Bar. In lieu of a promised Brigade command post exercise, Mike Kefford had written a Battalion 'table top' equivalent. 'As we're at sea I've invented a new concept,' he said briskly, 'instead of a "Tactical Exercise Without Troops", you're going to have a "Tactical Exercise Without Land" i.e. a TEWL instead of a traditional TEWT!'

When the laughter died down he added, 'So during the next three mornings we'll brainstorm plans for inserting the Battalion onto the Falklands from *Fearless*. And this'll keep everyone busy!' An abundance of helicopter availability had been discussed incessantly at Brigade HQ level and influenced our thinking. This was reflected in Mike's scenario, 'We'll be planning a four-phase Battalion helicopter assault on Teal Inlet in the north of East Falkland. So sharpen your pencils folks, as you'll be working out the detailed movement tables for this notional operation!'

'Is this a realistic method for us to land on the Falklands?' I wondered as the planning complexities were revealed. Although minds were flexed, nobody considered a landing craft alternative deployment. External lecturers also taught us the characteristics of specialized weapons. Two Gunners gave briefings on the 105-mm Light Gun, then, shoulder-held Blowpipe launcher and ground to air missile. Once on the Falklands a nil 'fire and forget' capability would provide its firer with insurmountable problems, unlike the superb artillery piece. Major Mike Hughes' briefing was the most interesting. Attached to us at Sennybridge, the tall Welsh Fusilier FAC described his equipment which would mark Harrier laser-guided bombs onto their targets.

'The Ferranti laser target marker designator is top secret and so new that its service issue date has been brought forward for Operation CORPORATE. My job is to lead a four-man Tactical Air Control Party who'll "ground-lase" the selected target with a "laser spot" which the RAF Harrier GR3's Laser Range Finder and Marked-Target Seeker will pick up at five miles out. I'll be talking direct to the pilot whose two 1,000 pound "dumb" bombs have been converted into "smart" ones by Paveway II Texas Instruments modification kits to give them precision accuracy . . .'

Fifteen minutes later, the FAC's enthusiastic exposition of his baby's impressive merits ended with a dubious claim, '. . . and it'll be the first time RAF Harrier ground attack pilots will launch this bomb, so this'll be a case of "on the job learning" for them! Any questions?'

This *Star Wars* technology that might save British lives, including mine, was fascinating. But the bomb had never been used operationally by British Harriers so I asked naively, 'OK, I hear you – but is this bit of kit going to work on the big day?'

Red Dragon treated my doubt with the fiery contempt it deserved, 'Yes, of course! And don't forget the bomb's explosive effect is equivalent to one salvo from an artillery battery's six Light Guns!'

After lunch Bill and I moved to the Midships Bar, now the Brigade training conference and Battalion's early-evening O Group venue. The same afternoon, on Ascension Day itself, *QE2* arrived at a position fifty nautical miles west of Ascension Island. Unlike *Baltic Ferry* and *Nordic Ferry* moored there, most did not see land as we loitered under the Island's 100-mile radius Terminal Control Area umbrella for the next fifty hours to avoid Soviet Bear aircraft overflights and spy trawler. The TCA had been implemented ten days before to aid the air defence organization and air traffic control of overflights and Hercules, Nimrod, VC10, Vulcan, Harrier, helicopter and other military aircraft movements to and from the world's busiest military airfield at Wideawake. A lucky few were flown off *QE2* to carry out superficial cross-loading of stores. The offshore patrol cum supply vessel HMS *Dumbarton Castle* also made a rendezvous to cross deck other reinforcements and stores which included seventeen Gunners for us from the appropriately titled 132 Field Battery (The Bengal Rocket Troop) of the Royal School of Artillery, thereby bringing our total of British attachments to thirty-nine.

On board, eating and drinking continued. So did fear of the unknown, the entertainments and family yearning – throughout that day and into the evening. At his O Group, the Commandant then announced, 'Once beyond latitude ten degrees south, active service living conditions will apply. But an enemy propaganda victory of sinking us must be avoided, so air defence stations of heavy machine guns will be manned soon on *QE2*'s bridge wings as well as Blowpipes and GPMGs around the funnel. Also our course'll be altered constantly as a counter-torpedo measure and a night-time blackout enforced!'

His seriousness was reinforced with a post-dinner BBC World Service report of a Sea King crash into the drink near the Falklands during a cross decking operation. Twenty-one, mostly SAS, died – to remind us again of our mortality. Familiarized with this helicopter type at Freetown, our crash drill had consisted of the comical instruction, 'After ditching just wait inside until it stops rolling in the sea, before kicking out the escape hatch!' It seemed even more unlikely now that the South Atlantic would oblige with such a textbook sea surface prior to any future need to evacuate.

Battlefield fantasies continued. International diplomacy had failed. So did the black plastic sheeting now pinned up over all our room windows. Exposed to a night helicopter flight's visual check, they were rated ineffective. Someone knocked on the door and I opened it. Outside was a Royal Navy officer. '*QE2* is like the Royal Yacht entering Portsmouth Harbour on Coronation Night decorated with all of Blackpool's illuminations,' he snapped. 'So it's lights out in here, gentlemen, until you're light-proof!'

Our mission was accomplished before retiring to bed. Living cheek by jowl, one had become accustomed to others' personal habits. That night, though, the ripple of cannon fire and bomb explosions from the 2IC sahib's bed increased alarmingly in strength. Lacking only the 1812 overture, this cacophony of battle could have beaten any *Aerea Fuerza Argentina* air strike. 'Gosh . . . what a useful live-firing exercise to compliment our on-going TEWL!' I concluded before drifting off into the land of nod.

Our TEWL, the Battalion's intense training programme and psychological pressure continued next morning. Ascension Island remained below the horizon throughout 21 May as *Baltic Ferry* and *Nordic Ferry* departed to the Theatre of Operations, steering east of a straight line to avoid the enemy Boeing 707 reconnaissance flights. Major General Jeremy Moore, his Land Forces Falkland Islands HQ and stores, mail and reinforcements were flown out to the *QE2*. Once aboard, the General's title of Commander Land Forces Falkland Islands (CLFFI) was reduced to a more manageable Cliffy. The Battalion's new arrivals consisted of Major Mike Fallon, the Battery Commander, accompanied by his four-man BC's party, and Captains Gus Pugh and Keith Swinton, Mike's Forward Observation Officers otherwise known as FOOs. They also had five men apiece in their FOO parties, their only shortfall being a lack of 105-mm Light Gun ownership. Tools of the trade would be needed in a shooting war but then this *was* just one more signal from an Army top brass convinced 5 Brigade would not fight. This logic defied description. Mike and I had been on the same Norwegian winter warfare course fifteen years previously which led to my first meeting with Tove. She continued to write about the mounting pressures and her psychosocial support strategy with the other wives:

I'm still waiting for the good news in spite of the world telling me it's not going to happen. I just grab the paper every morning wanting to see to see PEACE splashed across the front page. This constant one more chance, one more day, is terribly wearing and I still want to cling to the hope . . . But then that would mean that you'd be going to Belize, and then we'd have another eternity of separation. I just can't win! . . .

. . . I have gradually started to think of this place as <u>home</u> now. This is where I can best be in touch with you and the news about you. There are other wives with whom I can associate, friends for the girls and lots of routine must-do-that to take my mind off things. I'm at home here and can do precisely what I want . . . even though it gets very lonely at times. But going to Oslo isn't going to make you feel nearer – possibly on the contrary . . .

There are a lot of grim faces and voices on the media today. Everything still hanging by a thread. Desperate attempts still being made for peace . . . I shudder in horror over the visions of war that even I have been forced to realize thanks to all the programmes on the 'box'. They send lots of 'these are the possibilities of a re-invasion' . . . Galtieri's remark about being willing to sacrifice 40,000 lives, also hit me with its sudden realistic implication . . . Surely there therefore will be heavy losses on your side? . . . However as the days slowly tick by, maybe your predictions will be correct after all.

They were, because the landings had taken place that morning and the Battle of San Carlos Water had now started between the Royal Navy and *Aerea Fuerza Argentina.* That evening the quarterdeck state board was updated by another sixteen splashed enemy aircraft and adjacent Falklands' map adorned with numerous white cardboard military symbols. One Harrier had been shot down. The BBC TV programme *A Queen Goes To War*, reporting our Southampton departure had also arrived. This and the landings had put the Guards into a festive mood and hundreds of them gathered in the Queen's Room that evening where the programme was shown on a big video screen. Most booed, catcalled, and V-signed interviews of demonstrating war protesters and the left-wing politician, Tony Benn, but those Gurkhas present watched only with phlegmatic interest. None displayed any macho tendencies either then or later. Even Guardsman Simon Weston of the Welsh Guards observed, 'The Gurkhas were . . . unbelievably amiable.'[2]

The BBC World Service was also reporting air attack damage on Royal Navy warships. 'So what the hell's it going to be like at San Carlos when we arrive there?' I wondered, getting into my campbed for a worried night's kip.

Next morning, 22 May, while Gurkha BIT continued to throb around the prom-enade deck, the Cunard container ship cum aircraft transport SS *Atlantic Causeway* with her Brigade cargo of twenty-eight Sea King and Wessex helicopters arrived alongside. Stores were 'vertreped'[3] on board *QE2* and our heavy machine gun Small Arms Service Corps instructor flew off UK-bound. More mail was received for us and another eighty-one Task Force ships. It would be the last for twenty-two days. One letter was pinned up outside the Field Post Office near the Sergeants' Mess:

Dear British Task Force,

I am writing to wish you good luck in regaining power over the Falkland Islands and South Georgia. I don't suppose you are enjoying yourself, but I hope you all return to Britain safely. Don't worry though, one way or the other you will get the islands back. You have a very good crew and it is the BEST. No matter who is reading this can you (if possible) let the whole task force hear this letter. GOOD LUCK.

Signed
Alan Johnston
Age 10

P.S. Best of luck from me and Britain.

At mid-morning we started our next cruise leg beyond Ascension. The TEWL ended at lunchtime, but the Liffy requisition of the Midships Bar caused an even more cramped situation on board. I peeked through the green curtains drawn permanently over its glass walls. Inside the staff were intriguingly busy so I wondered, 'What *are* they doing?' Perhaps it was a good question because, unbeknown to us, direct Liffy communication was non-existent with British forces on the Falklands. Because of this takeover Bill also informed me, 'The Brigade training conference has had to move back to the Double Down Bar and our O Group to the ante-room, alias the Queen's Grill Lounge.'

After our O Group the quarterdeck state boards' figures remained the same and my bedtime story was the BBC World Service's report that Harriers had attacked Goose Green and the frigate HMS *Ardent* had sunk. Next morning, 23 May, the air was muggy at latitude 35 degrees south, midway between Rio de Janeiro and Buenos Aires and the sea like a mill pond. Rifleman Baliprasad Rai maintained that, '. . . sometimes (on board) it was hotter than Dharan during the summer, so much so that we frequently had to take refuge in the air-conditioned lounges.'[4] The black plastic taped over the windows was causing *QE2*'s internal temperature to rise uncomfortably. So did mine as the numbers on the state board increased by another ten splashed enemy aircraft. As a debit, the frigate HMS *Antelope* had been damaged. The Commandant also announced to our evening O Group, '*QE2*'s now under command of the Carrier Battle Group commanded by Rear Admiral Sandy Woodward on his flagship, HMS *Hermes*. We'll cross deck to *Fearless* on Friday, 28 May and land on the Falklands by the 30 or 31 of May.'

The deduction was that, politically, *QE2* could not be risked in the uncomfortable San Carlos Water environment. Cross decking our stores with *Baltic Ferry* and *Nordic Ferry* would take place the following day 1,000 nautical miles north of the Falklands. However the rendezvous was cancelled without explanation. On *Baltic Ferry* young David Wright was the ship's Adjutant. He and his small band of Gurkha drivers had been enjoying independence, even though they had been shadowed by a Soviet trawler for days. The crew were more concerned about their cargo of 500 tons of white phosphorous bombs, tracer rounds and 105-mm shells: a juicy target for any attacking aircraft. Although the amount of enemy aircraft shot down at San Carlos eased their worries a little, *Antelope*'s sinking after an undetonated bomb had exploded aboard her, provided another reminder of *Baltic Ferry*'s vulnerability. It also gave the chaplains extra business on *QE2*. 'So perhaps the salve to such festering fear,' reasoned my logic, 'could be a quick-fix communion.' But I had pestered the clergy too much already to dare participate, even though life would become busier as 5 Brigade's daily routine orders *At Sea* on Monday, 24 May warned in an Anglo-Spanish footnote on prisoner taking. Between its lines and under the final humour was pessimism about the enemy's numerical superiority:

Surrender – Rendase.
You are a prisoner – Esta un prisinero.
Hands up – Manos ariba.
I am wounded, help me – Estoy merido ayudame.
Where is your officer? – Donde esta su official?
Where is your HQ? – Donde esta su Cuartel General?

Where is your minefield? – Donde esta su campo de minas?
Have you got food? – Tiene Comida?
How many men are over there? – Hay cuanto's hombres alli?
example:

Hay cuanto's hombres alli? – 100,000.
Adios.

Despite the BBC news of more Harrier attacks on Stanley Airport and one Harrier lost at sea, there were also optimists. The Education Corps personnel on board had held Progressive Qualification Scheme tutorials for Staff College candidates, a soldiers' Education Promotion Certificate course and exam and even resettlement interviews for those who knew the grass was greener on the other side and intended to become civilians after Operation CORPORATE. The same daily routine orders had christened all participants in these activities as the Defence and Employment Platoon and published two sample questions for the entrance exam to this make believe unit of soldiers who would be concerned with the taking of life shortly. One question was about biology and, indirectly, the politicians who had sent us to war to sort out their sloppy mistakes. The other alluded to Operation CORPORATE's astronomical cost of £1.6 billion, plus an eventual £2 billion post-war for creating 'Fortress Falklands':

Create life. Estimate the differences in subsequent human culture if this form of life had developed 500 million years earlier, with special attention to its probable effect on the English parliamentary system. Prove your thesis.

Develop a realistic plan for refinancing the national debt. Trace the possible effects of your plan in the following areas: Cubism, McDonetist controversy and the wave theory of light. Outline a method for preventing these effects. Criticize this method from all possible points of view.

Our training juggernaut rolled on. The programme that day was typical. BIT with Sergeant Durkin on the upper sports deck had progressed to instruction in 'pokey drill' – an exhausting blend of PT and SLR drill to strengthen the arm muscles. There was Gurkha training on the upper and quarterdecks. The officers attended an intelligence lecture at 09.00 to 10.00 hours in the Queen's Bar; the Commandant addressed the British Other Ranks at 09.00 until 09.30 hours and the main cinema showed Hindi films from 14.00 to 17.30 hours. Rifleman Baliprasad Rai assessed that, '. . . we were all geared up mentally and physically for any action'[5].

After I attended the Brigade daily training conference, another Battalion O Group was held in the ante-room at 17.15 hours. There the Commandant issued yet another change of plan with a first indication that a helicopter assault might not be our method of landing on the Falklands. '*QE2*'s destination, gentlemen, will now be the Island of South Georgia where the Brigade'll cross deck to Royal Navy ships. . . .' There was stunned silence, but he continued, 'We're also going to bomb-up the Battalion tomorrow. Ram's department will organize this initial distribution of live ammunition plus three 24-hour ration packs per man. 7.62-mm ball and link will be issued for SLRs and GPMGs, and 9-mm for Sterling sub-machine guns and Browning pistols – in addition to the 66 and 84 anti-tank ammo. Training Officer, you'll take down the Company Commanders' ammo orders.'

I made ready with pen and notebook. The most popular item was the 'throw away after use' 66-mm light anti-tank weapon – a Lester Holley priority. The SAS were always on the offensive. 'B Company needs twenty-four of these,' he demanded as I scribbled with restaurant waiter dexterity. The mathematics were an infernal chore, but weight of firepower would win Falkland battles and attention to detail was necessary.

'I haven't any faith in the proposed resupply system so, once on the Falklands, our riflemen must carry a minimum of 200 rounds each,' insisted the Commandant, knowing that a Gurkha was bred on manpacking seventy kilos of weight over some of the most difficult terrain in the world without blinking an eyelid. It was therefore diffi-cult to overload such soldiers with extra ammunition, so the problem revolved around exactly *where* on each man this should be carried. 'This amount is, of course, equiva-lent to ten full rifle magazines. It is double the normal number carried, and there must also be link ammo for the extra GPMG in each rifle section. So I want C Company to be issued now with 100 rounds per man more than the others, and your company, Taj, are to find the best method of carrying all this extra weight,' he ordered.

There was a buzz of excited conversation as officers shuffled out of the ante-room to prepare and issue their own company orders. There had been reports of more aircraft splashed at San Carlos so I took another turn past the quarterdeck state board. Its numbers were unaltered. Enemy losses were so breathtaking that their attacking momentum could not possibly be sustained. It also led to the board suffering indiges-tion from the situation's dynamics. Acquisition and onward transmission of updated, real-time intelligence to front-line units would be unsuccessful throughout the campaign and an omen of things to come was now illustrated by a minor incident. An irritated Brigade Commander passed by an Intelligence Corps Corporal responsible for updating the board.

'Get them right!' snarled his boss wagging an accusing finger towards the numbers.

'Yessir!' replied the hapless junior NCO.

His amendment was incorrect. He needed help and my source was the early evening BBC World Service News:

> . . . Another eight Argentine aircraft are claimed shot down, making a total of more than thirty aircraft lost in the past seventy-two hours . . . British ships have been damaged . . . Argentine soldiers taken prisoners were starving and suffering from exposure . . . and the next British target appears to be the Argentine battalion at Darwin and Goose Green. . . .

So I returned to the state board and corrected it.

Tomorrow would be Argentina's National Day and a rumour circulated that the enemy might engineer a 'big' strike against the Task Force. There had been no sign of any destroyer escort the Commandant had talked about before Ascension Island and we might be in the firing line – but soon, from 19.00 to 23.00 hours, the upper sports deck's fresh air would become the Battalion's property again. This was priority number one after company, platoon and section orders had been completed, so many grabbed this chance to vacate *QE2*'s suffocating confines and relax up there in the dark before bed.

The Harriers had attacked Stanley Airport that evening, but next day the Gurkhas celebrated the 25 May by bombing-up in the Double Down Room. My personal quota of pistol ammo was equivalent to eight magazine clips. Not the same as a Gurkha carrying ten full SLR magazines in addition to other kit, my paltry 100 rounds were enough. 'Indeed, perhaps they might come in useful for any possible last-ditch, back against the wall situation,' I fantasized while also receiving three 24-hour ration packs. Thankfully there would be no requirement to backpack that seventy kilo Gurkha 'standard' which would have posed chaotic problems for this BO mortal.

The wane in training and now bombing-up activity might have accounted for the upsurge in Holy Communion services. These nearly equalled the number of final planning conferences. I attended four of the latter and also briefed Tac HQ on our expected tasks, organization, procedures and defensive layout. With such conference proliferation there was a tendency to forget their content quickly. Yet, accompanied by the RSO, I still recall one – for two reasons. First, the briefer's message on enemy electronic warfare countermeasures. 'From Day One on the Islands pay attention to your signals security. Keep transmissions short and concise. The enemy *will* be listening to you continuously. They *will* be attempting to jam and locate you. Don't compromise your operations. Be professional. Use the codes and change them at the appointed times of the day.'

Major Mike Forge, the Brigade HQ and Signals Squadron Commander made an impression on me. Not only by his charisma, but also because of the second reason. It cancelled his trip home because, in less than two weeks, he would be killed on East Falkland.

Information continued rolling out to us punch-drunk recipients. At the evening's O Group, Taj back briefed his ammunition trial results, 'OK, we've decided on the following. With one magazine on the SLR, our belt pouches will contain four magazines, link ammo and one ration pack. The remainder'll be put in the bergen. Prior to going into battle a magazine from the pouches will be taped onto the one already on the SLR.'

The Commandant approved and threw out more information with yet another change of plan, 'The entire Brigade will now be cross decked at South Georgia to *Canberra*. So we should be on the Falklands on 30 May, five days from now. Prior to the next phase, when we'll become part of the Amphibious Task Group, the Brigade Commander will address each unit in the main cinema tomorrow. Also as part of our battle preparation, Brigade has ordered all bayonets to be sharpened . . . but personally I'm not so sure this is wise.'

His doubt led to refusal. Sharpening bayonets would strip the metal's protective parkerization and lead to rust in the Falklands' damp climate. To any Gurkha or Guardsman this was anathema. An urgently required bayonet stuck fast in its metal scabbard could not be risked. 'And neither is sharpening really necessary,' as my Sandhurst platoon had once been told by its Woodentop instructor, 'because in hand-to-hand fighting a really determined thrust to the guts of a heavy SLR fixed even with a blunt bayonet, followed by a quick twist on extraction should be sufficient, gentlemen, to achieve the aim.'

Regardless of the merits or otherwise of such a solution, our reliable kukri arsenal had no rust or other incurable problems. Each was blessed with a wood and leather scabbard and every owner had also expended much effort in honing his blade to razor sharpness. It might be needed. Next morning the BBC were reporting the sinkings of the destroyer HMS *Coventry* and another Cunard aircraft transport containership SS *Atlantic Conveyor*, as well as six more enemy aircraft splashed and renewed Royal Navy bombardment of the Port Stanley area.

Live-firing on deck took place throughout 26 May, but the principal event occurred on the main cinema's stage. The spotlighted Brigade Commander gave the Gurkhas a twenty-minute pre-battle speech in classic 'dress up, stand up, speak up, keep the end as close as possible to the start, shut up, and sit down' Churchillian style. The Gurkhas followed the concise monologue with rapt attention as he started with Argentina's President, 'Galtieri's a madman! He continues fighting, but is in a hopeless situation and cannot win . . . He's made no regard for the fact we'll inflict terrible casualties on his forces . . . you can be proud of your training standards achieved at Sennybridge and on *QE2* . . . now we're ready and'll soon join 3 Commando Brigade . . . to start joint operations to recapture the islands . . . it is too early to issue a detailed plan, but when we do it'll be a good one . . . we'll win this game by good teamwork . . . I look forward to the Brigade getting this job done . . . then we can return home with our heads held high . . . you are part of history in the making which your grandchildren will talk about . . . so good luck and *Jai Seventh*!'

The ending drew a vociferous ovation from his motivated audience. And, as if to reinforce the message that business neared, two training films were shown that afternoon entitled *Captured* and *The Hidden Enemy*. My identity card was also exchanged for a white 'British Forces Identity Card' in compliance with Article 17 of the 1949 Geneva Convention. Only showing my number, rank, date of birth and name, on its back was a bleak message for me:

> If you are captured, you are required to give your captors the information set out overleaf so that your capture may be reported to your next-of-kin. When you are interrogated, but not before, tear off the duplicate portion and give to the interrogator. GIVE NO OTHER INFORMATION.

Graham Stewart-Smith also became involved in these days of final preparation. With distinguished grey sideburns and photogenic face, he exuded an artifical aura of awe-inspiring professional coolness. As Paymaster he controlled the Battalion's Gurkha Pension Fund, and therefore was regarded as a military-type 'godfather' by the Gurkhas. Income for their fund came monthly from a compulsory sum deducted from each man's pay. Invested in various Hong Kong gilt-edged companies, it totalled several million Hong Kong dollars. Such responsibility was not enough for Graham because, like my father who was the RAF Command Cashier on wartime Malta, these gentlemen of military finances always seemed to be looking for a slice of the real military action.

It was agreed therefore that within Tac HQ Graham would coordinate and compile the Battalion's resupply demands, known as supdems and opdems, which had to be flown in by helicopter. He would also have to grapple with mesco – a code to send radio messages, and nuco – a new numbers code introduced for the Falklands' War to be used for grid references and signal frequencies. His assistant was the youthful Lieutenant Chandrakumar Pradhan, otherwise known as Chandra sahib, whose MT Platoon had been converted into the Machine Gun Platoon. Being a Newar and also a bright officer, meant the QGO was tailor made for the number-crunching of logistics resupply. Both lacked experience, but the Paymaster was as keen as mustard. 'I wouldn't have missed this trip for anything!' he enthused. 'So come on Mike, give me the griff on these bloody supdems, opdems and all those awful codes – and then I'll be operational!'

Although this was admirable, Graham still had to solve his problem with the large amount of money Gurkhas still possessed on *QE2*. He made a final plea that more be returned to him for safe keeping before disembarkation and recommended each man keep £40. But his message became corrupted. It resulted in only another £27,000 arriving from the 630 Gurkhas – an average of £40 returned per man, making this Gurkha battalion the wealthiest ever to go into battle. However a few did hand back exceptionally large sums, including one of £1,200 to which the astonished Paymaster exclaimed, 'Goodness me man! You're just about to fight for your life against the Argies on the Falklands under *dreadful* weather conditions. And yet you were *still* planning to carry all this money into action?'

'Yes, sahib!' replied the highly optimistic, but equally startled Gurkha.

'What on earth, then, had you planned to do with it all?' asked Graham.

The embattled *sipai* answered with that curious Gurkha pronunciation of the letter S, 'For shopping in Port ish-Stanley, sahib!'

And that evening Tove was providing me with some wishes of her own in a 'pre-battle' epistle about my participation in this operation to stop our friends . . .

. . . the Argentines taking something that isn't theirs. I do understand even though I am against war – all war. Aggression like that should be stopped somehow, and it is perfectly true that if democratic countries like England didn't show the world that one cannot just take and call it mine – where would we be? If the Argentines got away with no opposition, then it would simply mean another country tomorrow and a third the day after that somewhere in the world. It is very, very sad that my husband has to go and show them that it simply won't be tolerated. But you are fighting a just cause, of that there is no doubt.

It is an irony that as this world of ours gets smaller and people intermingle more and more – there seems to be less justice and less peace. Countries are fighting 'forgotten' wars everywhere. I know we said that this particular war was stupid and needless and was of principle. It still might be that; but nevertheless you are fighting for justice and a simple human right to remain what they have always been – British (whether we like it or not!)

So, my love, I'm with you all the way and Galtieri's talk about cease-fire now makes me sick. The whole Junta system is sick of course – but you just show them!

I slept soundly as Captain Jackson worked hard throughout the small hours to prevent *QE2* from becoming the *Titanic* of the South Atlantic by navigating a desperate slalom course through an enormous pack of icebergs. The liner survived to rendezvous with HMS *Antrim* at noon the following day, 27 May – my tenth wedding anniversary. Maybe this was *QE2*'s so-called destroyer escort that the Commandant had talked about. Late austral autumn temperatures were just above freezing. We were now ninety nautical miles from South Georgia as a large number of khaki-clad spectators gathered on the starboard quarter of the boat deck to witness the cross decking operation by Sea King helicopter and two *QE2* launches of Major General Moore's and the Brigade Commander's advance parties. With them went £500 worth of Mars bars to replenish *Antrim*'s stores. Maintaining a distance of one nautical mile, the destroyer's upperworks displayed 30-mm cannon strikes from enemy aircraft attack.

Our first sighting of war damage quietened most. Captain Les Peacock, the No. 2 Quartermaster, was the sole Gurkha representative to be cross decked and, apart from one man who broke his leg clambering on board the warship, the advance party survived despite a heavy sea swell which the official Brigade account described later as 'putting hearts into mouths'. Although Les would be the first from our Battalion onto the Falklands, *Baltic Ferry* arrived in San Carlos Water the same day with its complement of Gurkhas. They did not land until five days later as their floating ammunition bunker moved in and out of the Falkland Sound to avoid enemy aircraft detection.

Retiring to our room, I listened to the BBC World Service for the last time on board. It irritated me. I had ordered some wedding anniversary red roses for Tove, but this broadcast would be mentioned in my anniversary day letter to her. That cliché 'The first casualty in war is truth' had become, by now, a recurrent problem:

Never have I had a more strange anniversary than in this place. We are now just about arriving at South Georgia, and I would reckon that we will be here a couple of nights. We shall transfer to the *Canberra* from here and then move in under cover of darkness to the Falklands. Landing place is San Carlos – a bit hairy, but it will be OK. Feel strangely very confident that everything is OK and will be OK. Heard (on the radio) that the Paras and Marines have been on the move all day today. So maybe we won't have anything to do!

Also heard on the radio that the Argies have claimed to have sunk the *QE2* off South Georgia. Absolute bunkum. The only thing that we have seen so far is HMS *Antrim* taking off Tony Wilson to the flagship (*Hermes*) and a few icebergs. The whole thing is really ridiculous. Those Argies are a load of lying bastards. Don't ever believe what they say.

That afternoon's O Group venue was the Trafalgar Suite, the Brigade Commander's ex-residence. This double-tiered lounge and bedroom had a splendid deep pile golden carpet and matching curtains, in contrast to the quarterdeck where wear and tear had led to the carpet being rolled back, exposing a steel floor. After we sat down on the sofa, chairs and floor, the Commandant addressed us, 'Welcome, gentlemen, to this last O Group on board. To celebrate the occasion I've a bottle of *tato pani* and some empty glasses, before the IO gives us a latest update on the enemy and we go through the Battalion disembarkation plan!'

We sipped the *tato pani* as Paddy Redding stepped forward to give his briefing. It was the eve of the battle for Darwin and Goose Green with the BBC World Service trumpeting that British Forces were closing on these twin objectives. With a theatrical flourish Paddy unfurled his map. There were so many red chinagraph enemy military symbols dotting East Falkland that one could be forgiven for believing that this had been an invasion carried out by the entire Soviet Red Army. The IO provided the facts with a solid dose of black humour, 'It looks as if Galtieri has been equalizing numbers since we received our marching orders. The result is that the enemy garrison strength is now at 13,000 and their in-theatre air capability has also increased. So watch out, for I've been told that their Pucará ground attack aircraft can eat helicopters for breakfast!'

His final remark achieved a deafening silence. Then the Commandant moved on to the next day's events, 'I'm pleased to inform you that the plan, gentlemen, has changed yet again! On arrival at South Georgia, only the Scots and Welsh Guards will be cross decked onto *Canberra*. We'll now have our own ship to share with 16 Field Ambulance. This'll be *Norland*, the same North Sea ferry that took 2 Para to San Carlos. So here's how the Battalion will disembark *QE2* . . .'

Afterwards most left the suite intent on disseminating this latest 'gossip' to their men. Later some enjoyed a final drink on board. I joined Graham Stewart-Smith in the Q4 Room night-club. An acquaintance of his, an Intelligence Corps officer on the staff of Liffy and past participant in the Northwood briefings of 'Memsahib *Thatcher le Thecharyo*', sat at our table. The sexy black colour of our tablecloth was symbolic of his prophecy and insight into the enemy's fate that provided a counterbalance to the facts that Paddy had presented in the Trafalgar Suite. 'Don't worry. The whole thing'll be sewn up within two to three weeks. The Gurkhas will be pushed through in the final phase. As far as West Falkland is concerned, this'll be allowed to wither and die. But if there's one thing that's coming out of Buenos Aires at the moment, then it's questions about your Battalion. They're scared stiff of you!'

The Gurkha reputation was at work. That letter on the eve of the 1915 Gallipoli landings from the Expeditionary Force Commander stating, '. . . each little "Gurk" might well be worth his full weight of gold . . .' applied already for the 1st/7th Gurkha Rifles long before their 1982 San Carlos landing. So maybe the *QE2* British Forces' Post Office number of 666, which seemed initially inappropriate with its correlation to the Bible's Book of Revelation, Chapter 13, defining this as the mark of Satan's Apostles, had now begun to mirror the enemy's perceptions of the Gurkhas with its further references to 'a beast riseth out of the sea' and 'another beast cometh out of the earth'.

There was also a change in *QE2*'s motion. No more vibrations. We had arrived at South Georgia, dropping anchor in Cumberland Bay East off St Edward Point near the disused Norwegian whaling station at Grytviken. Much later that night the BBC World Service reported Harriers had attacked Stanley Airport and Goose Green again, and one had been shot down. There had also been enemy air attacks on supply dumps at Ajax Bay and nearby San Carlos causing twenty-six British casualties[6] while two more enemy aircraft were splashed.

And soon we would begin our final cruise leg to East Falkland – and San Carlos.

Chapter Ten

TOWARDS SAN CARLOS

We held the boat up to the gale during that day, enduring as best we could discomforts that amounted to pain. The boat tossed interminably on the big waves under grey, threatening skies. Our thoughts did not embrace much more than the necessities of the hour. Every surge of the sea was an enemy to be watched and circumvented. – Sir Ernest Shackleton

Next morning Bill Dawson rolled out of bed to stomp into the loo for the last time declaring robustly, 'Right, girls! The party's over. It's from here that the real fun's about to begin!'

After breakfast we emerged on deck to admire the deep green sea, snow, glaciers and jagged mountains surrounding the Moraine Fjord. *QE2* was anchored off St Edward Point where the small collection of buildings lay that made up the derelict Norwegian whaling base of Grytviken, a name derived from the Norwegian words *vika* (bay), and *gryte* (pan or saucepan), because nineteenth century seal hunters had cooked seal fat there in colossal iron cookers. There was plenty of helicopter and small ship activity in the 'Bay of Pans' because the total of fourteen vessels there outnumbered the shipping in San Carlos Water. Three stood out. *Canberra*'s enormous rust-streaks belied her nickname of 'The Great White Whale', whilst the flame-red of the Royal Navy's ice patrol vessel HMS *Endurance* endorsed her nickname of 'The Red Iceberg'. Both made the squat blackness of *Norland*, anchored further to the west, singularly dreary. Disappointingly, I was unable to locate the enemy submarine because the Navy had beached her underwater.

Gurkha riflemen viewing the stunning scenery were horrified at the Antarctic winter. So they asked their usual question, 'Are we there yet?'

Trying to reassure their apparently worried men, the NCOs replied, 'No *keta*. Some days still remain of the cruise.'

However yet another question was put, 'But why has the Battalion's preparation for this war not included training for fighting on skis?'

The NCOs now understood, but shrugged their shoulders in secret glee. Jokingly they did nothing to alleviate these riflemen's fears, leaving quite a few to believe for a while they would have to operate on the snow-covered Antarctic 'Foklands' without either the benefit of ski training or winter warfare ski equipment. But the unreliable weather and being within enemy aircraft range[1] had started the Gurkha exodus already, so there was limited time for last-minute packing in an overloaded bergen while I listened to the BBC World Service and news that the UN Security Council had passed its Resolution 505.

'Nope, stop listening to this waffle,' I chastised myself, 'getting to an early lunch now is much more important than listening to any vague talk on the radio from the diplomats in New York trying to breathe life into a ceasefire possibility that doesn't even exist!'

Our suitcases were stacked together so they could be crossed decked and stored on 'The Great White Whale'. We would now live on the contents of our bergens. The tug *Typhoon*, which had been the first surface ship to depart UK for Task Force duties, and trawlers *Junella* and *Northella* would cross deck the Battalion. In B Company, Rifleman Baliprasad Rai was about to disembark regretfully as he later pointed out, 'We were all sorry to leave the great ship and her staff with whom we had made friends'.[2] However his OC sahib, Lester Holley, realized that the cross decking operation would take too long in the available daylight and with the allocated shipping. So the former SAS trooper improvised, and . . .

. . . just before noon the Queen's launches began to load the (B Company) Gurkhas and their nearly overwhelming bulk of equipment. When the boats reached the *Norland*, they found that she had no pontoon alongside and that her hatch, normally used for disembarking cars, was eight feet above the water and higher than the Gurkhas were tall by a very good measure. There is no question that the Gurkhas are amongst the finest fighting troops in the world, but this represented a very substantial challenge. The troops could not even see the *Norland*'s deck, let alone reach it, from the *QE2*'s launches. The solution was to use the cab of the launch plus a good boost to get the soldiers on their way.[3]

I snatched a quick lunch whilst listening to Bill talking to Lieutenant Keith Mills, a Marine Commando officer on a visit from 'The Red Iceberg'. He had led the defence of South Georgia with only twenty-one men on 3 April, an action that would lead to his being awarded the Distinguished Service Cross. They had shot down a Puma helicopter, and damaged an Alouette helicopter and a frigate. 'Despite,' as he said, 'receiving information from the opposition that the invasion of South Georgia was part of a UN peace deal!'

Afterwards, Tac HQ and C Company proceeded to the *QE2*'s starboard shell door just above the waterline. *Typhoon* had arrived, but we had to wait as her passengers, the survivors of the frigate *Antelope* sunk in San Carlos Water, embarked onto the liner. Wearing white anti-flash hoods for protection against the cold, they all clutched a black plastic gash bag containing replacement clothes for those lost at sea. As they shuffled past us, one of them broke their silence by muttering, 'Give 'em hell, boys.' Déjà vu from many a war feature film – except there really *was* a war now. *And* it was coming closer.

It took thirty minutes to embark 150 soldiers onto the tug but, another ten minutes later, we were approaching the starboard shell door to the aft of *Norland*. Then we scrambled aboard the 12,988 ton Hull-Rotterdam 'Ro-Ro' ferry to become part of Amphibious Task Group 317.1.2. Ascending the car and lower decks' steep stairs was a wearying test of strength as I was loaded down by my bergen and equipment. Mark Willis and I were to double up in a cabin and, after locating it, I slumped onto one of its two bunks to recover.

Later over a cup of tea in the restaurant, we listened to the crew's tales of being attacked by enemy aircraft in San Carlos Water. 'The place's become known as Bomb Alley!' said one Merchant seaman. 'On our second sortie in there four days ago, *Norland* was lucky not to be hit by bombs that detonated in the water near us. On the top deck 2 Para's B Echelon Rear Party fired 1200 rounds from their GPMGs and SLRs at incoming aircraft. Even their Paymaster drew his 9-mm Browning pistol and hopefully banged away at a Skyhawk. It flew below *Norland*'s bridge. Then there was an explosion which showered the firing party with shrapnel and aircraft wreckage!'

Being on board *Norland* compared with *QE2*, was the difference between night and day. Her spartan accommodation had a homely feel with its permanent blackout created by black plastic bags stuck over portholes and windows. There was a bar in the Officers' Wardroom and by the dartboard hung a blackboard on which had been hastily scribbled an 'HMS' *Norland* score from her previous game. 'They've claimed a Skyhawk *and* a Mirage as well as two seagulls and one whale!' noted Kit.

Besides 2 Para's Rear Party still on board providing their Battalion's resupply, there were other reminders of the previous occupants. In the main foyer outside *Norland*'s only shop was a comprehensive 2 Para picture gallery of the Falklands' countryside and outskirts of Stanley – vital training items we had sorely missed on board *QE2*. There was also a 2 Para caption glued to the bottom of a large travel poster displaying a South American folk dance group. The four lavishly-dressed gentlemen carried an empty wicker basket in one hand and, in the other, held up an orange with the caption mercilessly declaring: 'President Galtieri and his Junta approaching the USSR and trying to trade oranges for dysentery tablets.'

Waiting for the remainder of the Battalion to come on board *Norland* had also provided me with an opportunity to write home as there were a pile of blue virgin aerogrammes on the foyer information desk. 'Last bag of mail's about to go,' a crew member warned, so I scribbled three epistles in rapid succession. 'Perhaps my last chance, ' I thought. It was too, because these reached London on 8 June, compared to one written two days later which did not arrive until 22 June. Hunger now drove me to the crowded restaurant for supper and Mark sat down at my table. *Roti* (orderly) and food were on the agenda.

'Have you sorted out your Gurkha orderly problem yet, Mike?'

'Nope, not at all. I've still managed to fail on that one.'

'Don't worry. It'll be more effective if you share mine when we're on the Falklands. Rifleman Bis Bis is OK and does what he's told with the minimum of fuss.'

'Bis Bis? Never heard of such a Gurkha name before. What part of Nepal is he from?'

'Like most of the others – East Nepal! Don't get misled. Remember what I told you at Church Crookham. The last four numbers of his regimental number are used to address a Gurkha soldier. So Rifleman Rankeshar Gurung has 2020 as his last four, and "Twenty Twenty" translated into Gurkhali is "Bis Bis"! And he can make a good curry and rice from a compo ration pack!'

Others were also talking about their stomachs. With his easygoing but decisive personality, Lester Holley had already made a significant start to his new command. He was also able to equate with his soldiers and, standing in the queue, Lester commented to his Company's British medical orderly, Private Baldwin, 'It's quite plain food, but there's plenty of it. So what do you think Baldwin?'

The squaddie had no doubt about the quality of his pie, beans and chips compared with Cunard's culinary delights. 'Sir,' he said with bastion-like judgement, 'I can assure you *Norland*'s grub is much better than all that fancy rubbish on *QE2*!'

By 18.00 hours cross decking had been completed. We were lucky. The temperature outside was falling and sea state rising. After a drink in the bar, most retired to their cabins. As we slept, our last lap began from South Georgia accompanied by 'The Great White Whale' and auxiliary ship RFA *Stromness*. There was also another silent change because, time-wise, Northwood, Ascension and the Falklands had to be aligned to avoid operational confusion. We were therefore moved onto Greenwich Mean Time or Zulu Time which would mean operating four hours ahead of local time. The practical consequences were that next day's dawn would be at 11.00 hours, and our last meal of the day at 22.00 hours.

It was an uncomfortable night in my rocking bunk, but *Norland*'s method of starting the new day was worthy of an Academy Award nomination. We awoke to music piped over the Tannoy, and London West End musical star, Elaine Paige, singing *Don't Cry for Me Argentina*. A member of the Naval Party 1850, Lieutenant Commander Ian Hughes, was next with the first of his rise and shine messages:

D'ya hear there? *Ram, ram* (hello) 1st/7th Gurkhas, *ram ram*! The ship's company hope that you've slept well and are looking forward to your first morning on this cruise of a lifetime to the wind-beaten Islands of kelp, penguins, sheep, and Argies! We can offer a varied cruise programme for you today.

For the lucky few on top deck we've replaced deck quoits and volleyball with the distinct possibility of practising your shooting skills against the winged machines of Dago Airlines. For the not-so-fortunate below deck, there'll be organised games of defence and muster station drills, which'll be followed tomorrow with assault boat station drills. On offer in the restaurant is plenty more no-nonsense food. But have your sea-sickness tablets on stand-by. The weather forecast promises a stronger north-westerly wind and choppier seas.

We rose from our pits to meet these challenges. 'Whoops!' I gasped at Mark, clutching the edge of my bunk. 'We've started! That's proof there are definitely no stabilizers fitted!' The Roaring Forties lived up to their name as those notorious Cape Horn rollers increased in height and prophesies of those more knowledgeable than myself became true with the South Atlantic taking its toll on Gurkha stomachs. Other unpleasantries were the assumed sub-surface threat and growing air threat as the distance between ourselves and the Falklands diminished. Furthermore at this time of year, these latitudes had eight to nine hours of daylight in every twenty-four – more than enough for enemy aircraft to locate and attack us.

Norland was not fitted with any rapid firing Phalanx guns to engage an inbound AM-39 Exocet or any Protean dispensers to discharge decoying clouds of 'chaff', or any electronic countermeasures. Nevertheless her upper deck was ready. It now bristled with an air defence umbrella of two Blowpipe missile launchers, two Browning heavy machine guns and ten GPMGs mounted on louch poles to facilitate rapid swivelling from one fast moving attacking aircraft onto another. The GPMGs' rate of fire was such that their gunners could put up a barrage of 12,000 rounds per minute if required. In comparison the upper decks of 'The Great White Whale', which was three times the size of *Norland*, boasted forty GPMG positions. With *Stromness* also possessing eighteen, this meant that 5 Brigade had a total of sixty-eight instantly available GPMGs to repel any potential air attack.

Norland's weapons were manned by a Gurkha defence platoon during these daylight hours. These men had plenty of time to get up, eat breakfast and be in position by 11.00 hours, but their watch duties had to be rotated frequently to counter the unpleasant and increasing Roaring Forties wind. Combined with the cold air, this caused an additional chill factor and meant those manning all these weapons had to wear protective eye goggles. When the defence station drill was the first procedure to be rehearsed on board, they remained at their posts while the Navy voice on the Tannoy recommended to all others: 'The safest place for all embarked troops during a red air alert will be on the bottom deck below the waterline!' With that, the exercise started by jangling alarm bells and a more urgent pipe: 'D'ya hear there? For exercise! For exercise! Air raid warning red! Imminent attack! All personnel take cover! Defence stations and damage control parties close up at the rush!'

All machine guns were test-fired and, much to Gurkha consternation, shelter positions taken up below the waterline. But this first red alert dry run revealed an impossible lack of space in the narrow corridors. 'OK then,' decreed the next pipe laconically, ' for the next exercise and also the real thing, everyone instead will lie on their bunk wearing a helmet!'

Nobody informed us at the time that such a position would reduce whiplash from a bomb detonating in the ship. Perhaps it was just as well we did not know, after all I preferred to sleep on my bed rather than use it to avoid the worst effects of an enemy 1000-pounder. But there would be no rest for us maritime-tortured Gurkha soldiery. Muster station drill for evacuation to our lifeboats and fire drill had to be practised, once in the morning and again early in the afternoon. The relevance of these rehearsals had already been underlined on that first day. As I was nearly blown away by the wind in a late afternoon stroll on the top deck and was taking photographs of an exceptionally choppy sea, Steve Crowsley suddenly appeared. Running past en route to his heavy machine guns he glanced at me with some alarm.

'Better get back below!' he panted. 'The tanker *British Wye* has just sent out a mayday call that she's been bombed by an Argie Hercules transport. Apparently the bombs have been kicked out of the back of the aircraft by a Mark One Argie boot. She's only forty miles away, and now there's a yellow air alert!' And with that he ran off to inform his storm-battered Gurkhas manning the guns. Stress contributes to creating fog of war. Steve's information was corrupt, for the support oiler *British Wye* had been attacked several hundred nautical miles further to the north-east and the attacking aircraft had used wing bomb racks. Nonetheless it was proof enough of the air threat which led to another enemy Dagger splashed in San Carlos Water that day.

By now, the Gurkhas were engaged in a different sort of battle inside the ferry which they would be doomed to lose. Gone were those *QE2* days of carefree running on deck and intensive weapon training. 'There're already many empty chairs in the restaurant at lunch – and even more at supper,' observed Mark.

'Yes,' I agreed, adding, 'and prostrate bodies to be found in cabins and other areas of the ship, as well as pools of vomit on every deck!'

The men in blue were also alarmed at the Gurkhas' lack of seamanship and consequent internal state of their boat. So when one of *Norland*'s three Lieutenant Commanders, during a frantic hunt for any available BO, finally buttonholed me, he issued a fierce reminder of the golden rule aboard any Royal Navy ship, 'For Christ's sake, this is too much! Can you *please* remind your men over the pipes that the person who's sick, is the one that also clears it up!' Mark Willis was to become heavily involved in the Gurkhas' attempts to adjust to life on the ocean wave. I was also getting to know him better. A sensible, intelligent and proactive Adjutant who would turn down a place at Staff College to retire from the Army a couple of years later, his latest challenge was the taking on charge from the 2 Para party of seven Argentine prisoners of war who had been captured on the Fanning Head cliffs above San Carlos. This entailed providing a Gurkha guard and ensuring these POW's well-being.

'There's only one who can be described as a tough case, all the others are simply frightened teenagers. But, boy, do they all smell!' complained Mark. Despite his daily visits and insistence that Gurkha-provided soap, water and cleaning tools be used, the prisoners' strong body odour was to remain undiluted. If this was bad, conditions three weeks later, when 2,047 POWs were stuffed on board *Norland* about to depart Stanley on a repatriation voyage to Puerto Madryn in Argentina, can only be imagined.

In a side office the 18.00 hours Battalion O Group was gathering and I picked up a typed document lying on the table. Signed by 2 Para's CO, Lieutenant Colonel 'H' Jones, its detail revealed this to be a copy of his complicated landing orders for the San Carlos Amphibious Operating Area. Our meeting began. Planning the following evening's assault station drill rehearsal for the Battalion's landing had priority, but portly Lieutenant Commander Hughes suddenly poked his head around the door to say, 'Sorry to disturb you folks, but I thought you'd be interested to hear the good news. 2 Para has captured Goose Green and 1400 prisoners. The bad news is that their CO, "H" Jones, has been blown away.'

The victory wiped all the red hieroglyphics surrounding Goose Green off Paddy's map. But the fate of 'H' caused the Commandant's face to blanch. He had been well acquainted with this later recipient of a posthumous Victoria Cross. 'Christ!' arrived my sudden appalling thought, 'And *I'm* the Gurkha officer who's witnessed our Commandant's signature on *his* Last Will and Testament!'

After the O Group, I wandered along the corridor leading to the Officers' Wardroom and its snug bar as *Lillibulero* was piped over the Tannoy. Swaying and listening on this Argentine National Army Day to the BBC World Service News reporting the details of the Battle of Darwin and Goose Green, where several other 2 Para officers had also died, and being told by the news reader that 'The Great White Whale' and *Norland* were now sailing towards San Carlos became a surreal experience. My thoughts, as usual, spun in all directions. 'So would we be involved in something similar

123

to the Paras?' I worried. 'If so, when and where would it take place? And what would it be like?' There were, of course, no answers. Just waiting, as usual, and continuing yet more intensive pondering on an exceptionally uncertain future.

The bar was the venue where a favourite, but morbid, conversation topic on *QE2* for the younger Gurkha BOs had been fanned into life again on board *Norland*. The need to verbalize a stiffening of their mental preparedness for the challenges ahead, after the latest BBC news, had become essential. One subaltern was in full flow as I entered the beer and cigarette-smoke tainted atmosphere, further enhanced by the stuffiness resulting from the black plastic bag-draped portholes.

'So what d'you think the chances are of promotion on the battlefield by taking over a sub-unit of a superior officer who got unlucky by being wasted in a firefight?' he was fantasizing.

His conversation partner replied, 'Well, I know it's a case of dead men's shoes, but perhaps the eventuality of us becoming company commanders now doesn't seem to be so far-fetched as on *QE2*, once we get our feet onto dry land!'

Fed up with listening to further power aspirations of these two youthful Napoleons, I retired early to my cramped bunk and unpleasant dreams of another North Sea ferry and my crossing to Oslo at Christmas 1967 with the jovial Simon Garthwaite, a Sandhurst officer cadet friend.

Our cabin became an evil-smelling refuge as, for thirty-six hours, we suffered an awful bout of seasickness. There was also a visit to his parent's Sussex home where he went hunting and, much to Tove's disgust, shot a squirrel, skinned it and fed it to his dog. Then Simon, an Irish Ranger who became an SAS captain, took life to extremes by going to war in the Oman – where he was killed attempting to rescue a soldier wounded from enemy fire. I cried when father, after reading a *Daily Telegraph* article about the ambush, rang to tell me. Simon would have enjoyed the Falklands, as would my fellow 2LI D Company subaltern. After Londonderry and another emergency tour in West Belfast, Nigel Loring became a Sultan's Armed Forces contract officer in the Oman War. But in January 1975, less than a year after Simon's death, Nigel's Company was also ambushed and he became the first of thirteen to die.

Elgar's *Pomp and Circumstance* belting out of the Tannoy woke me next morning, 30 May, and the nauseatingly cheerful Lieutenant Commander Hughes seemed optimistic there would be a land of hope and glory with his announcement: 'D'ya hear there? *Ram, ram* 1st/7th Gurkhas, *ram, ram*! Here's the weather forecast! There's now a high pressure over Goose Green, and the outlook is good . . .' It did not alleviate the gloom for us on *Norland*. Hope and glory would be replaced by the day's intake of Stugeron seasickness pills, which had little of the desired effect. Winds developed into a Gale Force Ten. Dark-green waves crashed over *Norland*'s twenty-three metre high bridge as she dawdled along at a speed reduced by a third to eleven knots. A fortnight before in these latitudes 'The Great White Whale' had only experienced Storm Force Seven twice. I wrote to Tove:

> About 400 nautical miles off the Falklands now. The seas are pretty rough, and all the Gurkhas on board are puking like crazy. Vomit everywhere! I can under-
> stand it when they said that the Gurkha is a bad traveller by sea. Amazingly

enough I am personally not affected by the sea swell. Don't know why, but it must be because I found my sea legs already aboard the *QE2*.

Together with the RSM, Mark's next challenge was to embark on his self-proclaimed 'worst job of the campaign' – a regular seasickness patrol checking the ship's cleanliness or, rather, lack of it. Rifleman Baliprasad Rai provided a description of this never-ending nightmare which had changed his attitude towards life on the high seas:

> . . . never once while on the QE2 did I have to resort to the sea sickness pills we were issued in abundance. This happy state of my health was soon to change however when . . . (dressed) in our full compliment of Arctic gear, we swayed, shook and rolled towards, as we were told, East Falkland. It was only about 800 miles away but to me it seemed to be 8,000 miles as my stomach remained in a constant state of turmoil and no amount of sea sick tablets could settle it. Oh, I am not so very lucky this time, I thought, as I fervently prayed for dry land. All around me I could see the same scenes, people huddled . . . straining to gain some semblance of balance as we were bounced and buffeted like rag dolls. I would have willingly sat through hours of Argentine torture than go through another minute of this ordeal![4]

The oh-so-ill Gurkhas were assaulting the communal washrooms, but failed to launch their attacks into the proscribed target areas. *Norland*'s Senior Naval Officer, Commander Chris Esplin-Jones, had introduced a system of water rationing on board where, during the day, water was unavailable in two periods totalling six hours, with another period of three and a half hours late at night. This made a bad situation absolutely horrendous and resulted in the RSM's ever strident: '*Sunnuhos*! (Pay attention!)' pipes on the Tannoy, followed by severe Gurkhali exhortations to fatigue parties requiring them to generate more effort in the battle against the evil smell. Other memorable pleas by One-Ton included this polite reminder: '*Tapain haru wakchha bhane mukdhune bombama nawaknu. Tatti gherma waknu hos. Dhanyabad!*' (You who are vomiting please don't vomit in the washbasins. Please go in the toilet and vomit. Thank you!)

During all this, the fastidious Adjutant continued with his daily visits to the POWs, and received one benefit from this irksome chore. 'You should see them, Mike. My morale's lifted sky-high whenever I clap eyes on them!' Mark exclaimed after wading back through shoals of seasick Gurkhas from his visit, thoughts uppermost of forthcoming combat against his prisoners' colleagues. But I never took advantage of his invitation. Perhaps reading might have helped. A relevant book could have been *South* written by the Antarctic explorer Ernest Shackleton, and his description of these waters sixty-six years before in one of the most harrowing survival stories of all time.

Meanwhile enemy air activity continued in this gale-torn voyage towards San Carlos. Just after 17.30 hours, a final air-launched Exocet attack of the war intended for HMS *Invincible*, but mistakenly targeted on the frigate HMS *Avenger*, proved unsuccessful as was a follow-up bombing run from four enemy Skyhawks which resulted in two crashing. The attack took place approximately 200 nautical miles south-west of

Norland's location. A deceptively safe distance as it was equivalent to a Super Etendard flight time of only twenty minutes. But now, thirty-six hours away from embarking into landing craft bound for Blue Beach at San Carlos, there was still no other information on our immediate Falklands' task.

'So much for all that helicopter assault training on WELSH FALCON and *QE2*,' I commented to Mark.

More muster station and defence station drills also provided a reminder of the assumed sub-surface threat. One enemy submarine had already been captured at Grytviken last month. But the question, 'Was there another?' remained unanswered. We were able therefore to sample in miniature the practical effect of that Second World War Norwegian Merchant sailors' assertion, '. . . the worst torpedo is the one that doesn't arrive'. Also added to that evening's programme was the assault station drill rehearsal for moving 662 Gurkha and British soldiers, less those too sick to participate, from their cabins down to the bottom car deck.

Without equipment they assembled in the rear cafeteria, then companies moved off in the correct order of battle – A, Tac HQ, B, C, D, HQ with Support Company detachments absorbed into the rifle companies – to take the route down to the car deck. Once there we shuffled along in the semi-darkness. Placed along the deck, a line of lanterns provided a ghostly glow of red light to preserve our night vision. This illumination handrail ended at the ferry's rear ramp where, at San Carlos, two landing craft would be waiting to take aboard the Gurkhas and commence their shuttle trips to the shore. But the time taken to complete this rehearsal had been too slow, and everything would have to be repeated again the following evening with full kit.

These preparations meant spare moments for relaxation were rare. But one had now arrived. It was late evening. 'A beer might be welcome,' I decided. However on entering a relatively empty bar, I found a concentrated RSO amid a mound of paperwork grappling with his private writing war. Our subsequent conversation revealed Kit's acute need for a Battalion Signals portable computer system. It had been a major disadvantage for him that military information technology *anno* 1982 was a relatively primitive affair.

'What's that you've got there Kit?'

'I'm making out the Battalion CEI from the Brigade document.'

'The . . . what?'

'It's the Battalion's "Communication Electronic Instructions" for all our radio operators which includes all the necessary codes, and is applicable for the first five days of our operations on the bloody Islands!'

'But that's a phenomenal amount of paperwork to be distributed to them. Why's that?'

I recalled Mike Forge's *QE2* signals security briefing as the harassed Kit replied wearily, 'Because a new set of coded call-signs and codewords will be required not just daily, but every twelve hours once we set foot on the Falklands!'

Little surprise, then, that Kit was working in the bar. It was assessed a Battalion would require 3,000 sheets of paper for this data since signallers at all levels – company, platoon, and section – had to copy out the information in laborious longhand every fifth day. This self-imposed peacetime bureaucracy would be a nightmare in a battlefield environment, and unworkable if the CEI became compromised. 'But we do have a secret weapon,' I half-joked to myself, 'because in the event of such a situation, and unlike any British unit on the Falklands, at least our Battalion has its reserve code of Gurkhali which no enemy would ever crack in a month of Sundays!'

Also present relaxing with a quiet beer were a few 16 Field Ambulance officers, including their dark-haired 2IC, Major Roger Nutbeem. He was a pleasant officer but, like Mike Forge, an unlucky one because his next voyage in ten days would also be his last – aboard the good ship RFA *Sir Galahad.*

That same night at home, Tove wrote about how the pressures were also affecting her. Not normally someone to complain, she had begun to develop breathing problems. They were purely psychosomatic, but a visit to the doctor resulted in a prescription for an inhaler:

> The 'box' is full of the Pope's visit and he too makes me cry. The man really has a magic something – in spite of all he represents – and I find myself wishing to pray for peace with him. There's been enough bloodshed on both sides now – it's all too terrible for words and turning into a nightmare. I sometimes don't go to sleep until the small hours just thinking about you being involved in all that awfulness.

I retired after downing a single can of Budweiser. My head seemed to have hardly touched the pillow of my bunk, when life's realities were put on temporary hold with the gradual onset of more restless sleep.

Next morning I awoke to a Beatles' tune being piped throughout the ship. Though the awful gale around us continued, turning a two-day voyage into one of more than three, Lieutenant Commander Hughes had chosen George Harrison's inapplicable composition *Here Comes the Sun.* George was followed by the inevitable Lieutenant Commander disc jockey's salutation: 'D'ya hear there? *Ram, ram* 1st/7th Gurkhas, *ram, ram . . .*'

His update provided his hapless passengers with more information on the extended cruise itinerary, '. . . *Norland* will shortly arrive at the "trala" situated east of the Falklands. Here we'll marry up with our Naval Grey Messenger of Death which will then escort us on our final approach into "Bomb Alley".'

The messenger frigate might be needed because the enemy had switched to bombing San Carlos by night and, earlier that morning, a quartet of enemy Canberra bombers had carried out one such raid 200 nautical miles away. The Royal Navy acronym TRALA had been born a few days before out of LOLA – the 'loitering and logistics area' – located at the far end of the 170 nautical miles of seaway leading into San Carlos Water. Pronounced 'trah-lah' as if it were the opening two bars of a sea shanty, the TRALA's translation was 'Tug, Replenishment, and Logistics Area' – home for damaged warships, merchantmen and other shipping not required inshore, and a forming-up area for the likes of us Gurkhas aboard inbound convoys.

'However with ninety-two ships in the Task Force, could some of these vessels actually be visible now in the TRALA?' I wondered with growing curiosity.

So after having tucked into a plate of *bhat* for breakfast and writing a letter home,

127

the Training Officer sahib ventured up on deck once more. 'Perhaps, also, *Invincible* could be around here somewhere with a few Harriers taking off and landing!' my hopes continued as, Nelson-like, I peered through my small army binoculars at an angry green sea for the first of several attempts during that day to witness such a phenomenon. The carrier was, after all, affiliated to The Light Infantry. All the same, disappointment prevailed. The TRALA's vastness meant that the only floating objects in our vicinity were a few icebergs. So there was a temptation to hum 'trah-lah, trah-lah' in frustration as I walked up and down *Norland*'s deck trying to spot an otherwise invisible British Armada. 'No wonder the Royal Navy's known as "the Silent Service"!' was my final thought on the matter, once safely below deck.

We were, however, quite close to the Carrier Battle Group and forming up into our convoy for the passage to San Carlos. This comprised *Baltic Ferry*, aircraft transport container ship *Atlantic Causeway* and fleet oiler RFA *Blue Rover*. 'The Great White Whale' and *Stromness* would not sail for San Carlos until the following day, but *Norland* would be the first to run the gauntlet of 'Bomb Alley' because she had been earmarked to start embarking POWs from Goose Green. The other ships of our convoy sailed in the late afternoon, but *Norland*'s departure would be delayed for several hours because a Royal Marine and sailor contingent of *Hermes*' 'Blue Beret Platoon' had to be embarked by helicopter to take over the guarding of Mark's POWs. The new guards were appreciative of *Norland* and one later wrote,'We quickly settled into our quite luxurious cabins and found the routines and food very much to our liking.'[5] This was more a comment on their spartan lifestyle aboard the carrier. Conditions would soon become more cramped. During the next fortnight another 1,009 *chicos de la guerra*, half of them from the battle at Darwin and Goose Green, would join the original seven before *Norland*'s departure on 12 June to deliver them all to the Uruguayan port of Montevideo.

It was our final evening on board. That day there had been little activity because of the Gurkhas' seasickness. Not even the lure of *bhat* could tempt them to the restaurant and, if they managed to struggle out of their cabins, many were unable to get back unassisted. The extent of the problem was exemplified by A Company which had thirty soldiers affected. Two were so ill they had been attached to saline drips in their bunks. The assault stations' drill dress rehearsal remained but, prior to this, the Commandant held his own pre-battle speech to the Battalion, paraded by the RSM in the rear cafeteria. From the outset, standing on a chair to let the final message be heard clearly, he held his audience in the palm of his hand and, unlike British soldiers, they responded interactively to this military evangelism several times with cries of, 'Ao, sahib! Sahib! Ao, sahib!'

'Bless my soul, was not this scene reminiscent of the film *Zulu*,' I thought, 'and the Battle of Rorke's Drift 103 years ago when eleven Victoria Crosses had been won?' And mentioning the word 'medal', as I had already observed, would make the eyes of a Gurkha glint. Such a prize after a conspicuous act of heroism on the battlefield was for him the only concrete proof of his bravery. His *gora sahibharu*, the BOs, were the only ones meant to be courageous. A subtle difference. But the mysteries of the Commandant's Gurkhali speech were also being liberally peppered with the sinister word *dushman*. It was yet another turning point in my Falklands' adventure since, as from now on, I would become accustomed to hearing *dushman* used frequently by the Gurkhas or, as their BOs preferred to say, the *dush* (pronounced as in bush and not hush). Yet my frustration remained in neither understanding what this meant, nor the Commandant's general urgings to his Gurkhas. Mark noticed the problem, so he drew closer to whisper, '*Dushman* means the enemy, Mike. And the boss is wishing the *keta* good hunting in their forthcoming operations against the *dush!*'

Shortly after Mark's simple explanation, the Commandant's triumphant, '*Jai Seventh!*' ended his ten-minute oration and Gurkha *josh* (enthusiasm) burst again into life with a sustained ovation for their *gora* sahib. The characteristics between a Gurkha and British Battalion were becoming, for me, even more dissimilar. Once again, British soldiers would not have responded in such a manner, but then the Brigade of Gurkhas' straightforward motto of *Kaphar hunu bhanda marnu ramro* (It is better to die than be a coward), is well in keeping with the uncomplicated thoughts of a Gurkha soldier. Mix in *josh*, as I would later learn, and such a combination becomes irrepressible.

The assault stations drill dress rehearsal completed our landing preparations. At San Carlos, still 170 nautical miles distant, there was a red air alert. *Norland* began the last leg of her journey from the TRALA later that night escorted into the TEZ by HMS *Active*. She would hand over her duties to another frigate, HMS *Penelope*, once north of East Falkland. Most officers gathered in the wardroom to enjoy an appropriate appetizer for the following morning's work – the video film *Chariots of Fire*. Afterwards the B video film was, indeed, a frightfully boring video of anatomical art between man and woman. We remained together and watched, mesmerized by the artistes' gymnastics on the big screen.

Nonetheless it did contrive after a while to make me miss my wife – and I became sad with the pessimistic thought that this might be the absolute final visual reminder in my life of the matrimonial bed's safety and mutual warmth. But such intimate comforts would now be only reserved for the protected. Whatever awaited us, that bizarrely uncomfortable cocktail of celluloid patriotism and sex that evening was a final prologue to the next fortnight when familiar norms in everyday life would no longer be valid. Afterwards everyone retired to a twitching sleep. Time horizons had contracted even more, and a successful disembarkation of *Norland* without casualties was the only current aim. All else was irrelevant. Blue Beach at San Carlos had been again confirmed as our landing area but, with *Norland* moving towards 'Bomb Alley' for the third time, nobody knew what to expect. At least the seasickness would end soon, although the two Gurkhas anchored to their drips remained so ill they would be left on board.

But the worrying fact also remained that, so far, there had been about 140 *dush* air strikes into the anchorage of San Carlos Water – and tomorrow morning might well bring more.

PART III – IN-THEATRE

Chapter Eleven

WARNING ORDER, COUNTER-ORDER, DISORDER

Disembarkation was completed before dawn. While it was still too dark for artillery observation by the enemy, the Battalion assembled in a covered position behind the line held by the 29th Brigade of which it now formed part . . . But during the day . . . the Turks from their position on higher ground, were able to overlook and command with fire the whole of our areas, even the sea beaches. By daylight no ship could approach the shore without coming under heavy artillery fire. On land no movement could be made that was not in full view of the Turks. At Anzac the beaches were actually under the enemy's rifle fire. – From an account of the 1st/4th Prince of Wales' Own Gurkha Rifles' landfall at Anzac Beach in September 1915, five months after the Gallipoli Expeditionary Force's main landings.[1]

'So Les, you're deserting us at last to join your red-bereted friends! What's wrong? Aren't we bloodthirsty enough for you?'

Captain Les Peacock, the pencil-thin running fanatic ex-RSM of 3 Para had been the butt of many such typically good-natured remarks from his fellow 1st/7th Gurkha Rifles' BOs on board *QE2* after being appointed the Gurkha representative in the Brigade Advance Party. Early on 29 May he had cross decked again by Wessex helicopter from *Antrim* to *Fearless* 300 nautical miles east of the Falklands to become, next day, the first Gurkha to land on the Islands. His former Battalion, 3 Para, had already left Port San Carlos three days before. With a 'yomping' 45 Commando they were on a tactical advance to battle or 'tab' (tactical advance to battle) towards the other side of East Falkland, so Les had no chance to swap war stories. Instead, the No. 2 Quartermaster became heavily involved in preparing for the Gurkhas' reception at Blue Beach 2, San Carlos.

5 Brigade's plan was to land the Welsh and Scots Guards first from 'The Great White Whale' followed by the Gurkhas from *Norland*. Our mission was to relieve 40 Commando guarding the Force Maintenance Area at San Carlos, originally an early nineteenth-century penal settlement whose Spanish place name had been given by the Gauchos of the River Plate area. Sleeping on *Fearless* by night and working on shore by day, Les had reconnoitered all the Marine Commando positions that the Battalion would occupy. However his plans were to founder thirty-six hours before *Norland*

dropped anchor. 5 Brigade had now been ordered to advance on a southerly axis to Stanley with 2 Para and 29 Field Battery under command, and our ferry would arrive first so that some of the many POWs could be embarked onto her. One Gurkha Company was to relieve B Company, 40 Commando on the 270-metre high Sussex Mountains, while most of the Battalion would fly to Goose Green and relieve 2 Para. The remainder of the Brigade would land at San Carlos the next day, dig in, and eventually follow up.

This revised plan was the first 'embuggeration' of many to hound the Battalion throughout the land campaign's next fourteen days. Les was horrified at the news. His own plans needed revising rapidly. A glass of *tato pani* from the Welsh Guards 2IC made a good start and, by dint of working all day and evening, Les completed his preparations. Ninety minutes were then spent locating a boatman to ferry him at first light from *Fearless* to the San Carlos jetty. There he would meet and brief the Battalion before guiding them to their assembly area. Satisfied, he had returned to his cabin for a doze.

Some time later at 06.30 hours *Norland*, escorted by *Penelope*, was sailing down the Falkland Sound towards the two-kilometre wide entrance to Bomb Alley. Up to 27 May, the latter had been known as the AOA. 5 Brigade's impending arrival meant this 'Amphibious Operations Area' had to be converted with effect from midnight to a less glamorous 'Transport Area' because, except for our landing craft crew, there would be no Marine Commando involvement in our administrative TA landing. On board, a cacophony of bagpipe music blared out of the Tannoy. Anxiety had prevented sleep, but *Scotland the Brave* was a fitting touch to the end of our maritime adventure and prelude to Lieutenant Commander Hughes' final message:

D'ya hear there? *Ram, ram* 1st/7th Gurkhas, *ram, ram*! Wakey! Wakey! We're now some way along the Falkland Sound. The Navy's Grey Messengers of Death continue to steam nearby as we make our run into San Carlos Water. Thanks to calmer seas we're a little earlier than anticipated and hope to begin our disembarkation at 09.15 hours.

The weather outlook locally is promising, even though there's a continuing low depression over Buenos Aires. The high pressure over Goose Green will quickly spread to Stanley and soon you'll be enjoying a much-needed Falklands holiday. This does not, of course, prevent air defence personnel closing up to their defence stations at 08.00 hours. On behalf of the crew, may I take this opportunity to say we hope your South Atlantic cruise has been an invigorating experience and whetted your appetite for more. We wish you all a sunny time ahead, and look forward to having you on board with us again soon.

In the neighbouring cabin Mike Kefford's guffaw signalled appreciation of this black humour. Our Naval informant had forgotten to add that the day was also the 188th anniversary of a naval battle known as 'The Glorious First of June' when the British Admiral Earl 'Black Dick, the sailor's friend' Howe had crushed the French fleet by destroying seven of its ships and dismasting ten others in the Bay of Biscay. With these historical omens on our side, the bagpipes increased in volume and I climbed out of my bunk to shave. This was also Day One of the austral winter. I eased into my virgin thermal underwear and familiar combat kit, as Mark put on a sensible lightweight smock made out of parachute silk before donning his outer combat jacket. Perhaps we should have clad ourselves in something more imposing as the 3 Commando Brigade HQ had been talking about two things the *dush* feared most – Gurkhas and chemical warfare. Apparently one plan discussed was to send us 'ashore amidst lots of publicity and wearing NBCD (Nuclear, Biological, and Chemical Defence) suits.'[2]

The engines slowed to a barely discernable vibration. *Norland* passed through the entrance of San Carlos Water and turned southwards into its long landlocked corridor. Once past Ajax Bay to starboard, she dropped anchor opposite Blue Beach 1 where 40 Commando had landed eleven days previously. I hurried to breakfast of bacon and eggs, washed down by a cup of hot tea; the traditional British Army final meal before action. A sensible start to a busy day but, on the way back to my cabin to complete bergen packing, alarm bells rang. It was 08.00 hours. Minus humour, the Tannoy also burst into life: 'D'ya hear there? Air raid warning red! Air defence personnel and damage control personnel close up at the rush! Air defence personnel man defence stations! All other personnel not on duty, move to your cabins! Lie on your bunks and put on your helmets!'

Maybe: '. . . and wait for your salvation!' would have completed the ending. I rushed into the cabin and found my helmet. Mark came in to look for his. We lay on our bunks. This procedure had been practised several times before, but a live event was different. 'Should I brace my body for the impact?' I mused stoically. 'But from what and where?'

My heart thumped loudly. Two minutes passed. Nothing. Five minutes. Still nothing. The situation began to be ridiculous. 'Enjoying your lie-in with our first red air alert, Mike?' I enquired. Priority must be disembarkation from our vulnerable ship. More minutes ticked by. This imposed Egyptian PT was an irritation and the next pipe more than welcome: 'D'ya hear there? The red air alert is still in force and all defence personnel are to remain at their stations. All other personnel, however, stand down and continue landing preparations.'

Dush Canberra bombers again had been trying to penetrate the air space over San Carlos, but were chased away by a Harrier closing to within four miles of these bandits. Red air alert or not, at 08.30 hours the final move began to our assault boat stations in the rear cafeteria. Draping webbing, helmet, pistol, battle map and bergen around my body, I made my way down the ship into the dimly-lit room already full of Gurkhas. A heavy air of anticipation for land hung over them. Disembarkation began with Rory Stewart's order on the Tannoy: 'Assault boat stations. A Company and Tac HQ move now!'

A Gurkha Signaller then approached me. 'Training Officer, sahib! This has arrived from Brigade HQ!' He thrust a piece of paper into my hand. 'Shit! What the hell's this?' I swore through my teeth.

Accustomed already to little or no information and many rapid changes in plan, I looked at Mark who seemed equally suspicious. Eyes down, and the signal's contents were scanned. It should have been sent at least twenty-four hours before and contained all the necessary planning information for our landing operation that had already begun. The temptation to stuff it into a pocket was stopped by Mark who said, 'You'd better show it to the boss, Mike.' I moved across to the Commandant with the anti-quated epistle. 'Colonel, better late than never. Here's our warning order for deploying the Battalion into the San Carlos bridgehead!'

He grabbed it, read and snapped, 'Make sure this one goes into the Battalion scrap-book, will you? I've just received a message as well! The Brigade Commander's coming out here by boat to give me a revised set of orders and I've got to remain on board to meet him. So just carry on the disembarkation without me.'

'Tac HQ move now!' Rory's insistent pipe cued the thirty-eight man Tac HQ less Commandant to disappear through the swing doors and rear stairway, followed by B Company, while on *Fearless* the plans of Les had been wrecked again. Just before first light and through the labyrinth of corridors, he had made his way onto the top deck in order to relocate his boatman. But a shadow materialized in front of him. It was the Brigade Commander. He had seized the No. 2 Quartermaster's landing craft in order to rendezvous with *Norland* and personally give the Commandant his revised orders. So Les had no alternative but to accompany his hijacker.

Back on *Norland* Tac HQ lumbered awkwardly down the steep internal stairs. 'My punishment for packing too much,' I cursed before logic returned. But although my bergen and equipment was a dead-weight, it did take my mind off the red alert and any possible *dush* air strike.

The car deck was reached in the ferry's bowels without mishap. Ahead stretched a long line of Gurkhas bathed in a subdued red glow from the lanterns. At the far end was blackness towards which we silently moved. The ferry no longer swayed. Thoughts strayed towards my family and home. It was an hour before dawn. Nearer the lowered ramp I peered into the blackness and made out the outline of a hill crest against the starry heavens. A shout broke into my thoughts. 'Come on! Get in and push on down!'

Below was the seventy-five ton Landing Craft Utility designed to take either 100 tons of cargo, two main battle tanks or 140 men. We were going for the latter option – plus an overload of sixty. Standing room only. I stepped awkwardly into the LCU and onto its tank deck. My heavy bergen made such a manoeuvre doubly difficult. The other 199 Gurkhas and attached British troops packed more tightly around me as though we were in a super king-size carton of cigarettes. The darkness diluted feelings of vulner-abilty, but did not alleviate the pain that cut into my shoulders from the bergen's straps.

'Push on down! Get a move on!' The Marine Commando skipper above me had become more irritated. He was not going to hang around. There was an air threat. 'Come on! Hurry up!' he roared. 'I wanna put to sea ASP, and get well away from this ship!'

A Gurkha in front of me shuffled forward a few more feet. I moved into the gap he had vacated. Others climbed down on board as we continued to press further along the twenty-five by six metre deck. Getting into a rush hour train on the London Underground was easier. We inched forward and more space was made for those behind. This loading procedure lasted another half-hour until the final man pushed himself on board. With no more room the skipper was satisfied, ropes cast off and slowly the LCU with its 200 tightly packed soldier cargo slid away from *Norland*. The next moved alongside the ferry which began disembarking her second batch of Gurkhas with Rifleman Baliprasad Rai among them:

136

I don't know after how long my prayers were answered but they finally were. We climbed off *Norland* with shaky feet into smaller craft called assault ships . . . (to) disembark at the British bridgehead . . . (and) gratefully set foot on terra firma again.[3]

It was still dark. Just. I looked around. 'So where *are* the *dush* aircraft?' I wondered. 'This is a golden opportunity to strike.'

The first smudges of dawn appeared to throw the crest lines of hills around the bay into greater relief as we slipped past a line of anchored ships and into mid-stream. Our destination was Blue Beach 2 – the same as 2 Para who had completed their landing by 07.30 hours; in the dark. It was now 10.00 hours and the breaking of dawn threatened more. Still no hostile aircraft. This 'Transport Area' was definitely a euphemism for an 'Amphibious Operating Area' when, as part of this 'administrative landing', we had to to wait silently for the next forty minutes as the craft chugged on. Her top speed of nine knots was unobtainable because of the overload, neither could the bergen load be relieved. Unable to sit or turn, one could only bend forward to spread weight more evenly across the back. It was an eternal lose-lose situation because even this new stance quickly became uncomfortable. The only advantage was psychological as physical effort conquered fear.

We neared the dark headland of Little Rincon. Behind lay Bonners Bay, Blue Beach 2 and the settlement of San Carlos. Jubilation would be an understatement to describe dry land. Our MTO and Battalion's expert in Egyptian PT, David Wright, must have already arrived from the *Baltic Ferry*, judging by the description of a '. . . young Gurkha officer, straight from Eton and Sandhurst by his accent . . .' in a later light-hearted account of the Falklands' War. The following Gurkha anecdote from it might have been likely, knowing David:

'How do you reckon your lot will get on here in the freezing deep south?' inquired a friendly Marine officer . . .

'Might have a bit of trouble if comes to a bayonet charge,' said the Gurkha officer. 'They're not awfully good at that.'

. . . beaming with pride, (he) explained. 'You see . . . once they've set off, bayonets fixed and all that, you can't stop them. There's absolutely no point in yelling "right wheel" or "halt" or anything. They just keep on going, destroying anything in their way. Bloody good, actually, but as you can see, it does have its drawbacks.'

As he was speaking, the first LCU drew up by the jetty at San Carlos. Inside were rows of little Nepalese men, eyes sparkling.

'Jesus,' said the Marine. ' I see what you mean.'[4]

It was 10.45 hours. One by one, men climbed out. Five minutes later, my turn came. Bent double by my bergen, I heaved myself onto the jetty's rickety planks. Twenty consecutive maritime days of liner, tug, ferry and landing craft gave an involuntary sway to my gait. Following the line of shadowy figures towards wooden buildings at the end of the jetty, I was unaware there lay, in its crater, an unexploded *dush* bomb on the beach a short distance away. Suddenly a voice called out, 'Ops Officer?' 'This is not Les!' I thought. Another revised plan was imminent.

In the dark grey of an embryonic East Falkland's dawn a dark blue beret and cap badge of my past materialized. An RCT Movements officer stood in front of the San Carlos wool store building. His task symbolized why my career in that Corps did not last long as he gave me a sheet of paper saying, 'Here, this is for you. A revised grid reference for your Battalion's assembly area. Just continue along this track and you'll arrive at it.'

I left the RCT messenger boy because, with Paddy Redding leading, Tac HQ were already moving up the muddy track past some nissen huts. The climate was mild and thermal underwear a mistake. Daylight made its unwelcome arrival as the other Gurkha companies began their embarkation from *Norland* into the returned LCUs. We stopped to allow A Company to move through, then continued southwards parallel to San Carlos Water that lay to the west. A wall of hills surrounded us with, on their tops, a protective umbrella of twelve air defence Rapier missile sites; a comforting thought in our exposed position. Across the bay stood a small red-roofed building, accurately named Head of Bay House. Near its garden was positioned a 105-mm Light Gun of 29 Field Battery. Further south lay the Sussex Mountains on which 2 Para had been replaced by the 40 Commando Company. Now on the Falklands more than two hours, our frequent stops and starts, tussocky grass braking our progress once away from San Carlos settlement and constant battles against heavy bergens and other kit, meant only three kilometres had been put between us and landing at the jetty. Ahead of us lay our grassy plain assembly area remarkable for its Sennybridge resemblance.

After another thirty minutes' tab, I positioned Tac HQ in a small gully. Not waiting for further orders, we quickly dug shell scrapes deep enough to accommodate a prone body. Transported from *Norland* in broad daylight, the rest of the Battalion were already moving up and soon a Gurkha army of gardeners began landscaping the nearby countryside effectively. They were back in their natural element of the khuds, well away from the South Atlantic's incapacitating moods. My Signaller, Corporal Chris Aslett, had established communications on the Brigade net. Mark was on the Battalion command net exercising his Gurkhali expertise. Things seemed to be going well. Brandishing his silver-topped walking stick, the Commandant approached us sixty minutes later at 14.00 hours. He had received his orders from the Brigade Commander and was impatient and irritated. He issued more orders counter to those given on *Norland*. 'Get the Company Commanders in here so I can hold a quick O Group,' he shouted at me. 'We've got an new plan! And Tac HQ! What the hell are you lot doing? Move your shell scrapes further apart! It looks like the final five minutes of Custer's last stand the way you're so closely grouped together!' The silver-topped Excalibur described a violent arc towards the hillsides ringing the south-eastern reaches of San Carlos Water. 'One of the main flight paths used by *dush* aircraft in the last few days has been from over *there*! If they attack now, they'll fly right over us. There's no cover here. We're highly exposed! So move apart and get digging again!'

He was right. There was a high cloud base, fine weather, excellent visibility and, unknown to us, 'air attack probable'[5] had been judged by the Commander of the Amphibious Task Group, Commodore Michael Clapp. Tomorrow, though, would be a different story as fog would bless the arrival of 'The Great White Whale' and her Guardsmen cargo. Whilst still digesting the implications of constructing further earthworks and a new Battalion plan, I listened to the strained voice in my radio handset from Force HQ on *Fearless* and its short but meaningful message: 'Hello all stations, this is zero. Air Raid Warning State Red! Over.'

The first of many I would receive during the next fortnight, this red air alert might delay the Commandant's orders, but would provide better motivation for planning future Tac HQ defensive layouts. That this was happening on land and not in *Norland*'s claustrophobic confines, provided little consolation. 'Roger, Out!' I acknowledged and Mark repeated the message over the Battalion's command net. Everyone took what limited cover was available in our hastily dug shell scrapes. Flat on my belly for ten minutes, I sampled the aroma of East Falkland's peat and swung anxious eyes southwards. No longer being in personal charge of one's fate was unhealthy.

At last the *Fearless* watchkeeper's voice declared: 'Air Raid Warning State Yellow.' Stand-down and anti-climax. 'Second false alarm of the day,' I muttered, getting to my feet. On the contrary, a *dush* Hercules transport aircraft on its return run to Rio Gallegos from Stanley had popped up above the radar horizon to make an unauthorized and unwise radar sweep. The frigate, HMS *Minerva*, had spotted the intruder and a Sidewinder missile fired from a Sea Harrier had splashed the 'Herkey bird' into the sea some seventy to eighty kilometres north-west of our location.

The Company Commanders arrived at Tac HQ and the Commandant started his O Group. It did not last long. 'OK gentlemen,' he said in a voice hoping for a smoother future, 'the plan has changed yet again. Brigade's ditched the idea of a Battalion defensive position around the San Carlos Force Maintenance Area. D Company will now take over from the Commando Company dug in on the Sussex Mountains, while we'll have a more exciting helicopter trip southwards to the Goose Green air strip. Only one helicopter's available. Of the four Chinooks on board the *Atlantic Conveyor*, it's the only one that didn't go down with the ship after the Exocet hit her. So get organized into "sticks" for the flight!'

Mike Kefford's Company with a mortar section of two 'tubes' left shortly afterwards to make the laborious six kilometre tab over bog and thick tufts of grass before climbing the Sussex Mountains. 2 Para had experienced this route as a nightmare, but the Gurkhas were later described as moving along like 'heat-seeking ferrets'[6]. Mike was the most experienced Company Commander and would monopolize all the major Battalion 'pathfinder' tasks in the campaign. The Sussex Mountains objective was the first that the Commandant bestowed on him. Ten years later Mike would lead a Joint Services' expedition that only just failed to reach the summit of Mount Everest, so there was no doubting his toughness and professionalism. But I could not claim any affinity towards this future 7GR Commandant. Sometimes dogmatic, he commented later that my voice as Ops Officer had been heard too often on the radio. This implied bad delegation. Admittedly old habits die hard as a former Brigade watchkeeper, but the real reason for my monopolizing the air waves was that few QGOs had been trained in the arts of Battalion HQ watchkeeping.

A Gazelle helicopter touched down nearby. The Brigade Commander alighted and strode towards us putting on a red beret. His incongruous olive-green wellingtons did

139

not match his headwear but obviously he was taking no chances in exposing himself to the agonies of trench foot. 'Seen your Chinook yet?' he asked, full of expectation.

'No, sir,' I replied.

This did not stop his optimism. 'It'll be here soon enough to fly you all to Goose Green,' he said, and began conversing with the Commandant. Their chat revolved around our task at the settlement and 2 Para's recent battle, in which four of their officers died. Then the chirpy senior officer turned to go, categoric about *his* immediate future, 'And I assure you I've absolutely no intention of getting myself killed in this war!'

He was soon airborne again as the enormous double-rotored Chinook rumbled down from the sky, like a flying Panzer Tiger tank, to land near us. Call-sign Bravo November, otherwise known as the 'Flying Angel', was the only one of its type available in the war. Flying six hours daily for nineteen consecutive days, this helicopter was used alternatively as a troop, POW, casualty evacuation and cargo transport[7] despite defects such as no spare parts, no tools, no servicing manual, no heating, inoperative gyrocompass and broken windscreen wipers. It had nearly crashed into a lake two days before. Using the map, we briefed the pilot carefully where each of our companies should be dropped off while the first 'stick' of Tac HQ and good portion of A Company were assembled.

'We'll take at least seventy men in each stick, maybe more. Ignore peacetime flying rules! There's no seat belts to put on – because we've taken out all the cabin seats! So just load and go!' screamed the helmeted CrabAir loadmaster at me during his losing battle against the deafening 'chop, chop' of the beast's whirling rotor blades.

We marched up the rear ramp to jam ourselves into the cabin just like our landing craft departure from *Norland*. Standing room only again. More bergen-humping Gurkhas piled in from behind. The combination of no standard load of bergens piled onto the floor and small stature of the Gurkhas saved vital internal space, thus enabling the loadmaster to achieve his passenger load goal. Normally the helicopter took forty-four fully equipped troops seated. Our stick numbers were difficult to gauge, but probably eighty Gurkhas had become sardines in an exclusive flying tin can. Logic demanded that if passengers could be lifted vertically then they could be flown horizontally. The Chinook was built for flying large external loads such as the huge 155-mm howitzer *and* fly at 260 kilometres per hour, yet it had been so overloaded that the Commandant would enjoy the flight with his feet off the cabin floor.

'Considering the weight we were carrying,' he elaborated later, 'this meant I had a comfortable journey – whilst some poor bugger supported me and my bergen!'

Our altitude was an understandable twenty metres, contour hugging all the way. Clutching the starboard hand rail and looking down through the window at the Falklands countryside flashing by, I recalled Paddy's claim on *QE2* that the *dush* ground attack Pucará aircraft could 'eat helicopters for breakfast'. Two Pucarás had done just that to a Scout helicopter during 2 Para's battle and a thought crossed my mind, 'Wouldn't it be silly if we were gobbled up now for a late lunch with nearly all the command element of the 1st/7th Gurkha Rifles aboard?'

The surprise, though, came at the end of the flight – to be followed rapidly by several more. We had landed on a hill and deplaned from the Chinook's lowered rear ramp.

'So where's the Goose Green airstrip?' I asked, trying to orientate myself with the panorama below. It was not Goose Green. We had incorrectly touched down close to the northern settlement of Darwin where a sweet smell of burning peat assailed the nostrils. Devoid of trees, the tufted-grass countryside and dejected group of six houses were dominated by this central feature of Darwin Hill. Covered in still smouldering gorse bushes from a fire started in the battle, this was where 2 Para had been held up by *dush* machine-gunners and near where Colonel 'H' had gone down. Much further to the north-east were the snow covered slopes of Mount Usborne dominating the Darwin Isthmus.

Tac HQ eased down the hill towards the tiny settlement in the wake of our gung-ho Commandant, hunting for immediate Gurkha operational tasks against the doomed *dush*. An uneasy calm pervaded this part of the six kilometre-long by two kilometre-wide battlefield. Outside 2 Para's HQ located in one of the red-roofed houses, stood the silver-haired Major Chris Keeble. He was the Paras' 2IC who had assumed command during the battle. Beside him stood the Commandant. He was excited.

'OK, the remainder of 2 Para'll be moving out of here soon into Goose Green,' he informed us rapidly. 'A Company'll take over Darwin from them with C Company positioned to the north. Tac HQ'll move southwards to the north of the Goose Green airstrip whilst J Company of 42 Commando south of Goose Green will be handing over to our B Company. Everyone must dig in at these locations.'

Then the silver-topped drill bored into the soft, peaty soil with anticipation, 'And there's a good probability we'll be committed soon to a helicopter *coup de main* operation onto Bluff Cove further along the coast!'

This was not what the Intelligence Corps officer had crystal gazed in the Q4 room during that last night on *QE2*. However, the Paras must still have been exhausted and passing through fresh Gurkhas, to advance further up the coast, seemed logical. Yet despite these possibilities now for his Battalion, the Commandant retained his irritation. 'But the bad news is that Tac HQ has landed in the wrong place! Goose Green's two "clicks"[8] down that track,' he exclaimed as the silver-topped diviner twitched ferociously in a southerly direction, 'so we'll just have to get back into the damned Chinook when it returns with the next load and trust that the pilot, for a change, can map read correctly and fly us on down there!'

Unfortunately this would escalate the military disorder in addition to threats against psychological equilibrium. Turning back to the landing site to organize the move, a crack of small arms' fire rang out. I clicked into my Northern Ireland autopilot to prepare for an emergency bellylanding. It proved unnecessary as the perpetrators were friendly forces and easy to locate. A small group of paratroopers north of the tiny settlement were testing their marksmanship against geese, floating in an expanse of water known as Darwin Pond. The fall of shot whipped up the water's surface, causing startled birds to flap their wings fiercely and escape skywards. Correspondingly my landing was aborted, undercarriage retracted, and jangled nerves subsided.

Driven by a kelper, a tractor lumbered into view with a bedraggled but grinning red-bereted Para sitting on the back. Hitched to it was a trailer with five subdued and scared-eyed olive green clad figures perched on its sides. They were teenage *dush* POWs, a living testimony to Napoleon's accurate observation, 'There is not much difference after a battle in the material condition of the victor and vanquished: but the morale difference is immeasurably great.'

As the trailer went bouncing past I peeked inside. On the floor was a tangled heap of combat clothing similar to that worn by the prisoners. 'Odd,' I thought, glancing again at the load which could have been discarded leftovers from a junk shop. Boots and a hand stuck up from the jackets and trousers. A sensible Mark then said, 'Come on, let's get out of here.' The POWs had been collecting their battlefield dead and, walking away with my back safely to the receding tractor and trailer, I forced myself to think, 'OK, just forget what you've seen.' But that image of the tumbril's living and dead passengers remains razor sharp in my mind even today.

Back at the helicopter landing site, feelings had been placed on an unhealthy, but necessary, neutral hold. Ten metres away, two objects stirred up my anxiety again and made me wish for Bravo November's speedy return. We were standing in a redundant minefield because, marked off within a circle of white tape, the 250-pound dark blue aircraft bombs had been mixed with anti-personnel mines in the *dush* perimeter defence line on Darwin Ridge. Nobody went near them and one of our party asked suspiciously, 'Are those things safe?' 'Dunno. A couple of Argies tried to defuse them with a pair of pliers. God knows if they succeeded. We're just waiting for explosives ordnance disposal to give 'em the once-over,' was the nonchalant reply from a passing Para more concerned about the disappointing outcome of this second Battle of Darwin and Goose Green, when the mission had been to exterminate the pond's geese. After having had live military ordnance flung at him in the first battle, his threshold of tolerance to such objects as benign bombs was now much higher. A primitive instinct of satisfying hunger had priority. I would also experience later exactly such a phenomena – whilst this insignificant Darwin incident would become yet another crystal-clear East Falkland snapshot in my mental library.

We were soon whisked away by the Chinook to land at the Goose Green airstrip. The Commandant deplaned and moved on ahead to speak to a small group of sappers standing by a hedgerow. The silver-topped spear worked overtime as it thrust towards the adjacent hedgerow. 'Don't for God's sake tread near there,' warned its owner to us, 'because I've just been told that the ground is still chock-full of Argie mines!'

More than eighty hours old, the battlefield remained in disarray. A dirty yellow coloured goon tower stood in the centre of the airstrip which had presumably been utilized to provide warning of any approaching British aircraft. Its occupants were successful. Pieces of the first of nine Harrier fighters to be destroyed during the war were strewn near another fire-blackened and still smouldering hedgerow. The burial of its pilot, Lieutenant Nick Taylor, by the *dush* had been shown on television before we left the UK. Like chaos personified, many boxes of aircraft ammunition and rocket projectiles lay strewn everywhere. Nearby a loosely stacked napalm bomb pile, were three wrecked Pucará aircraft on the airstrip. One stood with its nose down in surrender and tail pointed drunkenly to the sky. Another remained in a normal parked posture, whilst the tail fin of a third was its only part that had not survived, as the black ashes and burnt grass in front told a grim story.

I was about to challenge the IO's Pucará predatory theories by commenting, 'Hey, Paddy, d'ya see that over there! It looks as if it's the Paras now who've managed to enjoy a tasty breakfast of Pucará!' when two Sea Kings suddenly swooped overhead towards the nearby settlement on a casualty evacuation mission. Just before our arrival some POWs had been clearing up a pile of artillery shells when there was an enormous explosion. 2 Para's Medical Sergeant had to shoot dead one of the four casualties, a horribly injured prisoner engulfed in flame. Another later died in the Commando Logistic Regiment's Medical Squadron Field Surgical Centre at Ajax Bay. The shells had been booby-trapped as some Gurkhas, probably from C Company, later found a grenade pin attached to a line which led from the incident site to the prisoners' accommodation in the spacious sheep-shearing sheds.

It was now mid-afternoon and more helicopter loads of Gurkhas began arriving. Some were from A Company – they were supposed to be at Darwin – others were from C Company. B Company was nowhere to be seen. There had been enough foul ups behind us in the execution of our landing on East Falkland and onward move, to have made the Muppets look like well organized beings in an orderly environment.

'Has everyone landed now?' enquired the Commandant, obviously expecting a rapid and professional briefing off my virgin battleboard on the precise location of each arriving sub-unit. His mood was not benevolent when the quaking 1st/7th Gurkha Rifles' Ops Officer prattled about the mounting disorder and runaway antics of Bravo November. This unacceptable situation was, without question, worse than that of the Grand Old Duke of York's 10,000 men when they arrived at the top of their hill.

'*What* did you say?' demanded the Commandant, ripping off his helmet and flinging it down onto the airstrip. Mud splattered everywhere as his simultaneous bellow, 'Christ! This is supposed to be *war*!' echoed around the lower end of the Darwin and Goose Green battlefield. Unfortunately chaos was to remain on our agenda, for the Devil himself was about to push the button to activate even more problems he had programmed for the Gurkhas' dreadful first Falklands' War day.

Chapter Twelve

GARRISONING GOOSE GREEN

War is a profession of positions. – Napoleon Bonaparte

At the end of the war Bravo November had its nickname of 'The Flying Angel' replaced by 'The Survivor' painted on its nose. 'So will I survive the Commandant's wrath?' was my equivalent thought now. Alas, the chaos continued as unhappy Taj Lewis and his twelve-man Company HQ deplaned from the Chinook to find they had been separated from the rest of C Company. The saying, '*Aba mare pani larhain garera marinchha*' (We will fight even if we have to die), was currently unrealistic, and his party would have to tab another wearying four kilometres through unknown countryside. There was little information available on the *dush* and, for all Taj knew, some might be nearby. It would be nightfall when his HQ became reunited with their main body.

I had learnt already that plans often do not work in war. Unexpected events can occur rapidly in a frightening environment and, to counter this, improvisation is required. Our Bravo November flights were a classic nightmare. Being the Ops Officer I felt guilty even though no radio means existed to talk directly to the pilot and make corrections. Trying to forget the cock-up, I tabbed with Tac HQ 500 metres northwards up a track from the airstrip, encircled by six abandoned anti-aircraft guns, to a bridge crossing a stream. The latter led to an inlet on the eastern coastline of the Darwin Isthmus. Nearby was a hut. This area had been the forming up point for the final phase of 2 Para's battle, the attack on nearby School House. Carcass Creek's name was given extra meaning by a bloated black and white cow lying motionless on the other side of the track from us. An innocent battle victim, its four legs stuck up grotesquely like flagpoles. Nobody took much notice. A major effort was now required to confirm and correct the companies' locations, and Mark worked on the radio like a Trojan using his Gurkhali to good effect. B Company's 6 Platoon guarded the airstrip, with the balance of the Company located further north up the track from us.

A Company remained at Darwin, C Company being north of them. A mortar line also was established a few hundred metres south of Darwin in an ideally situated re-entrant from where targets could be reached both north of Darwin and south of Goose Green. The lack of helicopters meant that obtaining ammunition for the four tubes was a problem. However 800 mixed smoke and high-explosive rounds would be eventually borrowed from 2 Para. We also dug furiously at Carcass Creek to establish the first Gurkha Battalion Tac HQ on the Falklands. The Paras drove up and down the muddy track that bisected our position in two kelper Land-Rovers mounted with a GPMG on each. Our trenches were getting deeper so Paddy Redding and I took a break to carry out a private recce of the battlefield. We quickly found a sledge which had been used to move ammunition up to the anti-aircraft guns, and then Paddy pounced on an object lying nearby, exclaiming, 'A-ha! This looks interesting. An Argie grease gun. Wonder how it works?' Paddy was curious. Too curious. Before the IO could be stopped, he was firing a few *pistola osino* bursts into the airstrip.

'And what the hell were you doing?' demanded Mark when we got back.

Paddy showed him the machine pistol and limply explained, 'Just testing out this liberated *dush* weapon. It might come in handy later on.' Ignoring Paddy's treasure find, Mark exclaimed, 'We stood-to because of your bloody shooting! For God's sake, next time you're tempted to do some target practice, clear it beforehand with Tac HQ otherwise there'll be a nasty blue-on-blue!'

This expression emanated from the SOP chinagraph pencil colour used for marking friendly forces on a battle map, as opposed to red for the enemy. Mark had every right to be annoyed. Already there had been a number of such incidents between friendly forces on the Falklands, some resulting in casualties. Paddy's indiscretion and my passiveness could have led to another blue-on-blue which would have been the final straw on that fraught day.

It was just after 19.00 hours and last light. The vulnerable time when a *dush* attack might be mounted. We stood-to – a standard defence routine of putting on webbing and helmets, climbing into our trenches and standing alert with weapons ready for use. Quiet descended, sharpening our senses. Then, after half an hour, we stood-down to continue establishing radio communications with the scattered companies. This was more difficult than we originally thought but, during the frustration, Bis Bis approached.

'Ah! What have you got there Bis Bis? Our evening grub?' asked Mark.

The grinning Gurkha held two mess tins full of steaming food, our first hot meal since *Norland*'s breakfast. His stew and rice concoction made from our ration pack contents showed that the Gurkha orderly system was operating satisfactorily.

'*Chiya*, sahib?' queried Bis Bis to me, cocking his head to one side in that quaint universal Gurkha mannerism while pushing a life-giving mug of hot tea into my hand.

The end of the meal was marked by another red air alert due to a *dush* aircraft contact near Pebble Island. It was a long way off to the north-west and we soon received the stand-down. Although uncomfortable and cold, there was no rain. BOs, BORs and Gurkhas had all worked hard on trenches which, by now, had reached acceptable depths. Updates on all the companies' locations and situations were received on the radio from company locstats and sitreps. These were then included in the midnight consolidated Battalion situation report sent to Force HQ aboard *Fearless* before I clambered into my sleeping bag for two hours prior to being next on radio stag duty.

It had been quite a day. Three red air alerts, *dush* bombing, a quasi-amphibious landing, a *dush* aircraft shot down, a hairy Chinook tactical flight, encounter with *dush* POWs and stiffs, unexploded bombs, the mess of a battlefield, exploding booby traps, lost Gurkha Battalion, angry Commandant, dead cow and irritated Adjutant. The variety was infinite.

'So what would tomorrow bring?' I asked myself. 'Oh, yes! Something about a heli-copter *coup de main* operation. . . .'

I tried to catch forty winks. But lack of information about the Battalion had been causing much worry among our next of kin. Tove's letter, which she wrote that same night not only described this, but also how their mutual psychosocial support had developed:

> We are still being denied reports about what is happening . . . One day I read that *QE2* troops have been landed on the Falkland Islands – the next day that they have not. You warned me before you left about non-communication, but I find it very hard not hearing from you regularly. It is a great comfort though, to have the other wives around. Today Libby Stewart and I had lunch with Meg Lewis . . . I've been baking tonight, and think I will send you something yummie to munch in your trench.

Just before dawn we got back into our trenches to stand-to again. Quiet and alert senses again as we waited for the *dush*. It was 10.15 hours Zulu time on Tuesday, 2 June. First light arrived slowly. There was a low mist, but no rain. At 11.00 hours we stood-down, had breakfast and continued to consolidate by increasing the depth of our trenches and improving overhead cover. 2 Para's GPMG-mounted Land-Rovers drove up the track to Goose Green before the large frame of Bill Dawson materialized leading the twenty Gurkhas of Alternative Battalion HQ. A few minutes later the Gurkha Major was walking around Tac HQ talking to our Gurkhas while Bill gazed around to find a suit-able place for his HQ.

'It's got to be on the other side of the Darwin Isthmus at Boca House,' he pondered while consulting his map. 'After all, it's important that Tac and us are kept as far apart as possible. No point in both HQs being blown away in the same *dush* air strike. So come on Geronimo! Let's move out.' Lalbahadur sahib nodded, following Bill. The Battalion had to devise its own radio appointment title for the Gurkha Major, and Geronimo was a humourous choice.

To counter our vulnerability from air attack required imaginative thinking, so our attached British artillery personnel, Bombadier John Batchelor and Lance Bombadiers Joe Jackson and Alan Gibson, began tinkering with a *dush* German-built Rheinmetall twin-barrelled anti-aircraft cannon on a promontory 200 metres to our north. Sited with a commanding field of fire over the eastern approaches of the Darwin Isthmus, the weapon would have had several seconds' window of opportunity to engage any attacking Harrier. I wandered across, and Batchelor's replies to my questions revealed good artillery and air defence knowledge.

'Any possibility of getting the thing to fire?'

'Well sir, I'm having problems with opening up the breech on one barrel, but reckon we can carry out a shoot with the other.'

'What's the chances of hitting a fast moving jet?'

'Oh, none at all, sir. The range of this thing's about 2,000 metres and just a prox-imity air-burst will be sufficient to start stripping the aircraft's skin in mid-flight. Its speed will complete the job.'

'You fired this type of gun before, Bombadier?' I asked, more impressed by the minute.

'If I haven't, sir,' he grinned, 'then there's enough loose and boxed-up 20-mm shells the Argies left behind here to enable me to become word perfect until Christmas!'

I looked at the ammunition. No wonder these Gunners were on a high. Five minutes later they were ready. Batchelor pointed eastwards and said, 'OK! Imagine an aircraft attacking on a flight path from over there. Load! Ready? Fire!'

Shells fired from the usable barrel burst in vicious patterns over the large inlet to the north of Goose Green. The cannon's stopping power was undeniable and a triumphant Batchelor declared, 'That's good enough. Betcha this caught that Harrier when it attacked here last month. You can see the result, sir. It's lying in hundreds of bits and pieces near the airstrip!' He started firing again. The Gunners were lost in paradise.

A Gurkha section commander of C Company became equally impressed and his men later took a leaf out of the *Little Red Book* of Mao Tse-tung: 'Replenish our strength with all the arms . . . captured from the enemy. Our army's main source of material are at the front' by dragging the cannon to their position. But there would be no red air alerts that day and Batchelor's assumption was wrong. For Taylor's Harrier had been hit by one of two brand new 35-mm Oerlikon anti-aircraft cannon sited on the western side of the small Goose Green peninsular.

Meanwhile Bill and his Gurkhas arrived at a small rise on which Boca House had stood years ago. Its flattened foundations, the only visible part remaining, had been a site of hard fighting during 2 Para's battle. Discovering the bodies of some Pucará pilots and not insensitive to this carnage, these Gurkhas conducted a death ceremony in honour of them and the dead Harrier pilot before digging their trenches. Destroyed *dush* bunkers there also demonstrated the Milan anti-tank missile's sledgehammer effectiveness. It was a lesson quickly absorbed by the Commandant who made a decision about the future deployment of his Anti-Tank Platoon. 'Our Milans are going to be used in exactly the same way if there's a need to crack any nut blocking our advance,' he said grimly. 'Have no doubt about that at all.'

But before setting out on any major advance we would need ammunition and rations. At San Carlos *Baltic Ferry* and *Nordic Ferry* were offloading these items, other stores and men. Ram and his B Echelon party[1] who had set up their base in the Brigade Maintenance Area would soon be able to resupply the Battalion. Concurrently 'The Great White Whale' had begun offloading the two Guards battalions earmarked to join D Company on the Sussex Mountains. Because this area would become dangerously over-populated and the intelligence received of a counter-attack threat on Darwin from the West Falkland *dush* 8th Infantry Regiment at Fox Bay, the Commandant was forced to review his force dispositions.

'D Company'll now have to reinforce us and must be prepared to move by helicopter. So send a radio warning order to Mike Kefford, and a helquest to Brigade,' he ordered. Mike was warned and Brigade received the helicopter transport request as another thought lurked at the back of my mind, 'So when are we going to mount that helicopter *coup de main*?'

But nothing happened because local cap badge politics had triumphed. There would be no fresh Gurkha reinforcements passing through a Para battalion which, although having achieved superhuman feats, had been compelled to evacuate twenty-seven sick and injured men from their six days on the Sussex Mountains and which had also taken forty-seven battle casualties. The traumatized and exhausted survivors were also riddled with trench foot, the first of seventy Brits suffering from this condition compared with a *dush* campaign figure of 290 in their much longer average sixty-five day ordeal.[2]. Nonetheless I witnessed some Paras that afternoon taking off in a couple of Scout helicopters to fly to Swan Inlet House further up the coast. Freelancing had started in earnest.

Later when Bravo November landed by the settlement, it was immediately 'requisitioned' by the Brigade Commander. The pilot applied the lessons learnt twenty-four hours earlier with us, but no new passenger record could have been set since only sixty-two Paras boarded the first flight with full kit[3], and the second must have had a similar load. It pays to be a small Gurkha when cabin space is limited, although the Paras became the helicopter *coup de main* force flown even further eastwards to seize Fitzroy and Bluff Cove unopposed. To the Brigade Commander it was a 'great fifty-five kilometre jump forward', but his unauthorized operation left a few senior staff officers at San Carlos twitching in their seats, and relegated Gurkhas to playing second fiddle and in the wrong position to attack the *dush*.

Orders had been received that we had to take over the following morning as Goose Green's garrison. Prior to this the ops cell of Tac HQ requisitioned the Carcass Creek hut. While we were moving in that afternoon, I spied a Para officer accompanied by a Warrant Officer walking down the track. He quickly approached, but his simple question seemed out of place, 'Excuse me, but can you tell me the way to Goose Green?'

It was Lieutenant Colonel David Chaundler, the replacement 2 Para CO. Twenty-four hours before he had parachuted out of a Hercules aircraft from Ascension Island into the sea off the Falklands. Having flown to Darwin and tabbed to Goose Green, he was about to hitch a ride on Bravo November that evening to Fitzroy. But our Commandant was now focusing on his new task. To ensure an organized move into the settlement, preparations commenced for the first formal Battalion O Group on the Falklands. The venue was our Carcass Creek hut, normally the settlement's dairy. It had also been used as a shelter for three 2 Para casualties during the attack on the School House, where Para white phosphorous grenades and *dush* 35-mm Oerlikon cannon fire had reduced this building 300 metres north of the settlement to a twisted mass of scorched steel girders. Rain fell as the O Group started, so it was fortunate there was overhead cover to protect Paddy's model of Goose Green and the nearby terrain.

The Commandant outlined his plan. 'B Company are to move first, followed by Tac HQ and C Company. A Company are to remain where they are to become Darwin's garrison. On arrival, B Company will relieve J Company of 42 Commando, and both B and C Companies will guard Goose Green's southern and northern fronts respectively. You are to dig in and establish defence routines. Battalion HQ'll be located in the settlement. There's no helicopter lift to move us towards Stanley, so we'll have to remain here for a few days. And that's why D Company'll have to tab off the Sussex Mountains at first light tomorrow and rejoin us on foot here.'

After a meal, stand-to, company locstats and sitreps received and midnight consolidated Battalion sitrep transmitted, we slept comfortably on the dairy's hay. Next morning we stood-to again, breakfasted and packed kit before tabbing the one and a half kilometres to Goose Green in single file. The Gurkhas seemed to disappear under their bulky bergens during the twenty minute march but, once in the settlement, my immediate challenge was to find accommodation for Battalion HQ. Home to eighty kelpers and 100 sheepdogs, it was an obscure dot on the atlas which overnight had been transformed to a household name in Britain. We passed a small hedgerow behind which was a line of innocuous looking dark bundles. 'Must be Argie stiffs,' remarked somebody dispassionately behind me.

Such an objective attitude was necessary because violent death mixed bizarrely with teeming life as, turning the corner of the waterlogged track, we were met by the sheep-dogs' barking and the omnipresent tang of burning peat. The settlement comprised twenty buildings, mostly private homes. By its entrance was a large garage and long, black-painted sheep-shearing sheds. Three 105-mm pack howitzers stood outside with many empty shell cases piled up by a wall. Hastily painted large POW white letters were daubed on the roof, side and front of the sheds which accommodated remnants of the 1300-odd strong ex-*dush* garrison guarded by a section of Paras. Two-thirds had been already transported to Ajax Bay, but some of those remaining emerged to observe us sullenly as we moved past. Many seemed to be only teenagers.

Most of the red-roofed properties were grouped around a green at the settlement's centre. But for the bustle of military activity it would have been a tranquil scene. Helicopters either stood silent on the grass or were taking off. The deafening chop-chop of their accelerating rotor-blades provided an illusion of even more chaos to that which already existed. *Dush* weapons and military ordnance lay everywhere. Besides FAL and FAP rifles[4], there were GPMGs, a variety of mortars up to 120-mm in calibre and Browning heavy machine guns so new that some had not been unpacked from their greaseproof wrapping. Napalm bombs were stacked up by a fence and, nearby, 81-mm mortar bombs, hand grenades, loose small arms ammunition, surface-to-air missiles, air-to-ground rockets, 105-mm and 155-mm artillery shells, anti-tank rockets . . . the inventory was endless.

'2 Para's located its Battalion HQ over here Mike!' Mark called out, waving at me. The Paras had set themselves up in a house whose outbuildings had been converted by the *dush* into a store to stack wooden boxes of 7.62-mm ammunition for FAL rifles and boxes of 9-mm dumdum bullets outlawed by the Geneva Convention. The British popular press insisted the *dush* had been issued with only fifty rounds per man, but the evidence in Goose Green that day belied such stories and provided a lesson. In crisis situations never believe what journalists write. Only believe what has happened when, and if, you have seen it with your own eyes. I poked my head into the small building's ops room where Paras scribbled messages and listened to radio headsets. My question was more in hope than anything else, 'Um . . . 'scuse me! I understand you'll be leaving soon. OK then if we locate our Battalion HQ in here after you?'

One officer looked up. 'No way! We're not leaving yet. Looks as if you'll just have to find lodging elsewhere.'

Nobody budged. Annoyed, I emerged to look elsewhere on the Goose Green property market. Nearby was Major Tony Rice, the 2 Para Battery Commander who had been in their Tac HQ during the battle. Like me he had been in Sandhurst's 41 intake and we recognized each other. Our conversation quickly focused on the *dush* Pucará aircraft capabilities. 'It's slow,' he said with the confidence of one exposed to the recent 'hands-on' experience, 'and easy to hit with small arms fire or Blowpipe. But, true to its name, the Pucará can puke little bombs at you from under both wings. I suggest you duck because, once these things hit the ground, they make a bit of a bang.'

He forgot to add that I ought to watch out for a bit of flame as well, because the bilious machine had also dropped napalm on the Paras. Informed about its capabilities, my attempt continued to find a suitable home for Battalion HQ. Accommodation was steadily being vacated as more Paras flew by helicopter to Fitzroy and Bluff Cove. I tried my luck again at a small house opposite their HQ, and entered to find half a dozen young Para tenants sitting in the easy chairs and sofa of the front living room. They gazed silently at me. I tried to ignore the hostility and asked, 'You lot going soon? I'm on the lookout for a place to house the Gurkhas' HQ, and this could be a possibility.'

More silence. An unwelcome stranger had wandered into this Para section's midst. It did not matter he was an officer. Indeed this made the situation worse. He represented authority. The collective body language spoke volumes about their prevalent mood. If they had voiced their thoughts, then these certainly would have been, 'Big deal! Bleedin' officer! Naff off! A base for 'is Gurkhas? So what? Wot does 'e know about coming under fire? Of being shit-scared? Of having to fight through them Argie trenches? Of surviving – but only to start fighting an' killing again?'

Like in Homer's *Iliad*, their silent combat veteran, existential authority stemmed from having risked all in battle and, six days afterwards, their cohesiveness was like cement. The difference between us was that they had seen 'the elephant' and I had not. They had tabbed on the planet Mars whilst we others remained virgin earthlings. To add insult to injury I was still wearing my tin hat indoors. They wore their red berets. That gave them status – and invincibility. They were the kings of Darwin and Goose Green. Anyone else was a pretender; an impostor. Nobody said, 'Piss off!' but the atmosphere could have been cut with a kukri.

Their Corporal shook his head. 'Dunno, you'd best ask 'im as he owns the place.' He nodded towards an old man with a grey straggly beard who carried a small white plastic bag. The kelper had no intention of remaining and was about to leave his home again.

'Do you mind if we use your house for our HQ?' I asked the third time that morning.

'No!' he replied, 'don't worry about me. I've just collected my toothbrush and pyjamas, so now I'm off back to my neighbour's house!' Disappearing like shit off a hot shovel, he had been affected by the Paras' 'blanking' as well.

I used two minutes to go through the motions of looking around the house. The tenants remained seated, their irritated eyes following my every move. Nobody twitched a muscle. This was *their* house. I gave up. Not only was it much too small, but also a relief to remove myself from the presence of that Para section.

'What now?' I wondered, 'back to the estate agents?'

Setting foot in the mud outside and inhaling that tang from the distant peat fire again, my trudge continued towards the settlement's green, at its centre. 'We should have done a recce yesterday to avoid this bloody time wasting nonsense,' I moaned to Mark standing nearby.

150

'Yep,' agreed the Adjutant, 'time spent in a recce is seldom wasted. But how about the shop? I've just heard the Paras have made the prisoners clean it up after the Argie garrison left the place knee-deep in rubbish.'

The shop was by the green. Inside was a single large room with rows of open wooden shelving along which customers could browse and select their groceries and other household purchases. The few there today could only chose from a few items perched on otherwise bare shelves. Behind the counter at the far end was the manager. He was also the postmaster. On one shelf a lonely box of chocolates caught my eye. 'Could they be sent to Tove for her birthday in a couple of weeks?' I wondered.

Making a beeline towards this stockily-built man with unkempt hair, I asked my well worn question, 'Hello, I'm with the Gurkhas. Is there any possibility that we can use your shop for our Battalion HQ?'

He replied with the air of one used to taking instant decisions, 'Yeah, should be no problem.'

My instant reaction, 'Thank God for that,' and follow-up request, 'Is there anywhere in here then which can be used for sleeping accommodation?' brought forth an equally terse answer.

'Yep. The name's Keith Baillie. Follow me.'

He guided me to a storeroom at the back of the shop which, although crammed with mountains of British Army compo ration boxes and freshly baked bread on a wooden pallet that had been helicopter-delivered from *Hermes* for the settlement's consumption, would make an adequate sleeping area for Battalion HQ personnel. I was then escorted to the side office used by 2 Para's Support Company HQ. Large enough to convert into a Gurkha ops room, two Paras still manned their radios there.

'We're leaving soon, so you can take over here,' was their uninterested comment.

This was our new home. I went back into the shop to organize Gurkha muscle power for clearing the storeroom. Keith was dealing with a few more new customers. The cleaning materials had been in great demand and these female kelpers were being handed out a limited free ration of washing powder and furniture polish. 'The Argies left my place in a terrible mess,' despaired one Goose Green lass. 'It's going to take another four days to finish cleaning up. So can't you please give more than this, Keith?'

He behaved like one who had heard this request many times before and his reply, made with a commendable grain of humour, had nonetheless a weary tone, 'Sorry love, there's simply nothing else other than this. I've got to continue the rationing. But next time I ring *Hermes* with the grocery order, I'll include a crate of furniture polish!'

Outside the shop a little later, we hoisted the Battalion's black flag. Emblazoned with a threatening pair of white cloth kukris, their handles crossed in saltire and numeral seven ensigned with the cipher of HRH the Duke of Edinburgh in between the blades' cutting edges, the flag had a strong resemblance to the Jolly Roger when viewed from a distance. In the context of 'psyops', no *dushman* could fail to notice that we blood-thirsty pirates had arrived. Had I realized though that the forty-five-gallon drum of JP 1 petrol standing outside the main entrance was booby-trapped, there might have been second thoughts on the choice of Battalion HQ's residence. A hand grenade with its pin removed had been placed under the drum with the weight of the latter pressing down on the striking lever. Only after we had walked past this into the shop that afternoon did our attached 9 Para Squadron Sappers led by no-nonsense Sergeant Ron Wrega discover this improvised explosive device. They promptly made it safe and then removed the drum.

Meanwhile work progressed in our ops room. I noticed an antiquated telephone by the window and picked up the receiver. Dead as a dodo. A pity, for communications to an Ops Officer is the mother and father of command and control. Kit Spencer and his Gurkha Signallers lost no time in setting up two radio sets. One was for the Brigade net and other for the Battalion command net, but our pool of Battalion HQ watch-keepers was mainly limited to the four BO staff officers of the HQ – Mark, Kit, Paddy and myself. Our official radio appointment titles resembled something out of Winnie-the-Pooh books, namely: Seagull, Pronto, Acorn, and Kestrel. Maps were also pinned up on the wall which displayed the Goose Green area and Lafonia, that enormous tract of countryside lying due south.

Afterwards the Commandant appeared. So did the silver-topped never-resting ultra-long conductor's baton. Satisfied with the location, he made a predictable demand, 'And now I want an all-singing, all-dancing ops room right from the word go!' So did the silver-topped baton as it rapped menacingly on the floor.

Mark had also been busy. His experience with the few POWs on board *Norland* had not been wasted since 2 Para's Provost staff made him sign for his next 471 customers still packed together in the sheep-shearing sheds. They would have to remain there. The sinking of *Atlantic Conveyor* and all her aviation cargo meant no helicopters for either our D Company's advance, or these POWs back-loading to Ajax Bay for further processing and interrogation. Unlike D Company, marching them there was no option. Rifleman Baliprasad Rai had some comments about these gentlemen:

> I saw my first Argentine soldiers at Goose Green. Prisoners-of-war, they were made to clear up all the rubbish they had created while occupying the settlement. They looked uncomfortable, ill-kept and ill-disciplined, like Mexican bandits in the cowboy films I had seen on the video. Some of them looked even younger than me![5]

A Gurkha guard for these POWs also had to be organized before Mark's return to the Battalion ops room where Bis Bis produced two tumblers of hot sweet *chiya* and, from thin air, chocolate bars for his two *gora sahibharu*. He was on the ball.

'Your mess tins, sahib?' he enquired.

'They're in my webbing,' I told him.

A little later the efficient Gurkha orderly served up a piping hot dinner in our tins with his usual all-in stew heavily laced with curry powder. His culinary expertise kept up our morale and, while we were eating, Keith Baillie poked his nose and long side-burns around the door.

'Everything all right in here, then?' he grinned from ear to ear. 'Are you sure that there's nothing else you guys need?'

'It's OK,' I replied, 'we've got our maps up, established radio communications, so all we've left is to sort out a watchkeeper roster.'

'Well, here's something you've definitely forgotten,' announced Keith. He pulled a bottle of gin from behind his back and put it down on the table. 'Sorry there's no tonic, but have this on the house and compliments of the Goose Green shop!'

Out came some tumblers, the gin was poured out and Keith proposed a toast which seemed surreal. 'To the Gurkhas!' he proclaimed waving his tumbler, 'and their next stop – Stanley!' Life had, at last, become a little more civilized and we listened for the next fifteen minutes to Keith, an ex-Marine Commando who had lived in the Falklands for twelve years after marrying a kelper, as he told us about life under the *dush* regime.

Initially after the invasion things were OK, and we got on with our life, and they theirs. About 200 officers and senior NCOs led the conscripts, some having been taken from schools in Argentina, given a rifle, and told to go and fight for *La Patria* – 'the Fatherland'. The Argies built up their defences, air strength, and logistic supplies which included a vast quantity of aviation fuel. They renamed Goose Green *Puerto Santiago* and their air base here was christened *El Condor de las Malvinas*. It had many helicopters – three Chinooks, three or four Hueys and a Bell-Agusta. As for Pucará aircraft, that was something else – because on 29 April I counted fourteen dotted around the airstrip! Later half of these with their Naval personnel were relocated to Pebble Island where they got knocked off by the SAS.

It all changed on 1 May when the shit hit the fan with the Harriers attacking Stanley Airport and airstrip here. We all got shoved immediately into the Community Centre at the top end of the settlement. One hundred and fourteen people, including sixteen from Stanley and thirty-nine children, were crammed into a building the size of an average British pub for the next thirty days. Our ages ranged from four months to eighty-two years, and we were guarded by six to eight soldiers armed with rifles and fixed bayonets. There were only two WCs, so you can imagine the stink when the fresh water supply failed for five days. We'd only one method to flush the toilets when they got full and that was to chuck sea water into them. At least the Argies allowed us to refill our buckets.

We needed shelter in which to take cover if the British forces started any attack, but the only way to get it was to dig! So we dug like blue crazy and made five shallow holes in the floor of the Centre. Three days before the battle, on 25 May, the Argies received a resupply drop from a Hercules aircraft of eight parachute loads which landed on the western side of the airstrip. They probably contained extra ammunition because their pack howitzers and mortars were in constant use during the battle. We also received 'overs' from the Paras' return fire when the battle got nearer us, and it was a good job that we had dug our shelters as quite a fair amount of flak flew around. Even one Para sniper successfully managed to drill one of our Argie guards standing outside the Centre!

'So what were the Argies like then at Goose Green?' I asked.

Yeah, I can tell you about them all right. When we were released by the Paras we'd found that they'd messed up our homes good and proper. Not only had they looted and vandalized, but crapped and pissed into everywhere there was space

153

available to crap and piss into. I assure you that my bath, bed and garden weren't exactly places of heaven on my first day of freedom! They'd also carried out the same trick in my shop, as well as turning over all the shelving and shopping articles onto the floor. It took six prisoners guarded by 2 Para's Support Company clerk a whole day to clear up the mess.

The Paras nicknamed them 'spics' – a shortened version of 'Hispanics'. But, to be honest, that's incorrect. Sure, many looked like Spaniards, Italians or Mexicans – however I've never met such a mix of different types. Some from Patagonia were descendants of Welsh immigrants and spoke Welsh! Others resembled Germans or Scandinavians with their blonde hair. Many were Indian peasants from Argentina's sub-tropical north. There was even a Jap equipped with a Samurai sword, but the conscripts' officers didn't treat them at all well. For example, at the surrender ceremony one conscript fainted and was kicked by an officer until he got up again. However they were good at improvising. 2 Para had rockets fired at them from launchers removed from a damaged Pucará and strapped to the children's slide. More were fired from the top of a tractor which'd been used to tow Pucarás around the airstrip!

Keith then left us and finishing touches were made to the ops room with everyone in Battalion HQ staking out an individual sleeping place in the storeroom. Elsewhere, B, C and Support Companies had also found accommodation in Goose Green. Their Gurkhas soon endeared themselves to the kelpers who provided warm mugs of tea and coffee for the Nepalese inner man because the grim, cold weather had become even grimmer. Never-ending rain and sleet lashed down. An unpopular and thankless task, Gurkha sentries had to man their trenches because the counter-attack threat from West Falkland also continued. 'However did the *dush* have the capability to mount such an operation?' I wondered once or twice.

Chapter Thirteen

DELAYED

If our task is to cross a river, we cannot cross it without a bridge or a boat. Unless the bridge or the boat problem is solved, it is idle to speak of crossing the river. – Mao Tse-tung

The first Battalion O Group at the settlement convened in our spartan little ops room at 20.00 hours and a determination for his Gurkhas to stamp their mark immediately on the Falklands shone through the Commandant's opening 'state of the Battalion' address. He had made another proactive strategic decision which did not permit rest, as his outline of sub-unit dispositions and tasks had a Himalayan ambition-level.

It seems we'll be staying here for a few days as Brigade's given us the task of garrisoning Darwin and Goose Green. However we'll do more than that and won't be underemployed whilst we're here. Aggressive patrolling is the only recipe to counter frustration with this delay in deployment eastwards. We've also received useful intelligence. Today 2 Para captured three *dush* in a stolen Land-Rover at Fitzroy who've provided information that a total of six *dush* ten-man 'stay-behind' parties are to be found somewhere in the northerly part of Lafonia. Here, due south of the Darwin Isthmus and south-west of Goose Green.

B Company have been active already in checking out two abandoned *dush* locations which are two to three kilometres south of Goose Green. One had twenty bunkers covered with corrugated iron sheeting, and the other position had sixteen bunkers with tents. The ground was littered with blankets, webbing, clothing, ammunition, and weapons so there could be some substance to the intelligence we've got from 2 Para. B Company's task will be to follow up, investigate Arrow Harbour House, and then fly twenty kilometres south-east on a similar mission to the areas of Torcida Point and Rush Valley Hill.

There was no let up in the intelligence information or taskings dished out by the Commandant. A and C Companies would be fully employed.

There've also been local reports of a *dush* radar position on Lively Island situated off the north-east Lafonian coastline and other eyewitness reports of at least one *dush* Chinook and a Skyhawk crashing there. It's claimed that a pilot of one of these aircraft is still alive. To the north of Darwin on Mount Usborne it's thought that a *dush* observation post exists in a small wooden hut or tent that had been spotting for their artillery during the recent battle against 2 Para. Brook Hardcastle, the General Manager of the Falkland Island Company who lives at Darwin, has also backed up this theory by claiming he saw a *dush* Chinook flying near this suspected OP location some days ago. I want A Company to mount an operation against it with helicopter fire support. As for C Company, they'll guard Goose Green and its airstrip as well as conducting their own patrol programme along the East Falkland southern coastline.

The O Group finished an hour later. By now 2 Para had nearly vacated Goose Green, leaving only their A Echelon behind and Gurkhas, at last, as the garrison. To broadcast this to the world and its wife, the Commandant decided time was ripe for initiating some Gurkha public relations with the Pipe Major's skills. So he told me, 'Mike, I want the Pipe Major to play *Black Bear* on the settlement's green at last light. Get him warned off about this, will you?'

A little later, Pipe Major Meherman Tamang appeared in front of me, saluted smartly, and asked innocently, 'Yes, Training Officer sahib?'

'Ah! Pipe Major, there you are! The Commandant sahib wants you to pipe *Black Bear* on the green outside the shop shortly. OK?'

The Gurkha Warrant Officer's face dropped and he replied sheepishly, 'I am sorry sahib, but piping this evening is not possible.'

'Why? What's the problem?'

'I cannot do this task because my bagpipes were flown by helicopter to *Canberra* at South Georgia. And I still have not been able to get them off that ship, sahib!'

More disorder.

Horrified at the possible reaction, I informed the Commandant when he reappeared shortly afterwards. In response the silver-topped sledgehammer nearly crashed through the closed door of the ops room accompanied by unprintable remarks. Thus neither the kelpers nor POWs were to enjoy any stirring tunes on Gurkha bagpipes then or, indeed, the following five evenings of our wartime garrison duty.

However, there was other Gurkha activity elsewhere on the Falklands. The Exocet that sank *Atlantic Conveyor* had presented D Company with far more serious consequences than those for the waiting POWs at Goose Green. Among the container ship's lost cargo had been three Chinook and six smaller Wessex helicopters, and they were assets which Mike Kefford sorely needed now. The weather on 3 June had also been a negative factor on the Sussex Mountains which cut across 5 Brigade's line of communications. Swirling mist and fog curtailed flying-time of Bravo November and remaining thirty-seven Wessex and Sea King helicopters which were prioritized elsewhere in moving forward the two British Brigades' artillery guns and ammunition. The Commandant had been left with no option but to order the D Company tab. The only Gurkhas spared this arduous slog with full kit over difficult ground were the mortar section. Less their two Mortar Fire Controllers who tabbed with the Company, the section were flown to Goose Green in a series of shuttle flights by a helpful Scout helicopter. Unlike 2 Para who had centralized and left their bergens behind before starting out along the same twenty kilometres of difficult terrain, D Company would backpack theirs of fifty kilos apiece. Indeed some Gurkhas with extra GPMG link ammunition and mortar bombs would be carrying sixty-five kilos which was in excess of their own body weight. With the onset of darkness it had taken two and a half hours for their single file to close up for a wet and windy night halt.

Meanwhile the Welsh Guards, located on a northern reverse slope of the Sussex Mountains, had also set out optimistically on 2 Para's and D Company's route towards High Hill, five kilometres north-east of Darwin. The Guards, though, had decided to travel first class and ordered three local tractors and trailers to transport their bergens. They must have had friends in high places for their Recce Platoon was also flown to Goose Green. However, when their only tractor became stuck in the mud, the Guards gave up after only a hour or so's tab and returned home to Sussex Mountains. A later deliberately light-hearted account of the war contained more than a grain of truth, nonetheless, of the subsequent comparisons:

> ... things were not going so smoothly with the Guards and Gurkhas of 5 Infantry Brigade. On the one hand the problem seemed to be to stop the Gurkhas hurtling off on their own, taking Stanley single-handed and then swimming the South Atlantic and taking Buenos Aires as well, while on the other, it seemed impossible to get the Guards to move fast enough to keep up with the rest of the land forces.[1]

It had also been a busy time for the Gurkhas lodged in the sheep-shearing sheds at San Carlos. The low cloud base precluded any low-level day air attack, but arguably the greatest threat to the Gurkhas' security here came from the Task Force journalists. Their night-time antics of lighting fires to keep warm and cook also provided homing beacons for the *Aerea Fuerza Argentina*'s aircraft which had become more active during the fourteen hours of darkness in every twenty-four period. Les Peacock, now indoctrinated in the methods used to mess up things for others, and the Battalion's Army Catering Corps chief cook, Warrant Officer Jack Massey, were therefore fully employed with kicking out the flames while hurling suitable expletives at the offenders.

In the Goose Green ops room our first night passed by peacefully. After being relieved from my watch at midnight I got my head down for a few hours in the shop's storeroom. The roster system seemed to be working well, even though sleep was disturbed by the changeover of outgoing and incoming watches. A concrete floor was under my wafer-thin karrimat mattress, on top of which I had rolled out my sleeping bag. By definition the surface was rock hard. But it was also dry. Although surrounded by snoring Gurkha Signallers and other Battalion HQ staff in addition to the kelpers' piles of compo ration boxes, this still provided a living environment of luxury compared with a trench dug into Falklands' mud from which water had to be bailed out continously. There was even an adjacent loo and washbasin. Despite the Gurkha queue, it guaranteed a proverbial shave and shit. Shampoo was more difficult to engineer. Shower was impossible. Others, though, managed more upmarket accommodation such as Graham Stewart-Smith, who had acquired a billet in Keith Baillie's home.

I woke early on the morning of 4 June. Rain was still pouring down, it being the hallmark of the next three days. Rifleman Baliprasad Rai described the Gurkhas' stoicism:

> The weather had become absolutely terrible. There was rain so heavy at times that we could hardly see ten yards further anywhere. Mist and low clouds added to the gloom. All our kit and clothing were soaked and remained soaked, and the icy wind of the Antarctic would chill us to the bone no matter how many woollies we wore. It was colder and wetter than ten English winters combined and they (the Goose Green kelpers) said this was just for starters! However we gritted our teeth, pulled our Arctic caps (everyone's favourite) over our ears and carried on.[2]

Battalion HQ personnel were lucky to have a roof over our heads and we girded ourselves to meet the operational 'G' challenges as the weather did not prevent implementation of our comprehensive patrolling programme. I had to coordinate this and we acted on 2 Para's intelligence by sending out Gurkha patrols to hunt for the *dush*, reminiscent of 'farmers' daughters' patrols in the bandit country of Northern Ireland. Unlike the remainder of East Falkland, Lafonia was a tract of flat countryside with similar dimensions to the English county of Surrey. More than ninety-nine per cent of its population comprised Goose Green's 110,000 sheep with a corresponding total of thirteen isolated shepherds' houses in the northern part of Lafonia. All could provide shelter for possible *dush* 'stay-behind' parties, and seven – Arrow Harbour House, Bodie Creek House, Orquera House, Brenton Loch House, Paragon House, Tranquilidad House and Dos Lomas House – were within fifteen kilometres south of Goose Green. The other six – Island Creek House, Upper Walter Creek House near Walter Creek settlement, Trap House, Old Drone House, Hope Cottage and Egg Harbour House were within twenty-five kilometres.

Army Air Corps Scout helicopters of 656 Squadron would also be utilized. One pilot of 'Teeny Weeny Airways', as it had become affectionately known, appeared in the ops room to be briefed. Captain John Greenhalgh was a dynamic officer whose gung-ho flying during the Battle of Darwin and Goose Green to remove battlefield casualties had earned much admiration. The Battalion regarded him almost as one of theirs for, during a late-seventies' tour of duty with the Gurkha Transport Regiment in Brunei, he had been attached to 7GR as an infantry officer for six months.

The Commandant wasted no time. 'A Company will be investigating a possible *dush* OP on Mount Usborne. So can you support this mission by two Scout helicopters armed with SS-11 missiles? Look at the map. It's supposed to be a possible wooden hut or tent location nearly 700 metres up just under the summit and, a little further away, there's a possible radar site.'

John bubbled with enthusiasm with the thought of more missile firing as he had done for 2 Para on Swan Inlet House. 'Yes, no problem, Colonel! Send in the helarm request, and I'll be on immediate standby for your guys,' he confirmed. The other B Company tasks with the isolated shepherds' houses in Lafonia were also explained before John disappeared, a happy man, into the cold and rain as I sent the SOP four-point 'armed helicopter' request to Brigade.

Meanwhile C Company would continue to guard the POWs and keep a platoon-strength Quick Reaction Force on immediate standby for any unforeseen threat. They would also start their patrolling eastwards towards Mount Misery and Fox Point, thirty kilometres distant, while the sixteen-man A Company fighting patrol led by the tough QGO platoon commander, Captain Hombahadur Gurung, and which included the 9 Para Sapper Sergeant Ron Wrega and a British medical orderly, left Darwin to mount their possible attack against the suspected Mount Usborne *dush* OP.

The remainder of A Company would send a patrol to Knob Point on the easternmost tip of Lafonia, and continue to clear the battlefield by emptying twenty-two *dush* bunkers full of grenades and ammunition. '*Grenade haru alu chhare jhain bhuinbhari thiyo*' (grenades were scattered on the ground like potatoes), was my QGOs' description to me of this mess after I became A Company Commander later that year. A number of bunkers were back-filled with earth while other Gurkhas removed a large ammunition and mortar bomb dump. They also built an improvised rifle range and got some useful target practice by firing some of the *dush* ammunition. Normally a Gurkha cherishes his rifle but, with no accommodation available at Darwin, A Company demonstrated contempt for the discarded and poorly maintained *dush* FAL rifles by using them as supports in strengthening their makeshift shelters. The Mortar Platoon could claim similar success:

> By now all four mortars south of Darwin had also been well dug in, complete with two command posts, shelter and ammunition bays, and GPMG trenches. Superb camouflage was achieved by transferring large prickly bushes from their natural positions, to sit on top of the trenches: indeed people were later to pass through the mortar line without realizing its presence . . . The mortar section (from the Sussex Mountains) set up a second mortar line on the outskirts of Goose Green from where it was possible to reach further out to the south. This also freed (the Darwin mortar sections) to concentrate on the north.[3]

The bad weather also meant warm rations became vital, but still no fresh water had been supplied from Brigade resources. Sometimes Gurkhas make too literal interpretations and, for one rifleman, the Darwin Pond on his map indicated a convenient water supply for a brew of tea and cooking up some food. He chose powdered soup from his ration pack and mixed this with water from the pond, heating it up on his hexamine stove. His section commander, Corporal Harkabahadur Limbu, received some of the steaming soup, only to spit it out because of its powerful salty tast.

'So where did you get this water from?' asked a surprised Harkabahadur.

'From the big pond over there *hajur!*' replied the equally surprised rifleman, not realizing Darwin Pond was, indeed, a sea inlet.[4]

A Company also carried out normal defence routine. Those bunkers not filled in, were improved. A methodical system of clearing patrols and listening posts was established in the awful weather to ensure the security of the nearby ground. They also found the first of more victims of British shelling in the recent battle. This would become almost a daily occurrence as the news arrived on the Battalion radio net to me in the ops room. Typical that June morning was the laconic message of Major David Willis,

159

the A Company Commander: 'Hello zero, this is one. Just found a stiff located under a gorse bush at Grid . . .'

This personnel challenge, however, was not so great as our current major logistics 'Q' shortfall – an acute rations shortage which also affected the prisoners. Like the Gurkhas, they could not be moved out of Goose Green because helicopter transport had been prioritized elsewhere. It meant Ram's B Echelon at San Carlos was suffering from the non-tactical loading of supplies on the *Nordic Ferry* and *Baltic Ferry* at Southampton and failure of Brigade HQ to implement its promise that stores on these ships would be restowed correctly at Ascension Island. Consequently the Battalion's rations, which should have been sent to Rory Stewart's A Echelon establishing itself at Goose Green, could not be found.

'No ration resupply means that we're going to have to live off the land. Get Warrant Officer Massey sent forward from San Carlos so that he can begin the supervision of the cooking of *dumba* centrally here at Goose Green,' ordered the Commandant using this appropriate Gurkhali word for an animal not renowned for its intelligence.

The kelpers, though, had an alternative '365' nickname for Falklands' mutton because of its availability throughout the year. So immediately after his arrival at the settlement, Massey began to cook vast quantities of mutton stew for the hungry Gurkhas. 'Here you are, get your teeth into this!' exclaimed the chief cook whose face and drooping moustache was reminiscent of Walt Disney's 'Captain Hook'. He had caught his 'crocodile' and, with an encouraging, 'There she goes!' to his hungry customers, the huge saucepan of stew thudded onto an ops room table. We were soon tucking into the steaming food.

However Massey was not the only newcomer to visit us in the ops room, which had become like the crossroads of Rome. Time and effort was needed to establish every visitor's identity and what he required. One was a short but stocky Royal Navy Lieutenant from HMS *Fearless*. The dark blue bereted officer introduced himself and the civilian ship he was now commanding with a cheerful, 'Morning! My name's Ian McClaran. I'm the Senior Naval Officer of the Falkland Island Company's ship *Monsunen* which is moored at the jetty here. She's now operational after her period of Argie ownership and beaching on Lively Island after a couple of our frigates challenged her in the Choisel Sound. The Argies towed her back to Goose Green afterwards. There was a rope twisted around her propeller, but this has been removed by some Royal Navy divers yesterday assisted by a lass from the settlement. We're available for possible future tasks in moving stores and equipment by sea to Fitzroy.'

The Battalion would become better acquainted with Ian's vessel the following week. Another visit that day was from an Ammunition Technical Officer. Better known as an 'a-toe', his warning was to prevent any unnecessary alert of the heavily armed Gurkha garrison. He had spotted their impatiently sheathed kukris. 'Eh, just thought we'd inform you that we're about to start destroying some of the more unstable Argie ammunition found in the settlement,' he carefully informed the ops room staff. 'This'll occur during the next few days. So don't worry, if you hear a few bangs. You've not been attacked. It's just us.'

He and the other ATOs began their work later that day. The daily explosions that rocked Goose Green provided more realistic battle sound effects than those experienced two months before in Bovington's Battle Group Trainer. It also reminded us we were at war, but the results of that first day's patrolling did little to alleviate the general Gurkha frustration. B Company had failed to locate any *dush* as Rifleman Baliprasad Rai would later describe:

> Each day we would smear ourselves with camouflage cream, climb into Scout helicopters and scour the East Falkland (Lafonia) hills for Argentines. Mostly we would find only abandoned positions with arms and ammunition intact. Their trenches were always poorly dug, inadequately sheltered with only a tin sheet or a tarpaulin overhead and a couple of blankets below. Some even had webbing, clothing and various oddments of war in them. We could only shake our heads in wonder at the sheer waste.[5]

A Company had also drawn a blank. Captain Hombahadur Gurung's fighting patrol reached its target area, only to be disappointed in discovering that the suspected OP tent was nothing more than an enormous rock. This severely disappointed John Greenhalgh whose helarm missile tasks were cancelled and Hombahadur sahib's patrol continued its search for the *dush* OP further eastwards. Ironically, however, it had been the three *dush* captured by 2 Para who had manned this particular OP, *and* also had provided the intelligence for the B Company operation in Lafonia. So the only good news at the end of that dull afternoon was from Mike Kefford. His D Company had arrived at 2 Para's first battle objective which was the isolated Burntside House, at the northern end of the Darwin Isthmus. It had been a trial of strength even for an officer of Mike's calibre, and there was fatigue in his voice as he reported on the radio: 'Sitrep. Now arrived at our final objective. No casualties to report. We're going to brew up, and establish ourselves at this location.'

The twenty kilometres from the Sussex Mountains as the crow flies had taken the fully-loaded Gurkhas only thirty hours including a night halt. It was an achievement demonstrating again the Gurkhas' collective strength and endurance, for an Army unit is as fit as its weakest man. They occupied some old *dush* trenches and dug others before taking a well-earned rest. Mike, understandably, would not be present at that evening's O Group scheduled to start at 20.00 hours, one hour before last light. Hors d'oeuvres arrived at 19.00 hours.

'Air raid warning red!' enunciated the Brigade watchkeeper on the radio.

'Helmets on!' I ordered the ops room staff in compliance with the strict red air alert routines laid down by the Commandant.

There was an air raid shelter built of peat sods located outside at the back of the shop, but we never used it. The radios and ops room had to be manned at all times. That familiar anxiety surged through one's body as the alert was repeated on the Battalion net. But there was no danger. The *dush* aircraft had already passed Goose Green to the north, disappearing towards the north-east. After stand-down, the O Group began with a displeased Commandant saying, 'There'll still be no move out of Goose Green to the front line being established in the hills around Stanley until, at the earliest, 7 June. The reason is lack of helicopters. However other alternatives are being considered. One is to put back into service a *dush* Coast Guard patrol craft with the name of *Islas Malvinas*.

It was damaged by a Harrier attack soon after the San Carlos landings and has been found beached further up the coast at Buttons Bay. Also the Falkland Island Company's motor coaster *Monsunen*, still moored at the Goose Green jetty for eventual Brigade stores transportation forward to Fitzroy, might also be a possibility.'

The Blohm and Voss patrol craft was only eighty tons and one third the size of *Monsunen*. However with a top speed of twenty-two knots it was nearly three times faster than the coaster and could partly provide a solution to our transportation problems. 'Until this can be examined to establish its seaworthiness, though, the Battalion's patrolling strategy will continue,' said the Commandant. 'Hombahadur sahib's patrol will remain out in the khuds because there's a suspicion that his original *dush* OP target might be located further east on Wickham Heights. C Company will continue with its clearing patrols along the East Falkland southern coastline, while B Company maintains its patrolling of Lafonia.'

The B Company Commander, Lester Holley, then announced that two patrols would investigate Arrow Harbour House again and Walker Creek Settlement, with the concept of operations for one of these patrols breaking new ground. 'It'll be supported by an 81-mm mortar put on a trailer and drawn by a Goose Green tractor! We're going to do it like this, not only because there'll be more firepower available,' he said before his classic SAS contradiction, 'but also because this'll be a fun way of going to war!'

David Willis was most preoccupied with implementation of an effective password system as he had to tab the three kilometres from Darwin to attend the 20.00 hours O Group, but Gurkha sentries straining at the leash for a first *dush* contact made him anxious. 'I'm running the gauntlet during daylight as I come into Goose Green,' he said, 'but more so when returning to Darwin in darkness, and there's no way I want to be a blue-on-blue victim!'

The Commandant provided an instant international phonetic alphabet solution. 'OK, this'll be our system,' he replied. 'As from tomorrow, 5 June, sentries observing anyone approaching their position will challenge with: "November November". The response'll be: "Foxtrot Foxtrot". These will change daily at 12.00 hours. So, for the following day, 6 June, they'll be: "Alpha Alpha – Tango Tango". Passwords for the 7th will be made known at tomorrow's O Group and so on. Happy now?'

Suddenly this mundane task of remembering the day's passwords, taken for granted on exercises and often treated as a bit of a joke if one got it wrong, had became one of potential life or death importance – as we were to discover in ten days during the climax to our operations. However the A Company Commander's fears had been allayed as a second red air alert interrupted the O Group at about 21.00 hours. *Dush* Canberras had taken the same flight path as their colleagues' two hours before to bomb the Mount Kent area and 42 Commando. A red air alert situation remained a nerve-racking affair despite our distance from the target, but the stand-down arrived shortly afterwards and the O Group broke up. Mark then made a sensible proposal, 'There's not only Gurkhas in Goose Green but also the kelpers. We get the warnings about the red air alerts, but they don't. I suggest therefore that a general warning of future alerts be broadcast within the settlement.'

So Keith Baillie was contacted. He later produced Goose Green's portable fire alarm siren which was positioned outside the shop's main entrance. Mark was satisfied. 'One of the Gurkha Signallers on duty here in the ops room can swing the handle on this whenever the next appropriate opportunity arrives,' he said, giving more instructions in his impeccable Gurkhali to the Gurkhas as to how the machine worked. Their practice drill produced a siren wail that would have woken the dead and guarantee an authentic London Blitz atmosphere to Goose Green's next red air alert.

I had scheduled myself to continue my watch until midnight and decided to write a quick letter to Tove. Thoughts continued afterwards about my home and girls at Wakefords Park in that quiet hour before going off duty as, outside, the rain continued to hammer down. Quite a difference from last summer's family holiday in the little Italian seaside resort of Pietrasanta not far from the town of Pisa and its leaning tower. Those lazy two weeks in the sun, sand and sea when both Victoria and Emily were stung frequently by mosquitos, and poor little Emily kept slipping and hitting her head on the wet marble floor of our rented house, seemed to be prehistoric events that had occurred on a different planet.

Such domestic images were interrupted by Mark arriving to start his watch. I snatched a few hours of fitful sleep on our storeroom concrete floor before Bis Bis gently shook my shoulder to hand over a life-giving mug of hot sweet tea and a cheery, '*Chiya, sahib!*' Afterwards a post-breakfast red air alert was accompanied by the siren's wail. The *Aerea Fuerza Argentina* seemed to be taking advantage of the slight weather improvement but, although the threat's reality and repeated wailing shook the tiredness out of my body, the *dush* pilots did nothing more than create that expected surreal blitz ambience. We also continued to follow the general war situation on our high frequency Clansman radio set. While the BBC World Service reported on the UN Security Council's latest resolution from the previous evening for ceasefire initiatives, B Company's Lafonia tour for that day was drawing another blank. However the tactics were original:

> Saturday, 5 June saw an interesting and somewhat comical experiment in which one mortar became for a while 'mechanized'. A platoon-sized patrol moving south to clear part of Lafonia was provided with a single mortar that followed approximately one kilometre to the rear. Due to the extremely boggy ground the only vehicle capable of negotiating the watery, soft peat was a tractor. Driven by the platoon commander the tractor drew a trailer containing one mortar with a No. 1 and 2, a CPO with plotter and two radios, 20 mortar bombs and a GPMG. As the Rifle Platoon reached each report line in turn, the mortar would be deployed by the side of the tractor ready to cover the patrol forward to the next bound. No contact occurred however and the detachment returned to Goose Green.[6]

Captain Nigel Price had enjoyed himself on this four-hour mission behind the wheel of his improvised machine of war, despite its large wheels forever throwing up large clumps of mud as he motored around Lafonia. After some time, Nigel looked behind to check on his four-man Gurkha crew sitting quietly on the trailer. Covered in mud from head to toe, in typical Gurkha fashion they had made no complaint and grinned back at their astonished OC sahib. In the meantime C Company had also maintained both its patrolling activity and vigil on the Goose Green POWs – while, to the north-east, Hombahadur sahib's patrol suddenly sent an excited radio report: 'Have located target of enemy Oscar Papa!'

This had to be the much sought-after OP, and a radio request was made to Brigade for a Harrier fighter ground attack strike. Somehow 2 Para in their command post at Bluff Cove became aware of the air strike request and intervened. If implemented, it could have caused a disaster. The proposed target was no *dush* location, but a 2 Para small radio station party set up to relay messages between Bluff Cove and their A Echelon still at Goose Green. Protected by four members of the Paras' Defence Platoon, they were located halfway between the two settlements. Another potential blue-on-blue incident had been averted but, by now, Hombahadur sahib and his men had been in the khuds for two nights. It was so cold Sergeant Ron Wrega and the accompanying British medical orderly began suffering from exposure; however, the QGO drove on his patrol despite an acute shortage of rations.

Our problems in Battalion HQ continued by unannounced visitors harrassing the ops room staff. A Company's daily dose of death messages on the radio was further underlined that day by two officers visiting from *Fearless*. One was a Marine Staff Captain who had to coordinate the following day's burial of the *dush* dead still lying behind the hedgerow. His partner, a padre on the same mission, then held up in the palm of his hand the bloodstained flying helmet of Lieutenant Nick Taylor, the dead Fleet Air Arm Harrier pilot. 'I'll make sure that'll be washed off before the helmet's returned to his widow,' he promised quietly.

Wanting solitude after that, I left the ops room in the afternoon and, despite the dreadful weather and squelching mud, the fresh air was a godsend. I promenaded past the 471 POWs enjoying their eighth day of captivity. Only a section of eight Gurkhas was needed to guard these docile *dush* who had food and a roof over their heads. But the hackles on the back of my neck rose a centimetre as they slouched in the doorways of the sheep-shearing sheds and gazed sulkily at their guards and anyone else who walked by. These men did not begin to compare to our Gurkhas' professionalism, and would have benefitted from adopting Gurkha methods of behaviour and standards – including perhaps a similar digital address system to tackle their plethora of common surnames such as Gomez, Lopez, Ramirez, Riveros, Sanchez etc. Indignation oozed out of them – to manifest itself in little more than two weeks time when, on board the *Norland* en route to Puerto Madryn and repatriation, their plan to hijack 'our' former ferry was fortunately foiled.[7]

A few must also have read the article in the Buenos Aires weekly periodical *Flash* which had been found in the settlement's bunkhouse for batchelor shepherds. This described the Gurkhas as 'famous for their bestiality' and the kukri as being their 'thirty-centimetre dagger', and was our first evidence that the 5 May press call at Church Crookham had begun to produce fruit. Perhaps, however, the general *dush* passivity could also be explained by the following 'psyops' story – even though part of it should be read with a pinch of salt:

Before they left, 2 Para had told the prisoners that the Gurkhas were cannibals and ate people they did not like. The Argentinian conscripts believed what they were told without question, as rumours about the Gurkhas were already rife.

The Gurkhas had no trouble. They had been told to smile at the prisoners every time they looked like getting out of hand. A Gurkha's smile is a terrifying thing. It looks as though he is about to do something dastardly. The prisoners behaved themselves immaculately every time a Gurkha bared his teeth, believing that one false move, and he would leap forward and eat them.[8]

The officers were certainly Gurkha aware. On 21 May the Goose Green manager, Eric Goss, was talking outside his office to a Captain Raullo whilst *Ardent*, on station in Grantham Sound, continued to bombard the airstrip. There she reduced the air threat against the San Carlos landings by destroying a second Pucará aircraft that day; but Raullo, a military/civil liaison officer, seemed more concerned about our imminent arrival.

'The Gurkhas are bad for our health,' he said. 'I understand they are very silent, so how do you know when they're about?' Goss did not miss his chance. 'When you wake up in the morning. Shake your head. If it falls off, they've called!' Raullo was impressed. 'So how much does the British Army pay them?' he enquired. 'A bowl of rice a day!' joked Goss. The response was a commendably quick, 'Please tell them, then, we will provide two or three bowls of rice a day, if they come and fight for us!'[9]

Further away from the prisoners of war accommodation and on a little rise, was the hedgerow near the settlement's entrance. The twenty dark bundles behind this still awaited their burial next day. Viewed closer they were not a pretty sight, with some just mangled lumps of flesh. I could never understand why other British soldiers had taken photographs of them or, indeed, other battlefield dead. Ghoulish souvenir hunting like that only signalled the perpetrators' poor upbringing. In war the dead on both sides should always be respected.

Not lingering there, I tramped across to the rear of a house south of the settlement where the two inanimate *dush* 35-mm Oerlikon cannon were located. This double-barrelled weapon had the capability of firing fifty-six shells in a single magazine, and could penetrate forty millimetres of armour at a range of one kilometre. Curious, I climbed into the vehicle containing its Skyguard computerized radar fire control system. The smashed computer screen indicated a *dush* information technology spiking operation on the guidance system. Shells were so plentiful though, that a rumour spread of a recommendation which had been sent to the Ministry of Defence urging the purchase of a similar weapon system so all this ammunition could be fired.

On return to the ops room, I was informed by an excited Gurkha Signaller of the Battalion's first wartime shooting incident. My radio appointment title Kestrel gave the Gurkhas some pronounciation difficulties – and this soldier was no exception as he tried to brief me. 'Krystal sahib!' he exclaimed. 'There has just arrived a report that one of our men in Support Company has been shot and wounded!'

My instant reaction that the *dush* could be now launching a counter-offensive to drive the Gurkha invaders from their *Islas las Malvinas* receded just as quickly when, after further questioning, I learnt that an attached British Sergeant belonging to Battalion Headquarters had fired a negligent discharge in a house taken over by Support Company. The scene of crime received my visit where the senior NCO, on past record a highly dependable and intelligent man, was still present. In a state of shock, his information was limited to a disconsolate, 'I was just cleaning my Sterling sub-machine gun, sir, when it accidently fired.'

The rogue burst of automatic fire had hit Rifleman Kamalprasad Limbu three times in the backside, but his injuries were not serious, although the potential results from such a scenario could, nonetheless, have been a lot worse. The Gurkha and his wounded posterior had to be 'casevaced' to SS *Uganda*, the Task Force hospital ship. Regardless of any quick recovery, this meant there would be one Gurkha less for the war. Once a soldier arrived on board the Red Cross registered and, therefore neutral, ship – the rules of this game implied that his return to the Theatre of Operations could only be via the UK.

Any 'ND' is a serious disciplinary offence. The Sterling had a notorious reputation in the Emerald Isle for causing such incidents, but clearly these rarely, if ever, occurred in Gurkha battalions as the Commandant asked me in the shop's entrance, 'Can you give me an idea of the severity of punishment meted out in Northern Ireland for an ND?'

My reply, 'When I had been serving there it was an automatic twenty-eight days in jail, sir,' made me feel, for once, something of a combat veteran. It also proved to be a sentence impractical to impose in a Goose Green where there existed enough prisoners in captivity already. So the Queen received this particular British Sergeant's Falklands' War services free of charge via the Commandant's fine which was equivalent to twenty-eight days' pay. By coincidence 2 Para suffered two such NDs forty-eight hours later at Fitzroy, one of these also involving a Sterling which seriously wounded another soldier.[10] Our blue-on-blue which had caused one totally unneccessary Battalion casualty would not, however, be the last – and would include near misses of the same category.

The O Group that evening was informed that the beached *Islas Malvinas* patrol vessel would be examined the following day by a Sapper search team and Spanish-speaking staff sergeant with two sections of the Recce Platoon placed on standby to provide local protection. 'But it looks as if *Monsunen* is still the best option for any Battalion move eastwards, although the earliest date for starting any such operation is Monday, 7 June,' sighed the Commandant.

That evening I dozed in my sleeping bag for a few hours before going on watch at midnight. The stillness was deafening, similar to that on night duty in the ops room of 39 Infantry Brigade HQ at Lisburn where the West Belfast PIRA had a habit of springing nocturnal surprises during my watchkeeper's job there. So I was on my guard as an opportunity to write arose. Impressions of the settlement were included in my letter to Tove:

> This Goose Green place is most remarkable for being unremarkable. Very simple, unsophisticated people who really just want to be left alone. I hope I don't sound converted or anything, but they have been through a bit of an ordeal with these Fascist pigs (dear oh dear, I sound terribly political now, don't I?).

The night dragged on. Still quiet. I looked at my watch and noted, 'That's it, soon 04.00 hours – dead man's hour.' Outside a starting helicopter engine and whomp, whomp of rotor blades interrupted the peace. Within a few minutes, the Gazelle was airborne. 2 Para's new location at Bluff Cove and Fitzroy had necessitated establishing some Brigade forward communications, and so a rebroadcast radio station had been placed halfway up Mount Pleasant at Wickham Heights midway between Goose Green and Bluff Cove. We received no information of this facility, however the station had developed a malfunction. In the Gazelle I had heard taking off were two signals specialists who would attempt to effect repairs. One was the Brigade Signals Squadron Commander, Major Mike Forge.

Ten minutes later a message from the re-bro station of: 'Just seen a sudden orange ball of flame which has exploded and fallen to the ground!' crackled faintly through on the Brigade command radio net.

Chapter Fourteen

ON THE MOVE

These (Gurkha) soldiers – typical cannon fodder . . . as experts in deploying in moun-tainous regions, they have an almost animal training in which they treat the lives of others or their own where death is the logical escape. They fight for pay – nothing else – and always to serve 'their British comrades', the purest type from the golden age of the last century when the pirate's flags fluttered in numerous captured territories on top of the mountains of corpses of these conquered areas. – Flash periodical.[1]

Off East Falkland's southern coastline the Royal Navy were shooting first and asking questions afterwards. But I was unaware that the soldier who had observed this spec-tacular blue-on-blue of Major Mike Forge's helicopter shot down by two Sea Dart missiles fired from HMS *Cardiff* had been the NCO in command of the two-man 5 Brigade re-bro station. Fatigue made me unable to put two and two together. Then he sent another radio report: 'Will move out from my location shortly with one other to try and locate the crash site.'

The darkness prevented them from finding anything, and later before dawn, I briefed the incoming watchkeeper about the incident before going off watch. While I slept there was a red air alert with high-altitude *dush* Canberras dropping bombs near San Carlos, that must have woken the B Echelon Gurkhas. The weather was frightful with a gale of Force Eight to Nine, but the Commandant still had not been informed by Brigade of the re-bro station's existence at Wickham Heights. Nonetheless after an air search revealed the helicopter's wreckage, he was then tasked to check the area with a patrol as the speculation was that a *dush* stay-behind party had been respon-sible. So C Company's QRF was alerted and the Commandant gave their commander, Captain Belbahadur Rai, his mission, 'Escort the Battalion's doctor to the crash site and check the surrounding countryside for *dush*. All movement there is to be regarded as hostile!'

This meant, to quote the Commandant's standard terminology that any *dush* forces found were to be 'zapped' immediately. So perhaps the Gurkhas' luck would now change as this platoon and doctor were flown to the crash site. After the airframe remains had been examined and Martin Entwhistle had noted the condition of the four dead, it was deduced the crash had been caused by the impact and subsequent ex-plosion of a surface-to-air missile. Meanwhile some of Belbahadur sahib's patrolling riflemen began to hear voices nearby and reported, '*Dush*, sahib!' to their QGO.

Gurkhas react instinctively in such circumstances. They prepared to attack whilst Belbahadur moved forward to make one final recce of the objective. Suddenly he heard English spoken and a closer investigation revealed the re-bro station's location. Another potential blue-on-blue had been prevented. Yet the threat of the *dush* stay-behind parties remained and, despite the weather, Belbahadur and his men continued to patrol around the area all that day. Their search was to be in vain.

Representatives from the media missed this story when they visited Goose Green that day. Just after lunch their minder, Lieutenant Colonel David Dunn, stuck his head into the ops room, and saw me. The official guidelines came for yet another job. 'I've got a dozen or so of the press outside, Mike,' he said urgently. 'Can you give them some information now on the way things are going for the Gurkhas? You know the policy. Just concentrate on describing the condition and general attitude of the prisoners at Goose Green, but give them nothing about your Battalion's future operations.'

We had been spared the attentions of these gentlemen since arriving in the Falklands, and this had led to an attack of Alzheimer's Lite regarding my other role as the Battalion Public Information Officer. Within five minutes the shop became the venue for an impromptu press conference. Bill Dawson also arrived. Lieutenant Colonel Dunn's public relations' guidelines written on board 'The Great White Whale' a few days before had forbidden the prisoners to be described as prisoners of war. This was another UK politically dictated method of manipulating the truth. There the Falklands' campaign was still labelled as a euphemistic conflict and not realistic war despite the prisoners' de facto POW home address painted in those large white letters on the sheep-shearing sheds.

One journalist present at the press conference was the BBC's Brian Hanrahan. His following day's optimistic report included points from our briefing, a few of which had been presented with, maybe, an excess of bravado:

> Privately, the British officers doubt that the men in the hills are likely to do anything except surrender. They say that the Argentine soldiers who gave up at Goose Green seemed happier in captivity than they were in their army. According to them the ordinary Argentine conscript was left very much to fend for himself while the officers and NCOs did all right. Among the professionals of the British Army there's amazement that no cleaning kit for their weapons was found on the 1400 Argentine prisoners, something borne out by the state of their guns. Many are so rusty that they're unusable. One (Gurkha) soldier who spent two hours cleaning up a captured rifle said that when he began he couldn't move a single part, not even the safety catch.
>
> The feeling among the British officers is that the lack of motivation among the Argentine soldiers explains their failure to do anything to check the rapid British advance. They say that if the defending forces were pushed forwards to face the British troops the evidence suggests that they would surrender once they're away from their commander's influence.[2]

Hanrahan's cameraman then filmed the Gurkhas, and the correspondent noted the detail of their patrol preparations:

... they fly out daily in Army Scout helicopters looking for groups of Argentine soldiers who were outflanked in the main advance . . . I watched one group preparing for their airborne patrol being briefed in Gurkhali by one of their officers. As he talked softly to them, one produced his kukri and slit open a tube of camouflage cream which they passed around, smearing it on their faces and exchanging banter. Then they mounted their helicopters and left, setting down from time to time to check a cottage or an abandoned tent. But this patrol, like the others for the past few days, failed to discover anything except abandoned arms and ammunition.[3]

Little, if anything, had been mentioned about the Gurkhas in the news until then, as my father wrote that day in an understated letter:

Life seems to be one long round of listening to the radio, watching television, and reading the newspapers for news of the Falklands in general and 5 Brigade in particular. On the latter there is virtually nothing, which may be perfectly correct strategy, but exasperating for fireside Blimps like myself and virtually everyone else in UK. Your dear mother, directing the entire operation from her armchair, has to be heard to be believed. Not that I am any better.

However life here, and at Church Crookham, I think, also goes on pretty much as before. I find that I am a shade more acid towards councillors who ask stupid questions about housing matters in committee, and I have noticed your mother is less tolerant than usual with the stupider ladies of her Art Society . . . Finally may I say that as far as one can judge from here, the whole Falkland operation is very well handled, and if it were not for you, I should be almost lost in admiration.

The British media, though, had started to spread the message to the *dush* of us being on the Falklands because Tove saw Gurkhas on her TV that evening, and wrote:

Tonight I watched the Gurkhas on the Falkland Islands! How long you've been there for I don't know, maybe a week. But now I know you are there, and I'm surprisingly calm. Think I'm just relieved to hear news of you – and at least you landed safely and are now out of range of Exocets etc. The message still is though for you to keep your head down. It looked dreadful on the box, mud and fog and water and yukky slush everywhere.

That afternoon, Sunday, 6 June, Hombahadur's empty-handed patrol, after sixty hours of effort, was returned by helicopter to Darwin. A Company's next task was to fly another patrol to Lively Island, but its subsequent search only located an abandoned camp, white *dush* flying helmet and aircraft wreckage. Shortly after the patrol returned to Darwin a Brigade intelligence report was received at Goose Green which gave Battalion HQ exactly the same Lively Island information: a precursor to every later intelligence document we received throughout the campaign which would be invariably late or of hopelessly poor quality.

These lack of results merely increased the Commandant's agitation to move his Gurkhas out of Darwin and Goose Green because any meaningful action for them would be found forward of Fitzroy and Bluff Cove, where 5 Brigade was now converging. So he had been pleased that day to receive a warning order for him to draw up preliminary plans for a night attack on the third, and inner, ring of high ground around Stanley. Our objectives were two features – the Tumbledown and Mount William where a *dush* Marine Infantry unit had dug a defensive position. One Gurkha company was earmarked as a Brigade sub-unit patrols company, so Mike Kefford received his second major task. Despite his Gurkhas' laudable Sussex Mountains tab, a similar operation from Goose Green to Fitzroy was not feasible. They had to be trans-ported to Fitzroy and then tab forward before mounting reconnaissance patrols onto these objectives. But only one means of transportation existed.

Not only D Company, but other Gurkha sub-units would have to return to their least-favourite natural element of the sea – and ships. Instructions were therefore sent to B Echelon at San Carlos for logistic resources to be dispatched as soon as possible to Fitzroy because of our imminent move. Two Battalion Land-Rovers and their drivers – a British Signaller attached to the Battalion and Rifleman Bhairabahadur Rai – were embarked upon the landing ship logistics RFA *Sir Tristram* as part of a seventy-strong Brigade party. The ship, loaded with ammunition and stores, would depart later that night and was scheduled to arrive at Fitzroy by first light. Ram and eleven of his B Echelon men would also move from San Carlos to Fitzroy the following day – on board *Sir Tristram*'s sister ship, the RFA *Sir Galahad*.

The evening's O Group at Goose Green began with Paddy Redding's information which would restrict the number of Battalion sub-units eventually moved into the front line near Stanley. 'We've received intelligence from Brigade HQ of a *dush* heliborne or parachute assault threat from the Argentine mainland onto the Goose Green airstrip. The source is graded as A2 category, a category reckoned to be most reliable,' intoned the grave-faced IO. Paddy had, by now, become used to his role as the constant bearer of ominous tidings to the Battalion. He also revelled in it.

The threat of a counter-attack from West Falkland also still existed, so the Commandant decided on some operational freelancing with his 'eyes and ears' sub-unit. 'OK, in that case it'll be prudent to deploy elements of the Recce Platoon to the west coast of Lafonia at Dos Lomas House and Egg Harbour House,' he told his listening officers. 'These two locations are fifteen and twenty-five kilometres respec-tively from Goose Green, and the Recce Platoon's task'll be to put out two OPs at these locations sited towards the west and Falkland Sound in order to give advance warning of any attacking forces that the *dush* might deploy.'

His continuing impatience had found no relief during the day as he now divulged more bad news about ending the Battalion's enforced stay at Darwin and Goose Green, 'Unfortunately the Sappers' examination of the beached *Islas Malvinas* has established she's badly holed and unseaworthy. This means we cannot use her for transporting Battalion sub-units closer to Stanley. So for present, most will have to continue to sit tight here.'

It was a classic case of mistaken identity brought about by fog of war. This was, in reality, the GC 83 *Rio Iguazú*. Her sister vessel, GC 82 *Islas Malvinas*, had beaten off a

British Lynx helicopter attack three weeks prior to three Harriers strafing the *Rio Iguazú* loaded with two 105-mm howitzers for the *dush* Goose Green garrison. The cannon fire holed the craft which was then beached, but not before her Browning machine gunner had shot down a Harrier.

'As for D Company, we're just going to have to jam even more men onto the *Monsunen*,' continued the Commandant. 'They'll be accompanied by 2 Para's A Echelon and both will embark and sail on her to Fitzroy tomorrow evening. This is fifty kilometres down the coast as the crow flies and about sixty-five kilometres or forty nautical miles by sea. The sixteen hours of daylight will be sufficient for *Monsunen* to deliver her cargo and return to Goose Green by first light. B Company with Bill Dawson and the Alternative Battalion HQ, will then embark on her the evening after tomorrow. I just hope she'll be big enough for that number of passengers. And to spare D Company, can we also find out if *Monsunen* is able to embark their men at Darwin?'

But before the O Group dispersed it was decided that D Company would tab another seven kilometres down the Darwin Isthmus from Burntside House and embark at Goose Green. Afterwards the ops room staff continued their duties until relieved at midnight by the incoming shift. Nigel Price, the Mortar Platoon Commander, paid a visit. We talked for a while about the outlook for the Gurkha exodus out of Goose Green. 'Anything's better than us remaining holed-up in this place,' declared Nigel. 'We've just got to be moved up to the front line as soon as possible in order to get on with the fighting.'

I remained silent. Nigel was a decent person, but his enthusiasm was suffocating and it set off a chain reaction of personal thoughts. 'How can Nigel bang on so much about *wanting* to move pronto up to the front line?' was my spontaneous inner reaction which smouldered on for some time after he left the ops room. I was scared about the likelihood of being involved in a full-scale infantry battle – a scenario I would have contemplated as ridiculous while watching childrens' TV with Victoria and Emily less than three months ago. Although I had been a pessimistic Tommy Atkins during the intervening period, my point of no return had long since passed last autumn, when I had accepted this secondment. So now, alone with the radios and two Gurkha Signallers in the ops room, my brooding continued unabated, 'If we have to go, we have to go – but those expressions Nigel was using really belong to the bad manuscript of an overstated Hollywood war-film. And even now, here in Goose Green, everything remains quite unreal – a fresh battlefield virtually outside our front doorstep, stiffs, POWs, and leftover rubbish from the fighting still being cleared up. As for moving up to the front line, as Nigel puts it . . . well, even that seems surreal. Indeed, everyone acts as if they're extras in a Falklands' War feature film!'

At midnight and off duty once more, I returned to the store room and the cosy little world of my sleeping bag. The night would be quiet operationally, but my planned kip was interrupted by severe stomach pains. Staggering into the loo, no relief was forthcoming. So, hooking up my combat trousers, I staggered out again into the ops room where Paddy Redding was on watch. He was reading a paperback. 'Can you help me to the quack so I can get some pills for this?' I mumbled, doubling up.

With Paddy's assistance, I reached Martin Entwhistle's requisitioned house further along the settlement. His RAP was also located there and the medicine handed out. It worked and a follow-up visit to the shop's loo proved such a great success that, by daybreak, my system had returned to normal. Others also experienced this affliction locally dubbed as 'Galtieri's Revenge'. Later, however, I suspected that my so-called *Galti garyo* bug could have been a similar pre-action psychosomatic stress symptom which a 1LI subaltern in my Company experienced in Northern Ireland seven years before. He went one better and fainted just before moving out from our base to a border operation.

Dawn on 7 June brought a transformation in the weather. No cloud, no rain, no wind – just sun in the cold blue sky. On the ops room radio D Company reported their imminent departure from the Burntside House area and yet another visitor arrived in my little kingdom. The bearded Surgeon Commander Rick Jolly had arrived from Ajax Bay and the Commando Logistic Regiment's Medical Squadron, where no wounded British soldier who entered his surgical centre there for treatment during the war died. The facility's nickname of 'The Red and Green Life Machine' referred to the colour of the Para and Marine Commando medics' berets. A good omen for the Gurkhas because their berets were also green.

Jolly, in accordance with his surname, announced his presence by a cheery, 'Hello, just arrived here at Goose Green in order to check on the local medical situation.' His main task that morning was to check out the 2 Para trench foot cases and, once this had been accomplished, he returned to the green and his waiting helicopter. Fortunately he arrived in the nick of time as the Brigade Commander was about to hijack it.

Meanwhile Sergeant Ron Wrega had made a quick recovery from his Mount Usborne exertions and started on his next task. Leading his small team of attached 9 Para Sappers in clearing the small and large minefields located around the airstrip and settlement, the ops room and shop would rock frequently during the next two days with the explosive results of their work. The ATOs also gathered together the leaking *dush* napalm bombs and these would be detonated later in a controlled explosion which threw up an enormous mushroom cloud of oily smoke and flame. Then at around midday, the Brigade radio spluttered into action with an urgent: 'Air raid warning red!' It was our seventh red air alert of the campaign, and the Gurkha Signallers galvanized themselves into action.

'*Chitto! Chitto!*' (Hurry! Hurry!), urged the senior of the two as his subordinate ran out of the ops room to crank the handle of the siren. Its shrill wail lasted several minutes, before the cranker returned to his radio set. A quarter of a hour later, Bill Dawson from outside the shop's entrance yelled, 'Look at this!' Many of us rushed outside to gaze upwards into that blue sky as he remarked, 'That's one more we don't need to worry about!'

I felt no pity when spotting the white contrails, remains of the mid-air explosion, and broken smoke trail of the stricken photo-reconaissance *dush* Learjet. Shrugging shoulders, I withdrew back into the shop. This was simply one less aircraft on the *dush* inventory list, and type at the time unknown, which indeed would not bother us again. It had been hit at an altitude of 40,000 feet by one of two Sea Dart missiles fired from the destroyer HMS *Exeter* in San Carlos Water. However the B Echelon Gurkhas incorrectly believed it to be a Mirage. And they were not impressed by how the aircraft, minus its tail and still containing the five doomed crew, drifted down like a sycamore leaf to crash onto Pebble Island. 'It doesn't look like that when you're at the movies, sahib!' they complained bitterly to Ram while waiting on the San Carlos jetty at Blue Beach to embark on board the equally ill-fated *Sir Galahad.*

Two small cabins had already been allocated to the twelve Gurkhas on the LSL which was also to embark two companies of the Welsh Guards and 16 Field Ambulance. But a short time later the Commandant changed his mind after the failure of another request to airlift the Battalion forward by helicopter from Goose Green. Mark was manning the Battalion radio net in the ops room, and the Commandant's subsequent order to him gave rise to my later suspicion that he possessed clairvoyant powers, 'Inform Ram *not* to move now to Fitzroy. He's better off remaining at San Carlos until we can sort out our helicopter transport.' The Adjutant sent this order which was received at San Carlos as the twelve Gurkhas were about to embark onto an LCU to take them out to *Sir Galahad.* Barely twenty-four hours later, Ram would get to know the true extent of his men's luck and that of his own as a result of the Commandant's decision.

More BBC World Service reports on our Clansman radio indicating the UN Secretary General had failed to mediate an Anglo-Argentine truce, meant there could be no doubt. We would be deployed to the front line soon. So later that day at Goose Green, Mark Willis, Kit Spencer and I found time for a brief visit to the *Monsunen.* The RSO had already been a visitor. Fed up with *dumba/*'365', he had increased the variety of his diet by finding a rod and line to fish from the coaster's stern during his off duty hours. On board, Senior Naval Officer Ian McClaran, was preparing for D Company's voyage. With three ratings also from *Fearless,* they had the honour of forming Naval Party 2160 which was the smallest of the Task Force. Despite being new to his ship, Ian sounded confident.

'She was in a dreadful state when we came on board. The Argies had crapped everywhere. Anyway, she's been cleaned up now and her propeller's working OK,' he said with a good portion of Navy pride. 'So I should be able to get her statutory eight knots or so out of her even though it's thought that her keel's bent after the Argies' had beached her at Lively Island. According to her civilian skipper the local name for this type of vessel appropriately is a "puff-puff"! I report direct to the Commodore Amphibious Warfare himself, and we're under strict orders not to let this ship be hijacked by 5 Brigade or sail during daylight hours. Should be an interesting trip later this evening.'

He showed us the hold where sheep, bales of wool and other freight were normally stowed, then added, 'We'll put your people down in there, so if the weather gets bad like last night they'll be nice and snug.' There would be about 150 Gurkhas and Paras crammed into the 130 feet by 20 feet space which had no heating. So, recalling the Gurkha orienteering exercises on *QE2* and rumours of a land-based Exocet threat, I asked *Monsunen*'s Senior Naval Officer, 'And so what'll they do in a worst case situation?'

His reply was a straightforward, 'I can't see that there'll be too many alternatives for them. They're going to be below the waterline, have no life jackets or life rafts, the water'll be bloody cold and it'll be as dark as hell – so, basically, I just hope there won't be any worst case situation!'

However D Company was about to embark on a most vulnerable voyage. During the day *dush* OPs on Mount Harriet had seen the approach of *Sir Tristram* towards Port Pleasant. The increased radio activity in the Fitzroy area was also a give away sign of a British forces' concentration there and air strikes from Stanley Airport had already been requested.[4] The Brigade party disembarked from *Sir Tristram*, but priority was given to the offloading of ammunition rather than other stores and vehicles such as the 1st/7th Gurkha Rifles' Land-Rovers. The two Battalion drivers on board were therefore in a situation of growing danger.

That afternoon's drama, though, belonged to the Gurkhas' Recce Platoon which was led by twenty-year old Second Lieutenant Quentin Oates, who was fresh from commissioning and eager to learn. He appeared to be a shy person, but was known to be temperamental. The Commandant had no doubts about his Recce Platoon Commander. 'He's a good egg,' confided the senior sahib to me. Sixteen years later Quentin, who was Australian, swam the English Channel in a highly respectable time of thirteen hours and eleven minutes demonstrating a more than abundant amount of determination.

His platoon had been split up into three patrols of four men per patrol for the task in Lafonia. He would take his patrol and set up an OP in the deserted building known as Egg Harbour House from where, on a fine day, West Falkland could be observed. The operation, seemingly straightforward enough, was not without incident. Quentin and his men were flown out of Goose Green aboard two Scout helicopters each carrying two men. A third Scout armed with wire-guided SS-11 missiles, acted as their escort. On reaching the area of their objective a report was received from the escort helicopter, 'Number of enemy seen running from the building. Engaging with missiles!' Two were fired from the escort Scout, and the other two helicopters landed immediately to deplane the Gurkhas. The latter chose a vantage point from where any further *dush* movement could be observed and radioed for the QRF platoon to be flown out from Goose Green. Quentin's helicopters had already returned to the settlement where, shortly afterwards, two Sea Kings also landed. A hurried briefing then ensued in the ops room between the pilots, Commandant and Captain Indraman Rai who had been ordered to lead the C Company reinforcements. The Commandant gave the QGO his orders in a non-stop stream of unintelligible Gurkhali which terminated with just one English word to which all Gurkhas respond as though placed on auto-pilot – 'Attack, sahib!'

Suitably directed, the QGO ran out, gathered up his men, charged into the Sea Kings, flew to Egg Harbour House and, in the subsequent follow-up operation, captured seven *dush* without a fight. Back in the ops room we monitored the incident and contemplated the accuracy of intelligence that had insisted on another five such *dush* groups in Lafonia. Quentin's adventures, however, were far from finished. The POWs had been flown out, leaving his section to continue their mission but, during the stand-to at last light, one of his soldiers reported seeing three men approaching the house. As these strangers neared it became obvious they were armed, however the Gurkhas waited in ambush. When the three reached an exposed position twenty metres away, Quentin challenged. They were the rest of the *dush* who had run from the house but, realizing there could be no escape, dropped their weapons and surrendered.

175

The excited Gurkhas ordered their prisoners to lie on the ground so they could be searched. Two obeyed, but the third, a Lieutenant Jaime Ugarte commanding the detachment, refused. His later account revealed the difficulties his men had experienced and poor morale:

> We ran out of food on the third day so we caught a bustard – a bird similar to the goose. As we feared being discovered if we made a fire, we heated up bits of its flesh with our cigarette lighters and ate them. We did the same with mussels and other sea food. We even ate a cabbage which we found in a deserted garden. It was so cold that one soldier began to show symptoms of gangrene in his foot; he was forced to stay in the refuge all day. I felt weaker all day but tried to appear confident so that my subordinates would not lose heart. At night, however, I used to walk some yards away to be alone. There I smoked a cigarette and then prayed while a few tears of helplessness ran down my face. This made me feel relieved and ready to face the struggle again. Being undernourished in such cold weather weakened us so much that we constantly felt dizzy, and our heads ached. We had enough food but it was unsuitable, the main problem being the impossibility of cooking it.
>
> Our hopes vanished when we listened to the news on the radio of the British advance on Puerto Argentino. As days went by, we felt worse. The snow fell, there was a strong wind, and our weakness increased.[5]

Lance Corporal Sukrim Rai went for overkill and, although holding a perfectly servicable SLR, drew his kukri with a flourish even Errol Flynn would have admired. In no uncertain way he told Lieutenant Ugarte what he thought of *Galti garyo* and his Army, and that any escape attempt would be stopped by active use of his kukri. This monologue was, of course, delivered in Gurkhali none of which the Lieutenant could understand, but the body language of an agitated Gurkha wielding a menacing kukri worked wonders. The officer joined his men on the ground, and all three looked pleadingly at Quentin to prevent this five-feet two inch madman from decapitating them.

It had been a most bizarre reenactment of David versus, not one, but three Goliaths minus the blood, and Quentin had great trouble in keeping a straight face. Later in the year, as a worthy footnote to this incident, Sukrim's kukri became one of the 728 items of Falklands' War memorabilia which fetched a total of more than £52,000 at the Great Falklands' Charity Auction held in London. But eyebrows were raised a little more when, certified by the Commandant as: 'The only kukri drawn in anger against the Argentines', it became known that this had fetched the impressive price of £1,200.

After searching their prisoners, the Gurkhas entered Egg Harbour House to find six shoulder-held Soviet SAM-7 anti-aircraft missiles. Ugarte and his men, however, were a 'left-behind' rather than a 'stay-behind' group. Flown by helicopter from the *dush* garrison in the Fox Bay settlement of West Falkland, they were inserted into Lafonia just before the Darwin and Goose Green battle. Their task was to hand over the missiles to a Goose Green Army detachment designated to intercept Harrier aircraft flying up the Falkland Sound to strike Fox Bay. No detachment, though, had arrived to take over the missiles, and no helicopter had returned from Fox Bay to pick up Ugarte's group the day after their arrival in Lafonia. But Quentin's Gurkhas discovered that one missile had already been armed for firing. If these *dush* had then stood their ground and engaged the much easier targets of the three approaching Scout helicopters, then this tale might never have been told.

The capture of the *dush* at Egg Harbour House and receipt of another intelligence report of the mainland threat to capture Goose Green's airstrip was the O Group's main subject that evening. With D Company having sailed, the Commandant announced his next move to counter this threat. 'When the remainder of the Battalion are moved to the Fitzroy and Bluff Cove area, C Company and the Assault Pioneer Platoon will be held back in reserve. Their tasks will be to maintain the garrison in Goose Green and, in particular, provide the defence force for the airstrip. So C Company,' and he looked at Taj, 'now need to develop their defence plans as the threat has to be taken seriously.'

Recalling my initial interview with the Commandant, I thought, 'Well, this was, after all, one of our tasks envisaged in 5 Brigade's out of area role.'

'There's also another reason why the airstrip here is so important,' we were then told. 'If Stanley Airport remains in the *dush*'s hands, there's a school of thought that the QOH, who're the UK Strategic Reserve, might have to fly by Hercules from Ascension Island and attempt to land on the airstrip. However it's not known yet if such an operation will be feasible.'

The O Group broke up and I stayed in the ops room until midnight. It was quiet, except for another red air alert probably caused by more ineffectual high-altitude *dush* Canberra aircraft activity, and I wrote a short third and final letter to Tove in this period at Goose Green informing her of the imminence of our move to the front. Afterwards the storeroom and my sleeping bag awaited. Meanwhile D Company on board *Monsunen* had been accompanied by the BBC/ITN TV team, and Brian Hanrahan made this subsequent report:

> With a company of Gurkhas crowded into the hold, sitting on their packs on the drums of fuel and even on Land-Rovers (the tracks are too bad for speedy driving) we set off for Fitzroy across the vital bridge from Bluff Cove. For the Gurkhas, who had already marched for two days to reach the ship, it was a useful lift, but whether they appreciated it was more doubtful – they're dreadful sailors. But as soon as they got aboard they slept, stretched out across the foothills of packs on the floor of the hold. It was an uneventful journey, with the flag of the Fifth Infantry flying in the sunset as the Task Force's most improbable ship went to war, part of the private navy of the Fifth Infantry Brigade.[6]

Monsunen was not spotted by the *dush* observers on Mount Harriet as she chugged along the coastline and into Port Pleasant that night. She disembarked her passengers at Yellow Beach and then departed for Goose Green again after 02.00 hours accompanied by the LCU *Foxtrot 4*. D Company moved into Fitzroy to spend the remainder of that night in the settlement's community centre. Before dawn Mike was briefed on his task and the Gurkhas set off northwards along the track leading to Bluff Cove. They crossed Fitzroy Bridge connecting the two settlements, which had recently been repaired by the attached Sappers of 2 Para, to continue along the track to a 200 foot-high ridge line known as Little Wether Ground.

Secured by a sub-unit from 2 Para, this feature was three kilometres from Bluff Cove settlement. Two hours and five kilometres after setting out they began to dig in on the ridge that overlooked Port Fitzroy and, six kilometres to the south, Port Pleasant. *Sir Galahad* had arrived there just before dawn and anchored 600 metres from her sister ship, *Sir Tristram*. Captain Tomás Fox, a thirty-five year old officer from the *dush* 3rd Artillery Group had just arrived on the summit of Mount Harriet on a visit to the 4th Infantry Regiment there with some new radio batteries from his location at Moody Brook, just outside Stanley. The two grey LSLs had already been spotted by this Regiment's soldiers who showed them to 'Tommy' Fox. This pleasant officer had been pulled out of his Staff College course in Buenos Aires, Argentina which he had only just begun, in order to be deployed to the *Malvinas* – leaving behind, like me, his wife and two children aged four and two. We had also been born on the same day. His great-grandfather was an Irishman who had emigrated to Argentina in the 1840s and grandfather lived for thirteen years in Manchester, England during the early part of his life. It was ironic therefore that this particular Tommy had no hesitation in radioing a request to Stanley for air strikes on the two ships and British Tommies aboard them. The D Company Gurkhas would have a grandstand view of the consequences in a few hours.

The night of 7–8 June had also been hectic for Quentin Oates and his men. After locking up their POWs in Egg Harbour House and placing a guard on their room, they prepared to spend an uneasy night alert for any possible *dush* counter-attack because radio contact with Goose Green had been lost. No report of their success could be made and, more seriously, they would be unable to request reinforcements if these became needed. At first all was quiet but, during the small hours, a loud commotion outside made some Gurkhas fear the worst. The kukri-wielding Lance Corporal Sukrim Rai woke Quentin with an insistent, 'Sahib, sahib, the *dush* are here and about to attack!' His platoon commander leapt up from his sleeping bag with the speed of light, but soon discovered that Falkland wild horses were incapable of mounting a *coup de main* attack.

The following morning, contact with Goose Green was regained and information transmitted about the latest batch of POWs. While waiting for a Wessex helicopter to pick them up, the Gurkhas collected the *dush* equipment and folding-stock FAL 7.62-mm rifles so that these could also be flown out. The weapons possessed both an automatic and single-shot capability. This gave Quentin an overwhelming temptation to test-fire one, so he picked up the nearest and drilled several rounds harmlessly into a nearby stream. He was then called away to answer the radio by an NCO who, having seen Quentin fire, requested also to test the weapon. But another Gurkha spotted a potential target. *'Hags!'* he shouted.

A flock of geese and potential tasty ingredient for the NCO's *bhat*, happened to be passing overhead. Like his contemporaries, the Lance Corporal loved hunting and let rip with a burst of fire skywards. His marksmanship fell short of those standards that regularly generate the individual winner of the Army Shooting Championships at Bisley, and only resulted in diverting the lead bird's track. Simultaneously, however, three Goose Green shepherds on horseback were also approaching Egg Harbour House. Hunting lost sheep in the tranquillity of the Lafonian wilderness, they had reached the crest of a nearby hill to hear suddenly the crack of a fusilade of bullets passing overhead. Spinning round, they then galloped non-stop all the way back to Goose Green. According to some, it took days before the traumatized shepherds recovered.

Others would not be so lucky. Extra communication resources were a prioritized requirement at Fitzroy and nine British Signallers had driven their six Land-Rovers and trailers from the Brigade Rear HQ established at Darwin to the Goose Green jetty where they waited overnight for LCU transport. During that morning of 8 June *Foxtrot 4*, escorted by *Monsunen*, arrived to embark the Signallers and their vehicles. Without waiting for darkness and its relative safety, the LCU departed that afternoon. This was, initially, as dull as ditchwater. In the ops room Mark and I were keeping watch on the Battalion and Brigade radio nets as HB sahib made an appearance to break the monotony. My Assistant Training Officer had been attached to the Machine Gun Platoon, and given the task of siting the locations of three heavy machine guns and a few Milan anti-tank missile launchers which were to cover the threatened airstrip. C Company also had at its disposal eighteen GPMGs as well as a section of mortars, so their total firepower would be considerable to meet any *dush* airborne assault.

'Is this alright, sahib?' HB sahib asked. He put his design for death paper in front of me. It contained the most perfect set of geometrical calculations and diagrams of multiple inter-locking fields of fire that mankind had ever seen.

'Perfect sahib! *Shyabash*!' gushed forth my immediate praise. No airborne assault force could have survived that quality of mutual support. He left the ops room looking as pleased as punch. Another example that positive BO feedback to a Gurkha was always appreciated. Shortly afterwards the afternoon's activities began. At 16.50 hours Mark acknowledged a message on the Battalion net. The short conversation finished, he half swivelled around in his chair to call out, 'OK everyone, that's Quentin Oates with his Recce Platoon patrol at Egg Harbour House. They've just sighted five *dush* aircraft, possibly Mirages, flying northwards over the Falkland Sound towards San Carlos!'

'Was this then,' it occurred to me, 'the start of that long awaited *dush* offensive on Goose Green?'

Chapter Fifteen

RED ALERTS OVER TROUBLED WATERS

The Gurkha soldiers were quite extraordinarily polite and a delight to draw. Once, when I'd been bundled into a trench during an alert, its rightful occupier crouched on the edge to request, please, if it would be alright if he could get in too . . . I had a problem with hats. The Gurkhas thought my civilian issue woollen hat inadequate and were inclined to thrust theirs on me at dangerous moments, leaving themselves exposed. Fortunately a Bombadier found an Argentine cast-off tin hat for me, and everyone was happy. – Linda Kitson, Falklands' War Artist.[1]

The aircraft, in reality five Daggers from Rio Grande, were thirty-five kilometres south of the frigate HMS *Plymouth* positioned off Chancho Point and closing. This was the start of a final all-out effort from the *Fuerza Aeria Argentina*. The combat intensity would match anything achieved in the Battle of San Carlos Water fought immediately after the British landings. Including tanker transports, a Learjet pathfinder and decoy and aborted sorties, a total of forty-one *dush* aircraft would be involved and the doomed LCU, *Foxtrot 4*, now making its way at a maximum speed of nine knots into the Choiseul Sound, was to become one of four British vessels that afternoon subjected to their attacks. Forty years before, my father had experienced the climax to Malta's siege on 'the Glorious 10th of May' when the Luftwaffe was beaten back. Conversely, that day on the Falklands should have been labelled 'the Disasterous 8th of June'.

But before there was a chance to pass on Quentin's report, a Brigade Rear voice popped up on my radio handset. 'Air Raid Warning State Red!' confirmed another impending incursion west of West Falkland. However that familiar acid cocktail of adrenalin and fear had already surged into the pit of my stomach with Quentin's report of the five Daggers. The ops room drill was initiated – helmets on, crank the siren handle, alert passed by radio to the companies and ears glued to handsets for further contact and situation reports.

There was a lull. I hated wearing my helmet in the ops room. It was cumbersome, a distraction, and my vanity felt threatened. So I took it off. 'Perhaps a stand-down would be called?' I thought but, already alerted by the red air alert, D Company on Little Wether Ground were about to engage five Skyhawks with small arms fire. These aircraft were from Rio Gallegos and shot past the Gurkhas from a westerly approach. Over Port Fitzroy they banked towards the sea to launch their easterly attack run on the *Sir Galahad* and *Sir Tristram* in Port Pleasant. No contact reports arrived at Goose Green and I could not speak to Brigade HQ at Fitzroy because the distances prevented radio transmissions as the re-bro station had still not been repaired. We relaxed as the minutes ticked by.

Half an hour later Linda Kitson, the Falklands' War Artist, entered the ops room. Strange to see a woman in these circumstances. Like HB sahib she wanted an approval also, in this case to continue with her particular scribbling mission. 'Hello, are you busy?' she asked. 'I arrived at Goose Green from San Carlos yesterday and hope you don't mind if I start drawing what's happening in here. I won't interfere, but just remain in the background.' My mother is an excellent artist too, so there could be no question of refusing Linda's request. Regardless of the medium used, recording historic events for posterity was an important task. 'No, no problem,' I replied.

She moved into the ops room, took out her large sketch pad and started to work. Shortly afterwards the Brigade Commander arrived, having flown in from HMS *Fearless* at San Carlos. He was accompanied by the Commandant and Bill Dawson. There were now about nine or ten persons present including Graham Stewart-Smith, Nigel Price and Bombadier Batchelor. The Brigade Commander appeared motivated even though he was probably aware that *dush* aircraft had attacked the shipping at Port Pleasant, but not of the results. He had some paper under his arm, and was conversing with the Commandant.

'I've got a trace of an Argie map here captured on Mount Kent some days ago,' he said with the intensity of one not about to let such an opportunity slip. 'You'd better take a look, because there's been marked some interesting information on it regarding the Tumbledown and Mount William objectives.'

The senior officers gathered around the wall map and the Brigade Commander put the trace over this and their discussion continued. Linda Kitson continued to sketch. Only then did fragmented reports of an incident begin to arrive in my handset. The words: '. . . fire . . . attack . . . aircraft . . .' indicated something significant, but this verbal picture being drawn further down the coast was not encouraging. I twisted round in my chair, got up and sat down on the table beside the radio set.

'Wait one,' I said deliberately, 'there's been an air attack on 5 Brigade forces – possibly at Fitzroy or Bluff Cove.'

The Brigade Commander stopped talking to the two senior Gurkha BOs and came across to sit on the chair next to me. His face was passive. The radio reception was poor and information fragmentary. Listening hard to my handset, every ounce of concentration was needed to understand the transmission's detail so as to provide further updates to the room. Then a message arrived from Brigade Rear concerning the Dagger incursion that had flown up the Falkland Sound:

Enemy aircraft have attacked one ship off San Carlos and set it on fire. Smoking badly from her funnel. Vessel now attempting to return to San Carlos Water. One enemy aircraft splashed.

Between radio static interference arrived other near-incoherent particles of information from further along the coast:

> Have been under enemy attack . . . my call sign one is still on the ship . . . both ships on fire . . . there is chaos on the beaches . . . many casualties . . .

Standing on the afterdeck of *Sir Tristram*, Rifleman Bhairabahadur Rai was among a number of men thrown overboard by the force of one Skyhawk bomb exploding near the stern. The other from the same aircraft careered right through the vessel but failed to detonate. A second Skyhawk strafed the LSL with cannon fire. The other three Skyhawks had attacked *Sir Galahad* and three of their bombs detonated inside the ship. Bhairabahadur was rescued from the sea by a Wessex helicopter and the two undamaged Battalion Land-Rovers eventually would be recovered from the vehicle deck. It was the twelve-strong Gurkha B Echelon party, though, that had the greatest luck when their cruise on board the doomed LSL had been cancelled at the last moment. Ram realized how lucky they had been when the Welsh Guards' Quartermaster told him that their allocated two small cabins had been among those completely destroyed.

In our ops room during the next three-quarters of an hour, I fed the growing dimensions of the situation to the Brigade Commander from information that continued to crackle intermittently into my handset:

> Starlight is requesting more medical supplies . . . common wounds are from burns . . . require helicopter casevac . . . ships still burning . . . there are 150 casualties plus . . . advanced dressing station now set up at my location . . .

The senior officer's face had turned pale. He said nothing. Linda had moved to the other end of the room for another angle and continued recording the tense scene and stunned Brigade Commander. Perhaps his reaction was from a realization that luck had deserted him with his 'great jump forward'. It was not for nothing that, nearly 200 years before, Napoleon Bonaparte's job description for his generals had also required them to be lucky. Today's disaster was the culmination of a series of unlucky incidents that had contributed to stretching the vital air defence umbrella to breaking point over Bluff Cove, Fitzroy and Port Pleasant – and which the *Fuerza Aerea Argentina* exploited to the full.

About 19.15 hours Brigade Rear's watchkeeper declared yet another red air alert. This was different. His voice possessed an emphatic doomsday tone: 'A heavy air raid warning red. Echo Tango Alpha nine enemy aircraft in your area figures two zero minutes!'[2]

The next wave was coming. I informed the ops room staff. Mark relayed the message into the Battalion command net, a Gurkha Signaller ran out to hand-crank wails out of the siren and Linda continued looking up from, and down to, her sketch pad. A nimble pencil kept pace with people's movements. Another page of her pad was turned and, five minutes later, another. In an artistic paradise, she drew frenziedly. Her subjects were interesting. Minutes ticked by, then Mark called out, 'Report from A Company at Darwin. They've just sighted *dush* aircraft flying from west to east!'

Many reacted differently. The Commandant and silver-topped blowpipe dashed out of the ops room anticipating to spot the winged *dush*. Grabbing his rifle, Bill followed. Diving to the floor, the Brigade Commander shouted out, 'Everyone get down!' The ops room staff did likewise as, pointing to the wall near the door, the senior officer barked to the artist, 'Linda, get under there *now!*' Without hesitation, she shot into a small space between the fitted waist-high cupboard system that ran around two walls of the ops room. Her eyes were wide open with fear. Poor lady. For an artist it could not be fun caught up in this situation. I was also afraid but, in addition, felt sorry for her. This seemed a perfect opportunity to get rid of that bulky contraption which restricted listening to my handset. So I offered her my helmet. In silence my offering was accepted as a flicker of appreciation ruffled her face. Putting on her newly-acquired bonnet, she simultaneously made herself even smaller in the small hole.

I slid down onto the floor with handset clamped to my ear still monitoring events of that dreadful afternoon. Whilst the floor was still carpeted with bodies, the moment of truth had arrived for Bill to prove the accuracy of his liberated folding-stock FAL against game more dangerous than geese. He heaved himself up onto the shop's roof to select a firing position from where he could confront the incoming flock of Skyhawks with his fowling piece. Alas, the heady ascent proved in vain as his quarry was destined for Fitzroy and Bluff Cove areas.

'So to where did you disappear in such haste during our moment of crisis?' we asked the 2IC later on return from his private expedition, and then laughed heartily at Bill's unsuccessful climbing 'n' hunting war story.

Meanwhile D Company on Little Wether Ground were engaging this next wave of aircraft from San Julián. The Skyhawks had approached from the west just after 19.30 hours – two hours and twenty minutes since the previous strike force had bombed *Sir Galahad* and *Sir Tristram*. Alerted, D Company's Gurkhas, elements of the Welsh Guards and 2 Para at Fitzroy put up another of automatic tracer and rifle fire at the aircraft as the latter raced off in the direction of Bluff Cove. As they made a port turn to line up for a north-easterly attack run into Port Pleasant and the burning ships there, the Scots Guards and others retaliated with more small arms fire and Blowpipe and Rapier missiles flew everywhere. The low-flying aircraft were deflected off course and screamed back past the Gurkhas who retaliated again. In total they had fired 4,000 rounds of ammunition that afternoon, proportionally equivalent to the 18,500 expended in thirty seconds by the entire Scots Guards battalion.

Even Mike Kefford's voice on the Brigade radio net was ruffled as he sent his sitrep: 'Hello zero, this is four nine alpha. One bomb exploded 100 metres from my call sign four one's location. No casualties. Out.'

Later accounts of the war cast doubt as to whether these Skyhawks dropped their bombs, but the Scots Guards maintained that they had been bombed with five 500-pound parachute-dropped retarded bombs and the Skyhawk's fuel drop-tanks. The Gurkhas were so near 'their' detonating bomb that one rifleman from 10 Platoon had his hand slightly grazed with flying shrapnel. They were also 'bombed' with a Skyhawk duck-blue external fuel drop-tank that missed them to land in a valley 300 metres to their north.

In the Goose Green ops room combat reports arrived. They were wildly over optimistic: 'At least three aircraft shot down. One was a Mirage with a wing ripped off by small arms fire. A further two aircraft observed flying south-west with smoke trailing from them.'

In reality all four Skyhawks, albeit badly damaged, only just managed to return to their mainland base with the Gurkhas having contributed, possibly, to their difficulties. We got up, dusted ourselves down, and breathed again. But the *dush* were still flying. A fourth Skyhawk strike force had been active over the Choiseul Sound. Yet another, six Daggers covered by three high-altitude Mirages, turned away before arrival at their target area. Soon afterwards Brigade Rear downgraded our alert status to a cooling: 'Air raid warning yellow'. We stood down just after 20.00 hours and, a few minutes later, another report was made: 'Four enemy aircraft splashed!'

My reaction was an immediate, 'That surely's got to be the final score!' The main event of 'the Disasterous 8th of June' had lasted more than three hours. The Brigade Commander and Linda vacated the ops room – with Bombadier Batchelor probably responsible for eventually resolving her millinery problem. She would remain at Goose Green for another six days, whilst the Brigade Commander flew forward to Fitzroy to continue his battle planning. I continued to monitor the situation. Forty-eight had died on *Sir Galahad*,[3] two were killed on *Sir Tristram* and a total of another 135 casualties had been treated in three hours by twenty-seven men of 16 Field Ambulance's Advanced Dressing Station at Fitzroy. The Advanced Surgical Centre had not yet been established there, so these wounded were then evacuated by helicopter to the Ajax Bay Field Surgical Centre and from there to the hospital ship SS *Uganda*. This greatest British disaster of the Falklands' War had severe ramifications for us because no Gurkha helicopter lift would be available now until at least the following day.

The problem would be exacerbated by another; the removal from this area of the unwounded Welsh Guards survivors and others who had been on board the two ships. As they had lost all their personal weapons and equipment, these soldiers were now de facto non-combatants. The only solution was to prioritize their evacuation in the next round of helicopter tasking which would further complicate the Gurkha deployment. We had no alternative but to proceed with our original plan and press *Monsunen* into its nocturnal sea transport service again. The passenger manifest this time would be pure Gurkha, and no Task Force merchantman could claim to be nearer to the truest definition of a STUFT ship than *Monsunen*'s that night. Her cargo would be the largest so far with 180 soldiers stuffed into the hold comprising Bill Dawson's Alternative Battalion HQ, B Company, A Echelon and elements of the Mortar Platoon. They would embark later that evening, but the BOs scheduled as passengers for this particular voyage were concerned. Faced with a continuing air threat there remained a dearth of life jackets and life rafts on board. A couple of weeks later Tove wrote:

I watched an extended news on TV covering the awful tragedy of *Sir Galahad*. Unbearably sad and gruesome. We saw the 7th Gurkha Rifles on board the *Monsunen*. You might have had a less luxurious hitch, but by God were you the lucky ones. Just dreadful, dreadful to think about.

184

Monsunen's real luck, though, had not yet begun – and neither was that late afternoon's tale complete. I began picking up faint radio transmissions on the Brigade net of a vessel in trouble: '. . . some dead and wounded on board . . . stern shot away . . . am taking in water . . . request immediate Hawkeye assistance . . .'

LCU *Foxtrot 4* and its cargo of Signallers and vehicles had been attacked by the rockets and bombs of the fourth, and last, Skyhawk strike force in the Choiseul Sound. Only one of the seven crew members on board had survived. One Signaller was wounded and the craft's wheelhouse and port engine had ceased to exist. Two Harriers, though, had shot down three of these aircraft and also claimed the fourth, but this managed to return to its Rio Gallegos base. Responding to *Foxtrot 4*'s radio request, a Sea King evacuated its ten survivors, but soon this drifting hulk would jeopardize all hands on board the now departing *Monsunen.*

Quiet had arrived and a delayed evening O Group was convened. The Commandant had only one theme. 'We must now get this Battalion forward,' he declared. 'Get Quentin and his men withdrawn from Lafonia and back to Goose Green. As we've seen, the *dush* are now launching a counter air offensive and the use of *Monsunen* by day is totally ruled out. So, Ops Officer, send another helquest to Brigade Rear at Darwin demanding that this callsign be moved tomorrow in order to join up with D Company.'

Afterwards the helicopter request was sent before a worried Commandant approached me, map in hand. 'I need help to plan our attack,' he said. 'Here's the information from the Brigadier's trace on the Tumbledown and Mount William *dush* positions. We'll have to work out the map intervisibility problem between these objectives. It's a bit of a headache.' He shoved the map in front of me. The military symbols on it indicated no potential walk-over. Facing north were a couple of machine-gun positions on the western end of the Tumbledown and two company positions in its centre and east end. Another company was located on the south-east saddle between the Tumbledown and Mount William. The latter feature was, in turn, defended by a fourth company. A further two companies had been placed, respectively, less than one kilometre to the south and two kilometres south-west of Mount William and both overlooked the Darwin-Stanley track. The grand total was six *dush* companies plus – double our Battalion's numbers.

The Commandant continued talking, almost to himself, as I looked at the map, aghast at the challenge facing us on paper, 'There are two options. Either we attack from the south-west and roll up each sub-unit one after the other. Or,' and he placed a finger on the map, 'if we attack from the Tumbledown's western end and swing down onto Mount William, perhaps we can bypass that unit on the saddle and the other two near the track.'

He did not sound too convinced himself and his listener was too tired after concentrating on the events of that afternoon and early evening to make any sensible comments. This was a tough nut to crack even if we attacked by night, and the Battalion would only have three rifle companies available for the job, instead of the Gurkha standard four. 'It's too much for just one battalion – even if it's a Gurkha one,' I reasoned to myself but, making an excuse to the effect of, 'I'd better sleep on the answer to that one, sir,' beat a retreat to the storeroom and my sleeping bag.

Despite a bad conscience in not being more productive during the boss's brain-storming, my light doze lasted a couple of hours. A Gurkha Signaller woke me by a shake on the shoulder and I returned to duty at midnight. It was idiotic to take on so many late night watches. I was feeling whacked already but the lack of sleep would become worse. Far worse. The situation was not helped by Warrant Officer Jack Massey bursting into the ops room half an hour later more concerned with operational matters than cooking his *dumba/*'365' all-in stews.

'Have you heard, sir?' he asked, his moustache bristling.

'No. What?' I asked, mystified.

'I've just come from the home of a kelper, and there's a lass in there crying her heart out. Her son is one of the civilian crew on board *Monsunen* which has left for Fitzroy. We were listening to the BBC World Service when it broadcast that the *Monsunen*'s making twice daily runs between Goose Green and Fitzroy ferrying troops and supplies!'

I shut my eyes. What had occurred with 2 Para was now happening to us. 'Hell, first *Plymouth, Sir Galahad, Sir Tristram,* the LCU – but surely not *Monsunen* as well?' I despaired. If ever there was a first time in my life to start praying, then it had to be now. She was chugging towards Fitzroy, but her operation had been compromised by the damned British media. *Monsunen*'s self-imposed radio silence meant nothing could be done and a long night awaited. Worse, not only her crew but the Argentine media had heard the BBC broadcast and her role and activities would be published in Argentina next day.[4]

However that night passed by peacefully enough and in the morning, after break-fast, the Commandant visited the ops room. I briefed him about the BBC World Service broadcast. His response was a predictable, 'OK. We can't use *Monsunen* today during daylight, because it's simply too dangerous. But the Battalion *must* be moved forward. So, Mike, I want you to leg it down to Darwin right now and insist to Brigade Rear in person that helicopter transport *has* to be provided as a high priority for the Battalion – today!'

Suddenly an angry Bill Dawson entered the ops room. Everyone stared at his flushed face. 'But – we thought that you would've been at Fitzroy by now!' was the astonished reaction from the Commandant, Mark, myself and others.

Bill blurted, 'Well, you'll never guess what we've had to deal with, and why we had to return here! So just listen to this!' He began recounting in detail *Monsunen*'s busy night, 'Early on our voyage in the Choiseul Sound, we were directed by the Royal Navy to *Foxtrot 4* in an attempt to salvage the Brigade Signals vehicles aboard. The drifting hulk of the LCU was eventually located and we put a boarding party on her to assess the damage. One soldier's body was found on the tank deck awash with freezing cold sea water. The Signals Land-Rovers and trailers were intact, so we attached a line and began towing the LCU to Fitzroy. After a while it became obvious she would sink and the line had to be cast off at 03.00 hours.

'Sod's law then intervened,' continued Bill. 'If it was to go wrong, then it really did go wrong. The rope became entangled around *Monsunen*'s propeller. We tried to free it, but failed. So with 180 Gurkhas in the stinking hold, we began to drift towards the Navy's gunline between Port Pleasant and Stanley twenty nautical miles away and definitely no place for an unarmed civilian coaster!'

Bill had every right to be concerned. Seventy-two hours previously one of two *dush* improvised land launched MM-38 Exocets had been fired out there, only to miss either the frigate HMS *Yarmouth* or HMS *Cardiff*. And two nights later another pair of MM-38 missile launchers were flown to Stanley. As well as the constant threat of *dush* air attack on the gunline, their 155-mm artillery had also been counter bombarding Royal Navy warships. The 2IC elaborated further to his listeners, 'So we broke radio silence just after 03.30 hours and a request for assistance was sent by our Senior Naval Officer on board to the Commodore Amphibious Warfare at San Carlos. Some time afterwards the frigate, HMS *Yarmouth*, hove-to by us and, standing-off, she fired a star shell for illumination purposes.' *Yarmouth* was taking no chances in sighting an unidentified vessel – despite this being the second occasion she had intercepted *Monsunen*, the first having been her involvement in the coaster's beaching at Lively Island seventeen nights before. The frigate had just now completed shelling *dush* land forces and duelling with their 155-mm artillery, so her crew's nerves must have been in high spin. Bill reached his war story's climax. 'Eventually two of *Yarmouth*'s divers were sent across to us, and they disentangled the rope from around our propeller by cutting it with a borrowed kukri. By then it was 06.30 hours, and dawn only four hours away. Unaware of what had been happening, the *keta* remained asleep in the hold. This meant we wouldn't arrive at Fitzroy until daylight and I couldn't risk exposure to a possible air attack. So discretion had to be the better part of valour and that's why we're now back here to await further *hi-hukums*,' he finished with the Gurkhali colloquialism of 'orders from on high', adding as a weary afterthought, 'and you guys simply don't know how lucky we've been!'

Monsunen's Senior Naval Officer then entered the ops room remarking, 'Bloody hell, that was a bit of a night and a half – and a good job that I managed to persuade *Yarmouth* from blowing us out of the water!'

'What on earth are you talking about?' demanded Bill.

Lieutenant Ian McClaran replied with a deadpan face, 'It's obvious that the Navy's become a wee bit trigger-happy these days. They signalled to us that we had to recognize ourselves. I discovered later that when an immediate reply was not received, they were about to open up with their 4.5-inch gun which was on action stations! Luckily I had this in my pocket.' He produced a small hand torch, held it up, and said, 'So I managed to catch their attention by flashing a signal in morse to them several times!' Pride was in this Senior Naval Officer's voice as his tale ended, 'And that stopped 'em!'

'Jesus Christ!' exploded Bill at this information he had not been party to previously. 'That's it! I'm off to get some kip!'

He stalked out of the room, shaking his head at Ian's action which had prevented the campaign's biggest blue-on-blue so far. Rifleman Baliprasad Rai, also on board the coaster and probably fast asleep, never did get to know the true story of what occurred in the Choiseul Sound that night as his brief account portrayed:

. . . we again loaded onto a ferry ship named 'Monsunen' . . . The Coy 2IC, Capt(QGO) Dalbahadur Sunwar, informed us that we were going to a place near the capital, Port Stanley, called Bluff Cove. We were about ten minutes on our way when the ship was turned back and we were taken back to Goose Green. This sudden change of plan we learned later was because of the Argentine air attack on two LSLs, *Sir Galahad* and *Sir Tristram.*[5]

The little gathering in the ops room slowly disappeared, leaving me alone with my radios and a Gurkha Signaller. I was now about to pay dearly for being on duty all night. No Land-Rover meant a round-trip five kilometre tab to Darwin, but just before departure more radio messages arrived. The first from Brigade Rear was a familiar: 'Air Raid Warning State Red!'

The Signaller ran out to crank the siren handle. My task at Darwin was more important than taking evasive action so, as the siren wailed, I put on my belt and pistol holster and prepared to leave. The Signaller had returned to his radio again and I was on my way out when Quentin Oates at Egg Harbour House sent message number two. Alarmed, the Gurkha looked up from the radio to gasp at me, 'Krystal sahib! The Recce Platoon patrol are hearing sounds of helicopters maybe approaching Goose Green!'

With this information passed to the companies and Brigade Rear, I started out on my lonely trek. Come what may, the Battalion *had* to get its helicopters today. Turning northwards to tab up the Darwin track, my worry remained that the much publicized *dush* assault had begun on the Goose Green air strip. Checking my pistol in its holster provided little comfort as I continued along the track with the vulnerable air strip on my left. Every so often I glanced up to confirm no *dush* helicopters or parachutes were descending from the blue sky. Thirty minutes later from the top of the gorse covered Darwin Hill, I looked down at Darwin's few houses where its twenty-five settlers and 5 Brigade Rear HQ were accommodated. The latter's Land-Rovers and trailers had been parked up outside a house so I tabbed down the hill and entered the building. Inside the improvised ops room, its personnel were also battling with the effects of sleep deprivation. The air attacks of yesterday had generated extra work for them and now, once more, they were manning their positions.

'We're on full alert,' explained the alarmed CrabAir Brigade liaison officer who was controlling the Brigade helquests. 'The red air alert and your Recce Platoon's reports of helicopters flying could mean a possible imminent enemy airborne assault!'

'I know,' I replied through a fog of tiredness and beyond caring about his worries. 'And that's exactly what is needed. Choppers to move us. So what's the chances, d'you think?' Our mutual fatigue produced a quality of communication between the Gurkha BO and Squadron Leader that resembled drunken goldfishes attempting to converse under water. Slowly his message sank into my head that such a personal request could not be handled at his level. 'You'd better speak to Arthur,' he said wearily.

Upstairs I located the Brigade Ops Officer, Captain Arthur Petrie, and began my cajoling. The descendents of William Wallace and Robert the Bruce are not, after all, renowned for their generosity. 'Come on, Arthur,' I asked sweetly, 'can you pull the stops out for us? I know you've been working hard, but we've had to sit on our butts for nearly a week now. We Gurkhas have been good boys and haven't hijacked any helicopters as yet, but my boss wants us on the move to the Fitzroy area. And that means today. So, can you give us priority?'

'I'll try,' he said after listening to this covert but oh-so-friendly hijacking threat. We went downstairs and he spoke to some other of the staff officers, then turned to me. His Scots accent, as sharp as a kukri, had a ring of confidence – and with every reason, too, because another four transport helicopters, and more air and ground crews were arriving in-theatre that day. Thirty-nine Sea Kings and Wessex plus, of course, Bravo November would now be available for both Brigades including the Gurkhas.

'Don't worry,' he comforted me, 'something'll be flown to you later on. And we've just heard from Brigade HQ at Fitzroy that helicopters are now moving the unwounded Welsh Guardsmen from Fitzroy to San Carlos. That must have been those your Recce Platoon had heard. So we can stand-down with regard to any enemy counter-attack for the time being!'

'Arthur, you're a good man!' I exclaimed and clapped him on the back, not with joy at the prospect of being moved up to the front line, but from his optimism that might brighten up my boss's day for a change.

I tabbed back down to Goose Green as quickly as possible, confident that something positive might occur and informed the expectant Commandant, 'It looks as if we're going to get some helicopter lift later this afternoon, sir!'

Then, as promised by Arthur, things *did* begin to happen. First Quentin and his men were flown back to Goose Green. Still flushed by recent triumphs, but unaware that any of the settlement's sixteen shepherds had been near Egg Harbour House, he was met by a faintly amused Battalion IO and an irate Commandant. In unison they demanded, 'And what do you think you were doing shooting up civilians near your OP location, then?'

Puzzled, he mumbled something to the effect that, 'It couldn't possibly have been us because we've only seen *dush* in the area,' and then beat a hasty retreat from what seemed to be a looming inquisition into his mysterious misdeed.

Subsequent attempts to maintain a low profile were in vain. *The Daily Telegraph* learnt of the shepherds' bushwhacking and an article appeared in the newspaper under a headline of: *Gurkhas Ambush Civilians.* A pity the journalist A.J. McIlroy did not acquire the full facts of that Gurkha's attempt to 'splash' the airborne goose to give more balance to the story.

Ironically, a meeting in Buenos Aires scheduled for the following day would discuss the possibilities of launching Operation BUZON (Mailbox).[6] Quentin's Egg Harbour OP had been one site for a possible amphibious landing by the *dush* 8th Infantry Regiment from Fox Bay. It was the preliminary phase of the subsidiary Operation TUCUMAN whose aim was to capture Darwin, followed by supporting an airborne drop of *dush* forces onto Wickham Heights, but not the Goose Green airstrip.[7] The Gurkhas' defensive work had been partially in vain, although this was not the first time, or last, we would receive inaccurate intelligence of a perceived threat. Additionally, San Carlos was a counter-attack target of the *dush* 5th Infantry Regiment at Port Howard. With only our C Company and Assault Pioneers at Goose Green, and two 40 Commando companies reinforcing the Welsh Guards at Wether Ground near Bluff Cove that day, British forces in the rear were at their most vulnerable at any time of the war. But the Buenos Aires meeting decided on cancellation as the *dush* did not possess either the logistic capability, shipping, air superiority or, it must be said, even the will to carry out such a complex operation.[8]

After lunch there was news from Brigade Rear that the Gurkhas could soon be flying, albeit with only enough helicopter capability to lift Tac HQ, A Company and elements of Support Company. B Company could not be flown. No more delay would be tolerated so, regardless of the danger, the Commandant decided to transport Lester Holley's men to Fitzroy by *Monsunen* during the night. We were at the start of a new and decisive phase. Time was short as I did a quick ops room handover/takeover with Taj Lewis. His Company and Assault Pioneers were now Goose Green's garrison, but he did not seem too enthused whilst wishing the outgoing ops room staff a terse, 'Good luck'. His pregnant wife Meg, who had become friendly with Tove during the last few weeks, was perhaps a compassionate factor in choosing C Company as the garrison company.

I rushed out of the ops room, through the shop, and into its back storeroom to throw on my thermal underclothing, combat clothing, rubber overboots and other equipment for a week's survival in the Falkland winter. Two twenty-four hour ration packs were stuffed into the top of my bergen. Strapping myself into my bulky heavy webbing that included a pistol holster, full ammunition and kidney pouches and respirator bag large enough to take both respirator and personal camera, I squatted down with my back to the bergen, put my arms into its shoulder straps and, assuming a weightlifter's stance to avoid toppling over, heaved myself into a standing position. Reality had arrived with a vengeance. The battle board was the final item to be slung around my body. I walked back into the shop past all the wooden shelving, now stacked with cans of food and other items for the settlement and out into fresh, cold air and its tang of burning peat.

We had been kept waiting in suspense too long, but now our phoney war had ended. Nigel Price was granted his wish. We were moving up to the front line to get the job finished as fast and efficiently as possible with, perhaps, achieving Memsahib *Thatcher le Thecharyo*'s political aim of us taking a minimum of Gurkha casualties. History had shown, however, that Gurkhas prioritized other matters than politics to ensure victory in any battle they fought. Despite fear, now I would be truly part of their Eastern culture and way of fighting.

We tabbed to the landing strip to await the helicopters in our allocated sticks. I looked at the mix of Tac HQ's Gurkha and British faces. Nobody said much and, outwardly, none seemed concerned of confronting the *dush* in the Falkland khuds. The way to success was obvious, just as Tove had written at Church Crookham two weeks before in response to the letter she received from my spiritual sparring partner on board *QE2*, Padre Peter Brooke:

> I also got the letter from the chaplain – and need I say what ran through my mind when I saw who that was from. I ripped his open first . . . My God, that frightened me . . . I know neither you nor I have a strong faith, but I think that men of the Church have changed – and I'm certain that Army padres are tough and rational and used to a lot of counselling. It was the best thing you could do – speak

to a neutral third person . . . you owe it to me and the two girls upstairs to do your bit and come back in one piece . . . All you've got to do is to dig up your famous stubborness and determination, do your job, and then come home to us.

Unfortunately there would be no guarantee at all of being able to return home to 80, Wakefords Park some 13,000 kilometres away to enjoy, once more, a normal family life.

PHASE IV – AT THE FRONT

THE BUSH WAIT

Chapter Sixteen

DISTANT GUNS

Meanwhile the military chiefs arrived at the conclusion that the decision to hand over to the Theatre of Operations expert fighters with daggers in close-combat against the fire of modern arms already deployed to oppose them in numerous battles, meant that (the Gurkhas) can only respond to newly-introduced ideas. One could be to use them as a first target, and therefore human shield, to secure adequate cover for the 'Royal Marines'' landing in a remote area of the Islands' territory. – Flash periodical. [1]

It was early afternoon when Tac HQ moved to the Goose Green airstrip to wait as the four Sea Kings and Wessex arrived first at Darwin to fly out A Company before returning for us and elements of Support Company. We quickly climbed aboard our Wessex which then flew for twenty exciting minutes at grass-cutting height to avoid *dush* radar detection. On touching down at Little Wether Ground, I struggled past the loadmaster with my bergen to drop down onto the tussocky grass below. Moving clear of the rotating blades, warmth of exhaust outlets and wash of sickly-sweet smell of aviation fuel fumes, I looked around. Some D Company Gurkhas were nearby and, at distant Port Pleasant, smoke still rolled up from the hulk of *Sir Galahad* and still intact *Sir Tristram.*

We tabbed down off the ridge northwards into a valley. Then Mark shouted, 'D Company are telling us on the radio to get out of here fast. We're under the direct flight path of yesterday's air attacks on them!'

The jettisoned Skyhawk droptank lay a short distance away to prove the point. In accordance with those principles of the Grand Old Duke of York, we hastily moved back up the hillside to rejoin D Company on the exposed ridge adjacent to its position and began constructing stone sangars for protection against more air attacks, as my radio transmitted: 'Air Raid Warning State Red!' for the thirteenth time of our Falklands' campaign. This alert also applied to a possible *dush* counter-attack in the Fitzroy area. Meanwhile the Little Wether Ground population was further swelled by the RAP's doctors and medics, whilst the Recce Platoon and elements of the Mortar, Anti-Tank and Machine Gun Platoons also moved into position to begin their construction work in the remaining hour before dark.

As D Company departed to secure its patrol base on a ridge south of Mount Challenger I realized something was wrong and asked Mark, 'Where on earth's A Company?'

His Gurkhali ability meant that he manned the Battalion command radio net, whilst the Brigade net was my responsibility. The ensuing dialogue he had with A Company revealed a recurrance of the problems that had beset the Battalion with Bravo November during our first day on the Falklands. 'Oh, hell! Some of A Company have landed at Fitzroy settlement, while others have been deposited two kilometres south of us!' exclaimed a head-shaking Adjutant after the tirade of Gurkhali questions and answers had ended.

Hitching a lift on other helicopters or tabbing enabled the missing Company to regroup eventually at our location. Nothing had materialized from the red air alert, so we made ourselves as comfortable as possible and prepared for a cold night. We were twenty-six clicks, or a little more than sixteen miles, from Stanley and there was much to do. 'Kit? Where are you?' asked Mark to the RSO. 'Can you give me the nuco and mesco sheets? I've got to prepare the Battalion's sitrep for the last twelve hours.'

The Brigade SOP demanded that in every twenty-four hour period two new sitreps be encoded into these cumbersome codes before transmission. Correspondingly any received mesco and nuco message had to be decoded. It sucked up time and effort. 'Message coming in from Brigade now,' said Corporal Aslett, writing furiously. Decoded, it revealed the planned third Gurkha voyage of discovery aboard *Monsunen* from Goose Green had been cancelled. Boating trips to Fitzroy had become too dangerous. Instead B Company would fly by helicopter in the morning. He looked up at me from the radio again, 'Sir! Brigade want to speak to Sunray.'

The Commandant came across, picked up the handset, exchanged a few words and announced, 'OK, I've got to fly to Fitzroy to take part in the planning for the Brigade's attack. Where's the BC? He'll come with me and we'll return here sometime tomorrow.' Shortly afterwards a Gazelle helicopter arrived to spirit the Commandant and Major Mike Fallon, his artillery Battery Commander without gun portfolio, away to Fitzroy and Brigade brainstorming of how the Gurkhas should take on the Tumbledown and Mount William. Last light was approaching, but my mind remained in neutral as Lieutenant John Palmer, the Anti-Tank Platoon Commander came up to me. He seemed concerned and demanded, 'Are we standing-to soon, Mike? Who's making out the sentry rosters? And who's sending out the clearing patrols?'

John was a keen young officer and a thinking one too; pertinent questions to my unforgivable lapse. I had forgotten the basics on our first night out in the khuds after the week of comparative luxury in Goose Green and consequently felt most stupid and unprofessional. We stood-to immediately.

Afterwards the other routines were carried out including transmitting our sitrep. Only after midnight did I crawl into my sleeping bag. Logic dictated that two hours of sleep in the last forty would guarantee an express departure to the land of nod. But this was no ordinary situation, and I began to think a thousand thoughts. Childhood, home, my girls, the war bubbling round in my head for the past ten weeks, and future – which, aside from the operational situation, had become restricted to activities related to the next twelve-hour period only. The prize for survival would be to look forward to the next twelve . . . my light doze was interrupted by the hollow thump of gunfire. It made me twitch. 'Christ! Are we now under attack?' I thought.

More gunfire. Thump! Thump! The 4.5-inch gun which fired one round nearly

196

every two seconds gave away its Royal Navy ownership. Far out at sea on the southerly Stanley gunline, *Yarmouth*, the *bête noire* of *Monsunen*, had begun its digital-computerized bombardment of *dush* positions on nearby Two Sisters, Mount Harriet, Mount William and elsewhere. I glanced at my watch. 04.00 hours. 'Impressive hearing what the media have reported for the past six weeks, yet it's disturbing this live gunfire is now being aimed at live targets,' I brooded. 'What's it like on the receiving end? Surely we'll find out soon.'

Such a train of thought washed waves of anxiety down my spine and into a nervous stomach. After an hour the gunfire stopped, but whilst *Yarmouth* again intercepted *Monsunen* minus Gurkha passengers and with only bulk cargo, en route to Fitzroy, my apprehension spun to new heights. It ensured no oblivion in my sleeping bag that, by now, had the appearance of an outsize green slug – and the following five hours of cold darkness crawled by.

In the meantime D Company had arrived at its position further up the coast un-detected by the large *dush* force on Mount Harriet five kilometres to the north-east. Mike Kefford then sent out a small recce patrol which approached within three kilo-metres of Mount William. Based on the information received from this patrol, he made his plan. Two half-platoon strength fighting patrols would move forward again the next night on 10–11 June from a south-westerly direction and work their way around the southern side of Mount William to ascertain detailed *dush* strengths and positions.

The current Brigade plan dictated that both the Scots Guards and Gurkhas should assault the Tumbledown from this direction in a coordinated double battalion attack at first light on 12 June, with the Gurkhas also seizing Mount William. Based on the experiences of Exercise WELSH FALCON such an unrehearsed manoeuvre would be, at best, exceptionally difficult to execute. A Guards Battalion fresh from public duties and a Gurkha Battalion in a highly advanced state of training was simply not the correct mix. However the planned Gurkha patrolling would be a classically simple affair, and the aggressive mountain men armed with rifles and kukris were adept at the sneaky tactics required to test the defenders' mettle. We stood-to in our positions again just before dawn at 10.15 hours, but were still unaware of the counter-attack threat in the Fitzroy area. 10 June would be a long day which, for others and myself, would not end until 04.00 hours the next morning. Stand-down came as well as a cold, clear day of bright sunlight. Forward of us, D Company observed four *dush* Pucará aircraft supported by 155-mm artillery fire attacking 3 Para's locations at Estancia House out of the early morning sun. There was no *dush* activity in the Fitzroy area. In the mean-time B Company arrived by helicopter to take up defensive positions. An underslung load of mortar ammunition was also flown in a little later as we improved our positions and continued to await the Commandant's return in the sunny afternoon.

Then the radio reported: 'Possible chemical attack threat in the San Carlos area!' Trying to reassure myself, I tapped the large pouch on my belt containing my respirator and personal camera. Since we only possessed the standard bag of fuller's earth as a decontamination kit, the lack of NBC 'noddy suits' led to my adoption of Gurkha fatalism for these circumstances. It seemed the most effective countermeasure as we had too much on our plate already to worry about another morsel.

By mid-afternoon the Commandant and Mike Fallon returned with the four-man

197

joint BBC/ITN TV camera team led by the reporters Brian Hanrahan and Mike Nicholson. The latter had secured some great footage of the Port Pleasant disaster two days before and now wanted more. Perhaps I should have been more active in my Battalion Public Information Officer's role, but operations and eating had priority with Bis Bis preparing Mark's and my meal while the Commandant held his O Group.

The silver-topped staff took a rest on the ground as he opened his notebook and looked at the pages packed with spidery hieroglyphics. 'OK, gentlemen, the situation's as follows,' he began in a standard mode of dynamism. '3 Commando Brigade will carry out a major Brigade attack in thirty-six hours on the *dush* in the second line of hills near Stanley. The revised plan is that we'll be launching our attack the night afterwards on Mount William after the Scots Guards have secured the Tumbledown. We'll be approaching from another direction than originally planned because Scots Guards' patrolling further up the coast at Port Harriet House has revealed an enormous minefield south-west of Mount William. Its area measures at least two kilometres by two kilometres and indicates the *dush* are expecting a major attack from that direction. D Company are therefore to be withdrawn 1,000 metres westwards and there must be no further movement forward of the VC1234 Eastings. Tac HQ are to inform D Company immediately after this O Group.

'We'll be leaving here shortly after the evening meal has been finished, so all sub-units must be ready to move in fifteen minutes. Due to all helicopters lifting artillery ammunition forward, there's no assets available for us. Our task therefore will be to advance on foot seven kilometres up the coastline to an area south of Mount Challenger where an artillery gun position is being assembled. We'll meet up with D Company there, dig in, and act as the Gunners' local defence force while we get ourselves sorted out for the attack. A Echelon will move into Fitzroy, and the Machine Gun Platoon remain here until helicopters are released to move them, their three heavy machine guns, and the mortar ammunition up to us.'

At 17.30 hours our meal was interrupted by Corporal Aslett. 'Sir!' he called to me, 'Brigade have just come up on the radio with an air raid warning red!'

The *dush* could be attempting to exploit the disaster forty-eight hours ago which had involved our D Company and where smoke still drifted upwards from *Sir Galahad*'s pyre in Port Pleasant. *Bahia Agradable* was the Spanish name for this inlet, but nothing could be agreeable with its sights. This was the TV team's chance. The cameramen took up a position to the right of my sangar, shouldered his camera like a Blowpipe missile launcher, and practised some horizontal panning towards Port Pleasant. We waited in anticipation.

Twenty minutes later another Brigade message arrived: 'Stand-by for imminent low-level air attack!' I remembered the 2 Para Paymaster's initiative on board *Norland* against incoming Skyhawks and my Browning found its way into my hand to be pointed skywards.

'Whatya got there? A pistol? You're optimistic! You'll never hit anything with that!' smirked the cameraman, Bernard Hesketh.

Irritated with this comment I retorted, 'Well, it's better than nothing,' whilst also thinking bitter thoughts, 'and at least I'll be a trifle more effective than you and your precious shoulder-held camera.'

Psychologically I felt good about my defiant little gesture to the *dush* and mighty BBC. The chance might come to loosen off a few of my 100 rounds of ammunition. The Fleet Air Arm had also taken up station and a pair of Harriers were on combat aircraft patrol, otherwise known as CAP, above Fitzroy. A couple of white contrails in the blue sky indicated another pair acting as top-cover for the first as we waited for the air strike, but apprehension finally melted with the soothing Brigade message: 'Return to alert status Air Raid Warning State Yellow.'

There was a strong feeling of anti-climax. 'So do you actually feel now a tinge of disappointment with the *dush* non-appearance?' I asked myself as the TV team beat a retreat back to Fitzroy and we began our advance. A Company were the point company. Tac HQ, accompanied by the RAP, Recce, Mortar and Anti-Tank platoons, followed with B Company taking up the rear. Our progress was slowed by the weight of our bergens while the Anti-Tank and Mortar platoons were engaged in a battle with their Battalion support weapons. The four Milan firing-posts were sixteen kilos apiece. Each of the four 81-mm mortars included the base plate and tube that, together, weighed nearly sixty kilos. In addition the length of a mortar tube was four feet and the Gurkhas who were backpacking these boasted an average height of five feet and two inches, thereby generating a totally disproportionate sight. Three days later after they had been married up with their three Browning guns of fifty-eight kilos each, the Machine Gun Platoon sections would also perform similar prodigous portering feats. The Commandant ignored the impressive spectacle of these mountain people utilizing their innate strength and stamina on such heavy loads over this rough terrain. He was irritated and the silver-topped windmill's gyrations increased in velocity.

'Spread out more!' he yelled. There's *dush* artillery up ahead, and I don't want an incoming shell to explode and cause a lot of casualties simply because we're grouped together too close! So spread out! Now!'

Tac HQ's formation had to be urgently revised and we took corrective action. It was early evening. The tab of two kilometres took us to a point due north of Bluff Cove settlement when an out of breath Guards officer's voice in my handset reported his problems in no uncertain manner: 'My forward callsign now under heavy mortar fire and being counter-attacked. Casualties have been taken and he has decided to with-draw from his current location at Port Harriet House.'

The Scots Guards' three-day reconnaissance patrol based in the isolated house had been compromised by the arrival of a Wessex helicopter bringing radio battery re-supplies. This action had taken place eleven kilometres further along the coast, providing a reminder to us that the *dush* were not asleep. Also busy were some 5 Brigade Snotrac vehicles. Capable of carrying a 500 kilogram load across country, they passed us with tracks flailing in the mud whilst Wessex helicopters clattered over-head in moving forward underslung loads of artillery, 105-mm Light Guns and their ammunition.

Ahead, A Company kept fanned out as the summit of Mount Harriet came into view. The officer who had requested the air strikes on *Sir Galahad* and *Sir Tristram* two days before, Captain Tommy Fox of the *dush* 3rd Artillery Group, had returned there that morning from Moody Brook in order to reinforce Lieutenant Tedesco, the lone FOO attached to the 4th Infantry Regiment HQ. These two officers were soon to become the *bête noire* of the Gurkhas for the next forty-eight hours. Two kilometres ahead, dull thuds sounded. I squinted through my binoculars. *Dush* shells called down by Fox and Tadesco were exploding on a crest line and their dark brown pillars of peat and smoke rose with surprising height. One minute later, puffs of smoke and thuds indicated where 4 Field Regiment's 29 'Corunna' Field Battery's gun position, which we had been tasked to protect, was being established at Wether Ground.

The results of this Royal Artillery fire were observed by Mike Kefford's reconnaissance patrol. His Gurkhas were close enough to Mount William to see the *dush* running around the feature trying to escape the effects of this harrassing fire. More explosions occurred near 29 Battery. Only then did I realize the size of gun calibre being used by the *dush*. The shells had not been 105-mm. They were 155-mm fired by two guns, one being located behind Sapper Hill and the other a little further westwards near the Darwin-Stanley track. These had given not only the Gunners, but also our D Company, a most uncomfortable afternoon.

Our tab continued towards the Royal Artillery gun position. More huge pillars of peat and smoke erupted in the distance, followed by the thuds. By now it had taken us four hours to tab five kilometres and we were well past Bluff Cove settlement. Our advance had been in parallel and to the north of the Darwin-Stanley track where work had begun before the war in improving its surface. Ahead by a small quarry near the track were two Portakabins in which the Welsh Guards' Tac HQ had taken up residence. Outside stood some of their officers including the CO, Lieutenant Colonel Johnny Rickett and his 2IC, Major Joe Griffiths-Eyton. Tac HQ walked towards them whilst the alert Gurkhas took cover and rested. The 155 shelling stopped any desire to talk.

Together with 2 Para, the Welsh Guards were under command of 3 Commando Brigade, and their CO had just returned from a Brigade Orders Group in preparation for the Brigade attack on Mount Longdon, Two Sisters and Mount Harriet. They were in pensive mood. Colonel Rickett's prophesy to me on board *QE2* before the start of the Gurkhas' Regimental birthday party had come true. It had been a tough war for his Battalion already but, despite the *Sir Galahad* disaster, he was determined to carry out business as usual. 'We've just been reinforced by a company from 40 Commando, and another's arriving tomorrow,' he informed us. 'The Battalion's in reserve for the 42 Commando attack on Mount Harriet in a couple of night's time, and our Recce Platoon has been tasked also to secure their start line. You'd better watch out for the Argie 155s. They've been pretty active all day and our motor bike dispatch riders have had to run the gauntlet of their shelling.'

A day or so later the shelling became too close for comfort and the Welsh Guards' Padre Peter Brooke would have to deal with yet another military soul when one of their dispatch riders was hit and mortally wounded. I was more concerned, though, with the information vacuum than any possible shelling. The Welsh Guards Ops Officer was the obvious man to ask, particularly since he must have received updated information from the Marine Commandos. So I approached the beige-bereted Captain with a hopeful, 'Have you any info on the status and location of friendly forces and the enemy in this area?

'Of course!' replied my Guards oppo. 'We've got an updated map from the

Commando O Group. It's inside this Portakabin, our temporary ops room. So be my guest.'

Tempted to exclaim, '*Carpe diem!*' I flung off my helmet and bergen to dive into the flimsy wooden structure. Helped by the Guardsman, I feverishly began marking my battle board with the new information displayed on their wall map. Five minutes passed in deep concentration. They were the fastest five minutes of my life. Too fast.

Crump! The first 155 shell called down by Captain Tommy Fox landed. I looked up.

Crump! Another exploded. Momentary panic. Shrugging my shoulders, the self-imposed updating task of enemy and friendly forces continued to have priority even in this situation.

Stupid me. Crump! Another explosion made the whole Portakabin rock. The moment had arrived to exit. We baled out of the doorway only to be met by a shout of, 'Watch out! Take cover, there's another incomer on its way!'

Flat on my stomach, I looked up.

Crump! The next incomer had hit the face of a sheer rock wall 150 metres away. Shrapnel and pieces of stone whizzed in all directions. There is nothing quite like a 'hands-on' experience to learn the art of survival. Rifleman Baliprasad Rai also had a vivid recollection of the incident, even though he mistook the 155-mm shelling for mortar fire:

> B Coy . . . advanced on foot . . . about six miles before we were spotted by the enemy. A fierce mortar barrage followed. The hills near us seemed to come alive as the shells exploded, but no one was hurt.[2]

The reality behind the innocent name 'incomer' had been assimilated. Their explosions were unlike anything I had ever experienced before. Observing the effect of shelling at peacetime firepower demonstrations within a strictly controlled range environment resembled bursting balloons at Victoria's fourth birthday party in comparison. We were frailty itself and a temptation to run from the probability of another incomer and its inevitable final explosion became almost overwhelming. 'How could we avoid them?' I thought and looked over my shoulder. And blinked. Right over *there* the solution stared at me.

'Get into the quarry! This way!' I yelled, and charged along the track leading into this rocky sanctuary. Others followed. A sensible decision.

Crump! Crump! More rounds of the 155 harrassing fire landed nearby. We were inside the quarry by then, hugging close to the red earth wall of our communal trench. Silence. The *dush*, by now, had taken a break. Our baptism of fire was over, but it had also marked the start of an uncomfortable *dush* 155 versus Gurkha relationship for the next forty-eight hours. D Company, 2 Para had been withdrawn from this area after being plagued by the 155-mm shelling. It was much worse than 105-mm fire which they 'tended to work through . . . but the 155-mm had a real punch to it . . .' commented their OC, Major Philip Neame.[3] The Gurkhas, though, would continue their advance eastwards at last light when we moved out of the protective quarry, got our kit together, and reorganized. The window of opportunity to collect more information from the

Welsh Guards Ops Officer had vanished and, strangely, I was more frustrated in not being able to complete my battle board map update than worrying about future confrontations with *dush* 155s. B Company was dropped off to establish a defensive position near the Welsh Guards' Portakabins. For the remainder of us there would be another hour's tab along two kilometres of the coastal track before arrival at Wether Ground and the semi-prepared gun position of 29 Battery.

It was 22.30 hours as the silhouettes of three 105-mm Light Guns resting under camouflage netting became visible against the starry heavens notable for the bright Southern Cross constellation. Luckily no more Gurkha movement eastwards would occur on the track because, after the war, a Royal Engineers 9 Para Squadron mine-field team discovered that the *dush* had buried two bombs in it some distance further along from where we had stopped. These had a TNT top layer on which were placed two anti-tank mines with five kilo weight fuses and, connected to a command deton-tation wire leading back to a firing point on Mount Harriet, this improvised explosive device was to have been detonated from there at an appropriate opportunity.[4]

Waiting for us was Mike Kefford. He had completed withdrawing from his patrol base after recovering the Mount William recce patrol and abandoning plans for his fighting patrols. 'Great to see you!' exclaimed Mike. 'And it's a good job night has fallen. It'll prevent the *dush* observers on Mount Harriet from bringing down yet more artillery and mortar fire on us. We've found an area which is effectively in dead ground to Mount Harriet, but have now got another problem because we've used up our rations and are in acute need of a resupply.'

The logistics cell of Graham Stewart-Smith and his QGO assistant, Chandra sahib, would have to collect the details of Mike's requirements and press Brigade even harder with another round of supdems and opdems later that night. The current challenge, however, would be to find suitable locations for Tac HQ, A Company and Support Company elements, because we were now within effective range of the *dush* 155s. Our hunt began. A Company had no choice other than to start digging their trenches forward of the artillery battery's guns, and the knowledge that they would be in full view of *dush* artillery observers on Mount Harriet at daylight provided additional moti-vation. Furious clinking of metal against rocks marked the start of Gurkha shovels and picks excavating that part of Wether Ground, with these backdrop sounds of trench construction continuing for the remainder of that night and into the following morning.

Meanwhile Tac HQ personnel continued their bumbling around in the dark. First into one area, and then into another. Nothing was suitable. 'No, this is absolutely hope-less, Mark,' I despaired to an equally demoralized Adjutant. We all felt foolish including the Commandant. As a last resort he gathered together four men, one of whom was Paddy Redding.

'Move out to the four points of the compass and find a suitable location for Tac HQ,' he briefed them, 'but you're to return back here within thirty minutes!'

Three of them came back from their mission within the time-limit, but reported that there was nothing in their path – just open grassland. Then with us on the verge of conceding and digging in the open country, Paddy suddenly sang out, 'I've found some rocks!'

The Commandant's instant groan of, 'God, that's all we needed!' reflected his pessimism which we all shared at that awful frozen moment of time.

However Paddy's further news on his discovery seemed better than a strike of gold that night as he reported, 'OK, come over here you guys! I've found a possible location for us a bit higher up here. It's on a ledge protected by a rock outcrop!'

At last, after three hours of fruitless searching this, maybe, was our stroke of much needed luck. We climbed up to join Paddy standing beside a massive tooth-like rock that jutted into the heavens. Moving around this monolith, I discovered a small hole in its base. 'OK, that's large enough to take one man working by torchlight to complete all necessary Battalion returns, before transmitting them to Brigade, ' I concluded. My relief was enormous as I then added, 'So well done, Paddy! Although we're still over-looked by the *dush* on Mount Harriet, this'll be good enough in the circumstances for Tac HQ's command post.'

It was approximately 02.00 hours. My radio operator, Corporal Aslett, exhausted from carrying the radio and his personal kit, gasped, 'Sir – thank God for that,' as he hauled himself onto the rock ledge. His thankfulness to rest from a wearying march encapsulated everyone's mood as we began the laborious tasks of compiling the companies' opdems, supdems, sitreps and locstats into consolidated totals and message texts before laboriously encoding these into mesco and nuco and transmitting the result to Brigade HQ. Concerned about our fast-dwindling rations and recent week's un-comfortable experiences of being unable to acquire transportation, we then needed a rapid response to the Battalion's opdems and supdems sent by Graham Stewart-Smith and Chandra sahib.

The QGO had worked diligently on this task. His 7GR family connections were impressive with past Regimental service of his grandfather and father, the latter serving in Burma during the Second World War. So being in the Falklands now for Chandra was, without doubt, also a matter of family honour.

In most critical condition was D Company. Two days longer in the field than the remainder of us, they were now without rations, hungry, and remained deficient of 4,000 rounds of SLR and GPMG link ammunition after their argument with the *dush* Skyhawks forty-eight hours previously. In addition our mortar ammunition had still not arrived, there were no augmenting cartridges to increase the mortar bombs' range, a general lack of pyrotechnics such as illuminating and smoke bombs for the platoons' two-inch mortars, shortage of medical supplies, and a looming requirement for fresh radio batteries. It was becoming increasingly obvious that battle preparations would not be complete prior to the planned deadline of crossing our start line on the night of 12–13 June.

The Battalion was now nineteen clicks, or twelve miles from Stanley. Without trans-port or resupply this distance might well have been like twelve days away as, in 1879, Lord Beaconsfield had intimated once during the Second Afghan War: 'We may be only five days march from Kabul, but that would be as bad as a great desert if we had no transport and adequate commisariat.'

'I'm sorry, Mike,' Graham complained to me after a while, 'these Brigade watch-keepers are totally unhelpful as to how and when all these shortfalls will be resolved.'

'Are you sure?' I asked.

'OK, listen to this then,' said Graham with a look that implied that he would be prepared to bet his entire Gurkha pension fund investment holdings in Hong Kong on the result. He picked up his radio handset and called Brigade, 'Reference last series of opdems and supdems from this call-sign. Please give estimated time of arrival at my location.'

This repetition of the Gurkha BO-QGO logistic cell's frequent request once again received its standard Brigade response: 'Roger, Wait Out!' – and these two men's eyes despairingly rolled upwards to the wonderfully starry East Falkland's heaven.

'See what I mean?' remarked an irritated Graham. 'Useless buggers, that's no solution to our problems at all,' then he added as an afterthought, 'and it's getting bloody boring as well!'

Thump! Thump! Our calculations and radio transmissions were suddenly disturbed by the first of that night's 189 incomers from the Navy's 4.5-inch guns out at sea on the Stanley gunline. The frigates *Active* and *Arrow* were bombarding *dush* locations on Mount Harriet and near Moody Brook, with the intention that the latter should not be given any night's sleep on the eve of 3 Commando Brigade's attack. They achieved their aim because Captain Tommy Fox never did sleep during his forty-eight hours on Mount Harriet. Neither did this bombardment or our current tasks give us any possibility for kip. At 04.00 hours I finally crawled into my green slug to stretch out, and listen to the Navy's noisy lullaby. The thin foam of the karrimat continued to be a lousy mattress, serving only to keep dirt off the bag. There was no point taking off my rubber overboots. Maybe a rapid exit from the bag might be required, and attempting to put these on again in the dark would be an impossible task. Bitterly cold, at least my feet were warm. Sleep was impossible. There was no need for a nocturnal shovel patrol because the Army compo rations guaranteed that constipation ruled – OK? That was the least of my worries. My system, awash with adrenalin that prepared the body to meet any potential emergency situation, kept me on the go and counteracted any sluggishness. Fear of the unknown nourished a fertile imagination. It also contributed to a vicious circle as this led to more anxiety which, in turn, gave even less chance of sleep.

At last the Jack Tar 4.5s fell silent. There were less than five hours to stand-to. If I had experienced the lightest of dozes for a couple of hours, consciousness seemed to return again almost immediately. I looked at my watch and quietly groaned, 'Bloody hell! Only 08.00 hours?' My total accumulated hours of sleep in the past sixty had amounted to five or so. 'Oh well,' I thought, shutting my eyes again, 'at least the pincers are closing around Stanley.' Curling up into a resigned foetal position to shut out the world and, in particular East Falkland, I failed miserably to generate even a modicum of warmth deep in the smelly recesses of my green slug.

When dawn arrived on 11 June at Wether Ground, the weather was surprisingly fine with a pleasant blue sky and a wintery sun. From Tac HQ's elevated position, even the cold blue sea to the south looked inviting. We stood down and breakfast was prepared with the last of our rations. Initially everything was quiet. Mark's radio came to life as radio checks were made and the Commandant borrowed his handset to speak to B Company. Lester's men had little room to move in an area overcrowded with the arrival of the second reinforcing 40 Commando Company to the Welsh Guards.

'Fetch Sunray,' snapped the Commandant into the handset. Lester came to his radio set and the Commandant continued, 'Roger. This is Sunray, callsign 9. I want you to move your call sign forward as soon as possible right away from your current location to a position adjacent to mine.'

B Company packed up immediately and were soon tabbing past 40 Commando's A Company. Lester Holley was obviously having a good influence on his Company, for one commando mistakenly wrote later that they saw: '. . . the awesome sight of a battalion of Gurkhas moving in file along the Darwin to Port Stanley road.'[5]

Despite their eye-catching appearance, it was not to be B Company's day. They arrived at their new location below and slightly behind Tac HQ, and began digging in next to the two Mortar Platoon sections. The Commandant and Mike Fallon flew back to Fitzroy for a confirmatory Brigade O Group on our forthcoming attack in thirty-six hours. We were far from ready, and the Commandant had become a worried man. Postponing the Brigade attack was now an urgent option to put forward at the O Group because still no resupply had arrived. Neither had any further recces of the ground been planned or even mentioned regarding the Battalion's advance and assault on the Tumbledown and Mount William. I called Brigade again on the radio to demand irritably, 'Why have we not received our resupply? Are you in a position to tell us when we can expect to receive it?'

And back came that inevitable response from our acquaintance, Captain 'Roger, Wait Out!' who must have been a polo-playing cavalryman judging by his plum in the mouth accent.

Meanwhile trench-digging continued unabated. Daylight's arrival had exposed all the Gurkhas, who did not need reminding how important good trenches would be on Wether Ground. When – and not if – the shelling resumed, the only cover available would come after a rapid dive into them. They worked as only Gurkhas can but, despite turf and stones placed in the bottom, the high water table caused many trenches to begin filling up with water levels of eighteen inches or more. Local rock had to be dug up and sangar walls built up around each trench to negate the pointlessness of ex-cavating further down. They did well. Trench quality was such that some of their Gurkha diggers found them intact on return more than a decade later during a peace-time operational tour of the Falklands.[6]

They had to work fast, though, to ensure even a modicum of personal protection on that Friday morning in 1982. Tac HQ had a grandstand view of the Gurkhas digging and the ground-hugging flying Wessex that soon appeared. The latter's priority task was the move forward of 29 Battery's remaining three Light Guns and its shells. Like giant grey dragonflies, these helicopters were busy darting from Fitzroy up to the Gunners' location with their underslung loads. Below us was the reason we had not received any logistic resupply.

Helicopter priority had gone to the Gunners because of their insatiable consump-tion of ammunition in providing harrassing and counter battery fire and supporting fire to patrolling sub-units. For the forthcoming assault on Stanley, it was necessary to bring forward another 12,000 artillery rounds from San Carlos. The requirement was to stockpile 500 rounds per gun at the gun position and another 500 rounds per gun in the Brigade Maintenance Areas. Even to fly thirty-six 105-mm rounds on a round trip from Fitzroy to the front line took thirty minutes. Refuelling helicopters could only be carried out at San Carlos, but when this, hours of darkness, bad weather, air raids, serviceability and frustrated units hijacking these machines had also been taken into account, other operational tasks, such as the replenishment of the 1st/7th Gurkha Rifles, was curtailed – to put it mildly.[7]

Moving an artillery battery took even longer. Six 105-mm Light Guns, their Gunners, one command post and 200 rounds of ammunition required forty-five Sea King lifts. This was never available. For example, three days were needed for 29 Battery to be moved from San Carlos.[8] It arrived at Bluff Cove on 5 June but even now, six days later, their last three guns were still being flown up to Wether Ground. The negative knock-on effect for the Gurkhas was considerable. No wonder our soldiers were becoming hungrier and forced to drink local water sources which, even with purification tablets, provided no guarantee against succumbing to the discomforts of 'Galtieri's Revenge'.

Captain Tommy Fox, Lieutenant Tedesco, and *Galti garyo*'s 155-mm guns, though, were about to deliver another much more dangerous threat to ruin our relatively idyllic sojourn at Wether Ground that morning.

Chapter Seventeen

SURVIVAL AT WETHER GROUND

If you have only six guns for each division that is not enough. You need a dozen. One wages war with artillery. – Napoleon Bonaparte

It was at midday that Captain Tommy Fox and Lieutenant Daniel Tedesco on Mount Harriet interrupted the digging on Wether Ground. The two *dush* FOOs had spotted the Gurkhas who, at that range, looked like mobile fence posts. Unaware that these enemy troops were Gurkhas, they brought down amongst B Company below us the first 155 salvo of explosion and flame which erupted into 100 metre pillars of dark brown peat and smoke.

'Jesus, some of them must have been hit!' reacted Mark with a mixture of dismay and horror. He echoed the sentiments of everyone in Tac HQ who felt like helpless bystanders.

'Perhaps some more incomers are on their way!' someone near me called out. Inspired by his logic and scared of the kinetic forces unleashed amongst a vulnerable B Company, I lunged head and shoulders into the hole at the base of our rock with all the speed of a striking king cobra. Others also took cover.

There was silence. Call it an instinct to obey SOPs but, shelling or no shelling, Brigade had to be informed. Pulling myself together, I crawled out of my funk shelter, grabbed the radio handset, and reported shakely, 'Now under heavy shelling!'

Graham Stewart-Smith and Chandra sahib had still not resolved their battle of opdems and supdems with Captain 'Roger, Wait Out!', but the latter's response was, nonetheless, a predictable: 'Roger, Wait Out!'

My inner reaction was an unfriendly, 'Hell, how I could scream at that man if he'd been standing in front of me now!'

Below us the three Light Guns of 29 Battery returned counter battery fire. Manning his radio at Tac HQ and oblivious to everything else, Mark mistook this as renewed shelling from the two *dush* 155s. 'This is no good,' he said, 'when the shelling starts again we've got to establish an internal Tac HQ system for warning those on radio sets and others engaged in other tasks.' He looked at the Commandant's orderly. 'And I know who to employ!'

Lance Corporal Dilbahadur Limbu received Mark's rapid Gurkhali instructions on this new procedure before us. 'OK everyone,' informed the Adjutant, 'Dilbahadur will now warn everyone in Tac HQ of any imminent threat of shelling. He'll do it like this.

To differentiate between *dush* and friendly forces he'll shout either "Incoming!" or "Outgoing!" dependent on which side's firing.'

But Dilbahadur was slow on the uptake when another salvo of *dush* shells exploded nearer us. His surprise manifested itself in a Gurkhali curse, and he tried to make amends immediately by yelling, 'Ingoing!' His originality caused much Tac HQ amusement, particularly when the gunners below us retaliated again and our Gurkha sentry responded with an equally loud, 'Outcoming!'

More explosions. Pillars of peat and smoke erupted around B Company to the rear and, 300 metres to their front, on A Company's position. It was like being trapped in a series of detonating PIRA car bombs during a potential Wether Ground Bloody Friday. From my vantage point B Company were worst affected. Gurkhas climbed out of their trenches and ran towards the comparative safety of ground nearer the coast-line away from the targeted area as more shells exploded to our front where Tac HQ had bumbled around during the hours of darkness. 'Thank goodness Paddy found this place we're in now,' I thought.

Such relief was not experienced by Nigel Price. At first light he had moved from his two mortar sections' harbour area south of the Darwin-Stanley track with his Signaller and two riflemen to recce a possible site for a mortar line close to Tac HQ. Leaving his three men at this site, he made his way back alone to the remainder of his platoon, but was caught in the open by another approaching 155 incomer and dived to the ground so fast that his helmet went flying. Worse still, the bottom of his SLR magazine then struck East Falkland and fell off, jettisoning its twenty rounds everywhere. Bracing himself, his only thought was focused on the vulnerability of his exposed back. When the shell impacted ten metres away, its explosive force threw Nigel a metre into the air. As he regained contact with terra firma, a white-hot fizzing piece of shrapnel ten centimetres long embedded itself in the ground only centimetres from his face as a postscript of peat and clods of earth cascaded down on him. Other pieces of shrapnel rang against boulders in the immediate area with a noise of snapping rings, and one of his mortar tubes still strapped to his men's equipment had its barrel dented by shrapnel strike.

'It wasn't a good day,' a lucky Nigel confessed later.

But Captain Fox and Lieutenant Tedesco on Mount Harriet could not bracket our Wether Ground positions to enable the firing of accurate salvos, and had to be content with calling in harassing fire missions only. Professional as ever, Bombadier Batchelor criticized the *dush* artillery and, in particular, that every fifth explosion or so came from an ineffective airburst round. 'Uh! Luckily they don't 'ave the technical expertise of Brit gunners,' he commented dryly in my direction. 'It seems to be observed fire all right, but it's gotta regular pattern, there's no multiple battery fire, your blokes are well-dispersed, and the peaty soil is absorbing a lot of the explosive and fragmentation effect. In fact, because of the peat, I would've thought that they oughta use more airburst. But what's being used by them Argies is exploding high up – perhaps as much as 300 feet. So they gotta be using MT fuses, instead of VT that our blokes would fire.'

'And what's MT, as opposed to VT fuses?' I asked, acting the stupid infanteer.

'Mechanical time fuses, sir,' he replied, 'which the Argies obviously have problems in setting correctly to make their shells burst at a lower height, and the second means variable time radar-controlled fuses which, as its name implies, is kit that's quite a bit more superior!'

Even a technical illiterate like myself picked up his message that the consequences could have been more serious if the Argies had more 155s, and VT instead of MT fuses. Current life was not amusing, and nor had we been the only attacked unit because *dush* shells had gouged out large furrows of peat near 29 Battery. Their seven-man gun detachments were lucky to escape injury and, like the Gurkhas, had combat kit torn by shrapnel. Everyone was now accustomed to the big cannons' acoustics. From the east and well behind the dush front lines on Mount Harriet would sound a muffled cough, followed by sinister pause. The shell was on its way. Fear wound up your guts as if they were on a fisherman's reel while a low whistle became louder – and louder. Yet these three seconds of waiting time for the inevitable sickening crump were invaluable as they gave an opportunity to seek cover either in the prone or kneeling position from this menace. Whatever took your fancy, for it had become part of the routine at Wether Ground.

Despite the shelling, 29 Battery continued receiving their underslung helicopter loads of ammunition and other three Light Guns. This first round of *dush* shelling was ended by the Gunners returning what we assumed to be several salvos of counter battery fire. However the *dush* 155 locations near Sapper Hill were approximately fifteen kilometres from Wether Ground. Belonging to their 3rd Artillery Group, their maximum range of 20,400 metres outranged 29 Battery's guns by 8,400 metres. The Light Gun maximum range of 12,000 metres could only be achieved if shells were fired on supercharge as witnessed by Captain Fox on 1 June when three co-located Light Guns with 42 Commando sub-units on Mount Kent had engaged the *dush* at Moody Brook. A 105-mm Ota Melará gun received a direct hit and was overturned, fortunately without any casualties.

So 29 Battery's tactic had been to bombard Mount Harriet seven kilometres away where the two *dush* FOOs were located. The 4th Infantry Regiment soldiers became concerned that their FOOs' radio transmissions were attracting British attention and causing the subsequent counter battery fire. This created a breathing space for us, however, as Captain Fox and Lieutenant Tedesco were forced to take cover in a small cave thirty metres below Mount Harriet's summit. Twenty minutes later they would reappear and then Dilbahadur's shout, corrected now to a terse, 'Incomer!' obliged us to become more intimate with East Falkland peat once again. In their trenches, the small men's anger grew. They hated this passive challenge of holding ground under shellfire. Grappling with active challenges was more in keeping with Gurkha attitudes – and no Gurkha was smiling at Wether Ground as yet another warning was shouted, '*Kankra jharnu shuru garyo!*' (They have started to drop their cucumbers!) Rifleman Baliprasad Rai, as the number one gunner on a B Company sustained-fire GPMG, found himself in the middle of another round of shelling which became:

. . . more intense and accurate by the minute, and it was increasingly difficult to poke our heads above our trench, crouched as we were in waist-deep muddy water. (155mm) shells whistled and whined above our heads and crashed around with a deafening noise, showering everyone with dirt. My ears ached from the terrible din but I could faintly hear the OC, Capt Holley sahib screaming for everyone to keep their heads down. I don't know if anyone else heard him. The shells seemed to come even closer and I would not be telling the truth if I said I was not at all frightened. I thoroughly was but I was also angry. This was no way to fight a fight I thought and a No. 1 Gunner was no use in this situation, no matter how good.[1]

Lester Holley kept his wits. There was no future in his Company 2IC, Captain Dalbahadur Sunwar, and himself continuing to share a trench. The next incomer could vaporize their home and, with it, the Company's command and control. If this happened, there was no possibility of replacement. Lester decided therefore that the QGO and he should part company, sending Dalbahadur to another trench further away. But as the latter was moving, yet another incomer screamed towards its impact point on the Company's position. Rifleman Baliprasad Rai described the result:

A shell landed periously near, about 20 feet away, and I heard my trench-mate, 21160801 Lance Corporal Gyanenda Rai cry out. He had been hit by flying shrapnel on his (right) shoulder (and on his left hip). I told him, 'There is blood pouring down your back.' He looked at me and replied, 'You are also hit. There is blood all over the back of your head!' Yes, (three) piece(s) of shrapnel had penetrated my tin hat (helmet) and lodged themselves in the back of my head. Only then did I feel the pain.[2]

Captain Dalbahadur Sunwar was also hit in the left thigh, and Rifleman Pranaya Rai of Support Company received a shrapnel wound to his left leg. The Company reported their casualties over the radio to Mark. In the brief lull that followed, Rifleman Baliprasad Rai's platoon commander, Lieutenant Garjabahadur Gurung, hurried over to the SF gunner's trench to administer first aid, whilst Lester Holley charged across to Tac HQ. He had a concerned look on his moustached face as he arrived at the top of the rise and panted at me, 'I've got four casualties in my Company area from that last lot of shelling. Can you get the doc to look at them and organize their evacuation?'

There was another muffled cough in the east, and he took cover as a couple more incomers in rapid succession arrived on target. He then returned to his position only to discover that the forward lip of his trench had been hit by shellfire. An unusually fearless person, it would have been in keeping with his character to have shrugged his shoulders, made a remark to the effect of, 'That's life!' and then devote his energies only to moving about his soldiers' trenches in order to encourage them and look after their well-being.

I briefed Martin Entwhistle on the radio, 'Can you move out to call sign two and assess the situation there with their casualties?'

Then Mark called Rory Stewart in command of our A Echelon at Fitzroy. Rory was on the ball: 'No Hawkeye lift is available, but we'll move up our Playtime resources here to the rear of your location for casevac puposes.'

The casualties would be loaded into Land-Rovers and driven back to Fitzroy via the Welsh Guards' location. Martin trotted off past Tac HQ and was ambushed immediately by more incomers as he moved from trench to trench treating the casualties. Like my uncle Percy Maides, a First World War Passchendaele medical orderly survivor, the 1st/7th Gurkha Rifles' doctor experienced that the military medical fraternity could find themselves exceptionally vulnerable to enemy fire. But despite these added complications, Martin evacuated his patients onto the Land-Rover. Irritated and shaken, he then scaled Tac HQ's minor hill to lodge his objections. There was no foghorn laughter as he politely confronted me. 'Mike, could I have a word? Look, it was pretty hairy out there with all that shelling just now. Could I remind you that there's only two doctors with this Battalion, and it's a wee bit difficult to get us replaced if we cop it? So, next time we're unlucky to receive casualties, can these please be central-ized at my RAP in order that I can treat them there instead of me having to scrabble around platoon and company locations?'

Martin had every right to be concerned. He withdrew back to his trench to recover. Guilty at initiating the incident which highlighted the lack of a procedure so basic to any Battalion defensive position, my lesson had been learnt the hard way. It would not be forgotten for the remainder of the campaign. Yet there would be a twist of irony in my stupidity because, later, Martin was awarded a Mention in Dispatches for his after-noon's work.

The shelling eventually ceased as the 155s signed off with two airbursts showering Tac HQ with shrapnel. Although the shells again exploded too high, only good fortune prevented casualties. A piece of shrapnel landed five feet away from Bombadier Batchelor's position, and a few minutes later he walked around Tac HQ's position to show me the wickedly jagged piece of metal nestling in his hand. 'What d'ya think sir?' he queried, not without pride at having survived direct *dush* artillery fire. 'Not bad, eh? When I'm back in Blighty this one's going to be put on the mantlepiece as my souvenir of the bloody Falklands!'

We picked ourselves up and looked in the direction of Mount Harriet where the two *dush* FOOs had been busy. A pair of the ten CrabAir Harrier GR3s flown in from Ascension Island to reinforce the Task Force climbed into the sky from behind Harriet. The jump jet ground attack fighters had been dropping cluster bombs on the Moody Brook and Tumbledown areas, and were now making their escape run towards the sea. A smudge of smoke burst above them. It was an exploding missile fired from a *dush* Blowpipe shoulder-held launcher. Both targets survived and one pilot waggled his aircraft's wings.

'He's just wishing those below better luck next time,' remarked the chirpy Kit Spencer. The two mortar sections had resited themselves at their new mortar line away from the exposed plain, and B Company also later were to follow suit. Meanwhile Graham and Chandra sahib continued the supdems and opdems war against Captain 'Roger, Wait Out!' To us it seemed that no senior officer at 5 Brigade was ever avail-able to make decisions or resolve priorities. Their organization lacked a Deputy Commander of the rank of colonel to resolve this problem, and Brigade watchkeepers' hours of duty should have been lengthened to provide more continuity and better service to units like ours. Despite these problems, our two 'loggies' had been efficient. Not only I, but other officers, had personal cameras with them, and one took a photo-graph of Graham speaking aggressively into his radio handset. This and a two-day face stubble made him the personification of true grit at a seemingly titanic moment. On return to UK, the photographer showed his result to a relative who exclaimed, 'Gosh! Is this your CO giving out his orders during a major Gurkha attack on the Argies?'

Although this particular confrontation had only been with 5 Brigade's logistics staff, the Graham-Chandra sahib team did eventually receive its due reward by the QGO's award of a Mention in Dispatches for his diligent work in Tac HQ. But the current logistic shortfalls were affecting the operational planning which had been taking place at Fitzroy. The Commandant, accompanied by the impatient silver-topped stick-in-lieu-of-weapon and Mike Fallon, returned by helicopter from the Brigade O Group there in the late afternoon. He had to be informed about the day's events and his Gurkha losses.

'Keep it simple,' I told myself as they both strode towards the beleagured Tac HQ personnel.

'Hello, sir!' I ventured with trepidation. 'I don't know if you know, but we've received some 155 shelling during the afternoon and B Company have taken four casualties.'

Having been involved all that day in the brainstorming of the Brigade's attack planning, the Commandant's mind was divorced from Wether Ground reality. It had been no safe place for his Gurkhas. A look of impatience immediately turned to one of worry as he snapped, 'What was that you said?' It was strange Brigade HQ had not informed him of the situation.

Repeating myself, I then added, 'Don't worry sir, it's all been sorted out, and the casualties have now been casevaced by Land-Rover back to Fitzroy.' After a minute the shock had been absorbed. Back to business. He required to brief us all and ordered, 'OK. Plans are getting firmer. I want an O Group here at 19.00 hours.'

A little later, the Company Commanders and other members of the O Group assembled expectantly at Tac HQ. It was the end of a trying day, but there would be a moment of pure SAS lighter relief as Lester Holley appeared wearing an empty circular grenade tin on his head. Everyone stared nonplussed at this apparition. He grinned. 'Do you like it?' asked the B Company Commander, whose leadership had undergone a severe test that afternoon. 'I've just developed a new type of helmet!' Typical Lester.

The desired effect was achieved and we all laughed. But reality quickly returned. Next would be the outline plan for 3 Commando Brigade's attack scheduled for later that night and the first details of 5 Brigade's follow-up attack, including our own. Tension returned in the evening air as people squatted down on grass tussocks and small rocks. Notebooks were produced from pockets and pens poised to attack paper. The scribbling started as Paddy made a meal of describing the ground. After his performance, an intense Commandant confirmed the Commando Brigade's objectives on the second ring of *dush*-held hills which ran from north to south. 'Gentlemen, 3 Para will attack the northernmost, Mount Longdon, to be followed by 45 Commando and 42 Commando taking on Two Sisters and Mount Harriet respectively,' he said gravely. One could not mistake that this was the most important set of orders he had issued so far in his military career. However one item critical to any attack is the H-hour: the time at which a unit plans to cross its start line to begin the advance towards its objective.

So I noted down carefully three timings issued, '3 Para – 00.01 hours, 42 Commando – 00.30 hours, and 45 Commando – 01.00 hours'.

This would determine the order of those on radio stag for that night. These battles had to be monitored and updates provided to our sub-units. Internal passage of information was vital, particularly as we would be the next to perform on the inner ring of hills.

'Doesn't sound, though, that there's going to be too many who'll be getting forty winks tonight!' I thought flippantly, as the Commandant continued with facts and figures on the planned artillery and naval gunfire support firepower demonstration against *dush* positions.

'Two 42 Commando companies will move through our location en route to their start line south-east of Mount Harriet. All five Commando and Royal Artillery gun batteries will be in support – a grand total of thirty guns that include 29 Battery's below us – plus naval gunfire support from HMS *Avenger*, *Glamorgan*, *Yarmouth* and *Arrow*. If the attacks are successful, then 3 Para will exploit forward to the next line of defence at Wireless Ridge, 42 Commando to Goat Ridge and 45 Commando to the Tumbledown. If that happens then this'll still leave us free to capture Mount William.

'5 Brigade's attack is still on for the night of 12–13 June. We've got the warning order, but with no recces mounted and our logistic resupply problems, the chances are that it'll be postponed twenty-four hours. The direction of our approach has also been altered due to the Scots Guards' intelligence info on mines. This'll now be from Two Sisters and along Goat Ridge rather than south-west along the Darwin-Stanley track. Since the Tumbledown is considered a lesser objective in terms of *dush* strength, the Scots Guards will secure this first. Then our B Company will assault the Tumbledown's north-east spur, before our attack on Mount William. This'll be D Company's mission, with A Company providing a fire base on the Tumbledown to shoot them in. Finally, all Company commanders, the BC, his FOOs, Mortar Platoon Commander and I will be flown forward as a Battalion Recce Group onto Two Sisters tomorrow to eyeball their objectives.'

He looked at us to say, 'I'll take questions, gentlemen, in one minute.'

We pondered over the plan. Despite his recent uplifting dance with the 155 shell, Nigel Price remained on the offensive after the pause. 'I've only got thirty-six large augmenting cartridges to increase our mortars' range,' he said, 'and must have more. This is a priority sir, because with the distances involved we can currently only give limited effective supporting fire to just one company during the attack. So will these be made available in time?' Nigel's insistence illustrated the importance of detail in planning the Battalion's attack, but the Commandant could not provide an answer. It only illustrated our dependence on an unreliable Brigade logistics resupply system before any attack could commence.

People returned to their locations and Tac HQ ate the last of its rations. With last light approaching, 250 heavily camouflaged and ammunition bedecked 42 Commando Marines marched past us and over the Darwin-Stanley track on a long sweeping manoeuvre to their start line near Pony's Pass, prior to advancing up Mount Harriet from its rear. Contrary to the universal belief that these Marine Commandos had been undetected they were, in fact, spotted by Captain Fox from his location on the summit of Mount Harriet. He estimated that the 4th Infantry Regiment would soon be attacked by a Regiment, but the problem was that the dark prevented them readjusting their defensive positions to face this new threat.

The Commando Brigade attack would be compulsive listening on my radio. Planning the various watchkeeper two-hour 'stags' had been so designed that mine would start at 02.00 hours, well after all three H-hours but, hopefully, when all battles were being fought. By now night had fallen. After four days of enforced abstinence since the visitation of 'Galtieri's Revenge' at Goose Green, there was a need for a private diversionary attack prior to the main event. A shovel patrol was the name of the game.

'Excuse me, gentlemen,' I informed those nearest, after borrowing the required implement. 'I'm leaving you now. Duty calls. But kindly don't shoot me as I return from such a dangerous one-man mission.'

This stupid little joke made me feel good. Clutching the toilet paper raided from an otherwise empty ration pack, I wandered away. Fifty metres later, having dug the hole, my posterior was bared to the cold Falklands' air. Afterwards I felt like new and returned to engage 5 Brigade HQ with the usual radio traffic of sitreps and locstats. These completed, I laid out my thin foam karrimat again and put the green slug on top. Countering the near zero temperature and, perhaps, a snooze were important basics to keeping my grey-matter faculties functioning. Chandra sahib had been assigned the job as the first watchkeeper. It was just after 00.30 hours. The deadlines for the first two H-hours had passed as battle was joined by gunfire support from *Avenger* and *Glamorgan* on the southern Stanley gun line combined with another Commando artillery battery to the north. Still cocooned in the warmth of my green slug, I nearly jumped out of my skin as 29 Battery's Light Guns below us fired a salvo of shells that spat flame and smoke. Thump! Thump! Out at sea the unmistakeable sound of the Navy's 4.5-inch guns beat an angry rhythm of up to twenty rounds per salvo.

'What's up sahib?' I whispered a little later to the QGO manning the radio. Chandra was not so buoyant as he had been before that first briefing in the Officers' Mess at Church Crookham two months ago. Reality, maybe, had sunk in with the realization of what we would be about to face in the following nights because his reply was subdued.

'3 Para are on Mount Longdon sahib. They have received one casualty from an anti-personnel mine explosion,' he whispered back.

'Have you informed the companies, sahib?'

'Yes, sahib.'

Another forty minutes or so passed. Including *Arrow* on the Berkeley Sound gun line, naval gunfire support as well as artillery fire increased markedly. No more waiting. My watch now showed nearly 02.00 hours. I got out of the green slug to relieve Chandra. Paddy was next on after me at 04.00 hours but I had decided already to stag on throughout that night and listen to all arriving sitreps. This self-imposed chore had its roots in a peacetime preference to experience the thrill of watching a big sporting event live on TV, rather than being content with the recorded highlights afterwards. In these Falkland circumstances it was amateurish behaviour as sleep for a front-line soldier is a vital commodity to steal in any war.

214

'But when would there be an opportunity again to acclimatize mentally to the Gurkhas' battle looming in forty-eight hours?' I asked myself. 'So get back again, Seear, into your smelly green slug, keep warm, and hang sleep!'

Listening during those next few hours to the artillery gunfire, explosions, naval gunfire support bombardment, radio sitreps, an air threat, Exocet attack and helicopter assault threat would become a mosaic of events which few in the British Army have since experienced. Awareness had become acute that a large number of men on both sides were, and would be about to be, killed and wounded. Psychologically, my monitoring this on the radio was one way of exercising solidarity with those fighting in the nearby hills that night. The discovery that I had become anxious for them surprised me. Any lingering Army career ambitions had become subservient in the past weeks to questions of human relationships and staying alive. In addition, the multi-dimensional cacophony of sound made me even more humble amid a growing personal fever of fear. Excluding figures in the post-battle shelling, the final friendly and *dush* casualty total of eighty-eight dead and 261 wounded would justify my concerns.[3] This radio stag would be, in a way, my little dress rehearsal for events in forty-eight hours time. Every radio report from Brigade would produce a reaction from me, whether it be a personal thought or requirement to relay information. I kept a constant eye on my watch. The next part of this long night began with positive news.[4]

'42 Commando has crossed its start line.'

It was considerably more than an hour behind schedule though, and still nothing had been heard about their sister unit, 45 Commando.

'Now under heavy mortar and machine-gun fire on Wireless Ridge.'

With this report, also 3 Para's good progress on Mount Longdon had been halted. The destroyer and two frigates on the gun line to my south and British artillery, including a violently noisy 29 Battery below me, increased their rate of shellfire which was being poured onto *dush* locations.

'Hand to hand fighting on 42 Commando's objective.'

Things were getting hotter. But at 02.45 hours came the first concrete success.

'42 Commando have secured eastern edge of Mount Harriet, but are under heavy machine-gunfire.'

Just before 03.00 hours, the Two Sisters' battle made its entry onto the air waves at last.

'45 Commando advance going well . . . meeting light opposition, but still advancing.'

Sound travels well at night – so the gunfire and explosions seemed to be quite close by, even though they were eight to nine kilometres away. Another twenty minutes passed.

'42 Commando captured one enemy 120mm mortar.'

Just after 03.30 hours there was more news of 3 Para on Mount Longdon.

'Close-quarter skirmishing continuing.' Some of the *dush* 7th Infantry Regiment facing 3 Para mistakenly thought they were being attacked by the Gurkhas during this fiercest land battle of the Falklands' War. Rumours of Gurkhas beheading men were prevalent. One conscript there by the name of Guillermo described them later as soldiers who . . .

. . . advanced listening to music on their 'walkmans'. They had been brainwashed and nothing mattered to them . . . The Seventh Regiment had its hospital zone, but it was a long way away, about two miles from us and even further from the boys in the front line. That was one of the biggest problems for those who were wounded at the front line. If they couldn't be brought back and the Gurkhas found them, they finished them off. When the Gurkhas found a trench, they'd order you to come out and once outside, even if you surrendered, they'd cut your head off. Once the Gurkhas had passed, the English came along behind and if some Argentine had not been discovered by then, there was nothing for it but to surrender. They'd already had you flat on the ground for hours on end with the artillery fire, they'd let loose the Gurkhas at you, and you'd run out of ammunition. Anyone who has survived all that and gave himself up to the English was very lucky and could begin to consider himself safe.[5]

Thump! Thump! Naval gunfire support to my south continued. It was now 04.00 hours.

'Attacking the western end of Mount Harriet. Fifteen prisoners taken.'

42 Commando were now totally committed, and things seemed to be going well – although that should never be taken for granted in a battle.

'Air Raid Warning State Red! Five hostiles approaching from the west. Time overhead 04.30 hours.'

'Heavens! This might affect us,' I thought, and grabbed the Battalion command net handset to inform all the companies.

'Major enemy activity west of Sapper Hill.'

'What were they doing now?' I wondered with some alarm and, once again, fed this news into the handset. Fifteen tense minutes ticked by.

'42 Commando now secure on the western edge of Mount Harriet. Little opposition.'

Another twenty minutes elapsed.

'Hostiles carried out a high level bombing run in the Mount Kent area.'

'Nowhere near us!' I sighed, and breathed out even easier with the next report.

'45 Commando secure on the western edge of Two Sisters.'

It was now 05.00 hours. Thump! Thump! More naval gunfire support. At the end of that night, a total of 684 rounds would be fired from the Stanley gun line.

'42 Commando under heavy counter-attack.'

The plot thickened as Cymbeline – the British artillery's radar locating system equipment with a Gunner Battery somewhere on that dark night in the East Falkland khuds – had begun to display on its screen an ominous picture. It was no static enemy artillery battery or mortar base plate location.

'Ten to fifteen helicopters identified as enemy at Grid 295701.'[6]

I got out my map. Plotting this location aided by torchlight in the wonderful safeness of my funk shelter was a minute's work. Then a shiver tracked down my spine. Another minute was used to double-check the frightening answer. 'Jesus, just southwest of Mount Harriet, and only seven kilometres from us!' I muttered to myself. 'Are the *dush* trying to counter-attack us?' Once again I passed the information on the Battalion net.

'42 Commando skirmishing on western edge of Mount Harriet.

216

More artillery gunfire. My watch showed 06.45 hours. Still sitting up in my green slug, I attempted to gain an overview from the confusing reports. 'Nothing more on the *dush* helicopter threat,' I concluded hopefully, even though this remained a niggling worry.

'Perhaps they landed somewhere behind their front lines to evacuate escaping men from the Mount Harriet area,' was my later speculation from a lack of further helicopter activity whilst, from his trench at A Company, David Willis observed an enormous explosion at sea. '*Yarmouth* was late to leave the gunline. Hit by land-based Exocet fired from south-eastern outskirts of Stanley.'

Yarmouth had been escorting the destroyer *Glamorgan*. Thirty minutes later came confirmation that the fog of war reigned supreme. The victim was *Glamorgan*. Thirteen dead and seventeen injured. The attack justified Bill Dawson's worries about a cargo of Gurkhas and him on board a drifting *Monsunen* three nights before.

'45 Commando firm, but under artillery fire. Enemy using airburst.'

'So Two Sisters has now been taken!' I rejoiced silently. But the 155s were back in action, meting out punishment that day on the audacity of attackers who had now become the victors. The sounds of battle continued to roll on slowly for the next hour like diminishing claps of thunder in a subsiding storm. Here and there were odd explosions from shelling and other ordnance. At 08.30 hours the final confirmation of a successful night arrived and the undeniable fact that we would be next on the battlefield.

'All positions now taken and mopping up operations continue,' informed my radio handset with British debit figures as a casual afterthought: 'Forty casualties on the northern objective, and twenty apiece on the two southern objectives.'[7]

45 Commando were refused permission to exploit forward onto the Tumbledown, leaving 5 Brigade's attack plan intact. 'But,' I continued brooding, 'when the hell, then, would this take place?'

The morning of 12 June dawned bright and cold. Some snow had fallen during the night and there were patches of the white dust everywhere, reminiscent of icing sugar sprinkled thinly on top of a cake. The rising sun soon restored the light tan colour to the thick grass tussocks. Psychologically this would be the most difficult day on the Falklands. Our attack might be tonight but, more probably, would be postponed for thirty-six hours. Anxiety grew throughout that day, my stomach feeling as if it could expand into my mouth. That no rations were available for breakfast mattered not a jot.

After first light and stand-down, the helicopters began resupplying ammunition to 29 Battery's gun position. Their work rate was intense for, in forty-eight hours, they had flown forward 5,000 rounds. Indeed the average Sea King had a total flying time of forty hours per week in the Falklands, which was the same figure it achieved during a month in peacetime. More Light Guns flying past underslung from the Sea Kings indicated that 4 Field Regiment's 97 'Lawson' Field Battery was being leap-frogged forward over 29 Battery to a gun position south of the recently taken Mount Harriet. Leaving our position, the Commandant and his R Group also flew up to the Two Sisters' battlefield to carry out a long-range visual recce of the Tumbledown and Mount William areas.

They timed their departure to perfection. A muffled cough sounded in the far distance. 'Incomer!' yelled the diligent Dilbahadur as the whistling signature of the unwelcome visitor marked a resumption of the shelling.

'Worst sound on the battlefield,' commented Graham. It was, but there is also a paradox to the unwritten law of the shell. If its whistle is not heard in the final part of its flight then the incomer is destined for you. Another explosion had just occurred 200 metres below me and near B Company's trenches when, in almost less time than Dilbahadur could call out 'Incomer!' a Sea King flew low over the still-smoking shell crater. Nothing, it seemed, could stop the resupply helicopters. Although we were still waiting for the fruits of our opdem and supdem requests made to Captain 'Roger, Wait Out!', a shout from a familiar figure of stout proportions indicated that at least reinforcements had arrived.

'Great to see you all! Thank God we're back with the Battalion again!' exclaimed Bill Dawson as he arrived at Tac HQ, giving a much needed vent to his bad conscience in having been forced to remain at Goose Green for the past few days. His Alternative Battalion HQ, including the ever-cheerful Gurkha Major, had now managed to rejoin us and would be needed as a command and control back-up for the Battalion's attack.

The Brigade radio net burst into life once more: 'Air Raid Warning State Red! High altitude aircraft moving from west to east!' We had become blasé to such a threat and, perhaps, it was the effect of yesterday's shelling that caused this reaction. Nonetheless I gazed up into the blue sky to observe the contrails of a high-flying aircraft. The helicopters ignored this and continued flying their ammunition loads to the Gunners stockpiling for the 5 Brigade attack. Resupplies for 29 Battery's guns were also being received from a couple of civilian tractors driven on the track below us by kelpers from Bluff Cove and Fitzroy. These lumbered slowly along, towing trailers on which were box upon box of artillery shells. The Battery was also engaging in harrassing fire missions after the previous night's attacks. They did not have to contend any longer with Captain Fox and Lieutenant Tedesco on Mount Harriet but, like the Gurkhas, still came under more intermittent 155 shellfire.

Bill was a novice to being on the receiving end, and his expletives, 'Jesus Christ! What the devil's that?' matched the force of the impacting *dush* meteorites. But I had already come to the same conclusion as General William Sherman of the American Civil War. He had not been exaggerating with his claim that war is all hell.

The *dush* 155s remained busy all that day. Their 3rd Artillery Group were using a spotter from an airborne helicopter to direct the shelling and, judging from the renewed accuracy of shelling on our positions, the same helicopter must have been utilized against us. Luck remained on our side. The peaty soil at our location absorbed the ground bursts, and the airbursts were again too high. At Mount Longdon, Two Sisters and Mount Harriet, the Paras and Marine Commandos were more vulnerable. Shrapnel exploding on rock and stony surfaces accounted for a total of six fatalities and fourteen wounded. At least we had no casualties that day. A few more shells exploded at Wether Ground as Bill became a popular man. 'I've got some mail for you guys!' he called out.

This included a few of several weeks' vintage from Tove. Only then did I appreciate the morale booster of four small blue aerogrammes after having been subjected to more than thirty plus 155-mm incomers for the past thirty-six hours. The 2IC also browsed through a copy of *The Daily Telegraph* in between shell explosions as I analysed my letters. We then received more local news. A decoded mesco message informed us of a twenty-four hour postponement of the Brigade attack. This would now take place on the night of 13–14 June. But still there was no resupply. Les Peacock had now been inserted into 5 Brigade's logistic organization at Fitzroy as a Battalion liaison officer to speed up the process, but the other Brigade watchkeepers did not provide any variation in their answers to those of Captain 'Roger, Wait Out!' Such inertia seemed to put our attack in jeopardy once more by causing increased pressure on a vital commodity commanders always struggle against, and on which Napoleon had elucidated: 'Ask of me anything but time. I will lose a man, but never a moment.'

An hour later another Brigade radio message warned: 'Some of the prisoners taken on Two Sisters and Mount Harriet are being moved along the Darwin-Stanley track to your location. They are to remain there until Hawkeye can provide them a lift to Ajax Bay!' These visitors would first arrive at D Company, who then had to provide escorts to guide them to Tac HQ. But a threat remained from shelling. We were committed to mounting a Battalion attack in thirty-six hours. Yet, of most concern, there was no sign of the vital logistics resupply.

Our current situation at Wether Ground that early afternoon was far from good.

Chapter Eighteen

UP AND AWAY

It is very necessary to attend to detail, and to trace a biscuit from Lisbon into a man's mouth on the frontier, and to provide for its removal from place to place, by land and by water, or no military operations can be carried on. – Duke of Wellington

A headcount of POWs took place between a Marine Commando and D Company QGO. This handover/takeover did not go smoothly as First Lieutenant Ignacio Gorriti of B Company, 12th Infantry Regiment, witnessed:

> . . . the frustrating attempts of a Royal Marine, an Argentine officer and a Gurkha, who attempted to count the prisoners in three languages and kept getting different totals. Finally, after half an hour, the Royal Marine selected one of the totals given to him and said that would have to do.[1]

Gathered on the Darwin-Stanley track, the bulk of 300 POWs were flown out to the Ajax Bay facility which would handle a grand total of more than 2,000 POWs. But these remaining eighty-three were then sent back to us, marching in file the eight kilometres to Wether Ground and, via A Company, arriving at Tac HQ dirty, dishevelled and exhausted. Lieutenant Colonel Diego Soria, the 4th Infantry Regiment's CO, and our artillery FOO tormentors, Captain Tommy Fox and Lieutenant Daniel Tedesco, were blindfolded and had their hands tied behind their backs. Fox had managed to burn the Regiment's documents before hiding in the entrance of his cave, then surrendered after 42 Commando had taken Mount Harriet. This was a tricky manoeuvre and, to avoid being shot in the confusion, he had demanded to be taken to a British officer. All three men were soon flown out in two Scout helicopters. Lacking suitable cold weather combat clothing, another prisoner resembled a third-class version of Batman. This caped crusader had cut a hole in an olive green blanket's centre. Putting his head through this, it now had become an improvised poncho. Two were wounded. One had his head wrapped in bandages and, at the rear, another nursed an equally heavily bandaged arm in a sling. Exhausted, he sank down opposite me to regain a little strength for the final 200 metres of this first leg of his journey back to Argentina, as the long line shuffled down the hillside. They sat down to wait for their helicopter transport. I saw no gaucho knives on these 'boys from Corrientes' which *The Daily Telegraph* in our Officers' Mess at Church Crookham had intimated they might carry.

Then D Company sent a radio message: 'Return eight prisoners to carry another badly wounded man from our location.' These were selected by the Gurkha detachment commander and they set out, one limping badly. Perhaps it was faked but, annoyed only at the QGO's apparent bad choice and indecisiveness to intervene, I barked out, 'For goodness sake! Can't you see the state of that man? Exchange him for someone who *will* be able to carry the damned stretcher!'

The QGO blinked at the Training Officer sahib's irritability that also surprised me. Although a classic post-traumatic stress reaction symptom, it felt good to vent my wrath on the poor QGO after our pasting from the *dush* 155. The POW gave me a weary thumbs-up and his replacement joined the original seven who all slouched off to D Company. Most of them came from B and C Companies of the 4th Infantry Regiment stationed, in peacetime, in Argentina's northern sub-tropical province of Corrientes. This unit had completed its move from the mainland as part of 3 Infantry Brigade on 29 April and, less one company remaining in Stanley, had been deployed as Task Force Monte Caseros in reserve at Wall Mountain, with one platoon on Mount Challenger. Acclimatization problems had been dreadful and were exacerbated by them being located furthest in the Outer Defence Zone around Stanley which had the minimum of logistic resupply.

Post-hostilities, a Gurkha foraging party led by Mark Willis visited Two Sisters and Mount Harriet in search of *dush* souvenirs among the detrius of battle. Both my radio operator, Corporal Aslett and Corporal Anandkumar Rai of the Battalion Intelligence Section were soon busy. Equipment was strewn everywhere. From the eastern side of Two Sisters, items such as helmets, weapons, and webbing were picked up by the two corporals, as well as the backpack and full kitbag of one particular 4th Infantry Regiment soldier, *Cabo* (Corporal) Nicolás Urbieta, the *grupo de apoyo* (support section) commander of eleven soldiers in 2 Platoon, C Company.

'Why have you collected so much?' I asked Anandkumar later.

He replied seriously, 'To gather intelligence on the *dush*, sahib – for the next time.'

Among other items found in Urbieta's equipment were two rolls of undeveloped film and a training manual which stated the mission of his section in defence as: 'Fight the enemy as soon as they are within the reach of the section's firepower, putting them under an increasing volume of fire with the aim of smashing their attack.'[2] There were also identification papers and five unposted letters which revealed the dark-haired handsome nineteen year-old had joined the Army in March 1981 and had completed his first year of NCO training at the Buenos Aires School of Infantry in Campo de Mayo. He had started his second year but, after eight weeks, was pulled off the course and mobilized because of the retaking of *Islas las Malvinas*. His new unit was the 4th Infantry Regiment in Corrientes. They were soon deployed by train to Rio Gallegos from where they flew to the Islands. There, Urbieta would soon put his training as a leader into practice. His platoon commander was the determined *Teniente* (Lieutenant) Jorge Perez Grandi whose name Urbieta had included on a piece of paper depicting the *'Rol de Combate'* Company order of battle organization. As a good section commander, he had also noted down on a piece of toilet paper the names and home addresses of his men. Perez Grandi became quickly impressed by the qualities of this young *Cabo* even though life was hard for their month's stay on *Monte Wall*

(Wall Mountain). They were reminded of the war on 12 May when a Skyhawk crashed into the nearby hillside, victim of a British warship's missile. Their critical problem was lack of food, so Perez Grandi ignored the order that no *oueja* (sheep) be shot and Urbieta went about the business of trying to ensure a twice-daily hot meal for his starving men. The platoon commander also secured a supply of onions to augment the mutton which he had put into some kitbags to be naturally frozen by the bitter cold, and is why the Gurkha foraging party found Urbieta's stuffed with half a *dumba*'s carcass.

Most of this had been recorded in the *Cabo*'s letters. Three had been written on 26 May, five days before his Regiment was redeployed to *Dos Hermanas* (Two Sisters) and *Monte Enriqueta* (Mount Harriet) in order to reinforce the defences there which faced the westerly British threat post the Battle of Darwin and Goose Green. A vivid pen-picture is painted of both life in the *Isla Soledad* (East Falkland) hills and a soldier wrestling with chameleon-like moods. One letter of understandable bravado had been addressed to his cousins:

First of all I want to tell you that I'm not a soldier anymore. I have been a corporal for two months. My destination was RI 4 (Regimento de Infantria 4) Monte Caseros, Corrientes. It's a pretty town. As soon as I arrived there the regiment was mobilized and that is why I'm here now. There is very little fighting. Occasionally they come to bother us. But they retreat quickly. We are about 3 km away from the sea. From the top of a mountain we can see everything that takes place at sea or on the coast.

Army life is excellent. I like the fighting. I am the leader of a 12-man support section. My soldiers are worse than me, but our relationship is very friendly. Life is hard mainly for one reason: lack of supplies. Our section steal sheep from the English. We hunt them with FAL or shotguns or we even catch them with our hands.

I'm fed up with eating mutton, though that's how we manage to get by. Thank God. . . . Here, it's so cold, it drizzles all day long and it's foggy.

He exhibited a similar mood in a letter to his aunt:

I've been here now for almost two months, things have been pretty rough but on the whole the weather is bearable. We sleep in tents. We're on Monte Wall, it's very rocky, there are no plants. The only animals I've seen are sheep. I don't think this situation will last for long if the war continues. We captured 8, we killed 4 and the rest, we kept just in case . . .

This is the beginning of my Army life, I think it's wonderful. As an NCO I have a good time. Maybe I'll come back, maybe I won't. Only God knows. I trust I will, and hope to see all of you very soon . . . you will see the news in the papers. This is a dirty war we're going through, I don't know how to explain it to you, maybe one day I'll try to, if I come back!

Extracts from two letters to his mother revealed grimmer realities:

The war is hard and painful but we're feeling really angry. I hope no Englishman tries to come anywhere near us because I can't tell you what we would do to him. It would be a massacre. We're all right, but we must be alert every day and night. Army life is hard, but I like it . . . We have faith that God will help us and we shall soon be back . . .

I'm well, thanks to God and the Virgin Mary nothing has happened to me so far. It's just that I'm so cold. We don't eat much here. There's a wind of about 120 km per hour. Mother, I want to ask you a favour, send me a parcel with some drinks to keep my body warm: coffee, vitamin C, sugar – the one in little bags, chicken stock or soup and mother, that woollen hat of yours, send it to me. If we get back I'll buy you a new one.

There's so much I would like to ask you for, but it's impossible . . . answer my letter so I that know something about what's going on . . . I know nothing about the outside, tell me what people say, what the telly says. I'm writing the way I am because my fingers are stiff with cold, I can't even do up my buttons . . .

I'm glad to be able to communicate to you through this piece piece of paper and as a last word I would like to thank you, Mother, for all you've done for me.

And finally there is downright depression in his letter to Elba, a girl friend:

Maybe you're asking yourself why is he writing to me? Sometimes I think about this myself and I don't know what to answer . . . This week I've written twelve letters . . . after all these long days and nights . . . this seems to be the end of life, of everything . . . and what hurts even more is to have to write with this writing, it really is horribly cold here.

I hope you will answer me and in this way make me feel better in this solitude I'm in which is dragging me into an abyss.

You might say, what can I tell him? That's simple, just write and I will write back. I have faith in God and believe I'll be back.

Another letter had been sent to Urbieta from eleven year-old Christian Fabian Lopez who lived at Tandil in the province of Buenos Aires. The boy's sentiments, addressed to *Uno soldado de la Patria* were strikingly similar as those in ten-year old Ian Johnston's letter to the Task Force displayed aboard *QE2*. Christian's letter also illustrated the depth of patriotism Argentine children viewed 'their' *Islas las Malvinas*:

Dear Soldier of the Fatherland,
I'm writing this letter so that you should know that all the people in our country are thinking of you, and are praying for this battle to end quickly, and that God and the Virgin should protect you because it's we who are in the right. And I want you to know that we all feel very proud of the way you are defending our Islands.

My mother has asked me to pray for you in my prayers, and to ask that none of you should be wounded, and that you should all come home triumphantly, after defeating the English. Your name will remain written in the glorious history of our country. I am a boy scout and I belong to the Union of Catholic Scouts of Argentina. We have a song that's very attractive. Here's a verse of it, I want to send you:

The patrols advance

The patrols advance in the distance, forward march!
The patrols advance to the beating of the drum, forward march!
Let's climb that high mountain together
Let's climb right up to the blue peaks.
Only the falcons above our heads
Wheel majestically in the blue sky.

   I think it's pretty, so I'm sending it to you as a souvenir. I also send you and all the other soldiers warmest best wishes and embraces from all my family. Strength and Bravery and we'll triumph! May our beautiful, free Fatherland always be sovereign!

Nicolás Urbieta would need Christian's good wishes. Most of the 4th Infantry Regiment were moved by truck from *Monte Wall* via *Puerto Argentino* (Stanley) to *Monte Enriqueta* and *Dos Hermanas*, the exception being Perez Grandi's platoon which tabbed direct to the latter, and defensive positions were prepared on these two features from 1 June with C Company on *Dos Hermanas*. Treating his men well during their ordeal, he had fostered a good *esprit de corps*. Despite being frightened, starving, sick, without artillery support and possessing only three night sights, 2 Platoon virtually fought alone against 45 Commando's night assault twelve days later and received heavy casualties. After they ran out of ammunition Perez Grandi ordered Urbieta to lead his platoon off their position. Not shirking his responsibility, the officer then covered their withdrawl alone. But, as they began to move down Moody Valley, a mortar bomb exploded by Perez Grandi. Shrapnel tore into his right arm, legs, and thighs – smashing bones and slicing off chunks of flesh. He ordered his men to continue their withdrawl, but one volunteered to remain with him. Perez Grandi's men managed to escape but, on reaching an Argentine Army artillery battery three kilometres away near Moody Brook bridge, south-east of Mount Longdon, Urbieta asked for a stretcher and, accompanied by three men, made his way back to *Dos Hermanos*. Like frozen mutton, his platoon commander's bleeding had been slowed down by the cold. Perez Grandi was put on the stretcher, covered with combat kit and, despite lack of morphine, survived the agonizing trek to a waiting truck at the artillery battery. Urbieta had tabbed more than nine kilometres to rescue his officer who, that same day, underwent an emergency operation in *Puerto Argentino*'s military hospital before being flown out on the last Hercules to Rio Gallegos. Perez Grandi contracted gangrene and was hospitalized for a year. Urbieta remained in defence around the battery, only to withdraw to *Puerto Argentino*'s Racecourse just before the ceasefire – but would receive no decoration for his outstanding bravery.

Many other 4th Infantry Regiment soldiers had also escaped. Two reached *Puerto*

Argentino and met another conscript, Santiago of the 3rd Infantry Regiment. Both claimed they had been their section's only survivors, and Santiago's subsequent account, although a total fabrication, reveals how unbalanced psychologically the uneducated *dush* had become about the Gurkhas. According to Perez Grandi though, the educated men did not have this problem and merely regarded the Gurkhas like the squat mountain inhabitants of Bolivia:

> They were two kids, soldiers from the Fourth Regiment . . . in an area at the front which met the Gurkha advance . . . It had been a terrible battle with lots of dead and wounded on both sides. It seems that the Gurkhas advanced doped, stepping on Argentine mines, yelling like madmen. There were eight of them (Argentines) in a trench set back a bit behind a ridge. At one point, a group of eight or nine Gurkhas had approached them laughing and screaming. They (the Argentines) threw grenades at them and fired their FALs and downed five or six, and those left alive screamed as if laughing at what had happened and finished their wounded mates off themselves. They jumped up and down, laughed and shot them all at the same time. The boys also killed them in the end. They finally ran out of ammo and saw that the Argentines in positions further forward were beginning to surrender. They stayed hidden in their trench and from there they watched a Gurkha make an Argentine who had surrendered strip naked and walk across a field while they kicked him and hit him with their rifles. A bit later they saw a sergeant come out of his trench. He had run out of ammo and he threw away his helmet, his belt, his rifle, everything and surrendered. But the Gurkhas grabbed him by the hair, pushed him down on to his knees and cut his throat. They did the same with four or five boys from his position. Some of them wept, begged them not to kill them, but they slit their throats anyway.[3]

The Gurkha threat also made even Stanley Airport's 25th Infantry Regiment defenders change their sentries far more often than usual. At Wether Ground the stretcher party had taken thirty minutes to carry Lieutenant Jorge Echeverría, 4th Infantry Regiment's IO, into Tac HQ's location. He had bloodstained bandages wrapped around five chest and leg bullet wounds. Two Sea Kings arrived shortly afterwards and the prisoners wandered down the hill with their wounded, to be shuttled back to Ajax Bay. The irony would be found later in Urbieta's training manual that contained an anecdote from the Battle of Chacabuco fought on 12 February 1817 against the Spanish Army:

> At the end of the battle the obstinate persecution of the beaten realists began. Sergeant Toro captured a Spanish officer, who offered him a pocket full of gold not less than sixty ounzes for his freedom. The brave man smiled ironically, and giving it back to him said arrogantly: 'Sir, I do not need gold. I have come to fulfil my duty by taking you prisoner. Next time you will know that we, the Argentines, aren't for sale because we have no price.'[4]

It was a different situation now on Wether Ground and I felt pity, but Sergeant Deoman Limbu of A Company did not. He had conversed in English with one POW and afterwards stood by me as we watched their departure. The puzzled Gurkha shook his head, pondered a while, then said, 'Training Officer sahib, I just cannot understand why these men are here in the Foklands. One of them told me that he had only joined the Army a few weeks before being sent here. He had never cleaned his rifle, nor ever received any instructions in how to do this, did not enjoy the fighting, and did not want to come to his Malvinas Islands anyway!' For a professional Gurkha this must have, indeed, been one of life's great mysteries. Another, also in the same casualty evacuation chain as the *dush* wounded, later described his experience. Rifleman Baliprasad Rai:

> We left (Wether Ground) to a rear position where the Welsh Guards were dug in. A helicopter then evacuated the wounded back towards San Carlos . . . (and disused refrigeration plant at Ajax Bay which) had been turned into a field (surgical centre) . . . it was crowded – Guardsmen, Marine, Para and even Argentine wounded lay about as teams of medical men and doctors worked on them. I had the dubious distinction of being the first Gurkha casualty to be treated there. I did not have to stay long because the next day I was put on the hospital ship *Uganda*.[5]

Meanwhile the Battalion R Group had landed near the twin-peaks of Two Sisters defended by Perez Grandi and his men. Evil smelling human excrement lay amongst discarded weapons, clothing, sleeping gear, rations, ammunition, cooking utensils and other rubbish. Climbing up onto this feature they observed the Battalion's objectives five kilometres away. Some *dush* could be seen wandering around casually to the rear of Mount William in an administrative area. Current intelligence indicated they belonged to a Marine battalion better trained than other conscripts and would, it was assumed, fight harder. The R Group agreed that the expansive areas of open ground and rocks going in and around the Tumbledown and Mount William made our task a daunting one. It was imperative to reduce the odds that favoured the *dush*, but this could only be accomplished by us attacking at night. The worry about time had been temporarily dispersed with the twenty-four hour postponement of the Brigade's attack, but our logistics resupply problem remained.

At Wether Ground nothing had materialized. Tac HQ were also waiting for the R Group to return from Two Sisters, for only then could the Commandant convene an O Group for the impending operation. Suddenly Graham Stewart-Smith spotted a Sea King. 'At last!' he exclaimed. 'Our resupply!'

The helicopter landed, but expectations were dashed. From under whirling rotor blades ran the combat kit attired BBC/ITN team of Brian Hanrahan, Mike Nicholson and two cameramen. Captain 'Roger, Wait Out!' had failed to deliver.

The helicopter took off, leaving us dumbfounded. Ejected earlier that day by Major General Moore from the Brigade Commander's final briefing at Fitzroy, the TV team had been flown to the Gurkhas instead. It was an alternative accepted with reluctance. Unlike newspaper war correspondents, such as the legendary Max Hastings whose only requirement was to write, thereby permitting him mobility when attached to a unit, the two TV correspondents needed accompanying pictures with their verbal reports. Despite this built-in logistics burden of their cameramen hauling around cumbersome cameras, these gentlemen intended to acquire good footage of the Gurkhas. They did not anticipate Bill Dawson's reaction. Nicholson backed off as the Gurkhas' 2IC, jaw protruding, took several menacing steps towards the black wollen-hatted war correspondent and began to fire on all guns, 'What the hell does Brigade think they're doing in sending the media to us instead of our resupply?' Alarm registered on Nicholson's face. A veteran of thirteen wars, he and Hanrahan froze solid confronted by this Gurkha BO red-mist. Bill continued to roar, 'You're not what we've been asking for! What we need right now are rations, water, our mortar ammunition and augmenting cartridges, Milan missiles, heavy machine guns, pyrotechnics, radio batteries, new signals instructions and medical supplies to name but a few! Without these things there's going to be no battle tomorrow, and you're not going to get any TV pictures! Just wait until we get home to UK, when people there start finding out what's going on down here!'

The media will always attempt to seek conflict between people or groups of people and another crisis within the main crisis will always sell well. Fortunately the TV team's camera did not record Bill's tirade. Nicholson and Hanrahan understood they were not the Battalion's priority and, although being acutely unwelcome for the second time that day, wisely rode out this Gurkha storm by saying little. Perhaps they realized the real reason for Bill's anger was the continued blocking of our entry into the fighting by a non-functioning logistics system. We could have worked wonders with the first Chinook that would land on the Falklands in forty-eight hours from the nearing third container ship cum aircraft transport MV *Contender Bezant.*

Calm began to descend, although the 2IC continued to snipe, 'OK, now you're here, you'll have to stay. You'd better start digging in over there!' Pointing out to the guests their positions within Tac HQ's location, he added, 'And don't delay! Just like us, you'll all be smack in the path of any incoming Argie 155 shell!'

With a look of alarm, they complied and I decided my Battalion Public Information Officer role would be activated at an appropriate opportunity. Our innocent 'visitors' had a rotten start to their second Gurkha field visit and the balance had to be redressed. Meanwhile a Gazelle helicopter landed nearby to return some of the R Group.

'The pilot's saying he'll take any letters back with him to Fitzroy,' Mark informed me. This was an opportunity to scribble on a moth-eaten aerogramme to Tove. It might be my farewell note. The time was 16.00 hours. I had one minute. Reading the text, nobody would have been aware that this, the only battlefield letter I ever wrote, was composed after forty-eight hours of intermittent shelling and thirty-six hours before going into battle. My address proved a teaser. Wether Ground seemed inappropriate, and a grid reference plain stupid. So in the interests of Task Force security and my desperation, it became:

On a hill near Stanley,
Just a quick line to tell you I am OK. No problems. Someone is going back to
Brigade to post this – must write quickly. Go round to Mark Willis' bird. Tell her
he is OK. A lovely afternoon believe it or not. The sun is shining! It snowed this
morning! Kiss the girls and tell them I'm coming back as soon as possible. Got

four letters from you yesterday. A lovely surprise! Two and a half weeks old. It's rare to get letters! I'm OK – don't worry.

Others in the Battalion were also OK, although a few needed Lady Luck's assistance. For example when David Willis and his FOO, Captain Gus Pugh, reached A Company's location after the recce trip to Two Sisters, they discovered that their trench and personal equipment had been totally destroyed by a 155 shell. The two officers remained outwardly unperturbed because collective battle preparations were more important than individual concerns. They were not alone in having such luck. On Mount Harriet Lieutenant Tedesco had once left his trench to relieve himself. He made a smart decision. In his absence the British shelled his position and, on return, he found lying on his sleeping bag, a large piece of shrapnel which would have cut him in half.

To assist our matters, a couple of Wessex helicopters now arrived at last with the Machine Gun Platoon and their weapons, Milan missiles and a couple of underslung loads of 800 smoke and high-explosive mortar bombs and many ten-man boxes of rations. In one stroke, several pieces of the logistics jigsaw puzzle had been fitted into place and dialogue with Captain 'Roger, Wait Out!' dried up temporarily. Most thankful were D Company who had not eaten for three days. Our A Echelon at Fitzroy had also sent a ration box only containing dozens of curry-powder tins. So Mark called out, 'Where's Bis Bis? We can now gorge ourselves on his all-in curry stew this evening!'

But as we continued distributing these boxes to the companies, Bill pointed out the delivery's disadvantages, 'OK, we've got our rations at last, but all this is unsuitable for troops who'll shortly be getting ready to move out from here and then go into battle.' Our sub-units found that breaking these bulky ration packs down for distribution to individuals consumed much time, and the different tins and other items also meant each man received unequal amounts and types of food. Neither were there any hexamine cooking blocks. And the current quietness indicated something else was also missing.

'The shelling's stopped!' I observed as if a rain shower had ended. Gurkhas make dogged defenders – like in 1944 when the 1st/9th Gurkha Rifles were shelled and mortared for nine consecutive days on Hangman's Hill in front of the monastry at Monte Cassino. But their instinct is to attack rather than endure the incomer's whine and explosion. Also they did not now have to wade in the calf-high water of their trenches. A Company had been worst affected because their sojourn at Wether Ground, added to their week in the open at Darwin wearing the wretched British Army DMS boot, had accounted for several cases of trench foot. 'Or in Gurkhali,' commented Mark, '*Khutta hilole khayo* – the mud has eaten the foot!'

The reasons for this unexpected quiet were threefold. Counter battery fire from British artillery batteries which had moved forward after the successes of the previous night was now having an effect but, of more significance, the *dush* had virtually consumed their stocks of 155 ammunition during the past ten hours. However our attached FAC's news was the most satisfactory. Major Anwell Hughes had arrived late that afternoon by helicopter with the other three members of his 602 Tactical Air Control Party. He was a colleague of 'Red Dragon' Mike Howes, who had been attached to the Battalion on Exercise WELSH FALCON and participated in the *QE2*

TEWL. A jocular officer, Anwell was in his early 'fifties, always preferred to wear an arctic cap rather than a tin hat, and proudly owned a tradename even more bizarre than Mike's when in radio dialogue with the Harrier pilots.

'I'm Rubber Duck' he informed us, 'and will be directing the Harrier GR3s' laser-guided bombs onto selected targets tomorrow so as to soften up the Argie defences prior to your attack on Mount William. And the good news is that we've got a possible eighteen such sorties lined up for you boys between now and then!'

Listening sympathetically to our shelling experiences before rejoining his team, Rubber Duck's weathered face was aglow when he returned later. 'Hey boys!' he exclaimed. 'I've just heard on my FAC radio frequency that a Harrier cluster bomb strike behind Sapper Hill has just taken out one of your dear Argie friends – a 155!' However Anwell's information of RAF Flight Lieutenant Mungo McCleod's attack was incorrect. His and his colleague's total of four bombs did not hit their target, with McCleod's combat air report revealing that this sortie had developed complications which led to him being awarded the Queen's Commendation for Valuable Service in the Air:

Mission tasked as a pair against a 155mm gun position on Sapper Hill at VC 388716. Ingress to the target was at low level through the hills to the west approaching Sapper Hill from close abeam Mt. Harriet and Mt. William. Smoke was seen coming from the first SF of the target UTM and an attack was made on this position. During the attack MacCleod's aircraft was hit by shrapnel which penetrated the rear equipment bay area of the aircraft and fractured the aft reaction control air pipe. On decelerating to the hover, during the recovery, this caused a fire to start in the rear equipment bay and smoke was seen coming from the aircraft. Fuel indications suggested a considerable fuel leak at the same time. MacCleod executed a very quick and professional landing in worrying circumstances. Having landed-on the fire was extinguished by the ground crew.

Time to call in the O Group. Company commanders and other officers required 'need to know' information for the Battalion's attack on the third, and closest, ring of hills to Stanley. Paddy had constructed a good model of the Tumbledown-Mount William-Sapper Hill area by utilizing piles of stones and his poncho cape. It was correctly aligned in the approved manner to the ground and direction from which our attack would be made. He could be quite pompous . . . and I hallucinated mildly by returning, in spirit, to a Sandhurst military history period. Paddy was Napoleon Bonaparte during the latter's opening sequence of orders prior to the 1805 Battle of Austerlitz. He was perfect in this role: 'Gentlemen, examine this terrain. It is going to be a battlefield, and you will have a part to play on it . . .'

After describing the ground, Paddy provided the Brigade's latest intelligence, 'Apparently there's still a *dush* Marine company in the centre of the Tumbledown and a company on its eastern end and north-east spur. Another's on the saddle between the eastern end of the Tumbledown and Mount William, and one more on Mount William itself. Two others are located one kilometre south, and two kilometres south-west of Mount William respectively. All this indicates a strongly reinforced battalion.

In addition there's an OP, mortar-base plate position, three or more 105-mm guns in the Mount William area, and strong Regimental position on Sapper Hill four kilometres to the east which can, if required, counter-attack forward!'

I was not the only one to blink twice at the opposition's numbers. Because of them the Commandant had rightly judged Mount William, rather than the Tumbledown, to be the tougher nut of the two to crack. An appropriate objective for his Gurkhas. How it would be taken became apparent by his outline of 5 Brigade's plan of attack, 'Gentlemen, I should point out first that 2 Para, under command of 3 Commando Brigade, will attack Wireless Ridge to the north whilst 5 Brigade will carry out a three-phase attack. Phase one – 2 Scots Guards will secure the Tumbledown feature, with the exception of the north-east spur. Phase two – 1st/7th Gurkha Rifles will capture the north-east spur of the Tumbledown and Mount William. Phase three – 1 Welsh Guards and D Squadron, Royal Horse Guards are to be prepared on orders to clear the axis of the Darwin-Stanley track and secure Sapper Hill.'

Tight cooperation would be required between the Scots Guards and ourselves. However we were the only unit required to capture their objective, whilst the others had to secure theirs. Our mission from the Commandant was clear-cut, 'To capture the north-east spur of the Tumbledown and Mount William,' and then, in accordance with that time-honoured British Army SOP, he paused – to repeat with greater emphasis, 'To capture the north-east spur of the Tumbledown and Mount William.'

In summary, the Battalion would form up on the western end of Goat Ridge whilst the Scots Guards carried out a diversionary attack south-west of Mount William before their main attack. At 03.00 hours we would start moving along the two kilometres of the ridge's southern side. Our start line was at its eastern end, with H-hour at 04.00 hours. We would then advance another three kilometres behind and around the Tumbledown's northern slopes before plunging into the area secured by the Scots Guards. If all went to plan, four hours of darkness would remain in which to capture the north-east spur and Mount William.

The Commandant elaborated further, 'Our attack'll be split up into four phases. First A Company will move through the Guards and set up a fire base on the Tumbledown's eastern end. This'll require concentrating all our long-range weapons there – the heavy machine guns, Milans and sustained-fire GPMGs – to support the assault on Mount William. B Company will then capture the Tumbledown's north-east spur.'

Unbeknown to us, this spur was important for 3 Commando Brigade because they planned to use its base as the start line for their next operation – the southern envelopment of Stanley. The Battalion's third phase entailed D Company assaulting Mount William. They would employ an inverted triangular formation of two platoons up and one back, the choice dictated by the possible use of one of the forward platoons to screen off the *dush* company thought to be on the saddle between the Tumbledown and Mount William.

The Commandant's concept of operations for Mike Kefford was a simple, 'Use your 66-mm anti-tank launchers to engage *dush* rifle fire. The shock of explosions by night near their trenches and in such an enclosed rocky location should allow your riflemen, covered by GPMG fire, to close with the *dush*. But remember we've only got four 66s per section, and this isn't enough for a protracted operation. Once you've captured

Mount William, A Company will roll up the remaining two companies to the south and south-west by attacking from east to west in the final phase.'

Having described the attack's execution, he turned to other details. 'The Battalion'll be flown by helicopter up into its assembly area near Two Sisters at 12.00 hours tomorrow. We'll carry out our final battle preparations there. Ops Officer,' he looked at me, 'you and the Paymaster will organize this move. We've not received any new signals instructions, so Gurkhali will be used on the Battalion radio command net. It's as good as a code because there's no way the *dush*'ll be able to understand us. The Adjutant therefore will continue manning the Battalion net in Tac HQ, so he'll fly first with me up into the assembly area. As for the fire plan, it'll be a noisy night attack. Apart from the TACP guiding the first Harrier laser-guided bomb strike on the Tumbledown tomorrow at 15.00 hours, other details haven't been coordinated yet. But there'll be an opportunity to inform you about them at the final confirmatory O Group tomorrow night. Gentlemen, that's it. Questions in one minute.'

There were hardly any. The litmus test was negative: a good set of orders. And even Nigel was able to provide better mortar news. 'Although still no augmenting cartridges have arrived, I'll be able to borrow thirty-six from 40 Commando's Mortar Platoon who've reinforced the Welsh Guards,' he informed us. Support from the Gurkha mortars was vital for D Company's attack and that of the Scots Guards. Due to the open terrain, our four mortar base plates had to be positioned on the western end of Goat Ridge to avoid being made too vulnerable to *dush* fire, and therefore were out of range to Mount William, more than five kilometres distant. The augmenting cartridges enabled firing on charges six and seven. This increased range, but continuous use would damage base plates and bipods. The platoon's other two mortars were not available as replacements. Supposed to be in reserve at A Echelon, due to non-tactical ship loading at Southampton they would never see the light of day until our return to UK.

The O Group ended, but Paddy was keen to throw more light on our objectives whose detail remained a mystery. 'Don't leave, because I've received some air photos from Brigade,' he said, handing them out.

'Ah! These must be of Mount William,' I concluded and grabbed two. 'Now at last we should get a better idea of the terrain and *dush* positions.'

Heads bent down. Then cynical laughter broke out. 'Oh boy! Par for the course again,' said someone.

'These aren't of Mount William or even the Tumbledown!' exclaimed another.

'You're right!' I agreed. 'Because, believe it or not, mine are of Stanley Airport!'

I looked at all the photos. Not one was of Mount William. The point of providing them was lost on me. At least six photos of B Company's objective on the eastern end of the Tumbledown had been taken by camera pods fixed to Harriers during attack runs in the past few days[6], but they were of dubious quality and never did reach us. There was no dedicated photo reconnaissance aircraft to the Task Force, and Harriers prioritized air strikes rather than recce missions. Morale sank with our inability to eyeball these unfamiliar objectives. As we were to discover, the *dush* strengths and sub-unit locations on the Tumbledown, Mount William and Sapper Hill also differed wildly from the intelligence given to Paddy.

'Not for nothing,' complained the IO later, 'will I remember the Falklands' campaign as the mushroom war when lack of hard intelligence caused rumours to grow like mushrooms!'

After the O Group had dispersed, I walked over to Nicholson and Hanrahan. They had not been allowed to attend the orders, so now could be an opportunity for some efficient Gurkha public relations. The ITN war correspondent's low-style basha had been constructed from a poncho cape and, putting the finishing touches to the peat-sod camouflage on its top, Nicholson had started cooking an evening meal over his portable hexamine cooker. In the fading light he and Hanrahan seemed relaxed as I introduced myself, 'Hello, I'm the Ops Officer. Would you like to hear details of our battle plan for tomorrow night?'

They looked up. 'Of course,' replied Nicholson.

So I began. 'OK, our main objective is Mount William and we've chosen to carry out a noisy night attack . . .'

Nicholson was more inquisitive than his colleague and interrupted, 'So what's the difference between that and a silent one?'

'The artillery support,' I replied, 'with the guns firing as we close onto our objective.'

They listened carefully to my briefing. Nicholson wanted to make up for the disappointments with Brigade HQ, so he asked at the end, 'I've got one question. Can we accompany your Tac HQ and film you during the battle?'

My inner haughty reaction, 'What? Media? With us? They'll get in our way as we crisis-manage and fight onto the Tumbledown's north-east spur and Mount William!' was camouflaged by a verbal polite refusal of logical simplicity, 'Sorry, the fighting's going to be carried out in darkness. So there's no point at all you coming along with us as there won't be any light to film. I suggest you stay with our Alternative Battalion HQ and TACP which'll be located near Two Sisters and not far from our assembly area. You'll then be guaranteed some good daylight shots of the Harrier strikes on the Tumbledown and Mount William.'

Nicholson replied with a satisfied, 'OK. Thanks for your briefing. It was most useful.'

'My pleasure,' I said, 'it's only my other job as Battalion Public Information Officer.'

He looked at me in the darkness and commented, 'Well, you do it jolly well!'

This positive feedback from a professional of thirteen previous wars was pure oxygen to an officer whose performance had been degraded in the past weeks' atmosphere of stress and fear. Nicholson's remark was more a comment though on the sparse information received from the campaign's media 'minders'. Following my suggestions, the correspondents would acquire an excellent sequence next day for the last programme of the BBC documentary series *Task Force South*. I had enjoyed this little self-imposed job which had occupied me constructively instead of brooding about the following day. Our preparations were complete as an all-stations radio call arrived from the Brigade Commander: 'Are there any further requirements that call-signs wish with regard to this formation's planning?'

It provoked a laconic reply from Lieutenant Colonel Mike Scott, the Scots Guards CO, who would be awarded a Distinguished Service Order for his forthcoming night's work – 'No, I'm perfectly content with what I've seen,' possessed cool understatement which caught my attention at the end of a long day. After transmitting the midnight sitrep, sleep became the most important consideration although fear remained. The waiting would soon be over also for Tove who was on a visit to my parents' West Sussex home. She wrote in a letter that night:

> Talk about watching telly for telly's sake. No idea what's happening on the screen – just switching knobs to catch all the news flashes. The battle for Port Stanley has begun, they say, but no details of course.

With the opposition having been ejected from the outer ring of hills there was no Royal Navy activity on the Stanley gun line, and we heard little of *Active* and *Arrow* bombarding the Moody Brook and Sapper Hill areas from the Berkeley Sound gun line. This would guarantee no sleep for the *dush* on the eve of our battle.

That night was bitterly cold and my green slug failed to provide any warmth for frozen bones. This and the adrenalin produced from pessimistic thoughts made sleep impossible. Snow began to fall and, by daybreak, the ground was covered with a thin layer of white flakes. With air temperature at freezing point, we ate a quick breakfast before the Commandant and Mark flew out in their Gazelle. They had to join the Scots Guards south of Goat Ridge who were already being flown to their assembly area there. After coordinating final planning details between both Battalions, the two Gurkha BOs would then move to our assembly area near Two Sisters and await our arrival.

Meanwhile Graham and I sat down to make the necessary calculations for the 467-man fly out from Wether Ground. My pen flew over the page in my notebook, but more changes of detail came over the radio and the first plan had to be rewritten twice during the next hour. Finally it was ready. Perhaps that TEWL on *QE2* had been useful after all.

'OK, the entire operation will take two and a half hours as sixty-four sticks of soldiers have to be moved. Order of march will be Alternative Battalion HQ, TACP, TV team, A Company, Gunners, Machine Gun Platoon, Tac HQ, RAP, Recce Platoon, B Company, D Company and last will be the Mortars including us two!' I told Graham.

Six Sea Kings and Wessex would be used in a continuous shuttle. Due to start at midday, the whole operation would be terminated by the Milan missiles and mortar bombs being flown up in underslung loads. The Alternative Battalion HQ, TACP and TV team had to fly first to prepare for that afternoon's Harrier LGB strikes. The TV boys walked down to the Darwin-Stanley track to wait. They whiled away their time filming a Blues and Royals troop of Scimitar and Scorpion light tanks moving up the track to position themselves for the night's attack. These would provide fire support not only for the Welsh Guards, but also for the Scots Guards' diversion. Then helicopters began arriving from the Fitzroy area and I marshalled in the first.

As it landed I ran to the Sea King. Pointing on the map to our assembly area and a 175-metre contour ring one kilometre south of Two Sisters, I yelled into the boom mike of the headset given to me by the helicopter's helmeted loadmaster who peered through his dark plastic visor, 'That's where our landing site is! OK?'

He nodded and up went a thumb. The noise was deafening as the first Gurkha sticks emplaned. Our marshalling continued and, one by one, two or three sticks tumbled into either the larger dark blue Sea King or smaller dark grey Wessex to fly out. Rotor blade down-draught made marshalling difficult. While other incoming flights stacked themselves above us, turning one's back to an aircraft during its touchdown phase was the only method of avoiding being blinded by violent gusts of air and, worse, blown over.

With thirty sticks left, one pilot climbed out of his cockpit to speak to me because no means existed for a pilot sitting up there to talk direct to those on the ground. Nonetheless this manoeuvre was unusual. As rotor blades turned, familiar sickly-sweet warm fumes of burnt aviation fuel wafted up my nostrils and a stick emplaned, the concerned aviator pressed his mouth up against my ear, cupped a hand over his mouth and yelled, 'You're going to have to choose another landing site! The present one's under heavy mortar and artillery fire! So where d'ya want us to land now?' The Battalion's fly-in had alerted the *dush*, and his question demanded a response impossible to give immediately. I also experienced an acute twinge of fear.

Chapter Nineteen

BATTLE PREPARATION

The other idea consists of transferring (the Gurkhas) to submarines and disembarking them to act as 'suicide commandos' so they can kill in night-fighting and so, in this way, undermine the high morale of the Argentine soldiers. During the day they will try to conceal themselves in the uneven terrain of remote areas. Whatever the alternative possibilities, they only demonstrate again Thatcher's profound scorn for humans, taking into account that today there can be only one end for these 'fierce mercenaries of white skin': the grave. – Flash *periodical.*[1]

I took a deep breath and shoved my finger onto an arbitary location north of the 175-metre ring contour on the map, then yelled back at the concerned aviator, 'Here!' with as much force as possible to convince him some grand alternative plan existed. He nodded and turned to climb back up into his cockpit. However my answer had been mere bluff, triggered by a requirement to maintain the Battalion's fly-in momentum to its assembly area. Simple to provide a solution from the map, it was much more difficult to solve the resulting problems. My fear also remained of *dush* unpleasantries at Two Sisters.

We kept to our helicopter loading schedule and so, just after 14.15 hours when the first two Mortar Platoon sticks had flown, I was hooking up the mortar bomb and Milan missile underslung loads under two Sea Kings. Some optimistic Gurkha had placed the ten-man box of curry powder tins on top of the last load, but this was impossible to fit into a full net. 'Damn the bloody thing,' I thought, 'the Battalion will just have to go without its *bhat* until after the battle!' So the Training Officer sahib picked up the precious curry powder and slung it away.

Our job completed, Graham and I ran to board the last Sea King for its seven-kilometre contour-hugging flight up to Two Sisters. It landed and we jumped out to dive into all-round defence. The *dush* shelling and mortaring had temporarily lifted from our landing point and, as the engines increased their roar to drive whirling rotor blades into a frenzy and waft invisible clouds of burnt aviation fuel fumes everywhere, the Sea King started rising to fly away towards the coast. I pulled my bergen from the pile that the loadmaster had thrown out and Mark Willis appeared from an outcrop of rock. He grabbed my arm to guide me into the location he had chosen for Tac HQ.

'We're getting Quentin's men to run around and collect up the companies,' he yelled above the roar of the departing Sea King, 'come on, we're over here!' Lugging my cumbersome bergen, I ran after him to a large outcrop of rocks where the Commandant was waiting. There was now silence – except for the occasional Crump! of distant artillery. Located in the rear of a 45 Commando objective seized two nights previously, we were now eleven clicks, or seven miles as the crow flies from Stanley whilst our objective, Mount William, lay six clicks to the south-east. Given the appropriate code name of Long Toenail by the Commandos, 'our' rock feature ran one and a half kilometres from west to east and lay 500 metres south-west of the 280 metre-high twin-peaked Two Sisters feature. Sited in Long Toenail's centre and facing south towards Goat Ridge, our exposure to shelling would be minimal in this location. But there were other threats to concern us.

'Brigade have warned that there's a red air alert in force, sir,' Corporal Aslett called out to me after setting up the radio.

'Good job then that we've now arrived at our new location!' I replied, getting out my battle board. Unfortunately the Battalion had been infected again with that Bravo November disorder syndrome of our arrival two weeks ago at Darwin and Goose Green, and had been deposited in penny packets over a wide area. So the next three hours would be busy for the twelve-man strong Recce Platoon as they earned their day's pay and miserly Falklands' allowances many times over by marrying up scattered company groups and guiding them into their correct locations.

'I'll try to get my board updated with the Battalion's positions,' I informed Mark more in hope than optimism. My plotting of sub-units began within the one square kilometre assembly area on this seventy-second and penultimate afternoon of the Falklands' crisis.

Bill's Alternative Battalion HQ, Anwell Hughes and his Tactical Air Control Party, and the BBC/ITN TV team were co-located 500 metres from Tac HQ on the extreme eastern end of Long Toenail. Their 350-metre high perch gave them an excellent view eastwards towards Stanley which was vital for the planned laser-guided bomb strikes. The first to land in the assembly area 500 metres to the south of Long Toenail had been A Company and their Support Company assets for the Tumbledown fire base. Another 500 metres south lay the 175-metre ring contour hill. On its forward slopes B Company dug their shell scrapes while D Company, being the last company to land, took up a similar position on its reverse slopes. The Machine Gun Platoon remained south of these two companies as there was no point moving its heavy weaponry up to A Company. Instead, the latter two sub-units would eventually marry up in the Battalion's forming up point on the western end of Goat Ridge not far from where the two Mortar Platoon sections had established themselves between that feature and Mount Harriet. Some distance to the south of the Gurkha mortars were those of the Scots Guards, three sections in all, one of which had been detached from the Welsh Guards. The *dush* kept up a steady rate of artillery fire during this period. Several rounds landed near the mortar line, but no casualties were taken. The Gurkhas' ammunition had been initially dropped in the wrong place, but was eventually lifted to the mortar line where the men worked flat out to break open boxes, prepare the ammunition and, at the same time, continue digging.

The shelling made battle preparation for all a tense affair, but at 15.00 hours Anwell's laser-guided bomb strike was scheduled to commence. The first four sorties of the

RAF's No. 1 (F) Squadron from *Hermes* had been unsuccessful a few days earlier because the laser target marker parties on the ground were unable to achieve coordination with their attacking Harrier GR3 aircraft. The results of the fifth sortie guided in by Red Dragon and his 601 TACP on Mount Harriet that morning had been better. One hit and one miss on the Tumbledown.

Suddenly Mark called out, 'Look up over there! It's the laser-guided bomb strike going in!' Eyes turned skywards to witness the first bomb release of the sixth Harrier GR3 Paveway II bomb sortie of the war. With the Harrier wheeling away after its 3g climb, the 1,000 pound bomb resembled an oversize model aircraft which wobbled to acquire the laser 'basket' at 1,500 feet and then flew smoothly away to disappear over Goat Ridge.

High up on the eastern end of Long Toenail were Bill's Gurkhas, the TV team and Anwell's TACP. They had been plagued since their arrival with incomers from unobserved *dush* artillery fire and time was overripe for retaliation. These artillery positions were on Stanley Common ten kilometres away and the white low houses of the capital in the background, provided a reminder of the accuracy required from the Paveway bomb and its ground laser designator. Rubber Duck's tripod-mounted camera-like laser target marker was pointed at the target, but Anwell's commentary with the Harrier pilot and his TACP personnel demonstrated the operating complexities of this top-secret equipment.

'Stand by, Rubber Duck . . . Roger! . . . Bomb's gone . . .'

'There's the bomb! Got it? . . . OK, switch on! Switch on! Switch on! . . . Where was that?

'Rubber Duck, I didn't see the bomb . . . it may have gone . . . Ah, yes! Got it! Just a little bit over from where I was aiming. An absolute beauty I would say . . . probably where there's a defensive position . . . Roger, I can now confirm that the bomb actually landed on the mark!'

The billowing column of greyish white smoke was from a direct hit on a 105-mm gun position. A second bombing run of this sixth Paveway bomb sortie came shortly afterwards as the same aircraft whipped past us at an altitude of twenty metres and 500 kilometres per hour. Another body-crunching climb achieved the correct loft profile and release of its bomb which glided away towards its target.

'Everyone a winner!' yelled Kit Spencer, punching a clenched fist into the air. After being told what was happening, one of our Gurkha Signallers in Tac HQ also pointed a finger to the sky and rejoiced in a flood of unintelligible Gurkhali.

'What's he babbling on about?' I asked Mark.

'Oh, that,' replied the busy Adjutant nonchalantly about to answer another message on his radio net, 'do you mean, "*Akash bata bomharu pharsi jhare jhain jharyo*"? Well, he's only letting his agricultural instincts come to the fore by commenting, "Bombs are being dropped like pumpkins from the sky!"'

I laughed. Mission 3K513 had been flown by attack mission leader Squadron Leader Jeremy Pook, later awarded the Distinguished Flying Cross for missions that included attacking the Goose Green anti-aircraft guns under heavy fire and being forced to eject from his Harrier, and his number two, Flight Lieutenant Mike Beech. But Kit's wish was unfulfilled. The later combat report revealed that Pook's second bomb had missed:

Mission tasked for LGB delivery using LTM against enemy positions in the area of Tumbledown Mt. (VC 3372). The run in was made from Bluff Cove and first bomb was a DH (direct hit) on enemy position. The second bomb fell short by 400 yds. Both bombs were delivered from 30 degree Loft Profile. During the attacks Beech gave cross-cover to his leader. No AAA or SAMs seen, although Super Fledermaus audio was heard.[2]

The cross cover Beech gave to Pook was necessary for, at about this time, the red air alert had materialized into a gaggle of seven Skyhawks which crossed the East Falkland southern coastline east of Fitzroy. They must have passed close to the Gurkhas' assembly area prior to their parachute-retarded bomb attack from the east on 3 Commando Brigade's HQ at Bluff Cove Peak. This lay west of Mount Kent, seven kilometres from our Tac HQ where a message on my radio handset informed me: 'Sunray of this formation will be arriving shortly at your location.'

Kit and I emerged from the security of the rocks to guide the Brigade Commander into our location. He had flown from Mount Harriet where the Brigade's forward Tac HQ had been set up prior to its attack and we climbed up to meet his Gazelle helicopter which had landed on a higher piece of ground above us. Together we moved back to Tac HQ. 'Good luck for tonight. Do you have any outstanding problems?' the Commandant was asked.

After a short conversation to satisfy himself that everything was ready, the one star staff officer turned to go. Suddenly a Harrier GR3 from the LGB sortie screamed past, twenty metres above us and a surprised Brigade Commander took evasive action by diving to the ground. Nobody followed suit and, as he dusted himself down, my indiscretion was total. 'We're used to it at the sharp end, sir,' I cheerfully informed him.

His reply was unprintable as he strode back to the waiting Gazelle. To our front, Major General Moore was also out and about giving his troops encouragement during their final preparations. The Gurkhas also received a visit that late afternoon which impressed most as the occasional incomer continued to land into this area. It was 19.00 hours and the light had begun to fade. The Argentine national football team were to lose 0–1 against Belgium in the World Cup that evening and the Pope had now completed his two-day visit to Argentina. Its people would need to draw some comfort from the Bishop of Rome because we were gathering together to receive our final orders that would ensure yet another Argentine defeat tomorrow – in the Falklands. This third and confirmatory O Group at Tac HQ would etch more fine detail into the overall attack plan.

First the Commandant updated the situation, 'Nothing new on the *dush* positions on the Tumbledown and Mount William area. The Scots Guards will attempt a diversionary attack on the Marine company south-west of Mount William. Its aim is to give the impression that the main three-phase Guards' attack will be mounted from the Darwin-Stanley track.' This piece of Brigade intelligence about Mount William which the Commandant had received would, however, prove to be inaccurate as it was not known at the time that the *dush* had moved only a reinforced platoon into this south-west position.

'Once we go firm on the Tumbledown's eastern end,' he continued, 'there'll be considerable artillery and naval gunfire support for our assault on Mount William. The architect of this fire plan is Mike Fallon and he'll provide the details.'

Mike stood up to brief us on the Gunners' plan. It was simple but comprehensive. 'We'll be getting the two batteries of 4 Field Regiment and a battery of 29 Commando Regiment in support. They've five primary targets. The west-end, centre, east-end and north-east spur of the Tumbledown, plus Mount William. They'll also engage in a long counter battery and harassing fire programme,' he said.

The explanation, an oasis of fact in a desert of uncertainty, had a captive audience. One of Mike's FOOs, Captain Gus Pugh, had also been busy during that sunny afternoon of intermittant incoming *dush* artillery fire. This officer in a balaclava was suitably armed with a pump-action shotgun for the night's expected action in the Tumbledown and Mount William rocks, and had whiled away his time by adjusting fire onto opportunity targets from his vulnerable perch on Long Toenail. After Mike's briefing, he succinctly described the climax. 'By the size and strength of the bonfire,' mused the elated FOO, 'I'm sure it must have been an Argie fuel dump.'

More points were added to the fire plan as Nigel Price chipped in, ' Because we've not received any resupply of large augmenting cartridges as promised, Mount William will be our only Battalion target, and so B Company's attack will have to be supported by artillery fire only. I can confirm that our mortars, who are also in support to the Guards, have now managed to adjust onto three of their five mortar targets on Mount William with white phosphorous smoke rounds.'

This adjusting shoot had been carried out by the MFC attached to D Company from an OP on the slopes of Mount Harriet. Nigel was then followed by Anwell Hughes who confirmed, 'Only two of the promised eighteen Harrier offensive air support sorties with laser-guided bombs have been committed so far. So we'll be clear for further tasking once daylight is upon us.'

The Battalion's mission and company tasks were confirmed, but the Commandant pointed out an unforeseen problem that caused most to miss a heartbeat. 'The 9 Para Squadron Sappers think there's a *dush* 500 square metre minefield at the north-west base of the Tumbledown,' he said. 'Its perimeters aren't known, but circumnavigating this obstacle to the north will lose us valuable time. I'm therefore going to risk a direct easterly approach along the northern contours of the Tumbledown after the Guards have completed their attack. We'll have some Sappers upfront though, who'll search for mines during our advance.'

His coordinating instructions for our attack contained the vital timings, 'Most important is our H-hour at 04.00 hours when we *must* cross the Guards' start line. This must occur in darkness to negate the lack of cover once we are through the Tumbledown to attack its north-east spur and our main objective of Mount William.'

Then came the final section of his orders that included the Battalion's vital code-words and password. The Guards were a festive 'Fat Goose' whilst 1st/7th Gurkha Rifles would be known by the belligerent 'Rose Thorn'. This regimental rivalry continued with 'Circus Flea' – indicating the Guards had taken and gone firm on all their apportioned areas of the Tumbledown – whilst 'Clown Paint' stood for our capture of the Tumbledown's north-east spur and Mount William. The spur was important as it would be used for 3 Commando Brigade's start line in their next phase to Stanley.

Selection of a password was most important as Guardsmen and Gurkhas would be working closely in the dark, and any mistaken identity could be disasterous. Careful thought had been therefore applied to the problem so that 'Jimmie' of Scotland and 'Johnnie Gurkha' of Nepal could enjoy a simple system. The *dush* would have difficulties in the English pronounciation of the first letter, J, to these two nicknames as 'Jimmie' and 'Johnnie' in Spanish become '*H*immie' and '*H*ohnnie' respectively. So, using this common denominator, a supposedly ingenious procedure was devised. The Guards' CO's understanding was that his men would use 'Hey Jimmie!' to identify themselves and, correspondingly, the Gurkhas would use 'Hey Johnnie!' It was too ingenious. The Commandant had come away from this tête-à-tête believing that the Gurkhas were to challenge with the words 'Hey Jimmie!', and the Guards' response to this would be 'Hey Johnnie!' Any Guards' challenge would reverse these passwords so that 'Hey Johnnie!' should produce a Gurkha response of 'Hey Jimmie!' A further compounding muddle now occurred at our O Group because the only password given by the Commandant was 'Hey Johnnie!' The more complicated and ponderous NATO password system should have been used, but this was a NATO out of area theatre so the short cut became applicable. Designed to avoid a nocturnal blue-on-blue clash, the system had become a potential death trap, and even more so when combined with a lack of inter-unit communication about headgear. For, despite every prospect of the unlimited use of artillery, mortar and small-arms fire, the Guards, unlike the Gurkhas, were ordered not to wear steel helmets. So in the interests of aiding night-time sub-unit identification and boosting morale, they would wear berets with cap badges displayed. The Guards were also informed that anyone seen wearing a helmet would be, by definition, an Argentine and, therefore, a bona fide target. However no attempt was made to discover the Gurkha order of dress regarding steel helmets, even though the Commandant and Mark Willis had been wearing theirs that afternoon with the helmeted Guards' CO and his bereted Ops Officer while coordinating both Battalions movement which included passing the Gurkhas through the Guards on the Tumbledown at night. So the Gurkhas were already at risk before the battle started. Common sense dictated that the Commandant's Battalion followed his example of wearing a steel helmet, and all Gurkhas wore this even though vision was restricted and one's hair felt like a Brillo soap-pad which had scoured the pan used for cooking the Sunday roast. Many military casualties in Northern Ireland have been caused by a soldier not following his unit's SOPs but, by following the 'rules', the chances would be reduced of a Gurkha being killed or wounded after a bullet or shrapnel strike on the helmet.

The final summing up was interrupted by three or four *dush* shells exploding an uncomfortable 100 metres away. Unwittingly we had been vulnerable to such harassing fire throughout the O Group and was why the latter ended abruptly just before 21.00 hours. As everyone stood up to return to their positions two Marine Commandos appeared out of the deepening gloom. Lester Holley stood up and, moving across to them, the ex-SAS trooper clapped them heartily on the back saying, 'Hello, you guys! Good to see you again!'

Obviously during his service in the Regiment he had previous dealings with Lieutenant Haddon and Sergeant Wassell of the Marines' Mountain and Arctic Warfare Training Cadre. The latter consisted of thirty-six instructors and pupils who had been converted into a special recce unit in the UK and attached to 3 Commando Brigade. Sergeant Wassell would act as the Gurkhas' guide up to the eastern end of Goat Ridge after his platoon commander had carried out the same task for the Guards. Four days previously these two and their patrol had spent all day behind enemy lines concealed in the centre of Goat Ridge observing positions and movement to the rear of Mount Harriet and Two Sisters as well as on the Tumbledown and Mount William. Wassell had actually moved along the Battalion's entire route, parallel to Goat Ridge and was therefore superbly qualified for phase one of our tab.

Company Commanders then vanished into the darkness to brief their subordinates in the Battalion assembly area. The companies, in the order A, D and B respectively, were lined up south of Tac HQ behind the Scots Guards' assembly area. Located at the 175-metre ring contour this, in turn, was less than one kilometre west of Goat Ridge. Some Gurkhas in D Company had taken the opportunity during those final hours to recce forward and take a closer look at their objective, Mount William. They were in no doubt as to the challenge's severity. At least five riflemen in one of the D Company point platoons tasked to assault Mount William had written farewell letters to their relatives in Nepal. These were given to their British platoon commander sahib, Lieutenant Jeremy McTeague, for eventual onward transmission either by himself or, if circumstances should so dictate, by someone else.

Ten weeks of intensive preparation for this particular night were completed. 1st/7th Gurkha Rifles were ready. If 2 Para and 3 Para were set aside with their specialized airborne role, the Battalion had been the first pure infantry of the line to land on the Falklands since the 11th Battalion, West Yorkshire Regiment's autumn 1942 arrival as the Islands' garrison for a short period. The Gurkhas were ultra-competitive and now also wanted to be the first pure infantry of the line to go into action in the Falklands. A five-hour wait prior to moving off to the forming up point on the western end of Goat Ridge began but, suddenly, Paddy prised himself away from an intensive conversation on his radio and ran up to me.

'Mike!' he gasped. 'For your info I've just received a message from Brigade. They say there's possibly two *dush* anti-aircraft guns sited on Mount William! As you know, they can be used in the ground role and might well engage us with direct fire à la Darwin and Goose Green. Perhaps you should inform the Commandant!'

The little battlefield intelligence received in the past had proved unreliable, so we decided to treat this latest tit-bit with a degree of scepticism even though the unsubstantiated claim would lurk in my mind throughout that long night. Mundane tasks had to be prioritized as Mark Willis and I agreed on our duty roster duty for the radio. 'It's OK,' I said to him, 'you get some shut-eye for a couple of hours, and I'll take the first stag.'

After returning to the radio set placed in a convenient cubicle of rock I decided to stag on there for the rest of our stay at Long Toenail. It was not through lack of trying, but blame for my last four near-sleepless nights lay in the tension of being on the battlefield. Besides I was fed up with the ineffectiveness of my green slug. So Mark was left undisturbed as, based on my track record, there would be little probability of me achieving a similar state of rest prior to fighting in a Gurkha infantry battle. My assumption, though, that this would be a quiet period turned out to be wrong.

Tac HQ had settled down for a few hours of restless sleep, although a few began to snore so loudly they would have won any competition against a *dush* 155-mm exploding shell. Time passed. At 21.45 hours looking northwards, a myriad of stars twinkled at me. Higher up I observed again the Southern Cross constellation; the northernmost of its two northerly stars was the brightest. Mimosa, 490 light years away from this fracas on the Falklands, is used by air and sea navigators so perhaps it would also be useful for the Battalion after our guide had left us. Mimosa is also the family name of a strange plant in Malaysia. After a flying insect lands on one of its leaves, the plant then traps its victim by closing the leaf around it and, during our childhood in Kuala Lumpur, my twin and I would play for hours touching the leaves of this plant to initiate such a reflex action. The *dush* waited also to trap the Gurkhas but, unfortunately for our opponents, we were about to land on another leaf from the one they had planned to use.

Such was the personal day-dreaming which diverted my mind from the crucible of battle that soon would start on terrain similar to Salisbury Plain. There were also professional thoughts about this climax to my insignificant military career. So many years of military training under my belt was undoubtedly the reason for such a strange feeling of déjà vu on this special night of my life, in preparing for battle that seemed so routine. I racked my brains for any previous occasion, apart from Exercise WELSH FALCON, when I had participated in a battalion attack on training. Horrified, I realized this was twelve years before on Exercise GRANADA and a 2LI daylight attack in north-east Malaysian jungle on a bunker system of Viet Cong-inspired design from the Vietnam War. There, amidst the green and red clouds that billowed out of hissing smoke grenades, an umpire had notionally 'killed' me as I led my platoon's charge on a bunker. My frightening conclusion now to such a memory recall was that this live Gurkha battalion attack about to be executed on East Falkland would be, indeed, my first at night.

Soon other diversions caught my eye as the Royal Navy began to fire star shell. Exploding intermittently, these illuminating flares were too high to be effective and only partially lit up the desolate terrain. Tempted to use both eyes, my training told me to keep one shut in order to preserve night vision. Shadows danced eerily as the flares, suspended by small parachutes, were caught by the wind and moved across our front. If I had been in the opposition's boots this would have made me nervous, particularly since the Gurkhas were poised to start their attack. *Dush* shelling began to range onto Goat Ridge seeking out the Gurkha mortar line with blinding bursts and one eye had to be shut again. British guns behind us replied, emphasizing that artillery fire is also an effective psychological neutralizer and sleep depriver. With that, my previous mood of comfortable familiarity became one of controlled fear. Radio business then began for the Training Officer sahib as Brigade called me: 'Require that you relocate your Lima-Sierra for Hawkeye casevac. Current location is far too close your objective.'

Initially I was pleased to get my teeth into something worthwhile as these final hours ticked by. It would also give Captain 'Roger, Wait Out!' a taste of his own medicine.

Out came the nuco codes, and soon a six-figure grid reference for the revised helicopter landing site to pick up Gurkha casualties was encoded. 'New Lima-Sierra location now Romeo-Juliet, Echo-Whisky, Uniform-Yankee,' I informed my masters diligently.

But a frustrating time had begun as Captain 'Roger, Wait Out!' was about to get his revenge. Five minutes later he made yet another call: 'Reference last Lima-Sierra. Negative, this remains too close for Hawkeye. Move this further back again!'

It was still too dangerous for the helicopters, so the grid reference had to be then altered not once, but another three times in an attempt to arrive at a suitable compromise. In the end, a location was mandatorily imposed on me – 100 metres north from where I was now standing and six kilometres away from the point of attack. This was too far even for a team of four fit Gurkhas struggling with not only a stretcher and heavy casualty in pain, but also his rifle and kit. The effort required to traverse such demanding terrain was not being factored into the overall equation, yet no amount of arguing could reverse the decision and later this caused severe problems. My arguing had contributed to keeping Nigel Price awake pondering over the great questions of life before his four-man Platoon HQ accompanied Tac HQ into battle. The following month during the return to UK, he would write a poem entitled *Before Battle*, about this awful wait. Here is the first part:

> All is done.
> Perched against the frozen stars
> A radio is friend,
> Muffling voices into urgent words
> Leaving those who cannot sleep
> To play the night for thoughts.
> Tumbled into rocks they lie
> Burdened with each curve of stone,
> Sleeping-bags drawn tight against the cold.
> Dreams are scarce
> Sucked white like breath, pulled from lips.
> Could no other method bring
> To hearts like these
> The urgency of life and play?

I surprised myself by my reaction to the perceived Brigade intransigence to life or death. Their unwillingness to accede to my requests only underlined the Battalion's vulnerability – and my anger exploded. Normally the most patient and phlegmatic of persons with an over-cautious approach to authority, a fundamental change started occuring in me that night that led to a diluted respect for superiors in general, which on more than one occasion later in life would cause severe problems. It reflected a shortfall in our Falklands' training as we had not received any information in basic self-help or buddy-buddy techniques regarding stress reactions and management of traumatic stress.

Concurrently I was also holding a running dialogue on the radio with a sailor. He was the naval gunfire support forward observer for the night's attack and had just departed from the Scots Guards' position, but the man had now become lost in the rocks and began to ask for assistance: 'Am attempting to reach your Sheldrake to discuss your call sign's fire plan. Can you guide me into your location?'

'Roger, send location and I'll give you directions,' I advised.

But as he moved we lost radio contact. Fortunately two other Gurkha BOs heard the problem and helped the sailor by navigating him through the dark and over his unnatural element of land. One of these was the Recce Platoon Commander, Quentin Oates, who had become our Gurkha liaison officer in the Guards' Tac HQ. The other was Bill Dawson with his Alternative Battalion Headquarters on Long Toenail. Bill's location, much higher up than Tac HQ, was invaluable as it would provide a much needed radio relay facility during the night and following morning whilst we moved in terrain that had many radio dead-spots. 'Roger,' confirmed Bill after a number of calls had been made between the two, 'you're nearly there now.'

Stumbling over the rocks, the sailor suddenly arrived at my location out of the Falklands' darkness. 'Welcome to the Gurkhas,' I said, extending my hand.

'Good to be here,' replied the sailor standing before me in his thick white wool roll-top sweater.

'Heavens above, would the Navy never learn about the necessity of camouflage when in the field?' I thought as he shook my hand more from relief in finding Tac HQ than anything else.

The introduction over, I led him over to Mike Fallon's cramped shelter in the rocks where they could begin to debate the fire plan. A painful lesson from Gurkha history concerning the coordination of naval gunfire support had shown the necessity of such a pow-wow. Nearly seventy years before at Gallipoli, the 1st/6th Gurkha Rifles had been hit by six Royal Navy monitor shells during a vital attack on the Sari Bair Ridge. Now, on the Falklands, every effort was being made to prevent similar incidents and ensure that naval firepower would this time be used effectively on the *dush*. We were not to be disappointed, although the ultimate touch that night would have been for the frigate HMS *Gurkha* to provide us with naval gunfire support onto our objectives. Alas, she had been in the Standby Squadron at Rosyth, Scotland and the decision to prepare her for South Atlantic operations was taken on 26 May but was too late for active participation in what remained of Operation CORPORATE – and which had a 20 June deadline as the Royal Navy warships at sea required urgent maintainance work after their battering from the South Atlantic storms.

It was midnight. Towards the west, British artillery gunfire increased tempo as *dush* positions on Mount William were neutralized prior to the Guards' diversion. At 00.30 hours which was their H-hour, the thirty-man Guards' fighting patrol made contact with a *dush* position south-west of Mount William. After a welter of explosions the Guards' Tac HQ sent a report on the Brigade command radio net: 'My call sign has taken casualties. Two dead.'

'Unpleasant listening but, nonetheless, interesting being a fly on the wall,' I concluded to myself. The diversion continued as the lead Guards' unit, G Company, crossed their start line at 01.00 hours to begin the advance and main attack on the Tumbledown. Simultaneously our mortar line, being the first Gurkha sub-unit earmarked to go into action, started firing in support of the Scotsmen. Just like my body, all personal thoughts remained numb and cold. So were Nigel's:

> Within each breast
> Slowly now the questions fall,
> Like the sticky flakes of snow
> That fall on stone
> On butt, pack and breathing man
> Fall through dark, the waiting dark,
> To lure into a single blend of form
> The agony of shapes that cross the plain.
> Time, persuaded into nervous hours, passes;
> Movement pulls the group awake
> And night has no more sanctuary,
> No more dreams to give.

Concurrent with G Company's H-hour, our departure preparations began. We stripped down to light assault order by centralizing bergens in a pile to be picked up later by helicopter. Removing these was not enough in lessening each man's load because we still carried far too much. If the move-up of the latter could have been guaranteed, which it never was, we should have discarded everything but the belt, a pick or shovel, kukri, one pouch plus five magazines of SLR ammunition, one meal, two field dressings in the pocket and GPMG link ammunition carried in another pouch. This would be yet one more lesson of the many learnt from that night and the following day. And we had forgotten another item – so I asked Mark, 'Is there any cam cream on offer? We should put it on now before moving out.'

Camouflage cream was a necessary infanteer accessory to blot out white faces and hands which otherwise would glow like beacons in the dark. Mark asked a Gurkhali question to our Signallers if they had any, but nobody in Tac HQ could find even one green tube of that thick dark brown ointment with its sickly scent.

'Looks like we'll have to make do another way,' said Mark after a few minutes and spoke again to the Gurkhas who began digging with their hands in the ground to manufacture a surrogate version from Falklands' peat lubricated with their spittle. My finger was one of many that dipped into this improvised face pack applied to cheeks, foreheads and hands. Alas, there would have been little point to take out a patent because the revolting mixture quickly dried to a faint greyish colour, leaving us no better off than before. But there was a positive spin-off. Most of us had stopped shaving because of the cold. The deliberate disobedience of this Sandhurst sacred cow retained a miniscule of facial warmth. If we had applied the real stuff it would have stuck most uncomfortably to the considerable stubble on our faces.

Immediately south and nearest us, A Company had been moving from their location to join the other two Gurkha companies already on Goat Ridge. Our waiting, so we thought, was over. At 01.40 hours and twenty minutes before Tac HQ's move out to Goat Ridge, I returned to my position in the rocks where Corporal Aslett was packing up the radio. A faint sound hit my ears. Seconds later a low-flying jet aircraft flew overhead.

'Was that one of ours?' I asked myself, peering hard into the night sky and black terrain before me. The answer came soon enough. I must have missed on the radio our seventeenth and penultimate red air alert warning of the campaign, and a series of crimson flames from ordnance dropped by a *dush* Canberra bomber aircraft stabbed into the darkness to the north. Dull thuds from this final air raid of the campaign then rolled across the few kilometres of night separating the explosions from Tac HQ.

'Surely the target was then Teal Inlet?' was my doubtful deduction.

Another was made as I got out my map and shone the red light of my handtorch on it. 'No, that position's further to the north-west, so the bombs probably landed there – in the area of Mount Kent.'

Two high-flying Canberra bombers escorted by a pair of low-flying Mirage III fighters had been attempting to attack the Commandos' Brigade HQ located west of Mount Kent – a hill that, eleven and a half years later, on a January afternoon, would become the site of the first Falklands' Gurkha Khud Race during a 7GR company four-month operational tour of the Islands.[3] The bombs landed north of 2 Para's position on Wireless Ridge, some kilometres away from the relocated 3 Commando Brigade HQ which had already been subjected to the Skyhawk attack earlier that afternoon. Turning away to leave my position and join the remainder of Tac HQ, I missed witnessing one of these Canberras being shot down south of Fitzroy when a Sea Dart fired by the destroyer *Exeter* on station east of Stanley hit the bomber at a height of 40,000 feet. Its pilot, Captain Roberto Pastrán, ejected to safety. His navigator, Captain Fernando Casado, did not. *Cardiff*, stationed as another anti-aircraft guardship off the Berkeley Sound, had also fired a Sea Dart at one of the escorting Mirages. The missile detonated north of Stanley, but its target was not hit and subsequently escaped.[4] Nor was I aware of another alleged raid, again off the Berkeley Sound, when the frigate *Penelope* claimed to have become the target of an unsuccessful air-to-surface missile attack.[5] This might also have been, however, a near blue-on-blue incident involving a Sea Dart missile.

I took a final look around the relative safety of our base before moving down towards the assembling Tac HQ BOs, Signallers, Gunners and Gurkha other ranks. But there was a delay because the routine for locating every man prior to our initial move out proved to be flawed. One of Kit's Gurkha Signallers was missing and frustration grew. Already we were five minutes late with our planned departure time. More minutes ticked by. Other Gurkhas were running around trying to locate the absent Gurkha still enjoying his forty winks whilst his angry RSO sahib groaned loudly, 'So for God's sake, where the bloody hell *is* he then?'

Their efforts revealed nothing. More minutes ticked by. Suddenly the hunt ended with Kit's voice hissing venomously, 'Christ, man! You're just about to go into battle and you've overslept! You dozy idiot!'

'Yes, sahib! Sorry, sahib!' In making amends, the sleepy culprit thrashed around like a bull in a china shop trying to locate his kit. This response to the sahib's oaths proved so effective that the Gurkha's lie-in only caused a few minutes of extra delay. In his poem's conclusion, Nigel describes the stumble out of our location just after 02.00

hours in the wake of the Commandant who, unaware of the missing Gurkha, was already well ahead setting a fast pace:

> A trick of dark becomes a line of men,
> Rest gone, peace gone,
> 'Move now.'
> Strung with belts of ammunition,
> Heavy under all the load of war,
> They trudge, hunched like peasants
> With slow and measured step
> Called by their fields to work.

But we could not become separated from yet another Gurkha who was determined to be at *his* battle start line punctually so, to catch up, Tac HQ had to run the first 200 metres before beginning the '. . . trudge . . . with slow and measured step . . .' towards our turn to rock 'n' roll and, maybe, die.

Chapter Twenty

QUEUING-UP FOR
THE TUMBLEDOWN

The Gurkhas came at us all fired up, high on drugs. They came tearing towards us, screaming, not trying to protect themselves. It wasn't difficult to shoot them, but there were so many. You could shoot one or two but the next one in line would shoot you. They were like robots. One Gurkha trod on a mine and was hurled into the air, but the man behind didn't take the slightest notice. He just carried on, on the same path. Some of the Gurkhas came at us with heavy machine guns, and it didn't matter who got in their line of fire, us or the other Gurkhas. – Guillermo, an Argentine soldier on Wireless Ridge during 2 Para's assault there on the night of 13–14 June.[1]

A stronger wind whipped up once we distanced ourselves from the protective lee of our rocks in the Two Sisters area. Speed became dictated by the atrocious terrain and our pace slowed. This would be a laborious fight across the one kilometre of frozen ground to the western end of Goat Ridge and the Battalion's forming up point. We reached the first of six stone-runs fifteen to twenty-five metres wide, that consisted of tightly-packed angular quartzite boulders. Each had to be traversed with care and I cursed silently as conditions were not good. Concentration was needed to avoid slipping but, even so, I nearly turned turtle several times on the thin layer of snow covering each rock. It was bitterly cold, but a layer of thermal underwear and my exertions caused sweat to trickle down my face and back in the most uncomfortable fashion. Predictably the shadowy Gurkha figures ahead made light work of the energy-sapping stone run as distant artillery gunfire on targets in the Tumbledown reminded us of our tasks ahead.

An hour was needed to cross that dreadful one kilometre to Goat Ridge. Its western end was one of 42 Commando's objectives two nights before when they had launched a minor attack to clear out the *dush*, but now the remainder of the Battalion sat there as if on the starting grid of a Formula One Grand Prix. Altogether we were 406 Gurkhas, BOs and attached British soldiers, though this total did not include the two Mortar Platoon sections preparing their four mortar base plates for action nearby.

I looked at my watch. 03.00 hours. The unflappable Corporal Chris Aslett placed my radio on a nearby rock and I sat down beside it while small-arms fire echoed from the direction of the Tumbledown. A trained ear could differentiate between the crack of friendly rifle-fire against the thump of *dush* Browning heavy machine guns as, with an increasingly cold posterior, I monitored the Guards' progress on the Brigade command net. While the diversionary attack was being made south-west of Mount William, their G Company's initial approach had secured the first third of the Tumbledown without any *dush* contact. Thirty minutes before our arrival on Goat Ridge, the Scots Guards' Left Flank Company were passed through G Company to start the second phase. Their advance had been quickly halted by *dush* snipers and machine guns, and the continuing exchange of fire would mean a delay to our departure from the Battalion's forming up point.

Difficulties were being reported by the Guards' Battalion Tac HQ: 'My call sign now under fire from enemy snipers and machine-gun fire. Our two lead call signs are pinned down and unable to move. Situation now being assessed.'

On my radio Captain 'Roger, Wait Out!' had given way to the Brigade Commander located at Brigade Tac HQ near Mount Harriet. 'Remain at your current location,' he instructed me.

The start of our tab had been formally postponed and our long wait began. I looked into the inky blackness. One and a half kilometres north lay the Two Sisters' battlefield whose Brigade nickname was Rock Trunk, and three kilometres south was the Mount Harriet battlefield of Still Concorn. Of more interest was the *dush*'s third line of hills in their Inner Defence Zone lying before us.

According to later British accounts, the Scots Guards' diversion south-west of Mount William had diverted the 5th Marine Infantry Battalion's attention away from the Guards' main thrust on the Tumbledown, the net result of this preliminary operation being surplus to the effort required to mount it. *Capitán de Fragata Infanteria de Marina* Carlos Hugo Robacio, the Marines' *senor jefe*, believed however that the *'Galeses'* (Welsh Guards) were attacking.[2] Later in life he became a Rear Admiral and wrote a book about his unit's war experiences in which he took a contrary view to the British claim:

> This was a costly and incomprehensible ruse, intended to induce us into believing that the British effort would be focused on that mountain (William). This did not happen, nor did they succeed in influencing us into distracting efforts already planned. The only effect was to make us repel strongly the senseless simulated attack. The crude realism of this action, from our point of view, was that it prevented the enemy from detecting beforehand the position of O Company (-) that we had advanced north-east of Pony's Pass.[3]

Robacio was, '. . . a very nice chap, a classical naval officer of the old school . . . sports-loving, tough, democratic, liberal, with wit, (and) with . . . much initiative.'[4] Of the opinion that Argentina 'will never resign willingly the Malvinas, whose sole position on the map clearly signals our right over them'[5], he had been able to analyse previous British attacks against Army units to get an idea of our procedures. His Marines were well-prepared. They had been the first reinforcing unit to arrive on the Islands from their peacetime base at Rio Grande in Tierra del Fuego in response to UN Resolution 502, deploying to the Tumbledown and Mount William area on 7 April. However in contrast to the 4th Infantry Regiment from sub-tropical Corrientes, they were used to operating in extreme climates and would be the only *dush* unit equipped, trained and environment-ready for the engagement, exemplified by the fact that, during the average seventy-one day exposure to the adverse conditions, only one of its 707 men suffered from severe trench foot. He required a right big toe amputation.[6]

The *dush* would be 'very well supported by fire from battalion guns (one 105-mm battery, six 81-mm mortars, and six 106.6-mm mortars) and the Army's artillery'[7] in their defensive layout which originally comprised N Company and O Company on the Tumbledown, and M Company with 81-mm mortars on Mount William. But the outer defence zone's fall had required a reassessment of the threat and expected direction of 5 Brigade's follow-up attack. Escaping Army units from the Two Sisters and Mount Harriet battles also provided Robacio with unexpected reinforcements to make a drastic redeployment of his Battalion. He had ordered O Company, in reality a platoon reinforced by an Amphibious Engineer platoon, forward to block Pony's Pass south-west of Mount William. 2 Platoon of N Company was moved onto the Tumbledown-Mount William saddle, and M Company withdrew to Sapper Hill to be reinforced by C Company, 3rd Infantry Regiment and a 4th Infantry Regiment platoon. On Mount William another platoon from 4th Infantry Regiment was joined by N Company's 1 Platoon, and a 602 Commando Company assault platoon sited in anti-tank defence on the south-west shoulder.

N Company retained three platoons on the Tumbledown. 3 Platoon was located on the north-east spur, a composite 4 Platoon of Marines and remnants of a 4th Infantry Regiment platoon defended the summit centre. Behind them 5 Platoon, another composite sub-unit comprising Amphibious Engineers and a depleted 12th Infantry Regiment platoon was sited on the north-west summit. Including N Company's HQ, approximently 100 men defended the Tumbledown. B Company, 6th Infantry Regiment was also in reserve near the eastern end. In summary, *dush* sub-unit strengths and dispositions differed considerably to those given out by Paddy Redding at our O Group thirty hours before. Such flawed intelligence was not his fault.

Suddenly a message arrived on the Brigade net which did not bode well for the Guards: 'Information received that the enemy on your objective have now been re-inforced by another company.' A SAS OP on the coast at Seal Point must have been responsible for providing the information that Robacio had pulled back his O Company.

'How then would the Guards cope if the *dush* dared to carry out a determined counter-attack?' I wondered as goose pimples ran up and down on my spine, 'and could this mean we might be fighting on the Tumbledown after all?'

Thoughts of a personal nature were now replaced by only professional proactive ones. I was still concerned at the lack of a helicopter casevac landing site near the Tumbledown. This provoked a fresh, and more alarming, deduction. Current *dush* resistance might mean a Gurkha resupply of ammunition, water, and rations – in that order – would be needed sooner rather than later. 'However if the helicopters were to approach the battlefield,' I reasoned, 'to where and how could our resupply be made in time?

Soon it would be 03.30 hours and another fire mission had been called. Above us whistled a stream of 105-mm shells towards Mount William as the eighteen guns in support of the 5 Brigade attack increased their rate of fire. Regular drumbeats could also be picked out amongst the British artillery's cacophony. They belonged to the 4.5-inch gun of the frigate *Active* which was to fire 220 high-explosive shells and eight star shells on the Tumbledown. Another, the *Avenger* on the Berkeley Sound gunline, also fired 156 shells onto this target while the frigates *Yarmouth* and *Ambuscade* engaged Wireless Ridge. A further 4,500 rounds were to be fired by the Royal Artillery. The latter's ammunition use represented the equivalent of one artillery Regiment's training ammunition allocation for four years, but despite such disgraceful training quotas created by politicians' ill-advised policies, the Gunners were doing well. Including the Commando Brigade's batteries, approximately 7,000 rounds were to be fired during the next twelve hours at *dush* positions located within six square kilometres.

Meanwhile the Guards' fighting patrol had broken off their diversionary attack more than an hour before at a cost of two killed and six wounded. During their tactical withdrawl they were mortared, and an urgent radio request was made by the Guards to Brigade: 'Require Hawkeye now for casevac task.'

The response, though, exemplified how non-attention to planning detail for such a casualty evacuation situation as this could mean the difference between life and death: 'Not possible. Papa November Golf is not available to Hawkeye.'

The Brigade Air Squadron helicopters did not possess passive night goggles which would enable pilots to see in the dark so that my earlier argument with Brigade about the Gurkhas' casualty helicopter landing site was irrelevant now. No helicopter would arrive even if requested. The military 'first-class bog-up' colloquialism to describe such situations, where the right hand (controlling landing sites) did not know what the left hand (knowledge of logistic limitations) was doing and vice-versa now applied. This did not help the soldier on the ground that night, when *not* becoming a casualty seemed to be the only answer.

The fighting patrol's situation had become more complicated. 'They've been slowed down by their dead and wounded on their way out, and the call-sign's now entered a minefield,' reported my radio. 'They've received at least four further casualties. One has had his foot blown off and, another, a leg.' To me, a passive radio listener, this frightful situation seemed to be getting worse rather than better and, even more so, as one of the four Scorpion and Scimitar light tanks from the Blues and Royals' troop in support, had been abandoned after being badly damaged by a mine explosion when moving eastwards on the Darwin-Stanley track.

It was now 03.50 hours and the artillery quietened. Unlike the rear platoon of the Guards' Left Flank Company waiting to go into action, who ran around trying to keep warm, the Gurkhas below and in front of my elevated position barely twitched a muscle as they listened impassively to the battle ahead. Their behaviour was derived from 7GR Regimental *kaida* which brought about an automatic self-imposed collective discipline. Some were aware that *kaida* could be construed by outsiders as being an outdated quality; but becoming a modern military force is important to the Gurkhas, embodied by one QGO's remark I would read later that, '*Kaida* can be interpreted as "keeping all in the dark ages"'. Paradoxically just such a quality, however, contributed significantly to a unique 'psyops' mysticism that the *dush* held only for the Gurkhas and no other Falklands' British ground-force modern unit.

Time ticked on as a whisper went slowly round the ranks of cross-legged hillmen sitting and listening to the crackling machine-gun fire. '*Makai bhuteko jastai!*' (It's just like the sound of frying maize!), was their description of the fighting. But my radio reported more gloomy news from the Guards' fighting patrol: 'Roger, yes. My sub-unit has a further two casualties, and we require Hawkeye.'

We should have moved more than an hour ago at 03.00 hours. Information on the Brigade command net was not encouraging, and reasons for the delay became more obvious as the Brigade Commander, located on an outcrop of rock between Goat Ridge and Mount Harriet, began to apply the pressure. The Scots Guards' CO gave as good as he got:

'Send sitrep!'

'Attempting to continue our advance.'

'Why aren't you moving forward?'

'We're under fire from snipers and machine-gunners!'

'Your delay's holding up this formation's entire attack. Can you try an outflanking manoeuvre?'

'No. Impossible. Am attempting to get Sheldrake to adjust onto enemy machine-gun positions with individual rounds.'

'Have you used grenades?'

'No. We're not close enough.'

'Have you tried your 66s and 84s?'

'Yes!'

'So when do you estimate you can begin moving forward again?'

'Sheldrake is still adjusting!'

This dialogue continued to snap backwards and forwards. The Guards' CO kept his cool and his superior's aggressive questions and hopeful suggestions slowly petered out. Time dragged on. On the ether came another report on the Guards' fighting patrol withdrawl: 'Our call sign not yet out of the minefield. Holdfast is providing assistance.' Another two long hours would be needed before the patrol, which received nearly fifty per cent casualties, could be extracated by their Sapper. Forthcoming Gurkha casualties on the Tumbledown would not have the benefit, however, of the Guards casualties' luxury of travelling on the back of a Scorpion light tank to 42 Commando's RAP at Port Harriet House.

The Brigade Commander's voice suddenly popped up again: 'Send sitrep!'

Enough, apparently, was enough. A Guards officer's voice rapped back: 'Nothing heard, out!' and there was a click.

I heard nothing more from the Scots Guards' Tac HQ until some hours later because they had switched off their Brigade command net radio. This was unprofessional since it denied us periphery information and meant we had to indulge in guessing games about the evolving situation in front us. The battlefield had also become quieter as the eye of the artillery typhoon had arrived in the attempt to flush out the defenders. Using artillery like a sledge-hammer to crack a nut would also eat even more into our Battalion's precious time, and impact negatively on our H-hour. A flurry of snow hit my face as the wind gusted more strongly than ever. I tugged up my parka hood as protection against the ever-increasing cold. Every so often an adjusting shell was fired, providing ominous signals that our planned night attack might now have to be undertaken in broad daylight. The Gurkha Tac HQ's patience began to run ragged with the fumbling Scots Guards.

'Maybe they might want some assistance from a few kukris,' I thought.

'What the heck's going on? We've got to get moving soon! Otherwise we're going to wait here until the Woodentops march out on Horseguards' Parade for next year's Trooping of the Colour!' was a typical reaction from another BO and, since that year's parade had been held only thirty-six hours previously, this implied a considerable wait.

In the Tumbledown, the Guards' Left Flank 'FOO' had been located with the platoon elevated in the rocks, and it had taken him some effort to scramble down to the Company HQ. Once there, he began adjusting artillery fire onto a machine-gun post facing the platoon on the low ground. The distance between these two locations was a mere 250 metres and that esoteric Gunner shooting procedure of 'danger close coordinated illumination' had been initiated. One incorrectly firing 'rogue' gun of the battery engaged in this drawn out shoot dropped rounds on the Left Flank while the other five continued their pedestrian adjusting that led to even more delay for us.

Patience now ceased to be a virtue in our Tac HQ. The Woodentops were ruining the Gurkha show because the Victoria Cross is not won by warming one's bottom sitting behind the front line. The Brigade attack momentum had to be maintained, so the Commandant marched up to me and demanded, 'Give me your handset!'

Acutely aware of our exposed current location, time, and need to balance the relative safety of dark between the dangers of daylight, he asked his superior, 'Request permission to move forward so we can be better positioned to commence our attack when required.'

The negative response made him fume. More precious minutes passed as Murphy's Law stared at us. If it was going to go wrong, then it *will* go wrong, at the worst possible time, with the worst possible result. Frustration was his driving force, and the senior sahib again hijacked my handset to repeat his request. This time he succeeded. 'OK! Wind up!' he snapped. 'Ready to move in five minutes!'

Corporal Aslett heaved my radio up onto his back and, as I held to my ear the handset attached to the connecting lead and started to move off, he began to follow me like an obedient labrador. So at 04.45 hours and 105 minutes behind schedule the Gurkhas had started their overdue tab along the southern side of Goat Ridge. The first part of this would be in single file, with Tac HQ taking up a position behind A Company who were leading. Having dumped their bergens, the Gurkhas were now in assault order and at the lightest they had been for any Falklands tab. Nonetheless kukris, rifles, machine guns, M-79 grenade-launchers, throw-away rocket launchers, to say nothing of bandoliers of heavy machine-gun and rifle ammunition, bedecked the small figures which began to move carefully along a narrow shepherds' path, parallel to the rocks of Goat Ridge on our left.

The intention was to move up behind the Guards and manoeuvre ourselves nearer our twin objectives of the Tumbledown's north-east spur and Mount William. This would marginally reduce the dreadful disadvantages of an attack in daylight over terrain devoid of cover. But our initial pace out of the forming up point was painfully slow as frozen muscles had to adjust to the unaccustomed movement. We were not alone with this problem as the waiting Guards in the Tumbledown could later testify.

The two Gurkha mortar sections' base-plate locations were passed on our southern side. Boxes of mortar bombs had been stacked neatly up against the Goat Ridge rocks and the Gurkhas manning their tubes were ready to slide more bombs down them. They would have to wait. The long line of silent marching Gurkhas was already the cause of frequent stops and starts.

'Ah, no – shit! Not another halt,' I moaned yet again and sat down on a nearby rock. Kit Spencer was just ahead of me and had also stopped. Confident nobody could see him, he hid in the wall of rock and lit up a well camouflaged cigarette. He was a naughty boy, but got through half his smoke before A Company ahead of us began moving slowly forward again.

'What *is* the problem?' I wondered, 'there can't be any map reading problem. Goat Ridge's rock line has a really good directional handrail for our Marine guide up front.'

Soon Tac HQ was tabbing slowly again towards the Tumbledown. Picking our way silently through the snow we passed by a tent where shadows stood and talked quietly. One leant on a walking stick. He was probably the Adjutant trying to exhibit Guardsman-like coolness in a tense situation. One or two men lay stretched out in sleeping bags. More than likely medical orderlies, they resembled, nonetheless, frozen mummies. 'Must be the Guards' RAP,' I concluded. 'Lucky buggers, they seem blissfully unaware of activities further eastwards. Never mind, they'll soon have their hands full of casualties.'

With that final mean thought I continued my tab into the inky dark. Perched on the rock line was a storm lantern marking the end of the Guards' forming up point and start of their path towards their attack start line. Its soft green light lured us gently on towards the sounds of battle. I looked at my watch. The hands had slid past 06.00 hours. There were less than four hours to first light and more than five kilometres to Mount William – but these facts in such an equation did not include the time required for the Guards to engage in any likely fighting. We continued to tab in fits and starts down a gradual incline. Every so often there was a familiarly irritating halt. Men sat in the snow to take advantage of these, only to move on again after five minutes. As the height of the Goat Ridge rock line diminished, so a glow began appearing on the eastern horizon. Some pointed in puzzlement at this phenomena, then suddenly a whisper came down the line. The Gurkha ahead of me turned and, with teeth flashing an excited grin, hissed softly, 'Lights of Port ish-Stanley, sahib!'

I nodded in agreement.

We tabbed on. The lights of the town twinned with Whitby in North Yorkshire in recognition of the West Yorkshire Regiment's garrison of the Falklands during the Second World War became brighter. These had been kept on to prevent unnecessary damage and casualties from British shelling, and slowly it became possible to define buildings and roads. Created from Article 15 of the Fourth Geneva Convention, this neutral zone consisted of a rectangular area of ground measuring five acres from the central point provided by the Anglican Christ Church Cathedral and included a number of other buildings in which were housed civilian non-combatants and sick or wounded Argentine servicemen and civilians. Although the zone was still not operational, Navy gunfire accuracy prevented widespread damage. The statistics were compelling. Twenty-four days of shore bombardment, forty-three separate fire missions and 10,000 4.5-inch shells fired – of which 2,800 were expended in the final eight days. Despite this, only three civilians had been killed out of the capital's 1,000 population and, exclusive of Moody Brook Barracks, only eight buildings hit with seven others burnt down by unknown causes. The police station had received a direct hit from a missile fired by a Wessex helicopter. According to the local Falklands' news magazine *The Penguin News*:

> . . . few people were able to sleep soundly for the continous 'crumps' and whistles (of) the artillery exchange (which had been) frightening and depressing although everyone knew that the end of the conflict could not be far away. One elderly gentleman expressed a common view: 'If I'd known this was going to happen,' he said, 'I'd never bothered living to eighty-three!'[8]

Such accuracy was soon to bear fruit in the Tumbledown's crags as the occasional whistle of a British shell overhead reminded us of the general direction in which our *dush* lay. The eye of the artillery typhoon would soon complete its pass over the Tumbledown as we neared the eastern end of Goat Ridge having, by now, tabbed only one and a half kilometres. I looked up as my boot trod on the heel of the Gurkha's ahead of me.

'So what's happening now?' was my irritated reaction. 'Slowing down yet again? Oh, no! Not yet *another* sodding halt!'

This one was different. At a natural gap in the rock line huddled a group of figures. The Guards' Tac HQ. In terms of numbers, they seemed to be half of ours. The Commandant approached the Guards' CO. Their dialogue did not last long, but neither Regimental pride was at stake nor rivalry to the fore, because the Guards faced a difficult situation. 'Can your men help us to get to our objectives?' asked their CO to an equally pressed Gurkha Commandant reassessing his own plans in a losing battle against time.

It must have been tempting to oblige the Guards CO's request for here was the chance to commit the Gurkhas to a certain Falklands' battle. Logic prevailed. Night and darkness is no time to marry up two Battalions in an unrehearsed joint assault on dug-in enemy positions. 'Sorry,' said the Commandant against his instinct. 'There'll only be muddle and disaster committing our men and mixing them with yours, so we'll just continue to move forward behind your companies as time is now becoming critical for our own attack.' Soon the ensuing daylight chaos, when friendly forces moved closer together during the battle, would prove his decision to be a wise one.

The Guards' delay was causing us so many problems that all of our plans would require adjusting once we arrived in the Tumbledown. 'OK,' said their CO, 'but move with caution because the *dush* are continuing to resist with snipers in the Tumbledown's centre and Left Flank's FOO is still adjusting artillery fire prior to their attack.'

As agreed, our Marine Commando guides then left us as we passed through this gateway in the rock and beyond into the unknown. To the north lay Moody Valley, running from west to east. On the far side was 2 Para's objective, Wireless Ridge, and to the east and forming the southern side of Moody Valley, loomed the darkness of the Tumbledown. There in the course of the next six hours or so, the Gurkhas would sight the soldier's equivalent of the holy grail, an experience that changed my values in life. Others on that tab should perhaps judge for themselves whether they have been similarly affected.

Our boots continued crunching on the frozen tufts of grass as we began to edge eastwards along the northern side of Goat Ridge. In the distance, Mount William's cone structure came into sight. Its ghostly appearance, illuminated by Royal Navy star shell, made the grey rock shimmer. But there appeared no sign of life on its western slopes as the *dush* must have taken cover because of the shelling. On the western side of the Tumbledown, more star shell bathed friend and foe alike in light as we closed on its satanic mass. I was so fascinated that the drill of shutting one eye to preserve night vision had been forgotten whilst the *keta* probably began sensing that their contribution to the Falklands' War could soon become more meaningful.

We had reached the Brigade report line of Pear Tree and I forgot to report this over the radio. But at 06.30 hours the artillery typhoon began to blow in full strength again as Left Flank's FOO started reaping his long awaited harvest. The lull ended with three salvos of five shells that each smacked into the Tumbledown's centre with a succession of sickening crumps and a reciprocating burst of *dush* tracer. Then another and another. The artillery rounds fired for effect on the machine-gun post signalled the start of a Guards' left-flanking platoon attack on it. My radio handset burst into life with a demanding Brigade Commander's voice: 'Send location, and keep moving forward!'

'Damn!' I blamed myself, 'you, Seear, can't get much more stupid in this situation than to forget the codewords to the Brigade report lines of our advance!' So a deliberately vague reply was made to the Brigade Commander: 'Now approaching the first objective!'

Though there was a desire to pull out my torch from my combat jacket top pocket in order to check the map, I refrained. Now was definitely *not* the moment to become non-tactical. Odd how this ingrained drill from basic training surfaced at such a moment. Meanwhile more flares and tracer rose from this battlefield. The *dush* were firing high and tracer from several machine guns clawed and arced into the heavens before hitting high ground west of Mount William. The cork was now being extracted from the bottle at last. In the far distance 2 Para committed themselves to their Wireless Ridge objectives. As we moved across the valley floor, they seemed to be fighting their battle in silence. But this ghostly effect was caused by the strong wind which blew away the noise of combat before it could reach us.

These ethereal mysteries of the 2 Para battlefield contrasted to the shelling and mortar acoustics in our area. It made the rifle, machine-gun and mortar live firing during our final Sennybridge battalion exercise six weeks ago sound like the pop of .22 rifles at a shooting gallery. Like a high-pressure hose turned on for maximum effect, tracer from the Paras' Machine Gun Platoon and Rarden cannon of the other Blues and Royals troop spewed out parabolic streams of bright red beads that vanished into the darkness. A similar visual effect came from the fire of *dush* anti-aircraft guns which were being used in a ground-mounted role from the Moody Brook area of Stanley.

There was that sneaking thought again, 'Would we be subjected to similar treatment with those two reported guns on Mount William? And, if so, how would we all react?'

We tabbed along the north side of Goat Ridge parallel to Moody Valley. Unlike the Guards, I continued to listen to Brigade radio transmissions by holding the handset to my right ear. I looked across at the valley and, away in the distance, Mount Longdon – 3 Para's forty-eight hour old battlefield. The moon was bright but often covered by thick cloud as snow squalls blew in off the sea. Oblivious to the freezing cold, it felt as though one was walking to a normal day's work on the Ash Shooting Ranges at Aldershot. A strange absence of fear prevailed as attention focused on 2 Para's spectacular battlefield effects.

We descended gradually from the eastern tip of Goat Ridge to lower ground towards a large flat bowl of terrain that would lead the Gurkha column nearer the Tumbledown's western end and its initial slopes. To accomplish this, the Battalion would have to cross the Guards' start line which had been secured by their Recce Platoon. This was a waist-high stock fence that restricted the movement of sheep. It proved also an obstacle for us for as we had to queue up by kneeling on the frozen ground. More time was consumed by each soldier's efforts to climb over the fence and avoid the sharpest of barbs on the top wire.

My turn came.

'Dammit!' I muttered in attempting to swing my left leg over after my right.

Trying to hold the wire down by pressing my battle-board on it instead of an SLR stock I did not possess, this piece of improvisation led instead to impalement. Jerking the trapped leg forward and away again from the barbed wires's clutches, I tore a hole in my combat trousers.

'Shit!' I swore again, this time at the noise of the ripping in the trouser leg.

This was clumsy: stupidity and irritation nearly consumed me. Any prospective battle against the *dush* melted into oblivion for several minutes as concern about the trifling hole in my uniform increased to mountaineous proportions. Stress was to blame with these perceived personal priorities that had now become totally out of proportion.

The shelling eased again. With our Assault Pioneer Platoon at Goose Green, the Battalion was being led by a team of three Sappers that included Sergeant Ron Wrega. He had worked non-stop in disarming Goose Green booby traps and munitions and was available again as the minefield was supposed to lie on our line of march approaching this north-west side of the Tumbledown. Armed with long wire probes at the van of the Battalion, the Sappers' task, therefore, was to clear this route for mines and possible tripwires connected to booby traps. It was a nerve-racking job.

They were accompanied by the A Company rifle section of Corporal Khemkumar Limbu. He was an excellent soldier and considered leading the Battalion and safeguarding it from wandering into a minefield to be an honour. Both the Sappers and Khemkumar carried out their duty to perfection. Arriving in the lee of the Tumbledown had been far from simple, as the light-hearted account of one the Sappers, Corporal A. Iles from 3 Troop, 9 Parachute Engineer Squadron, described. His young partner, Sapper Seth Roose, had only just celebrated his eighteenth birthday on *QE2*:

It was known from Intelligence that there was a minefield on their (A Company's) planned route. They needed a section from the troop to lead them and I had been given the task by the troop commander. 'Can we take our trench with us, sir?', I asked.

. . . Myself and Sapper Seth Roose were leading (he had the white handkerchief!). The Gurkha recce element were fifteen to twenty metres behind and the rest of the section, under Lance Corporal Shankland, in immediate reserve. We made good ground over the first 800 metres and were still 200 metres from the start of the minefield, but then I experienced a coldness I have never known before. We had come close to a bird's nesting place and they let us know it with a hissing sound. Seth and I hit the ground, fingers tightening on the safety catch. We honestly thought that it was the enemy saying, 'Psst.'

Pushing on we came to the start of the minefield. With a bit of patience we managed to find a safe route around it. Meanwhile the battle for Tumbledown was going on. The Scots Guards had taken the first part of the ridge and were moving on to the centre.[9]

They quickly took the obstinate *dush* machine-gun post while other Guardsmen, high in the rocks, moved forward flushing out snipers. The defenders did not appreciate the use of the bayonet, but a kukri would have been even more unpalatable. It must have been at this point that the *dush* spotted us. Near Moody Valley's Felton Stream five kilometres away, Robacio concluded in his command post, which would be 'engaged in an intense fight due to the fire from 2 and 3 Para . . . at our flanks'[10], that the Tumbledown was now being subjected to a classic pincer manoeuvre by the *Nepalese* and *Escoceses* (Scots Guards):

> The 5th Brigade of the Royal Army (The Queen's Guards)[11] . . . converge(d) a Battalion of the Scots Guards from the south-west towards that point where 4 Platoon was located, and the Nepalese Guards Battalion (Gurkhas) from the north-west from an almost inaccessible place to where 5 Platoon was located,[12] . . . The enemy attack concentrated generally over the heights of Mount Tumbledown, for it was here that the Scots Guards and Gurkhas attacked. We think it is a virtue of our enemies to aim decisively towards an important objective.[13]

Also a post-war sketch of the Tumbledown battle, possibly used in an internal regimental enquiry and depicting the same theory, was seized from special category POWs on board the Townsend-Thoresen ferry MV *St Edmund* returning them to Argentina and Puerto Madryn.[14] But now, with friendly and *dush* small-arms fire crackling above us, I tugged on the radio handset. The dutiful Corporal Aslett, still lagged behind me and, impatiently, I whispered loudly, 'Come on! Close up a bit!' while tugging on the handset yet again in my attempt to reel in the Signaller.

A bright idea that this would be an excellent debriefing point, after this night and coming day of the necessity to provide a longer radio lead for future wars, was interrupted abruptly. The Brigade Commander's voice boomed in my handset: 'Send location!'

'Not so easy without those damned report line codewords, and I still can't read a

258

grid reference from the map in the dark by using torchlight,' I cursed to myself. 'Wait a minute, though, there's an alternative. Use veiled speech you idiot!' So I trusted my luck and reported back: 'Now at the base of the first objective of our friends from the hills!'

This Scots Guard's description would be understood as they had been known as such on the radio throughout to differentiate them from the corresponding description: 'Our friends from the valleys' for the Welsh Guards. As I sent the message my eyes looked down. Perhaps they were playing tricks, but ten metres away appeared to be a prostate body. Its dark outline seemed to be separated from the shape of what appeared to be a rifle. There was also a large circle of freshly-burnt grass and the unmistakeable tang of cordite and my imagination began working in overtime again. 'So could this have been where one of those Harrier laser-guided bombs had landed yesterday afternoon?' I wondered.

The daydream was over as quickly as it had started. A muffled cough sounded behind the Tumbledown. I looked up. The gun barrel was trained on us. A familiar whistle grew in intensity. My reflexes took control of my body. We were about to see 'the elephant' in this pre-selected *dush* defenders' final protective fire artillery target area – otherwise known with dread as 'the DF(FPF)'. With binoculars still slung around my neck, a perfect horizontal landing onto East Falkland was achieved so quickly that even an Exocet in full cry towards its target would have had difficulty in beating me. My binos hit the frozen ground simultaneously and the right eyepiece rim contrived to ram itself into the corresponding upper bone of my eye socket. Surprisingly there was no sense of pain then or in the immediate hours afterwards. For I had only one priority at that moment. Survival.

Chapter Twenty-one

UNDER FIRE AGAIN

When first under fire an' you're wishful to duck,
Don't look nor take 'eed at the man that is struck,
Be thankful you're livin', and trust to your luck
And march to your front like a soldier.
Front, front, front like a soldier.

Rudyard Kipling

Eighty metres away, the Tumbledown's western slopes erupted with thunderclaps into multiple showers of peat. Like a photograph ingrained into my mind, the explosions are crystal clear even today from that 'fight or freeze or flee' moment.

The enemy barrage, fired by six Italian-made 105-mm Ota Melará field guns of B Battery, 1st Marine Field Artillery Battalion located near Felton Stream east of the Tumbledown at 5,500 metres range, moved rapidly towards us. Making a virtue of necessity, this was no occasion to remain in the open. Lewis Carroll's white rabbit in *Alice in Wonderland* would have lost in any race against me as I scuttled towards the dubious shelter of the nearest rock. To my rear, forty metres away, was an explosion amongst the shadows of men. Then immediately to my front twenty metres away, another. We were being 'bracketed'. Others had also gone to ground. Ten metres behind me, Nigel Price heard the next incomer which encouraged a doomsday vision. Kneeling down with one hand on the ground, he was transfixed at the whistling shell and thought, 'Jesus, is *this* the way I'm about to go?' But the blind crashed harmlessly into the ground ten metres from Tac HQ. A second incomer hit the same spot. Another blind.

The irrepressible Bombadier Batchelor glanced at the horrified Nigel to remark with sublime understatement, 'I think we would have felt that one, sir!'

Tove's talisman worn around my neck had done its job, but there was a seemingly never-ending chain of explosions, to our left, right, front and behind, twenty, thirty, forty and fifty metres away. More shells crashed down again among A and B Companies as dark figures were silhouetted against the blinding dazzle of explosions. Like a swarm of metallic bees in flight, the hum of shrapnel enveloped us. The momentary silence of shock was then filled by Gurkhali screams of pain, '*Madat dinu!*' (Help me!) '*Madat dinu! Madat goli lagyo!*' (I got hit!).

For several minutes confusion reigned as shells continued to rain down on us. The numbers and extent of our casualties were not immediately known. Spotted high in the

Tumbledown by Second Lieutenant Marcelo De Marco, this *dush* N Company's artillery FOO had called down the fire to halt our advance. He succeeded in temporarily neutralizing the Gurkha threat. Most of Tac HQ found cover under a rock overhang that afforded the barest of protection and, as we crouched down, more shells exploded seventy, sixty, fifty and forty metres away. With the exception of the Royal Artillery's rogue gun, the Guards' Left Flank Company had never been exposed to such near-proximity shelling during the 'Danger Close' procedure prior to their attack. Coming frequently under fire from 155-mm *dush* shells at Wether Ground had been an enlightening experience, but surviving such an intense and accurate barrrage as this was quite another and, as the metallic hum continued to cut through the cold night air, the vulnerability of the Battalion's predicament was obvious to all. To my fellow students who attended that Warminster platoon commanders course a decade before, I can confirm once again that the day at Bovington, when we experienced live shell-fire from within the safety of shut down tanks, was nothing in comparison to this night.

Raising my headset yet again I yelled into the mouthpiece, hopefully, direct to the Brigade Commander himself: 'Advance now stopped! Under heavy artillery fire and taken cover!' As yet another shell crashed down nearby, I screamed a postscript: 'And you should have been here!'

'Amazing! Why am I being *so* cheeky with higher authority? What is happening?' I asked myself. The answer was simple. Exposure to these exploding shells *and* surviving them gave me not only the existential authority to make the remark, but also the basic need to ventilate my stress of that moment to somebody. Indeed, anybody. That it had been directed at the Brigade Commander himself was coincidental. But he made no reply. Perhaps he was too shocked at his subordinate's death wish for him. I was not the only one to think like this. Nigel Price later described his feelings with those two infamous Tac HQ blinds:

> Things were out of control – not with the Battalion or Brigade, but in the universe. Human groupings and organisations had become a pitiful joke. Brigadier, General, Prime Minister, all just pathetic dupes. And in truth we were completely on our own. We were like a flesh-and-blood limb that a farmer or factory worker has accidently caught in a piece of machinery and the cogs rip it off and grind it to pulp. No rationale about it, not even particularly sad – that's what cogs do. And I felt the hopelessness of our position at that split-second moment. The pity of the human condition, if you like. To find ourselves conscious, supposedly rational beings in a blind universe of whirling stone planets.[1]

Coming under heavy bombardment caused an inability to move and my body stiffened. It demanded action in response to the sudden adrenalin, but my brain insisted that I remain under cover. The conflict produced more stress. A temptation to seek even more shelter was averted by the requirements of one's job. Mine was to relay information to and from the Brigade Commander. Others had their men to consider. Some like Mike Fallon, who coolly began to call down counter battery fire, also carried on with their particular jobs. But illogically I still retain a guilty conscience for not having thrown my handset to Corporal Aslett, and then charged out into the open

261

ground to assist locating the wounded like a stooping Martin Entwhistle who called out, 'Right then, I need someone to come with me!'

Nigel answered Martin's call for assistance and also moved out. 'Cometh the hour, cometh the man' now applied to A Company. They were the trailblazers but, if their column had broken, our tab might have been impossible to restart. Their Company Commander, Major David Willis, was up at the front and some distance away from those who had been hit. His 2IC, Captain Narainprasad Rai, was nearer and called on his twenty-odd years of military experience to exhort with Gurkhali expletives his men into cover. He pushed those that moved slowly and then, single-handedly, located his two company casualties while under fire. This QGO's determination and bravery had ensured that his Gurkhas did not buckle at their moment of truth.

Back at Tac HQ Martin Entwhistle had managed to move back by somehow dodging around the explosions. 'OK!' he called out, 'I'm establishing a makeshift RAP just behind Tac HQ! I need two orderlies here and all the casualties to be sent to me now!' The doctor was not going to repeat Wether Ground errors by running around to give first aid and Mark passed this information on the radio to the companies. Tac HQ was worst hit with four casualties that included two British Gunner NCOs. A few metres in front of me an HQ Company Signaller, Lance Corporal Gauriman Limbu, had been hit by shrapnel in the chest and abdomen. He was pulled unceremoniously past my location. Martin, assisted by some of his medical orderlies, got to work a few metres behind me and non-tactically flicked on his torch. Psychologically it was a smart move. The beam of artificial light cut through the dark and chaos to give a much-needed impression to those nearby that someone had taken charge in this emergency situation.

Also hit by shrapnel, both A Company casualties were helped past me. One was moaning and clutching his bleeding chest. Nigel and three Gurkhas were carrying the other, Corporal Gyanbahadur Rai, by his legs and arms. The badly wounded man had been talking calmly and coherently, directing his helpers to get him and themselves into cover. Imagination plays tricks in such situations. The BO had become more than worried at the weird crunching sound which he thought was shattered leg bone being rubbed together. But he soon realized his mistake. It was their boots crunching on the icy bracken and tussocky grass. 'Here, take this!' Martin commanded an orderly and handed him his torch when they arrived at the RAP. Morphine syrettes were injected into limbs. The doctor then began the laborious job of stuffing exposed gut back into a stomach.

'For Christ's sake, I can't see! Get the bloody thing nearer the wound!' he snapped to the orderly as he finished his operation on one casualty, then turned to the others while orderlies started bandaging and two more groaning casualties from B Company were helped into the RAP.

The ferocity of the shelling made the Commandant believe that many other Gurkhas had been hit. Losing control of his Battalion at this critical stage of its advance to battle had been a distinct possibility, but the worst case of all was uppermost in his mind. 'Christ, I've only been in command for eight months,' he remonstrated to himself, 'and yet I've written off the whole bloody Battalion in one night!'[2] His bad conscience and powerful guilt feelings were working overtime in this unbelievably

262

stressful situation. It also demonstrated the extent of the psychological responsibility factor which had been burdened on this officer in overall command. Fortunately he had been and still is, in his own words, the proverbial pessimist, because we had taken only eight casualties. Once again the soft peaty ground had absorbed much of the explosive effect. Indeed one B Company Gurkha, after being treated on the spot, was able to return to his platoon almost immediately.

'Require Hawkeye at our current location for Starlight task,' I requested on my radio in a further bid for a casevac helicopter.

The reply: 'Negative, Hawkeye cannot be provided' was predictable.

Another forty-five minutes had been lost and now it was 08.15 hours but, despite the shelling and casualties, the Brigade Commander's voice insisted: 'You must keep moving forward!'

He was influenced by the Guardsmens' progress in the Tumbledown. Of the forty who had stormed along the Tumbledown, only four were left standing because casualties and guards for POWs had accounted for the rest. By 08.20 hours the centre of Tumbledown had been secured at a cost to Left Flank of five dead and twenty-one wounded, a third of their total strength. Although killing a dozen of the opposition, Left Flank had taken six hours to move 600 metres thereby creating a serious time problem for us. But before we could continue, our casualties had to be evacuated. The consumption of field dressings on the wounded was such that we concluded four, not two, should have been carried per man throughout the Battalion. Head, chest, back, arm, abdomen and leg shrapnel wounds meant that twenty-eight stretcher-bearers, equivalent to a platoon, were now required to remove seven casualties[3]. Most severely wounded was Corporal Gyanbahadur Rai of A Company. Two days previously his sangar had taken a direct hit from a 155-mm shell when he was fortuitously not in it. Now he had no webbing as this had been also shredded by the Wether Ground shell. Other A Company Gurkhas had exchanged fatalistic looks when Gyanbahadur had been hit, rather along the lines: 'If your number's up, you can't avoid it.' His injuries led to an eventual medical discharge from the Gurkhas and qualification for financial compensation from the post-war South Atlantic Fund. As his next Company Commander I was to become involved in his case and he would be awarded a derisory £2,000, but not until after yet another fight through the bureaucratic red tape that administered this charity money.

The bandaged casualties were packed into sleeping bags and attached to saline drips to reduce shock as, with the barrage lifting, stretcher-bearers gathered from B Company and the Recce Platoon. They would need strong arms since the casualties' personal weapons and equipment also had to be carried. Lightweight collapsible stretchers would have been invaluable, but none was available for these Gurkhas' trek back to the Guards' RAP beside Goat Ridge. Meanwhile Nigel Price had moved forward again to locate his two MFCs attached with A Company and check radio communications. He also found Narainprasad sahib perched cross-legged on a flat-topped rock speaking calmly into a radio. The QGO was not aware that his combat jacket left shoulder had been shredded by flying shrapnel as if a tiger had taken a wipe at it. 'Look at this sahib!' exclaimed a worried Nigel pointing to the ruined outer layers of cloth. 'Are you OK?'

The surprised QGO was miraculously unhurt, but all Nigel could hear from him in reply was a strangulated, 'A-a-h . . . !'

Reduced now by thirty-five men, the remaining 371 regrouped. Our advance had been delayed more than an hour, but we prepared to move forward. After lying in water amongst snow and falling shells, the rear Company Commander, Mike Kefford, was relieved our tab began again. His Company was unscathed, but he had to shake two Gurkha Signallers either side of him because, like British soldiers expert in utilizing periods of inactivity, they had fallen asleep. A bizarre mixture of fear, excitement and sense of survival had drained emotions so much that the minefield threat twenty metres away was now forgotten. Reality returned with an easing of shelling, crack of more rifle and machine-gun fire above us, and a hint of first light, grey and cold, that began to seep through the darkness as the precursor to a reluctant dawn. It might even clarify the confusion. We ascended the shepherds' path along the Tumbledown's northern slopes as snow blew around us and the *dush* resumed their shelling more sporadically. Perhaps even then they were having ammunition resupply problems. Nigel looked at the face of Sergeant Krishnaraj Rai. The Signals Platoon Sergeant's face was white and traumatized from the effect of the past hour or so. He saw the BO looking at him, then shook his head and, muttered un-Gurkha-like in limited English, 'I am not a well man, sahib.' Coming under that weight of accurate *dush* artillery fire had not been any fun at all.

To our disadvantage the Battalion's attack would now have to take place in daylight, over open terrain, and under *dush* artillery fire. Of even more significance, our Gunners' ammunition stocks were dwindling fast. At that moment the Guards' Tac HQ radio operator suddenly reported news of Left Flank's success in the Tumbledown's crags: 'Have now secured centre section of the objective. Commencing next phase shortly!'

The crumps from anti-tank 66-mm rocket and 84-mm rounds, laced with rifle fire, indicated a different story. We halted another twenty minutes as A Company began to exploit forward and the firing slackened. *Dush* snipers were still active and the Guards' Right Flank Company took an hour to prepare themselves for their first platoon attack. A Company could not wait, and overtook Right Flank to begin establishing their fire base in preparation for D Company's assault. The voice of Quentin Oates, our Scots Guards' liaison officer, then popped up on the radio. 'Twenty-seven prisoners have been taken by my call sign and include the enemy company's Sunray. They've indicated that there's just one company on your call sign four's objective!'

No time could be wasted in passing on this vital information. 'Mark!' I called out to the busy Adjutant, 'tell D Company there's probably only one *dush* company located on Mount William. That should make their task a bit easier!'

'Roger!' he replied, and his Gurkhali dialogue continued on his overworked radio net as the Commandant insisted through half-clenched teeth, 'Come on! Come on!' The silver-topped piledriver thumped a tattoo into the ground as he waited for news of A Company's progress.

Although the Gurkha fire base's firepower was impressive, the weight of the weapons and ammunition had slowed them down considerably. In addition to three Browning heavy machine guns and eight sustained-fire GPMGs commanded by my Assistant

264

Training Officer, HB sahib, four Milan anti-tank launchers with their eighteen wire-guided missiles were controlled by John Palmer. To 'manpack' this arsenal to the Tumbledown's summit had cost much sweat. Each Browning weighed so much that it had to be broken into four parts and, given to every member of the gun team, each weighed fourteen kilos. The ammunition was the main problem. 4,500 belted rounds per gun had to be split into individual belts of fifty rounds before being given to A Company's riflemen who wore two belts slung around their shoulders as bandoliers and which weighed seven kilos. Every Milan missile carried up the Tumbledown also weighed fourteen kilos, but the Gurkhas' supreme fitness made light work of this and other extra loads. Their BOs also had to be fit fighting alongside the Nepalese – but John, just like Steve Crowsley with his Brownings, held admirable qualifications as a sub-two hour and forty-five minute marathon runner.

At last Mark said, 'A Company's reported their fire base has been secured and everyone's in position!' The Commandant's impatience ceased as we continued up the narrow shepherds' path whilst the Scots Guards began the last phase of their attack against two *dush* platoons. Nigel gabbled Gurkhali into his handset to the Goat Ridge mortar sections, updating them of the fire base's readiness which was the agreed signal for his tubes to go into action once again. It was 10.30 hours. The two sections' limited supply of thirty-six large augmenting cartridges now had to be treated like gold dust. In reality use of these would only enhance the range of less than four per cent of the 800 bombs originally stockpiled the afternoon before.

On the Tumbledown A Company were keen to witness the outcome of their labours, and began to scan the countryside for the *dush*. Captain Hombahadur Gurung's platoon had the best view out to the north, even though the light was still poor. With a face that resembled three kicks in a mud pie, this tough, squat, quick-witted QGO who could munch through a whacking big green chilli as easily as if it was a spoonful of corn-flakes, saw the *dush* running from 2 Para on Wireless Ridge. In addition he detected the threat of an unidentified low-flying helicopter coming towards his platoon.

'*Dush!* Open fire!' yelled the QGO at the Gurkha manning the heavy machine gun attached to his platoon. There was an immediate rattle of shots but, fortunately, the Gurkha gunner missed the vital parts to this aircraft of Teeny Weeny Airways – even though the British crew on board did complain later of how draughty the interior had become with the sudden appearance of some ventilation holes. Including the Goose Green ND incident, this was the fifth near-miss or actual blue-on-blue incident that involved the Gurkhas and for which the fog of war had been responsible. More were to come. The helicopter then fired a missile at the retreating *dush* near Moody Brook and disappeared quickly, but business had only just begun. It reappeared with two others to fire five more missiles at three bunkers containing *dush* 105-mm guns and four hits were recorded. Possibly these were the guns that had fired on us a few hours previously. Driven away by incoming *dush* mortar fire, these helicopters had been led coincidentally by the same pilot and ex-7GR officer who had assisted us at Goose Green. Captain John Greenhalgh had remained enthusiasm personified in these last hours of the war, and was later awarded a Distinguished Flying Cross.

The twenty-five Gurkhas on the mortar line were not enjoying the same success. After only eight to ten rounds fired from each mortar, frantic digging was required as each round fired drove the base plate further and further into the soft peaty ground. The base plates could not be moved away to be repositioned as this would have required them to be adjusted onto their targets again. With the proximity of the Battalion's forward troops to the *dush* positions on Mount William, yet another blue-on-blue could have been a real possibility. Indeed, early on, several rounds fell so close that some Gurkhas had to dive for cover. The firing led to an inevitable encounter with buried rocks which bent the base plate rims and, in a couple of cases, completely fractured them, thereby rendering their tubes useless. One mortar also had its tripod bent. The third, damaged by the Wether Ground shrapnel, was non-operational at the start of this engagement because rounds could not be slid down its barrel. It left only one mortar firing throughout. During the execution of its fire missions, the mortar line also came under fire from *dush* artillery and one shell actually landed in the line but, the reverse slope being relatively steep, it was difficult for the *dush* to acquire an accurate range. Fortunately no casualties were taken. Hits were scored mainly on the forward slopes of Mount William and a total of 272 Gurkha high-explosive mortar rounds would be fired that day; nonetheless, with its maximum range of 8,380 metres, the larger *dush* 120-mm mortar would have been a more suitable weapon to use against this feature.

By now we arrived at the eastern section of the Tumbledown as *dush* 81-mm and 106.6-mm mortar bombs began exploding nearby. Some of A Company's riflemen came into view. I passed by their anxious Company Commander who was sitting under the protruding lip of an isolated rock which, shortly afterwards, received a direct hit. Asked later for an assessment of his Falklands' experiences, the former Oxford University rowing blue's bland reply, 'Oh, it was without doubt the artillery that worried me the most!' disguised the fact that David Willis had been arguably one of the Battalion's luckiest to escape injury.

We passed through the rear A Company platoon and then headed up a narrow re-entrant into the centre of the Tumbledown and recent battle. A steep slope took its toll on weary legs. Movement was made even more difficult by small and large boulders on the ground. 'Come on, what's your worry?' I chided myself, to add philosophically through gritted teeth as the steep ascent up and into the Tumbledown bit into thigh and calf muscles, 'The Khud Race in Hong Kong is much worse than this little lot!'

Four Guardsmen in a small rock recess were busy tending another who had been shot in the left ankle. His foot, still in the blood-soaked sock, was being wrapped up in a field dressing and the four looked up as we passed by, their faces betraying fatigue and shock. A dead Guardsman was wrapped in a green poncho cape a short distance away and further along lay a sergeant face up amongst the rocks. A sprinkle of snowflakes covered his body. Hit in the left knee, an attempt had been made to wrap a field dressing over the wound but bandages trailed from either side of his leg. His rifle had been rammed, muzzle first, into the rocks to mark the owner's location but, for some reason, the stretcher bearers had been unable to reach him and death must have been caused by shock, exposure and loss of blood. Someone from our Battalion eventually placed the Guardsman's beret over the dead man's face. But no time was available to dwell on this strangely serene tableau as a job still remained and, as the

Scots Guards' CO passed by with his entourage, the Commandant rushed to a location just below the Tumbledown's summit. The rest of Tac HQ followed, reaching a sheer rock wall with convenient overhang that towered over us at 250 metres above sea level. 'OK everyone, we'll stop here. This is as good a place as any to set up a temporary command post,' I shouted breathlessly with my heart pumping overtime and leg muscles suffering from a lactic acid overdose. We were now five and a half clicks, or three miles away from the outskirts of Stanley. Mount William lay less than one click to our south.

'We'll have to alter the timings for B and D Companies' crossing of their start lines!' ordered the Commandant a few minutes later before making a rapid recalculation for B Company.

'Roger, new time for B Company is 13.00 hours. I'll send that info to all three companies now,' confirmed Mark and the Battalion command net vibrated with the Adjutant's fluent Gurkhali instructions.

It was 12.00 hours. The British artillery and Gurkha mortars, with the attached D Company MFC directing mortar fire from an OP, continued to provide an unpleasant time for their customers on Mount William. This was also observed by the first Gurkha platoon on the Tumbledown, commanded by Lieutenant Tekbahadur Limbu. Tumbledown's loss made Mount William untenable and they saw the *dush* running first one way and then the other to avoid incoming shells. Trapped, some even ran into the sea to escape. No counter-attack could have been rehearsed from Mount William and a few *dush* stood there in demoralized groups. One of their MFCs was still directing mortar fire onto us in the Tumbledown and a convoy of three Guards' stretcher bearer teams, blowing two stretcher bearers to pieces. About twenty Mount William *dush* then began moving towards the Tumbledown, but it was unclear if they had surrendered. Two Gurkha mortar bombs exploded near them, and they dived to the ground when two Gurkha GPMG(SF) bursts of fire sent them running into Scots Guards' arms. The Ministry of Defence official post-war dispatch on the South Atlantic campaign by Admiral Sir John Fieldhouse could not resist telling the story:

> Some (Argentines), ejected from Tumbledown by 2nd Battalion Scots Guards, realised that they must pass Mount William, now firmly in Gurkha hands. They chose instead to retrace their steps and surrender to the Guardsmen.[4]

Its understatement contrived, however, to get the detail of this contact wrong – the only occasion during the war when Gurkha small-arms fire had been directed at *dush* ground forces. Enough was enough for those few who had remained on Mount William because when push really came to shove there had been no contest. The Gurkha irresistable force had overcome the *dush* immovable object without any kukri-wielding charge. *Dush* expenditure of artillery and mortar ammunition on us also contributed greatly to ending any potential resistance because, without ammunition replenishment, battles cannot be fought. Mortar bombs continued to land near Tac HQ, as well as a couple of bombs which exploded fifty metres below us on the route we had climbed to this vantage point.

To the north of the Tumbledown lay Moody Valley, along whose southern side we had moved a few hours before. Beyond, forming the valley's northern side, lay Wireless Ridge. It led westwards to the Mount Longdon battlefield that the *dush* Tumbledown snipers had targeted after 3 Para had taken their objective, whilst below me lay the interior of this eerie place where flushing out the *dush* had presented the Guards with such great difficulties. The Tumbledown, which is the correct local name for this area, was marked on *dush* maps as *Cerro Destartelado*, a Spanish name meaning untidy or tumbledown hill. Although the latter name had been derived from an incident when a herd of wild horses once stampeded over the north-east escarpment, untidy appeared more appropriate for the entire feature as, looking westwards, I gazed down into its long jumbled formations. Along the north side ran two parallel rock walls fifty-feet high in places where the floor in between was not more than fifty-feet across. Such terrain enabled construction of well-prepared positions sited in underground caves big enough to take two to four *dush* and where, outside, some fought from two-foot high sangers, slit trenches and well-made stone bunkers. Wire was not used as part of a positional defence concept and lack of aggressive patrolling, not keeping minefields covered by fire, and an unwillingness to take calculated risks were other elementary mistakes. Even so, the motivated *dush* in the Tumbledown had been above average.

As shells continued to shriek overhead and explode along both sides of Moody Valley kicking up showers of peat which left brown scars on the frozen tan coloured landscape, radio requests for casevac helicopters were being made by the Guards' Tac HQ: 'This call sign has now collected many casualties at our current location. Several are seriously wounded. One has been shot through the neck, and he's in need of urgent treatment. I say again: it is of utmost priority Hawkeye begins casevac ops!' But the shelling prevented helicopters from flying and much time was being lost. The urging became more intense: 'It's vital that Hawkeye evacuates our casualties to Starlight higher formation immediately. I say again – immediately! If this does not happen now, then lives will be lost!'

The Brigade Commander, still near Mount Harriet, took the hint and, joining in the general chorus of agitation for TWA action, barked at Brigade Main HQ in Fitzroy: 'For goodness sake, where on earth are these damned helicopters? Get them into the air now!'

As if to underline this emergency, the Guards' Tac HQ radio operator then reported: 'It's now confirmed that the casualty with the neck wound at our location has just died.'

Listening to this radio chat of pain and death, I became a useless witness by my inability to provide assistance – not that this was my job to do so. News of the wounded Guardsman's alleged death was taken personally as if he had been my close friend. Worse than witnessing it, my imagination ran riot with the unfolding scenario below me. It was unprofessional, but I had become involved emotionally and took out my binoculars for a better view. A distant clatter of rotor blades indicated that at least one pilot was willing now to ignore the dangers. This former Scots Guards Colour Sergeant proved Regimental blood was thicker than water as his Scout landed and, with rotors still burning and turning in the bitter cold air, casualties began to be lifted carefully into the small helicopter.

During a lull in the mortaring, more helicopters landed. Still using my binoculars, I made out the blue of woollen balaclava helmets which probably belonged to the two men of the Marine Commandos' Mountain and Arctic Warfare Cadre who had been the guides for both battalions. They walked slowly, circumnavigating the many rock obstacles, to disappear from view down and along our approach route to this battlefield. A few Guardsmen were also moving up towards us and the Tumbledown's eastern end. Out of curiosity, I tabbed down the steep slope a little and one of them, an officer, stopped me.

'Do you know the whereabouts of my CO?' he asked.

I was a little shocked. It was the first time I had met Major Iain Dalzell-Job since our platoon commanders' course ten years before when we were members of the same syndicate, and only illustrated how the Brigade's battalions had kept to themselves on board *QE2*. We were too traumatized by the previous night's experiences to acknowledge each other openly but, after a silent mutual recognition, he wandered away as I gesticulated vaguely towards the east.

'B Company's still moving, sir,' one Tac HQ British Signaller informed me when I got back to our perch in the rocks. Then he asked almost tenderly, 'Fancy a brew, sir? We're making a cuppa when we've melted some snow.'

'Don't see why not! Thanks a lot,' I replied to his generosity. A life-giving cup of tea was a good British tradition in a tricky situation and would be wonderful now despite the odd mortar bomb or two exploding nearby. There was no water so he and Corporal Aslett gathered up handfuls of snow and then put it into a pair of mess tins soot-blackened from previous meals. These were then heated up on the small blocks of flaming hexamine placed in the equally small portable tin cooking stoves. This insignificant, but laborious, job exposed hands to the vicious cold which meant that the thick woollen inners of our arctic gloves had to be put back in double-quick time afterwards. Without these, our hands would have quickly frozen into chunks of numbed flesh but, even wearing them, it took several minutes before even a little warmth was restored.

Meanwhile the voice in my radio handset insisted: 'Little opposition left on Mount William. More enemy are standing in groups on Sapper Hill, but most are heading towards Stanley.' I failed to register the significance of this news as hot tea was more important than anything else, including shelling and mortaring. Perhaps I was in denial. Focus was on the black masking tape stuck around the top of my metal mug as insulating material – but it did not prevent my lips from being scalded with every sip.

By now, at 12.30 hours, with the fire base ready to support the assault onto the Tumbledown's north-east spur, Lester Holley and his FOO had already arrived at their start line twenty minutes ahead of the Company's main body. The two officers called for a harassing fire mission against a *dush* platoon of B Company, 6 Infantry Regiment running from the Tumbledown. The leading platoon of the Guards' Right Flank Company had only fifty rounds between them plus fixed bayonets ready to resist any possible counter-attack but, confronted by the Gurkha-directed shelling, the *dush* continued their escape along Moody Valley towards Stanley. Lester's artillery bombardment packed quite a punch. Arguably the last of the war, it was fired by no less than three batteries with one combined salvo from these eighteen guns equivalent to three exploding Harrier laser-guided bombs. On Wireless Ridge, Brigadier Julian Thompson, the Brigade Commander of 3 Commando Brigade, mistakenly thought that the *dush* were responsible for this shelling on his Commandos' forming up point for the next phase of the battle that night.[5] It would be also commented upon by the *dush* platoon commander, Second Lieutenant Augusto Lamadrid:

> . . . we fell back; it was starting to get light. The whole hill had fallen by then, and we were on lower ground, just south of Moody Brook. We eventually got through to Stanley, through what I would like to say was a perfect barrage fired by the Royal Artillery. We had to wait for breaks in the firing, but I still lost a man killed there. I had thirteen men at the end, from the forty-five I started with, but another seven men joined us later.[6]

The hands on my watch had moved to 12.50 hours. There was little time remaining as the agitated Commandant became concerned at B Company's slower than wished for progress. As the Gurkhas filed past, his impatient cries of, 'Come on B Company! *Chitto, chitto!*' were made in an attempt to provide more impetus to the riflemen in their stumbling and slipping over the sea of rock. They came closer with rifles, and kukris clanking on webbing equipment. Their faces were impassive as dozens of Gurkhas passed by me. I took a second glance at each of them. No sign of the red mist yet as they ran on – and then *through* an anti-personnel minefield to join up with Lester some distance away. But they were thirty minutes too late as their imminent arrival had halted a *dush* N Company platoon counter-attack. This unit pulled back, leaving only these disappointed Gurkhas to find three terrified *dush* of B Company, 6th Infantry Regiment, hiding in a trench that also contained the body of a fourth killed by shellfire.

These promptly surrendered and were relieved to be back-loaded by helicopter to Fitzroy, but the Gurkhas could not be placated by this success. Their prisoners had been probably left behind to cover their platoon's retreat. One was an English speaking 5th Marine Infantry Battalion medical orderly who promptly told his captors, 'There were three things that the British had which were most feared by us Argentines. The Harrier aircraft, artillery and – you Gurkhas!' And neither could any Gurkha consolation also be found in another 6th Infantry Regiment soldier's conviction that every Gurkha on the battlefield was capable of hurling his kukri with devastating accuracy from a range of 100 metres.

Determined not to let the *dush* off the hook, the Commandant moved forward to assess the situation prior to D Company's assault. Behind him stood Mike Fallon with A Company's FOO, Captain Keith Swinton, and the latter's Bombadier Signaller. Nigel Price was ten metres away. The Gunners were rejigging the artillery fire plan when they and others near them came under heavy small-arms fire. Further behind, Tac HQ was still preparing for the assault when the air cracked above us and, with a ping, a few of these rounds struck rock. We were below the line of fire but, insignificant to previous events, it had been ignored and I foolishly returned to my tea. Ahead, the situation was serious. It was assumed that the firing had come from *dush* snipers and, to counter the problem, an 84-mm anti-tank launcher from A Company had been ordered forward. Meanwhile Steve Crowsley had already begun crawling forward to get into a position near enough to throw some *dush* hand grenades he had purloined at Goose Green. Suddenly he identified the real cause of the problem and yelled at the Commandant, 'The fire's coming from the Scotsmen, Colonel!'

As the silver-topped propeller rotated at full bore signalling *extreme* impatience and one of the many Scots Guards' high velocity bullets contrived to miss the Commandant's helmet by a mere inch or so, the latter yelled back, 'So get off your bloody arse then, and move forward to stop them!'

In the heat of the moment he forgot that the harassed Machine Gun Platoon Commander's priority was, in fact, to direct Gurkha covering fire for the D Company assault. Nevertheless in all this chaos Steve obeyed the order and courageously jumped up, waved his arms and screamed at three myopic Guardsmen, 'Stop firing! Stop firing immediately, you bloody stupid idiots! Can't you see we're on your side? We're the Gurkhas!'

His vocabulary of expletives fired off at the Guards' Right Flank Company was quite astonishing, but did not include any passwords. The blue-on-blue that both Battalions had sought to avoid during the confusion of darkness now occurred during the hazards of daylight. There were no John Wayne histrionics of the wounded with the victim, Keith Swinton, as he merely turned to his Bombadier who stood on his right to remark, 'I think I've been shot!' The NCO replied with a matter-of-fact, 'Well, turn around, sir, and we'll have a look.' Keith complied and, sure enough, there was a bloody mess on his back. The surreal dialogue continued with the Bombadier's eminently sensible recommendation, 'I think, then, that you ought to lie down, sir.'

The manner in which this conversation was conducted between these two men provided a comforting structure to a frightening situation. Keith, once more, did as he was told. His legs crumpled from under him and he sat down – while Mark received a report about our latest casualty on the Battalion net. The Adjutant then informed the doctor and updated me, 'Keith Swinton's been hit! Can you organize a chopper to evacuate him?'

As I made the radio call for a helicopter, the firing ceased and wounded FOO was examined by Martin Entwhistle. Keith was sucking in his breath because a lung had collapsed. The over-worked doctor found that a ricochet had passed through the one and a half-inch diameter area where there are no vital organs such as the heart. In other words, one inch had made the difference between life and death. There was no exit wound. Martin administered morphine, bandaged the wound, put the FOO onto a saline drip and into a sleeping bag where he winced and, in suppressing the pain, complained not unnaturally, 'It's getting a bit sore now.'

Casevaced out in the helicopter, Keith received his further treatment as if this had been a minor wound. Up and about after two weeks, he made a miraculously fast recovery – although nine months later came a psychological reaction. But the fog of war surrounding this incident prevailed as Captain Tim Spicer, the Scots Guards' Ops Officer, wrote incorrectly seventeen years later: 'One of the Gurkha soldiers did not know the password and was wearing a helmet so, taking him for an Argentine in the early-morning gloom, one of our soldiers shot him dead.'[7]

Meanwhile the Guards were counting their final total of nine dead and forty-three wounded. A 'no-helmet' policy had not only contributed to the blue-on-blue, but also to their own casualties. The possibility of self-inflicted disaster in all this confusion had been ever present because *dush* sniping was to account for two dead Guardsmen, both shot in the head through their cloth cap star. These made good aiming marks because a sniper's bullet also caused the severe head injury of Right Flank's Lieutenant Robert Lawrence. If only they could have learnt from the lessons of Northern Ireland where, for example, Light Infantry battalions painted their silver bugle cap badges black in order to reduce such a risk. Lawrence's bravery on the Tumbledown was recognized by his award of a Military Cross but, although his appalling incapacitation, medical treatment and other long-term consequences were described graphically in a book and BBC television film[8], the possibility of preventing such a wound was never mentioned. Ironically, the book's front cover misleadingly portrayed two Paras wearing GPR (glass reinforced plastic) helmets which could brake the effect of a hit from a high-velocity round. Indeed on Wether Ground three days previously, Rifleman Baliprasad Rai could acknowledge conclusively that his life had been saved by the wearing of the older model 1944 helmet and its braking qualities on flying shrapnel.

H-hour had been now readjusted for 14.00 hours and fire plan altered accordingly, but Mike Kefford's men had to negotiate more problems. As they moved around the eastern end of Tumbledown the persistent *dush* 81-mm and 106.6-mm mortar fire, probably coming from Sapper Hill, became heavier. Hunting for the D Company Gurkhas who had taken cover amongst the rocks, the bombs were more unwelcome than the artillery. They fell from a more vertical trajectory than 105-mm shells and, with a correspondingly slightly less shrill sound, had greater accuracy. The *dush* mortar base plate crews pumped in these rounds as if they had already decided to bug out of their current location once all ammunition had been exhausted. One of Mike's QGOs, Captain Bhuwansing Limbu, turned round in the middle of this *feu d'enfer* and, through the dirt, mud and noise a huge grin split his face. Then, in a moment of Gurkha innocence, he shouted in his perfect Oxford accent to Mike, 'Jolly exciting this, isn't it sahib?'

The explosions reached a crescendo after twenty minutes, when they suddenly stopped. There were no casualties and D Company prepared to advance. Almost simultaneously, at 14.00 hours, the Brigade Commander rapped out on the Brigade radio net I was still monitoring: 'Warning order. This formation be prepared to attack Port Stanley!' From the sound of his voice he meant business, too.

THE BAILLIES' HOME.

PHASE V – AFTERMATH

Chapter Twenty-two

ON MOUNT WILLIAM

... attaining one hundred victories in one hundred battles is not the pinnacle of excellence. Subjugating the enemy's army without fighting is the true pinnacle of excellence ...
Sun Tzu

'When, apart from Exercise WELSH FALCON,' I asked myself, 'had I last been in a FIBUA exercise?'

The answer was only twice, as a cadet at Sandhurst, and then Imber Village on Salisbury Plain a decade before. My personal knowledge of 'fighting in built-up areas', the acknowledged worst phase of war for a fighting infantry soldier, was therefore decidedly limited. A 15.30 hours Harrier laser-guided bomb strike on Sapper Hill, four kilometres away to the east was also confirmed, with our Rubber Duck FAC still co-located with Alternative Battalion HQ on Long Toenail likely be involved. Then the Welsh Guards were given their radio warning order: 'Prepare to move forward to secure Sapper Hill.' This was the last high ground before Stanley and the implications percolated into my punch-drunk brain. Meanwhile D Company moved, only to be delayed yet again when confronted by the anti-personnel minefield which B Company had previously walked through. Mark informed the Commandant. Another change of plan.

'OK. Slip D Company's H-hour back another sixty minutes to 15.00 hours,' Mark was ordered. He, in turn, relayed this to Mike.

Sergeant Ron Wrega and his two men from the Royal Engineers' 9 Parachute Squadron then worked feverishly for another forty-five minutes to clear a path through the minefield by removing tripwires, booby traps and detonating five anti-personnel mines. It was the culmination of a fortnight's work for Ron Wrega who, post hostilities, carried out further minefield clearance at Port Howard on West Falkland. Later awarded the Military Medal, he would modestly describe it as, 'an embarrassment'.

D Company were able to move forward again through the path cleared for them by the Sappers and at last they crossed their start line. The mortars had prepared smoke rounds to cover the Company's advance where Mike Kefford's plan had been to attack with two platoons up and one in reserve. Once the northern slopes of Mount William was seized, the third platoon would then hook around from the east and take the southern slopes. But their position as the British point sub-unit was to be cruelly taken from them because, just after 15.00 hours, a helicopter filled with some of the Welsh

Guards' Royal Marine Commando reinforcements flew overhead as part of the operation to secure Sapper Hill. By error, the aircraft landed on this objective defended by the 5th Marine Infantry Battalion's M Company and other units. The campaign's ensuing final firefight produced two British casualties and three *dush* dead, but there was, of course, no reaction from Mount William as D Company advanced into the open.

Tac HQ now experienced a rapidly evolving order, counter-order, disorder situation as, like the tail end of an exercise, odd radio reports on the *dush* status began to be mingled with strange orders. One about the Harrier GR3 strike at 15.30 hours began the confusion: 'Foxtrot Golf Alpha on Sapper Hill is to be cancelled!'

Eagerly awaiting this first ground attack sortie of the day, we had been disappointed with the overall lack of action because, according to Rubber Duck, another fifteen could have been flown. Both TACPs had been requesting GR3 launches during the day, but 5 Brigade's operational rigidity only demonstrated lack of experience in controlling offensive air support assets. The pilots' frustration in having to wait on fifteen-minute cockpit alert during those last seventy-two hours was confirmed three weeks later by Captain Lynley Middleton, the Flag Captain of *Hermes*, during a visit to our Goose Green ops room.

'What *are* they thinking about at Brigade?' I wondered at our Tumbledown command post.

'Sounds like the exercise is coming to an end,' remarked Kit Spencer, 'better get someone to tune into the Gunners' radio net as they're always the first to get new ops information.'

The Commandant then cheated in anticipating D Company's seizure of its real estate as he seized my handset to report to the Brigade Commander: 'Mount William is now secured!' Apparently he received the reply: 'OK, the town's yours!'

Our next move would be to Stanley in which nearly 10,000 *dush* were milling around and who outnumbered British ground forces by two to one. Suddenly another voice in my handset countermanded the Brigade Commander's invitation to a night-time rendezvous with the *dush*: 'Firing is only permitted in self-defence!'

It was Brendan Lambe, his Brigade Major at Fitzroy. A playful Don Macauley, our attached Royal Signals subaltern, then acted strangely by snatching my handset to transmit an anonymous off-the-cuff remark: 'Why's that? That's not why we're supposed to be here!' Being under fire for the past four days had also, perhaps, smitten Don with that existential authority bug.

The BM, who would receive a Mention in Dispatches for his work in the HQ, countered such a smart-arse question and comment with an understandably savage: 'Shut up, and keep off the bloody net!'

I looked across at Moody Valley where 2 Para were marching down in file from Wireless Ridge towards Moody Brook and Stanley with four Scorpion and Scimitar light tanks of the Blues and Royals to the rear. This was most odd. My handset provided another update: 'Enemy have moved away from Mount William towards Sapper Hill and Stanley. 200 enemy now standing in groups on Sapper Hill.' Yet another made us wonder even more: 'Roger, air strike on Sapper Hill now confirmed cancelled and the aircraft placed on hold.'

'What was that? What is going on now?' I asked out loud, glaring at the handset and wondering who in the hell had chosen to put *yet* another spanner in the works of the Gurkha assault on Mount William. The answer was, simply, the *dush* themselves. Still not grasping the significance of this message and 2 Para's exodus from the Wireless Ridge area, I listened to the BM's orders which were to end the day's and campaign's operations:

> Hello all stations, this is zero. A white flag has been seen flying over Stanley. Higher formation requires that everyone stands fast. I say again. All call signs of this formation must remain in their current location until further orders. There is to be no exploitation forward beyond the 39 Easting. Cease fire and check all weapons.

Such instantaneous lifting of the fog of war felt like being on Fantasy Island rather than the Falklands. The mind had become so tuned to our impending task, that it was difficult to interpret, let alone believe, the message's consequences – but then life is all about change. 'OK! It must be a ceasefire!' I had to repeat out loud to ensure some feeling of reality. Relief then arrived in capital letters and, with it, my inner reaction, 'So is this how it feels to have, at a stroke, one ton of bricks falling off one's shoulders?'

Elation was tempered with fatigue as I passed this news to the Commandant. He was not amused. Neither was D Company who saw no *dush*. Another update arrived of even more significance:

> The Argentine forces on the Falkland Islands are about to surrender. Negotiations will commence this evening. However you are reminded that at the moment we still remain at war with Argentina, and 'cap' – Charlie Alpha Papa – will continue to be flown. Normal air precautions against anything happening in Argentina should be continued.

'Endex confirmed, folks!' sang out the chirpy Kit Spencer to Tac HQ.

The bare-headed Commandant squatted down by the side of my radio set. He conferred with the Brigade Commander again. 'Roger, out.' He looked at us. There was a sudden change of mood akin to a sinking feeling. 'It's all over,' murmured Colonel David, acute disappointment on his face, and shoulders suddenly slumping. The dream of Gurkha glory had gone with the wind. He, and we, had approached to the extreme edge of Pandora's box only to have the lid shut just at that moment. There would be no close quarter battle. Did he now have any tinge of regret with his courageous refusal to assist the Scots Guards earlier that morning? Hopefully not. After all, the decision of his life had been proved right by their daylight blue-on-blue.

'They're talking about white flags over Port Stanley,' he said slowly as if not believing reality, 'so we're to remain here. Mark, give me your handset. I must update D Company.' He decided to ignore the Brigadier's order to remain in our current locations with his follow-up radio orders to Mike Kefford: 'A ceasefire is now in effect. Fire only in self defence. The enemy will be negotiating for a surrender and we must not jeopardize these negotiations. Continue to the objective. Clear it and go firm. Confirm when completed, then this call sign will join you.'

D Company took Mount William unopposed just before 16.00 hours. Indeed, the Gurkha UK Rear Party, acting as extras in the John Cleese film being made at Church Crookham had more success in their kukri charge than Mike's men. The latter checked empty trenches in this abandoned portion of *Islas las Malvinas* and, soldiers being soldiers, there was also some souvenir hunting. But a unique prize lay in one of these nineteen trenches dotted around the western and southern slopes of Mount William. It was unseen by most until the observant Jeremy McTeague spotted the Golden Fleece for which the Battalion had strived for so long. He snapped up the crumpled blue and white Argentine national flag emblazoned with a grubby golden sun. The following year it would be packed into his main baggage sent by sea as part of the Battalion's move from the UK to Hong Kong. It was an attractive item because, after his baggage arrived, Jeremy discovered his battlefield booty had vanished and, incensed at the theft, promptly lodged a £200 insurance claim.

As snow swirled around them on the bitterly cold wind, D Company's frustration grew. They confirmed that no minefields were in the immediate area, then sited themselves in all-round defence and began to dig. To emulate the deeds of their fathers they and the remainder of the Battalion had trained zealously for the fight of their lives. They had suffered on the final leg of a long sea voyage, had withstood the Argentine shelling at Wether Ground for forty-eight hours, and then had been attacked by the latter's last shell reserves during that tab to Mount William. Displaying courage while on the receiving end had been too abstract for them. They were more concerned with losing an opportunity to achieve *bahaduri* i.e. killing the *dush* and being awarded a gallantry medal. There could be no substitute for this, the only reason why the Gurkhas had participated in the 'Foklands' War. One QGO knew why the Battalion had not managed to close with the *dush*. 'I think, sahib,' HB sahib later told me sadly, 'the necessary *bhagya* (fate) to achieve *bahaduri* had been lacking.'

However a few Gurkhas seemed pleased with the result when ITN's Mike Nicholson recorded Bill Dawson's spontaneity at the Alternative Battalion HQ's location on Long Toenail:

> At five to four that afternoon, our major came running excitedly out of his bunker towards us: the radio message had just come through.
>
> 'There's a white flag flying over Stanley. It's all over. Bloody marvellous . . . bloody, bloody marvellous!'
>
> It was a wonderful way to end the war, but it had happened so suddenly that Bernard (Hesketh) had not captured it on camera. At this juncture, that could not be allowed to happen. So we asked our major to go back inside his bunker and do it all over again. Which he did . . . four times and three times something went wrong, first with the camera, then with the microphone, then he fluffed his lines. On the final attempt with his Gurkhas cheering him, we had a take.
>
> Faked or not it did not matter, then or now. There was a white flag over Stanley, and it *was* bloody marvellous![1]

278

But Gurkha disappointment was again reflected by the unrehearsed disgust on Captain Khile Rai's weathered face as he listened to Bill's Gurkhali explanation of the cease-fire. The Alternative Battalion HQ 2IC glowered into the camera lens as he turned to walk away in disgust. His action personified the general Gurkha mood while, in this late East Falklands' afternoon of lost opportunity, Colonel David continued to readjust his Gurkha locations – but quite contrary to the Brigadier's orders.

A Company went firm on the eastern section of the Tumbledown and B Company moved down to its western end, while Tac HQ began tabbing to Mount William. Once there, Bill's Alternative Battalion HQ would marry up with us. In a cold, inhospitable environment that the *dush* had endured for the past ten weeks we followed the route already taken by D Company past abandoned tents, bunkers, weapons and other equipment. I took out my camera to begin taking photographs of everything and everyone. Recording this scene was personally important. At the end of the path, having carefully avoided the anti-personnel minefield carelessly marked with a single strand of green wire, a panorama came into view. There, nestling beside Stanley Harbour seven kilometres away was Stanley, the goal the Gurkhas never reached. Through my binoculars I searched for the famous white flag, but there was nothing to be seen this Monday. Perhaps a white sheet hanging on a line during this washing day in the capital had caused yet another fog of war muddle. Indeed the white flag vision emanated from our A Company. They had informed Bill Dawson on Long Toenail, who then relayed this message to Brigade HQ. Memsahib *Thatcher le Thecharyo* used the Gurkha error effectively in her House of Commons statement later that day.

We passed through B Company who were moving back in the opposite direction to meet a tired and subdued Scots Guards' Tac HQ. Although in a similar state, the blue-on-blue incident did not prevent us from congratulating them on their work which eventually was to become a new Regimental battle honour. A request would be made that the Tumbledown battle should also become a 7GR battle honour based on the logic that we had contributed to the final outcome. This would be refused, even though the Gurkhas had validated a central tenet of Sun Tzu's ancient, but universal, book on the art of war. The Guards had lost men, however neither pity, euphoria, dis-appointment or fatigue dulled wits so much that none remained unaware of the current threat which Mark voiced for us all, 'Watch out for mines everyone!' We had witnessed that these could be in places least expected and our tab across the same saddle of ground D Company had traversed was therefore carried out cautiously.

'Hello, what's this?' I called out, alarmed at black wire on the ground. My fears were quickly dispelled when realizing it formed part of the Argentine communication system between the Tumbledown and Mount William.

Our safe arrival at D Company's location was only one small part of the reshuffle of units into their final locations. Most Paras and Marine Commandos continued to converge on the outskirts of Stanley while the depleted Welsh Guards, who with their reinforcement of two 40 Commando companies had failed during the night to find a way throught the minefield south-west of Mount William, secured Sapper Hill by 16.57 hours. The Brigadier had achieved his goal despite senior Marine Commando oppo-sition, but whether he would have succeeded in pushing up the 1st/7th Gurkha Rifles to compete with 3 Commando Brigade in the retaking of Stanley against *dush* opposition is debatable. Instead our A and B Companies continued the mundane job of consolidating on the Tumbledown whilst the Scots Guards occupied its centre section. Tac HQ, meanwhile, had climbed the bleak northern slopes of Mount William to rejoin D Company contemplating what might have been.

Under a canopy of dark clouds that scudded along in the wind and threatened another uncomfortable East Falklands' night, I selected another Tac HQ location. Nearby amongst the rocks was an Argentine Marine. 'The elephant' had charged right over him and only the lower part of his legs and boots protruded from under a dark grey blanket speckled with snowflakes. Sixteen Argentines had died and sixty-four had been wounded[2] defending the Tumbledown and Mount William area. He was one of them and had been killed only hours before. A small pool of blood near his head, FAL rifle shattered in two, and adjacent mortar bomb crater were the clues which made Colonel David remark to a solemn Nigel Price, 'That one's yours!' It was an irony the dead Marine also had been a mortarman.[3]

I felt no anger, only pity. His tragedy underlined our luck with the Argentine shelling, and information soon circulated around Tac HQ of another body on top of Mount William – maybe it was the MFC who had directed mortar fire onto the Tumbledown. I informed Brigade HQ of these stiffs' locations for later collection as Captain Khile Rai, fresh from his experiences with the Argentine artillery and joint BBC/ITN TV camera team on Long Toenail, arrived with the Alternative Battalion HQ. His annoyance at the ceasefire knew no end as, with macabre humour, he poked the barrel of his rifle into the Marine's side and barked, 'Eh! Stand-to!'

Most ignored this symbol of the final outcome of the junta's adventure – and dug. We needed shelter as the weather was worsening with alternating sleet and snow showers. Then Corporal Chris Aslett, on radio watch, called out, 'Sir, I've just received a red air alert from Brigade!'

'Shit, that's the last thing we need now,' I complained, 'ensure that info's passed on to the companies, Corporal Aslett.'

Bill Dawson commented dryly, 'Sounds as though they might go for an air counterattack. I haven't heard anyone say anything about them surrendering their Air Force or, come to think of it, their Navy. And don't forget that they've also still got their forces intact on West Falkland. I bet that some sort of preliminary planning is already being carried out for a counter-invasion there.'

'So will the Gurkhas become involved in that, as we've missed out on things here?' I asked without expecting any answer in return. There was none as lookouts became posted and our shell scrape excavations speeded up. The weather then really went sour, frequent snow squalls blowing up to gust continually into our faces.

Another message on the Brigade radio net momentarily made us forget these appalling conditions: 'Negotiations will begin tonight in Stanley for an unconditional Argentine surrender of all their forces in the Falklands.' But although it was tempting to contemplate our rapid removal from this godforsaken place to decent accommodation, the capital was certainly one place not to be as Robacio, the Argentine Marine CO, later described:

280

The place lived on the legend made bigger by fear. Fear of the British Commandos, fear of the sophisticated weapons, of the Gurkhas, fear of the fear in Puerto Argentino, where many unnecessary men were kept and where, at sunset, it was incredibly dangerous to be found, for at the sound made by the wind or at the imagined movement of a shadow, the shooting would start.[4]

Helicopter assets also remained unavailable, except for the Gazelle which approached from Mount Harriet and landed nearby. 'It's Sunray from higher formation!' observed Mark as a figure clambered out of the cockpit.

Despite his setbacks the Brigadier seemed a happy man. He strode up to us. 'Everything all right here? Everyone OK? Congratulations! You did well last night.' He looked at me and smiled again. 'Well done!'

Never *ever* a blue-eyed boy of his, I was surprised at this unexpected positive feedback and merely continued my digging into the Falklands' peat while the Commandant talked to him. The Brigadier was proud of his formation's achievements. More than 3,000 men and 460 tons of stores had been moved from their landing place at San Carlos by sea, air and land to Fitzroy and Bluff Cove sixty kilometres distant and from where, only eleven days later, the Brigade's night attack was launched. Including its original units of 2 and 3 Para, the Brigade suffered ninety-eight killed and 244 wounded and would receive 116 individual gallantry awards and eleven for meritorious service. So the Brigadier later sent a signal to all Brigade unit UK Rear Parties:

Would you kindly inform all Commanding Officers' wives and all Rear Parties that we are in very good shape. The Brigade was second to none in the role it played to force the enemy into total surrender. Let them all be proud of their men whose determination and bravery carried each day against odds of 3 to 1 and an enemy who fought at times to the last man. Inevitably we have taken casualties. We shall take great care of our wounded and even now we mourn our dead. Our sympathies go to all those whose husbands or sons have been lost. Will you also let all wives know that we have not received any letters dated later than 21 May. It is important that we now stay in touch and I propose to send a sitrep daily to this end which I would be grateful if you could repeat to families. You can be proud of the Brigade. It has shown itself to be a fighting formation in every sense of the term. The men you see when we return will walk in the way that only those who have been through such an experience can walk. They have proved themselves. They are men of some consequence and stature now. They are soldiers who have fought and won their war.[5]

After his departure, two Wessex delivered Tac HQ's and D Company's bergens, and some much-needed compo rations. Although ensuring minimal comfort, this also indicated a delay to our departure, to be confirmed by the Adjutant's return from the helicopters' drop-off site in the shallow valley between the Tumbledown and Mount William.

'What's the matter Mark?' I asked as he was shaking his head.

'Uh! One pilot must be pessimistic over the outcome of the ceasefire,' he replied, 'because he's also delivered a large consignment of small-arms ammunition to us!'

Whatever the reason for this aviator's generosity, no air counter-attack from the Argentine mainland was launched that evening or night. This threat, the Falklands' winter environment, and Gurkhas' depressive reaction, prevented us from celebrating but, although awake throughout that night under an irritatingly flapping poncho cape and in my revolting green slug that continued to provide no defence against the cold and wind, did not prevent my private rejoicing. The sudden transition from war to peace had breathtakingly expanded into infinity from previously contracted time horizons. It marooned one in a psychological and emotional limbo, and took more than a while to become accustomed to this new situation as I began to contemplate life without war. This included my girls in UK where Tove had been recording her reactions:

> I don't know if I'm laughing or crying, in fact I do both . . . I'm so, so tired. Yet so awake. The ceasefire news has just come through on the TV, and the telephone went three times in the last hour . . . Is it really true? No more fighting? Does this mean you're safe from now on? Does it mean you will be coming home soon? Sorry about the writing – had nothing to eat – but two stiff whiskies. Oh dear. Then Emily and Victoria <u>both</u> woke up half an hour ago – just put them back. I swear they <u>sense</u> it all. Anyway – the whisky will make me sleep . . . Ceasefire means no shooting tonight – but will it bring you home? Sorry to ramble – but you're getting a good impression of how I feel. Confused. Elated. Trying to be calm.

Next morning my steel helmet had been replaced by an arctic cap whose inner woollen lining side flaps made effective ear warmers. Over this went my parka hood when weather conditions deteriorated even more with the snow blowing into our faces and settling on everything. A and B Companies on the Tumbledown had not received any of their bergens the previous evening and their Gurkhas, minus sleeping bags, had been forced to take refuge in the abandoned Argentine Marine tents and crude rock shelters. We also received a visit from an incensed Lester Holley who made our ears even warmer.

'You blokes in Tac HQ should get your act sorted out! My company's had an awful night because of your lack of organization. So now I'm having to send some of my men back to the Two Sisters area and gather up bergens and sleeping bags that we left there!' he complained bitterly before turning to fight his way back through the gusts of yet another snow storm to B Company's position. Everyone, including him, had been under considerable stress for twenty hours so his anger was understandable, but complaint misdirected. We *had* tried to coordinate the collection of his kit, but the required helicopter lift had been unavailable.

On the Brigade radio net an all-stations call informed us: 'It's now confirmed that a surrender document has been signed for all Argentine land forces on the Falkland Islands.' To be followed later by: 'Plans are now being made to retrieve your call sign back to Fitzroy!'

The surrender, and perhaps thoughts of warm accommodation, had inspired our Mortar Platoon Commander. Nigel had been understandably pleased with his men's performance, writing later:

> During this time the mortar line remained in situ beside Goat Ridge, with the prime concern now of surviving the atrocious weather conditions that had suddenly arisen. To say that the Platoon had 'fired in anger' would be to do them an injustice. Indeed for the mortarmen, anger was the lesser of the many emotions prevalent at the time. Rather they worked with a dedicated, cool thoroughness, their minds too fully occupied with the tricky business of keeping the mortars in action on difficult ground whilst under fire.
>
> A baptism of fire perhaps, but one thing is clear: the platoon that returned from the Falklands' campaign is not the same one that sailed from Southampton on the *QE2*. The single word 'experience' stands between them as they were when leaving England for the South Atlantic and the mortarmen that returned three months later . . .[6]

His last paragraph contained a shrewd, and maybe unconsciously prophetic, assessment of his men. Nigel was also a Philosophy and English language graduate who, after his Army career, became a film playwright and novelist. Writing poetry is an efficient method of catharsis after experiencing a traumatic event as he demonstrated with his poem *Before Battle*. On learning I had started to write this book at Goose Green, he shoved a piece of paper into my hand and said, 'I've written something too. It's nothing much. But if you don't think that your book will be spoilt by this, I'd like you to put it somewhere into the narrative.' He was more than generous in handing over a subtle poem *On The Surrender of Port Stanley: 14 June 1982* which also reflected the numbness caused by the effect of war and weather enveloping most:

> Grey with light,
>   morning wandered from the hours
> Sunless, sucked from dark,
>   strange with whine and rush;
> Pocked with burst,
>   shell-scabbed, coaxed with mortars tread
> Slowly looms the span of hills,
>   lulled to sight.
> Disturbed from heights that lately bent the dark
> Tracer dark,
>   night worn thin by flash and flare,
> Houses clenched,
>   sparse beyond the shallow plain
> Hands clasping tight the waters sullen stretch.
> Fumbling with taunts,
>   sky-spun,
>   leaned from the wind

> A flag enjoys the gull-creased air
> > and stills
> The vague and tumbled dreams of jagged men.
> And there below,
> > what cities forge as news
> Is toiled from words.
> > Cloud-hung,
> > > winds idly curve
> A waste of snow
> > and shame the rocks with ice.

This deliberately jarring masterpiece also described some of the split-second images of danger during the war's final hours which had been lasered forever into that part of his mind responsible for hyper reflex reactions, as they had been into mine. Like me, he would never forget these past few days, and even felt guilt for wanting to peek into Pandora's box. Like one 'old fart' to another, he wrote to me two decades later:

> Unlike the Scots Guards, Commandos, and Paras . . . ours was not a clear-cut experience. This was undoubtedly a good thing, because had (the *dush*) stuck to their ground and forced us to cross to Mount William and push them off it, we would have suffered very high casualties . . . Had we been in a battle, or hadn't we? I suppose the answer, unsatisfactorily, is 'Yes, but . . .'[7]

The first Gurkha to leave Mount William was Colonel David. A Gazelle helicopter flew him to the Task Force hospital ship SS *Uganda* so he could visit the Battalion's wounded on board. These included Rifleman Baliprasad Rai:

> I do not remember much about (*Uganda*) except for the care and warmth of the many nurses and doctors who looked after me. I constantly thought about my friends in B Company and what they were going through, and I wished I could go back to them.
>
> But after three days on the *Uganda*, instead of being sent back to the front line, I was transferred to another (ambulance) ship, the *Hecla*, which took me and many other patients to the Uruguayan port of Montevideo.[8]

Years later, a yarn containing a blue-on-blue theme and which bore all the hallmarks of Gurkha soldier black humour, emerged from this visit of Colonel David's:

> Everyone was . . . distressed to hear that the worst had happened, and a 7GR sentry had, somewhere between Mount William and Tumbledown, shot a Scots Guards Sergeant in the leg. The unfortunate sentry was quickly brought to see the Commandant sahib. The sentry confirmed that he had, thrice, challenged the shadowy figure he had seen approaching in the darkness and mist, but when he refused to halt or even respond, he had no choice but to open fire. Congratulating

the sentry for his vigilance and marksmanship, the Commandant left for (Ajax) Bay to see the guardsman in the (Field Surgical Centre) and to try to discover what had gone wrong and why. The Sergeant amazed the Commandant by confirming that he had heard the sentry challenge him.

'Then why didn't you halt as ordered?' asked the puzzled Commandant. 'I could nae do that sorr,' said the man pulling himself ramrod straight, as befitted a Scots Guards Drill Sergeant. 'Your wee man kept giving the order on the wrong foot, sorr!!!'[9]

But the Scots Guards were now expertly monopolizing the Brigade radio net. 'Watch out! The Woodentops'll be the first unit to be flown out of the battlefield, and we'll be doomed to yet another night in the khuds before we get to Fitzroy,' predicted Mark. To celebrate this unwelcome reality, soothing mugs of tea were brewed up by Rifleman Bis Bis, as Kit Spencer noticed my insignificant injury. 'What's happened to you Mike?' he exclaimed, 'you've got a bit of a shiner!'

I looked in a mirror and felt the tender skin around my right black eye. Then came memory recall of that evasive action from the shelling behind the Tumbledown. Combat stress had caused the brain to produce its own morphine known as endorphins which, in turn, act as a natural painkiller. Only after Kit's observation did the eye hurt.

In the late afternoon, those helicopters started arriving – but were not the Gurkhas' salvation. After watching them flying out the lucky Guardsmen to Fitzroy and eating a Bis Bis curry powder all-in stew, I decided to implement two vitally important initiatives for my future personal comfort in this wilderness. The first was to terminate my battlefield constipation. The other would be to change my sleeping quarters location for this second night, as anything was better than lying awake under that flapping poncho. Achieving the former was dependant on finding a location to carry out the deed. It proved nearly as challenging as our tab to Mount William the previous day since the results of the Argentine decentralized latrine system made even walking around 'our' Mount a most hazardous and disgusting activity.

With oncoming darkness threatening, I also succeeded with task two by finding and crawling under a long slab of rock between two large boulders which was barely high enough to accommodate one man lying down. My green slug accompanied me in this maneouvre. The rock must have been used as a shelter against the British shelling although, once under it, claustrophobia would have become a secondary enemy to fight against. Ten metres away, my Argentine sleeping partner remained under his blanket. Supervised by Robacio, he and others would not be interred until twenty-five days later on 10 July. More Argentine bodies from Mount Longdon and the Tumbledown would be found and buried on 28 July[10] because there were 111 minefields around the Port Stanley area including Tumbledown and Mount William, and this threat led to battlefield burials receiving a low priority. The Training Officer sahib was the lucky one and, thinking about the Argentine and the penalty he had paid two nights ago for not reaching my current residence in time, I tried to sleep. But the below-zero temperatures and my numb emotions prevented this whilst, in Church Crookham, Tove wrote:

285

On this the 'Liberation Day for the Falkland Islands' – quote from Robin Day on 'World at One'! – there is this unexpected feeling of anti-climax. The rest of the nation rejoices – the media is full of Falkland Island extras – I'm waiting here for a one and a half hours of it on BBC1. But we, the wives here, are quiet. No street parties as the others suggest, no champagne corks popping. We feel tremendously relieved that you are not being fired at etc. at the moment. So, so grateful that the war is over. But while I thought that would be enough, it plainly isn't. We won't feel the jubilant joy until we have you home . . . Meg wants Alan back for the birth of the baby by early September. I want you home <u>now</u>.

I told the girls this morning that all the British soldiers had frightened the Argentinians away – and Victoria wanted you home for tea-time. I'll be prepared to wait a bit longer . . . in the meantime it's back to waiting time. But obviously things are different and I don't feel this all-consuming fear for your safety. It's now 11 p.m. and I've sat through all the news and interviews! On ITV they say that the Gurkhas and Paras would stay behind to garrison the place. So there! Boom! I knew I was right in not being ecstatic yet. However I shall be watching developments closely and, with a bit of luck, maybe it won't be too long. In the meantime it's back to waiting time here; but where the hell are you? The paper said Fitzroy.

That night the snowstorms and cold claimed a Gurkha exposure victim on the Tumbledown. These conditions continued next morning as forty-knot winds prevented our helicopters from reaching us and little consolation was to be gained from the magnificent view of rolling countryside where most of the recent battles had been fought. Instead I whiled away the time touring the abandoned Argentine positions on *Cerro Guillermo*, the Spanish name for Mount William, first with Mark Willis and then Kit Spencer. These promenades were unique, for it is not often a private TEWT can be carried out on your former enemy's location. Mount William and Tumbledown lay near Stanley so the logistics of resupply would have presented them with few problems. Behind the Tumbledown's east end had been located a food store in a cave plus two field cookers and, on Mount William, was another tented store which contained enormous quantities of food cans, carrots, potatoes and onions. Personal items such as clothing, sandals and gym shoes lay everywhere. We even found inflated air beds in the bottom of bunkers as our hunt continued for the anti-aircraft artillery positions reported to Paddy just before our move from Two Sisters. Despite our efforts, none were to be found. 'The Intelligence Corps must have been looking at Wireless Ridge with their maps upside down,' I quipped to Paddy.

Mount William was a minor fortress, an appropriate objective for the Gurkhas and me because Fort William had been the original Honourable East India Company name for Calcutta where my grandfather had worked as Chief Architect in a sister company, the East India Railway Company. Months later, Sappers needed two weeks to clear away the military bric-a-brac that included several abandoned recoiless anti-tank guns, SAM-7 Russian rocket launchers, as well as thousands of rounds of rifle ammunition and some grenades. The Argentine platoon manning a position with two Browning heavy machine guns on Mount William's south-west shoulder which commanded the approach along the Darwin–Stanley track and any 5 Brigade daylight advance up it, would have been easily visible and within range. South-west of the Tumbledown and west of Mount William lay the main killing area into which ten sustained-fire GPMGs had been zeroed and many artillery defensive fire pre-planned targets plotted. Placed unprotected in exposed locations, seven of these GPMGs had been destroyed by the material effect of the intense shellfire but, although the British artillery's neutralizing effect had a more significant negative effect on Argentine morale and will to resist, its lethal effect remained unimpressive. Major Jonathan Bailey of 4 Field Regiment wrote later that month at Fitzroy:

> Many fire trenches had deep bunkers attached to them and these often burrowed under the natural overhang of rock. This offered a peat surface to absorb the impact of the shell with several feet of rock protection under that . . . not one man in these well-prepared (Tumbledown) positions was wounded by the British artillery . . . The (Argentine) detachments hid in their rock-roofed bunkers, often firing their guns on fixed lines, remotely by string . . . It was only this bunker protection that enabled the Argentines to fire their weapons and survive . . . one such deep bunker actually had a table in it with a pack of cards – an echo from the Somme![11]

Even the main minefield discovered by the Scots Guards' Recce Platoon extended into this killing area. Their reconnaissance revised 5 Brigade's original attack plan, and prevented us being caught in the open with an Argentine-rehearsed counter-attack moving down from the Tumbledown's eastern end. Although the latter's snipers had a significant effect, there appeared no ability to coordinate infantry action above company level and use of artillery was limited to firing one battery onto one target at a time. Conscripts also have an inherent disadvantage against a combination of regular troops and effective leadership as, two millenia before, Euripides' simple maths had stated: 'Ten good soldiers wisely led – will beat a hundred without a head'. Thus only *static* defence was uppermost in Argentine minds as they had also prepared to counter an expected amphibious assault landing with another two Marine platoons dug-in on Mount William's southern side. It had been the Royal Navy who deceived them by mounting Operation TORNADO along this coastline during the previous weeks with naval bombardments, radio transmissions and other measures to camouflage San Carlos as the real landing area.[12] This succeeded beyond the Navy's wildest dreams too, judging by the Argentine trench from which I peered through the cross sights of one of six Swedish-manufactured missile launchers that had their wire-guided missiles targeted onto the two kilometre distant landing beach.

Two decades later I enjoyed the privilege of a fascinating correspondence with Rear Admiral Carlos Hugo Robacio who resolutely maintained that the Gurkhas were the Tumbledown battle-winning factor in his Marines' 'delay position'.[13] His description of Gurkha action against his 4 Platoon in the following summary is incorrect however, because the latter was outflanked by the Scots Guards. Such mistaken identity is easy to make in darkness when explosions, gunfire and hand-to-hand fighting cause mounting casualties, and shouting, stress, fear and fatigue contribute to the confusion.

This is probably why Sub-Lieutenant Carlos Vázquez, the impressive 4 Platoon Commander who would be decorated later for gallantry, had remarked, 'I was able to see several Nepalese.'[14] Robacio nonetheless provides a revealing Argentine perception of the Gurkhas and their role in the battle:

... the selected area of action (for the 5th Marine Infantry Battalion) was far too large, three times the size accepted in the Regulations and advisable through experience ... a Company of the Argentine Army (A Company, 3rd Infantry Regiment) should have been positioned on the (Tumbledown's) north-west summit. Unfortunately this Company took up a position somewhat to the rear, two or three kilometres closer to Moody Valley ... things would have been different if the original position had been occupied ... Regrettably I was able to concentrate only twenty men there (Amphibious Engineers), as well as an element of Advance Artillery Spotters.

The above resulted in a significant reduction of forces at a place that justified its protection by a Battalion-force unit, for it was the key point for the defence. Being able to hold it, the fight could have been prolonged significantly and the cost to both sides would have been greater.

But the most important consideration I have to make ... is that although the Scots (their attack concentrated on 4 Platoon) attacked obstinately, they would not have advanced nor conquered the Tumbledown had it not been for the direct action of the Gurkhas ... Some of these ... later took the rear cooking facilities of N Company. The effective Nepalese forces, very well led by their British officers, simply reached an inaccessible position by crossing a mined area, then climbed on in spite of our pre-planned (artillery) fire and pushed my Amphibious Engineers back, conquering the highest and most dominant part of the mountain. They grouped and efficiently fired their weapons on the rear of ... 4 Platoon, causing it to collapse at that point of the defence ...

Sub-Lieutenant Miño (of the Amphibious Engineers) was able to see your men climb at the wall (almost inaccessible in daylight, much more difficult by night) in order to reach a higher position. This was done in spite of his men's fire and the concentration of 106.6mm mortars and our own artillery. We tried an offensive reaction with men from the 5th Marine Infantry Battalion and with officers and regulars from B Company, 6th Infantry Regiment, including Second Lieutenant Lamadrid. This attempt was insufficient, for those of you who had succeeded in setting foot on that part of the mountain did not yield ...

As for the (Gurkha) manoeuvre ... of attacking Mount William ... I had made an appreciation that this could be easily out-flanked despite my Battalion's M Company and C Company (-), 3rd Infantry Regiment that had joined us ... We recognise the valour and bravery of the Nepalese troops, which is an example of conscious sacrifice, and we do not pay attention to the perversity that psychological warfare assigns to them: beheadings, executions etc. (invented history for cowards). Their main virtues are their strength of mind and spirit for sacrifice and, moreover, they do not like to show their backs, they want to march ahead, they are simply true soldiers, experienced and bold, they are men![15]

Despite all our discoveries on Mount William, morale deteriorated during that final Wednesday as cold winds drove sleet into our faces. We observed many helicopters flying *empty* from Stanley, just as they had done in the previous thirty-six hours, and my temper became frayed with repeated radio requests to Brigade HQ such as: 'Where the hell are our helicopters?' These mood swings could be blamed on a post-traumatic stress reaction. Chaos, too, was occurring at home as Tove observed:

> Well, the news continues to pour in about this strange surrender. Nobody seems to know if the war is actually over – as yet no final words from Buenos Aires. There are lots of reports though of foul weather, shortage of housing/tents etc., what to do with the prisoners-of-war. I only wish I could do something: send you warm clothes or a little house for you to keep warm in. I am desperate to hear exactly where and how you are. No communication at all from the camp at Church Crookham . . . We're all resigned that, bar a miracle, you'll stay behind as the garrison. Things seem to be in a muddle however, with the politicians arguing and not knowing what to do until the bastard Junta says what's on it's mind.

Existential authority, yet another stress symptom, was now planted firmly in my mind – and, in exercising this, I did not care about my behaviour or, indeed, any logical reasons for the helicopter shortfall. Never before had I been so outspoken on a radio net to a superior headquarters as my pithy transmissions increased in volume during those final hours on Mount William. 'Is there, once again, any chance of sending helicopters to pick us up today? Weather conditions are deplorable. We've suffered one exposure victim already, and soon there'll be others if you can't coordinate these flights better,' I complained bitterly. 'Your planning is dreadful – and making our situation absolutely critical!'

My anger, further intensified by the inevitable response from Captain 'Roger, Wait Out!' and his Brigade HQ cronies, was not placated by a later vague reply indicating possible transportation: 'Roger to your last. We're trying to secure helicopters to move you back now to Goose Green and not, I say again, not Fitzroy. Unable to give you a pick-up time at present.' It was only when the first helicopter arrived at the battlefield that a semblance of sanity also returned. Two hours later, when climbing aboard the last in that late afternoon of Wednesday, 16 June 1982, I was not unthankful to leave for those heavenly comforts of Goose Green.

It had been a busy week, but there would be no relaxation as the Gurkhas began their next task of winning the peace.

Chapter Twenty-three

WINNING THE PEACE

During their short stay at Leslobes the men made many friends. At first the farmers' wives of the district had been terrified at the idea of sheltering Indian troops in their houses. They soon discovered, however, that Gurkhas know better than most people how to behave, and they were immediately astonished and pleased when the men brought in to them eggs which they found around the farms. 'What good men,' said one old lady. 'Our boys would have had those eggs in their soup in no time.' – An anecdote from the 1st/4th Prince of Wales' Own Gurkha Rifles during their stay at this village near Neuve Chapelle in December 1914[1]

The flight back to Goose Green reunited us with C Company. 'We got really concerned when we lost radio communications with Brigade and you guys in the first forty-eight hours after you left, and never regained it!' was Taj Lewis' first comment after our arrival. Faced with an airborne assault threat, they had improved defences and David Grey, Goose Green's civilian electrical engineer, was involved in some of their schemes:

> Beyond the large garage building on the west side of Goose Green where the Darwin road enters the settlement, they put a ring of mines in front of the outer defensive position and I found some cable for them and a battery so that the mines could be detonated en masse. We had a Milan position at the backdoor of my house and a Heavy Machine Gun outside the sitting room window. My two daughters, Andrea and Johan, used to take drinks and cookies to the lads manning the positions and sit with them when they test-fired the guns, which they were allowed to do at 4.00 p.m.
>
> The defensive positions stretched out to the Puzzle gates which were on the road to Port Stanley just above Burntside House (north of Darwin) ... South-west from Goose Green is Egg Harbour and a patrol of Gurkhas set up a defensive position to watch westerly to Fox Bay to give warning of a counter-attack from the Argentine troops stationed there.[2]

C Company had also continued patrolling in the Mount Usborne and northern Lafonia areas. One weapon system at their disposal was Blowpipe. It had less than a mediocre war reputation but Taj needed an air defence capability so, shortly after we departed for the front line, he approached the detachment commander to ask, 'How's your marksmanship?'

The Gunner Blowpipe teams had been training intensively in their simulator set-up on *QE2*, but Taj was horrified with the reply, 'Dunno sir, we've never fired it live!'

The ground to air missile might be expensive and simulator firing an admirable money saver, but preparing for an imminent airborne assault on the grass airstrip was something else, so Taj did not hesitate. 'Fire three missiles now!' he ordered.

Soon the airstrip would become the Gurkha collection point for Argentine military ordnance, weapons and equipment of every quantity, quality and variety. Goose Green had already become wildly overcrowded because of the loss of *Atlantic Conveyor*'s 4,500 winter tent cargo, some of which had been earmarked for the Gurkhas. So at our first O Group in the shop we weary BOs were informed of A Company's immediate return to Darwin, and Tac HQ and two other companies' redeployment to outlying settlements on West Falkland. 'Not only help with the clearing up is required, but there's also a need for a military presence since hostilities haven't been officially terminated,' said Colonel David.

After the O Group Graham Stewart-Smith approached me to say, 'The Baillies have invited some of us to stay with them, so why don't you come along?' We walked towards the jetty and into the home of Keith and Ginnie Baillie and their noisy children, Kim and Diana.

'Go upstairs and sleep in our bed,' insisted the couple to me, intimating that the Second Falklands' War would break out if I refused. Careful to bathe and change into clean combat kit, I tried sleeping on the double bed for a couple of hours. I gave up and wandered downstairs to find Bill Dawson and the 5 Brigade FACs Rubber Duck and Red Dragon alias Anwell Hughes and Mike Howes had also been included in the guest list. The Baillies had coped with much. They had first endured Argentine vandalism and then housed some of 2 Para. Whilst we had been at the front line, Keith had given a daily bottle of rum to a C Company platoon; now it was our turn for their support. Uncomplaining, they were concerned a blue-on-blue had led to one of their Para tenants, a Private Parr, running out of luck. 'During our local battle his belt stopped an Argie bullet that lodged in his stomach button, but we've just heard he was killed by British shellfire on Wireless Ridge,' Keith sadly informed me.

Next day our ops room moved to the bunkhouse. Located further up the settlement, normally this was accommodation for all the batchelor shepherds employed by the Falkland Island Company. Sleeping quarters were also made available and a room converted into an Officers' Mess, but the Argentines had left the place in too filthy a condition to house many. So the Gurkhas began spring-cleaning and painting it in their general assistance with the settlement's recovery. Regaining personal equilibrium also began as lethargy, a light depression and psychosomatic flu symptoms continued throughout 17 June which was also Emily's second birthday. I went on full alert at any unusual sound, the word 'gun' was repellent and my hands shook slightly. Keeping emotions under wraps during the Wether Ground and Tumbledown shelling now produced these reciprocal post-traumatic stress reactions.

'In Second World War Gurkha circles,' Colonel David said as an off-the-cuff remark, 'this was known as "the blue period" and lasted three or four days.' It would be the only form of anticipatory guidance information given on such psychological matters. No disaster psychiatrist could have bettered the Baillies' psychosocial support except for one item because, unlike survivors from civilian aircraft, ship, train, bus and other types of disasters, there was no telephone to ring home afterwards. Keith and Ginnie lavished kindness on the five of us. A can or two of beer, '365' meal and chatting about our experiences continued the process of thawing out emotional numbness. We did not receive mail, so I began writing daily letters again to Tove. This also served as therapy in removing some frustrations:

Just heard that General Galtieri has resigned. I wonder what other dosser they are going to put in his place? It certainly will be interesting. At the moment we just don't know when we shall be leaving these wonderful islands. With any luck it won't be a stay for 6 months. The rumour has it that it might be between 2–3 months. But I wouldn't gamble on that one.

My bed that night was on their living room floor. In a light doze I dreamt badly, so Bill shoved a Valium pill down my throat to stop the muttering. Next day Tove wrote:

The big question is of course how long you'll have to stay down there. I have no idea <u>where</u> or <u>how</u> you are at present. Is there anything at all I can send you to make life a bit easier? Anything. Surely the mail should be getting into a regular routine soon, so we don't have to wait so long? I 'rush' downstairs every morning to make tea – grab the paper and turn on the 8 a.m. news on the radio. I only wait for the voices to say that the whole Task Force is coming back – no more hostilities – with all the papers signed!

Another stress reaction manifested itself on 19 June but, after the attack of those stomach cramps at 05.30 hours, an effective cure came with pills from the doctor and sitting on the loo. My flu was also receding, although fear seeped through me on recall of battlefield images and sounds. The personal challenge was in contributing to a return of 'business as usual' as the Gurkhas continued to clear local battle debris. All immediate resupply had to be flown as there was a transport shortfall. We had only eleven Battalion Land-Rovers; *Monsunen*, now under Brigade control, had not yet become available and our REME-attached Sergeant Jim Turner and two Gurkha vehicle mechanics were still repairing four Argentine immobilized Mercedes vehicles, one of which had been earmarked as Colonel David's staff car. My task was to coordinate a daily helicopter flight programme, so I designed a fancy flight state board and pinned it up on an ops room wall. 'That's more like it!' enthused Colonel David as the silver-topped wand rapped on my art work approvingly.

Even though ten helicopters daily would land and take-off at Goose Green, they remained in short supply despite another three Chinooks arriving in-theatre. As the Argentines had named their helicopter landing site *Helipuerto Santiago*, I felt justified in calling ours 'Goose Green International' and the kelpers became used to seeing all types of Task Force helicopter – first the smaller Scout, Gazelle, Wasp, Lynx variety and then, later, Chinook, Sea King and Wessex. They also realized increased possibilities of hitching a lift to other parts of the Islands so, as potential passengers waited coyly outside the ops room, 'Any extra seat on a helicopter today, Krystal sahib?' became a daily Gurkha question inside it.

At 02.00 hours on 20 June, our clocks went back to local time and those three extra hours were killed in bed. A sports idiot but never churchgoer, my attendance, nonetheless, that Sunday with a few other BOs at the inter-denominational memorial service for the Islands' liberation in Stanley's red-bricked Christ Church Cathedral seemed more pertinent than listening to the BBC World Service broadcast of England versus Czechoslovakia in football's World Cup. We flew there in a Wessex. Some Argentine Hueys had been parked near our racecourse landing site as well as a Chinook on adjacent playing fields, but none were in working order. All equipment was stripped out, leaving only the airframes intact. Passing an Argentine Sea King helicopter lying beside the roadside, we walked through a sea of mud, filth and soldiery to observe a few burnt out houses and piles of ammunition everywhere. The packed Cathedral's understated service for the fallen did not glorify in a traumatic past and successfully closed that chapter, although others of a long-term nature remained open.

Outside, our only hope of seeing Stanley was to thumb a lift. Once aboard a British Army Land-Rover, we seemed to pass commandeered new Argentine Mercedes vehicles and Chevrolet trucks everywhere. At the quayside Royal Military Police were searching hundreds of prisoners prior to repatriation. Judging by a warehouse we entered, no town-based Argentine could have had malnutrition problems. British soldiers scavanged in mounds of food whose variety was enormous and even included toiletry items such as disposable razor packs. Nearby were another two warehouses and line of containers filled with rotting meat. The Argentine logistic failure lay in a system of distribution not equal to the size of the task, unlike the British system's efficiency as a CrabAir twenty-six hour Hercules return flight from Ascension Island appeared in the wintery afternoon sky and, unable to land at the wrecked airport, circled twice to drop a twin parachute attached mail load.

The town's chaos jarred the senses. We were better off in Goose Green where, that evening, I received a morale-boosting windfall of eight letters and food parcel from Tove. Phase two of churchgoing was next morning when Padre Peter Brooke held a BO and BOR church service in the Community Centre. Afterwards the Welsh Guards' Chaplain offered communion. It was my rite of passage – a group transition ritual from chaos to a more structured existence, but this must have been a sign of the times because I have, shamefully, never indulged in such an event since. As I left the Centre he told me, 'I've received a super letter from Tove!' His message demonstrated, just as on *QE2*, that the good padre knew much about the unknown and how to tackle it. Two days later he would be leading the *Sir Galahad* and *Sir Tristram* memorial service at Fitzroy.

The ops room staff also began to be updated with events from the outside world via newspapers and BBC World Service on our Clansman radio. Strangely, more significant to me than Argentina's new President, General Bignone, announcing all their forces would observe the ceasefire, or Marine Commandos retaking the Island of South Thule during Operation KEYHOLE, the South Atlantic campaign's final operation, was the news of Israeli shelling of the PLO in Beirut. It provided a nerve grating flashback to recent events.

293

Signals also arrived and one was from an exceptionally senior British Army officer with congratulations about our '. . . heroism in seizing our objective on Mount William against overwhelming odds'. This was embarrassing so, to fill the information vacuum, Colonel David began to draft a signal in reply. Unbeknown to us there were also rumours circulating in Nepal's eastern hills that the 1st/7th Gurkha Rifles led by Major Lalbahadur Rai had been wiped out by the Argentines. Similar stories were being published by the local Buenos Aires' press claiming that the Argentine 5th Marine Infantry Battalion had buried 180 Gurkhas, and also that our men, having fought drugged, had killed each other in battle.[3]

But Graham Stewart-Smith, returning to his Paymaster role, had been quietly efficient. 'I've acquired a supply of 26p stamps from the Force Paymaster in Stanley,' he said, 'so the *keta* can now send their letters to Nepal free of charge!' His initiative hopefully made a contribution to silencing the extermination rumours as did, likewise, Colonel David's understated text in his signal. It hid a hundred stories:

> Most grateful for your signals and apologies for not keeping you informed. Battalion in fine fettle including wounded who are all progressing well. Enemy ran before we could get near to engage at close quarters. It is now confirmed that our reputation did our work for us. Although frustrating this must be the best way to win battles! Future intentions not yet known. Jai Seventh.[4]

On the afternoon of 21 June Warrant Officer Jack Massey entered the ops room determined to improve the Battalion's diet. The Gurkha-type compo ration pack had not been available in the Falklands, so high on his shopping list had been the reintroduction of *bhat*, but the ingredient he needed desperately was rice. Understandably his eyes had gleamed on hearing of Stanley's bulging Argentine food warehouses.

'Sir, can you get me a chopper tomorrow so I can go rice hunting?' he requested.

So next day, when the Brigadier's welcome news was received that we would arrive back in UK by mid-August, Massey made his flight and found Argentine treasure in their ex-capital of *Puerto Argentino* because, not only did his team of Gurkhas carry away fourteen 50lb bags of rice, but they also 'liberated' many packets of pasta and noodles, and cans of tomatoes and peas. The Wessex cabin was filled and excess put in a net as an underslung load, however weight calculations were awry because the helicopter could hardly struggle off the ground. A short distance out of Stanley it failed to surmount Sapper Hill and so began the most bizarre air raid of all with bags of rice and tin cans flung out to enable a return to Goose Green. Wise to such problems, another half-dozen resupply flights during that week ensured enough rice for the remainder of the Gurkhas' stay. Mail was also collected and brought back, including a letter my Aunt Nancy wrote on 23 June from her London flat:

> We all listened to the news pretty breathlessly, and the week before Stanley fell there were people shoving for room round the ticker-tape in the House of Lords all the time. You must have been absolutely thankful that they surrendered before fighting had to start inside the town. From all accounts you must have had the most hideously uncomfortable time and I can't imagine how you are surviving.

I gather the Gurkhas didn't exactly take to the sea, but I suppose the mountaineous regions are rather more like home for them.

Now of course there is the tricky business of what sort of a permanent arrangement can be fixed – even an interim arrangement is difficult enough. It's not going to be helped by Haig's resignation which few people had expected. Meanwhile we here have our assorted selection of strikes. The tube strike last week was a good time-waster. It took me two and a half hours on Friday to get back home from Waterloo. And we are expecting next week the total rail and tube strike to be one long obstacle race. But you are far more uncomfortable and we shall survive.

My first notes for this book started as a subconscious surrogate for a psychological debriefing. They became expanded at the Baillies' home where we five officers were far from being uncomfortable. An entrepreneurial square peg in the round hole of Goose Green's feudal society, Keith confided to me, 'I'm thinking of starting a Stanley fish and chip business to cash in all the UK reinforcements.' The Postmaster's speculative approach was also reflected in Falklands' philately ambitions. Receiving letters from all over the world with requests for Falkland Islands' stamps, he was also a member of the 200-strong Falkland Islands' Stamp Study Group. Philately was a local industry second only to sheep farming and, in 1981–82, grossed £255,000. After displaying a suitcase brimful with stamps and first-day covers, Keith declared, 'One day I'll make a fortune from these!'

His other hobbies were fishing, hunting and beer, while Ginnie made simple food taste delicious and took pride in her home where, similar to the 'kaida' in Norway, she made us remove our boots in the entrance of their house. She rode her horses around the 'camp' because their expensive UK Land-Rover had been damaged by the Argentines. Keith had claimed compensation for this and other damage to their little home warmed up by a large oil-fired Aga stove in the kitchen. There, the two-metre band radio set was essential for socializing and one evening we engaged in radio chat with a Fox Bay kelper who told us: 'The Argies were thankful the surrender came because one of their officers knocked on our door and, when we opened it, he stood smiling with a bottle of champagne in his hand!' We also heard about the more obscure invasion details. 'Of course,' said Keith, 'the Argies made radio broadcasts. Their propaganda was not only meant for us, but also the garrison – to whom they gave an impossible task.'

'How did they do that then?' asked Bill Dawson, sipping from another generous tumbler of *tato pani* Keith had poured out. 'By telling them that they weren't allowed to die until the last drop of blood had flowed from their veins. Impossible!' the Postmaster chortled.

'The four-hour broadcast always started at half-past six in the evening with the announcement 'This is the free voice of the Falkland Islands' People', followed by martial music and issuing of regulations in English and Spanish. There were also unplanned commercial breaks, because HMS *Endurance* must have been responsible for playing those recordings of *Land of Hope and Glory* and *Rule Britannia* which always broke into the programmes. And, look over there,' he said glumly, pointing to a large colour TV in the living room, 'because Stanley didn't broadcast TV before the invasion I joined an English video club and bought that. It meant missing out on the Argies' offer a month after the invasion because, having started to broadcast TV propaganda programmes, they gave TVs away at £110 apiece!'

He had also collected a large stock of Argentine radio sets and arsenal of weapons. Stanley's constabulary had already issued instructions that all firearms had to be handed in to them, but Keith was in no mood to follow their dictates. 'I'll stash everything away if they come looking,' said the ex-Marine darkly, 'and there's no way they'll find my little treasure trove,' and he even refused Bill's £100 for a superb Argentine Army Mauser sniper rifle.

Elsewhere David Grey, his boss Eric Goss, and their wives, Patricia and Shirley, were invited to a farewell dinner given by Taj Lewis because C Company would shortly leave for West Falkland aboard *Monsunen*. David appreciated the Gurkhas' efforts:

> We were delighted, although the location of the dinner was somewhat strange – the Blacksmith's workshop. The last time I'd looked in there, it was wrecked. With some trepidation we set off to the venue and were surprised to see this workshop transformed – cleaned, festooned with camouflage nets and candles lit, with the drills, anvils and bending machinery decorated in some way. It was a nice meal, drinks and wine. A really pleasant evening. I asked what the meat in the main course was, and the steward said, 'Ducks.' That's how we found out where the Logger Ducks had gone to from the beach. The duck numbers soon recovered.[5]

Others in the UK were also grateful and their letters would daily arrive in the ops room, such as that from Mrs Dianne Morris of Bristol:

> Hello Beautiful,
>   I've never met any of you, but you are all bloody fantastic, you are a credit to those islands. I hope this little gift (a balaclava helmet) will come in useful and no. 2 is in the making . . .
>   This one is coming courtesy RAF Lyneham. I'm not very good at much, but I can knit. It's impossible for me to put into words what the Task Force has done there in the South Atlantic, and if I wrote a book full of your praises it would still not be enough. I didn't have anyone on that Task Force to worry about. I wish I had, so I just worried about everybody. I watched every news bulletin and bought newspapers like they were going out of fashion . . .
>   Two things I shall never forget. No. 1, within one day we were at war I always thought it was something we would see coming and, no. 2, the speed at which the Task Force was brought together which brings me back to repeating myself – you are the best in the world and let no one doubt it. I thank every one of you for putting the GREAT back into Britain and I look forward to hearing from one of you, and hope some of you will soon be home. Take care and tread lightly, remember the mines.

Mrs. Georgina Wood of Taunton sent a more personal Gurkha letter, despite its Ascension Island address:

> To the Men of HM Gurkha Reg., English Bay, BFPO,
>
> Our thoughts go out to you all, with them go our heartfelt wishes for a quick completion of your task, and a speedy return to all your loved ones, who I know await your safe return. My husband who is now a pensioner speaks so highly of you all, not only as men but as soldiers also. I shall always have a light burning in my window, and the flags flying, until that not too distant day when you all return to that and those most dear to you.
>
> May God Bless you, one and all, that is my constant prayer.

Possibly both ladies had experienced similar premonitions. The Gurkhas' work included local battlefield clearance and more back-filling of Argentine trenches, and at midday on 24 June I was on duty in the ops room when a radio report arrived from Lieutenant Jeremy McTeague of D Company: 'Explosion just occurred at my call sign's location. Three casualties. One dead and two wounded. Request Starlight immediately!'

With Lisburn ops room golden hour reflexes, I leapt up and plotted the Burntside House grid reference, then passed vertical and horizontal information by scrambling the doctor, alerting a casevac helicopter and contacting Colonel David flying nearby in a Gazelle. Buried in front of a trench, a live 2 Para M-79 grenade had been hit by the spade of the Signal Platoon's Lance Corporal Budhaparsad Limbu. The resulting explosion removed half his head and wounded D Company's Corporal Chandrabahadur Tamang and HQ Company's Rifleman Dipmani Rai in the legs. The lesson was obvious. Sapper specialists would be needed to deal with battlefield clearance and formidable Falklands' mine threat, as we infantry 'grunts' were redundant in such work.

Two days later in the rain and wind GM sahib led Budhaparsad's death *puja* ceremony at the Darwin cemetery whilst the Gurkha Firing Party performed smartly and Pipe Major piped the lament *The Flowers of the Forest*. Beside me stood an unusually silent and pale-faced Brigadier. 'Post-war problems with higher command?' I wondered as he stepped forward to throw the first handful of earth on the coffin before everyone else. The kelpers had already erected the Goose Green and Darwin memorial for 2 Para's dead from an idea by Eric Goss, and it now also became an official memorial for the Gurkha. In addition GM sahib decided that the Battalion would plant a tree to honour him[6]. It might have been this post-war blue-on-blue that started my worst short-term stress reaction of a fortnight's insomnia. During the second week I feared this condition had become chronic but, being stubborn, never asked the doctor for sleeping pills. Operations had priority as redeployment became more extensive than first planned with B Company embarking onto *Monsunen* and departing to their new North Arm base in Lafonia and A Company rotating platoons for periods of time on Lively Island.

West Falkland received many sub-units. C Company had already sailed to Port

Stephens, D Company and the Anti-Tank Platoon now flew to Fox Bay on 27 June, followed by the Mortar Platoon to Chartres, Assault Pioneers to Weddell Island, and a brief deployment to New Island was led by Rory Stewart to observe some of the Falklands' six million penguins. Thankfully, Tac HQ's move to Port Howard was cancelled. Fourteen days' rations were taken by all, but helicopters had to be coordinated carefully because of further resupply flights that included newspapers, NAAFI essentials and *tato pani* deliveries. Stanley Airport had also opened again and, the same day as D Company's deployment, the Goose Green ops room was visited by the Director of Army Public Relations.

Major General David Ramsbotham, late of the Royal Greenjackets and my previous boss at 39 Brigade, stared at his ex-watchkeeper before asking carefully, 'How are you?' If a follow-up, 'And did you put a foot wrong?' had also been asked, then this Light Division combat veteran's answer would have been a categoric, 'Yes, sir. Often!' Seeing this first post-war face from UK made a change. My moods could also swing as, later that day, a British NCO passenger on the daily Stanley 'milk run' flight forgot to collect the Battalion's mail bag. He did not forget me afterwards.

Seventy-two hours later I decided that my insomnia might be cured by an afternoon walk to the 2 Para memorial on Darwin Hill. Outbound on the eastern side of the airstrip I stopped to look at a trench and, with curiosity getting the better of me, climbed down into it. As at Mount William, there was personal and military equipment strewn everywhere including unposted letters. One had been written on 27 May, the eve of the Darwin and Goose Green battle, by a Corporal Jorge Zarate serving with a platoon of C Company, 25th Infantry Regiment from the southern province of Chubut. I picked up his letter as a souvenir and later, once back in the UK, had it translated before redirecting it on to Argentina via the Geneva-based International Committee of the Red Cross. Corporal Zarate '. . . would have give(n) anything to be back there (in Córdoba, Argentina) drinking maté and eating tortilla.' He was also pessimistic to his friend, Martin Perez, about the outcome of meeting 2 Para in battle:

> We are alright in spite of the exhausting night we just had. The English want to come closer to the coast but we are keeping our positions. We are one of the best units and so far we haven't had any losses. But things are not looking good, the other day they shelled us in the morning and then the aircraft started. But it's clear that God is always with us.

After writing this he would, that same day, also have experienced yet another Harrier cluster bomb unit attack. Twenty-four hours later, towards the end of the battle, three more Harriers had carried out further attacks near the settlement. Evidence of rocket and cannon fire was clear to see as, not far from Corporal Zarate's trench, enormous divots had been torn out of the closely-cropped turf bordering the airstrip. 'The absurdity of this,' I contemplated when back in the UK, 'was not needing God with him to survive, but that he needed our mutual God!'

Climbing out of his trench, I continued my walk. Further on was a small badly damaged house which had been occupied by the Argentine garrison's Roman Catholic priest, and a source of replenishing Corporal Zarate's faith. Scattered on the floor inside was a sea of paper sheets printed with a Virgin Mary colour picture and, underneath it, a simple prayer. Distributed to many Argentine soldiers, it was read out by a Spanish-speaking British Army officer at the burial of Argentine dead on the Tumbledown a month later. Translated, the prayer's title was *The Blessing of St Francis* and its text read: 'The Lord Bless and protect you showing you his face and having mercy on you, giving you his countenance and his peace. The Lord Bless you.'[7] Not to labour the point, this would have been familiar to those VIP Church of England members present at the following month's controversial St Paul's Cathedral Memorial Service in London where some were against the gesture of a prayer to the Argentine dead. The Book of Communion Prayer's version is: 'The Lord bless us, and keep us; the Lord lift up the light of his countenance upon us, and give us peace, now and evermore.'

I reached the iron cross and brick plinth memorial to surprise myself by muttering a prayer. Inbound to Goose Green I was caught in a frightful snow storm but, although the snow had disappeared by next morning, my insomnia continued. This was linked to festering battlefield memories, however revisiting the Tumbledown and Mount William as a passenger aboard the 2 July Stanley 'milk-run' flight made them less awesome in daylight. The pilot was an obliging soul, and I guided him over both objectives to take photographs. My timing was fortunate because, twelve hours later, heavy snow fell everywhere to cover war's ugliness with a serene white blanket of peace. That day my father wrote about his own post ceasefire:

> You may not realise the intensity of interest with which the entire country has been following the campaign, and the fortunes of every ship and battalion involved. Mother and I mentioned, but certainly did not broadcast, the fact that you were serving in the Gurkhas, and we are constantly having enquiries about your safety from people who have been told by others.
>
> For example, you know the little arcade of shops near Angmering Station where we do a great deal of everyday shopping? One is run by an ex-Sergeant who had served at Bielefeld a few years ago. We chat a bit, and I mentioned you. Now other shopkeepers and assistants ask your mother if you are alright. One old lady serving behind the counter whom I have known vaguely for twenty years told me the whole shop were looking for Gurkha casualty lists and were keeping their fingers crossed for you.
>
> In the Council offices I am deluged by enquiries, not only from Councillors, but from the staff, from the Chief Executive down to obscure typists. 'Oh Mr. Seear, is your son safe? Oh good, we're all so glad.' That sort of thing. Almost embarrassing . . . We attended a West Sussex County Council function and even then no less a personage than the Duchess of Norfolk, with whom your mother is on friendly terms, has expressed her hopes that you will be restored to your family safely. It's all quite remarkable.

The day after the snow's arrival we 'Baillie five' bade farewell to our hosts. I was reluctantly redeployed to spartan sleeping quarters in the bunkhouse – although compensation for this return to the 'real' world came with Colonel David's announcement that our autumn Belize tour had been cancelled. However Bill and Graham were the winners. They achieved their great escape from Goose Green to fly out from the repaired Stanley Airport by Hercules via Ascension Island as part of the Battalion's UK Advance Party. One already back at Church Crookham, though, was Rifleman Baliprasad Rai. Nearly three weeks before he was on board one of *Uganda*'s three ambulance ships, the *Hecla*, bound for Montevideo:

> This voyage took four days and I was gradually getting used to proper square meals and dry clothes again, and the wet of the days and nights and soggy compo dinners was fast becoming a memory.
>
> A waiting RAF VC-10 at Montevideo Airport jetted us to Brize Norton via Ascension and on 21 June I was back in Britain, lying in an air force hospital at Swindon. Within another few days I had sufficiently recovered to make the trip to Church Crookham as I longed to see some familiar faces again.
>
> As I relax and enjoy my sick leave here in my own barracks room in Queen Elizabeth Barracks, my mind retraces the long journey I have made – from the quiet stillness of Bagsila to the blood and thunder of the bombardment at (Wether Ground). Yes, it has been an incredible journey – and yes, I have been lucky again![8]

Meanwhile C Company's redeployment was quiet at Port Stephens. Except for two helicopter visits, the Argentines had ignored this settlement where everyone opposed the Argentine invasion vehemently like the school teacher who had painted pro-British slogans on her tiny school's walls. Delighted with their temporary garrison, thirty-five kelpers turned out on the small jetty to welcome the newcomers' arrival and, although dour and insular, were pleasant enough. The Gurkhas dug trenches, went patrolling, constructed a rifle-range, and shot. This captivated one local nineteen-year old who participated in all their activities. Although uphill work, Taj Lewis continued to socialize and one tête-à-tête with a shepherd put perspective into the busy pace of life at the Port Stephens metropolis.

'Well, where do you spend your holidays, then?' queried the Company Commander in a brave attempt to open up the near one-way dialogue. There was a pause.

'Oh, yuh,' replied his reluctant conversation partner, finally remembering the exciting experience, 'I quite enjoyed my holiday at Stanley thirteen years ago, thank yer very much!'

B Company had also been well received at North Arm and became even more popular after a liaison was set up with Navy helicopter pilots who regularly flew in NAAFI deliveries. The subsequent Gurkha-organized parties in the local Community Centre led to its being renamed The Kukri. Apart from a visit by two Argentine helicopters on a head-counting operation and overflights of aircraft en route to attack British forces at San Carlos, the sixty kelpers had seen little of the war. Nonetheless they were proud of their contribution in defending the Islands because the settlement manager had not only instigated a programme of daily horseback and Land-Rover patrols hunting for Argentines, but also masterminded an ingenious plan after a pair of Harriers intercepted a flight of Skyhawks and shot one down nearby. Some days later the bedraggled pilot was picked up by local shepherds who found his cockpit

SARBE beacon still on him. The manager decided to position this in a valley, hoping its distress signal would lure an Argentine rescue helicopter to where some North Arm kelpers had also been placed in ambush. Although they waited in vain, there had been good cause for the manager's optimism because the kelpers were capable marksmen and on a local Gurkha-built range B Company only just managed to beat them in a shooting competition.

D Company were presented with severe challenges that limited their training. Fox Bay was the Argentines' premier base in West Falkland where the 8th Infantry Regiment from Comodoro Rivadavia, elements of 9th Engineer Company and 3 Infantry Brigade HQ had been located. Their 889 soldiers had an unhappy stay. Only 882 surrendered and, of the remaining seven, one had drowned, two succumbed to illness, another two were burnt to death in a fire, one blew himself up after treading on a mine and the last committed suicide. Divided by a 400-metre stretch of water, both Fox Bay East and West accommodated the Gurkhas. But there was distrust between the two settlements because East thought West had been over-helpful to the occupying invaders and diplomacy had to be used by the Gurkhas to soothe feelings. They established themselves quickly, becoming owners of twelve sabotaged Argentine Mercedes vehicles and four Mercedes Unimog trucks. With engines full of iron-filings, employment was guaranteed for REME mechanic Lance Corporal Nigel Hughes, ex-Machine Gun Platoon. After repair, these vehicles were used by D Company to collect vast quantities of surrendered small arms. These were then tied into bundles and back-loaded by helicopter to Goose Green.

Other more dangerous tasks awaited. Any British attacking force would have had a few problems to resolve before becoming the new landlord of Fox Bay. Argentine defensive positions were mutually supporting and trenches well-sited with excellent fields of fire that covered the nine anti-tank and anti-personnel minefields that their Engineers had laid. Six of these were uncharted and required careful reconnaissance before approximate perimeters could be located and marked. Of the remainder, small red triangular signs hanging from the top of wire fences delineated the Argentine side and many forty-five-gallon oil drums filled with petrol marked the outer perimeter. With six-foot high iron pickets also strapped to their sides and a two-pound explosive charge attached to the rear, it took the Gurkhas six days to clear away these obstacles and many improvised hand grenades made of Coca-Cola cans filled with a half-pound of explosives and iron nails.

D Company also placed a guard on the ARA *Bahía Buen Suceso*, an abandoned Canadian-built 3,100-ton Argentine Naval transport ship which had landed the scrap metal merchants at South Georgia. Loaded with unstable explosives and ammunition, it had been strafed on 16 May by Harriers and, afterwards, the beached and rat-infested vessel had been looted as it lay by the West jetty. A Gurkha guard put a stop to that. They also offloaded and distributed a flour and rations cargo to the kelpers before a tug arrived to tow the ship to San Carlos. Such acts made the highly popular Gurkhas so supreme in winning the peace that some Fox Bay kelpers organized a petition to demand their continued retention on the Falklands. At this or other Gurkha settlements, there were no discipline lapses as with other British units in Stanley. The Gurkha standard was so high that courts martial did not seem to exist in their vocabulary and even appearing on disciplinary charges at the Commandant's Orders would be so unusual that it excited much Battalion comment. A company commander could consider himself highly busy if he had to discipline more than three men in as many months. Graham Bound, the Stanley-based editor of *The Penguin News* who interviewed several Gurkhas and BOs at Goose Green, later provided me with a well-rounded local impression:

> Falklanders were, I think, quite charmed with the Gurkhas. They were always friendly and seemed to be perfect gentlemen. The paradox of this side of their nature and their ferocity in battle, for me at least, is fascinating.
>
> As I am sure you are aware, the deployment of the Gurkhas had a powerful psychological effect on the Argentines. They could not understand why these Nepalese men should be fighting with the British, and, having heard the many rumours about them, were terrified.[9]

The trump card Colonel David played in this 'hearts and minds' work was the P and D's Beating the Retreat performances at Fox Bay, Port Stephens, North Arm and Goose Green, an idea that came from Borneo when their predecessors had toured around the local kampongs. He gave me the job of coordinating the logistics by demanding, 'We need transport assets to move the P and D and I want *Monsunen* to be made available. So sort it out Mike!'

The coaster became a Gurkha showboat and successful landfalls were made at Fox Bay and Port Stephens. The master plan seemed to be working but, on 8 July, while Battalion HQ entertained five UK and seven foreign journalists, the outlying platoons on West Falkland were being recovered to Goose Green, and nine Battalion Land-Rovers were being driven to Stanley to board the *Nordic Ferry* for Southampton, Sod's Law intervened again during the P and D's penultimate leg to North Arm. The Falkland Island Company had claimed that *Monsunen*'s keel was broken and propellor shaft bent by the Argentines when they had run the coaster aground, so the Royal Navy suddenly decided to inspect her.

With 5 Brigade's blessing, her Senior Naval Officer received orders to execute a 180-degree turn in the Falkland Sound and proceed to San Carlos with the Gurkha musicians in her freezing hold. On hearing of this hijack after the journalists' Goose Green visit, the silver-topped harpoon became violent and threatening gestures were made at the Falkland Island Company and all in higher command as Colonel David demanded, 'Make sure, Mike, that the P and D and their remaining performances are rescued!' This became *the* priority and a hectic succeeding day resulted in not only apologies regarding the lead-swingers' act of piracy, but also Sea Kings to hoist up and fly off the shivering Gurkhas to Goose Green.

These logistics operations were not the only ones. Many rumours regarding our imminent UK return had necessitated Kit Spencer driving to Stanley to become our liaison officer monitoring these ever changing developments. *Norland* was one possibility and *Uganda* another, but on that 9 July he supplied firmer information, '250 Gurkhas will embark the Townsend Thoresen ferry *St Edmund* on its return from repatriating the 593 special category prisoners to Argentina!'

Meanwhile D Company had begun to train again and the Anti-Tank Platoon participated in their Company firepower demonstration at Fox Bay. They had carried more than their own bodyweight in manpacking the Milan launchers and missiles up to the top of the Tumbledown, and were frustrated in not being given the opportunity to open fire on Mount William. A consolation prize was needed, so I included in the Battalion's final post-war ammunition return to Brigade a report of the necessary 'destruction' of six highly expensive missiles because of 'war shrapnel-damage'. That is why the Anti-Tanks launched their missiles that day and, at 1400 metres range, engaged a rock and peat Gurkha-built bunker with full overhead protection. To their joy it was totally destroyed.

Another demonstration took place the following evening at Goose Green, now the penultimate venue for the P and D since their North Arm gig had been postponed for three days. Every settlement kelper and two prospective Knights – Mr Rex Hunt, now Civil Commissioner for the Falkland Islands and Major General Jeremy Moore were in the audience that also included the Brigadier and war artist Linda Kitson. Against a background of Argentine exploding para-illuminating flares, these must have been arguably the strangest circumstances in which a British military band has performed. The occasion captivated David Grey:

> It was a marvellous thing to see. Remember most people had not seen the like before. The lads built Edinburgh Castle with oil drums on the green, and I put floodlights around it. They built seats for all the guests and VIPs, with braziers and torches. It was well planned, and then it snowed. A real blizzard. The sudden bad weather did not deter the men. With coal swiped from the galley for the fires and oil for the torches, and the driving snow, what a splendorous sight to see the band, pipes and drums, with troops of Gurkhas marching through the back-lit snowflakes. The most memorable sight was of the lone piper atop his Edinburgh Castle, tied on because of the wind, playing laments. People will talk of this night forever. After the Retreat we were led by torchlight to the transit shed which had been turned into a restaurant and theatre where a meal and drinks were served to all and we were treated to a show of Gurkha culture.[10]

The *nautch* overflowed with bonhomie. Gurkhas had been shooting the abundant local geese throughout their stay at Darwin and Goose Green to augment the monotonous diet of compo rations and *dumba/*'365', and there was most certainly a goose ingredient served in the delicious *bhat*. This topic popped up between GM sahib and Colonel David as they ate.

'Sahib, I have been thinking that the pretty name of this settlement is now quite incorrect!'

A mystified Commandant sahib asked, 'What *do* you mean, sahib?'

Major Lalbahadur Rai's eyes twinkled as he replied, 'Well, we must be realistic, sahib. The *keta* have hunted and eaten so much *raja-hags* (goose) that Goose Green should be renamed "Green"!'

Their meal was followed by ninety minutes of Gurkha entertainment, but they missed the real drama. A worried Gurkha Signaller hurried into the transit shed. His breathless report ended my *bhat* enjoyment, 'Krystal sahib, I have just been ordered by the ops room watchkeeper to find you immediately – because an air raid warning red alert has just been sent out by Brigade!'

That familiar adrenalin surged through my stomach.

Chapter Twenty-four

RETURN

The biggest marathon in the history of foot-running is some scene to steal but that, precisely, is what the small brown men of the Himalayas achieved through the streets of London yesterday. Fresh from their last foray into British history – on Mount William . . . in the Falkland Islands – they yomped the 26 miles and 385 yards in a manner never seen before and most likely never to be seen again. They smiled as they ran. They ran as they smiled. And amid the milling crush of 18,000 fellow runners they kept their military formation as though this were some high speed Trooping of the Colour. No question about it. The Gurkhas . . . took the London Marathon by storm . . . To their battle honours from the Indian Mutiny to the Falkland Islands they added a postscript that London will long remember. – Extract from an article written by Ian Wooldridge in the *Daily Mail* – 18 April 1983.

Mark and I hurried through the snow ready to crank the siren handle. 'It is OK, Training Officer sahib,' said Lieutenant Manbir Limbu in the ops room, 'a stand-down from Brigade has arrived!' Cause and effect was later reported by *The Penguin News*:

> An unidentified aircraft was spotted on radar at about 7.00 p.m. on the 10th July, and, as the 'plane had intruded about twenty miles into the total exclusion zone, the message 'air raid warning red' was flashed to all units and ships around the Islands. Ships in Stanley Harbour and Port William were blacked out, and army patrols on the streets urged people to return to their homes and extinguish their lights. However within minutes the aircraft had left the zone, and it appears that it was flying south and strayed into Falklands' air space. It is possible that the aircraft was a C130 Hercules of the Argentine Air Force which was on its way from Buenos Aires to a base in the Antarctic.[1]

No red air alert could stop a *nautch* that spellbound the kelpers with its Nepalese dances, songs and comedy acts. One was a revolting performance that occurred in a field hospital operating theatre where props included artificial *dumba* private parts and *the* silver-topped surgical instrument. Captain Hombahadur Gurung was a clever *jadu-wallah* and no magician could surpass his gluttony in devouring electric light bulbs. Afterwards most, including the General and Commissioner, danced with the Gurkhas to P and D tunes that inevitably included the majestic tones of *Black Bear* whilst I neared

305

the Brigadier. He nodded towards Linda Kitson and said, 'Why don't you ask her to dance?' I wanted something else. She was sketching a Gurkha thumping on his *madal* and so, instead, the artist was asked cheekily, 'May I have it?' Linda kindly signed the unique two-minute scribble that hangs today in my office: 'Love from Linda, to quote *Private Eye* "Kitbags" '. When the Brigadier retired in the small hours, three grinning Gurkhas assisted him into Colonel David's Argentine Mercedes. He was driven to the Darwin house of Brook Hardcastle, Manager of the Falkland Island Company, to sleep away the remainder of that night and retire from the Army in December. Another dazzled by the *nautch* and his Gurkha hosts was David Grey again:

> Most finished up a little drunk, but what the hell. What a night. What great and charming people. Ask the people who were there in Goose Green 1982. We remember them all.[2]

His opinion was similar to a Spaniard's who had visited us with eleven other journalists sixty hours before, and flew on 10 July back to the UK from Stanley Airport. Andrés Ortega, whose country had abstained from voting on UN Resolution 502, had written notes and taken pictures for a colour supplement article in the national newspaper *El País*:

> The famous Gurkhas . . . sleeping quarters were the cleanest in all the Malvinas. Before going into their rooms one had to clean one's boots with a brush and water. Their food was the best. We never had the opportunity to try their curry, but they are given the same rations as British soldiers. They just knew how to cook them better. So their famous 'spam', a kind of pig's cold meat which is rather revolting for those who know Italian chorizo or German sausage, was served fried with Argentine 'tagliatelle' to accompany this delicacy.
>
> They were simply charming, until the word 'mercenaries' was used. But no, they were loyal to their Regiment and the Queen of England . . . The cold Malvinas climate was not unfamiliar to them: it reminded them of Nepal where they all came from. The land was similar to Wales where they had trained, but they preferred to fight in the jungle. It requires more intelligence.
>
> The Gurkhas were disillusioned with the Malvinas Conflict . . . they thought that the Argentines had behaved like cowards even though they had a great deal of equipment at their disposal. According to the Gurkhas' claims, each time they advanced the Argentines would hastily run away. This is what a reputation can do for you . . . The inhabitants of Goose Green were obviously charmed by these extremely orderly Gurkhas, who at the end of the battle had restored the military salute amongst themselves; the British were more relaxed.[3]

But life had become trivial. I continued my ten-day long assignment of enquiring into the whereabouts of the *Sunday Mirror* 6,000 bottle consignment of specially-brewed Task Force beer and mysterious crates of rum that the Caribbean island of Jamaica had also provided. The former would turn up in the Falklands at the end of July when we were in mid-Atlantic, but I would fail totally to locate the latter. The only sensible alternative on 12 July was to load myself aboard a helicopter and visit D Company. Impressions at Fox Bay were many. Union Flags fluttered at both settlements and the word 'civilian' had been painted on the roofs and white walls of certain houses to warn any attacking Harrier. Ringed by mountains, the scenery and snow-covered terrain possessed a Norwegian wintry ambience as, in contrast to the Argentine minefields, lined up mortars, recoilless rifles and anti-tank guns, the Gurkhas tobogganed with child-like enthusiasm down the slopes of Fox Bay East.

As Argentina recognized a de facto cessation of hostilities, 5 Brigade's two-day Battlefield Tour Party debriefing was fed at Goose Green that day, according to Linda Kitson, with 'a sensational Gurkha curry'[4] i.e. *bhat*, and Kit Spencer later broke the news of our departure over the ops room radio. We did not have to wait for *St Edmund*'s return from Puerto Madryn after repatriating her 'special category' cargo that included General Mario Benjamín Menéndez, the *Ex Gobernador de Malvinas*. 'OK, the decision's been made,' reported the RSO, 'the hospital ship *Uganda* is to become a troop ship, and on 15 July we'll start embarking onto her – for Southampton! ETA is 9 August!' The date concentrated minds wonderfully and, unwilling to lose his Mercedes, Colonel David demanded that this *and* the other three be shipped to the UK. Only his made the trip as our MTO, David Wright, risked life and limb by somehow getting it loaded aboard a vessel at Stanley.

Meanwhile the QOH's Advance Party had arrived to start taking over from Rory Stewart's small Rear Party which eventually flew back to UK to arrive before us, and there was a last drinks party given to the 1st/7th officers by the Goose Green kelpers in their Community Centre on 14 July. Only a 'two-hour job from 8 to 10' as I wrote to Tove, a QGO burst into the proceedings early on to yell, 'Fire! Fire in the bunkhouse!' I ran out to discover a Gurkha Signaller in 'my' ops room had mistakenly filled a paraffin stove with petrol and then lit it. Fortunately he was uninjured, the alarm given and the fire extinguished, leaving behind scorched walls in the newly painted ops room and corridor outside. *'Bujhno'* (understand)? was always asked by BOs and QGOs alike to the soldiers, but this accident was an example of 'bujability' falling below expected standards. Any Gurkha detractor would have seized on this final Battalion blue-on-blue as more proof why Gurkhas in the British Army's order of battle are 'nice to have' rather than 'need to have'. The remainder of this book, however, argues that the Army cannot afford to be without them.

Next day I said goodbye to the Baillies while waiting outside their home for our Chinook. They took holidays in South America, including Buenos Aires, but just before the invasion had visited Ginnie's relatives in Australia. 'We'll probably emigrate there soon,' were Keith's final words to me and, many years later, I received confirmation they did just that. Our flight to *Uganda* in Grantham Sound took twenty minutes. Able to accommodate 300 casualties, the 16,907 ton former P&O children's educational cruise ship and ex-Naval Ocean-going Surgical Hospital had operated from this NOSH designated area known as the NOSH-BOX. She had been converted into a troop ship to accommodate the Gurkhas which required dismantling her wards, operating theatre and burns, intensive-care, x-ray, opthalmology and dentistry units. Rust had gnawed at the white hull and, to indicate *Uganda*'s new status, her white funnel and its red cross had been painted in a buff colour. After landing on the flight deck at 11.40 hours, we

307

deplaned through the side door as the Chinook's rear exit was protruding over the sea, cleared weapons, walked down the steep stairway, and through the Triage Area where arriving casualties had been sorted. Once inside the ship, a cabin allocation was made and I found myself sharing with Mark Willis again. Fresh bed sheets, comfortable leather armchairs and waiter service in the oak panelled officers' dining room meant our spartan existence ashore belonged to history. Gurkha feeding arrangements were more complicated with three half-hour sittings each meal time.

Twenty-four hours later on 16 July the last two Gurkha companies in West Falkland were also embarked by 14.30 hours. On board were now 598 Gurkhas, 79 soldiers of 16 Field Ambulance and 136 members of Naval Party 1830 that included surgeons, nurses and a Royal Marine band cum stretcher bearer platoon. The BO newcomers were immediately confronted with an evening cocktail party where the small talk was flush with Exocet, shore medical facilities and NOSH tit-bits. 'Did you know that during a red air alert on 1 June two Exocets were fired at *Norland* in the Falkland Sound and your escort HMS *Penelope* threw up chaff to deflect them away?' remarked the Senior Naval Officer of Naval Party 1830 to me. Another officer countered, 'Come on! *Penelope* did have a bit of a reputation for shouting "Exocet!" at anything that moved, y'know.' The facts later spoke for themselves because the Argentines had exhausted their arsenal of five air-launched Exocets by 30 May. I circulated to a surgeon who had some insider information. 'Before the war as a goodwill gesture the Argies built a hostel in Stanley to be used as a weekend recreation facility for Falklands' children,' he confided to me. 'Its design, however, enabled a rapid conversion after the invasion to a military hospital as rooms could be used as operating theatres, and full electric wiring had been installed for specialist medical equipment such as x-ray machines!' Another boasted about NOSH business, 'On board *Uganda* we managed to carry out 504 surgical operations on 730 "in" patients which were mostly limb amputations!'

Next in line was a nurse of the Queen Alexandra's Royal Naval Nursing Service only too pleased to talk to a 100 per cent intact ex-Falklands' War soldier. Her patients' pervading black-humour eased their suffering. 'Just like those,' she said, 'who placed bets on who had the smaller leg stump! Also one of our 159 Argentine casualties lay next to an SAS trooper, but was afraid that his walking-wounded neighbour would eat him alive. My consoling didn't help, but then an urgent errand forced me to leave the ward. On my return, I found the trooper and his friends seated around the Argentine's bed with their quaking victim hiding under his sheets as they held their knives and forks at the ready!'

I also felt unusual relief in learning quite by chance, from another lady of the lamp, of the survival of 'my' Scots Guardsman who had been shot through the neck on the Tumbledown. But as we moved down to the dining room, *Uganda* was already underway on an easterly course for the Stanley Harbour outer bay of Port William in a storm Force Eight wind and some of the newly arrived BOs began to feel seasick. It was also Tove's birthday, so I decide to ring her afterwards on the telephone satellite facility. Zac, a straggly black bearded P&O officer in the Purser's Office, answered my questions. 'It costs nearly £6 for three minutes. You can book here and pay afterwards,' he said but, in the phone booth, panic struck. The previous weeks' stresses had caused me to forget my home number, so another booking had to be made five hours later and at 23.40 hours UK local time, my mother received my first next of kin phone call thirty-one days after cessation of hostilities.

My insomnia of the past weeks was now replaced by a deep sleep that night. Next morning I sent a telegram to Tove instead as we berthed alongside the tanker MV *Fort Toronto* at Port William to take on water and the Battalion's freight and suitcases. The latter's storage in a Stanley warehouse required me giving a thorough wash to my mildewed and stinking clothing. Another important task was, as per *QE2*, identification of suitable training areas on the various decks. Conferences were also on the increase and I participated in three that day. In the evening Tove rang *Uganda*, and afterwards she wrote about her lowered emotional trigger threshold similar to mine:

> I have just been sitting through three hours of the TV spectacular – A National Tribute To The Task Force. Wept non-stop, so now I'm completely drained and must go to bed! The whole of the British theatre and music world paid their tribute . . . it makes me think of the Second World War and what England must have been like then. Only the English could do it like this. Slightly pompous – extremely pompous in the eyes of a foreigner, but oh so beautiful and right . . . they had all the Services represented tonight who fought on the Falkland Islands – and when those four little Gurkhas marched on the stage . . . well, I just bellowed! Literally! It is a good way for you to unwind and relax to come home by ship – and what a homecoming seeing the ship approach Southampton. Since I deliberately missed out on *QE2* leaving, I have had a sneaking hankering for at least welcoming you home the same way you left.

I participated in another three conferences on Sunday, 18 July when we sailed for Southampton after *Hydra*, another of *Uganda*'s ambulance ships[5], had received stores from her 'Mother Hen' vessel. The following morning, a General Emergency Stations drill signalled we were well under way but, compared with *QE2*'s daily 600 nautical miles, *Uganda* could only achieve 350. Three weeks without land except Ascension Island would be tedious, particularly as the coloured pins on the promenade deck's sea chart crawled painfully northwards. Inside this decompression chamber, back to a normal life, the NOSH pathology laboratory had reverted to its original cocktail bar status. Propping this up was not my style. I did not mix much and, in a daily sub-conscious four-hour 'defusing', expanded my notes on the war. Gurkhas, by definition, were exempt any psychological debriefing on possible negative effects from traumatic war zone stress and useful preventive self-help techniques. Not that any psychiatrists were available for British Army combatants, nor were any systematic long-term follow-up procedures initiated for us combat veterans. Perhaps this was a fault but, unlike US Army soldiers trickle-posted as individuals in and out of units during the Vietnam War, travelling back to the UK as a cohesive group from our war seemed a great advantage and sufficient at the time. Support, if needed, was available from others in 'the same boat'.

I also ran before dinner. During daily thirty-minute sessions on the promenade deck which prevented depressive thinking, fresh ideas were generated about a Gurkha London Marathon team. Battalion training also had to be coordinated and published in a daily Inter-Platoon Sports Championship programme comprising hockey, tennis quoits, table tennis, deck quoits, tug of war, and water polo, training for the annual Cambrian Marches Patrol Competition, and five educational courses run by Manbir sahib, the Assistant Education Officer. My compulsive writing took up so much time that I refused when he asked, 'Can you talk to the *keta* in the English classes, sahib?' I still have a bad conscience about that.

BIT also started up again early every morning, with objections. 'You Gurkhas are making such a damned noise thumping on deck that we can't sleep!' complained the Naval Party 1830 representative to Mark and me at the daily training and adminis-trative conference. We soothed away this irritation by starting BIT later. Gurkha bridge and engine room visits, parties, tombola, video and film shows were organized and, on one evening, two Gurkhas in colourful costumes accompanied by a singing team and *madal* drummers even performed a Tamang dance in the Warrant Officers' and Sergeants' Mess. Mark explained the origins of this drag act to me, 'One's dressed as a girl and is known as a *maruni.* Her partner's a boy or *phursunge.* It's *kaida* from the last century when these *jhaures* were held beside night-time campfires at lonely outposts far from Nepal, to boost sagging morale with no girls available – as you saw at Goose Green's *nautch*!' A year later similar entertainment on board *Uganda* would be provided by Sandhurst's Gurkha Demonstration Company returning from Fortress Falklands garrison duties at Port Howard, West Falkland. But was it really true that the ship's officers thought that the composite company's dancing was better than 1st/7th Gurkha Rifles'?

In comparison to our men's performance, the Officers' Mess Royal Marine band concert and nightingale voice of Nursing Sister Liz Law singing from *Jesus Christ Superstar* were violently conservative. The General Memorial Service on Sunday, 25 July brought deeper reflection as the ship's Padre spoke about Paul Callan's courage. A young Marine medical orderly, he had been severely wounded by shrapnel when retrieving a casualty. I thought of my Uncle Percy at Passchendaele as the Padre read out an extract from a postcard Callan had written to his family: 'Just a touch of shrapnel . . . nothing to worry about . . . as long as you're alright.' He became only one of three to die on board and receive a burial at sea. Afterwards, a warm afternoon brought the welcome contrast of a boat deck Sunday *bhat* lunch for all officers on board.

Two days later, I assisted Colonel David to write another post-Falklands' War report. No debriefing had been possible on the Falklands because 5 Brigade had wanted a 'first impressions' report, but the Company commanders objected at their non-inclusion and carried out their own debriefing on board. Countless lessons learnt and demands made were included in this second report which included:

More imaginative and challenging training needed . . . Improve collective endurance and aircraft recognition . . . More night training needed . . . Radio communications and leadership are vital . . . The value of snipers cannot be stressed enough . . . Effectiveness of small-arms fire against low-flying enemy aircraft and corresponding requirement to improve aircraft recognition . . . The helicopter's flexibility and Battalion anti-tank weapon bunker-busting capability are battle-winners.

Next day, 28 July, we arrived in English Bay, Ascension Island to take on water and fuel from the tanker MV *Alvega* and transfer stores and personnel. Some went ashore on this arid volcano whose only vegetation grew on the aptly named Green Mountain. Lester Holley and I gazed up at it as we leant on the deck rail. The ex-SAS trooper's mind was thousands of nautical miles away southwards as he groaned, 'I've had a bad war, and'll never be able to face up to the lads at the Regiment in Hereford. Jesus, fancy not having fought in a battle!' Lester had clearly not read Sun Tzu's book, *The Art of War*. His SAS squadron had also missed out, because their perilous Operation MIKADO mission to raid the Super Etendard base at Rio Grande had been postponed several times and they only arrived by a sea parachute drop immediately prior to the ceasefire.

We raised anchor to continue the plod north as the pipe on the Tannoy declared: 'Zac'll be running a raffle competition in aid of the British Limbless Ex-Servicemen's Association. The winner's prize will be to cut off his beard!' I decided then my London Marathon team would run for BLESMA. Combat stress contributed to the growing irritation of confinement. I continued coordinating the Sports Championship and easing frustrations by writing. An annoyed Colonel David also picked up a pen on 31 July after reading an article in a back number of *The Penguin News*. His letter to the Editor was a new example of BO care for Gurkhas:

> I caught sight of your excellent paper whilst . . . on SS 'Uganda', and was disturbed to read a certain statement made on page 2 of your issue . . . dated 16 July 1982 concerning the death of my young Gurkha soldier while clearing trenches at Goose Green.
>
> It is my duty to correct the impression you give that Lance Corporal Budhaparsad Limbu 'picked up an unexploded grenade'. This is not true. He was a skilled and professional soldier and would not have committed such a careless act. The grenade which we suspect was a British M-79 round, the type fired from a shotgun like weapon, was buried deep in the earth protecting the front of the Argentine trench which Budhaparsad had been ordered to fill in. The grenade detonated when struck by Budhaparsad's spade, killing him and wounding two other soldiers working with him.
>
> I heartily endorse the warning you give to treat any suspicious objects with caution but feel very strongly that by misinterpreting the facts of this tragic accident you devalue this young man's life. He died helping to make the Falkland Islands safe and clean again after the war, not through error or stupidity, but by sheer accident. There is a vital and important difference which I would be grateful if you could correct.[6]

UK arrival plans were also being made and verbal warnings given and orders published threatening severe penalties for anyone retaining Argie weapons and equipment. Via the satellite telephone, Bill Dawson reported the local town of Fleet's need for a P and D led Battalion march down the High Street after our Southampton disembarkation. When the daily midday O Group was informed, a united but unsuccessful BO protest broke out, 'No way! Why must we do that? The Paras won it, all we want is to get back home!' However as a psychosocial support measure, it would prove to be no bad thing.

The last major entertainment was the 'Falkland Follies' review and I attended its final performance for officers and senior ranks on Wednesday, 4 August. With the programme displaying: 'Costumes by Rent-a-Tent, Hair by Wind and Rain, Make-up by Mud Factor, Lighting by 'Lectric and Music by Eine Kleine Nachtmusik . . . at no expense whatever' how could the evening go wrong? The Gurkhas contributed with P and D music that naturally included *Black Bear*, a Sherpa Dance, Hombahadur sahib's conjuring tricks in his 'Joker Act/It's Magic' and a Mortar Platoon song about Falkland *dumba* entitled *Lazy Bones*. Mao Tse-tung's concept: 'An army without culture is a dull-witted army, and a dull-witted army cannot defeat the enemy' had been validated, even though the programme's 'Press Comments' – 'This show should go far, the further the better (*Goose Green Times*)' and 'The audience were fighting in the aisle to get out (*Darwin Echo*)' – were untrue.

Our current Jack Tar antagonists also intended making PR hay whilst the sun shone, leaving us dumped behind the haystack. Notified that press and TV reporters would embark twenty-four hours before docking at Southampton, I sent out a Gurkha press statement before being caught up in press conference planning. Then rehearsals took place for 'Procedure Alpha' prior to the final ride up the Solent as BO thoughts turned to painting slogans on banners. The buff funnel also became a vulnerable potential 'tagging' site, but the daily *Troop Orders* from Naval Party 1830 were adamant, 'It has been decreed . . . NO BANNERS are to be displayed except for the Red Cross Banner. All other banners will be removed.' Exacting revenge, Mark and Kit wrote a Gurkha 9 August disembarkation day edition of the official *Today's Arrangements* newsletter and daily *Troop Orders*. Signed by the 'Officer in Command Matelots: H. Nelson', *'Today's Arraignments (Alias: Troop Orders)'* was distributed throughout 'SS *Uganda* – Totally at sea'. This is an abridged version:

THOUGHT FOR THE DAY.
(Sorry, couldn't think of one.)

FROM THE NAVIGATOR.
At noon today, with a bit of luck we shall be at the position that we were wishing we were in for the last three weeks – i.e. on dry land in UK. Our average speed was half as much it ought to have been, and the distance travelled since noon yesterday was slightly more than yesterday but still barely noticeable. If you look over the right (whoops, starboard) side of the ship even now you will notice that the illusion of movement still persists.

INTERESTING FACTS.
Some interesting facts about our embarked troops (Who?) are listed below.

STATISTICS.
Number of grains of rice consumed by 1/7 GR personnel since 12 May – 9,433,511.
Number of hot meals consumed in the field under enemy fire – 3.

Number of hot meals missed due to enemy action – far too many.

Days spent by 1/7 GR personnel on windswept hillsides with rain dripping down collars and feet in six inches of water at the bottoms of their trenches – lost count.

Number of artillery shells fired by enemy in spiteful and unsporting fashion directly at little brown men minding their own business and digging peat for reasons totally unconnected with hostile thoughts – hundreds (that means at least one for each of us).

Embarked troops have run 1,764 miles along wooden decking during periods of fitness training. It has been estimated this means a loss of 17lbs 14 ¾ ozs of wood from Uganda's all-up weight.

Number of times that the plan for disembarkation has changed in the last two weeks: 1830.

It has been estimated that 1.679% of Naval personnel now believe that *Uganda* is a Troop Ship.

HISTORICAL YESTERDAYS AUG 9TH.

On August 9th 1830 the Navy discovered the sea. As the Army did not want it and, as in any case the land was already in use by thousands of squaddies doing PT, they laid claim to it. This claim was not disputed.

NP 1830 SPECIAL TEMPERATE ROUTINE.

0600: 1/7GR (598) muster in Triage for transfer of stores from Verandah to No. 2 Hold and back.

1030: Duty Watch Muster.

1045: Hands secure for the day.

1400–1700: All deck space reserved for Senior Rates recreation (Twenty minutes each side, turn over and repeat).

2130-Midnight: Entertainment. The port (left) side of the promenade (walking) deck (floor) forward (towards the sharp end) is reserved for the use of the lower deck sweepers and stokers. Dress: 13As (casual), with Red Cross armbands. STRICTLY BY INVITATION ONLY!! Apart from the six 1/7GR Company parties and the 16 Field Ambulance Disco and the P&O Officers' wardroom cocktail party there will be no organised entertainment.

Life became busier. Zac made £300 for BLESMA, and on 7 August had his beard cut off. Next day we packed our kit, and the six company *nautchs* on the bridge and boat decks were filmed by BBC and ITN TV crews whilst the Battalion Public Information Officer sahib became press-ganged into a *jhaure* as a *phursunge* to an enticing *maruni*. Disembarkation day began with the press conference and predictably presented the feats of the Task Force Naval Ocean-going Surgical Hospital, but little of 7GR. The rest was a blur . . . flawless blue sky and the sun . . . photographers placing Sergeant Hem in a kukri decapitation pose with Mr John Nott . . . sirens blasting in the Solent . . . water fountain jets being sprayed from four accompanying tugs . . . 10,000 meeters and greeters at Berth no. 106 . . . *QE2* parked up nearby in her new livery of grey . . . flags and slogan-bedecked banners . . . meeting my family . . . a lager and lime in a nearby pub . . . crowds six-deep along Fleet's High Street . . . Colonel David, minus the silver-topped mace, decorated with the longest garland of gold tinsel ever made by the local Indian restaurant owner . . . and nearly tripping up on it . . . a camp muster parade . . . and, finally, home to a yellow-ribboned, flag-bedecked 80, Wakefords Park and a nice cup of tea. Fan mail continued to arrive at the Battalion and one letter, posted in Southend-on-Sea the day afterwards, was 'From English Citizens Everywhere'. It read:

> Well Done Gurkhas
> and
> Welcome Back
> So glad you're on our side
> We're Proud of You
> An English Citizen

The Gurkha Falklands' adventure was over. Or was it? The aftermath rumbled on as I watched the joint TV team's pictures on Long Toenail during the BBC's last programme of its *Task Force South* series. My twitches at the Tumbledown shelling indicated a need for leave. We got one month and the Gurkhas received a special dispensation to visit Nepal provided they paid the £400 airfare – a mean offer from those controlling the purse strings to defenders of Britain. Nonetheless thirty travelled. At Heathrow Hem was prominent on *The Daily Telegraph*'s front page picture of them dressed in an immaculate 'uniform' of pinstripe suits, white shirts, Regimental ties, black shoes and carrying furled umbrellas for the rainy season.

To Tove's irritation, I continued writing on our Corfu family holiday. This was selfish, but expanding on the fifty-five typed pages from *Uganda* overshadowed everything. I also sent a postcard and letter to Keith Baillie and, on return to Church Crookham, received a reply dated 20 September with a local impression of post-war life:

> Goose Green is slowly returning back to normal, with most of the slit trenches and debris of war being cleared away. Although people still feel wary when moving around the outer perimeter of the Argentine defence lines.
>
> The trout season has opened, and I have had a couple of good catches of 8lb and a few smaller ones . . . The extension to the airstrip (at Stanley) has been completed and I believe that the Phantoms (RAF fighter aircraft) could be there next week. There is talk of building an international airport between Goose Green and Fitzroy . . . We are due our first visit from the compensation claims people on Wednesday of this week, we have nearly forgot what we are claiming for.

Not unsurprisingly the settlers were worried about mines. I also received some back-copies of *The Penguin News*, and one described the fate of a 'Gurkha' Argentine Land-Rover:

Two soldiers were injured at Goose Green on 1st August when the long wheel base ex-Argentine Mercedes-Benz that they were driving backed onto an anti-tank mine left by the Argentines. The explosion threw the vehicle some distance. Both men were flown into Stanley by helicopter for treatment. Their wounds were not serious.[7]

Falkland thoughts continued during an Army friend's dinner party. I felt irritated and impatient with others incapable of understanding war's stresses at its sharp end. Discovering this bizarre world had changed me. 'So why not them too?' I wondered illogically. *Penguins Prefer Peace* was therefore an appropriate title for the second draft of my book and, during the next four months, I surfaced daily from my bed at dead man's hour to ventilate frustrations on paper before work at camp. On the surface, life there remained unchanged. Few enquired about our experiences, although one of these exceptions were two Ministry of Defence Royal Artillery staff officers investigating Falklands' War artillery, Rapier and Blowpipe performances. Anxious to prove the latter had not been as bad as its nine-hit result, they were delighted to hear of C Company's test-firing those three Goose Green missiles.

'Oh yes,' they assured us in the Officers' Mess whilst deleting these missiles from a list of assumed misses and misfires, 'this'll have a significant effect on the Blowpipe statistics! Clearly the previous century's statement by Prime Minister Benjamin Disraeli: 'There are three types of lies: lies, damned lies, and statistics' had not been part of their calculations.

In October I took over command of A Company and a disgruntled L-squared returned to his old job. My first parade was a BFT that demonstrated the Gurkhas' running potential as most needed only nine minutes thirty seconds or under to pass the one and a half mile test. Before asking for London Marathon volunteers, a final Falklands' pilgrimage with other Battalion officers was made to the *QE2* at Southampton where GM sahib presented her Master, Captain Peter Jackson, with a Nepalese silver kukri. At the pleasant ceremony three men shared an unusual common denominator from another island war. I was one because my father had served in Malta during its Second World War siege. Captain Jackson was another. With two years service on Malta convoys, he spent days in an open boat after his ship, the Blue Funnel Line's MV *Mentor*, was torpedoed en route to the Island. Colonel David, the last, had been born in March 1939 at Sliema where my father had lived. Son of the Royal Navy officer in command of the Grand Harbour dockyards and bombed out of three houses, three-year old David Morgan was flown to Gibraltar with his parents in the belly of a Hudson bomber after the siege had been lifted.

A few weeks afterwards I recruited my marathon team, and a phone call was made to Chris Brasher, the Olympic gold medallist Race Director. He had climbed with Gurkhas in the Himalayas, so I secured a Gurkha carte blanche entry and free running kit worth £1,500. Captain Hombahadur Gurung asked for volunteers at a muster parade and twenty-six accepted the challenge. Later I gave a forty-five minute briefing, 'This is a marathon. 26 miles 385 yards. It's run in London. A million people will watch the marathon – and you. TV will broadcast it live. You'll be the first Gurkhas ever to run a marathon. We must train hard. For five months. And we have to begin now. *Bujhno?*'

Despite rubber-faced Hombahadur sahib's interpreter skills, the Gurkhas' facial expressions and blank eyes still registered incomprehension even though they nodded in agreement. I tried explaining the entry form, 'Because of so many runners there are two start lines. The red's for the girls and those men who've never run a marathon. And the blue's for men who've run at least one!'

The information would be used as the basis for a computerized start list. I noted my 1981 Bielefeld marathon finishing time on my entry form. To make matters easier, the Gurkhas were told by the enthusiastic OC sahib, 'Now fill out yours by copying mine!' Receiving start lists and running numbers months later, I became puzzled that no Gurkha name was on the red start list. Then the penny dropped. They did not want to run with the girls and had copied my Bielefeld time, so the computer deduced that L. Rai, S. Rai, R. Rai, K. Rai etc. had already run a marathon before in three hours thirty-nine minutes, and put eleven Mr Rais, five Mr Limbus and three Mr Gurungs on the blue start.

The marathon party began a twenty-one week training programme that month. Daily they paraded in double file and diminutive Lance Corporal Sukrim Rai who had drawn his kukri in anger at Egg Harbour House would report, 'Marathon party is present, sahib!' They always ran in that formation smiling and laughing and then, with the run completed, Sukrim would ask for permission to dismiss. 'Marathon' remained untranslatable into Gurkhali, so their curiousity was increasing and Sukrim Rai explained later, 'I did not care about any other sporting exercise other than marathon training, sahib. I kept on thinking, 'What is the marathon? I want to know that, so I must do it.'

We continued to train in double file through Christmas and New Year, and by February ten miles was easy. Continuing on the Battalion's two-month Exercise TRUMPET DANCE at Fort Lewis in Washington State, USA, we practised mobile drinking on thirteen-mile runs, but a torn leg muscle, bruised heel and sore knees indicated the tougher demands. On one session a hobbling Gurkha fell back and I advised, 'Stop, if you've a problem!' In spite of a stress fracture of his leg, the Gurkha replied, 'No, sahib, I must go on.' He did too. A few days later my men were taught how to rapell backwards down a twenty-metre rapelling tower. All succeeded and, after our US Army instructors demonstrated a more daring technique of running forwards down the tower's face, many also did this without hesitation. 'Gee!' exclaimed one American to me, 'our soldiers have problems in rapelling backwards, but your men smile achieving that *and* the Australian rapell!'

In twilight during the final couple of miles of a training run back to camp afterwards, the OC sahib tripped up on an unseen pothole. The 'dancer's fracture' of my right foot required three weeks' enforced rest but my 2IC, Captain Narainprasad Rai, continued to crack the whip. He supplied all with an apple and raw egg at the end of each training session with stringent instructions that both were to be eaten immediately. Before another training run from a morning on the shooting ranges, a *bhat* lunch was delivered.

'Shouldn't we have ordered sandwichs, sahib?' I asked the QGO, frowning.

'No, sahib,' he reprimanded me, 'the marathon party need *bhat* to give them strength for running!' And he made sure they received a double helping before their thirteen mile run.

The Gurkhas attracted attention wherever they went, and I gave an impromptu interview about them with a local Seattle TV station. At the end of our USA exercise I travelled with eighty plus of my Gurkhas for a weekend of sightseeing and shopping in Vancouver, Canada. On arrival our hotel flung open their doors and provided a free drink to 'the famous Gurkhas' but, to reduce the cost of our stay, *QE2* standards were imposed as four Gurkhas were put in each room. I shared one with Narainprasad sahib and two other QGOs, dependable Lieutenant Tekbahadur Limbu and *khaini*-enthusiast Ratnabahadur Gurung. There was only one king-size bed, but large enough to take three comfortably. My 2IC would not entertain the chilling thought. 'You will sleep in the bed, sahib,' he ordered me sternly. 'And we QGOs will sleep on the floor!'

Returning to Church Crookham and frightful weather at the end of March, our runs increased to sixteen miles thereby achieving the barest weekly minimum required of sixty-five. After a final twenty-miler the marathon party ignored pasta and ate *bhat* instead. Public relations had been limited to a couple of newspaper pictures and captions but, two days before the event, Ian Wooldridge of the *Daily Mail* rang to ask, 'Chris Brasher has told me about your Gurkhas running on Sunday. Sounds as if it could be an interesting story on the men from the foothills of Everest. May I interview you at Church Crookham tomorrow?'

I agreed and, at the appointed time, met the well-known sports writer and TV broadcaster outside the Officers' Mess. We sat down in the ante-room and a Mess orderly appeared.

'Drink, sahib?' he enquired politely.

'What would you like?' I asked Mr. Wooldridge.

'A whisky with a dash of water,' replied my guest.

So I placed his order with the orderly, 'OK, a glass of whisky with water, please.'

The Gurkha's 'bujability' was on trial. 'Sorry, sahib?' he enquired apologetically.

Perhaps a dash of my limited Gurkhali was needed to reinforce my order, so I foolishly took the chance by repeating loudly, 'Whisky! *Tato pani!*'

Five minutes later there materialized a glass of whisky and silver jug filled with steaming hot water perched on a silver tray. I tried to explain the Gurkha's apparent faux pas, but Mr Wooldridge smiled and just said, 'These things happen!'

But in A Company's restroom afterwards we failed *our* 'bujability' test miserably when Colonel David, now an Order of the British Empire recipient for his Falklands' War service, made a cameo appearance to give a pre-battle Gurkhali speech to the cross-legged marathon party. It extracted unanimous compliance between every sentence with the *keta*'s responses of, '*Ao,* sahib!' . . . 'Sahib!' . . . '*Ao,* sahib!' The scene also conjured up a personal memory recall of that final evening on board *Norland.*

Afterwards he translated the theme of his speech. It had a strong hint of *kaida.* 'You'll finish. You'll run as soldiers, together. I don't care if it takes three hours or four days. The name of the Regiment is in your hands!'

Next day, six months after a Gurkha contingent had marched with the Task Force Falklands' Parade through London, we arrived in our coach at crowded Charing Cross Station to take the special train to Blackheath and massed start. The Gurkhas appeared

317

as bemused as at Southampton before embarking onto *QE2*. But in this Falklands-like cold and drizzle their reputation turned heads. 'Cor! Look, Sid! It's them! Betcha they win it,' was one remark.

After the short train journey, we walked in the crowds towards the white-mushroom shapes of marquee tents on Blackheath Common and the Blue Start. As before and after our landing at Blue Beach, disorder then occurred. Responding to an urgent call of nature, two Gurkhas were still missing after the Royal Artillery had fired their twenty-five pounder starting gun. Keeping together became a major challenge in the awful crush. A clattering TV helicopter overhead produced a flashback to Bravo November's flight. Others' shorts were grabbed for safety as we passed under the 'start' banner and TV camera perched precariously on a gantry. But the BBC failed to capture one million spectators' reaction to the Gurkhas that day. At three miles we were running along the wet road at our own pace to a 'Here come the Gurkhas!' 'Well done the Gurkhas!' 'Keep moving Gurkhas!' chorus en route. 'Three cheers for the Gurkhas!' shouted a fellow runner – and they smiled back.

Avoiding hundreds of trampled and crushed cardboard cups lying over Woolwich Road, a common water station hazard, we ran past another South Atlantic veteran, the *Cutty Sark*, at Greenwich to continue up Evelyn Street towards Southwark. Eight miles were behind us as the crowds, band music and runners in fancy dress contributed to the carnival atmosphere. Even John Conteh, the former world boxing champion, ran with us. A London Marathon cliché that participants 'run through a tunnel of emotion' had become a reality for the Gurkhas and by Tower Bridge and Cable Street we had reached the halfway point. My watch showed we were on schedule with one hour and thirty-seven minutes of running but, at seventeen miles in the Isle of Dogs, I hit 'the wall'.

They left me standing while Kipling's line: 'By the livin' Gawd that made you, you're a better man than I am, Gunga Din!' jogged tauntingly around my mind as spectators supplemented my water station refreshments with oranges, water, a foul electrolyte drink and bags of encouragement. Not even a loudspeaker piping *Chariots of Fire* music last heard on *Norland*, could motivate my leaden legs' tempo as Tower Bridge loomed again. With feet hammering on planks that covered the cobbles down towards the Tower of London's outer courtyard, I ran past two amused Beefeaters into Lower Thames Street towards Victoria Embankment. There was no sign of the marathon party. Someone saw the crossed kukris on my running vest and called out, 'Come on Gurkha soldier!' Never did I feel less like one.

Passing under Admiralty Arch and along the Mall, I caught up with four Gurkhas including Sukrim Rai. The main body, four minutes further on at Westminster Bridge, dismissed themselves in the military manner by halting and turning to the right thirty metres from the finishing line. An oversleeping Sukrim had missed breakfast that morning, but the effects of his hunger were now forgotten because, as he said, 'I got a medal with kiss from a beautiful girl!' whilst Sergeant Basantkumar Rai chose to write later in the *Regimental Journal* about the collective Gurkha reaction to that 17 April day:

> We felt like a centipede crawling slowly towards its destination. After seventeen miles we became tired with the loss of body fluid, but the tremendous encourage-

ment that we received from the cheering crowds on both sides of the street and that of our fellow runners kept us moving to our final destination . . . What beautiful people. At times so deeply moved we felt like crying with joy and pride for we found in the midst of London streets how close and near we were to the British people. Perhaps the streets of London might be busy with its usual hustling and bustling of city life now, but for those of us from the 7th Gurkha Rifles who took part in the 1983 London Marathon it will remain a most memorable and great experience in life even when we finally return home on pension . . .[8]

The Olympic ideal that to participate is more important than winning was a new concept for competitive Gurkhas. Although three hours thirty-seven minutes had not been a time of any significance, their medals were glinting proof of *bahaduri*. Rifleman Aitabahadur Limbu also wrote:

Even though I did not come in the top ten or one hundred, I very much enjoyed the London Marathon. The beauty of the game was that all competitors who succeeded in crossing the finishing line received a medal.

Unacquainted with the mysteries of sponsoring, my Gurkhas never did understand this part of the marathon, but letters containing unsolicited BLESMA donations of £650 arrived afterwards. One was sent to me from a Margaret Hofman of Heston, Middlesex:

We stood in the rain for two hours on Sunday, but it was worth it to watch you all run by. The Gurkhas looked as (if) they were enjoying every minute of it, but if I might say Sir, I thought you were showing signs of wear and tear by the time you reached Lower Thames Street!

Meanwhile my manuscript still needed an amendment and addition or two . . . including something about my Gurkhas running in the London Marathon. Most important though was a conviction that the Falklands' War had, at long last, been run out of my system.

I could not have been more wrong.

319

Chapter Twenty-five

CATHARSIS PROLONGED

. . . we must retain an ability to be able to react to the unexpected – for there is, paradoxically, nothing more certain than the unexpected – with all that implies in terms of organisation and training. – General Sir John Stainier, 1983 Chief of the General Staff, Ministry of Defence, London.[1]

The British Army's Movement Freight Organization always features large in a soldier's life. Stored in our garage were their ubiquitous collapsible MFO plywood boxes which, after the London Marathon, had to be taken out to pack for the move to Hong Kong at the end of April. But unlike the Battalion's freight that included Colonel David's Argentine Mercedes Land-Rover, we could not take the family car. 80, Wakefords Park had also been as much a part of our Falklands' War as anything else during that unique experience. After fourteen months stay, it was therefore a sad paradox to move out of it for long awaited Hong Kong and our fourteenth Army married quarter.

This move was not popular with the Gurkhas because, financially, they would be worse off.[2] It was therefore a further paradox that the sums in my bank account would be conversely increased by the Army's monthly Hong Kong local overseas allowance for British soldiers. My family was also scheduled to grow because Tove was more than midway through her third pregnancy when we boarded the British Caledonian aircraft at Gatwick Airport. Possibly many other veterans of the Falklands' Task Force had decided to reproduce as, psychologically, it seemed the natural thing to do after the intention to take life, witnessing death and then receiving that gift of survival.

I enjoyed being the A Company Commander to 150 Gurkhas who, during the next thirteen months on three one-month Sino-Hong Kong border tours of duty, would excel in catching plenty of Chinese illegal immigrants. Perhaps the Falklands' War should have materialized at the end of my tour, not the beginning, because life had also become anticlimactic. Energies were also being diverted dangerously away from my job to the unfinished book project which needed others' contributions. So once the Battalion had settled into its New Territories camp at Cassino Lines, war stories were systematically prised out of BOs and QGOs alike. Only Lester Holley displayed reluctance.

'The Falklands is in the past now, so let's get on with planning for future operations!' objected this future CO of 21 SAS while, nonetheless, grudgingly providing me with a few anecdotes. Unlike Lester's typical SAS attitude, I believed history was a valuable resource and its detail should be documented for future generations.

A third draft of *Penguins Prefer Peace* was completed by late summer but, dissatisfied, I began a fourth. Meanwhile married quarter arrangements in the New Territories at Sek Kong remained chaotic. With a few snakes we lived initially in a small dilapidated bungalow adjacent to the appropriately named Route Twisk, only to move after two months to a nearby safer high-rise block of flats. By August we had moved to yet another flat – our third home in four months. Tove's pregnancy was approaching termination and during the small hours of the 12th she started labour pains. Mark Willis and his wife in the flat below ours had agreed to look after Victoria and Emily in our absence, but my plan to alert Mark malfunctioned temporarily. Severely delayed with our eventual departure, the Keystone Cops could not have performed better as I drove through six sets of traffic lights on red to reach the Kowloon British Military Hospital just in time.

The birth went according to plan – but not the need to react to the unexpected as we noticed immediately that which the Chinese midwife did not. She was used to delivering Chinese-eyed babies.

'Your suspicions are confirmed,' said the doctor twenty-four hours later. 'Your daughter has Downs Syndrome. A standard Trisomy 21 type.' He did not add that nothing in our life would be standard any more because of this chromosome fault. The shock did not sink in until I returned to our Buffs Avenue flat where Victoria and Emily were informed.

'Why are you always crying, Daddy?' asked three year-old Emily as a fortnight's reaction set in for the mongol daughter I had not expected and the normal one that did not arrive.

During the next hospital visit I tried to comfort Tove by saying, 'The Falklands are to blame, because we would never have had a third child if it had not been for the war.' At the time it seemed to be a reasonable way of apportioning blame. Adjustment came when she returned home with the dear little baby, and even black humour by my suggesting 'Falklandia' as an alternative name for Kristina. I sent a letter to my family in the UK informing them of the situation. My father wept on reading it and declared clairvoyantly, 'This'll break them.' The unexpected also broke him. Three weeks later he had a heart attack and, less than five years later, died from heart failure.

Life continued. There was an Officers' Mess Regimental dinner night and Brian Hanrahan, BBC's ex-Falklands' War correspondent now working in Hong Kong, was invited. He sat next to me and I did my best to follow up my Wether Ground briefing the previous year by supplying him with more information on the Gurkhas. Surprisingly he seemed overawed with the occasion and said little, only to be even more bemused at the Gurkha BOs' violent competitiveness in robust Mess games of rugby and boat racing.

Back at work, exorcising the Falklands' experience continued as I took a break from my daily encounters with Downs Syndrome. *Penguins Prefer Peace* had become known as *P3*, but my job suffered, as writing and worries about Kristina were prioritized. Tove sought therapy treatment for her in Kowloon as I tended to isolate myself from the other BOs and felt impatience and irritation at irrelevant pettiness from some participants of

Battalion conferences. Maybe the Falklands' experience was to blame partially for my moods. Perhaps a few of the Gurkhas understood. Captain Narainprasad Rai was A Company's disciplinarian but, like most Gurkhas, also fond of children. He knew things were not right and once approached me to enquire gently, 'How is your daughter, sahib?' I tried to explain but then restricted myself with a cursory, 'She's mentally handicapped, sahib, and will never be normal.'

In late January 1984, A Company flew to Singapore's Changi Airport for our two-month Malaysian exercise at Kota Tinggi, Southern Johore. The P and D accompanied us on Exercise ORANG HUTAN III, as well as Quentin Oates who became my Company Training and Public Relations Officer tasked to exploit the P and D's talents. Commanding an independent company away from the clutches of Battalion HQ is a company commander's highlight in a two-year Battalion tour of duty. This would also give plenty of opportunity to become better acquainted with my Gurkhas and another Army as our sponsor was a Royal Malaysian Army Battalion. Its soldiers were excellent on the parade ground but, when invited to look around their nearby barracks, my QGOs turned up their noses at the filthy barrack rooms, unhygienic WCs and showers – an antithesis of Gurkha cleanliness.

At the midway point of our stay, we were placed under command of the Malaysian Battalion for a defence exercise. My Gurkhas surpassed themselves when, under a blazing sun and on a hill devoid of cover, they completed digging their trenches in thirty-six hours compared with the four days the Malaysians needed, in the shade. We focused on more Company shooting and jungle training in the remaining weeks. During one morning, I was at the local Uli Tiran shooting range observing one of my platoons on a live field firing exercise. Up-country at our jungle camp near Pulada, Narainprasad sahib was with the remainder supervising a minor patrols exercise. It was about midday that the unexpected happened. My Gurkha radio operator called me to the radio. The news that a concerned 2IC's voice reported was dreadful: 'One of our soldiers has had an accident here. He has been drowned in a jungle pond. His platoon are trying to get him out of the jungle and back to us, but then we will need transport to take his body back to Kota Tinggi.'

Swearing at a situation reminiscent of the Falklands' War, I requested a Malaysian Army casevac helicopter and jumped into my Land-Rover to drive the sixty kilometres north. As I arrived, the dead man's platoon materialized along a track carrying the body out of the jungle on an improvised stretcher. The dead Gurkha's face had a greyish-blue hue and Narainprasad sahib's head shook resignedly.

'When the man arrived at the pond with his platoon, he jumped straight in, sahib. He was dressed in full combat kit, and carried his large pack and rifle,' he explained, 'but never came to the surface again. His rifle got stuck under an underwater rock and, although others dived in to rescue him, it took ten minutes for the *keta* to fetch him up.'

I was obliged to ask the $64,000 question, 'But have you any idea as to why he did such a strange thing, sahib?'

'The man had not been to the Foklands, sahib, because he was on Nepal leave at the time,' replied the QGO. 'We think he had been trying to show to the others that he was just as good as them by trying to swim to the other side of the pond.'

If my 2IC's theory was correct, then the drowned Gurkha had become an indirect final Battalion casualty of the Falklands' War. This incident demonstrated the dangers of cumulative stress in not having participated in a war that your fellow soldiers had fought. The Royal Military Police in Hong Kong sent a Special Investigation Branch team to carry out an official investigation which I had to assist. There were also two choices to be faced. Either hold the funeral quickly in line with Hindu custom, or wait and prepare one which included a full military parade and honours. The British connection paid dividends as I consulted Narainprasad and my other QGOs. Our decision was clear-cut. We had the men. We had the kit. And, above all, we had the P and D. Not to have a funeral with all the trappings would be detrimental to Company morale.

I had the grim business of carrying out the official identification in the local mortuary and persuading the Malaysian staff there to keep the Gurkha's body in its refrigeration box for another week. Meanwhile my QGOs rehearsed the firing party, and the P and D practised. The result was perfect. We buried our Gurkha in a British military cemetery at Sungei Patani where other Gurkhas from the Malayan Emergency of the 1950s had been laid to rest. A Hindu priest hired from Singapore performed the death ceremony, the music of the white-jacketed and tartan trews clad P and D created that special 7GR atmosphere, each man in the Company threw a handful of earth on the coffin and saluted it, and a well-drilled firing party carried out their duties smartly. At the wake in our coach afterwards I praised my 2IC for all his work with a, '*Shyabash,* sahib!' He smiled quietly, cocked his head to one side Gurkha-style, shrugged his shoulders with fatalism, and handed me a can of ice cold beer. Sipping on it, I hoped this was my last attendance at a Gurkha funeral. They had occurred all too frequently during my secondment.

At the end of ORANG HUTAN I travelled with a coach load of Gurkhas on a day trip to Kuala Lumpur. I had an ulterior motive and this was to locate my childhood home of three decades ago. It had been, after all, where *P3* had its origins with my father's Gurkha connection. I found Damansara Road by instinct but, wandering up the long U-shaped driveway lined by tall trees to the vast bungalow, was bitterly disappointed to find only the bougainvillea bush at the top of this rise and, nearby, some modern houses. My old home did not exist any more and a little piece of my childhood died with that discovery.

The flight back to Hong Kong was a relief because a signal had arrived at Kota Tinggi to inform me that Kristina had contracted pneumonia. There had also been a letter from Tove that a medical check revealed heart irregularities with the little girl. Preoccupation with this, writing and achieving my ambition to organize the Khud Race on *Nameless,* were partly to blame for an unsatisfactory A Company result in Exercise CONCRETE JUNGLE, the annual Battalion internal security test exercise. Draft four of *P3* also ran into trouble. A proof was printed by a Chinese firm in Kowloon but, when returned, its 200-odd pages were so full of errors that the two BOs assigned to read it grew weary. Literary quality was also lacking and veiled suggestions made that another draft might be wise.

'Why not read Deneys Reitz's best-selling book *Commando – A Boer Journal of the Boer War?*' suggested Mark Willis, one of the critics.

I did, and *P3*'s title became expanded to *Penguins Prefer Peace – A Gurkha Officer's*

Journal of the Falklands' War. Reitz's manuscript, written in 1903, was not published until twenty-six years later. 'Maybe you should be thinking about that sort of timescale as well,' Mark commented. The thought made me shudder with its implications.

A change of Battalion command produced a new broom sweeping clean, and the incoming Commandant's signals grew stronger in wanting 'Falklands' removed from the Battalion's vocabulary. His attitude at the time seemed incomprehensible as *P3* also came under fire, and its Battalion-sponsored publication became a case of, 'Put your money where your mouth is!' I became depressed that the goalposts had been moved with the game in progress, but then grew philosophical. 'How could he be expected to understand the thoughts and motives of a combat veteran when not one himself?' I reminded myself, as that latent existential authority born on 14 June 1982 on the Tumbledown's north side bubbled up to the surface of my consciousness again. So after one final Company border tour of hunting and catching the elusive IIs, I decided secretly to shelve the project for the time being.

It was soon replaced by another, and my last, with the Gurkhas when Narainprasad sahib and I decided to enter several six-man teams to compete in the annual Hong Kong MacLehose Trail hike – a 100 kilometre race over the ridge of mountains that spans the New Territories from east to west. This was originally a Gurkha training exercise which some completed in twelve hours, but had now become an elongated cross between a London Marathon and a Khud Race in which hundreds of military and civilians participate. Although relatively unfit, I also decided to participate. Navigating through heat and oppressive humidity, we had far more hills to scale on the undulating course than a single *Nameless*. My team mates therefore became most concerned after the first sixteen hours of non-stop marching over this difficult terrain.

'Sahib, are you all right, sahib?' they eventually asked an ashen-faced OC sahib on seeing he could hardly put one foot in front of the other. After another ten hours, I crawled over the finishing line happy to have survived. There was also a bad conscience that, as the team's weakest link, I had applied an unnecessarily heavy brake on the Gurkhas' natural speed of foot. To rub salt into the wound, they smilingly did not appear to mind their *gora* sahib's physical weakness. 'Indeed, I've got an awful feeling they expected it,' I thought as Narainprasad sahib swept me up, bundled me into the Company Land-Rover, and drove me home – to demonstrate that a QGO sahib also looks after his BO sahib when required.

The end had also arrived for my secondment. At my Regimental dining-out night there would be the usual round of speeches for a departing officer. My Ops/Training Officer predecessor had been 'dined-out' the year before but, with retirement imminent, still had no civilian job. His speech was made in accordance with the Gunner custom of standing on a chair and a foot on the table. Bending forward with an elbow resting on his knee, he delivered an elegant dissertation on Gurkha virtues. The punch-line was an L-squared classic, '. . . Finally, I'm fed up with people asking what on earth I'm going to do when I've retired. Heavens above, I don't even know myself! Anyway – after the 7th Gurkha Rifles, does it really matter?'

I could not compete with L-squared's flamboyance, particularly when the new boss mentioned in his speech that *P3* still lived. This took the wind out of my farewell speech's sails and made listening to the P and D's rendition of *Black Bear* for the last time after the dinner even more unbearable than necessary. All this proved a blessing in disguise. The manuscript was never meant to be a Regimental History vetted by Regimental Committee and my decision would lead, in the long-term, to a much more personal version.

When June finally arrived, Colonel David's prophesy made more than two years before about the OC sahib's finale with his Company came true. At my farewell party amidst the basketball, beer and *bhat*, I received a gleaming Nepalese silver kukri from Narainprasad sahib. The theme of my little thank you speech, 'You Gurkhas must never forget that you're special soldiers because you've fought in the Falklands,' came from the heart and my Johnnie Gurkhas smiled and clapped politely. The last to shake hands and speak to me was the GM sahib at Kai Tak Airport two days later.

'I know you've had your problems,' said Major Lalbahadur Rai in his posh English accent which would have qualified him for residence in Windsor, 'but thank you, sahib, for serving with us. Our Gurkha soldiers have appreciated you.'

He did not have to say more. I was touched and, walking to the departure lounge, no quote other than: 'And that,' said John, 'was that' from A. A. Milne's poem, *Happiness* could have described the moment better. My feelings coincided with the valedictory part of a letter written to the Battalion some weeks later by Goose Green's Mrs. Eileen Jaffary:

> We were very pleased to receive the (Regimental) Gurkha plaque last week . . . (The) children were very excited as the Gurkhas were a great favourite with them. Likewise ourselves as we will never forget the way they helped us here in G.G. Good luck to the 1st/7th Duke of Edinburgh's Own Gurkha Rifles wherever they may go. They are proudly remembered here in Goose Green.[3]

One task remained. A manuscript about the Gurkhas and the Falklands' War was packed in my suitcase. It had to be rewritten and, indeed, the will to do so remained. The only uncertainty would be *when*, because my next job was at the NATO Allied Forces' Northern Europe HQ outside Oslo, and strategic logistics contingency planning in a Grade 2 staff officer appointment got in the way of my writing ambitions. More analytical thought was required than in a regimental job, and soon the Falklands' War slipped to the back of my mind. Esoteric projects such as the *Conceptual Military Framework for the Year 2000* became a substitute for my rejected *P3* manuscript that lay in a shoebox. My young family was prioritised, particularly when Kristina underwent two heart operations in successive years. Witnessing the post-operative care that included those twenty tubes dangling out of her little body not once, but twice, was unpleasant but the Falklands' War had inoculated me against the stress of such sights and, unlike Tove, enabled me to tune into a familiar military operational mode. I became emotionally detached during those nights of lying on a mattress beside her hospital bed on alert to provide support if necessary.

Both occasions felt like having been 'on exercise' after return to my job. I was also asked to lecture on the Falklands' War at the Norwegian Army *Krigskolen* near Kristiansand together with another Kolsås officer, Lieutenant Commander Andy Auld. A Fleet Air Arm Harrier pilot who had commanded 800 Naval Air Squadron on board

Hermes, this quietly spoken Scot led the first Sea Harrier bombing raid on Stanley Airport, shot down two Dagger aircraft and carried out sixty-three combat missions. His clinical description of reacting to the unexpected by 'how-to-proceed-when-an-Argie-air-to-air-missile-locks-on-to-you-in-mid-flight', followed by combat tactics and mechanics of 'how-to-fire-a-Sidewinder-air-to-air-missile-in-reply' enthralled the cadets and gave me another dimension to the war.

Then came the unexpected in 1986 with media reports of 1st/7th Gurkha Rifles soldiers on an Hawaii overseas training exercise, similar to ORANG HUTAN III, mugging Major Corin Pearce their OC, and Chandra sahib who had been in my Falklands' Tac HQ. One of this notorious incident's ringleaders had been in Nigel Price's former Mortar Platoon, and I knew Corin who, like me, was a seconded officer. From the Royal Anglian Regiment, he had not served in the Falklands' War. His attackers claimed he had belittled them in front of members of a foreign army during his farewell speech to their American hosts. On return to Hong Kong, 109 Gurkhas of Support Company, mostly Falklands' veterans who included some of Nigel's mortarmen on that Goat Ridge mortar line, were dismissed from the Army because they broke their *kasam khane* parade oath to the Regiment and its officers by not coop-erating with the official investigation. Shocked, I was also puzzled as to how such behaviour could be so contrary to that of my A Company Gurkhas. It is easy to specu-late. But might there have been another underlying reason, in addition to all the official ones of alcohol abuse as well as lack of knowledge of Gurkha culture and Gurkhali? Diluted respect for authority is a well documented after-effect that many acquire in the aftermath of a traumatic experience like war or peacetime disasters. So was this a case of so-called combat veterans' existential authority going too far? And, if so, could it have been prevented?

In 1988 I resigned my commission and acquired a civilian job in Scandinavian Airlines with responsibility for its operational security and emergency response arrangements within Norway. Parallels could be drawn with a Gurkha secondment, but *P3* initially remained in the shoebox as civil aviation enthralled me. By now the Falklands' War had converted my previously easy going professional attitude to the opposite of 'always-be-prepared-for-the-worst'. Comprehensive plans had to be written, organizations built up, expert assistance from the Office of Disaster Psychiatry in Oslo enlisted and training implemented in expectation for the unexpected to strike. It also included planning for the expected as, on behalf of the Norwegian Foreign Office, I wrote an operational security contingency plan for all Oslo hotels earmarked to accommodate foreign guests for the eventual funeral of King Olav V.

Special security measures were sometimes implemented to protect, for example, 'high-threat' passengers such as Salman Rushdie and Shimon Peres. The unexpected inevitably materialized with bomb threats on the ground and in-flight, strategic threats post Pan Am's sabotage disaster over Lockerbie and during the 1991 Gulf War, as well as involvement in crisis-managing an SAS aircraft accident near Stockholm's Arlanda Airport. General Dwight D. Eisenhower's principle: 'A plan is nothing, planning is everything', described perfectly my modus operandi and virtually became a personal motto. My ambition level was sky-high and the demands I made of myself ferocious and, on occasions, unrealistic.

P3 had also been taken out of my shoebox so that a long overdue fifth draft could be started. But I was realizing that a book about an infantry battalion in which the author had been a wartime member is never written – but rewritten and rewritten, again and again, as memories continued to be dug up. I had also built up a private library on the Falklands' War which, in the end, amounted to thirty-seven books. In addition to further *P3* research, reading them provided subconscious catharsis, but irritation came at the distortions. For example:

At William the Gurkhas, after being held back until Tumbledown was secured, were allowed to go forward. The advantage of using the Gurkhas in a daytime attack was that they would be seen, and their ferocious reputation would unnerve the opposition. To the Gurkhas' disappointment, they found the enemy melting away in front of them.[4]

And in another:

In both World Wars, the Gurkhas drew prisoners' blood with their kukris and cut off heads or ears. It is accepted by the Government that the Gurkhas do such things, but in the Falklands it was not only the Gurkhas.[5]

So as I strove to explain why a daylight battle where the Gurkhas could be observed attacking was the Battalion's *last* wish, and also became amazed at an ex-3 Para Lance Corporal's absurd insinuation that atrocities had been committed by the Gurkhas in the Falklands, the downside started in 1993. A collapse caused by chronic fatigue syndrome, a painful psychosomatic condition from self-imposed overwork and not listening to the body's signals, required five days' hospitalization and six months sick leave. The next year also provided the unexpected with a Bosnian refugee hijacking an SAS aircraft in northern Norway. Only a political demonstration against the Bosnian War that included bomb threats, the nonetheless exciting incident lasted just eight hours. No one was hurt, but all those plans and the emergency response organization had been successfully tested – although Falkland memories would be also revived with my stress reaction of five successive nights of insomnia.

The hijacking gave my work further momentum, but probably caused more problems for others trying to follow in my slipstream. So when twenty months later two minutes of innocent misjudgement occurred at an international security symposium in London, this 'misdemeanour' led to my becoming jobless by August. This punishment, tantamount to unlawful dismissal, far outstripped my 'crime' of posing two questions in open forum perceived as too provocative. Maybe that existential authority of mine was to blame, but I came to the conclusion it had been safer as a BO of a Gurkha battalion fighting in the Falklands' War than as a civilian working in the private sector of civil aviation.

The incident triggered latent war long-term after-effects. Post-traumatic stress disorder materialized with a typical symptom shopping list of guilt feelings, apathy, insomnia, self-imposed isolation, anxiety attacks, inability to concentrate and cumulative weight loss of eleven kilos, all of which overlapped into a severe long-term depression in which there were thoughts, but never plans, of suicide. This dual condition, known as a co-morbidity psychological problem soldiers can develop in both combat and post-war was, maybe, predictable with hindsight. It was also not entirely disassociated with a civilian job in which I had taken a second bite at an imaginary Falklands' apple – and gained total compensation for an indifferent war performance. Prince Malcolm's line in *Macbeth* summed up the next requirement: 'Give sorrow words; the grief that does not speak whispers the o'er-fraught heart and bids it break.' But taking this talking cure proved steadily more difficult in a wobbling marriage.

It led to a nervous breakdown so serious I was hospitalized again – this time for three weeks. Unexpectedly, the ensuing treatment principles were identical to those that Keith and Ginnie Baillie administered to us five officers at Goose Green after the Falklands' hostilities had ended. During this 'dark blue period' in hospital a memory returned of a conversation with Narainprasad sahib while on my final border guard duty in Hong Kong. A Company's hero of that never-to-be-forgotten Tumbledown night was worried. He was due to be posted from the Battalion to the Gurkha Demonstration Company at Sandhurst, but the previous day he had been driving the Company's Land-Rover and had dented its bumper in a minor accident. 'Sahib, my career is now over!' Narainprasad sahib agonized. It was not, because he had been an outstanding QGO. And although dented temporarily, neither was mine.

Unemployment continued throughout 1997 and my marriage collapsed as a final ignominy, but I was already well into writing the sixth and final draft of *P3*. During this catharsis prolongation, research was also renewed by reading yet more Falklands' War books in which the odd Gurkha distortion continued to materialize. For example: 'As the battle for Tumbledown came to a close, screaming, blade-waving Gurkhas . . charged up Mount William.'[6]

Now I only laughed – and wrote and researched even more. This included receiving confirmation that *Cabo* Nicolás Urbieta (Chapter 18) had continued his career in the Argentine Army after the Malvinas' War to become a *Sargento Primero*, stationed with the 24th Mechanized Infantry Regiment at Rio Gallegos. Married to Sara, he was also father to four children. Leandro Etchichury, the advisor to the Argentine National Congress representative, Marcela Bordenave, got hold of this story, checked out my background with the British Embassy's Defence Attaché in Buenos Aires, then wrote to me and asked:

> During the war, the media gave us in Argentina an image of the Gurkha battalion, like killer beasts, like merciless assassins. Is it real or is (it) a fable around this battalion? (this image has no connection with your . . . kind of mind) Did you know this fable? And if yes, why did you enter this battalion?[7]

I replied to point out the excellence and high professionalism of the Gurkhas, although this book does much more justice in responding to Mr Etchichury's questions. He tipped off *Clarín*, one of Argentina's more reputable newspapers and, without undertaking any interview with me, it published the story under the heading of *Cartas de Nicolás* (Letters from Nicolás). This was a title which belonged to a discarded *P3* chapter based on those five letters Urbieta wrote while surviving on East Falkland, but could not send and which, post-war, I returned to Argentina via the Committee of the International Red Cross.

Fourteen years before on 25 May, Argentina's National Day, *Clarín* had published yet another article on the Gurkhas by the novelist and Nobel Prize winner Gabriel García Márquez entitled *The Queen's Gurkhas*. This had described yet again the presumed savagery of the 1st/7th Gurkha Rifles during the Falklands' War, reinforcing his views from the previous month's *El Spectador de Columbia*. The 1997 *Clarín* article about Urbieta and myself was published the day after the fifteenth anniversary of the Falklands' liberation, but once more demonstrated that truth remains a casualty in Buenos Aires concerning the Gurkhas and Falklands' War with its extravagant claim that: 'The English ex-officer affirmed that whilst he was travelling to the Malvinas he was the manager of encouraging the psychological campaign that presented the Gurkhas as murderers.[8]

As the ex-Battalion Public Information Officer, I can only admit to organizing that press call day which had started the 'psyops' ball rolling. The rest was concocted by Argentina's media, assisted to a certain extent by their British counterparts and, not least, the Argentine soldiers' fertile imaginations. *Clarín*'s next assertion, though, was closer to the mark:

> His book seems to be for him the best opportunity in sealing his soldier's life. Urbieta seems to be uninterested in the possibility of a meeting (with Seear). His refusal can be for him like keeping a remnant of the beaten's dignity. The fact is that fifteen years later, the two men still fight for putting a final point to those battles.[9]

The article touched a raw nerve in Argentina, and the unexpected occurred again. Although Urbieta said he could not 'get in touch with someone who could have killed one of my partners'[10] I received a phone call from him nonetheless, but unfortunately in Spanish. Another call with Rear Admiral Carlos Hugo Robacio, the 5th Marine Infantry Battalion's ex-CO, surprisingly confirmed this officer's hope to meet me one day. There were also five conversations with Emilio Gimelez, a Buenos Aires Channel 2 TV producer who wanted me to discuss this 'hot story' live on his local talk show. My projected visit there did not materialize due to Urbieta's refusal to participate, but letters arrived from other Argentines including those of Malvinas' War combat veterans, such as Gabriel Sagastume of La Plata, Buenos Aires who had fought on Mount Longdon with the 7th Infantry Regiment. On return to civilian life he had become a lawyer, but also informed me that the subsequent writing about his war experience was 'an inconclusive task' that 'I never will end'. My advice to Gabriel Sagastume is to keep trying because, as I would later discover with a final seventh draft, there are only positive feelings when such a project is finished.

In the Autumn of 1997 I did something different. As a P&O guest lecturer during SS *Canberra*'s penultimate cruise to the Canary Islands before her decommissioning, I gave a series of Falklands' War lectures. This produced no longed-for job, but being on board 'The Great White Whale' gave me the chance to share memories of the amazing Gurkhas, their paradoxes, and of going to war with them. My main message was that their detractors had labelled them as a twentieth-century anachronism immediately prior to the Falklands' campaign, whilst in an era of computers on the battlefield a similar argument had been levelled at the bayonet – until the Falklands' land fighting started.

There was also a need to reflect on life during that cruise, which retraced the first part of the voyage I once took to the Falklands, and recharge batteries before continuing my search for a job and writing *P3*. It was not until April 1998 and after twenty months unemployment, I began a new career as an external consultant in emergency response and crisis management for industry. It included an SAS comeback with participation in a thirty-month emergency response project run by the airline's Head Office at Stockholm, Sweden. Organizations were created, plans rewritten, seminars held and training exercises run. Post-traumatic growth intensified and more inspiration came from my Gurkha service experiences. In October 2001, four months after the project ended, an SAS aircraft accident killed 118 people at Milan's Linate Airport in Italy. The airline's state of the art emergency response to the disaster vindicated my theory that the wheel does not require to be reinvented for crisis-managing such a disaster. Tried and tested British Army and Gurkha principles were sufficient.

A more pleasant accident occurred when I stumbled across *The Gurkha Spice* restaurant during a recent visit to Croydon. When the *bhat* was served I remembered to say, '*Dhanyabad!*' The waiter's Gurkha smile made me quite nostalgic. It was almost like being amongst Tac HQ or A Company again. Learning of my 7GR service, the hospitable proprietor then served a Nepalese cake dessert. 'I would like to give you this and a drink free of charge, sahib,' he said, 'as my cousin, a former employee of mine, also served with the Battalion's Rear Party at Church Crookham during the Falklands' War!'

Unfortunately, defence cuts led to the 7th Gurkha Rifles' disbandment in 1994. Three years later British Army troop levels fell below 100,000 only for the second time since the Battle of Waterloo in 1815 – also a year noteworthy for the first Gurkha recruitment into British ranks. With such a modern-day lack of British recruits for the Army, one wonders at the politicians' logic that insists on British Army Gurkha 'drawdown' when droves of the hillmen are queuing in Nepal to be enlisted. 7GR's descendants, the Royal Gurkha Rifles, have maintained that unique Gurkha professionalism during peacekeeping operations in Bosnia, Kosovo and East Timor. Even *Aftenposten*, the Norwegian national daily, acknowledged them during the 1999 Kosovo operation as being '*verdens beste infanterister*' (the world's best infantrymen).[11] So after 2001's 11 September terrorist attacks on civil aviation, New York's World Trade Centre and the Pentagon in Washington DC, there must surely be a Gurkha role in the long-term fight against international terrorism. I will follow their future successes.

Jai Seventh!

EPILOGUE

Ah, horrific war, amazing medley of the glorious and the squalid, the pitiful and the sublime, if modern men of light and leading saw your face closer, simple folk would see it hardly ever. – Sir Winston Churchill

I am remarried now. It is nonetheless my intention to maintain a dialogue with Tove about our daughters' well-being and futures. She still visits the UK occasionally and recently was reminded of her own Falklands' past. The incident caused her to put pen to paper:

> I've just spent some days at a rather posh 'do' in Yorkshire. The man next to me at the dinner-table was an ex-Scots Guards officer who just left the Army before the Falklands blew up. His remark about 'Didn't your ex-husband absolutely love going down there?' left me speechless for a second. God, there was so much I could have told him, but in the end I simply couldn't be bothered with shallowness like that!

But, for me, one item remained outstanding. During the absolute final lap of writing what was now no longer *P3*, but *With the Gurkhas in the Falklands – A War Journal*, I flew to Buenos Aires. My aims were to fulfil a twenty-year ambition of experiencing Argentina first-hand, and meet people who had written to me after publication of the *Clarín* article five years before. Perhaps the visit would also help cleanse my soul.

I arrived a few days before 2 April, the national Malvinas' War Veterans Day and twentieth anniversary of the invasion. My guide, the knowledgeable TV producer and political analyst, Alberto Peralta Ramos, arranged numerous meetings. The first was with a charming but defensive seventy-two year-old ex-Governor of the Malvinas, General Mario Benjamín Menéndez. His Malvinas' War shortages of ammunition, helicopters and general supplies still preyed on his mind. Asked about the Argentine soldiers' attitude to the Gurkhas, he shrugged his shoulders and, referring to the prospective Stanley battle instead, said, 'There was no third phase, because I stopped it. We had no more ammunition.' Nonetheless, he asked for a signed copy of this book.

We also met the amicable Lieutenant General Diego Soria, former Malvinas' War CO of Nicolás Urbieta. Next day Marisa Clausen de Bruno who was a teacher, local politician, active supporter of the Malvinas' War veterans and author of two books on them with a third in the pipeline, was waiting in the Plaza de Mayo as agreed.

Afterwards I paid my respects to the Argentine fallen at the Buenos Aires Malvinas' War Memorial. Later the welcome was overwhelming in Marisa's small town of General Roca and in the surrounding area of Córdoba, where 120 Malvinas' War veterans live. A local TV camera crew and radio reporter covered the short formal reception which included a speech by the youthful Mayor, Pablo Garbelotto. An emotionally charged atmosphere affected my translator, Natalia Alemanno, who burst into tears mid-way through translating my improvised 'from-the-heart' reply. The Mayor then presented me with a clock.

'I'm embarrassed,' I said, 'because I've no gift to give in return.'

'It doesn't matter,' was his generous reply, 'it's enough that you're here.'

The locals and media laid siege to Marisa's home in which I enjoyed her wonderful hospitality. Two live radio interviews between Urbieta and me were again facilitated by Natalia and her friend, Ligia Picardi. Both girls also wanted to learn more about the war as their knowledge was transparently thin, seemingly a deficiency shared by many others. Could a contributory factor be due to the repatriated Malvinas' War veterans being given a written order not to talk about the war – even to their wives? Such thinking runs directly counter to the basic method of treating post-traumatic stress i.e. the necessity of speaking out about such experiences. The order could also explain Urbieta's supposed reluctance to meeting me in 1997. Yet two long conversations about the war with ex-Marine Infantryman Juan Arias, who had been a member of the Malvinas' invasion force, produced a farewell bear hug from him that personified my reception from all Argentines I met. Perhaps that was how British and German soldiers felt when they fraternized at Christmas 1914 on the Western Front's no man's land.

Such feelings would be best summed up to me later by Rear Admiral Carlos Robacio:

I am very sorry for the language barrier (this is probably the one and stupid trauma left from that distant action), for I believe that in this Christian and Western world in which both us ex-adversaries belong, this kind of dialogue is enriching both our professional and personal experience. On top of that, it encourages us to get to know each other in a better way, for it is true that the world has to keep on being built and there will always be a need for good soldiers capable of keeping order and correct wrong-doings.[1]

Marisa also showed me her little plastic bottle containing a few specks of earth from her Malvinas. I respect her patriotic convictions, but disagree with the method used in attempting to regain the Islands twenty years before. She also was to inform me later, 'The word "war" is "hell": for many Argentine boys it is "Gurkhas"!'

Back in Buenos Aires, Lieutenant General Soria had made possible a visit to the flat of retired Lieutenant Colonel Tomás Fox who had once directed the 155 shellfire against the Gurkhas on Wether Ground. Tommy produced a razor-sharp Gaucho *Facones* knife for me, and I showed him Chapters 16 and 17 of this book describing the effects of his FOO work. But after four hours it was his English teacher wife who found the real common denominator before we all enjoyed a midnight restaurant meal together.

'You and my husband,' she said quietly, 'have the same way of speaking and looking when you talk about these things.'

There would also be a rendezvous with another Malvinas' War veteran, Lieutenant Jorge Perez Grandi, now a lawyer and once Urbieta's platoon commander. I returned Urbieta's training manual and personal photographs which the Gurkhas had found twenty years before on the Two Sisters' battlefield, and Jorge told me about his platoon's battle with 45 Commando and of Urbieta's deed in saving his life. But Jorge had still not completed his post-Two Sisters' catharsis, so I tried to assist by later sending him five different British accounts of his battle and a copy of my battle map.

I also attended the impressive War Veterans' Day Parade at which Mr Eduardo Duhalde, the President of Argentina, took the salute and where it was a strange feeling to watch the Malvinas' War veterans march past. Some were grey-haired and two hobbled on artificial legs. However a reassertion of the Argentine claim to the Falklands, South Georgia and South Sandwich Islands was low-key. The emphasis lay in thanking the veterans for their performance in a war which cost 649 Argentine lives. It is needed. At least 264 of their contemporaries have committed suicide[2] and some claim this figure is double – compelling facts when compared with the British Falklands' War veterans' suicides of 200 plus. Perspective is provided by the 1996 Argentine male suicide rate of 9.9 per 100,000 and corresponding UK rate for that year of 11.7.[3] Here is the mutual Falklands'/Malvinas' ground between Britain and Argentina in which not only more resources should be directed to solving a humanitarian problem that transcends the territorial dispute and squalid politics, but where also a formal Anglo-Argentine cooperation could be fruitful.

Via Dan Krishock, editor of the English-language newspaper *Buenos Aires Herald*, this thought would lead to my eventual contact with Dr Eduardo César Gerding – the Malvinas' War veterans' Medical Coordinator – and his health team at the *Subgerencia de Veteranos de Guerra* of the *Instituto Nacional de Servicios Sociales para Jubilados y Pensionados* of Buenos Aires. They were to become involved in planning a Malvinas' War veterans' traumatic stress research project to be implemented in 2003 which I would help coordinate, incorporating the international expertise of my Norwegian disaster psychiatrist colleagues, Professor Lars Weisæth – the world's first professor of traumatic stress – and Dr. Pål Herlofsen. Eduardo, a retired Naval Lieutenant Commander who had been the 5th Marine Infantry Battalion's Medical Officer from 1987–90, would also express his hope to me that the scientific conclusions might assist veterans on both sides of the Atlantic. But perhaps it is just wistful thinking that a corresponding British Falklands' War veterans' project could also be initiated afterwards, thereby offering the unique possibility of both sets of results being scientifically compared.

As for the Gurkhas in the Falklands' War, misleading statements about them by both British and Argentines inevitably continued during the period of my first visit to Buenos Aires. For example, on 30 March a two-page article by the UK journalist Patrick Bishop was published in *The Daily Telegraph*'s commemorative war supplement. His November 1982 letter to Brigadier David Morgan appears in this book's introduction, but in his article two decades later he commented: 'The Guards and Gurkhas of 5 Brigade who arrived at San Carlos at the beginning of June lacked their (Para and Marine) comrades' tungsten constitutions.'[4]

My plea to him is to read *With the Gurkhas in the Falklands* and, in future, not place the Gurkhas in the same Falklands' War category as the two Guards Battalions. Three days later another who failed to get his facts right was the ex-conscript Private Oscar Poltronieri who had fought with the 6th Infantry Regiment on Two Sisters and the Tumbledown. Subsequently awarded his country's highest decoration for gallantry, the *Cruz-La Nación Argentina al Heroico Valor en Combate*, nearly twenty years later and the day after he had been interviewed by an Argentine television programme on 1 April, a two-page *Clarín* article appeared about him in which he claimed the Gurkhas had attacked the 4th Infantry Regiment on Two Sisters and killed many of its soldiers. This made me think, 'If that is still Poltronieri's conviction, then what does the rest of Argentina believe?'

Finally, after arriving back at Heathrow from Buenos Aires, I exercised my habit of visiting an airport bookshop. A recently published book that caught my eye was written by John Nott, the former 2GR officer and Secretary of State for Defence during the war. In one of his final chapters he described D Company's advance towards Mount William as: 'When the Argentine troops saw the Gurkhas approaching, kukris drawn, they abandoned their positions and fled down the hill into the town (of Stanley).'[5]

My reaction was an inevitable, 'Goodness me! Seeing the Gurkhas approaching? With kukris drawn? Yet another guilty of an act of presumption. Well, one day Mr Nott might learn what it really was like to be with the Gurkhas in the Falklands when he reads this book – and war journal of one of them, Rifleman Baliprasad Rai.' The latter, who later became my Company piper, was to summarize his experiences as:

> Now I have been to that bleak and barren land, felt the cold of the wind and the snow, experienced the incredible hardship of an Antarctic campaign, the thump and thunder of battle, the comradeship of friends and the spirit of the regiment. From the hills of Sagarmatha to the seas of the South Atlantic is a long way, but I have travelled it and what a trip it has been![6]

His OC sahib agrees – although for many on each side it is a trip that never ends.

If a man will begin with certainties, he shall end in doubts; but if he will be content to begin with doubts, he shall end in certainties. – Francis Bacon (1561–1626)

NOTES

Introduction

1. *The Scars of War* by Hugh McManners, p. 5.
2. *Shell-Shock – A History of the Changing Attitudes to War Neurosis* by Anthony Babington, p. 173.
3. From an e-mail dated 28 January 2002 sent to the author from Denzil Connick, Secretary of the South Atlantic Medal Association 82.
4. *Regimental Association Journal of the 7th Duke of Edinburgh's Own Gurkha Rifles.* No. 6 2000.
5. *The History of the British Army* by Sir John Fortescue.
6. Extract from an article entitled *The Gurkha Myth* by Peter Osnos dated 4 May 1983.

Chapter 1

1. *From Bagsila to Bluff Cove – A Soldier's Story of the Falklands' War* by Rifleman Baliprasad Rai as told to RQMS Jasbahadur Gurung of the 1st/7th Gurkha Rifles' Quartermaster's Department in June 1982.
2. Ibid.
3. Ibid.
4. *East of Katmandu – The Story of The 7th Duke of Edinburgh's Own Gurkha Rifles Volume II 1948–1973*, p. 166.
5. *From Bagsila to Bluff Cove – A Soldier's Story of the Falklands' War.*
6. Ibid.

Chapter 2

1. *Urial-ovis vignei* – a reddish brown wild sheep of the northern India mountains and Tibet.
2. *Regimental History of the 3rd Queen Alexandria's Own Gurkha Rifles 1815–1927.*
3. In 1976 there were five Gurkha infantry battalions in the British Army. Three were stationed in Hong Kong, one in Brunei and one in the UK. The latter did not participate in the Khud Race. Transport, Signals and Engineer Regiment units gave a total strength for the Brigade of Gurkhas of 6,000 men. The Battalions were:
   – 1st and 2nd Battalions, 2nd King Edward's Own (The Sirmoor Rifles) Gurkha Rifles.
   – 1st Battalion, 6th Queen Elizabeth's Gurkha Rifles.

– 1st Battalion, 7th Duke of Edinburgh's Own Gurkha Rifles.*
– 1st Battalion, 10th Queen Mary's Own Gurkha Rifles.
* The designation, Duke of Edinburgh's Own was awarded in 1959. The 1st and 2nd Battalions amalgamated in Hong Kong to form a single Battalion on 1 August 1970.

Chapter 3

1. The original 7th Gurkha Rifles was raised from the 43rd Gurkha (Rifle) Regiment of Bengal Infantry in 1903. Four years later the 7th was redesignated as the 8th Gurkha Rifles. In the same year, 1907, the 2nd Battalion, 10th Gurkha Rifles received its new 7th Gurkha Rifles' designation (to be the forefather of 1st/7th Gurkha Rifles that fought in the Falklands' War). It was this Battalion, four years before, which had been raised from the original 8th Gurkha Rifles that, in turn, had been raised on 16 May 1902 by Major Vansittart from the 8th Madras Native Infantry. Not a simple birth.
2. When the Battalion had completed its next three-year tour at Church Crookham twelve years later in the renamed 5 Airborne Brigade, 130 7GR officers and other ranks had become parachute trained and qualified to wear the red beret.

Chapter 4

1. *Sandhurst Sketches* by General Sir John Blacker, p. 37.

Chapter 5

1. *Inside the British Army* by Anthony Beevor, p. 345.
2. 5 Infantry Brigade's organic units were:
   – Brigade HQ and Signal Squadron with Rear Link Detachments Royal Signals.
   – 2nd Battalion, Parachute Regiment.
   – 3rd Battalion, Parachute Regiment.
   – 1st Battalion, 7th Duke of Edinburgh's Own Gurkha Rifles.
   – Two squadrons of 36 Engineer Regiment, Royal Engineers (including 9 Parachute Squadron).
   – 407 Road Transport Troop, Royal Corps of Transport.
   – 10 Field Workshops, Royal Electrical and Mechanical Engineers.
   The additional units were:
   – 1st Battalion, Welsh Guards (replacing 3rd Battalion, Parachute Regiment).
   – 2nd Battalion, Scots Guards (replacing 2nd Battalion, Parachute Regiment).
   – HQ Battery, 97 Field Battery, and 29 Field Battery of 4 Field Regiment, Royal Artillery (with six 105-mm Light Guns each).
   – A Blowpipe troop of 43 Air Defence Battery, 32 Guided Weapons Regiment, Royal Artillery (with eight Blowpipes: a shoulder-held ground-to-air missile launcher containing one missile per launcher).
   – 656 Squadron, Army Air Corps (consisting of six Scout and six Gazelle helicopters).
   – 16 and 19 Field Ambulance, Royal Army Medical Corps.

– 81 and 91 Ordnance Companies, Royal Army Ordnance Corps.
– 421 Explosive Ordnance Disposal Company, Royal Army Ordnance Corps.
– A platoon from 160 Provost Company, Royal Military Police.
– 8 Field Cash Office, Royal Army Pay Corps.
– A detachment of 21 Postal Courier Squadron, Royal Engineers.
– Two Forward Air Controllers and their Tactical Air Control Parties: 601 and 602 TACP(FAC).
– Elements of 38 Group, Royal Air Force.
– Elements of the Joint Helicopter Support Unit.
– 825 Naval Air Squadron (with two Mark II Sea King helicopters on board *QE2*).
Later, on the Falklands, 5 Brigade was joined by:
– A troop from B Squadron, Blues and Royals (with Scimitar and Scorpion light tanks).
– A troop from T Air Defence Battery, 12 Regiment, Royal Artillery (with four Rapiers – a ground-to-air missile system with four missiles per system).
– 2nd Battalion, Parachute Regiment (for a short period only).
3. *When the Fighting is Over* by John Lawrence and Robert Lawrence MC, p. 12.
4. ARA *Santa Fé*, a thirty-eight year-old Guppy-class submarine was damaged by the Royal Navy, beached and eventually scuttled in 1985.

Chapter 6
1. The submarine was HMS *Conqueror*. Two other ships were hit by Sea Skua missiles fired from two Lynx helicopters – one being a patrol vessel and ocean-going tug *Alfred Sobral.*
2. *From Bagsila to Bluff Cove – A Soldier's Story of the Falklands' War.*
3. *Soldier* magazine, 17–30 May 1982, p. 9.
4. Ibid.
5. Edition no. 104 dated 18 May 1982, p. 3.

Chapter 7
1. The sunk Argentine naval transport *Isla de los Estados* was carrying 325,000 litres of aviation fuel and military vehicles.
2. *From Bagsila to Bluff Cove – A Soldier's Story of the Falklands' War.*
3. Ibid.
4. *Signals from the Falklands* by John Winton – *Five Star Wars*, p. 151.
5. *From Bagsila to Bluff Cove – A Soldier's Story of the Falklands' War.*

Chapter 8
1. From the Brigade of Gurkhas' newspaper *Parbate* (Hillman) Vol. 36 No. 1 dated 5 January 1984.
2. *The Falklands' War – A Visual Diary* by Linda Kitson, p. 27.
3. Extract from a post-war report entitled *Mortars in the Falklands Campaign* by Captain Nigel Price.
4. *QE2* by Captain Ronald W. Warwick, p. 124.

5. *The Falklands' War – A Visual Diary.* p. 26.
6. The actual number of Argentine mainland fixed-wing offensive aircraft now available for air strikes after the Pebble Island Raid were four Etendards, thirty-eight Skyhawks, twenty-four Daggers, six Canberras plus seven naval Skyhawks supported by two Hercules KC-130 refuelling tankers. Additionally, six Aeromacchi armed jet trainers, eighteen Pucarás, and twenty-six helicopters were based on the Falkland. These figures reflect that eleven aircraft were destroyed on Pebble Island – six Pucarás, four Turbo-Mentors and one Short Skyvan transport.
7. *From Bagsila to Bluff Cove – A Soldier's Story of the Falklands' War.*

Chapter 9

1. Edition no. 184 dated 18 May 1982, p. 3.
2. *Walking Tall* by Simon Weston, p. 113.
3. 'Vertrep' – vertical replenishment – the transfer of logistic supplies by helicopter.
4. *From Bagsila to Bluff Cove – A Soldier's Story of the Falklands' War.*
5. Ibid.
6. Actual casualty figures were thirty-three – seven dead and twenty-six wounded.

Chapter 10

1. *The Royal Navy and the Falklands' War,* p. 105. On 26 April a Canberra bomber raid on Royal Navy ships was aborted after reaching South Georgia.
2. *From Bagsila to Bluff Cove – A Soldier's Story of the Falklands' War.*
3. *QE2,* p. 133.
4. *From Bagsila to Bluff Cove – A Soldier's Story of the Falklands' War.*
5. *Globe and Laurel.* Royal Marine Commandos' Regimental Journal dated July/August 1982. Volume XCI, No.4.

Chapter 11

1. *History of the 4th Prince of Wales' Own Gurkha Rifles 1857–1937.*
2. *Reasons in Writing – A Commando's View of the Falklands' War* by Ewen Soutby-Tailyour, p. 247.
3. *From Bagsila to Bluff Cove – A Soldier's Story of the Falklands' War.*
4. *Don't Cry For Me, Sergeant Major* by Robert McGowan and Jeremy Hands, pp. 177–78.
5. *Amphibious Assault Falklands – The Battle of San Carlos Water* by Michael Clapp and Ewen Southby-Tailyour. Caption to illustration 19.
6. *Don't Cry For Me, Sergeant Major,* p. 179.
7. The impressive statistics were:
   – 1,388 personnel.
   – 555 POWs.
   – 93 casualties.
   – 458 tons of cargo (409 tons underslung and 49 tons internal).
8. One click is military jargon for one kilometre.

Chapter 12

1. Echelon – a French word meaning step. The Battalion operated with two Echelon parties for logistic resupply. A Echelon was forward at Goose Green and, later, Fitzroy.
2. *Trench Foot: The South Atlantic Experience* by Dr E. C. Gerding of Argentina for the *International Review of the Armed Forces Medical Services* – 15 September 1998.
3. *A Soldier's Song – True Stories from the Falklands* by Ken Lukowiak, p. 102.
4. The basic weapons of an Argentine Army rifle section were:
   - FAL (*Fusil Automatico Liviano*). The Argentine-manufactured standard 7.62-mm self-loading rifle of the Argentine Army. Effective range – 300 metres.
   - FAP (*Fusil Automatico Pesado*). A heavier version of the FAL mounted on a bipod. Effective range – 600 metres.
   - *Pistola osino*. A machine pistol known to British forces as a 'grease-gun'.
5. *From Bagsila to Bluff Cove – A Soldier's Story of the Falklands' War.*

Chapter 13

1. *Don't Cry For Me, Sergeant Major*, p. 190.
2. *From Bagsila to Bluff Cove – A Soldier's Story of the Falklands' War.*
3. *Mortars in the Falklands Campaign.*
4. *Regimental Journal of the 7th Duke of Edinburgh's Own Gurkha Rifles.* No. 44, 1990.
5. *From Bagsila to Bluff Cove – A Soldier's Story of the Falklands' War.*
6. *Mortars in the Falklands Campaign.*
7. *Nine Battles to Stanley* by Nicolas van der Bijl, p. 222.
8. *Don't Cry For Me, Sergeant Major*, p. 181.
9. Extract from a letter sent to the author dated 1 August 2002 by Eric Goss.
10. *2 Para Falklands – The Battalion at War* by Major-General John Frost, p. 118.

Chapter 14

1. Edition no. 184 dated 18 May 1982, p. 3.
2. *I Counted Them All Out And I Counted Them All Back – The Battle for the Falklands* by Brian Hanrahan and Robert Fox, pp. 66–67.
3. Ibid. p. 66.
4. *Signals of War – The Falklands Conflict of 1982* by Lawrence Freedman and Virginia Gamba-Stonehouse, p. 387.
5. *The Fight for the 'Malvinas' – The Argentine Forces in the Falklands' War*, p. 209–10.
6. *I Counted Them All Out And I Counted Them All Back – The Battle for the Falklands,* p. 74.

Chapter 15

1. *The Falklands' War – A Visual Diary*, p. 62.
2. ETA – estimated time of arrival.
3. Thirty-two Welsh Guardsmen, four Army Catering Corps cooks, two Royal Electrical and Mechanical Engineers mechanics, three 16 Field Ambulance soldiers including one officer, two 9 Para Squadron Sappers and five of the ship's crew died in the attack.

4. *Signals of War – The Falklands Conflict of 1982*, p. 450.
5. *From Bagsila to Bluff Cove – A Soldier's Story of the Falklands' War.*
6. *Nine Battles to Stanley*, p.167.
7. Ibid. p.168.
8. Ibid.

Chapter 16

1. Edition no. 184 dated 18 May 1982, p. 3.
2. *From Bagsila to Bluff Cove – A Soldier's Story of the Falklands' War.*
3. *A Fighting Retreat – The British Empire 1947–97* by Robin Neillands, p. 509.
4. *British Army Review.* No. 75. December 1983, p. 57.
5. *Globe and Laurel.* Royal Marines Regimental Journal dated July/August 1982. Volume XCI, No. 4.
6. *Regimental Journal of the 7th Duke of Edinburgh's Own Gurkha Rifles.* No. 44, 1990.
7. *British Army Review.* No. 73. April 1983, pp. 23–24.
8. Ibid. p. 24

Chapter 17

1. *From Bagsila to Bluff Cove – A Soldier's Story of the Falklands' War.*
2. Ibid. Corrections to his injury details have been made from Battalion medical records.
3. *Nine Battles to Stanley.* Accumulated figures derived from Chapter 9 (The Battle for the Outer Defence Zone) and Appendix VII (Orders of Battle). However some of the figures in this account are in conflict with each other.
4. To provide greater clarity to the reader, unit call signs and the nicknames of *Record Bill, Rock Trunk,* and *Still Concorn* for Mount Longdon, Two Sisters and Mount Harriet respectively used during the fighting have been replaced by unit and real place names.
5. *Los Chicos de la Guerra* (The Kids of the War) by Daniel Kon, p. 85. One of seven interviews with Argentine conscripts about their claimed, but untrue, combat with Gurkhas.
6. The sixteen Argentine surviving helicopters were two Chinooks, nine Hueys, two Bell-Agustas and three Pumas.
7. The finalized casualty figures were:
    3 Para: seventeen killed and forty wounded.
    42 Commando: two killed and twenty-eight wounded.
    45 Commando: four killed and ten wounded.

Chapter 18

1. *The Fight for the 'Malvinas'*, p. 243.
2. From the Argentine Army's 1981 infantry training manual entitled *Manual De Orientacion Para El Suboficial Recien Egresado*, p. 104.
3. *Los Chicos de la Guerra*, p. 36 and pp. 24–25.
4. *Manual De Orientacion Para El Suboficial Recien Egresado*, p. 13.

5. *From Bagsila to Bluff Cove – A Soldier's Story of the Falklands' War.*
6. From an Internet account (August 2001) entitled *Down South – A Pictorial Diary of My Falklands' War* by Lance Corporal Barrie Lovell, former member of HQ 5 Brigade's Intelligence Section.

Chapter 19
1. Edition no. 184 dated 18 May 1982, p. 3.
2. AAA – Anti-Aircraft Artillery.
   SAM – Surface-to-Air Missile.
   Super Fledermaus Audio – audio signal for lock-on radar guiding, probably, a Roland SAM system.
3. *Regimental Journal of the 7th Duke of Edinburgh's Own Gurkha Rifles.* Final Edition – No. 48, 1994.
4. *Blue-on-Blue in the Falklands. Proceedings/Naval Review* dated October 2000.
5. *The Royal Navy and the Falklands' War*, pp. 327–330.

Chapter 20
1. *Los Chicos de La Guerra.*
2. *Nine Battles to Stanley,* p. 198.
3. *Desde el Frente, Batallón de Infanteria de Marina No. 5 (From the Front Line – 5th Marine Infantry Battalion)* by Carlos H. Robacio and Jorge R. Hernández, p. 226.
4. Extract from a letter sent to the author dated 8 December 1997 by Alberto Peralta Ramos.
5. Extract from an E-mail sent to the author dated 7 August 2002.
6. *Trench Foot: The South Atlantic Experience.*
7. *Desde el Frente, Batallón de Infanteria de Marina No. 5*, p. 250.
8. From the first post-war edition – no. 20 dated 30 June 1982.
9. *The Sapper.* Vol. 20. No. 11, October 1982, p. 445.
10. Extract from an e-mail sent to the author dated 7 August 2002.
11. *Desde el Frente, Batallón de Infanteria de Marina No. 5*, p. 194.
12. Ibid. p. 260.
13. Ibid. p. 319.
14. Nine Battles to Stanley, p. 198.

Chapter 21
1. Extract from a letter sent to the author dated 16 April 2002.
2. Extract from an e-mail sent to the author dated 4 December 2001.
3. The casualties were:

Corporal Gyanbahadur Rai	– A Company. Seriously hurt with shrapnel wounds to his back, chest, left leg and foot.
Rifleman Harkaraj Gurung	– A Company. Shrapnel wounds to his left leg.
Bombadier Richard Bowley	– 132 Battery of Support Regiment, Royal School of Artillery. Shrapnel wound to his right arm.

Gunner John Williams	– 132 Battery of Support Regiment, Royal School of Artillery. Shrapnel wound in his head.
Lance Corporal Gauriman Limbu	– HQ Company. Seriously hurt with shrapnel wounds to his chest and abdomen.
Rifleman Bhairabahadur Rai	– HQ Company. Shrapnel wounds to his right leg.
Rifleman Tilbir Limbu	– B Company. Shrapnel wound to his right arm. He was subsequently treated on the spot and returned to his company.
Rifleman Jitbahadur Limbu	– B Company. Shrapnel wound to the back of his head.

4. Supplement to *The London Gazette* of Monday, 13 December 1982 containing the Ministry of Defence Dispatch of Tuesday, 14 December 1982 by Admiral Sir John Fieldhouse, GCB, GBE, Commander of the Task Force operations in the South Atlantic: April to June 1982, p. 16119.
5. *No Picnic* by Julian Thompson, pp. 154–155.
6. *The Fight for the 'Malvinas' – The Argentine Forces in the Falklands' War*, p. 262.
7. *An Unorthodox Soldier – Peace and War and the Sandline Affair*, p. 97.
8. *When the Fighting is Over* and BBC film drama *Tumbledown* by Charles Wood.

Chapter 22
1. *A Measure of Danger* by Michael Nicholson, pp. 262–63.
2 *The 1982 South Atlantic conflict's aftermath* by Dr E.C. Gerding, a paper submitted in 2002 for publication in the *International Review of the Armed Forces Medical Services*.
3. *Nine Battles to Stanley*, p. 203.
4. *Desde el Frente, Batallón de Infanteria de Marina No. 5*, p. 458.
5. Part I Orders of 1st/7th Gurkha Rifles Serial No. 13 dated 25 June 1982, para. 77.
6. *Mortars in the Falklands Campaign.*
7. Extract from a letter sent to the author dated 16 April 2002.
8. *From Bagsila to Bluff Cove – A Soldier's Story of the Falklands' War.*
9. *Regimental Association Journal of the 7th Duke of Edinburgh's Own Gurkha Rifles*. First Edition – No. 1, 1995. The factual inaccuracies have been corrected by the author.
10. *The Penguin News*. Edition no. 23 dated 30 July 1982.
11. *British Army Review*. No. 72. December 1982, p. 79.
12. *Amphibious Assault Falklands – The Battle of San Carlos Water*, pp. 100, 133 and 148.
13. *Desde el Frente, Batallón de Infanteria de Marina No. 5*, p. 250.
14. Ibid. p. 309.
15. Extract from an e-mail sent to the author dated 7 August 2002.

Chapter 23
1. *Regimental History of the 4th Prince of Wales' Own Gurkha Rifles 1857–1937*.
2. Extract from two letters sent to the author dated 21 and 26 June 1997 respectively.

3. Extract from two letters sent to the author dated 16 June and 14 July 1997 by Alberto Peralta Ramos.
4. Part I Orders of 1st/7th Gurkha Rifles Serial No. 13 dated 25 June 1982, para. 83.
5. Extract from two letters sent to the author dated 21 and 26 June 1997 respectively.
6. Budhaparsad's parents later insisted that his body be reburied in the UK Aldershot Military Cemetery. His name is among those of 255 engraved on the South Atlantic Roll of Honour in the Crypt of St Paul's Cathedral. Five months after this accident, Corporal Krishnakumar Rai of 69 Gurkha Independent Field Squadron, Queen's Gurkha Engineers, was also killed near Stanley by an exploding Argentine grenade placed as a booby trap under a SAM-7 missile. A short while later three others, Sappers Jagatprasad Gurung and Ghanendra Limbu, and Lance Corporal Chandrabahadur Gurung were all injured by shrapnel from an exploding 66-mm rocket fuse.
7. *The Penguin News.* Editions no. 23 and 27 dated 30 July and 30 August 1982.
8. *From Bagsila to Bluff Cove – A Soldier's Story of the Falklands' War.*
9. Extract from a letter sent to the author dated 7 September 1982.
10. Extract from two letters sent to the author dated 21 and 26 June 1997 respectively.

Chapter 24
1. *The Penguin News.* No. 21 dated 16 July 1982.
2. Extract from a letter sent to the author dated 21 June 1997.
3. *El Pais Semanal.* Edition no. 277 dated 1 August 1982.
4. *The Falklands' War – A Visual Diary*, p. 107.
5. *Uganda*'s third ambulance ship was the *Herald.*
6. *The Penguin News.* No. 27 dated 30 August 1982. Its editor added a note under the Colonel's published letter, 'We apologise for this mistake, and thank you for pointing it out to us.'
7. Ibid. No. 24 dated 6 August 1982.
8. *Regimental Journal of the 7th Duke of Edinburgh's Own Gurkha Rifles.* No. 38, 1984.

Chapter 25
1. From the Foreword of *The British Army in the Falklands* – a 1983 British Army publication.
2. The UN-ratified Tripartite Agreement of 1948 between Great Britain, Nepal and India established that Gurkha basic pay of the three Armies would be the same. Hence the rifleman's monthly pay in February 1983 was only £12. However there were a number of additional British Army Gurkha allowances, including those for married accompanied or married unaccompanied soldiers, which increased monthly pay dramatically. However the difference varied enormously between service in the UK/Falklands and Hong Kong, e.g. total monthly pay (February 1983) for a married unaccompanied rifleman with four years of service was £450 (UK/Falklands) and £147 (Hong Kong). Riflemen did not pay for food or accommodation and only paid tax when serving in the UK/Falklands. In Hong Kong married accompanied Gurkhas received subsidized rent, food and electricity charges.

3. *Regimental Journal of the 7th Duke of Edinburgh's Own Gurkha Rifles.* No. 39, 1985.
4. *Signals of War – The Falklands Conflict of 1982*, p. 399.
5. *Excursion to Hell* by Vincent Bramley, p. 178.
6. *Her Majesty's Interrogator* by Guy Bransby, p. 121.
7. Extract from a letter sent to the author dated 4 June 1997.
8. *Clarín – Segunda Sección* (Second editorial section) dated 15 June 1997, p. 14.
9. Ibid.
10. Ibid.
11. 19 June 1999 edition.

Epilogue

1. Extract from an e-mail sent to the author dated 7 August 2002.
2. From the front page of the Argentine national newspaper *La Nacion* dated 2 April 2002 quoting Héctor Beiroa, President of the Argentine Federation of Malvinas War Veterans.
3. *The 1982 South Atlantic conflict's aftermath.*
4. *The Daily Telegraph*'s Falklands' War commemorative supplement dated 30 March 2002. p. III.
5. *Here Today, Gone Tomorrow – Recollections of an Errant Politician* by John Nott, p. 316.
6. *From Bagsila to Bluff Cove – A Soldier's Story of the Falklands' War.*

BIBLIOGRAPHY

Abdela, L., *Women With X Appeal – Women Politicians In Britain Today* (Macdonald, London, 1989)

Adkin, M., *Goose Green – A Battle is Fought to be Won* (Leo Cooper, London, 1992)

Babington, A., *Shell-Shock – A History of the Changing Attitudes to War Neurosis* (Leo Cooper, London, 1997)

Beevor, A., *Inside the British Army* (Corgi, London, 1991)

Blacker, C., *Sandhurst Sketches* (Privately published, 1991)

Bramley, V., *Excursion To Hell – Death in the Falklands* (Bloomsbury, London, 1992)

Bransby, G., *Her Majesty's Interrogator – Falklands* (Leo Cooper, London, 1996)

Brown, D., *The Royal Navy and the Falklands' War* (Leo Cooper, London, 1987)

Caplan, L., *Warrior Gentlemen – 'Gurkhas' in the Western Imagination* (Berghahn Books, Oxford, 1995)

Clapp, M., and Southby-Tailyour, E., *Amphibious Assault Falklands – The Battle of San Carlos Water* (Leo Cooper, London, 1996)

Clavell, J. (tr.), *The Art of War* by Sun Tzu (Hodder & Stoughton, Sevenoaks, 1992)

Colbeck, G., *With 3 Para to the Falklands* (Warrior Publications, Thirsk, 1992)

Davies, P.E., and Thornborough, A.M., *The Harrier Story* (Arms & Armour Press, London, 1996)

Director Public Relations (Army), *The British Army in the Falklands 1982* (Main Titles, London, 1983).

Freedman, L., and Gamba-Stonehouse V., *Signals Of War – The Falklands Conflict of 1982* (Faber & Faber, London, 1990)

Frost, J., *2 Para Falklands – The Battalion at War* (Sphere Books, London, 1984)

Goleman, D., *Emosjonell Intelligens (Emotional Intelligence)* (Gyldendal Norsk Forlag, Oslo, 1997)

Gould, T., *Imperial Warriors* (Granta Books, London, 2000)

Jolly, R., *The Red and Green Life Machine* (Century, London, 1983)

Kitson, L., *The Falklands' War – A Visual Diary* (Mitchell Beazley, London, 1982)

Kon, D., *Los Chicos de la Guerra* (New English Library, London, 1983)

Hanrahan, B., and Fox R., *'I Counted Them All Out and I Counted Them All Back' – The Battle for the Falklands* (British Broadcasting Corporation, London, 1982)

Hastings, M., *Going to the Wars* (Macmillan, London, 2000)

Hastings, M., and Jenkins, S., *The Battle for the Falklands* (Pan Books, London, 1983)

Hutchings, D., *QE2 – A Ship for all Seasons* (Waterfront Publications, Blandford Forum, 1988)

Lawrence, J., Lawrence, R., and Price, C., *When the Fighting is Over – A Personal Story of the Battle for Tumbledown Mountain and its Aftermath* (Bloomsbury, London, 1988)

Lukowiak, K., *A Soldier's Song – True Stories from the Falklands* (Secker & Warburg, London, 1993)

Luvaas, J., *Naploeon on the Art of War* (The Free Press, New York, 1999)

Macdonell, R., and Macauley, M., *Regimental History of the 4th Prince of Wales' Own Gurkha Rifles 1857–1937, Volume I* (William Blackwood & Sons, London, 1940)

Mackay, J., *Regimental History of the 7th Gurkha Rifles Volume I 1902–1947* (William Blackwood & Sons, London, 1962)

Mao Tse-tung, *Quotations from Chairman Mao Tse-tung* (Foreign Language Press, Peking, 1966)

McGowan, R., and Hands, J., *Don't Cry For Me, Sergeant Major* (Warner Books, London, 1995)

McManners, H., *Falklands Commando* (William Kimber, London, 1984)

–– *The Scars of War* (HarperCollins, London, 1993)

Middlebrook, M., *Task Force: The Falklands' War, 1982 (Revised Edition)* (Penguin Books, London, (1987)

–– *The Fight for the 'Malvinas' – The Argentine Forces in the Falklands' War* (Viking, London, 1989)

Meerendonk, M., *Basic Gurkhali Dictionary* (Sen Wah Press & Co., Singapore, 1960)

Neillands, R., *A Fighting Retreat – The British Empire 1947–97* (Hodder & Stoughton, London, 1996)

Nicholson, M., *A Measure of Danger* (Fontana, London, 1992)

Nott, J., *Here Today, Gone Tomorrow – Recollections of an Errant Politician* (Politicos Publishing, London, 2002)

Parker, J., *The Gurkhas – The Inside Story of the World's Most Feared Soldiers* (Headline Book Publishing, London, 1999)

Reitz, D., *Commando – A Boer Journal of the Boer War* (Faber & Faber, London, 1983)

Rettersøl, N. (ed.), and Mortensen, M. (ed.), *Disasters and After Effects – Disaster Psychiatry in a Troubled World* (Atlantic Press, Bærum, 2001)

Robacio, C., and Hernandez J., *Desde el Frente, Batallón de Infanteria de Marina No. 5 (From the Front Line – 5th Marine Infantry Battalion)* (Editorial Solaris, Buenos Aires, 1996)

Sawyer, D. (tr.), *The Art of War* by Sun Tzu (Westview Press, Oxford, 1994)

Shackleton, E., *South* (Penguin Books, London, 1999)

Shephard, B., *A War of Nerves* (Jonathan Cape, London, 2000)

Smith, E., *East of Katmandu – The Story of The 7th Duke of Edinburgh's Own Gurkha Rifles Volume II 1948 – 1973* (Leo Cooper, London, 1976)

–– *The Autumn Years – Volume III of the History of the 7th Duke of Edinbugh's Own Gurkha Rifles* (Spellmount, Staplehurst, 1997)

Southby-Tailyour, E., *Reasons in Writing – A Commando's View of the Falklands' War* (Leo Cooper, London, 1993)

Spicer, T., *An Unorthodox Soldier – Peace and War and the Sandline Affair* (Mainstream Publishing Company, Edinburgh, 1999)

Thompson, J.H.A., *No Picnic – 3 Commando Brigade in the South Atlantic 1982* (Leo Cooper, London, 1985)

Various, *Serve to Lead (An Anthology)* (Royal Military Academy, Sandhurst, 1959)

Ward, N., *Sea Harrier Over The Falklands – A Maverick at War* (Leo Cooper, London, 1993)

Warwick, W., *QE2 – The Cunard line flagship, Queen Elizabeth 2* (W.W. Norton & Company, London, 1993)

Washington, L., *Ten Years On – The British Army in the Falklands' War* (National Army Museum, London, 1992)

Woodward, S. and Robinson P., *One Hundred Days* (Fontana, London, 1992)

Woodyatt, N., *Regimental History of the 3rd Queen Alexandria's Own Gurkha Rifles 1815–1927* (Philip Allan & Co., London, 1929)

Weisæth, L. (ed.), Mehlum L. (ed.) and Mortensen M., *Mennesker, Traumer og Kriser (People, Traumas and Crises)* (Universitetsforlaget, Oslo, 1993)

West, N., *The Secret War for the Falklands* (Warner Books, London, 2002)

Weston, S., *Walking Tall* (Bloomsbury, London, 1989)

Other publications and articles

British Army Review – December 1982, April and December 1983

Clarín (national Argentine newspaper) – 15 June 1997

El Pais Semanal (national Spanish newspaper colour supplement) – 1 August 1982

Flash (Buenos Aires periodical) – 18 May 1982

From Bagsilia to Bluff Cove – A Soldier's Story of the Falklands' War, RQMS Jasbahadur Gurung (the first Battalion account of the war) – 1982

Globe and Laurel (Royal Marine Commandos' Regimental Journal) – July/August 1982

Manual De Orientacion Para El Suboficial Recien Egresado (Argentine Army training manual) – 1981

Mortars in the Falklands Campaign – Captain Nigel Price (a post-war report) – 1982

Op Corporate 1/7GR Immediate Debrief Points – 10 July 1982

Operation Corporate 1/7GR Post Operation Report – Part II – 27 July 1982

Proceedings/Naval Review – October 2000

Soldier (Magazine of the British Army) – 17–30 May 1982

Regimental Journal of the 7th Duke of Edinburgh's Own Gurkha Rifles – 1984, 1985, 1990, and 1994

Regimental Association Journal of the 7th Duke of Edinburgh's Own Gurkha Rifles – 1995 and 2000

Supplement to the London Gazette – 13 December 1982

The 1982 South Atlantic conflict's aftermath (medical paper) Dr E.C. Gerding – 2002

The Penguin News – 30 July and 30 August 1982

The Sapper (Royal Engineers' Regimental Journal) – October 1982

Trench Foot: The South Atlantic Experience (medical paper) Dr E.C. Gerding – 1998

INDEX

Ranks and titles used are those at the time or on first appearance

350

351

359